W9-AYR-402

THE LIFE AND WRITINGS OF ABRAHAM LINCOLN

THE LIFE AND WRITINGS OF ABRAHAM LINCOLN

Edited, and with a biographical essay by
Philip Van Doren Stern

With an Introduction, "Lincoln in His
Writings," by Allan Nevins

THE MODERN LIBRARY

NEW YORK

1999 Modern Library Edition

Copyright © 1940 by Random House, Inc.

All rights reserved under International and Pan-American Copyright
Conventions. Published in the United States by Random House, Inc., New York,
and simultaneously in Canada by Random House of Canada Limited, Toronto.

Modern Library and colophon are registered trademarks of Random House, Inc.

LIBRARY OF CONGRESS CATALOGING-IN-PUBLICATION DATA
Lincoln, Abraham. 1809–1865.
The life and writings of Abraham Lincoln/edited, and with a
biographical essay by Philip Van Doren Stern; with an introduction,
"Lincoln and his writings," by Allan Nevins. — 1999 Modern Library ed.
p. cm.
Originally published: New York: Random House, c1940.
Includes index.
ISBN 0-679-60329-8 (alk. paper)
1. United States—Politics and government—1861–1865. 2. Lincoln,
Abraham, 1809–1865. 3. United States—Politics and
government—1845–1861. 4. Illinois—Politics and government—To
1865. I. Stern, Philip Van Doren, 1900– . II. Nevins, Allan,
1890–1971. III. Title.
E457.92 1999
973.7'092—dc21   99-12661

Modern Library website address: www.modernlibrary.com

Printed in the United States of America on acid-free paper

2   4   6   8   9   7   5   3   1

A NOTE ON THE TEXT

As CARL SANDBURG points out in the foreword to his *Abraham Lincoln: The War Years*, the total number of Lincoln's words preserved for posterity is more than one million—a figure greater than that of all the words in the Bible (including the Apocrypha) or of Shakespeare's complete works. Strangely enough, there is no adequate complete edition of Lincoln's works, nor is there likely to be until after 1947, when certain papers deposited by his son Robert in the Library of Congress will at last be made public. At present, the largest collection is the *Complete Works of Abraham Lincoln*, edited by John G. Nicolay and John Hay and published in 1905. This was issued in twelve volumes, and in 1905 could be considered a reasonably complete edition. Since that time much new Lincoln material has been discovered. In 1917, Gilbert A. Tracy edited the *Uncollected Letters of Abraham Lincoln*; in 1927, the *Lincoln Letters at Brown* was issued by Brown University; in 1930, Paul M. Angle's *New Letters and Papers of Lincoln* was published; in 1931, Emanuel Hertz, in the second volume of his *Abraham Lincoln: A New Portrait*, brought out still more new material.

All these sources have been carefully examined in compiling the present edition. This volume, of course, does not pretend to completeness, but it is the largest single-volume collection of Lincoln's writings ever published. The principle of selection used has been to include all those items which are of biographical interest or of historical importance. In order to bring within the covers of one volume a large and representative selection of Lincoln's writings, it has been necessary to print excerpts from some of the longer pieces. When deletions have been made, they have been frankly indicated either by asterisks or by ellipsis points. For the general reader these excisions should not be serious, for the material omitted has been left out because it is relatively unimportant, dull, repetitious, of ephemeral interest or because it pertains only to Lincoln's legal or business life.

A survey of Lincoln's life has been included in order to give the background needed to understand the full import of his writings. This biographical section is closely integrated with the Lincoln text and with the notes to the text. For quick reference, an extensive chronology is appended to this section so the reader can see at a glance the salient events of Lincoln's life and of the history of his time.

In compiling a volume of this kind, the author has had to call upon the services of many people to whom he gratefully acknowledges his indebtedness. In particular, however, he would like to mention the name of Mr. Paul M. Angle, Librarian of the Illinois State Historical Library, whose reputation as a Lincoln scholar is too great to need any comment here. He has been endlessly patient in answering questions and in giving advice. The invaluable day-by-day record of Lincoln's life from 1847 to 1861, edited by him and by Mr. Benjamin P. Thomas, has served not only as the basis for the chronology in this volume, but also as an authoritative guide to check the disputed dating of some of Lincoln's letters and speeches. Mr. Angle has kindly supplied a photostatic copy of the significant Kalamazoo speech of August 27, 1856, which has never before been printed in any collection of Lincoln's works.

PHILIP VAN DOREN STERN

Brooklyn, New York
December 24, 1939

TABLE OF CONTENTS

Table of Contents

x Table of Contents

Table of Contents

Table of Contents

Table of Contents

LINCOLN IN HIS WRITINGS

by Allan Nevins

"No LONELY mountain peak of mind," wrote Lowell of Lincoln in the "Commemoration Ode," emphasizing Lincoln's broad humanity of intellect and character; but a mountain peak of spirit he did represent, and as the years furnish perspective his countrymen more fully realize the fact. There was a time when Americans were too near Lincoln to comprehend his full greatness. To a traveler standing near a mountain range many eminences seem to have approximately the same altitude; it is difficult to disengage Everest from his lofty neighbors. But as the range recedes in the distance, the highest peak lifts more and more above its fellows, until it alone fills the horizon. So it has been with Lincoln. Of all the men whom Americans of 1870 or even 1890 placed near him—Douglas, Seward, Chase, Sumner, Grant—none but now seems small when measured against his fame. Or to change the simile, the Civil War era was a crowded stage on which many heroes strutted and struggled. To people of Southern blood and sympathies some of the scenes still show Robert E. Lee in the foreground. But to Americans, North and South, the drama as a whole has but one dominating figure, and all the *dramatis personae* are grouped about and subsidiary to the tall, gaunt form of Lincoln.

A study of Lincoln's writings obviously has two great elements of interest, one historical, the other biographical. To these might be added a lesser element—the purely literary interest of the latest and best of his work; but that actually belongs to the study of the man, for he never deliberately tried to be a literary artist, and wrote only to express his thought and emotions. Most men will read Lincoln either to find out what contributions he was making to his time, or to learn something about his mind, heart and personality. And of these two elements, the historical and the biographical, the latter is by far the more alluring and important.

It is true that even in 1844, when Lincoln was on the Whig electoral ticket and stumped Illinois for Clay, or at least in 1847, when he entered Congress, he was making some small contributions to American destiny; that after 1854 these contributions became important; and that beginning in 1861 they were of transcendent value. But after all, to study the history of the slavery struggle and Civil War we must go to far ampler sources than Lincoln's writings. Our principal reason for reading and re-reading them is to learn what Lincoln was thinking, feeling and hoping; to penetrate the lucid depths of his mind, to learn something of his wisdom and moderation, to refresh ourselves with his sensitive, lofty and sometimes half-mystical spirit.

The greatest statesmen, unlike the greatest artists and poets, seldom burst upon the world in full-panoplied strength; the William Pitt who dazzles all contemporaries in his twenties is rare indeed. One of the fascinations of a study of Lincoln's writings lies in the material they present for following the growth of a mind and a spirit that only slowly awoke to their full power. The process of this growth is half-explicable, half impenetrable. There is much in Lincoln's intellectual and emotional life which will forever remain mysterious. His moody changeability, the man now all extroverted activity, genial sociability and strong self-confidence, now all melancholy, self-withdrawal and irresolution, like a lake first irradiated by strong sunshine and then darkened by black clouds—this is mysterious. His combination of humor and poetry, of broad jest and sensitive emotion, a combination which explains his instinctive fondness for three writers who show the same traits, Shakespeare, Burns and Tom Hood—this equally goes to the very roots of his being. The contradiction between his stern common-sense sagacity or practicality, and his bursts of mysticism and superstition ("I was always superstitious," he wrote

Joshua Speed in 1842)—this is difficult to explain. Yet from lustrum to lustrum, decade to decade, we can see him growing, and in his writings we can divine something of the secret.

For Lincoln slowly developed great inner reservoirs of strength, which enabled him to meet each new demand, each fresh crisis of his life, not merely adequately but with inspiration. The awakened opponent of slavery-expansion after the Kansas-Nebraska Bill of 1854 was clearly greater than the man of 1850; the debater against Douglas in 1858 was clearly greater than the author of the Peoria speech; and the Lincoln of the Gettysburg Address and the Second Inaugural was greater—far greater—than the Lincoln whose silk hat Douglas held as he first took the oath of office. We can trace this development in his speeches and letters, and we can catch glimpses there of the deep springs which fed his inner reservoirs of power.

It is impossible, in dealing with a career so eventful, and in treating a personality so full of mysterious depths, of shrouded, reticent qualities, to lay down exact categories. Neither the man nor his life can be divided into neat compartments. Both were too rich, mutable and full of mysterious lights and shadows. The promise of Lincoln's ultimate greatness unquestionably lay in him from the beginning, and it is a significant fact that as an uncultured, uncouth country lawyer some intimates—including the woman who rather heroically became his wife—were confident that, given the proper opportunities, he would rise to eminence. But it helps to understand his growth if we attempt to fix some general divisions in his mental and moral development. And it is certainly roughly true to say that in the evolution of Lincoln as a leader, it was his greatness of character which first emerged to view; then the greatness of his intellectual faculties, his reasoning power; and finally, in combination with the two preceding, the greatness of his spiritual vision. Assuredly we can discern these three divisions in his writings.

There was nothing precociously brilliant in Lincoln's mind, or if there was, the circumstances of his early life were unfavorable to its expression. He went to school "by littles," hardly a good year altogether. He loved reading; he made extracts from books with a buzzard's quill pen dipped in brier-root ink, and omnivorously devoured even the Revised Statutes of Indiana. But his early precocity was physical—and above all moral. The young giant who tugged Denton Offut's boatload of provisions over the New Salem dam and outwrestled the "Clary's Grove Boys" had also gigantic traits of character.

We see even in Lincoln's beginnings his strong humanity, his kindliness, his simple sincerity, his strength of conviction allied with moderation of temper, and his courage. Though his early writings have the intellectual crudity of the country-store arguer and stump-speaking lawyer, these virtues glint through them. One of the turning points in his intellectual life was the result of a charitable act. He paid a Western migrant half a dollar for an old barrel not because he wanted it, "but to oblige him." In the rubbish at the bottom he found Blackstone's *Commentaries.* "The more I read the more intensely interested I became. Never in my whole life was my mind so thoroughly absorbed. I read until I devoured them." Even the letters on the sorry Mary Owens courtship, a wild reaction to the Ann Rutledge tragedy, reveal his sensitivity of feeling. "I want in all cases to do right, and most particularly so in all cases with women." His early political utterances are not distinguished by any special force of logic, much less felicity of expression. But they are distinguished by integrity, sense of balance, an instinct for compromise and a certain magnanimity; that is, by moral qualities. "If elected, I shall consider the whole people of Sangamon my constituents, as well those that oppose as those that support me." "I would rather die now than, like the gentleman, change my politics, and simultaneous with the change, receive an office worth three thousand dollars a year. . . ." "I want you to vote for me if you will; but if not, then vote for my opponent, for he is a fine man." Much of the powerful appeal which Henry Clay made to him lay in Clay's capacity for strong moral fervor; some of it in Clay's bent toward moderation and conciliation. But above all, Lincoln was always marked by a kindliness and sympathy which inspired his sociability and sweetened his humor. It was Joshua Speed who had shared his Springfield room with Lincoln when, in 1837, beginning to practice there, the rail-splitter was too poor to have a room of his own. "You know well," he writes Speed a few years later, "that I do not feel my own sorrows much more keenly than I do yours. . . ."

Yet intellectually he was growing. As he disciplined his mind by study and courtroom argument, his native sagacity was forged into a logical power as sharp and crushing as a battle ax, a power that by the middle fifties had become the most formidable weapon borne by any man in the American political arena. The process of molding and tempering this logical faculty can be followed with some distinctness from the later eighteen-forties. Even his statement of 1845 on the Texas question combines with clear moral conviction a simple but irrefutable dialectical power. A few lines of homely English, as lucid as a Euclidian demonstration, present both his characteristic mode of reasoning and his abiding belief as to the status of slavery:

I never could see much good to come of annexation, inasmuch as they [the Texans] were already a free republican people on our own model. On the other hand, I never could very clearly see how the annexation would augment the evil of slavery. It always seemed to me that slaves would be taken there in about equal numbers, with or without annexation. And if more were taken because of annexation, still there would be just so many the fewer left where they were taken from. It is possibly true, to some extent, that, with annexation, some slaves may be sent to Texas and continued in slavery that otherwise might have been liberated. To whatever extent this may be true, I think annexation an evil. I hold it to be a paramount duty of us in the free States, due to the Union of the States, and perhaps to liberty itself (paradox though it may seem), to let the slavery of the other States alone; while, on the other hand, I hold it to be equally clear that we should never knowingly lend ourselves, directly or indirectly, to prevent that slavery from dying a natural death—to find new places for it to live in, when it can no longer exist in the old.

This is not equal to any of a hundred passages which we could find in Lincoln's writings from 1854 to 1861. Nevertheless, it is a glimpse of the Lincoln that was to come. And as the years pass we can find in Mr. Stern's well-edited collection —much the amplest and best selected body of Lincoln's writings ever brought into convenient form—more and better specimens of his argumentative power.

If men had kept a fuller record of Lincoln's courtroom arguments we should doubtless be able to follow better the development of this faculty of close-textured and irresistibly logical reasoning. As it is, his mind seems to show a new energy and force in the year 1854; for the political crisis precipitated by the Kansas-Nebraska Act either awakened powers previously dormant or gave him an opportunity to exhibit to the general public powers theretofore used only in the courts. Probably it did both. After Douglas came home this year to face an outraged constituency, and found the Northwest burning him in effigy while a Chicago audience howled him from the platform, he visited Springfield to make the defense that he hoped would win back the downstate voters. The speech that Lincoln delivered in reply had a logical power that astonished even his admirers. Not many days later, Douglas spoke again at Peoria in defense of the Nebraska Act. The rejoinder which at once came from Lincoln revealed still greater scope, power and vision; it was not so much a speech as a closely woven political essay, such as no man in the country could have surpassed and few could have equaled. At last he had fully emerged intellectually. He was irrefutable in his opposition to the squatter sovereignty doctrine. "Whether slavery shall go into Nebraska, or other new Territories, is not a matter of exclusive concern to the people who may go there. The whole nation is interested that the best use shall be made of these Territories. We want them for homes of free white people." And the logical power of the speech was matched by its complete intellectual honesty. The candor and reasonableness of the passage on slavery beginning, "If all earthly power were given me, I should not know what to do as to the existing institution," came to reflective Americans like a cool and refreshing breeze out of the heated debates of the day.

Thereafter Lincoln never really faltered. From the increased positiveness of the Bloomington speech in 1856—"We will say to the Southern disunionists, we won't go out of the Union, and you SHAN'T!"—he went on to the irresistible force of the "house divided against itself" speech in Springfield the day after his nomination for the Senate in 1858; one of the political classics of the language. He was the least rhetorical of speakers, caring nothing for mere art, and everything for simplicity, directness, lucidity and honesty. These were qualities which, each seemingly commonplace in itself, his mind possessed to a degree which made it arrestingly individual and original. It was not the means which interested him, but the effect; he thought always of the minds of his auditors and readers, and desired only to reach these minds swiftly, candidly and logically. Few men understood the intelligent masses better than he, and the vocabulary and phrasing he had drawn from Shakespeare, the Bible and Blackstone were sufficient clothing for his honest thought in reaching them. For, above all, it was his thought which set him apart. He had perfected his logic until he could take a complex set of ideas, a jarring, confused array of facts, and, as shapeless globules of water are suddenly crystallized into ice, turn them into a diamond-clear pattern, which everyone saw to be Truth. People who were thinking crookedly heard him and were set thinking straight.

And when he met an adversary the edge of his logic was like a living sword. The Lincoln-Douglas debates were a battle of giants, but few have ever doubted which was the greater giant. The Cooper Union speech made, as the *Tribune* said, the greatest impression any political leader had ever produced on his first appearance before a New York audience. Not since Burke had so trenchant a political intellect appealed to the world in such forcible English.

But still a third Lincoln, as his writings show, was to emerge from the final stage of his career, a Lincoln who superadded to special moral qualities and special force of reasoning a spiritual quality which not even the great Edmund Burke had ever possessed.

Matthew Arnold said of Gladstone, whether justly or unjustly, that he failed in foresight because he failed in insight. It was precisely because Lincoln possessed so keen and sympathetic an insight into democratic strivings and hopes that, during the awful years of butchery and hatred after 1861, he rose to such a noble view of the nation's future—to such prophetic heights. It was a spiritual insight. The first touches of the new grandeur in his thinking and writing appear in the First Inaugural, in that closing passage which represents an amalgamation of his and Seward's thought. A half-practical, half-mystical sense of the true objects of the War—something far better than defeat of the South, far broader than emancipation—thereafter rapidly gained upon him. It was, he wrote even before Bull Run, "a struggle for maintaining in the world that form and substance of government whose leading object is to elevate the condition of men—to lift artificial weights from all shoulders; to clear the paths of laudable pursuit for all; to afford all an unfettered start . . ." A religious feeling as to the import of the War also grew upon him. It was, he thought, a testing by God of the purposes and devotion of the American people, a punishment by God for their past errors and an opportunity given them by God to re-create their life in a nobler pattern. In his daily work Lincoln could be very hard-headed, stern and even relentless. But he had a vision, and little by little he strove to lift the people to it.

Hence the noble eloquence of his greatest utterances, and hence their semi-religious tone. The Gettysburg address has two keynotes. One is the oft-repeated phrase concerning government of the people, by the people, for the people, and the necessity of maintaining it as an object-lesson to humanity, an idea that can be traced back to the Peoria speech of 1854, where he said that he hated the popular indifference to slavery-extension "because it deprives our republican example of its just influence in the world." The other keynote is his expressed hope "that this nation, under God, shall have a new birth of freedom" worthy of the sacrifice made by the heroic dead. It is this second keynote, the religious and prophetic chord, which should vibrate most strongly to later generations. That chord is touched in a different way in the letter to Mrs. Bixby. It sounds again in the noble letter that Lincoln sent to J. C. Conkling after the battle-summer of 1863, a letter that at times comes as close to poetry as prose well can. "The signs look better. The Father of Waters again goes unvexed to the sea. Thanks to the great Northwest for it." So he begins. He goes on to thank New England, and the sunny South too, "in more colors than one." They had helped to win the late victories. "Nor must Uncle Sam's web-feet be forgotten. At all the watery margins they have been present. Not only on the deep sea, the broad bay, and the rapid river, but also up the narrow, muddy bayou, and wherever the ground was a little damp. . . ." And finally the splendid ending: "Thanks to all: for the great republic—for the principle it lives by and keeps alive—for man's vast future—thanks to all."

And finally, as in some ways the finest utterance of this third Lincoln, the Lincoln who was not only a great moral leader, not only a great intellectual director, but a great spiritual monitor, we have the Second Inaugural. It is not so much a state paper in the ordinary sense as a bit of religious musing upon the past and the future of the Republic; and, long after the diapason undertone of cannon which accompanied it has faded away, it still rings in the nation's ears as a haunting and uplifting harmony:

The Almighty has His own purposes. "Woe unto the world because of offenses! for it must needs be that offenses come; but woe to that man by whom the offense cometh." If we shall suppose that American slavery is one of those offenses which, in the providence of God, must needs come, but which, having continued through His appointed time, He now wills to remove, and that He gives to both North and South this terrible war, as the woe due to those by whom the offense came, shall we discern therein any departure from those Divine attributes which the believers in a living God always ascribe to Him? Fondly do we hope— fervently do we pray—that this mighty scourge of war may speedily pass away. Yet, if God wills that it continue until all the wealth piled by the bondsman's two hundred and fifty years of unrequited toil shall be sunk, and until every drop of blood drawn with the lash shall be paid by another drawn with the sword, as was said three thousand years ago, so still it must be said, "The judgments of the Lord are true and righteous altogether."

With malice toward none; with charity for all; with firmness in the right as God gives us to see the right, let us strive on to finish the work we are in; to bind up the nation's wounds; to care for him who shall have borne the battle, and for his widow, and his orphan; to do all which may achieve and cherish a just and lasting peace among ourselves, and with all nations.

In that passage intellect, character and spiritual vision find their perfect fusion; and the writer of it distilled into a few lines of unforgettable eloquence all the sorrows, the chastened resignation and the passionate hopes of a great people emerging from such travail as nations seldom have to endure.

December, 1939

THE LIFE OF
ABRAHAM LINCOLN

THE LIFE OF
ABRAHAM LINCOLN

WHEN a man has become so famous that he is known to everyone, his identity as a person is likely to be lost. His most prominent physical features are emphasized by caricaturists until they come to stand for the man himself. A single adjective describing one phase of his personality is repeated until it takes on the value of a nickname. All the underlying subtleties and inconsistencies that go to make up the real man are forgotten or suppressed; finally he becomes as conventionalized as his memorial statue —and with no more insides to him than there is to the bronze casting.

No one in American history has suffered more from this process of oversimplification than has Abraham Lincoln. We think of him as a tall dark figure muffled in a shawl and wearing a high silk hat that is apparently never removed. We remember all the little things about his costume—the unpressed, ill-fitting clothes, the bulky umbrella, and the little black tie, always slightly askew. We know that his contemporaries considered him homely, but we are so used to seeing pictures of his face that we have come to consider it sadly beautiful. It is everywhere about us, and we must be poor indeed if we do not have Lincoln's portrait on our persons at this very moment, for it is stamped in copper on every penny that comes from the mint.

Long familiarity with his name and his appearance has made us feel that we know all about this man. His honesty, his kindness and his passion for justice have been described to us ever since we were schoolchildren. And all the things that have been said about him are true—but they are not true enough. The Lincoln we have so firmly fixed in our minds is not a person but a concept. The man himself lies deeper. His character was extraordinarily complex; his motives are not easily understood—and they have often been misinterpreted; contrary to popular belief, his rise to fame was neither accidental nor unsought for; and, more important than anything else, he was a human being like the rest of us, with all the weaknesses and faults common to mankind. It is a confirmation of his inherent greatness that despite the flaws he still seems great, and he grows more interesting on closer study.

There is only one way to understand this man as a person and as a force in history. No amount of reading biographical accounts of him will give the whole picture; no study of history or contemporary records will give as complete an understanding of his curiously complex personality as well as his own words do. We are fortunate in having a large body of his writings and speeches. Much has been lost, of course; carelessness, fire, time and deliberate destruction have taken their toll. But the material that remains is so rich that the man who emerges from Lincoln's own record of himself can be seen whole and true in an unconscious self-portrait that is sometimes most revealing when its author was most unaware of what he was saying about himself.

It is important, too, to understand the man as he actually was, for his reality as a person is fast disappearing behind the clouds of myth and fancy that have been cast around him. The Lincoln legend is not without its value as a part of American folklore but it has no place in history, except that the myth should be taken into consideration as a part of the deep impression made by Lincoln on the minds and hearts of his people.

The fact that the American people have made Abraham Lincoln into a hero and a god is not to be regretted. In their very act of deification the people have indicated what they themselves most admire in a man. A popular hero is the living embodiment of his people, with all their characteristics, good and bad. He is one of them, lifted up and made great, yet never divorced from their earthiness, rooted deep in the soil from which he sprang. That the American people have chosen this man from among all others to be their representative in world mythology is evidence of their attachment to the principles of liberty, peace and justice for which he stood. And it is remarkable, too, that they have seen through the apparent disparities in his career to the essential underlying truths. They remember him as a man of peace and good will, although they know that he was a wartime leader. They cherish the words he spoke for freedom and democracy, although they realize that he was compelled by the emergency of war to suspend many of their most dearly defended civil rights. They know that he saw beyond the temporary measures of his day to ideals of eternal importance. They remember that he and the men of his time had to fight to preserve those ideals; they remember the part he played in this struggle; they know what he did and they will not forget what he said. The words of his greatest speeches have become as much a part of our political heritage as the Declaration of Independence and the Constitution itself.

Now, three-quarters of a century after his death, Lincoln's memory, which had perhaps for a time become somewhat dimmed by long familiarity, has taken on a new meaning in a world where the things for which he fought are again being threatened. We have seen civil wars and international wars surge around us in the world at large, and the struggle which in his time was sectional for the rights of black men has extended until it has become national and international for the rights of all men regardless of the color of their skins. As a result of this mighty struggle now taking place there has been an amazing revival of interest in the details of Lincoln's career. Plays, motion pictures, books and stories about him have attained wide popularity. His words are quoted—with varying emphasis—by all parties from right to left. He has become a guide and a prophet to an even greater extent than he was before. Through the study of his life and his words we can arrive at a better understanding of the problems of our own time. The battle for democracy and freedom to which he devoted his life has not yet been won.

His life is one of remarkable interest not only for its personal and political importance, but for its dramatic values as well; it develops through a rising curve to reach a tremendous tragic climax at the end. It has all the narrative elements, and it should be more interesting to most of us than any tale of kings and battles long ago, for it is the story of a man who rose from lowly origins to high place and yet was so human that he is still remembered in his home town as a friend and neighbor rather than as a figure in a history book.

He was born on February 12, 1809, in a log cabin near the village of Hodgenville, Kentucky. His parents came from pioneer stock. His father's family had settled in Massachusetts in 1637, and moved ever southward and westward in successive waves of migration. In 1786, Lincoln's own grandfather met the traditional death of the pioneer, shot down by hostile Indians while he was planting a field of corn on ground that he had cleared in the forest. Lincoln's father, then a small child, was rescued from the marauders by an older brother who killed the kidnapper with a single shot from his long rifle.

An enormous amount of research has been devoted to establishing the facts about Lincoln's ancestry and early life. As a result of this research, we know a good deal about Abraham Lincoln's father, Thomas Lincoln. We know that he was a carpenter by trade and a farmer by choice, although he was successful at neither vocation. We know that he was legally married to his wife, Nancy Hanks, on June 12, 1806, by one Jesse Head, deacon in the Methodist Episcopal Church. The certificate of marriage is still in existence. Abraham Lincoln would probably have given much to see it, for all his life he was apparently afraid that he had been born a bastard, son of a mother who had herself been born out of wedlock.

This mother, Nancy Hanks, is a vague and shadowy figure who left no tangible record behind her. She was probably not able even to write her own name, for the few legal documents she signed bear only that shakily drawn cross that is the mark of an illiterate. We do not even know what she looked like, except that she was probably small and dark. After her son became famous, old settlers who had known her tried to remember as much as they could about this woman who had died obscurely many years before. They succeeded only in further confusing our knowledge of her, because they disagreed with one another on almost every point. The woman they described was a protean creature who ranged all the way from a Madonna-like mother to a slut whose casual infidelities would cast doubt on the paternity of her son. She herself was so unimportant that even the few people who knew her at all could not agree as to what sort of person she had been. And she was not only poor and obscure—she was a woman, a pioneer woman who could leave to posterity only one kind of record to indicate that she had lived, breathed consciousness of the world around her, been a part of her generation and her race. Her life work, the sum of her accomplishments, the living memorial of all her qualities, were her children. Whoever and whatever she was, Nancy Hanks Lincoln made her mark upon the world in this one record of her life. Reasoning backward from the kind of son she bore, she must have been a remarkable woman. Certainly her husband shows no trace of greatness in his character. The heritage he gave to his son was the heritage of weakness, of indecision, of slowness and of unceasing inner struggle.

The father, Thomas, a man and a property owner, is as clear to us as the mother is vague. He left a written trail through the records of the counties in which he lived. We can trace his career as a militiaman in 1795; we know to a penny certain sums that were paid to him for his work; we can follow the intricate legal transfers of properties that he bought, sold or abandoned. He lived until 1851. Many people remembered the father clearly when the son became so celebrated that investigators were trying to find every scrap of interest about his ancestry and the facts of his career. There is nothing unknown about Thomas Lincoln. He was the result that might be expected of his environment, no more and no less. He was uneducated, and inclined to look down upon book learning as useless in the hard battle for existence that had been his life. He worked as hard as he had to—and no harder. He never made much money, but he never starved. He got by in everything and he was content to eat, sleep and remain alive. He had the slow deliberate ways and movements that were to be characteristic of his son. He had dark hair and complexion, and so did his son. Otherwise there was not much in common between them, and the little we know regarding their personal relationship indicates that Lincoln had not too much affection for his father, and no more than a formal respect for him.

Thomas Lincoln took his bride, Nancy Hanks, to Elizabethtown. There their first child was born, a daughter whom they named Sarah. Shortly before their second child was due, they moved to a three-hundred-acre farm which Thomas had bought for two hundred dollars. This place was noted for its fine water supply, and was called Sinking Spring farm. In a cabin near this spring, Abraham was born in mid-winter in surroundings that were typical of the pioneer country, crude and primitive to our eyes, but not unrepresentative of the living conditions under which thousands of others dwelled in that new country.

The family stayed on this farm for three years. The land title proved to be defective, and Thomas Lincoln suddenly withdrew from his holding to take his family to another farm of only thirty acres ten miles away. This was known as the Knob Creek place, and its physical features were among the earliest memories of Abraham Lincoln. Here he played as a little shirt-tail boy; here he first came to knowledge of a wider world. He remembered the bright waters of the creek that ran through the farm. He remembered some of his first playmates, and he never forgot the names of the teachers whose ABC schools were his first encounter with education.

THE INDIANA YEARS

Title trouble again drove his father onward. He sold his rights to the Knob Creek farm and invested the money in portable merchandise—whisky. Then he built a raft, loaded his whisky and tools on it and went on alone to Indiana in search of new land. He returned for his family, and with them he started out in the late fall of 1816 for the spot he had picked in the forest wilderness to begin his life anew.

Winter was beginning when they arrived there. Thomas Lincoln built a half-faced shelter—a simple structure open on one side to face an outdoor fire that was supposed to heat the interior. Life in Indiana was even more primitive than it had been in Kentucky. Neighbors were few, and the country was in its virgin state, covered by endless forests that had to be cleared by hand labor. Winter came upon them. Somehow they managed to live through it, but the snow must often have drifted into the open-sided cabin. They got food from the forest, shooting the wild animals that were there in great numbers. Water was to be had by melting the snow. Like most wilderness creatures they probably spent much of their time sleeping, for in sleep one could forget the cold and the endless boredom of life under such conditions.

In the spring they were joined by two young men, relatives of Nancy Hanks. A new and more sturdily built cabin was begun with their help. Work on it progressed slowly, so slowly that it was not quite finished when winter was upon them again. Nancy Hanks' aunt and uncle, Betsy and Thomas Sparrow, came to join them. The newcomers took over the half-

faced cabin, while the Lincoln family moved into their unfinished dwelling to spend another winter in hardship and
cold.

During the autumn of the next year (1818) a terrifying
epidemic swept through the woods. "Milk sickness," the pioneer people called it, although most of them had no milk or
any way to get it. It carried off Betsy and Thomas Sparrow.
They were buried on a little hill not far from the cabin.
Thomas Lincoln made their coffins, cutting out boards from
a tree with a whipsaw and putting them together with wooden
pegs. He had hardly finished burying these two when his own
wife fell sick. She lingered for seven days, and then, early in
October, just as the woods were turning into the autumnal
colors that heralded the approach of another winter, she died.
Another coffin was cut from the living wood of the forest.
The nine-year-old boy and his sister followed the sledge carrying their mother's body to the hill that had become a wilderness graveyard. It was months before an itinerant preacher
came to conduct a funeral service over the lonely graves. The
living had another winter to face, and again they managed
somehow to survive it.

During that winter the son and the daughter of Nancy
Hanks went to a schoolhouse which had been opened in the
neighborhood. People were settling in the new country, and
schools and churches were beginning to arise in the woodland.
Life at the Lincoln home, however, became even more hap-
hazard than it had been before. There was no woman in the
house to keep order, to prepare food and take charge of the
growing children. Thomas Lincoln endured this for a year;
then, in November, 1819, he went back to the Kentucky hills
to find himself a wife. Before he had married Nancy Hanks,
he had courted—and been rejected by—a good-natured Elizabethtown woman named Sarah Bush. She had married meanwhile, but her husband had died. Thomas went to see the
widow to try his luck again. This time she listened more

favorably to his story, moved perhaps by the plight of his children, for she had three of her own. She promptly consented to become his wife; they were married the next day, December 2, 1819.

Thomas Lincoln returned to Indiana with his second bride, her children and a wagonload of household goods. His new wife probably received a rude shock when she saw the cabin and its squalid surroundings, but she was inclined to make the best of everything, and she quickly brought order and management to Thomas Lincoln's home. His children were fortunate in their father's choice of a wife, for she was a kind and sensible person who took the two motherless children to her heart and raised them as her own. Abraham became her favorite. He was bright—far brighter than her own children— and he turned to her for the affection that he had not had since his own mother's death.

The household things Sarah Bush had brought from Kentucky added some comfort to the sparsely furnished home. The men in the family were persuaded to finish building and flooring the cabin. The children were taken in hand, cleaned, dressed and disciplined. Existence in that Indiana wilderness was never to become easy for the Lincolns, but Sarah Bush Lincoln raised their standards of living and made things easier for them. She did her best, tried to make the men work, tried to cope with odds that would have been overwhelming to anyone not possessed of her calm good nature and indefatigable energy. Lincoln never forgot his substitute mother. He watched out for her interests when he became a lawyer. When he was elected President, one of his last acts in Illinois was to travel across the state by train and carriage to pay a visit to the woman who had raised him as if he had been her own son.

The Indiana years were the years of Lincoln's growth to adolescence and manhood. In Indiana he acquired an elementary knowledge of reading, writing and ciphering. This was all that schools ever taught him; his entire contact with formal education lasted for less than a year. Yet there was in him a passion for knowledge that was never to cease throughout his life. There are many accounts of his attempts to learn, of his borrowing books to read, of his efforts to work out problems on the back of a wooden shovel which he then shaved clean so he could use it again. And the young Lincoln had not only to learn about words and figures, he also had to prepare himself for the lot in life that a son of Thomas Lincoln must expect. He became expert with the ax. He worked in the fields and took farm products to the mill. His father hired him out to work for others. Manual labor was all that he could look forward to, for his father was incapable of imagining any other career for him. The son, however, did not take to the kind of life he had inherited. He worked hard with his hands but he never liked such labor; he was more interested in words and ideas.

During this period of his life, Lincoln seems to have been a simple, good-humored farm boy, noted for his kindness, his readiness to oblige others and his love for talking and listening to talk. He lacked the hardness that is so often characteristic of youths raised in such an environment and he sought to better himself and to learn—otherwise there was not much to set him off from thousands of other lads in the new country beyond the Alleghanies. No one seems to have noticed in him at this time any of the moodiness that was to mark his later years. One thing happened to him during this period, though, that may have had some influence upon his development. It was an absurd incident, almost farcical in its occurrence, yet it may have had far-reaching physical and mental effects.

He had to take his father's grain to the local mill to be ground, riding there on the family's mare with the grain tied in bags to the saddle. The mare was then hitched to a long pole and driven around in a circle to turn the mill that slowly ground out flour or meal. On one occasion the boy drove the animal too fast; she rebelled and lashed out with her hoofs, striking him on the forehead and knocking him senseless. The head injury may have been more serious than ·was suspected at the time. At any rate, the youth who had hitherto been so cheerful and casual grew up to be a man whose major characteristic was melancholy—a melancholy far greater than even the harsh and disappointing circum-stances of his early life warranted.

The Indiana years passed slowly as the boy grew into man-hood. His sister married and died in giving birth to her first child, leaving Lincoln alone among his foster-family. In the spring of 1828, he went on a flatboat voyage down the Missis-sippi to New Orleans, which was the first city he saw and the only one he was to see for many years.

THE LINCOLN FAMILY MOVES TO ILLINOIS

Gradually the land became more settled, but Thomas Lincoln did not prosper as the community grew larger. Finally, in February, 1830, dominated by the restless urge that carried America across a continent, he decided to move on again into new territory. All the household goods were once more loaded into a wagon; the Lincolns and their relatives set out for Illinois, where there were prairies instead of forests and rich black soil to be had for the asking instead of the stubborn wooded acres of southern Indiana that could be subdued only by back-breaking toil.

They traveled on into new country, crossing ice-laden streams where there were no bridges and where even the fords were uncertain and treacherous. Early in March, they reached a spot on a bluff above the Sangamon River, not far from Decatur, Illinois. Here a new cabin was built; fifteen acres of soil were put into cultivation; and everyone hoped that this was to be the place where the family would at last be able to make a good living. This was Lincoln's first sight of the Sangamon River. It was to become an integral part of his life; its lazy winding course runs through the years to come like a muddy brown thread, tying up all the events that were to lead him to fame and glory.

The first winter the settlers spent in their new location was a terrible one—one of the worst in the annals of Illinois. Snow fell until it lay four feet deep on the level prairies; it drifted into piles fifteen feet high along the hill rises and filled up the wooded ravines. All the land was covered under a thick blanket that brought starvation and death to animals and men.

Again the Lincoln clan must have slept through most of the winter, buried away and completely isolated under the white snow. Food was reduced to the slenderest rations. Only sleep could make the miserable people in the cabin keep down the hunger that could not be satisfied. Again they managed somehow to survive. Spring came, causing great floods to rise from the melting snow. Brooks and rivers ran high, sweeping over the land, tearing out trees and bushes, washing off the topsoil into the watercourses to be carried away to the sea.

The experience that Lincoln and his cousin, John Hanks, had gained on their flatboat journey three years before obtained them employment now. An enterprising promoter, Denton Offut, hired them to pilot a boat to New Orleans. They went down the Sangamon in a canoe, taking with them one of Sarah Bush's boys. They landed near the newly established town of Springfield, and walked there to find Offut. This was Lincoln's first entry into the place he was so long to be associated with. It was then only a small town, built among the great trees of a grove on the prairie. It was four miles from the river, far from any central point of communication, and there was no reason then to believe that it would ever amount to more than any one of a hundred other prairie villages that were springing up all over the state.

Offut had not been able to purchase a boat. His crew had

to build one for the journey, felling trees by the riverbank, sawing them out and pinning them together to make a craft eighty feet long, sturdy enough to stand the voyage through hundreds of miles of inland waterways. In six weeks they finished it and were ready to start on their journey. They loaded Denton Offut's merchandise on board and pushed off down the Sangamon. About twenty miles from Springfield, where the river bends around in a curve below a hill, a new grist- and sawmill had just been built. Above it, on the hill, was a recently settled village which had hopefully been named New Salem. The flatboat's progress was stopped by the milldam that spanned the river here.

Lincoln's ingenuity was brought into play. He had the merchandise removed; bored a hole in the bottom of the boat; let the water run in; then the back of the boat was lifted; the water ran to the front, weighting it down and thus permitting the boat to be pushed over the dam. This feat served Lincoln as a favorable introduction to the village in which he was to spend his next few years. For the time being, however, he proceeded down the river with the flatboat which made its way toward the Mississippi and eventually to New Orleans.

These two visits to New Orleans were Lincoln's only first-hand contacts with slavery. He had been a child when he was in the slave state of Kentucky; Indiana and Illinois were free states. In New Orleans he saw one of the most important slave markets in the country. John Hanks said that the sight of a young mulatto girl on the auction block horrified Lincoln and made him resolve that if he could he would "hit slavery and hit it hard."

The little party returned to St. Louis by steamer; Lincoln walked across country from there to rejoin his family at Decatur, but he returned only to bid his folks farewell. He was twenty-two now and he had a job. Denton Offut had promised to hire him to help run a store that he was going to start in New Salem.

In July, 1831, Lincoln arrived on the crescent-shaped hill above the river where the fifteen straggling cabins that made up New Salem stood. Life there was almost as primitive as it had been in Indiana, but it was the sort of life to which Lincoln was accustomed. He had never known any other. He fitted into the village immediately, making himself known by his stories and his cheerful willingness to do favors for people. Offut was late in arriving, but by the time he came, his employee had made friends with everyone in the place. The two men built a log shelter on the hilltop just above the mill. They stocked it with general merchandise and opened it for business, but conversation and human contacts were their chief profit from the venture. Lincoln learned a great deal about people but very little about business. Through his great physical strength and courage he endeared himself even to the roughest element in the section. His wrestling match with Jack Armstrong, the leader of the Clary's Grove boys, has become classic. He met all kinds of people and he was able to hold his own among them, either by his physical prowess or by his growing intellectual ability.

Even while he was a boy in Indiana, Lincoln had been attracted to the law as a profession. In New Salem he had plenty of time on his hands. He began his study of the law, and in addition read everything else he could get. In Indiana he had read the Bible, Aesop's *Fables*, *Robinson Crusoe*, *The Pilgrim's Progress*, and Weems' *Life of George Washington*. Now he read Shakespeare and Burns and studied English grammar. Mentor Graham, the local teacher, took him in charge and gave him private lessons.

Business at Offut's store went from bad to worse. There was very little trade to be had in the tiny community, and the store soon went under. Offut moved on to try his hand at other enterprises; Lincoln was left without a job. Instead of trying to find manual work—the only kind for which he had been trained—he was seized by a new ambition; he determined to run for the State Legislature.

He was only twenty-three at this time (1832) and he had never done anything that would indicate to the public his fitness for the office he sought. But he was exceedingly popular in his community, and no one could object to the platform he announced for himself. He came out for internal improvements, for better roads, canals, navigable streams and even a railroad—although he admitted that it was difficult to see how one could be financed. He stood for education, too, and better laws. Everything was carefully calculated to please everybody and antagonize no one. Everything was expressed in general terms with no hard and fast promises that might be difficult to keep. Lincoln showed his political ability early.

His lack of training for public office at this period of his life seems startling to us in an age in which education is taken for granted. He knew nothing about history or politics except what he had picked up himself in his own reading; his knowledge of law was very sketchy; economics, finance and business were unknown subjects to him; except for the few days he had spent in New Orleans, he had never seen a city or a factory or, in all probability, even one of the railroads about which he spoke so glibly in his platform speech. Yet his ignorance was no greater than that of most of the men around him, and unlike them he was willing to learn. Men were elected to public office in those days because they had many friends who could support their ticket, or because they could wield some power through organizations they controlled. Their ability to rule or administer was not questioned.

The boy candidate started his campaign for election to the State Legislature. He canvassed the people, spoke to them in person wherever he could and hopefully awaited the results of the election.

Before it could be held, war broke out—a miniature war as

history records it, but it loomed large in the minds of the people in Illinois in those pioneer days. An Indian chief, Black Hawk, led his warriors back into the state to recover land that had been taken from his tribe some thirty years before. Lincoln immediately enlisted in a militia troop. He was made captain of his company for thirty days, and he kept chasing Indians for three months, never coming into actual conflict with any of them, and not even seeing a live one, except once, when an old drunken warrior stumbled into camp and had to be saved by Lincoln from molestation.

In July, the young candidate was mustered out of service.* He went on quietly with his political campaign but he lost the election. The people of New Salem voted for him in an almost solid block, but he was still too new and unknown in Sangamon County to have made enough friends to elect him. He often proudly said that this was the only public office he ever failed to win by a direct vote of the people.

Having been unsuccessful at politics, Lincoln tried his hand at trade again. He had an opportunity to acquire an interest in a general store in New Salem without putting up any cash. In partnership with one William Berry he started out hopefully in his own business. Berry promptly drank himself to death, leaving Lincoln saddled with an $1100 debt that took fifteen years to liquidate. Economically this was the lowest point in his life. He worked in the fields, split rails, did anything to earn his keep. His friends—who were always loyal—pulled wires to get him the postmastership of New Salem, and on May 7, 1833, he assumed his first position as an employee of the United States Government. At this time he taught himself surveying, and in six weeks mastered the rudiments of the science well enough to make actual surveys.

* He was sworn in by Robert Anderson, who was later to be the hero of Fort Sumter. The story that Jefferson Davis mustered him out is probably apocryphal.

He succeeded in getting himself appointed deputy surveyor. In addition to this he continued his general reading, going through Gibbon's *Decline and Fall of the Roman Empire* and Rollins' *Ancient History*; he also kept up his study of law, reading Blackstone's *Commentaries* and the *Revised Laws of Illinois*. Since there was no attorney available in New Salem he was permitted to plead minor cases before the local justice of the peace, Bowling Green, who was one of his best friends.

Although Lincoln's earliest political inclinations were toward the Whig party—he always idolized Henry Clay—his first chance for political advancement came from the Democrats. He was invited by them to run again for the Legislature as joint candidate. He consulted with his Whig friends, was advised to accept the offer, and was elected on August 4, 1834, as Representative to the General Assembly of the State of Illinois.

Through all this New Salem period there runs a note of freshness, of aspiring youth. This was the springtime of Lincoln's career, and despite the financial setbacks and the political disappointments, it was the one period of real happiness that his troubled life was to have. The idyllic forest groves and rolling hills of the New Salem country formed a fitting background to it. The village itself was very new and crude, but everyone in it felt sure that it would become an important place. There was hope and vitality in the air, potential wealth in the soil and beauty in the wide horizon of fields and trees. It was in New Salem that Lincoln first experienced the love of woman. Here he met and wooed Ann Rutledge, the now almost legendary girl who has become the center of so much dispute and acrimony. Nearly everything we know about her has come to us through William Herndon, Lincoln's law partner and biographer. Herndon first announced the Lincoln-Rutledge love affair to the world in a lecture in 1866. The story, as Herndon gives it, is a very simple one, a tale that could have been told about many young couples in pioneer settlements.

Ann Rutledge was the daughter of James Rutledge, New Salem innkeeper, and owner of the local grist- and sawmill. All those who told Herndon about her testified that she was pretty and sweet-tempered, with blue eyes and light hair. She died before photography was invented; no wandering artist ever came to New Salem to sketch her portrait. Like the half-mythical Nancy Hanks she has faded into the mists of tradition, and although her name is familiar to every American, the facts about her life are few.

She was one of nine children, and she was four years younger than Lincoln. She had been engaged to a John McNamar, a New York farm boy who had come to Illinois to make a living. His real name was McNeil; he took the name of McNamar so his family could not trace him until he had made his fortune. He settled in New Salem, prospered there, and then, in 1832, he left to return east to get his parents. On the way he was delayed by sickness; Ann did not hear from him for months; when she did, his letters were infrequent and finally they stopped altogether. Ann fell in love with Lincoln and he with her. The courtship progressed slowly. In August, 1835, she sickened of "brain-fever"—probably typhoid —and after a short illness she died. That is all we know about Ann Rutledge and her relationship to Lincoln. Even this much has been brought into question as something thought up by Herndon, made public by him because, his critics say, he hated Mrs. Lincoln and wanted to hurt her.

What Herndon's critics have attacked is not so much his revelation of Lincoln's love for Ann Rutledge—although some of them deny that there was ever any love between them—as his story of the terrible effect Ann's death was supposed to have had upon Lincoln. According to Herndon, Lincoln almost went insane; his friends had to watch him lest he commit suicide; he haunted the grave in which his sweetheart was buried and he could not tolerate the thought that the snow and the rain should beat down upon the earth covering her. Herndon claimed that she was the one great love of Lincoln's life, and that the contrast between Ann Rutledge and the woman Lincoln finally did marry embittered him and was the root of his melancholy and his strangeness.

We shall never know the entire truth. Lincoln was singularly close-mouthed, and it is unlikely that he would even mention anything so intimate as this to anyone. Herndon's evidence did not come from Lincoln but from New Salem people whom he interviewed after his partner's death. An examination of his original material, which has recently been published,* makes out a very strong case for the essential truth of his story. He may have exaggerated, but what we know about Lincoln's character, as it later developed, seems not incompatible with the Herndon version of the Ann Rutledge affair.

Ann Rutledge, however, was not the only woman whom Lincoln considered as a possible wife during the New Salem period. The lonely, single man who had to live as best he could in other people's houses turned desperately toward the thought of some woman to brighten his life and share his troubles. Lincoln was strongly attracted to women, always afraid of them, but always drawn to them by some inward yearning that he could never understand. His ugliness, his ungainliness and his awkwardness made him timid. He was unsure of himself, uneasy in the company of women. He knew that he had little to offer a wife, but he seems to have wanted one terribly. His uncertainty of how to act with women made him a poor ladies' man, as the correspondence relating to the next woman in his life, Miss Mary Owens, brings out. She said about him, years later, that he was "deficient in those little links which make up the path of a woman's happiness."

* See the Rutledge correspondence in *The Hidden Lincoln*, edited by Emanuel Hertz, New York, 1938.

Mary Owens arrived in New Salem on August 1, 1836, less than a year after the death of Ann Rutledge. She came from Kentucky on a visit to her married sister and there can be little doubt that she was on a tour to survey the matrimonial prospects in Illinois. The woman-hungry Lincoln immediately began to pay attention to her, although she was rather stout and a year older than he was. He proposed marriage to her, but she delayed accepting him, perhaps because she had noticed that he was inattentive and careless in his dealings with women.

LINCOLN MOVES TO SPRINGFIELD

Time dragged on. Lincoln went away to attend the Legislature at Vandalia. New Salem's bright promises of growth dwindled, and the little village began to decline. In the spring of 1837, Lincoln determined to move to Springfield. He had had a hand in the effort to move the state capital there, so he could expect a warm welcome.

He rode into the public square on a borrowed horse, carrying with him everything he owned. Springfield was then only fifteen years old, but it already had a population of fifteen hundred. New houses were going up every day and there was an air of general prosperity about the place that should have encouraged the young lawyer who was going there to live. But the record we have of Lincoln's behavior that day shows only gloom and dark foreboding.

He was entering Springfield with the best prospects that his poor life had yet shown; he was a member of the Legislature; he had already arranged to become the law partner of a man he had met during the Black Hawk War, John T. Stuart, one of the best-known lawyers in the state. It is true that Lincoln was penniless, but his name was already known, and the whole reason for his moving to Springfield was to better himself. His friends, as usual, promptly came to his aid. One of them fed him in his own home for several years without charge; another offered to share his room with Lincoln so he would have a place to sleep. But this man, Joshua Speed, whom Lincoln came to know so well that Speed became the one person in his life to whom he ever unburdened his heart, said about his meeting with Lincoln that day: "I never saw so gloomy and melancholy a face in my life."

Lincoln shared Speed's room and stayed with him for nearly four years. Speed was a successful young merchant whose large and well-stocked store was the meeting-place for the young men of Springfield. There was a large fireplace at the rear of it, and around this the men would gather in the evening to discuss politics, women, literature and life. Among them was Stephen A. Douglas, then a rising young politician, a Democrat, as opposed to Lincoln who was a Whig. They first matched wits in Speed's store, and the political discussions they had there were an embryonic form of the famous series of debates they were to engage in twenty years later.

Another of the young men who took part in these historic meetings was Speed's clerk, William Herndon, the man who was to become Lincoln's law partner and faithful Boswell. He had been removed from Illinois College by his father because of the abolitionist sentiments he had expressed at the time of the murder of Elijah Lovejoy, editor of the Alton Observer, who had been killed by a pro-slavery mob during an attempt to destroy his printing press.

Lincoln immediately made himself at home in Springfield as he had done at New Salem. People were glad to befriend him. All his life men were willing to go out of their way to do things for him. Within a week after he came to the town, he had found a place to live, a business and friends.

He wrote to Mary Owens twice after he arrived in Springfield, explaining why she shouldn't marry him; finally the whole affair was broken off. During the next year (on April 1, 1838), he wrote a long letter to Mrs. O. H. Browning, the wife of a friend of his, in which he described the Mary Owens affair in detail. It is a cruel letter, ridiculing the woman he had once considered worthy of being his wife; it is also one of the most intimate and self-revelatory documents Lincoln ever wrote. It shows his indecision, his lack of ability to judge others, and, more than any other bit of Lincoln's writing, it offers a key to the psychological puzzle of his attitude toward women and marriage.

And so began the Springfield years—the quarter century that was to make this melancholy young politician President of the United States. He entered Springfield on April 15, 1837. He was then twenty-eight years old. He had just twenty-eight years—to the day—in which to live.

The town, which was to be the scene of his rise to power, was then an ideal location for a man seeking both political and legal advancement. For all its unpaved and unlighted streets, Springfield was an important place; it had the beginnings of a local aristocracy already established; as state capital it was sure to become a social center where useful contacts could be made. An ambitious man could hope to do well there.

The one thing in the Lincoln legend that is most untrue is the idea that Lincoln was not ambitious, that he had to be pushed over hurdles by his wife and his friends; that he was forced, almost against his will, finally to become President. It is true that he was lazy, that he was over-cautious, that he often lacked confidence in himself. The Thomas Lincoln strain was strong in him, but he overcame his inheritance; he wanted political advancement and he worked all his life to get it, bringing to the struggle one of the shrewdest and most gifted political minds in American history.

Each move in his life from this time on was based on political ambition. He made mistakes; sometimes he temporarily abandoned the struggle, appalled by its apparent hopelessness; but to say that he did not seek the career that was to be his is as unjustified as to say that Napoleon and Hitler were accidents of history or fate. Lincoln used different methods, more humane and less selfish methods, but he, too, had the determination that enabled him to achieve his goal. He would have gotten nowhere if the course of events had not been exactly right to bring him forward and make him great, but he was never lacking in the astuteness to foresee the correct move that would put him in each successive position to advance upward toward his final high place.

MARY TODD

Of all the influences in his life none was to be more important than the marriage he made—but for reasons different from those usually ascribed to it. It is true that Mary Todd, the Kentucky belle he was to marry, did set out to capture this young politician for herself—underneath his uncouthness she saw possibilities of growth that she was clever enough to recognize. But Lincoln, too, for all his hesitation and his doubts, did marry Mary Todd, and in doing so he could not have been entirely oblivious of the fact that he was forming an alliance with the most influential family in Springfield—the Edwards clan which was powerful in politics and society.

With Lincoln's entry into Springfield where he met his future wife, the first of the tangled threads of his career is woven into the complicated pattern of personal life, history and drama that makes his story so interesting and so strange. That she, the high-born Southern lady who came to Springfield on the usual matrimonial tour, should link her destiny with this backwoods lawyer was remarkable enough. But still stranger was the fact that among the eligible young men in Illinois who immediately surrounded her was Stephen A. Douglas, who was to run through Lincoln's life as a counter-foil. Douglas's career, plotted against Lincoln's, seems like some novelist's invention, a device of clever and ingenious fiction. Even Douglas's death, which occurred shortly after Lincoln took office as President, appears almost as if it were an artfully calculated move on the part of the author to clear the stage so his chief character could dominate the story during the important war years.

And Mary Todd herself is a character out of Thackeray. She is Becky Sharp—even to her knowledge of French—and Amelia Sedley, with her aristocratic background and silly Victorian notions of female propriety, both rolled into one character, inconsistent, puzzling and forever fascinating as a human being as well as for the part she was to play in history.

She had been raised in Lexington, Kentucky, where she had been well educated. She came to Springfield some time in the autumn of 1839, just before the Legislature first met there. She probably met Lincoln at a ball held in honor of the occasion. At any rate, during the year 1840 they became engaged.

Things did not go smoothly between them. Mary Todd was high tempered, imperious, used to adulation and having her own way. Lincoln was still in a psychological muddle about women. He was drawn to them as desperately as ever, but he was at the same time afraid of becoming married to one of them. Marriage had about it a terrifying state of permanence; he had his own way to make in the world, and even a politically advantageous marriage might hold him back in some ways as much as it might advance him in others. Beyond all these practical reasons was some obscure psychological inhibition, some holdover from his past—from his attachment to his dead mother perhaps, or from his love affair with Ann Rutledge that death had also terminated. Something made him regret the step he was taking. He wrote a letter to Mary Todd, breaking off his engagement. Speed persuaded him not to send the letter, but to speak to her in person instead. He did so and he was lost. She melted in tears, and he, moved by pity, effected a reconciliation for the time being, although his own doubts were by no means stilled.

Then on January 1, 1841, something else happened.* Just what it was we do not know. Herndon said that the unhappy couple had planned to be married on that day, and that Lincoln simply did not show up for the ceremony. He had been driven almost to the verge of insanity by his own indecision, and again he had to be watched lest he commit suicide.

Herndon's story lacks external corroboration. No Springfield paper printed a word about an expected marriage—and a marriage with a member of the important Edwards family would surely have been in the news of the day. Something did happen on January 1, 1841, as Lincoln's own letters testify, for he refers to this day in a letter to Speed dated more than a year later (March 27, 1842) as "the fatal first of January," and he says that he is still troubled because "there is one still unhappy whom I have contributed to make so."

There is no doubt, too, that what took place caused a terrible emotional upheaval in Lincoln. His correspondence at this time with his law partner, John T. Stuart, hints at it, and it runs through his letters to Speed again and again. The hypochondria he feared had returned in full force and he said that he was the most miserable man alive. Apparently he did not see Mary Todd all spring and summer; some time in August he went to Louisville to visit Speed, who had sold out his store on that same fatal first of January and had gone to Kentucky, where he also was contemplating marriage.

Joshua Speed was the one man in Lincoln's life who was ever really close to him. Herndon, who was actively associated with Lincoln for fifteen years in his law office, came to know his partner well, but only by observing him closely. Lincoln confided much of his political interests to Herndon, but he seldom spoke to him on terms of great intimacy about his personal life. Lincoln's friendship with Speed slowly cooled

* In their book, Mary Lincoln, Wife and Widow, Carl Sandburg and Paul M. Angle put forth the theory that Lincoln's attempt to break off his engagement took place on January 1, 1841, and that the ensuing period of emotional stress was a result of the still unsettled problem.

after his marriage to Mary Todd, but during the period just preceding the marriage, Lincoln poured his heart out to Speed in a series of letters that are without parallel in all the Lincoln correspondence. He had never written like this before; he was never to do so again.

Speed was the recipient of Lincoln's misery; to him and to him alone, Lincoln confided his next attachment to a woman, for immediately upon breaking off relations with Mary Todd he again needed a woman to whom he could turn. After Ann Rutledge's death he had sought the company of Mary Owens; now he switched his attentions to a young girl of seventeen named Sarah Rickard. This affair lasted for more than a year, but apparently it never became serious—any more than the Mary Owens affair had.* These were simply women sought for on the rebound, sought for in order to forget the women who had really counted.

During the year 1842, Mary Todd and Lincoln were brought together once more. The matchmaking wife of a friend, Simeon Francis, editor of the *Sangamon Journal*, served as intermediary; one of the most ridiculous incidents in Lincoln's life helped to throw him again into the arms of Mary Todd. This was a threatened duel with a rival politician, a comic-opera affair that Lincoln was later ashamed of and disliked to hear mentioned.

The political rival was James Shields, the Democratic State Auditor of Public Accounts. One of his rulings on a banking matter was made the object of an attack by the Whigs. Then a series of four letters lampooning Shields appeared in a Springfield paper. They were signed "Rebecca" and purported to come from the "Lost Townships." Actually they had been written by Lincoln with the help of Mary Todd and one of

---

* Sandburg and Angle say that Lincoln never wooed Sarah Rickard at all— that she was Speed's girl and that the references to her in Lincoln's letters are for Speed's benefit. Miss Rickard told Herndon in 1888 that Lincoln had courted her, but they claim that she may then have forgotten the truth, or that she may have wanted to associate herself with Lincoln's fame.

her friends.. They infuriated Shields. Egged on by his friends, he challenged Lincoln to a duel. Lincoln's seconds maneuvered him into a position in which he had to accept the challenge. Fortunately, some sensible friends interceded, and the affair was called off just as the contestants were getting ready to go into battle.

It was all very silly and stupid, but the duel apparently clinched the match between Lincoln and Mary Todd. Lincoln wrote one last desperate letter to Speed, asking how he liked marriage now that he had tried it. A quick answer was requested. We do not know what Speed said, but whatever it was, it did not delay the marriage. The farce-comedy of the duel had taken place in September. On November 4, 1842, Mary Todd and Abraham Lincoln were quietly married in the Edwards's home.

The marriage between Mary Todd and Abraham Lincoln has been much commented on by partisans of both sides who have been eager to make a good case for their own favorite by denigrating the other party to the match. The evidence, judged as impartially as one can under the circumstances, would seem to indicate that, although the abstracted and psychologically twisted Lincoln was probably difficult to live with, his wife was hardly an ideal companion for wedded bliss. Lincoln became broken to the harness, resigned to the perpetual differences between himself and his wife. In order to avoid trouble he simply let her have her own way in almost everything. Mary Todd, however, became not more easy to live with, but more difficult. As her husband rose to power she became more aggressive in her demands on life. As mistress of the White House she was one of the most domineering and headstrong women ever to have presided in that famous residence. Nor did she stand up well under the blinding light of national publicity.

Much of our information about the Lincoln-Todd marriage comes from Herndon, who hated Mrs. Lincoln. According to him she was "the female wildcat of the age," "a tigress," "a she-wolf" who "woman-whipped and woman-carved" her long-suffering husband. Yet Herndon said of her: "In her domestic troubles I always sympathized with Mrs. Lincoln. The world does not know what she bore or how ill-adapted she was to bear it."

One thing that must be kept in mind in judging the woman who was Abraham Lincoln's wife is the fact that she later became insane and some years after her husband's death was actually confined for a while in an asylum. The seeds of this dark malady may well have been present during her earlier life. She was, perhaps, not responsible for her erratic behavior, her wild bursts of temper and her unreasonably jealous attitude toward her husband.

Immediately after their marriage, the ill-assorted couple went to live at a tavern in Springfield where they paid only four dollars a week for their board and lodging. One week later, Lincoln, in a letter to Samuel Marshall wrote: "Nothing new here, except my marrying, which to me is a matter of profound wonder." This was the only written comment he ever made about his marriage.

Nine months after their marriage a son was born to the Lincolns whom they named Robert Todd Lincoln. The responsibilities that Lincoln had dreaded closed around him quickly. He was thirty-three years old when he married Mary Todd. His prospects were good but he was still terribly poor. His ambition, however, had never slackened. He had served four terms in the Illinois General Assembly. He now determined to run for the United States Congress. He had good reason to believe that he would be successful; he was already powerful in the Whig party in Illinois; he had friends and a following. He began to pull the necessary wires to obtain the nomination. In this he was bitterly disappointed. He twice saw the nomination given to others—one of them his close friend, Edward D. Baker, after whom he named his second son, born in 1846.*

Lincoln did not give up his Congressional ambitions. He devoted himself to law while he waited his chance, but meanwhile he kept in touch with every aspect of the political scene throughout the county and the state. While he waited he also indulged himself—as so many other disappointed men have—in the writing of poetry. He corresponded with a friend, one Andrew Johnston, and exchanged poems with him. Some of Lincoln's poetical attempts have been preserved. They are generally heavy with gloom—even his taste for the poetry of others ran to the more funereal kind.

It was during the period after his marriage that Lincoln formed his partnership with Herndon. He had broken with Stuart in 1841 to form a short-lived association with Stephen T. Logan which ended in 1844. Herndon had not yet been admitted to the bar when Lincoln asked him to join him; as soon as he was, Lincoln made him his partner.

Herndon was politically useful to Lincoln. He had many friends and he could make friends easily, so that he could rally even the "wild boys" of the town to Lincoln's support. Whenever Lincoln had to be away from Springfield, Herndon kept him posted on developments on the home front. He acted as Lincoln's publicity manager, as his scapegoat when necessary, as his political under-cover man and, finally, as the preserver of his life record, energetically seeking out everything that was of interest in connection with the man who had been his partner.

Of the two men, Herndon was unquestionably the more forthright, the more passionately idealistic. He was ready to fight at the drop of a hat, and equally ready to forget his quarrels as soon as they were over. Lincoln's slower nature,

---

* The Lincolns had four children, all sons. Robert Todd was born on August 1, 1843; Edward Baker on March 10, 1846; William Wallace on December 21, 1850; Thomas ("Tad") on April 4, 1853. Three of the children were dead by 1871. Robert Lincoln lived until 1926.

which required him to weigh every phase of any situation before taking action, seems less admirable than Herndon's
"happy warrior" attitude—but it was to take him farther. His
was a mind that could function over a long series of carefully planned moves; it was like his ability to learn and
memorize—slow, steady and sure. Lincoln never possessed
wide learning, but what he did learn he never forgot.

The slow but stolidly ambitious Lincoln bided his time during the years after his marriage. Then, on May 1, 1846, he
finally received the long-coveted nomination. His opponent
on the Democratic ticket was Peter Cartwright, picturesque
Methodist circuit-rider, who attacked Lincoln as an infidel
throughout the whole hotly contested campaign. The two men
met one day in Springfield. Cartwright hoped to embarrass his
opponent publicly. "If you are not going to repent and go to
heaven, Mr. Lincoln, where are you going?"

"To Congress," Lincoln said quietly. He was right, and he
was elected by a large majority.

THE CONGRESSMAN FROM ILLINOIS

Before he could go—before his election actually—war with
Mexico was declared. With its declaration, and with his election to an office in the Federal Government, Lincoln's career
became associated for the first time with national issues.
Hitherto he had been an Illinois man; his interests had never
gone beyond the borders of his own state; his experience had
touched local legislation only; his training had been provincial,
restricted to the narrow boundaries of one small segment of
the nation. He went to Chicago for the first time in his life to
attend the Rivers and Harbors Convention there. He met such
men as Horace Greeley, Thurlow Weed, Schuyler Colfax and
Dudley Field. The world was beginning to open up before
him, and his eyes reached beyond the horizon of the prairies
to see the problems that were confronting a nation.

The Mexican War was no isolated incident in American

history. It was fought not merely for patriotic reasons or to protect the lives and rights of American citizens in the newly admitted state of Texas. It was in reality a part of a great and tremendous movement that was to tear the country in two— it was part of the slavery issue that was then building up to the conflict that was to be fought fifteen years later under the leadership of this obscure Illinois Congressman who went to Washington late in 1847 to serve his first and only term.

The Mexican War was an imperialistic move on the part of the pro-slavery forces to gain more territory for their expansion. Cotton land was rapidly being depleted under slave labor, and fresh soil was needed to grow new crops. Almost instinctively, Lincoln seems to have grasped the essential nature of the Mexican War. He opposed it from the beginning, and his opposition nearly wrecked his political career..

Lincoln's sojourn in the nation's capital must have had an important influence on him. He left Springfield in November, 1847, in company with Mrs. Lincoln and their two sons, Robert and Edward. The journey to Washington gave Lincoln his first view of the eastern part of the country. In Washington he came in contact with slavery, for the District of Columbia was an important slave-trading center, and the auctioning of human beings could be seen from the windows of the Capitol itself.

On December 6, the new Congressman from Illinois took his seat in the House of Representatives. On December 22, he introduced a series of resolutions sharply questioning whether or not the "spot" on which the first blood of war had been shed was Mexican or United States territory. The border between Texas and Mexico was in dispute, so the question was not without significance. He spoke again on January 12. On this occasion he not only attacked the war policy of the President and the Administration but went on to generalize about revolution.

The Democratic newspapers in Illinois immediately seized

upon these two speeches and used them in an attack on Lincoln and the Whig party. Illinois had enthusiastically supported the War, sent armies and supplied leaders. Shields and Baker had gone to win glory on the field of battle. Mass meetings were held at which Lincoln was attacked and his "Spot" resolutions held up to scorn. The word "Spot" was to stick to him for many years in all sorts of derisory connotations, and his theories of revolution were to be used against him even during his campaign for the Presidency. His own native honesty and his inexperience had defeated him. It was obvious that he could not hope for re-election. He had been rash enough to oppose a war and support an unpopular cause without compromise or equivocation.

Nevertheless, during the remainder of his term in Congress, he threw his efforts into furthering the political cause of the Whig party. He worked for the election of Zachary Taylor; he traveled in New England; he wrote letters and kept in touch with party affairs throughout the country. The Whig party was dying. Its principles were no longer valid, for the issue of the day, rising steadily into greater and greater prominence, was slavery, and the issue could no longer be avoided. The Democratic party stood for the extension of slavery; the Whigs stood for nothing except opposition to the Democrats. A new party was being born, a party composed of all those who hated slavery. This was the Free Soil party, which was attracting all the liberal-minded people of the Northeast. The Free Soil party was short lived; it accomplished little of importance, but it was indicative of the revolt against the inaction in the old Whig party. It died out in 1852, and its members became absorbed in the new Republican party which was to sweep into power in 1860 with Lincoln as its Presidential nominee. Yet, by one of those curious turns of historical circumstance, Lincoln now went to New England to try to put down this revolt—to attempt to strangle at its very inception the political movement that eventually was to carry him to greatness. And to compound inconsistency he went there in behalf of Zachary Taylor, whose chief claim to the Presidency was his military record in the Mexican War that Lincoln had opposed.

During this political campaign in New England, Lincoln first met William H. Seward and heard him deliver a speech against slavery. Lincoln was not only impressed by the nature of Seward's argument, he was even more impressed by the manner of Seward's speaking, for he spoke quietly, without the flamboyance or rhetoric that was so popular at the time. Seward was a man of importance in the East; his star was rising daily as the political leader of the anti-slavery forces. Lincoln's own speaking technique shows Seward's influence from this time on. He had never been given to excessive rhetoric, but now his words became even simpler and more direct.

Lincoln went on to Springfield, where he made certain that his popularity with his constituents had vanished. Taylor was elected in November—an appointive Governmental office was all that Lincoln could hope for. He returned to Washington for the session beginning on December 7, 1848. During this session Lincoln sponsored an unsuccessful bill that was intended to restrict slavery in the District of Columbia; otherwise he took no part in the growing anti-slavery movement. Taylor was inaugurated; the session came to a gloomy close, and Lincoln returned to Springfield, hopeful that he would be appointed to the Commissionership of the General Land Office. Again he pulled wires. He even returned to Washington to further his claims, but again he was disappointed. The position was given to someone else, and Lincoln was finally offered a minor position as Secretary of the Oregon Territory. He had no heart for the job, and Mrs. Lincoln was inalterably opposed to moving to the far West. His political fortunes were at their lowest ebb. There was nothing left for him to do but return to the law.

In February, 1850, his second son, Edward, died after

four short years of life. Everything seemed to be crumbling away from this man who had got so far and who now seemed to be pushed back, losing ground at every step. He buried himself in his law practice, riding the circuit through the small towns of Illinois while Herndon held down the home office.

THE YEARS OF THE LOCUST

Lincoln was only forty years old when his term as Congress-man expired, but he already considered himself an old man. The next few years were to age him rapidly. Life with Mary Todd could scarcely have been pleasant during this unhappy period. Their friends and neighbors testify to her bad temper, her nagging ways and her impatience with a husband who was a failure and who was apparently reconciled to remaining one.

The circuit with its tenth-rate hotels and shabby lodging places, its miserable food and long hard jumps from town to town, became infinitely more desirable than his home. He stayed away as much as he could. When court was held in a town near Springfield, all the lawyers and judges would ride home to spend the week end. Lincoln would remain where he was, lonely and miserable, putting up with the discomforts of a boardinghouse in order to find peace and to be left to nourish his own sense of failure without being nagged about it.

When he had to be in Springfield, he spent much of his time at his office in company with Billy Herndon. Although Lincoln had been greatly attracted to the law as a profession during his early youth, by this time the law had become pretty much of a routine matter to him, a means of making a living and not much more. His liking for abstract thought, his skill at argumentation and his ability to analyze any situation until he came to the kernel of its being stood him in good stead in his legal practice. According to Herndon, he had no use for detail; he hated writing legal papers and was generally careless in his methods and in his advance preparation of cases. Yet he was a good lawyer—and an honest one. In 1850 he wrote out some notes for a law lecture in which he set down his profession of faith. In his conclusion he said: "Resolve to be honest at all events; and if in your judgment you cannot be an honest lawyer, resolve to be honest without being a lawyer. Choose some other occupation, rather than one in the choosing of which you do, in advance, consent to be a knave."

The law office he occupied with Herndon was Lincoln's headquarters, his place of refuge, his study hall and conversation center where he could do exactly as he liked with no one to criticize his actions or his manners. As a result the office was not only exceedingly plain and simple—it was also disorderly and none too clean. One of the men who served as a clerk there said of it:

> There was one long table in the center of the room, and a shorter one running in the opposite direction, forming a T, and both were covered with green baize. . . . In one corner was an old-fashioned secretary with pigeon-holes and a drawer, and here Mr. Lincoln and his partner kept their law papers. There was also a bookcase containing about 200 volumes of law as well as miscellaneous books. . . . Mr. Lincoln had been in Congress and had the usual amount of seeds to distribute. . . . Some of the seeds had sprouted in the dirt that had collected in the office. . . . There was no order in the office at all. The firm of Lincoln and Herndon kept no books. They divided their fees without taking any receipts or making any entries.

Lincoln had one favorite filing place for everything—the lining of his high silk hat. When he was through with current documents he stuck them away in mysterious places. After his death, Herndon came across a bundle of papers marked simply: "When you can't find it anywhere else, look in this."

Lincoln would often bring his children to the office. They were an unruly lot, since their father tried to exercise no more control over them than he did over his wife. "The boys were absolutely unrestrained in their amusement," Herndon said. "If they pulled down all the books from the shelves, bent the points of all the pens, overturned the spittoon, it never disturbed the serenity of their father's good-nature." The junior partner, however, did not possess such sublime indifference. "I have felt many and many a time that I wanted to wring their little necks," he wrote in a confidential letter to a friend.

Lincoln's apparent idleness in the office and at home may have seemed to be wasted time to a more energetic man like Herndon, yet Lincoln actually used his time well. During this period he took up the study of Euclid for mental discipline, and pored over the problems in his office and on the circuit until he had mastered everything in the first six books. He read a good deal, too, sticking to a few books to which he returned again and again. Shakespeare was his great favorite. He memorized whole passages and would quote them—if given an opportunity.

During these years of political retirement, Springfield came to look upon the familiar figure of Lincoln with that half-amused tolerance which small-town people display toward a person who has ability but who has never quite achieved success. The fact that he was somewhat eccentric in appearance and entirely unconscious of the condition of his attire probably influenced them in underestimating the ugly duckling in their midst. He was oblivious of everything that was not of major importance to him, and his mind often turned inward so completely that he was unaware of friends passing him on the streets. People shook their heads sadly as the tall shambling figure went by without noticing them. A story is told of his walking along near his home, dragging behind him a little cart on which one of his children had been riding. The child had fallen off and was lying on the sidewalk crying, but his father had not noticed what had happened and was calmly proceeding with the empty wagon.

Herndon has described in detail the odd appearance of Lincoln as he was seen by his friends in Springfield:

He was thin, wiry, sinewy, raw-boned; thin through the breast to the back, and narrow across the shoulders; standing he leaned forward—was what may be called stoop-shouldered, inclining to the consumptive by build. His usual weight was one hundred and eighty pounds. His organization—rather his structure and functions —worked slowly. His blood had to run a long distance from his heart to the extremities of his frame, and his nerve force had to travel through dry ground at a long distance before his muscles were obedient to his will. . . . The whole man, body and mind, worked slowly, as if it needed oiling. Physically he was a very powerful man, lifting with ease four hundred, and in one case six hundred pounds. His mind was like his body, and worked slowly but strongly. Hence there was very little bodily or mental wear and tear in him. . . .

When he walked he moved cautiously but firmly; his long arms and giant hands swung down by his side. He walked with even tread, the inner sides of his feet being parallel. He put the whole foot flat down on the ground at once, not landing on the heel; he likewise lifted his foot all at once, not rising from the toe, and hence he had no spring to his walk. His walk was undulatory— catching and pocketing tire, weariness, and pain, all up and down his person, and thus preventing them from locating. The first impression of a stranger, or a man who did not observe closely, was that his walk implied shrewdness and cunning—that he was a tricky man; but, in reality, it was the walk of caution and firmness. In sitting down on a common chair he was no taller than ordinary men. His legs and arms were abnormally, unnaturally long, and in undue proportion to the remainder of his body. It was only when he stood up that he loomed above other men.

Mr. Lincoln's head was long, and tall from the base of the brain and from the eyebrows. His head ran backwards, his forehead rising as it ran back at a low angle, like Clay's, and unlike Webster's, which was almost perpendicular. The size of his hat measured at the hatter's clock was seven and one-eighth, his head being, from ear to ear, six and one-half inches, and from the front to the back of the brain eight inches. Thus measured it was not below medium size. His forehead was narrow but high; his hair was dark, almost black, and lay floating where his fingers or the winds left it, piled up at random. His cheekbones were high, sharp, and prominent; his jaws were long and upcurved; his nose was large, long, blunt and a little awry towards the right eye; his chin was sharp and upcurved; his eyebrows cropped out like a huge rock on the brow of a hill; his long, sallow face was wrinkled and dry, with a hair here and there on the surface; his cheeks were leathery; his ears were large, and ran out almost at right angles from his head, caused partly by heavy hats and partly by nature; his lower lip was thick, hanging, and undercurved, while his chin reached for the lip upcurved; his neck was neat and trim, his head being well balanced on it; there was the lone mole on the right cheek, and Adam's apple on his throat.

Thus stood, walked, acted and looked Abraham Lincoln. He was not a pretty man by any means, nor was he an ugly one; he was a homely man, careless of his looks, plain-looking and plain-acting. He had no pomp, display, or dignity, so-called. He appeared simple in his carriage and bearing. He was a sad-looking man; his melancholy dripped from him as he walked. His apparent gloom impressed his friends, and created sympathy for him—one means of his great success. He was gloomy, abstracted, and joyous—rather humorous—by turns; but I do not think he knew what real joy was for many years. . . .

He was odd, but when that gray eye and that face and those features were lit up by the inward soul in fires of emotion, then it was that all those apparently ugly features sprang into organs of beauty and disappeared in the sea of inspiration that often flooded his face. . . .

Many of the people in Springfield had good reason to love this curious person who somehow stood apart from their lives in an inner world of his own. They knew that he would never refuse to do a favor and that he was always ready to defend the poor and the friendless in court. His court fees were notoriously low—so low that other lawyers complained of them—yet many of his cases were handled without thought of any fee at all, and often, of course, the money due him for legal services was never collected.

Although the law was a refuge to him during this period, to a man with Lincoln's ambition the enforced retirement from politics must have been irritating. However, he evidently believed that he would some day have another chance to re-enter the political field, for he spent his time reading, studying and keeping up with current issues. Herndon tried to interest him in world history, philosophy and general literature. But Lincoln would read only what he wanted to read; he could be influenced, perhaps, but he could not be led. Herndon's efforts to make an abolitionist out of him failed also. Lincoln simply did not have the makings of an abolitionist in him. His mind did not work that way.

He listened politely to his partner's abolitionist arguments but he would have none of them. He was willing enough to agree with Billy Herndon that slavery was an evil that must somehow, some day, be shaken off. But he could not tolerate the violence of expression and action that was associated with extreme abolitionism. He was essentially conservative, and the methods used by the abolitionists shocked and alienated him. Men like William Lloyd Garrison, Thomas Wentworth Higginson and Theodore Parker (who was a good friend of Herndon's and corresponded with him regularly) stood for principles of action that were repugnant to his cautious mind that had been devoted to legislation and that was trained in the horse-swapping policies of legal practice. He wanted to see slavery done away with just as much as they did, but he wanted to see it legislated out of existence, quietly, and over a long period of time, with some kind of compensation given to the slaveholders in exchange for their property. He knew that if slavery was extirpated suddenly, the whole economy of the country would be thrown out of joint; a billion dollars of American capital had been invested in slaves—the immediate destruction of such a huge investment would cause panic and disrupt the financial structure of the nation. The Abraham Lincoln of the fifties was no abolitionist, no advocate of violent measures of any kind. That he was to be the agent for emancipating the slaves and the leader in a war fought primarily over the issue of slavery is one of the great ironies of history.

The whole matter of slavery was becoming more important every day. A change was taking place in the organization of the country that was forcing the issue to a climax. Hitherto the South had held a dominant position, politically and economically, in the structure of the nation. During the first half of the nineteenth century, cotton had become tremendously important. The invention of the cotton gin and the improvement of spinning machinery had made cotton a crop necessary to the economy of the world. Cotton acreage had increased, and with it the need for more slaves. The founding fathers of the nation had believed that slavery would die out of its own accord; they did not foresee the growing demand for cotton that was to keep it alive and make it a more active force than ever.

Coincident with the spread of slavery in the South, opposition to it had increased in the North. The polite anti-slavery societies of early years were supplanted by militant organizations determined to eradicate slavery at any cost. Heart-and-soul abolitionists were willing to spill blood, dismember the Union and tear up the Constitution to see the sin of human slavery erased from the land. They spoke of a "higher law," of the God-given rights of freedom which were not to be compromised by any mundane devices of expediency. And, as abolitionists became more bitter in their denunciations of slavery, Southerners became more ardent in their defense of an institution of which they had once been rather ashamed.

The South had made money from slavery—but not much money. Slave labor was profitable only on the big plantations, and the wealth of the South was highly concentrated in very few hands. By 1850, the North had already surpassed the South in economic power; in order to keep on growing, the North had to gain political power as well, for the South, which held the reins of government by her control over the Presidency and the Senate, was naturally unwilling to pass legislation that would favor her rival section. The South was agricultural, the North industrial; at this time the South was favoring free trade, the North protective tariffs to safeguard her infant industries; the South was in constant need of fresh capital to finance her agrarian enterprises, the North had become the money center of the nation, and all sections had to go to her for business loans.

Owing to the peculiar structure of the American government in which each state, regardless of its size or importance, is entitled to send two representatives to the Senate, the South held a control over this important body that was out of all proportion to her population or wealth. In 1850, the South had a fairly static population of about nine million people (nearly four million of whom were slaves). The North had a population of almost fourteen million which was increasing rapidly. With her greater population, the North could control the House of Representatives; since the number of states North and South were evenly balanced, the South could sway the Senate, and with the help of the Northern Democrats, she could dominate it. Each state that applied for admission to the Union endangered a balance already too delicately poised to suit the South. Thus the admission of a new state became a matter of tremendous importance. In a situation in which voting was likely to be decided on a purely sectional basis, two new senators could swing power to the section that had succeeded in bringing in another ally.

In 1849, California applied for admission as a free state. Her entry into the Union would give the North sixteen free states to the South's fifteen. The South began to murmur threats of secession; she realized that in the battle of population and wealth she must eventually lose. If she were to become a separate nation she would be free from Northern restrictions; she could set up a form of government that would be planned to protect her "peculiar institution" of slavery. In order to appease the South and hold the Union together, the Compromise of 1850 was drawn up under the sponsorship of Henry Clay. It granted the North the admission of California as a free state and abolished the slave trade in the District of Columbia; it gave the South three concessions— the organization of Utah and New Mexico as territories that were to be permitted to enter the Union as either free or slave states as soon as they had sufficient population to warrant statehood; a satisfactory settlement of the boundary dispute between Texas and New Mexico, with Federal assumption of the national debt incurred by Texas during her brief existence as an independent nation; and, most important of all for its influence on future events, a new and harsher fugitive slave law. This law permitted escaped slaves to be retaken anywhere in the United States, brought before Federal courts where the slave was not to be allowed to testify in his own behalf, and then, if proof of ownership was established, the slave was to be returned to the South by Federal marshals who could call upon citizens to assist them if necessary. Anyone aiding a fugitive slave was liable to a fine of one thousand dollars and to a suit for damages which could be brought by his owner. This act, as the people of the North bitterly interpreted it, put the United States Government into the slave trade, and made it possible for anyone to be summoned from his home to help run down a Negro fugitive with dogs and guns.

The Compromise of 1850 served about as well as putting a stove lid over a volcano would. The aged Calhoun, who had once sponsored nullification, died denouncing the compromise measure. The North must guarantee the South perpetual equality in the government by constitutional amendment, he said, and she must stop this endless agitation over slavery. Let free speech be stifled if necessary—it was less important than preserving the property rights of Southern slaveowners.

Daniel Webster lost the respect of his New England followers when he spoke in defense of the measure on March 7, 1850. It was his farewell gesture. He died in 1852, only a few months after the death of his life-long rival, Henry Clay. The old order was passing; the great men of the second generation of American statesmen who had held the nation together by a series of compromises, made this one last effort to keep it intact by the only means they knew. They were commanding the sun to stand still. Geology, climate, mechanization and the drive for industrial expansion were forcing the sections apart. The quiet legislative give-and-take methods of the early half of the nineteenth century were no longer sufficient to overcome the tremendous disparities between the North and the South. And under all the economic substrata ran the still deeper current of the moral issue of slavery—an issue that divided churches, brought the intellectuals of the day into the struggle and added the emotional fervor of a holy crusade to the already explosive situation.

STEPHEN A. DOUGLAS

Yet for all its obvious shortcomings, the Compromise of 1850 held the two hostile sections together in a sort of armed peace for a period of four years. And then, surprisingly enough, the whole matter was thrown into open agitation again, not by a Southern leader, but by a Northern one. Stephen A. Douglas, Lincoln's brother alumnus of the political debating society that had had its headquarters in Joshua Speed's store, was the man who, more than any other one person, was responsible for the re-opening of the slavery issue.

While Lincoln remained in obscurity, riding the circuit to try petty lawsuits in provincial courts, Douglas had gone on from conquest to conquest. He had become judge of the supreme court of Illinois, Congressman, Senator and one of the outstanding leaders of the Democratic party. He was four years younger than Lincoln and his opposite in every way. He was as aggressive as Lincoln was reserved; as winning in speech and personal presence as Lincoln was awkward. He was an outstanding example of an extroverted personality—whereas Lincoln, for all his ability to mix with other men and hold them entranced by his stories, was basically an introvert.

Even in their physical appearance the two men were opposite types. Lincoln was six feet four. Douglas was hardly more than five feet high. Lincoln had a thin narrow face supported by a long scrawny neck. Douglas had a huge round head set close upon massive shoulders. Lincoln was slow in movement, heavy and difficult to get under way. Douglas was quick, excitable and filled with a vast energy. These characteristics are not unimportant in determining a man's attitude toward the world. Douglas had all the small man's urge for the power needed to satisfy his personal vanity. Lincoln had the casual tolerance of a tall man who can look down upon the foibles and weaknesses of his fellow men with as much ease as he can view the tops of their heads.

Douglas had been born in Vermont but had gone to Illinois at an early age and risen to prominence there. He had become a Westerner by sympathy and economic interest, and he had that curious attachment for the South which Westerners often have. His greatest ambition was to build up the new West, to see it civilized, crossed by railroads and made an important part of the country. His political acumen made it easy for him to see that in working for the West he would also be furthering himself—he might even obtain the Presidency as a result of his maneuvers. His defenders, however, steadfastly maintain that what he did in connection with the Kansas-Nebraska Act was completely divorced from all personal interest.

He was Chairman of the Committee on Territories, a position that enabled him to supervise any legislation regarding territorial matters, see that the act was written to suit his will and then be in a position to push it through Congress. The Compromise of 1850 had apparently settled for the time being the endlessly disputed question of the extension of slavery. Even the widespread opposition to the fugitive slave law had somewhat died down in the North by 1854. Douglas re-opened the whole matter. The Kansas-Nebraska Act, introduced into the Senate under his auspices, provided that the huge territory from which the states of Kansas, Nebraska, North Dakota, South Dakota, Montana and parts of Colorado and Wyoming were later carved out, was to be organized into two large sections, Kansas and Nebraska, and that the issue of slavery in these new sections was to be determined, not by Congress, but by the people who would settle there. This was in direct opposition to the principle laid down in 1820 under the terms of the Missouri Compromise which held that all the land acquired under the Louisiana Purchase north of 36°30′ (except Missouri itself) should be free from slavery. And it conflicted in spirit, if not in letter, with the intentions of the Compromise of 1850, which had been written to maintain peace between the sections.

The principle of "popular sovereignty," or "squatter sovereignty" as it was called in derision, seems at first to be a harmless enough political idea. Let the people who were to live in a new country decide whether slavery should exist there or not. Unfortunately, the plan did not work out so well. A mad scramble took place on the part of both slavery and anti-slavery men to control the new territory. Instead of orderly governmental processes and free elections, frontier violence and mob rule dominated.

The Act was put through the Senate under Douglas's skillful direction, but it met with great opposition in the House, and was finally passed there only by iron-handed party discipline in one of the most turbulent sessions in the history of that body. On May 30, 1854, it was signed by Franklin Pierce, New Hampshire-born President, who was willing to serve the political purposes of the South more openly than any Southern-born President would have dared to do. The bill became a law; Douglas won his victory—but it was a victory that was to ruin him politically, break the strength of the Democratic party, eventually make his rival, Lincoln, President of the United States and—more than any one act of legislation ever passed by Congress—it was to breed civil war.

Opposition in the North was immediate and violent. Even while the Act was still in Congress, hundreds of mass meetings were held in Northern cities. Editors, clergymen and other intellectuals denounced the measure. The populace was wrought up to a frenzy that spread across the land, growing in fervor and moral earnestness as it spread. The amazing success of *Uncle Tom's Cabin*, which had been published in 1852, and immediately had gone into printing after printing, had shown that Northern sentiment—in contradistinction to Northern political practice—was strongly opposed to the institution of slavery. Now that the issue had been forced upon the country by Douglas's ill-advised Nebraska Act, men who had hitherto been willing to let slavery alone were stirred into activity. Abolitionism became respectable. The fugitive slave law was openly defied. The North was in revolt against Southern aggression, for it was now obvious to everyone that the South had no intention of keeping slavery within its present bounds. The move for the annexation of Cuba with which Pierce had been toying, and the attempt of the South to meddle in Central American affairs in order to promote insurrection (and slavery), became apparent as imperialistic gestures of a Southern oligarchy that was on the march to obtain new areas in which they could carry on a type of economy based on human exploitation of the crudest and most naked kind.

Douglas was the originator of this move, but the slaveholders were quick to follow his lead. Whatever he may have hoped to gain in popularity in the South was more than offset by the hatred that rose up against him in the North. He was made the object of newspaper attack; ministers preached sermons in which they portrayed him as the incarnation of the devil; he was burned in effigy in dozens of Northern cities. A group of Ohio women sent him thirty pieces of silver. His own Illinois constituents turned against him. When he came back to Chicago to make an attempted extenuation, he was not allowed to speak. He tried vainly for two hours to silence a furious mob that howled at him until he had to give up in disgust.

THE RETURN TO BATTLE

Thousands of Northerners were compelled to realize that the issue of slavery could no longer be avoided. Among them was Abraham Lincoln, who rose up like a man awaking from a dream. He shook off his lethargy and began to take an active interest in political affairs. His first action was to take the stump to help Richard Yates be re-elected to Congress on the Whig ticket. But more important things were ahead for him. This was his opportunity and he knew it. Here was an issue— and an opponent—worth fighting against. And Douglas was an Illinois man whom Lincoln could meet on his own home ground.

The still-obscure Springfield lawyer neglected his own business to study American history and slavery as he had never studied before. He knew Douglas well, knew all his weaknesses, the chinks in the armor of his methods of reasoning, the manner of his speaking and all his tricks of oratory. Lincoln prepared himself to meet his adversary. He did not have to wait long for his opportunity.

There was a preliminary skirmish between the two men during the latter part of September, 1854. Then, on October 3, Douglas spoke at the State Fair in Springfield before a

large audience. The Democrats turned out in great numbers
to lend support to their discredited hero. His speech, according to contemporary accounts, was a good defense of his position. On the next day, Lincoln replied to him, speaking in
the Hall of Representatives in the State House.

The place and the time were ripe for a great speech, and
Lincoln made one, the first really great speech of his career.
In it he reviewed the history of slavery in the United States;
he presented his own carefully thought-out arguments and
marshaled facts and evidence against his wily opponent. What
he said surprised Lincoln's friends, who had not believed that
this lawyer who had retired to private practice had the ability
to oppose so successfully the leading political speaker of the
Democratic party. This speech made Lincoln; he was called
upon to repeat it, and he did so at Peoria,* twelve days later,
adding to it and replying to Douglas's rebuttal.

Meanwhile, in the wave of resentment that had swept across
the North as a result of the passage of the Kansas-Nebraska
Act, a great concourse of people had been called to meet
together in Jackson, Michigan, on July 6. On this occasion a
new political party had been formed—the Republican party.
It was from the very beginning an anti-slavery party, sectional
by nature. To it flocked the abolitionists, the dissatisfied
Whigs and the disaffected Democrats. It even drew some of
its strength from the short-lived Know-Nothing party which
had been organized as a chauvinistically native American
party, violently opposed to foreigners, Catholics and Negroes.

On October 5, the day after Lincoln's great speech at
Springfield, a meeting of this new Republican party was held
in that city. The organizers were eager to win Lincoln's support, since he was an influential Whig, but Herndon, although
he enthusiastically favored the new party, advised his partner
to leave town immediately so he would have neither to reject

---

* The speech has consequently become known as the Peoria Speech, and
is so entitled in this volume.

nor accept the Republican policies at this early stage. Lincoln took his advice and left town hurriedly the next day, bound for Pekin, ostensibly to plead a law case there, but actually to avoid the issue. It was as strange a political journey as he was ever to take, but now, having come out boldly against slavery in his speech, his natural prudence bade him not to commit himself too far.

But he had completely regained his interest in politics, and he wanted to be in office again so he could influence public policy. The autumn elections gave the Anti-Nebraska men in Illinois a much stronger position in the State Legislature which elected the United States Senators. Lincoln immediately began a skillful canvass of his friends and possible supporters in order to gain the Senatorship.

The election was held at the State House on February 8, 1855. Lincoln's opponents were James Shields (the man with whom he had almost fought a duel in 1842), Lyman Trumbull, one of his best friends, and Joel A. Matteson, then the Democratic Governor of Illinois. Lincoln received 44 votes on the first ballot against 41 for Shields. It soon became obvious, however, that Matteson was his real opposition. Lincoln's votes went steadily down as Matteson's went up; on the tenth ballot Lincoln instructed his followers to vote for Trumbull in order to stop Matteson. Trumbull was a Democrat but he was opposed to the Kansas-Nebraska Act, and Lincoln preferred to see him win, rather than let the pro-Nebraska Democrat, Matteson, be elected. Mrs. Lincoln was so incensed at her husband's defeat for office that she would never speak to Trumbull's wife again, although until that moment Mrs. Trumbull had been one of her closest friends.

Lincoln, again disappointed in his political ambitions, returned to his regular circuit-riding routine. But events were not to let him rest in inactivity and obscurity. The territory opened up to settlers under the Kansas-Nebraska Act was becoming a potential battleground for the opposing forces that were struggling to win the new land for slavery or for freedom. The South sent men into Kansas from Missouri and other slave states; the North, not to be outdone, financed anti-slavery settlers who wished to enter the new territory. An Emigrant Aid Society was founded in New England, and men, guns and ammunition were shipped to Kansas to win the state for the anti-slavery forces.

On March 30, 1855, an election was held in Kansas to choose the first legislature. There were no slaves to speak of in the territory, but the South was determined to hold Kansas for her own. Five thousand armed men from Missouri marched across the line to vote illegally. Seventy-five percent of the voting was done by these outsiders. A pro-slavery legislature was elected, but the anti-slavery men refused to recognize it. They set up a government of their own, and the territory actually had two mutually antagonistic governments for a while.

Violence naturally flourished under such circumstances. On May 21, 1856, seven hundred and fifty pro-slavery men entered Lawrence under the pretext of serving as a sheriff's posse. They sacked the town, threw newspaper presses into the street and set fire to several buildings. Three days later, John Brown of Ossawatomie (later to be heard from at Harper's Ferry), went into action and "sacrificed" five pro-slavery men in retaliation for the sack of Lawrence.

The news of the Lawrence outrage hit the country simultaneously with the news of another attack made on the North by the South—this time in Washington, on the floor of the Senate Chamber. Charles Sumner, ardent anti-slavery Senator from Massachusetts, had made a bitter speech during a debate on Kansas in which he impugned the character of Senator Butler of South Carolina. On the day after the sack of Lawrence, Preston Brooks, a relative of Butler's and a Representative from the same state, entered the Senate Chamber

and assaulted Sumner, beating the seated man over the head
with a gutta-percha cane until he fell to the floor almost unconscious. Sumner was severely injured—so severely that it
took him several years to recover.

These two events coming together, and so closely associated
with each other, threw the whole country into a turmoil of
angry discussion. The North was enraged at the destruction of
Lawrence, and even more furious at the attack on Sumner.
Brooks was dubbed "Bully" Brooks, and his act was cited as
an example of the South's readiness to appeal to violence
when provoked. The South looked with horror at the calm
and deliberate killings done by John Brown in the name of his
stern New England God. But the South made Brooks a hero.
He was fcted and honored in Southern cities, and deluged
with a flood of canes presented to him by enthusiastic com-
patriots.

Underneath the partisan demonstrations the nation stirred
in uneasy alarm at the course the slavery issue was taking.
Civil war was being waged in Kansas; blood was beginning to
flow as American killed American in the struggle over the
basic question of whether a Negro was a human being or
merely a piece of chattel property.

LINCOLN AND THE REPUBLICAN PARTY

During this period Lincoln took no political action, nor
was he even certain in his own mind just what course he
should take. In a letter to his old friend Joshua Speed, dated
August 24, 1855,* he explained his position on the problems

* This was the last confidential letter Lincoln wrote to Speed. After this,
their correspondence became infrequent and impersonal. The rift between
the two men was caused not only by their differences over slavery—Mrs.
Lincoln had much to do with it. She seems to have disliked Speed and perhaps was jealous of any intimate friendship formed by her husband. Shortly
after he was elected President, Lincoln wrote to Speed, inviting him to come
to Chicago. Speed visited the White House during the War. In 1864,
Lincoln appointed Speed's brother, James, Attorney General of the United
States.

of slavery, Kansas and Know-Nothingism. Speed had upheld slavery, but, as an enlightened Southerner, he opposed the way that Kansas was being administered. Lincoln, in reply to him, said:

I shall advocate the restoration of the Missouri Compromise so long as Kansas remains a Territory, and when, by all these foul means, it seeks to come into the Union as a slave State, I shall oppose it. . . . In my opposition to the admission of Kansas I shall have some company, but we may be beaten. If we are, I shall not on that account attempt to dissolve the Union. I think it probable, however, we shall be beaten. . . .

You inquire where I now stand. That is a disputed point. I think I am a Whig; but others say there are no Whigs, and that I am an abolitionist. When I was at Washington, I voted for the Wilmot proviso as good as forty times; and I never heard of any one attempting to unwhig me for that. I now do no more than oppose the extension of slavery. I am not a Know-Nothing; that is certain. How could I be? How can any one who abhors the oppression of Negroes be in favor of degrading classes of white people? Our progress in degeneracy appears to me to be pretty rapid. As a nation we began by declaring that "all men are created equal." We now practically read it "all men are created equal, except Negroes." When the Know-Nothings get control, it will read "all men are created equal, except Negroes and foreigners and Catholics." When it comes to this, I shall prefer emigrating to some country where they make no pretense of loving liberty—to Russia, for instance, where despotism can be taken pure, and without the base alloy of hypocrisy.

By May, 1856, the tide of public opinion in the North was moving so swiftly that Lincoln could no longer postpone his decision as to where he stood politically. A county convention of the Republican party was scheduled to be held in Springfield on May 24 to elect delegates for the state convention. Herndon signed Lincoln's name to the list of men making the call for the convention. When Lincoln's more conservative friends protested, Herndon telegraphed his partner, asking for his sanction. Lincoln wired back: "All right; go ahead. Will meet you—radicals and all." He was elected as a delegate to the state convention.

The die was cast. Lincoln had finally made up his mind to stand or fall with the new party. On May 29, the state convention was held at Bloomington, and there Lincoln went with many others who were still not sure just what attitude the new party would adopt. Democrats, who had revolted from their party because of Douglas's support of the Kansas-Nebraska Act; Whigs, who were desperately trying to find some raft of safety to which they could swim in the troubled sea in which their own party was rapidly sinking; abolitionists, who saw in the new party some hope for a strong political movement to which they could attach themselves—all came to Bloomington to see what would happen there. Curiously enough, the word "Republican" was never used at the convention. The term had been seized upon by the Democrats and branded with the curse of abolitionist radicalism; "black Republican" was already an epithet; and many men who were willing to oppose the Nebraska Act were still not ready to identify themselves with outspoken abolitionism. There was a good deal of pussyfooting on all sides. Everybody was trying to sound out everybody else's sentiments without revealing his own.

Lincoln could be of great importance to the new party. As a leading Whig he could knit together the strong body of conservative sentiment in the state. He was known, liked and respected throughout Illinois. He stood firmly on middle ground, so he would frighten no one by his views. He was opposed to slavery, sympathetic to the Free State cause but he had not been rashly outspoken about the struggle in Kansas. He could do a great deal for the new party. It was not yet suspected how much the new party could do for him.

Before Lincoln entered the convention hall, he made a purchase that carries with it a poignant personal significance. He visited a jewelry store and bought his first pair of spectacles. He paid thirty-seven and a half cents for them, and they were fitted to his eyes by the old-fashioned method of trying on all kinds until he found a pair that seemed to be right. His eyes had begun to fail; long study of books and legal documents had impaired the far-seeing range of vision that had been his during his youth on the wide prairie—and he was forty-seven years old.

Speeches at the convention were filled with references to Kansas and the assault on Sumner in the Senate Chamber. Men who had fought in Kansas were at Bloomington to relate their experiences to the delegates. Emotion ran high, yet it was essential for political reasons to hold the convention to a middle course. Lincoln played an active part in this. He guided the meeting through dangerous channels and kept public declarations of policy reasonably mild. He was called upon, too, to perform one very necessary duty. Someone had to address the convention who could rouse enough enthusiasm among the delegates to make them feel that they were joining a fighting party, but he had, at the same time, to do this in such a way that the more conservative element would not be antagonized. Unity had to be brought out of the warring elements present; agreement had to be established on those common points on which all could agree.

Lincoln was called upon to speak. His effort was probably the greatest achievement in oratory that he had yet made. He spoke on Kansas, denouncing what had taken place there; he pleaded for the restoration of the Missouri Compromise which had been repealed by the Nebraska Act; and he warned the South: "We won't go out of the Union and you shan't!" He ended on a plea for tolerance though, saying that "moderation and forbearance will stand us in good stead, when, if ever, we must make an appeal to battle and to the God of Hosts!" With this prophetic closing he sat down to a round of tremendous applause. Herndon said that on this day Lincoln was "seven feet high." His friends told Lincoln that the speech was the greatest in his career and that it would make him President. There is, in fact, good reason to believe that Lincoln's definite Presidential ambitions dated from this occasion.

The words of the great speech, however, were lost to posterity. No record was made as Lincoln spoke, nor did he ever write out the speech afterward. Various reasons have been given for not recording it. One was that the reporters present became so excited and moved by what Lincoln said that they simply forgot to put down his words. Another was that Lincoln, speaking extemporaneously on this occasion where he had to commit himself to statements that he might not want held against him later, persuaded the reporters not to publish it. At any rate, the words were forever lost. H. C. Whitney, who was present that day, attempted to reproduce the speech from memory forty years later. Whitney's record may be reasonably accurate as to content, but the words he reports are certainly not like Lincoln's; he never spoke in florid oratorical manner attributed to him in Whitney's reproduction of the famous "Lost Speech."*

Lincoln had made his mark at the Bloomington Convention, and it had made its mark on him. He was now publicly committed to the principles of the Republican party (whether it was called by that name or not). Actually, he had had very little choice in the matter—there was no other party to which a man of his beliefs could honorably turn. The old Whig party had become so moribund that it could not find a candidate for the next election; it had to adopt the Know-Nothing nominee, Millard Fillmore. Whigs and Know-Nothings combined were then able to carry only one state (Maryland).

The National Republican Convention was held in Philadelphia, on June 19, 1856. John C. Frémont was quickly chosen as its Presidential nominee, but in the ensuing scramble

---

* Whitney's version can be found in full in the appendix to Ida M. Tarbell's *The Life of Abraham Lincoln*, New York, 1900.

for the Vice-Presidential nomination, a new and significant
political move took place. Friends of Abraham Lincoln presented his name to the convention and succeeded in getting
one hundred and ten votes for him, although they were unable
to obtain the nomination. It was given finally to William L.
Dayton, Senator from New Jersey. The move to nominate
him was a complete surprise to Lincoln. When he first heard
of it, he thought some other man by the name of Lincoln was
meant. There was a well known family of Lincolns in New
England. It might be one of them, he said.

The publicity Lincoln received at the Philadelphia Convention made him better known in Eastern political circles.
It was to be useful at the next Republican convention in
1860.

THE ELECTION OF JAMES BUCHANAN

The bright hopes of the Republican party for winning the
election of 1856 were dashed to the ground as soon as the
returns came in. The Democratic candidate, James Buchanan,
received 1,838,000 popular votes and 174 electoral votes.
Frémont received 1,341,000 popular votes and 114 electoral
votes. More significant, however, than the number of votes
for each candidate is an examination of where they came from.
Buchanan, and even Fillmore, received a respectable number
of votes in every one of the thirty-one states of the Union.
Frémont did not receive a single vote in the states of Alabama, Arkansas, Florida, Georgia, Louisiana, Mississippi, Missouri, North Carolina, South Carolina, Tennessee and Texas.
His total vote in the four Southern states that permitted him
to be listed on the ballot (Delaware, Maryland, Kentucky
and Virginia) was 1,194. It seemed that the solid South had
such a strong hold on the elective powers of the nation that
it would be forever impossible to elect a Republican President.

The newly elected President, James Buchanan, had been
selected by the Democrats as their nominee because he was a

safe man on the slavery issue who came from a Northern state (Pennsylvania) with twenty-seven electoral votes. He had already demonstrated his devotion to the slaveowners' interests. When he had been Minister to England he had distinguished himself by sponsoring one of the most shameless declarations of imperialistic foreign policy that ever disgraced the history of the United States. This was the infamous Ostend Manifesto, which was an ultimatum to Spain, stating that if she would not agree to sell Cuba to the United States to be used as additional slave territory, the island would be taken by force. Few Presidents have had the verdict of history so unanimously directed against them as has James Buchanan. He was a weak man, an old man, tired, lacking in energy, ideas and administrative ability. That he should have been elected to the Presidency of the United States at this critical moment was a disaster for the whole nation.

In his inaugural address he made two serious errors, one of which damned him for his own time, and the other for all time afterward. He said incautiously that he did not stand for re-election, that he was not interested in a second term. This immediately rendered him useless as a political leader for his party. The implications in his other statement are more serious. After making the usual tributes to popular self-government, the new President went on to remark how fortunate it was that Congress had seen fit to use the same method of popular choice in establishing the status of slavery in the territories. Popular sovereignty was the rule of the day and it would solve all problems—even the difficult one of Kansas. As to whether the problem was to be solved when Kansas was admitted as a state or while it was still a territory was, he said, "of but little practical importance. Besides, it is a judicial question which legitimately belongs to the Supreme Court of the United States before whom it is now pending, and will, it is understood, be speedily and finally settled. To their decision, in common with all good citizens, I shall cheerfully submit, whatever this may be."

This was, on the face of it, a reasonable enough statement. It referred to a case then before the Court, the case of Dred Scott, Negro slave vs. John F. A. Sanford, his legal owner, in a suit for the freedom of the slave in question. But those who had little reason to trust Buchanan in matters regarding slavery wondered why he was so willing to submit "cheerfully" to the Court's decision, unless, of course, he already knew that the Court would uphold the slave status of Dred Scott. The Chicago Times had predicted several months before that the decision would go against the poor Negro whose name has become famous in the legal annals of our country. And go against him it did, only two days later, when Chief Justice Roger B. Tancy read the decision that made every Negro in the United States ineligible for Federal citizenship, and held that the Missouri Compromise had been unconstitutional from its very inception. Buchanan had evidently been informed of what the decision would be or he would not have been willing to submit to it so "cheerfully." (Later it came out that one of the justices had told him beforehand just how the Court stood.)

This decision was one more move in the series of moves that the anti-slavery men had seen made against them. In 1850, in order to make peace with slavery, they had consented to the passage of the Fugitive Slave Act; in 1854 they had seen a Congress subservient to the slave interests pass the hated Kansas-Nebraska Act; they had seen blood flow in Kansas under an administration that cynically favored the pro-slavery element there; in the election of 1856 they had seen that the Southern states would not even permit the anti-slavery candidate to be placed on the ballot, although there were certainly some people in the South who were opposed to slavery. The South had an iron hand on the government of the whole country. It elected Northern men as Presidents when they would favor its cause. It controlled the Senate absolutely, and even the House when necessity demanded. Now, with the Dred Scott decision, the South had apparently taken over the third and last branch of the government—the judiciary. Its victory was complete.

Charges of conspiracy were immediately made in the North about the decision and the way it had been handled. Five of the nine judges were of Southern origin; two of the Northern judges had dissented from the majority opinion. The power of the slaveholders had reached even into the Supreme Court of the United States—the one body that was popularly supposed to be above suspicion, influence or prejudice—and had dictated a legal opinion of sweeping importance.

Northern resentment again burned high. There was now as much talk of secession in the North as there had formerly been in the South. The abolitionists openly preached separation—slaveowners, they said, would hold to no compact, therefore it was necessary to cut loose from them so the North could build a new nation, free from all taint of slavery and having no compromise with it anywhere within its borders.

In the midst of all this controversy Douglas came to Springfield. Because of his eminent position with the Democratic party, he was asked to speak on Kansas and the Dred Scott decision. On June 12, 1857, he addressed a large audience assembled in the Hall of Representatives. He astutely tried to turn the Court's decision to his own benefit. He said that the fact that the Dred Scott decision had removed the question of slavery in the territories from the jurisdiction of the Congress simply indicated that resistance to the Nebraska Act was useless. Popular sovereignty was in the ascendancy—it was, indeed, the only way in which the status of slavery could be settled in any section. His doctrine of popular sovereignty was the one cure for all evils. The country was indeed fortunate that it had been devised.

Douglas hammered this point home. He went on to say, too,

that peace had come at last to bleeding Kansas. Things were quiet there, and popular sovereignty would now solve the problem of Kansas' status. Slavery could exist in any section only by the will of the people who lived there, since only they could make the necessary laws to support it. If Kansas—or any other section—did not want slavery, it was obvious that slavery could not be forced upon it. As to the Dred Scott decision, it was simply the duty of every citizen to abide by the law laid down by the highest tribunal of the land, otherwise the free institutions that had made America great could no longer exist. He attacked the principle of Negro equality that the Republicans were supporting. If Negro equality were to be carried out literally, he said, it would mean that every slave in the country must be freed, that Negroes could vote, hold office, and intermarry with the whites. Was Illinois willing to accept such a doctrine? Certainly, he insinuated, the Republicans would bring these things about if they got into power.

Lincoln was seated in the audience listening to Douglas and making notes on what he said. On June 26, he made his reply, speaking in the same place, but to a much smaller audience, for Stephen A. Douglas was then a very important man and Abraham Lincoln was not.

THE FATE OF A NATION IS DECIDED IN KANSAS

Lincoln's speech was a good one—one that adequately answered Douglas's charges in a temperate and logical manner. But the two weeks that had passed since Douglas had spoken had already made a difference in the situation. Things in Kansas were not going as well under Douglas's doctrine of popular sovereignty as its sponsor had predicted they would. The new turn in events had only begun when Lincoln spoke, but it was to make his well-reasoned arguments unnecessary —the whole course of history was moving against Douglas, and the doctrine of popular sovereignty that he had upheld was to break him and break the power of his party, too. The Nebraska Act was running to its logical conclusion, but the conclusion was so outrageously a perversion of justice that even Douglas himself was unable to stomach it.

A few days before Lincoln spoke, the Free State men in Kansas had refused to participate in an election of delegates for a constitutional convention. The convention, solidly composed of pro-slavery men, later met in the town of Lecompton to draft a constitution that upheld (in a non-amendable provisory clause) the right to hold slaves, prohibited free Negroes from residing in the state and pledged rigid enforcement of the Fugitive Slave Act. The people were to be given the privilege of voting for this constitution with its non-amendable slavery cause, or of voting for it without the slavery clause—in any case they must adopt the constitution as written, except for the one clause. It was quickly pointed out that the provisions covering free Negroes and fugitives were contained in the constitution itself, not in the slavery clause. The anti-slavery men protested against the trick and again refused to vote. The election was held without them, and the fraudulent constitution with its slavery clause was finally "ratified" on December 21, 1857, by a vote of 6143 to 589.

Before this one-sided election was held, the Free State men won control of the Legislature in October, putting Kansas in the curious position of having a free-state government and a pro-slavery constitutional convention both at work trying to defeat each other. The Lecompton constitution, however, was denounced even by the pro-slavery Territorial Governor, Robert J. Walker. Nevertheless, it obtained the tacit approval of the Buchanan administration.

Governor Walker resigned in disgust. Early in 1858, the free-state Legislature in Kansas resubmitted the constitution to a vote by the people with the additional provision that the whole constitution could be refused. It was—by a vote of 10,226 to 138. Yet even after this firm rejection by people who

were obviously determined to make Kansas a free state,
Buchanan persisted in his efforts to have the Lecompton constitution adopted. An amendment offering a large grant of
public lands was added, and the constitution was again put
to vote. Acceptance meant that Kansas would be made a
state; rejection meant that statehood would be deferred until
the Territory had a much larger population. Again the people
of Kansas rejected the constitution—and the free-land bribe.
On August 2, 1858, the vote against the Lecompton constitution ran 11,300 against to 1788 for accepting. Kansas remained
a Territory and kept her honor. She was not brought into the
Union until January, 1861, when she entered as a free state
into a country that was then on the verge of civil war.

In November, 1857, Douglas went to Washington to protest to Buchanan that his plan of popular sovereignty was
being used to cover an enormous fraud. Buchanan insisted
that the Lecompton constitution stand as written. Douglas
broke with him at once. Buchanan fumed and threatened, but
Douglas, who was an infinitely more powerful political figure
than the pompous old hack in the White House, laughed at
his threats and said that he would take the whole matter to
the public.

On December 9, 1857, Douglas spoke in the Senate and he
minced no words. He aptly compared the choice given under
the Lecompton constitution to a Napoleonic election, in
which Napoleon was supposed to have promised his soldiers
that they could vote as freely as they pleased, but that if they
voted against him they would be shot. Douglas also revealed
what was behind the peculiar manner of presenting the
Lecompton constitution to the people. "I have asked a very
large number of the gentlemen who framed the constitution,"
he said, "quite a number of the delegates, and a still larger
number of persons who are their friends, and I have received
the same answer from every one of them. . . . They say that
if they allowed a negative vote, the constitution would have

been voted down by an overwhelming majority, and hence the fellows shall not be allowed to vote at all."

Thus the slaveholders' methods were exposed by a man who had always been friendly to the South. It was made evident to the nation that the South had overreached herself in her desire to bring Kansas into the Union as a slave state by fair means or foul. But in his break with Buchanan, Douglas had broken with the Democratic party. He had deviated from the party line, and the party line, good or bad, honorable or dishonorable, had to be followed by a politician who wished to stay in the party. Douglas was made the butt of political vengeance; lesser men crept forward, eager to dethrone the "Little Giant." Douglas, however, still considered himself a Democrat. He had differed with the President and with the party on a matter in which his moral scruples were involved. His duty now was to make the party come over to his way of seeing things. Certainly there were many men who would follow his lead rather than Buchanan's, or, for that fact, anybody else's. He was not alone in his belief that the Lecompton matter was unfair and unjustified. Plenty of Democrats in the South as well as in the North agreed with him. They would form the nucleus of his following; others, perhaps, could be won over by the inherent justice of his cause.

So Stephen A. Douglas, late in 1857, broke away from his party as Theodore Roosevelt was later to do in his Bull Moose campaign in 1912—and with as little success politically. The combined effect of Douglas's revolt and growing sectional differences was to sweep the Democratic party out of power for twenty-four years. It is absurd, however, to suppose that if Douglas had remained meekly within the party fold, the South could have continued in its dominant position. The strength of the North was increasing too rapidly to be held in check by any more political maneuvers the South might devise. Another state was added to the Union in 1858—Minnesota, a free state. Population and wealth were predomi-

nantly in the North; the North had to control the national
Government in order to safeguard its vast interests. The Civil
War had to come—only bloody conflict could wipe out a
South grimly determined to hold on to her waning political
power while the bigger, richer North was equally grim in its
determination to break that hold. The real history of the
period was being written in drafting rooms, machine shops,
banks and brokers' offices. The speeches in Congress, the outdoor debates and all the other political gestures with which
Douglas was so familiar were merely shadow play that con-
cealed the more important, more earnest and more deadly
struggle going on underneath.

What Douglas did only accelerated the coming conflict.
Had he stayed with the Democratic party it might, perhaps,
have elected one more President;* it might have been successful in holding power for the South for four years more—
then we would have dated our Civil War as beginning in
1864, and our war President would almost surely not have
been Abraham Lincoln.

"A HOUSE DIVIDED"

Events took shape rapidly from this time on, with Douglas
and Lincoln pitted against each other in a campaign that
grew in two years from a local contest for the Senatorship of
Illinois to a national battle for the Presidency. At the Illinois
Republican State Convention held in Springfield on June 16,
1858, a resolution was unanimously adopted that read: "Resolved that Abraham Lincoln is the first and only choice of
the Republicans of Illinois for the United States Senate, as the
successor of Stephen A. Douglas."

And then, on that night, Lincoln made one of the very
finest speeches of his career, a speech that clearly defined the
issues before the country, hinted at conspiracy in the political

* Even this is doubtful, as an analysis of the Lincoln electoral votes in
1860 will show.

maneuvers of the slaveholders and presented in plain language the charge that Douglas was not to be considered as a possible ally for the anti-slavery forces. In characteristic fashion, and in the matured style that had by this time come to mark Lincoln's utterances, he began:

If we could first know where we are, and whither we are tending, we could better judge what to do, and how to do it. We are now far into the fifth year since a policy was initiated with the avowed object and confident promise of putting an end to slavery agitation. Under the operation of that policy, that agitation has not only not ceased but has constantly augmented. In my opinion, it will not cease until a crisis shall have been reached and passed. "A house divided against itself cannot stand." I believe this government cannot endure permanently half slave and half free. I do not expect the Union to be dissolved—I do not expect the house to fall—but I do expect it will cease to be divided. It will become all one thing, or all the other. Either the opponents of slavery will arrest the further spread of it, and place it where the public mind shall rest in the belief that it is in the course of ultimate extinction; or its advocates will push it forward till it shall become alike lawful in all the states, old as well as new, North as well as South.

These prophetic words were to be the keynote of the Lincoln-Douglas campaign. They run through the speeches of the next two years again and again, and Douglas was to quote them as often as Lincoln did, using them against his opponent on the charge that the prophecy was an incitement to dissension and civil war.

Douglas left Washington and returned to Illinois to begin his senatorial campaign. This time he was received everywhere in triumph—in strange contrast to his reception four years before when he had just engineered the Kansas-Nebraska Act through Congress. He spoke in Chicago on July 9 from the balcony of the Tremont House. Lincoln came up from Springfield to hear what his opponent had to say and sat behind Douglas, industriously taking down notes of his words.

Douglas, who had already declared in the Senate that he did not care whether slavery was voted up or voted down, made clear that he was opposing the Lecompton constitution, not because of slavery, but because it ran counter to the will of the people. He referred kindly to his opponent, and then sharply attacked his "House Divided" speech, saying that what Lincoln had predicted would require absolute regimentation throughout the country if it were to come to pass. Local laws would have to be the same everywhere once the differences in state laws regarding slavery were abolished. The original intentions of the founders of the nation, who had specified that each state should be sovereign over its own internal affairs, would be ignored. "Uniformity is the parent of despotism the world over," said Douglas, cheerfully distorting Lincoln's argument, ". . . then Negroes will vote nowhere or everywhere; then you will have a Maine liquor law in every state or none; then you will have uniformity in all things local and domestic by the authority of the Federal Government. But when you attain that uniformity you will have converted these thirty-two sovereign, independent states into one consolidated empire, with the uniformity of despotism reigning triumphant throughout the length and breadth of the land."

Lincoln's stand on the Dred Scott decision, he said, was wholly unjustified. The Constitutional guarantee of equality of privilege among the citizens of all the states applied only to white citizens; Negroes had no such guarantee, and the Supreme Court of the United States had just ruled that they were not citizens at all. "This Government is founded on the white basis," Douglas said. "It was made by the white man, for the white man, to be administered by white men. . . . I am opposed to Negro equality. Preserve the purity of our Government as well as the purity of our race; no amalgamation, political or otherwise, with inferior races!" Douglas used this point of white supremacy many times during the campaign. In Lower Illinois, where the people were almost wholly of Southern origin, he emphasized it with devastating effect upon his opponent.

Lincoln spoke the next night at the same place before an audience even more enthusiastic than the one that had listened to Douglas. Lincoln's speech was by no means one of his best, but in his reply to Douglas's stand on racial inferiority he came out with a declaration that is as valid today as when he spoke the words more than three-quarters of a century ago:

Now I ask you, in all soberness, if all these things, if indulged in, if ratified, if confirmed and indorsed, if taught to our children, and repeated to them, do not tend to rub out the sentiment of liberty in the country, and to transform this government into a government of some other form? Those arguments that are made, that the inferior race are to be treated with as much allowance as they are capable of enjoying; that as much is to be done for them as their condition will allow—what are these arguments? They are the arguments that kings have made for enslaving the people in all ages of the world. You will find that all the arguments in favor of kingcraft were of this class; they always bestrode the necks of the people—not that they wanted to do it, but because the people were better off for being ridden. That is their argument, and this argument of the judge is the same old serpent that says, "You work and I eat, you toil and I will enjoy the fruits of it." Turn in whatever way you will—whether it come from the mouth of a king, as an excuse for enslaving the people of his country, or from the mouth of men of one race as a reason for enslaving the men of another race, it is all the same old serpent, and I hold if that course of argumentation that is made for the purpose of convincing the public mind that we should not care about this should be granted, it does not stop with the Negro. I should like to know— taking this old Declaration of Independence, which declares that all men are equal upon principle, and making exceptions to it— where will it stop? If one man says it does not mean a Negro, why not another say it does not mean some other man?

He was to use this statement only a few months later, during his last debate with Douglas at Alton, Illinois. By that time the words had undergone a process of transmutation in the creative furnace of Lincoln's mind. The words had been purified of dross, put together with artistry into a brief statement that has the emotional appeal of great literature. It is interesting to note the transformation:

That is the real issue. That is the issue that will continue in this country when these poor tongues of Judge Douglas and myself shall be silent. It is the eternal struggle between these two principles—right and wrong—throughout the world. They are the two principles that have stood face to face from the beginning of time; and will ever continue to struggle. The one is the common right of humanity, and the other the divine right of kings. It is the same principle in whatever shape it develops itself. It is the same spirit that says, "You toil and work and earn bread, and I'll eat it." No matter in what shape it comes, whether from the mouth of a king who seeks to bestride the people of his own nation and live by the fruit of their labor, or from one race of men as an apology for enslaving another race, it is the same tyrannical principle.

Lincoln had been a long time maturing; his mind worked slowly in all things, turning over and digesting the material on which it worked, but never ceasing to wrestle with the problem that absorbed him. He grew slowly but he never stopped growing. His power over words became greater each day. His speeches from this time on show not only growth in ideational content but growth in phraseology, in word power, style. The Lincoln of the Second Inaugural and the Gettysburg Address was now in the throes of birth.

The political rival who was to make Lincoln great, not through friendship but through enmity, went on from Chicago to speak at Bloomington, and then at Springfield. Lincoln followed him, speaking after Douglas in Springfield, on July 17, 1858, where he renewed his charges of conspiracy, and made his first reference to himself in regard to the Presidency—although in a purely negative and self-deprecatory way. After pointing out that the Democrats benefited by having Douglas as their candidate because he was a person of great renown who might some day very well become President and hand out political patronage, he said: "Nobody has ever expected me to be President. In my poor, lean, lank face nobody has ever seen that any cabbages were sprouting out. These are disadvantages . . . that the Republicans labor under."

THE LINCOLN-DOUGLAS DEBATES

The campaign rapidly grew more bitterly partisan. The old Mexican War charges against Lincoln were hauled out, and he was again accused of having voted to prevent the army from getting supplies; the "Spot" resolutions he had made in Congress ten years previously were used to ridicule him; and the Democratic press in Illinois did its best to play Lincoln down and Douglas up, while the Republican press, of course, waged an equally vitriolic counter-attack. The Republicans were dissatisfied with the way their candidate had been trailing Douglas, speaking only after he had spoken. They urged that a joint debate be held so the candidates could both have a chance to address the same crowd. Lincoln sent a letter of challenge to Douglas, and Douglas was forced into a position where he had to accept, although he knew perfectly well that he had nothing to win and everything to lose by such an encounter. The debates would make Lincoln well known, whereas Douglas was already so famous that he needed no additional publicity; if Lincoln were to win it would be a great victory for him, but if Douglas won he would simply be eliminating a competitor who was of slight importance. Douglas foresaw and feared the results of such a campaign, and he was quite correct in his forecast—the debates made Lincoln, and in making him they broke Douglas, even though he won the Senatorial race which served as an excuse for holding the debates. Lincoln was out for bigger game. He saw the coming split in the Democratic party, astutely realized that it would give him his chance, and—if he could in some way obtain the Republican nomination in 1860—he would have a heaven-sent opportunity to become President of the United States.

Much against his better judgment Douglas accepted Lincoln's challenge. He was given the privilege of setting the time and place for the seven joint debates that were to be held. These were decided upon by Douglas as follows: Ottawa, August 21; Freeport, August 27; Jonesboro, September 15; Charleston, September 18; Galesburg, October 7; Quincy, October 13; and Alton, October 15.

All seven places were small towns; the largest of them, Quincy, had a population of not much more than 10,000. All the towns were relatively new. Most of them had been settled within the memory of living men. And their citizens were American to the core, American with the peculiar native passion for independence and individuality that distinguished the small-town dweller in the first half of the nineteenth century. Freeport was in the northern part of the state, north of Chicago; Jonesboro was in the extreme south, down in "Egypt," where the people were Southern by ancestry and tradition. But north or south, all these towns were alike in one thing—their passionate interest in politics. The debates were not simply one-day shows—they were important events to be talked about before they happened and then discussed long afterward, with endless elaboration of the points made by the speakers, and with great argument as to whether the "Tall Sucker" or the "Little Giant" was the better man.

Douglas traveled in a private railroad car, accompanied by friends and advisers as well as by the beautiful Mrs. Douglas who did yeomanlike service in winning over the ladies of each town to her husband's cause. Women could not vote, but they were an important influence in politics, and Douglas was clever enough not to ignore them. Mrs. Lincoln stayed at home; she heard her husband speak only once—at the final debate at Alton.

Douglas's train carried a flatcar on which a brass cannon was mounted. The cannon was fired at every stop; brass bands played; people cheered; influential citizens came to greet the celebrated Senator at the railroad station. Lincoln traveled modestly as an ordinary passenger on the regular trains. In towns where the Republicans were strong he was received with as much enthusiasm and fanfare as Douglas. Certainly he never lacked audience support. Even in the extreme south of the state there were some men who came to cheer for Lincoln, even though this expression of approval met with their neighbors' scorn.

Lincoln's stage presence on the speaker's platform has been recorded for us by Herndon who caught his partner to the life in his description of Lincoln during the debates:

When standing erect he was six feet four inches high. He was lean in flesh and ungainly in figure. Aside from the sad, pained look due to habitual melancholy, his face had no characteristic or fixed expression. He was thin through the chest, and hence slightly stoop-shouldered. When he arose . . . his body inclined forward to a slight degree. At first he was very awkward, and it seemed a real labor to adjust himself to his surroundings. He struggled for a time under a feeling of apparent diffidence and sensitiveness, and these only added to his awkwardness. . . . When he began speaking, his voice was shrill, piping, and unpleasant. His manner, his attitude, his dark, yellow face, wrinkled and dry, his oddity of pose, his diffident movements—everything seemed to be against him, but only for a short time. After having arisen, he generally placed his hands behind him, the back of his left hand in the palm of his right, the thumb and fingers of his right hand clasped around the left arm at the wrist. For a few moments he displayed the combination of awkwardness, sensitiveness, and diffidence. As he proceeded he became somewhat animated, and to keep in harmony with his growing warmth his hands relaxed their grasp and fell to his side. Presently he clasped them in front of him, interlocking his fingers, one thumb meanwhile chasing another. His speech now requiring more emphatic utterance, his fingers unlocked and his hands fell apart. His left arm was thrown behind, the back of his hand resting against his body, his right hand seeking his side. By this time he had gained sufficient composure, and his real speech began. He did not gesticulate as much with his hands as with his head. He used the latter frequently, throwing it with vim this way and that. This movement was a significant one when he sought to enforce his statement. It sometimes came with a quick jerk, as if throwing off electric sparks into combustible material. He never sawed the air nor rent space into tatters and rags as some orators do. He never acted for stage effect. He was cool, considerate, reflective—in time self-possessed and self-reliant. His style was clear, terse, and compact. In argument he was logical, demonstrative, and fair.

He was careless of his dress, and his clothes, instead of fitting neatly as did the garments of Douglas on the latter's well-rounded form, hung loosely on his giant frame. As he moved along in his speech he became freer and less uneasy in his movements; to that extent he was graceful. He had a perfect naturalness, a strong individuality; and to that extent he was dignified. He despised glitter, show, set forms, and shams. He spoke with effectiveness and to move the judgment as well as the emotions of men. There was a world of meaning and emphasis in the long, bony finger of his right hand as he dotted the ideas on the minds of his hearers. Sometimes, to express joy or pleasure, he would raise both hands at an angle of about fifty degrees, the palms upward, as if desirous of embracing the spirit of that which he loved. If the sentiment was one of detestation—denunciation of slavery, for example—both arms, thrown upward and fists clenched, swept through the air, and he expressed an execration that was truly sublime. This was one of his most effective gestures, and signified most vividly a fixed determination to drag down the object of his hatred and trample it in the dust.

He always stood squarely on his feet, toe even with toe; that is, he never put one foot before the other. He neither touched nor leaned on anything for support. He made but few changes in his positions and attitudes. He never walked backward and forward on the platform. To ease his arms he frequently caught hold, with his left hand, of the lapel of his coat, keeping his thumb upright and leaving his right hand free to gesticulate. . . .

As he proceeded with his speech the exercise of his vocal organs altered somewhat the tone of his voice. It lost in a measure its former acute and shrilling pitch, and mellowed into a more harmonious and pleasant sound. His form expanded, and, notwithstanding the sunken breast, he rose up a splendid and imposing figure. . . . His little gray eyes flashed in a face aglow with the fire of his profound thoughts; and his uneasy movements and diffident manner sunk themselves beneath the wave of righteous indignation that came sweeping over him. Such was Lincoln the orator.

The first debate took place at Ottawa on August 21; the other six followed at intervals until mid-October. Summer slowly turned into autumn; leaves drifted down from the oaks and walnuts of the prairie groves; crowds that had come in shirt-sleeves came in coats and shawls. History was being made in Illinois and the crowds sensed dimly what was happening. They saw Abraham Lincoln and they saw Stephen A. Douglas. Then they went home convinced that they had seen at least one great man.

The actual content of the debates is disappointing when first read in the full stenographic reports that were taken of every word spoken. There are many arid passages, and worst of all, both speakers repeat themselves again and again. It may almost be said that each speaker had one standard argument for which the other had one standard reply.*

The high point in strategy was achieved by Lincoln during the second debate at Freeport. Douglas had presented a set of questions for Lincoln to answer; Lincoln prepared a set for Douglas, the second one of which was:

* It is for this reason that the material reproduced from the debates reprinted in this volume has been carefully chosen to give Lincoln's most representative arguments and to avoid repetition as far as possible. The last debate, at Alton, which best summarizes Lincoln's position, is given nearly in full.

Can the people of a United States territory, in any lawful way, against the wish of any citizen of the United States, exclude slavery from its limits prior to the formation of a state constitution?

This was, of course, a very ticklish question for Douglas. If he answered in one way, he would lose the support of his own Illinois constituents and the race for the Senatorship; if he answered in another way he was sure to lose the support of the South.

Lincoln had already correctly forecast what Douglas's answer would be. In a letter to a friend, Henry Asbury, dated July 31, he had said:

The points you propose to press upon Douglas he will be very hard to get up to, but I think you labor under a mistake when you say no one cares how he answers. This implies that it is equal with him whether he is injured here or at the South. That is a mistake. He cares nothing for the South; he knows he is already dead there. He only leans Southward more to keep the Buchanan party from growing in Illinois. You shall have hard work to get him directly to the point whether a territorial legislature has or has not the power to exclude slavery. But if you succeed in bringing him to it —though he will be compelled to say it possesses no such power— he will instantly take ground that slavery cannot actually exist in the territories unless the people desire it, and so give it protection by territorial legislation. If this offends the South, he will let it offend them, as at all events he means to hold on to his chances in Illinois.

Douglas made the inevitable answer; his split with the Buchanan administration was widened still farther; he won the Illinois election and lost the Presidency in 1860, when Southerners flocked to his rival Breckinridge.

On October 15, the great debates came to a close at Alton, where the two candidates spoke in the public square overlooking the Mississippi River. Douglas had the final word, speaking in rejoinder to Lincoln, and when he had finished making an appeal to the voters to stand by old traditions, to avoid agitators and to let everything remain as it had always been, the campaign was over. Lincoln returned to Springfield, poor in pocket, and forced to concentrate his energy on his law practice which he had neglected for nearly six months. Everybody waited for the election that was to be held on November 2.

Election day was cold and rainy; Lincoln's heart sank as the returns came in. The Republicans gained in power and prestige, but the Democrats still held control in both Houses of the State Legislature, making Douglas's election practically certain.

Lincoln was disappointed. He had been willing to jeopardize his chance of winning when he had made Douglas commit himself at Freeport, but he still hoped that he might somehow win the Senatorship. Had he obtained it, it would have advanced his strategic position; it was an important post—one in which he might have made a name for himself during the two years before the 1860 Presidential election would be held. He was disappointed but determined not to give up the struggle. Two weeks later he wrote a revealing letter to his friend, Henry Asbury:

The fight must go on. The cause of civil liberty must not be surrendered at the end of one or even one hundred defeats. Douglas had the ingenuity to be supported in the late contest both as the best means to break down and to uphold the slave interest. No ingenuity can keep these antagonistic elements in harmony long. Another explosion will soon come.

The explosion predicted by Lincoln was purely a political one. A more important and devastating one had been forecast by another great political leader, William H. Seward. Speaking at Rochester, New York, on October 25, ten days after the end of the Lincoln-Douglas debates, Seward gave the coming struggle for power a name that was to stick to it. After drawing a comparison between the systems of free labor and slave labor, he said that their mutual antagonism was not "accidental, unnecessary, the work of interested or fanatical agitators and therefore ephemeral. . . . *It is an irrepressible conflict* between opposing and enduring forces. . . ."

The man who was to be the Northern President during this irrepressible conflict again had to return to his old life, riding the circuit, pleading law cases in country courts and staying at nights in small-town inns and taverns where he was still one of the boys. The next year—1859—was not one of outstanding achievement for him although he was called upon to speak several times at places outside the state.* He also made several unsuccessful attempts at non-political lecturing, but mostly he just waited with that vast patience that was his. He studied the situation as it developed, and he studied it until he was able to analyze its hidden meanings and so deduce its probable tendency and drift.

The year 1859 was a year of desperate measures on the part of individuals North and South. These individuals did not have the official approval of the communities they represented, but they expressed in action the most advanced ideas that were taking form in the two opposing camps. A few bold men in the South attempted to revive the slave trade from Africa, bringing back upon the high seas the horrors of the Middle Passage that had been outlawed for fifty years. One bold man in the North declared a private war on the slaveholders and took up arms against them in an insurrectionary attempt to seize the Federal arsenal at Harper's Ferry in order to arm the slaves.

Sporadic attempts to run slaves from Africa to the United States had been made for years, but the severity of the law and the vigilance of the navy had discouraged the trade from becoming general. Slave prices were on the rise in the South during the fifties; prime field hands had risen to the all-time

---

* In Iowa, Ohio, Indiana, Wisconsin and Kansas. Many of these speeches are devoted to a discussion of the value and importance of free labor.

high of $1500 to $2000 a head. Slaves were scarce and more slaves were needed. The very system was one that rapidly exhausted the soil and the men who worked it, consequently a fresh supply of both was continually needed. The demand for new soil gave rise to the territorial expansion program of the South; the demand for slaves gave rise to attempts to smuggle them into the country and to a movement to make the trade legitimate by repealing slave trade laws. At the Southern Convention held at Vicksburg in May 1859, a vote of 40 to 19 was cast in favor of a resolution recommending the repeal of all laws restricting the African slave trade. Slave ships were actually fitted out and put into service. The profits in the forbidden trade were enormous, since Negroes could be purchased on the African coast for $50 a head and sold in America for $500, even under the surreptitious conditions of sale made necessary by their illegal entry. Unscrupulous promoters—Northern as well as Southern—were willing to risk their capital for such tremendous possibilities of increase; ship's officers and sailors were ready to make a voyage that paid them many times more than any regular trading venture could. Death was the penalty for engaging in the slave trade*—the old piracy laws had been extended to cover it—but ships were bought, and men willing to sail them could be hired.

Douglas, who was emphatically opposed to reviving the odious trade and who was in a position to be kept informed of its progress, once said that 15,000 Negroes had been brought into the country in 1859—a figure greater than that of any year during the period when the traffic had still been legal. Douglas also said that if the Democrats made the

* One of the few men condemned to death whom Lincoln did not pardon during his Presidency was Captain Nathaniel Gordon, convicted slave runner whose ship had been taken with 600 child slaves on board. Lincoln postponed his execution for two weeks in order to give him time to prepare himself for death, but resolutely insisted that the sentence be carried out. Gordon was hanged in New York on February 21, 1862.

re-opening of the slave trade a principle in their party platform he would decline their nomination for the Presidency in the 1860 campaign.

The revival of the African slave trade was kept relatively quiet—so quiet in fact that its importance is sometimes overlooked in historical discussions of the events leading to the Civil War. Nevertheless, it was a move on the part of the South almost as desperate as the single-handed gesture made by John Brown at Harper's Ferry.

BLOOD AND IRON AT HARPER'S FERRY

John Brown's attempt was not so foolhardly as many have liked to believe. Fugitive slaves from the South had for years been taking refuge in Canada; they were a picked lot of men who had had the courage to break away from their masters and make the long difficult journey north. Brown was in touch with some of them and he had planned for them to come to Virginia to assist him as soon as he had captured the arsenal. He expected, too, that the slaves in the South would rise in one great insurrectionary movement to overthrow their masters. Slave revolts had been numerous in the South—more numerous than written history records, for they were put down with an iron hand and all news of them was suppressed whenever possible in order to prevent a local insurrection from spreading by example. The South was in deadly fear of an uprising of the slaves. It was something that haunted the mind of every slaveholder, and every plantation possessed its own private arsenal to be used in case the long-dreaded revolt ever broke out.

John Brown entered Harper's Ferry during the night of October 16, 1859. With a band of only eighteen men he seized the town and stopped the trains and telegraphs. He succeeded in holding the place for one day; then a force of United States marines under command of Colonel Robert E.

Lee put down the miniature rebellion, killing ten of Brown's followers and capturing the fierce old leader.

News of the insurrection brought terror to Northern and Southern people alike. The long breeding conflict had broken out into open warfare, and the spot picked for the initial battle was near enough to both Northern and Southern centers of population to make them feel that the battle had begun on their own doorsteps. This was no distant rumbling of the drum in far-off Kansas. It was a thunderbolt let loose in the heart of the East. Harper's Ferry was only fifty-three miles from Washington and only one hundred and sixty miles from Richmond. It was a small place, but it was a railroad junction with which thousands of people were familiar, for they had seen its wild gorges as their trains had passed through, bound for the South, the North or the West.

The interrogation of Brown and the testimony brought out during his trial caused a tremendous sensation. Although John Brown resolutely refused to reveal anything that might implicate the abolitionists who had backed him, some of these men took fright and revealed their own identity by fleeing to Canada and Europe in order to get beyond reach of the American law.

Brown himself was brought to trial immediately, being taken into the courtroom while he was still on a cot recovering from his wounds. His bearing during the trial was so fearless, so completely that of a man who felt that what he had done was right and who was perfectly willing to stand the consequences, that he won admiration even from those who were bent on sending him to his death. On December 2, 1859, he was led to the gallows, and there, surrounded by troops of soldiers, he was hanged. Among the uniformed men in a volunteer regiment from Richmond was a man who was to take an active part in another historic death. He was a young actor, intensely pro-Southern in his sympathies. His name was John Wilkes Booth.

John Brown hardened public opinion in both the North and the South. The South naturally poured out its wrath on his head; the North, although divided in opinion, nevertheless began to realize that the raid carried out by the stern old rebel was part of a cause that most Northerners considered a worthy one. He had fought for freedom, and his words at the trial had made it clear that he had fought without thought of personal danger or self-interest of any kind. The example that he had set was not forgotten. His deed had made a great impression on the Northern people, and his name became their rallying cry when they finally marched to carry on the battle he had begun.

His action, however, was a source of embarrassment to the still young Republican party. The Democrats attempted to make political capital out of his deed by placing the responsibility for it on the Republicans. Some of the milder abolitionists had flocked to the Republican party, since it was the only major party that came near to representing their beliefs. The Republicans tried to shake off their unwanted friends; they used every means at their disposal to disavow any connection with abolitionism or John Brown. Their leader in Illinois went out of his way in the most important speech that he had yet made, to emphasize his belief that Brown was an irresponsible fanatic, a madman driven to murder by his madness.

During the autumn of 1859, Lincoln received an invitation to lecture at Henry Ward Beecher's Plymouth Church in Brooklyn. When Lincoln arrived in New York, he found that the place where the meeting was to be held had been changed. He was to speak at Cooper Union instead, where a large and important audience could be expected to attend. He spent the next two days feverishly polishing his words to make them worthy of the occasion, and then, on the evening of February 27, he made the great speech that was to publicize his name in the East and go a long way toward making him President.

In this address, which was mainly an answer to Douglas's charge that the men who had written the Constitution of the United States had forbidden the Federal Government to exercise any control over slavery in the territories, Lincoln took the opportunity to reply to the Democratic accusation of Republican complicity in the John Brown raid.

You charge that we stir up insurrections among your slaves. We deny it; and what is your proof? Harper's Ferry! John Brown!! John Brown was no Republican; and you have failed to implicate a single Republican in his Harper's Ferry enterprise. . . .
Some of you admit that no Republican designedly aided or encouraged the Harper's Ferry affair, but still insist that our doctrines and declarations necessarily lead to such results. We do not believe it. . . .
John Brown's effort was peculiar. It was not a slave insurrection. It was an attempt by white men to get up a revolt among slaves, in which the slaves refused to participate. . . . That affair, in its philosophy, corresponds with the many attempts, related in history, at the assassination of kings and emperors. An enthusiast broods over the oppression of a people till he fancies himself commissioned by Heaven to liberate them. He ventures the attempt, which ends in little else than his own execution. Orsini's attempt on Louis Napoleon, and John Brown's attempt at Harper's Ferry, were, in their philosophy, precisely the same.

Yet, although Lincoln denounced John Brown, he condemned without equivocation the dangerous policy adopted by the South in its fiercely conducted campaign for the defense of slavery; he referred openly to the often-repeated assertion of Southerners that they would secede from the Union if the "sectional" Republican party elected a President; and, in a bold and uncompromising conclusion he appealed to the Republicans to stand firm in the face of increasing Southern aggression.

Even though much provoked, let us do nothing through passion and ill temper. Even though the Southern people will not so much as listen to us, let us calmly consider their demands, and yield to them if, in our deliberate view of our duty, we possibly can. Judging by all they say and do, and by the subject and nature of their controversy with us, let us determine, if we can, what will satisfy them.

Will they be satisfied if the Territories be unconditionally surrendered to them? We know they will not. In all their present complaints against us, the Territories are scarcely mentioned. Invasions and insurrections are the rage now. Will it satisfy them if, in the future, we have nothing to do with invasions and insurrections? We know it will not. We so know, because we know we never had anything to do with invasions and insurrections; and yet this total abstaining does not exempt us from the charge and the denunciation.

The question recurs: What will satisfy them? Simply this: we must not only let them alone, but we must somehow convince them that we do let them alone. This, we know by experience, is no easy task. . . . What will convince them? This, and this only: cease to call slavery wrong, and join them in calling it right. And this must be done thoroughly—done in acts as well as in words. Silence will not be tolerated—we must place ourselves avowedly with them. Senator Douglas's new sedition law must be enacted and enforced, suppressing all declarations that slavery is wrong, whether made in politics, in presses, in pulpits, or in private. We must arrest and return their fugitive slaves with greedy pleasure. We must pull down our free-State constitutions. The whole atmosphere must be disinfected from all taint of opposition to slavery, before they will cease to believe that all their troubles proceed from us. . . .

Wrong as we think slavery is, we can yet afford to let it alone where it is, because that much is due to the necessity arising from its actual presence in the nation; but can we, while our votes will prevent it, allow it to spread into the national Territories, and to overrun us here in these free states? If our sense of duty forbids this, then let us stand by our duty fearlessly and effectively. Let us be diverted by none of those sophistical contrivances wherewith we are so industriously plied and belabored—contrivances such as groping for some middle ground between the right and the wrong:

vain as the search for a man who should be neither a living man nor a dead man; such as a policy of "don't care" on a question about which all true men do care; such as Union men to yield to Disunionists, reversing the divine rule, and calling, not the sinners, but the righteous to repentance; such as invocations to Washington, imploring men to unsay what Washington said and undo what Washington did.

Neither let us be slandered from our duty by false accusations against us, nor frightened from it by menaces of destruction to the government, nor of dungeons to ourselves. Let us have faith that right makes might, and in that faith let us to the end dare to do our duty as we understand it.

"Let us have faith that right makes might, and in that faith let us to the end dare to do our duty as we understand it"—strange words for a man whose whole policy hitherto had been that of "groping for some middle ground"! Circumstances were transforming men and policies; the whole course of history now takes on a greatly accelerated pace as the nation, drawn up into two irreconcilably hostile camps, moves toward the final event that was to plunge it into civil war.

This event was the election of 1860, an election that had long been anticipated with dread as the signal that was to summon the slaveholders to armed revolt if they saw the votes of the people go against them. The issues involved in this election were not simply party matters—the growing cleavage between North and South had become so great that the election cut across party lines; the South was not able to dominate even its own party, the Democratic party that had hitherto been its willing tool.

The split in the Democratic party started by Douglas flared wide open at the very beginning of the campaign, and the division immediately took on a sectional nature. The sectionalism the Democrats had been charging against the Republicans now came home to roost in their own convention. At Charleston, South Carolina, where the Democratic National Con-

vention first convened on April 23, 1860, the delegates separated over sectional differences. The Southern wing split with
the Northern Democrats who were standing for Douglas, and
withdrew from the convention to meet later at Richmond and
then at Baltimore, where they finally nominated John C.
Breckinridge of Kentucky on June 28. On June 18, Douglas
was nominated by the Northern Democrats. The chance of
electing a Democratic President was made still slimmer by the
entry of a third party into the field, the Constitutional Union-
ists, descendants of the Know-Nothings and the Whigs, who
nominated John Bell of Tennessee as their candidate.

Under such circumstances it became obvious that the man
nominated by the Republicans would stand an excellent
chance of being elected. The Republicans, in the election of
1856, had won 1,341,000 votes in the North alone, against
the 1,838,000 votes obtained by the Democrats from the whole
country. Without the Southern Democrats, Douglas could
hardly hope to be elected; without the Northern Democrats,
the South could not muster enough votes to elect Breckinridge.

THE REPUBLICANS SEEK A PRESIDENTIAL CANDIDATE

All this, however, is much clearer to us looking back at it
than it was to the sorely puzzled Republican politicians then.
The Republican National Convention was to be held at Chicago on May 16—late enough in the year for the party leaders
to be able to take the Democrats' difficulties into account, but
not late enough for them to know exactly what would happen, since the final choices of the two wings of the Democratic
party had not been made by the time that the Republican
Convention was held.

In the spring of 1860 it would doubtless have been easy to
get takers for a hundred-to-one bet against the chances of the
relatively obscure Lincoln receiving the nomination for the
Presidency. A political friend, Jesse W. Fell of Bloomington,

Illinois, had urged Lincoln to prepare a brief autobiographical sketch (on December 20, 1859) which indicated that his hat was in the ring, but very few people knew it. Late in 1859, a book entitled *Presidential Possibilities* had appeared; it listed and described twenty-one potential candidates—Lincoln's name was not among them. The men who stood out in the public mind as really likely possibilities were William H. Seward, who was the most eminent leader of the Republican party; Salmon P. Chase of Ohio, who had been U. S. Senator and Governor of Ohio and who was a noted anti-slavery advocate; Edward Bates of Missouri, distinguished lawyer and also a prominent anti-slavery man; Simon Cameron of Pennsylvania, a machine-politician who could swing the numerous electoral votes of his keystone state. Beyond these were a host of other possible candidates, none of whom was outstanding, but nearly all of whom seemed to have a better chance for gaining the nomination than Lincoln did. Among them were John C. Frémont, who had been the Republican nominee for 1856; Benjamin F. Wade of Ohio; John McLean of the United States Supreme Court; and Senator William L. Dayton of New Jersey, who had nosed Lincoln off the ticket for the Vice-Presidential candidacy in 1856.

Yet for one reason or another all these men were passed over. There was something wrong with each of them in the eyes of the astute Republican campaign managers. Seward's very eminence stood in his way; he had made enemies—among them was Horace Greeley, editor of the influential *New York Tribune*; Seward's declarations against slavery were more radical than Lincoln's and they had been better publicized than anything that Lincoln had ever spoken on the subject; Seward was a man who had tasted power and he would be sure to want to have his own way as President. Chase suffered from all the drawbacks that Seward did, and he was less well known. Bates was a favorite son, established only in Missouri, which was a small state with many pro-slavery voters. Cameron would never pass muster before the critical eyes of Puritan New England.

Lincoln was a dark horse; he had made some name for himself but not too much of a name; he had stood firmly for the principles of the Republican party but he had had no dealings with abolitionists. The times were perilous—someone who would take orders was needed in the White House so the Republican leaders could tell him what to do. After much bickering, Lincoln was agreed upon as a compromise choice whose nomination should offend no one in the party. He was not looked upon as an absolute nonentity. He was merely considered "safe," with all the meaning that that term implies in American politics.

There was no doubt that he was popular in his own state and throughout the Middle West. Laboring men and farmers could be depended upon to support him. At the Illinois State Republican Convention held at Decatur on May 9, an incident had occurred which showed Lincoln's potential strength with the masses. His cousin John Hanks, with whom he had gone to New Orleans by flatboat many years before, entered the convention carrying two fence rails which Lincoln had split on the Sangamon bottom in 1830. Lincoln became "the Rail-splitter Candidate" for President. This was something for vote-hungry political managers to think about long and seriously.

Eager enough as Lincoln had been to attain the Presidency, he must have had cause to ponder hard over the matter during the weeks before the convention. Becoming a Republican President in 1860—even a "safe" Republican President—was very much like hammering on a stick of dynamite to see whether or not it was correctly labeled. The South had long threatened to secede the moment a Republican President took office. The only thing that lulled Northerners into believing that the dynamite might not explode was that it was old—

the South had made so many threats for so many years that no one quite knew whether to believe this one or not.

Lincoln's managers, in order to obtain the nomination for their man, at the last moment had to make promises that their candidate had specifically warned them not to make. They agreed to swap offices in exchange for delegation votes. They promised the backers of Simon Cameron—who wanted to be President, but who was willing to take the next best thing—that Lincoln would make their man a Cabinet member. This was to cause Lincoln much mental anguish, and bring about internal wrangling in the Cabinet during the early and most critical period of the War.

On the first ballot, Lincoln was in second place with Seward more than seventy votes ahead of him; he was only three and a half votes behind Seward on the second ballot after the Cameron deal had gone through. Then the landslide began—more votes from Pennsylvania, votes from New Hampshire, Rhode Island, Connecticut, Ohio, Missouri, Iowa, Kentucky, Minnesota, California, Texas, the District of Columbia, votes from the territories—"bleeding" Kansas, Nebraska and Oregon rapidly came in. The hall was in an uproar. Three hundred and sixty-four and a half votes! Someone moved that the nomination be made unanimous. The motion was carried. Abraham Lincoln of Illinois was the Republican candidate for the Presidency! Artillery in the city was fired. Cannon fire was an appropriate salute to the man who was to be the first Republican President. These Chicago cannon were the first guns of the War; they were to be replied to at Sumter, and their echoes were to shake the nation for four long terrible years.

The candidate had spent the day quietly in Springfield, where he passed some of the waiting hours playing handball. Dr. J. G. Holland describes Lincoln's reception of the news of his nomination: "A messenger from the telegraph office entered with the decisive dispatch in his hand. . . . Mr. Lincoln read it in silence, then aloud. After exchanging greetings and receiving congratulations from those around him, he strove to get out of the crowd, and as he moved off, he remarked to those near him: 'Well, there is a little woman who will be interested in this news, and I will go home and tell her.' " Mary Todd was about to achieve the goal of her social ambitions.

There were torchlight processions and wild celebration in Springfield that night. Again the cannon roared, and to the fifty-one-year-old man who must have lain awake questioning in his own mind the reality of what had happened to him, their roar must have been filled with dark significance, for he certainly knew what was ahead of him.

The campaign dragged on through the summer. It was picturesque and spirited, but Lincoln took no part in it, nor did he, in fact, even go outside the town of Springfield until after election day. On June 1, he wrote out a long autobiographical statement to be used for campaign purposes. He kept in touch with his political leaders throughout the country, but he declined to take the stump to speak in his own behalf, although Douglas was engaging in a whirlwind electioneering tour for himself.

In October Lincoln received a letter from a young girl, Miss Grace Bedell, suggesting that he grow a beard so as to appear more dignified for the high position he evidently was about to fill. He seems to have been influenced by her suggestion, for he began to let his beard grow, and the smooth-shaven Illinois politician became transformed into the familiar short-bearded Civil War President.

On November 6, the nation voted. Lincoln waited in the telegraph office until his election was assured. Then he went out into the streets that were filled with cheering townspeople. He stopped for a while to partake of a Republican ladies' supper, and from there he went home with Mrs. Lincoln, to enter his house for the first time as the President-elect of the United States.

When all the returns were in they showed that Lincoln received 1,866,000 popular votes—more than Buchanan had received in 1856. Douglas got 1,377,000 votes; Breckinridge, the Southern Democrats' candidate, only 850,000. The North had spoken in terms of its vastly greater population; the slave-holders would never again be able to win a national election.* They had long realized this, but they waited for election day, hoping against hope that something might go wrong in their political calculations. On October 5, more than a month before the election was held, the Governor of South Carolina sent a confidential letter to the Governors of the other cotton states, informing them that his state intended to call a convention to consider a course of action if Lincoln were elected.

As soon as the news of the election of a Republican President was made known, the South boiled with activity. Secession meetings were called; bills were passed to raise and equip volunteers; large sums of money were voted for the purchase

* Two remarkable facts emerge from a study of the election figures. Breckinridge, outspoken slavery candidate, failed to carry the solid South. In fourteen slave states (omitting South Carolina which had no popular vote) Douglas, Bell and Lincoln had 124,000 more votes than Breckinridge, indicating that the urge for secession did not have the wide popular support often taken for granted. Lincoln was a minority President in that he obtained only 1,866,000 votes to the 2,815,000 cast for Douglas, Breckinridge and Bell, but he showed remarkable strength in the distribution of his votes among the large, heavily populated states that had many electoral votes—he received no votes in ten slave states. Lincoln received 180 electoral votes; Breckinridge 72; Bell 39; Douglas 12. Nicolay and Hay have remarked: "If all the votes given to all the opposing candidates had been concentrated and cast for a fusion ticket . . . Lincoln would still have received but 11 less, or 169 electoral votes—a majority of 35 in the entire electoral college." The split in the Democratic party started by Douglas and then forced wider by sectionalism was not in itself a great enough factor to lose the Democrats the election; the issue was more complex—the Democrats not only divided, they drove voters out of their party by their stand on slavery in the territories, their threats of disunion and their lack of a positive policy on national affairs. All the responsibility for the Democratic party's failure cannot be placed on Douglas—events were more important than the man, but he did serve as a catalyst to bring it about.

of munitions; Southern sympathizers in responsible governmental and army positions did their best to strip Northern
armories by sending materials of war into the South; Northern men and women residing in Southern states were told to
return home. Everything was prepared for the waging of a
general war. Even possible foreign allies were approached. The
South made good use of the long interval between the election
and the inauguration of a new President. The North, still
deluding herself that all this furor was only another gesture
of defiance, waited. And the President-elect waited, too. He
had to remain silent, withholding himself from public affairs
while his predecessor was still in office.

Buchanan as President had hitherto simply been a fool—
now he became a public calamity. Revolt simmered under his
feet and he did nothing. He was advised by General Scott,
commander of the Army, to garrison the forts in the South
as President Jackson had done during the nullification controversy with South Carolina in 1832,* but he disregarded
Scott's advice. In his message to Congress on December 4,
1860, Buchanan denied the right of the South to secede, but
he refrained from any action as though the matter were a
purely theoretical one. He seems to have been motivated only
by one desire—to postpone everything until the end of his
administration so that all the problems engendered by the election of a Republican President would be dumped into the
Republican President's lap. However, he apparently doubted
that Lincoln would be permitted to take office, for several
times he said lugubriously: "I am the last President of the
United States!"

The North was by no means united on the question of

---

* The doughty Jackson had met threats with counter-threats and had put
the fear of dire punishment into the hearts of those who were ranting about
secession. "Tell them," he said in a personal message to the nullifiers, "if one
South Carolina finger be raised in defiance of this government . . . I shall
come down there, and once I am there, I will hang the first man I can lay
my hands on, to the first tree I can reach."

what should be done. Greeley came out with an editorial in the New York *Tribune*, saying that the Southern states should be allowed to go in peace; he was supported in this attitude by the abolitionists who wanted to be free from all alliances with slavery. Others felt that some kind of compromise should be arrived at, and the last few months of 1860 were given over to a desperate effort to reach such a compromise. Several proposals were made, the best known of which is the Critten-den Compromise, so called because it was introduced into the Senate by Senator J. J. Crittenden of Kentucky. It provided for an amendment to the Constitution which would practically restore the Missouri Compromise; in exchange for this con-cession, laws regarding personal liberty issues and the taking of fugitive slaves were to be made still more stringent. It was a complicated and tangled measure, but the essence of it was that the South was to be permitted to extend slavery anywhere south of 36°30'; the slaveholders were to be guaranteed by Constitutional amendment the right of holding human beings in involuntary servitude, and the North was to acquiesce in their bondage. Crittenden was no fire-eating Southerner—he was an ardent pro-Union man who remained loyal to the Union during the War. These were the most reasonable terms he felt he could get the South to accept.

While these attempts to effect a reconciliation were in progress, South Carolina held her convention. On December 17, 1860, the delegates met at Columbia, and three days later passed an ordinance of secession which announced that the state had withdrawn from the Union and that South Carolina was now a sovereign nation holding allegiance to herself alone —and to the principle of slavery which she was determined to preserve at any cost.

On this same day, December 20, while the telegraph wires of the nation were hot with the news of South Carolina's secession, the President-elect faced his first grave decision. Seward had been invited by Lincoln to become his Secretary of State. Thurlow Weed, Seward's political manager, went to Springfield to consult with Lincoln about Seward and also to find out exactly how the President-elect stood on the whole matter of compromise with the South. Any concessions that might be made by Republican Senators and Representatives in Congress had to have the support of the incoming President if they were to possess any permanent validity.

THE END OF COMPROMISE

Lincoln had already made up his mind, as his letters written earlier in the month show. He resolutely opposed the kind of compromise proposed by the South, compromise that would permit slavery to be extended to the territories and perhaps to Central America and the West Indies. He had written to Weed on December 17, saying: "I will be inflexible on the territorial question . . . either the Missouri [Compromise] line extended, or Douglas's . . . popular sovereignty would lose us everything we gain by the election—filibustering for all south of us and making slave states of it would follow. . . . My opinion is that no state can in any way lawfully get out of the Union without the consent of the others; and that it is the duty of the President and other government functionaries to run the machine as it is."

Developments during the past ten years had led Lincoln to make this decision, fateful as it was. He had seen compromise after compromise with the slaveholding interests fail as they greedily reached out for more territory and for more privileges. He had no intention of attempting to prohibit slavery in the states where it already existed, but he was determined to arrest its spread. And he was convinced that slavery itself was wrong, an evil thing that had no right to exist in a civilized world, although for expediency's sake he was willing to let it stand as it was. Yet in the basic moral issue he was as inflexibly convinced as he was in the matter of confining slavery to its already established borders. This was the real issue—

"the issue that will continue in this country when these poor tongues of Judge Douglas and myself shall be silent. It is the eternal struggle between these two principles—right and wrong—throughout the world."

Compromise at this time might have again postponed the struggle; civil war might have been staved off for another year or two. But it was evident that the South would never be satisfied—or the North forever willing to remain politically hampered in the natural course of her development. The issue had been joined, and the issue that was tearing the nation apart was slavery.* From this moment on, the nation was at war. South Carolina had seceded, and on the same day, the Republican President-elect had given the answer that he would entertain no compromise dictated by the South to extend her territorial control and to preserve her peculiar property interests by means of a law written into the Constitution of the United States.

Weed went back to the East, taking with him a declaration of policy written out by Lincoln's hand. This policy did much to shape the Northern attitude on coming events. Its actual wording, unfortunately, has been lost—perhaps destroyed. But the Republican leaders knew where their "safe" candidate stood now. Nor was this the last time they were to be sur-

---

* For seventy-five years historians and political observers of all shades of opinion have been trying to fasten the cause of the Civil War on anything except slavery. They have advanced theories putting the responsibility for the War on the violation of states rights, on widespread economic differences between the North and the South or on the natural conflict between agrarian and industrial interests. All these causes are correct enough. They did help aggravate the situation. They were involved in many of the events leading up to battle. The American Civil War was, of course, too complicated a movement to have been precipitated by any single cause. But it is undeniable that underneath all the political and economic moves were the four million enslaved blacks, omnipresent and inescapable, whose bondage was the keystone of Southern economy, whose bondage was equally a challenge to the free-labor economy of the North, and an affront to the moral sense of the world. The men who fought the Civil War realized this; they should be given some credit for knowing their own minds. Their rallying cry was "Preserve the Union!" but although they did not fight merely to free the slaves, they knew that there would have been no war if there had been no slaves.

prised by the firmness of purpose and unshakable conviction of this rail-splitter President who had come up from the people to lead them in battle against a principle which, if allowed to persist, could end only in making all men slaves.

The defiant attitude of South Carolina, "cradle of secession," was rapidly adopted by other states in the far South. Mississippi seceded on January 9; then Florida, Alabama, Georgia and Louisiana. On February 1, Texas seceded, making a total of seven states that had withdrawn from the Union. Delegates from the first six states met on February 4, at Montgomery, Alabama, to set up a separate national government for the South. The cornerstone of the new nation was announced to be "the great truth that the Negro is not equal to the white man; that slavery, subordination to the superior race, is his natural and normal condition. This, our new government, is the first in the history of the world based upon this great physical, philosophical and moral truth."

Meanwhile, the man, against whose election this philosophical and moral government had been formed in protest, had to watch the months pass slowly by until the time came for his inauguration. The maundering Buchanan was still presiding in the White House; the nation impatiently waited to be rid of him.

The Lincoln home in Springfield became a focal point for office-seeking politicians who hoped to get jobs in return for having supported the new party. The President-elect had not only to face the most difficult internal crisis in his country's history, he had also to meet, talk with and not unduly antagonize all the aspiring postmasters, customs officers and petty job seekers who came to him from a hundred cities and a thousand towns. They pursued him to Washington; they made his life a hell in the White House; they ignored the impending crisis of the nation in their own eagerness to shove themselves toward the hog-trough of political patronage.

The Lincolns prepared themselves for their journey to

Washington. Mrs. Lincoln left Springfield early in January for a hurried shopping trip to New York in order to outfit herself with the fine clothes necessary for her position as mistress of the White House. This was to be the first of many such expeditions.

At the end of the month, Lincoln went to pay a visit to his aged stepmother, Sarah Bush Lincoln, who was living near Charleston, Illinois. The President-elect missed connections and arrived in Charleston in the caboose of a freight train from which he had to make his way down the track through the winter mud until he reached the station platform. He spent the night at the home of a friend in Charleston, telling stories to the neighbors who dropped in to see their old acquaintance who had now become great.

In the morning Lincoln drove out to see his stepmother. Thanks to Herndon, who interviewed her in 1865 and recorded her words, we have Sarah Bush's own account of this meeting. "He was here after he was elected President of the United States." (Here the old lady stopped, turned around and cried, wiped her eyes, and proceeded.) ". . . I wish I had died when my husband did. I did not want Abe to run for President, did not want him elected, was afraid somehow or other, felt in my heart that something would happen to him, and when he came down to see me . . . I still felt that something told me that something would befall Abe, and that I should see him no more. . . ."

The superstitions of the forest folk rose up out of the past, out of the far-off days when Sarah Bush Lincoln had lived with her stepson in the great wilderness of Indiana where the phases of the moon, the call of an owl in the night and the spirits that dwelled in the darkness had been a real part of their lives. The old stepmother was not alone in her premonitions. Her foster child had received the dark warning; he, too, had had a presentiment of his destiny and his end. In Springfield, a few days after his election, he had risen from a couch one day to look at himself in a mirror. He had seen a double image in the glass, one clear and real, the other vague and shadowy, lurking behind the clear reflection. The incident made a great impression on him. He told it to his wife who said that she felt it was a sign that he would serve two terms as President but that he would not live to finish his second term of office.

There was good reason for his mind—and the minds of his stepmother and his wife—to turn toward thoughts of an untimely death for him. The bitterness of feeling raging in the country had concentrated itself upon the person of this one man who was about to take office as President. Threats of personal violence and of actual assassination had begun even before election; they were to continue all through his administration. The Lincoln family mail was never free from them. Mrs. Lincoln finally had to have someone open their letters to remove the abusive and sometimes obscene messages addressed to them both.

Before the month of February was out, Lincoln was to have his first experience with threatened assassination. Long familiarity with its ever-present possibility finally made him oblivious of danger. "I long ago made up my mind that if anybody wants to kill me, he will do it," he said. "If I wore a shirt of mail, and kept myself surrounded by a bodyguard, it would be all the same. There are a thousand ways of getting at a man if it is desired that he should be killed."

"HERE I HAVE LIVED A QUARTER OF A CENTURY . . ."

The time was now fast approaching when it would be necessary to leave Springfield for Washington. On February 6, a farewell party was given by the Lincolns in the house that had been their home for sixteen years. As soon as the party was over the furniture was sold and dispersed forever. Trunks and bags were packed for the long stay in Washington. The family went to a hotel on February 8. There Lincoln made out the baggage labels with his own hand and addressed them: "A. Lincoln, Executive Mansion, Washington." On the afternoon of his last day in Springfield (Sunday, February 10), he walked over to his law office to talk with Herndon.

After disposing of business matters, Lincoln lay down on the old sofa which had been his favorite resting place. He spoke for several hours, recalling scenes from the past and joking about some of the ridiculous incidents that had taken place during their practice together. Finally the time came for him to go. He mentioned the weatherbeaten signboard that carried the firm name. "Let it hang there undisturbed," he said to Herndon. "Give our clients to understand that the election of a President makes no change in the firm of Lincoln and Herndon. If I live, I'm coming back some time, and then we'll go right on practicing law as if nothing had ever happened."

The next morning dawned rainy and cheerless. The Presidential train was to leave early, and Mrs. Lincoln and the children were to be on it. Something went amiss. According to the story told by a New York newspaper correspondent, Mary Lincoln quarreled with her husband that morning over a political appointment she wanted him to make. When the time for departure came, she was lying on the floor of her hotel room, screaming with hysterical rage that she would not leave for Washington unless her husband granted her wishes.

The President-elect entered his carriage without his family. He was driven through the muddy streets to a railroad station that was only a few blocks away from his old home. This was supposed to be his day of triumph, the auspicious beginning of a progress toward fame and success. The rain poured down as he rode through the familiar streets of Springfield; it drummed on the roof of his carriage and streaked down the window glass, obscuring the faces of people who had gathered along the sidewalks to see him pass.

Many of his old friends were at the railroad station. Some

of them doubtless inquired about Mrs. Lincoln, and the man whose heart was breaking at this miserable farewell to his own past had to parry off their questions and explain elaborately that she had changed her plans. He went through the waiting room to the platform, where he was greeted with cheers. Soldiers lined his passageway; friends stopped him to shake hands for the last time.

Heavily, tiredly, he mounted the steps to the observation platform at the end of the train. He stood for a moment at the rail, looking in silence at the people he had known so well—people whose lives had been so long intertwined with his. Then he spoke to them out of the fullness of his heart:

No one, not in my situation, can appreciate my feeling of sadness at this parting. To this place, and the kindness of these people, I owe everything. Here I have lived a quarter of a century, and have passed from a young to an old man. Here my children have been born and one is buried. I now leave, not knowing when or whether ever I may return, with a task before me greater than that which rested upon Washington. Without the assistance of that Divine Being who ever attended him, I cannot succeed. With that assistance, I cannot fail. Trusting in Him who can go with me, and remain with you, and be everywhere for good, let us confidently hope that all will yet be well. To His care commending you, as I hope in your prayers you will commend me, I bid you an affectionate farewell.

The rain fell fast upon him, glistening on his cheeks as he spoke. The engine whistle blew. He turned and went into the car, and the train moved off toward Washington, toward civil war and death.

The people of Springfield waited, standing bareheaded in the rain, watching the train recede into the distance. They were never to see their fellow-townsman alive again.

The train bearing the President-elect and his party headed east, stopping on the way at Indianapolis, Cincinnati, Columbus, Pittsburgh, Cleveland, Buffalo, Albany and New York.

Mrs. Lincoln and the children joined the train at Indianapolis. Mary Todd was not to be done out of the glory of social receptions and kowtowing. The route had been carefully planned, and Lincoln had to speak at all the scheduled stops —and at some of the unscheduled ones, for huge crowds came to see the train even when it halted at some wayside station to take on fuel and water. The speeches he made on this journey are among the worst of his career. He was determined not to say anything that might be construed as a declaration of policy, so he spoke only a few banal words. The situation in the South was becoming more dangerous every day; he wanted to see what would happen; and he felt that he had to wait until he took office before he could express himself on any stand.

On February 18, when Lincoln was on his way through New York State, he received word that Jefferson Davis had been inaugurated President of the Confederate States of America. Lincoln made no comment, but rode on grimly, knowing that on March 4, he would be faced with a problem of a rival government already in power on United States territory. The slaveholders, whose reckless course of action he had observed all his life, had struck the long-threatened blow at the Union, and they had struck at a moment when the whole defense of the Union would be thrust upon him. He had already composed his inaugural address and was carrying it with him on the train. "Physically speaking, we cannot separate," he had written in Springfield. "We cannot remove our respective sections from each other, nor build an impassable wall between them. . . . Can treaties be more faithfully enforced between aliens than laws can among friends? Suppose you go to war, you cannot fight always; and when, after much loss on both sides, and no gain on either, you cease fighting, the identical old questions as to terms of intercourse are again upon you." And he had written, at the end of his address, a question addressed to the people of the South which he had couched in forthright and uncompromising terms:

In your hands, my dissatisfied fellow countrymen, and not in mine, is the momentous issue of civil war. The Government will not assail you. You can have no conflict without being yourselves the aggressors. You have no oath registered in Heaven to destroy the Government, while I shall have the most solemn one to "preserve, protect and defend it." You can forbear the assault upon it, I cannot shrink from the defense of it. With you, and not with me, is the solemn question of "Shall it be peace or a sword?"

New York City was a Democratic stronghold; the reception awaiting him there was a purely formal one, lacking in enthusiasm or spontaneous warmth. One man who saw him said: "As the carriage in which he sat passed slowly by on the Fifth avenue, he was looking weary, sad, feeble and faint. My disappointment was excessive; so great, indeed, as to be almost overwhelming. He did not look to me to be the man for the hour."

New Jersey, too, was hostile territory; it was the one free state that had voted against him. Yet, when he addressed the State Assembly in Trenton, he spoke more frankly than he had at any time on his journey. Events in the South were becoming more and more ominous, and he was evidently making up his mind as to what course he must take, for he said that he, a man devoted to peace and with no malice toward any section, might find it "necessary to put the foot down firmly." And he was cheered when he said this.

THE FIRST ASSASSINATION PLOT

When he arrived in Philadelphia he received word of the first of the many plots that were to be made against his life. Allan Pinkerton, the famous detective, was waiting for him. Pinkerton's agents had found out that the President-elect was to be attacked as he passed through Baltimore. Their information did not sound unreasonable; Baltimore was a city known for its Southern sympathies and its gangs of "plug-uglies" who could be hired for any purpose from illegal voting to actual murder. Pinkerton wanted Lincoln to proceed at once to Washington in secrecy. This Lincoln was unwilling to do, since he had speaking engagements the next day in Philadelphia and Harrisburg. It was agreed that he should leave Harrisburg the next evening and go on to Washington from there in order to arrive ahead of his scheduled time. Later in the evening, Frederick Seward arrived from Washington carrying messages from his father and from General Scott, commander of the Army, warning Lincoln of the Baltimore plot which they had heard about from other sources.

The President-elect attended a flag-raising ceremony at Independence Hall in the morning, and the words he spoke on that occasion indicate the threats of death that were hanging over him. He went on to Harrisburg, and there, as he had arranged, he left the Governor's dinner, took a carriage and was rapidly driven outside the town, where a special train was awaiting him. Telegraph wires were cut so no one could signal ahead that he was on board. As soon as he arrived in Philadelphia, he was put into a closed carriage and driven around the city until it was time for the Washington train to leave.

He entered the sleeping-berth and went to bed immediately. The train proceeded on to Baltimore, where it arrived at three-thirty in the morning. Baltimore, at that time, had a curious railroad situation which made it an ideal place in which to attempt an assassination. Trains coming from the north had to stop at a terminal on one side of the city; their cars were detached and drawn through the streets by horses to the southern terminal, making it easy for armed men to attack the cars while they were in slow transit through the roughest part of the city. (Less than two months later trains were held up at this spot, and men of the Sixth Massachusetts Regiment were killed as they tried to reach the southern terminal.)

No one knew that Lincoln was on the train this night, so the passage across Baltimore was made without trouble. The train pulled into Washington at six o'clock in the morning, and the man who was about to be inaugurated President of the United States entered the city unknown and unheralded. He was driven to Willard's Hotel where he was to stay until he went to the White House.

Mrs. Lincoln and the rest of the party came through Baltimore later in the day without molestation. The conspirators—if they did exist—had evidently found out that the President-elect was already in Washington. Just how real the Baltimore plot was we shall never know. Certainly there were men in the South who had openly discussed the possibility of preventing the inauguration, and in December, the Richmond *Examiner* had printed the query: "Can there not be found men bold and brave enough in Maryland to unite with Virginians in seizing the Capital in Washington?" All this may have been mere gasconade, but irrefutable and tragic stands the evidence of April 14, 1865, in denial of all theories that Abraham Lincoln had nothing to fear while he was President.

On the evening of Lincoln's arrival in Washington, Stephen A. Douglas called upon the President-elect to talk with him about the impending crisis. Just before he left, he took Lincoln's hand and said: "You and I have been for many years politically opposed to each other, but in our devotion and attachment to the Constitution and the Union we have never differed—in this we are one—this must and shall not be destroyed!"

Lincoln spent the ten days between his arrival in Washington and his inauguration conferring with members of his prospective Cabinet, calling on President Buchanan, and visiting the Supreme Court, the House of Representatives and the Senate. Some of the Southern Senators refused to be presented to him, but in general there was little unpleasantness, for the issues involved were too grave to be expressed in such petty ways.

He consulted with Douglas and with Seward on the wording of his inaugural address, and changed several parts of it in order to make it more palatable to the South. Notably he changed the ending, taking a suggested paragraph of Seward's and transmuting its dull language into poetry. The "peace or a sword" ending now became:

I am loath to close. We are not enemies, but friends. We must not be enemies. Though passion may have strained, it must not break our bonds of affection. The mystic chords of memory, stretching from every battlefield and patriot grave, to every living heart and hearthstone all over this broad land, will yet swell the chorus of the Union when again touched, as surely they will be, by the better angels of our natures.

Shortly before noon on March 4, the carriage of President Buchanan stopped in front of Willard's Hotel. The weak-faced old man, looking like a figure from one of Dickens' novels, went into the hotel to meet his successor. The two men came out together and rode down Pennsylvania Avenue under a cavalry guard that kept close to the carriage. Riflemen were stationed on housetops; soldiers lined the broad square in front of the Capitol and stood under the speaker's platform. Artillery pieces were drawn up in the streets around the Capitol, and a long covered wooden passageway had been built to protect the Presidential party on its way to the speaker's platform.

The Capitol dome was unfinished; huge pieces of iron needed in its construction were standing around the square; scaffolding ran across the front of the portico. On the platform the great men of the nation were assembled to attend the ceremony. Abraham Lincoln came forward to the front of the speaker's stand, looking very uncomfortable in his new clothes. He held his hat in one hand and a large gold-headed cane in the other. He managed to put the cane away in a corner; as he tried to find a place for his hat, Douglas smiled, took it and held it for him. Then, reading from manuscript, Lincoln began his carefully prepared inaugural address.

There were about thirty thousand people assembled in the square. They heard Lincoln's plea for peace and conciliation, and applauded without great enthusiasm when he finished. Chief Justice Taney, the eighty-four-year-old head of the Supreme Court, stepped forward in great agitation to administer the oath of office for the last time in his long career which dated from Jackson's administration. He was the man whom public opinion held responsible for the Dred Scott decision; he and Buchanan and Douglas had been named by Lincoln as conspirators in the effort to extend slavery into the territories. The ancient black-robed figure was shaking as he held up the Bible on which the oath was to be sworn. Abraham Lincoln spoke the words that made him President of the United States. A signal was given to a field-battery stationed a mile away. The distant guns roared out in celebration; the smoke from their firing drifted over the city; the crowds in the square dispersed; and the new President drove to the White House to take over the responsibilities of office.

The Lincoln who entered the White House that day seems at first like a very different person from the Illinois politician who had left Springfield a few weeks before. He had mingled with the leading men of the nation and been treated by them as a person of high importance; he had been exposed to danger and the possibility of sudden death; he had the biggest job in the country to fill under conditions that were without precedent—no other President before or since has had to face the problems awaiting Lincoln when he entered the White House. It is a mistake, though, to feel that he had suddenly become transformed into another person. Actually he was the same Lincoln, the same melancholy country man fond of jokes and story-telling, the same clever politician and lawyer who could hold his own in a debate or persuade a jury. The highest office he had previously occupied was that of Congressman and he had been not too successful in it. The great position of power that was now his was to call out of him all the ability that had so far been latent; he was to concentrate in the next four years what would amount to several lifetimes for ordinary men. He knew that he had reached the peak of his career; there could be nothing more ahead of him after the Presidency. No circumstances could be more favorable for testing the mettle of a man—strong men rise to the occasion and become stronger; the weak give way, as Buchanan had done, and become miserable failures. It was all or nothing now.

The first indication of strength that Lincoln showed was in the selection of his Cabinet. He surrounded himself with the best men he could get. The three most important men in his Cabinet had all been his rivals in the race for the Presidential nomination. His Secretary of State was William H. Seward and his Secretary of the Treasury was Salmon P. Chase. They were both far in advance of Lincoln in their attitude toward slavery; they were both positive men, strong-willed and ambitious. His Attorney General, Edward Bates of Missouri, was an elderly man with a great legal reputation. His Postmaster General, Montgomery Blair, also was famous in the law—he had been the attorney for Dred Scott, and had made a national reputation for himself as a fearless advocate. All these men had been chosen by Lincoln; the other three Cabinet members were necessary compromise selections. Gideon Welles, Secretary of the Navy, had been selected by the Vice President, Hannibal Hamlin, for geographical reasons—he represented New England in the Cabinet. Simon Cameron of Pennsylvania, as Secretary of War, and Caleb Smith of Indiana, as Secretary of the Interior, had been given their places to fulfill the unauthorized promises made at Chicago by Lincoln's campaign managers.

Someone from the Lower South was badly needed in the Cabinet, but Lincoln had found it impossible to get any prominent man to serve. This was a great disappointment to him, but he had done the best he could in selecting his Cabinet under the extraordinarily difficult circumstances of sectional dispute and political expediency. He had to work with the material he could get, and he had made his own selections without any fear of rivalry or any consideration of personal favoritism.

This willingness to work with the best man for the job was one of Lincoln's greatest political virtues. When he was thinking of using Chase in his Cabinet, a friend in Springfield had warned him that Chase considered himself a bigger man than Lincoln. "Well," said Lincoln, "if you know of any other men who think they are bigger than I am, let me know. I want to put them all in my Cabinet." When the time came for him to appoint a new Secretary of War to replace Cameron, he chose Edwin M. Stanton, despite the fact that Stanton had once treated him with contempt during a law trial in which they both served as attorneys on the same side, and had often shown that he had very small respect for Lincoln as President.

SUMTER AND SEWARD

Lincoln showed his strength in his Cabinet appointments; he showed his weakness and vacillation in the policy—or lack of one—followed during his first month in office. There can be no doubt that he seriously underestimated the degree to which secession had proceeded in the South. Even though a new government had been set up there and a Confederate President inaugurated, he still felt that it might be possible to save the Union, to hold the South by peaceable means. The whole spirit of his first inaugural address shows this. He believed the South felt the same veneration for the United States that he himself did. Love of country was strong in the generation of men that had followed the leadership of Jackson, Clay and Webster. But Lincoln did not take Calhoun, who had been the leading statesman of the South, into sufficient account. Calhoun had stood for his state rather than his country, and local attachments outweighed national patriotism among many Southern people.

A long controversy had been going on since the previous December between the Federal Government and South Carolina over the Federal fortifications around Charleston. The key to Charleston was Fort Sumter which commanded the entrance to the harbor. South Carolina was determined to take over this fort; the Northern Government was equally determined to hold it. An attempt had been made in January to send provisions to Sumter by steamer. This steamer, the *Star of the West*, had been fired upon by the Confederates and driven away from the port. Sumter had been holding out ever since. Its little garrison, under the command of Major Robert Anderson, was now nearly at the point of starvation. The fort either had to be supplied with provisions or surrendered.

General Scott had already given his opinion that it would be practically impossible to hold Sumter. On March 15, Lincoln asked advice from his Cabinet. Only Blair and Chase felt that an effort should be made to provision the fort. Nearly all the forts, navy yards and Federal buildings in the South were already in possession of the Confederates. Sumter was not of great importance, but the months-old controversy over it had given it an unduly prominent place in the news. The North could not afford to let the fort go because of the unfavorable publicity that would be incurred; South Carolina was eager to get possession of the key to her Charleston harbor—she could not be regarded as independent so long as the waterway to her major city was controlled by the North.

Lincoln still made no move. He could not decide just what should be done about the impossibly difficult situation. To send supplies was to invite armed attack and war; to withhold them was to starve out the garrison and compel surrender. Time was working on the side of the South. The matter could not be delayed indefinitely. The Confederate Provisional Congress had already authorized the raising of 100,000 volunteers, floated an internal war loan, established an official navy and was even sending a commission to Europe to seek recognition as a nation.

On March 29, Lincoln again took a poll of Cabinet opinion on Sumter. There was some shift in favor of reinforcement, but the Cabinet was still not in agreement on taking a definite stand. Lincoln himself was, however, by no means convinced that the matter could be settled simply by letting the fort fall into the hands of the rebels. In fact he had already given orders to prepare an expedition which might or might not be used. Then on April 1, he received a document which, if it did nothing else, made him realize that he would have to fight to hold the Presidency just as hard as he had fought to obtain it. This was a confidential memorandum from Seward discreetly entitled "Some Thoughts for the President's Consideration."

This subtle bit of prodding indicated that the administration had not yet adopted a policy domestic or foreign; that it would be tactically desirable to "change the question before the public from one upon slavery, or about slavery, for a question upon union or disunion." Seward's formula for accomplishing this very desirable end was to abandon Sumter but to "maintain every fort and possession in the South." Then came one of the most breath-taking suggestions ever made by a high officer of the Government. Seward calmly proposed that the United States should deliberately provoke a war with Europe in order to unite her own antagonistic sections.

Someone, of course, had to do all this—either the President or some member of his Cabinet. Seward modestly closed by saying: "It is not in my special province; but I neither seek to evade nor assume responsibility."

This ingenuous advice must have been galling to Lincoln. His Secretary of State was not only suggesting that the country be plunged into an utterly unjustified foreign war, but was intimating that perhaps it would be better if he, the experienced and worldly wise Seward, take over the absolute control of its destinies.

Actually this was not all that Seward was doing to bring added trouble to an administration already overwhelmed with disaster. He had been in "indirect" communication with three men sent as commissioners by the Confederacy to sue for peaceable separation. These men had no official standing in the eyes of the United States which was certainly not ready to consider the Confederacy as a nation with the right to send agents. Nevertheless, Seward had let these men believe that Sumter would eventually be surrendered, although no such policy had been adopted. There were two unfortunate results from Seward's rashness in dealing with the unofficial commissioners: a great deal of information leaked out and was transmitted to the South; when an attempt was made to provision Sumter, the South charged the Lincoln administration with bad faith, even though Seward, of course, had no right to make commitments of any kind.

Lincoln was probably uninformed as to how far Seward had gone with the Confederate commissioners, but Seward's "Thoughts for the President's Consideration" required an immediate and positive reply. Lincoln could not afford to antagonize his new and in many ways really capable Secretary of State, but he did have to put him in his place. The weakness Lincoln had displayed during his first few weeks in office immediately vanished. The answer he gave to Seward was a masterpiece of political strategy combined with unyielding firmness. He gently reminded Seward that his first inaugural address had been a statement of internal policy and that he meant to stick to it—particularly to the pledge "to hold, occupy and possess the property and places belonging to the Government." He said that he did not "perceive how the reinforcement of Fort Sumter would be done on a slavery or party issue, while that of Fort Pickens would be on a more national and patriotic one." He ignored completely Seward's suggestion about provoking a foreign war but said that whatever must be done would be done by the President himself. And then he very sensibly buried the whole affair so that no word of it ever came out while the two men involved were still alive. These tactics gave Seward a new respect for the President; the two men thenceforth drew closer to each other.

The problem of Sumter was more difficult than the one that had arisen with Seward, but it, too, had to be met and settled. Lincoln moved forward rapidly now. He determined to provision the fort, but he would send in no reinforcements or munitions unless the place was attacked. On April 6, he ordered a relief expedition to sail.* As a last-minute gesture of conciliation, he notified the Governor of South Carolina of his intentions. Instead of conciliating, however, this served only to warn. When the fleet arrived off Charleston in the early morning of April 12, the Confederates gave word to fire on the fort. At 4:30 A.M. a shell rose from a mortar battery on the shore, curved high in the air and exploded over the walls of Sumter. The American Civil War had begun.

The firing continued for thirty-six hours, strangely enough without loss of life on either side. On the second day, build-

* Even this was not accomplished without serious bungling on the part of the new and inexperienced administration. A large and well-armed ship, the *Powhatan*, was to accompany the expedition to Sumter. Seward sent through an order assigning the *Powhatan* to go to Fort Pickens instead, and Lincoln inexcusably signed his order without reading it. When Lincoln discovered his own blunder he commanded Seward to send the ship to Sumter. Seward followed his instructions, but signed his own name to the order. The captain of the *Powhatan* refused to accept the new order when he already had one signed by the President. Even if the *Powhatan* had reached Charleston it could not have prevented the outbreak of war. Once Sumter had been fired on, war was inevitable—if, indeed, not before.

ings inside the fort were set on fire by incendiary shells. In order to prevent the powder magazines from exploding, nearly all the powder had to be thrown into the sea. With ammunition almost exhausted, the garrison agreed to surrender. On the next day, Sunday, April 14, 1861, the flag was hauled down, and the fort passed into the hands of the Confederates.

On that day, in quick answer to the attack on Sumter, Lincoln drafted with his own hand a proclamation calling for seventy-five thousand volunteers and summoning Congress to meet in extraordinary session on July 4. Douglas visited him in the afternoon to pledge his active support of the Union in the war. The two men consulted on military matters—Douglas had an excellent strategic mind and might have risen high in the army. A few days later, the Little Giant left for Illinois to rally Northern Democrats to the Union cause. Hardly more than a month later he was dead; a mysterious malady, perhaps brought on by the physical exhaustion caused by his active pro-Union tour, cut short his life when he was only forty-eight years old. The stage was now clear for Lincoln to dominate the national scene.

THE WAR BEGINS

News of the firing on Sumter was received in the North with incredulity at first—then with rage. Over the week end the war news spread across the land, running along the telegraph wires to far-distant places, radiating out from towns to villages and thence to isolated farms, to logging camps, to wilderness huts. Men gathered at railroad stations where the rapid stutter of telegraph-receiving instruments brought the latest information from Washington. The President's call for volunteers, which was published on Monday, April 15, was responded to with enthusiasm—many more than 75,000 men came forward. Everybody felt that the war would be a short one; the rebellion of a few recalcitrant slaveholders would be put down quickly.

Men volunteered in the South as readily as in the North.

The South, too, expected to win quickly. She would have her independence and be able to lead her own existence as a new nation. Yet in neither the North nor the South were the people solidly united on the issue at hand. The great Appalachian mountain chain that runs down through the South was the home of people who held no slaves, who profited in no way at all from a slave economy. These people were fiercely individualistic, scorning plantation owners and city dwellers alike. They wanted no part in the War, and many of them were determined to stay with the Union—or in some cases—to remain stubbornly neutral.

In the North, along the edges of the border states, in the newer Middle Western sections where people from the South had settled in pioneer country, and even in such states as New York, New Jersey and Massachusetts, there were thousands of men who opposed the Northern cause, openly and secretly. In the capital city of Washington, there were hundreds of men in governmental positions who held allegiance to the South; the more honorable of them resigned from their posts immediately; others remained to send out information and to do all that they could to obstruct the Northern military campaign.

On the whole, the South stood together better than the North did, although most of the Southern people had nothing to gain from the war. Less than seven percent of the white population there held ten or more slaves—and only these large slaveowners had been able to make slave labor pay. Men who held a few slaves lived on the thin edge of bankruptcy. The poor whites who made up the greater part of the population lived at a low subsistence level. Yet all these disparate elements were by one means or another welded together to wage the war. Some men—the wealthier ones—joined the army because they were convinced that slavery was desirable; others joined because of the example set by their neighbors. The rallying cry of states' rights was a potent force among the more intelligent; the slogan "Fight to keep the niggers in their places" worked with the more ignorant. The real tragedy of the South was that so many of its people were willing to fight and die in a War that would benefit so few of them even if they won it.

In the South, only some of the people in the border states and in the mountain regions held out against secession after the shots fired on Sumter clarified the many counter issues and made war certain. In the North, for all its initial enthusiasm, there were men who fought the war policy of the Government through all four years of battle. For one thing, Northern men had been used to free speech, accustomed to violent controversy among themselves over political matters. The moral issue against slavery and anger against the South for breaking up the Union helped to unify the North, but there were still many Northerners who cared nothing about freeing the slaves or holding the Union together. Political ties formed during the Democratic party's long reign served, too, to make Northern Democrats feel that perhaps the South was not entirely unjustified in her stand on slavery and disunion. Areas that had been solidly in favor of the Democrats were disloyal areas in the North. Copperheadism flourished there; treasonable activities of all kinds were prevalent in these sections. Naturally there were many loyal Democrats like Douglas in the North— but there were no Republicans at all in the South.

The South lost no time in following up her victory at Sumter. Virginia passed an ordinance of secession on April 17; several thousand hastily assembled volunteers moved on Harper's Ferry to seize the arsenal there with its 15,000 rifles. On the eighteenth, the Federal officer in command of the arsenal had to set it on fire in order to prevent it from falling into the hands of the insurgents.

Virginia's secession immediately placed Washington in great danger. The city was open to easy invasion from the south; if Maryland also proved to be hostile to the Northern cause it would be almost impossible to hold the capital. Everyone in Washington waited apprehensively to see what move Maryland would make. The only railroad leading into Washington from the north passed through Baltimore—if this railroad and the telegraph wires that paralleled it were cut, Washington would be isolated.

Troops were badly needed to defend the city. There were only 16,000 men in the regular United States Army at this time, and most of them were in far-flung outposts in unsettled territory. On the seventeenth a few hundred militiamen from Pennsylvania reached Washington safely. Then, on the morning of April 19, a long train carrying one thousand armed men from the Sixth Massachusetts Regiment and nearly as many more unarmed Pennsylvania volunteers, arrived at the northern terminal in Baltimore. The first eight cars were drawn through the city streets by teams of horses while a huge crowd of Southern sympathizers gathered. By the time the ninth car came along, the crowd was in an ugly mood. Someone threw a stone at the windows of the slowly moving car. The sound of breaking glass inspired the crowd to pelt the windows with more stones. Revolver shots were fired. The soldiers, at their officers' command, lay down on the floor of the car and offered no resistance. The car managed to reach the southern terminal, but it was the last one to get through. The crowd piled stones and scrap iron on the right of way, making it impossible for any more cars to pass. The soldiers still left at the northern terminal had to march through the streets to force their way to the Washington station. The mob fell upon them; men on both sides started to fire—the militiamen, grimly fighting their way, reached the terminal only after they had left four of their comrades lying dead on the streets.

The train pulled out of the south station as a final burst of fire from the soldiers killed a prominent man in the crowd. The infuriated mob then rushed to the Philadelphia terminal, where the unarmed Pennsylvania volunteers were still waiting in the train. Some of these men jumped out of the cars and were attacked. The train was hastily backed out of the station in order to escape the shower of stones and brickbats hurled at it. Baltimore was in a turmoil for the rest of the day. A huge secession meeting was held that night, at which it was made evident that no more troops would be allowed to pass through the city.

The train carrying the Sixth Massachusetts arrived in Washington during the late afternoon. The wounded were unloaded on stretchers, and the survivors were marched to the Capitol, where they were quartered in the Senate Chamber. Even the White House was used as a barracks that night—a group of Kansas men recruited in Washington were placed in the East Room to serve as a guard.

This was the beginning of a week of terror the like of which Washington had not witnessed since 1814, when the British had captured and burned the city. Each day that went by made Washington's position seem more and more hopeless. On the nineteenth, Lincoln issued a proclamation of blockade, declaring that all commerce to and from Southern ports would be stopped. On the twentieth, the Gosport Navy Yard near Norfolk, Virginia, had to be burned to save it from the rebels. Most of the ships had already been scuttled by disloyal officers stationed there. The North was placed in the position of having issued orders of blockade without having a fleet adequate to enforce them. On this same day railroad bridges near Baltimore were destroyed; railroad traffic ceased, and then, on the evening of Sunday, April 21, telegraphic communication with the North was cut off. The last message to come through from Baltimore simply said that the insurgents were taking over the telegraph office there.

On Monday morning, Washington was entirely isolated, in immediate danger of attack from Virginia and without enough troops to be able to put up much resistance if invasion were attempted. The Lincoln administration seemed likely to be as short-lived as its enemies had predicted. The President paced anxiously up and down the silent halls of the White

House, occasionally going to a window to see if any relief ships were in sight. On the Virginia side of the river he could make out a flag flying from the top of a building there. It was a Confederate flag, and he had good reason to believe that a large body of men were gathering around it in preparation for an assault on Washington. As night fell, he could see the watch-fires of the Confederacy burning on the hills, twinkling brightly under the quiet April sky.

Washington slept on its arms. Men stayed at their posts in Government buildings lest an attempt be made to seize Federal property during the night. Sandbags were piled up around entranceways; barricades were erected inside the halls. There had been a general exodus of Southern sympathizers during the last few days, but no one knew how many of them might still be waiting in the city to rise and join a concerted attack on the capital.

News had been received that men from the Seventh Regiment of New York and troops from Rhode Island and Massachusetts had been sent by sea to Annapolis, and that they had arrived there on Monday. They were expected in Washington on Tuesday. The railroad had been put out of commission near Annapolis, but the troops had only to march twenty miles to Annapolis Junction, where they could meet the main line from Baltimore, which was still intact from this point to Washington. Tuesday, however, brought no sign of the expected troops. Nerves were overwrought from long waiting. The city streets were almost deserted; people stayed inside their houses not knowing what might happen; stores and business places remained closed. Even the President's strong will was cracking. During the afternoon, after the day's work was over, he resumed his worried pacing up and down the floor of the Executive office. Finally he went to the window, and oblivious of people still in the room, said out loud: "Why don't they come? Why don't they come?"

The next morning, some of the men wounded in the Baltimore riots paid him a visit. He received them kindly, making them at ease in the formal rooms of the White House. Before they left he said to them: "I don't believe there is any North. The Seventh Regiment is a myth. Rhode Island is not known in our geography any longer. You are the only Northern realities!"

On Thursday, April 25, the long vigil ended. The troops from Annapolis, who had waited there to put a damaged locomotive in order, so they could bring their cannon and equipment, finally arrived in the city at noon. An enormous crowd flocked to the station to greet them. The streets were lined with cheering people as the men of the Northern regiments marched triumphantly down Pennsylvania Avenue with bands playing and flags flying.

More men came through from Annapolis on the next day. The isolation of the city was over, and Washington again became the capital of the nation—or at least of that part of it which still held allegiance to the United States.

During the weeks that followed, more and more troops kept pouring into the capital until it finally became a huge armed camp. Tents were pitched in open spaces; cannon were dragged through the streets and mounted in positions where they would command the approaches to the city. As Washington thus fortified itself, and the determination of the Northern states to oppose secession became evident, resistance died down in Maryland. By the middle of May, the railroad through Baltimore had been opened, and a majority of the people of the state had made it clear that they had no intention of joining the South. Naturally a strong secession element still existed, but there were enough pro-Union men in the state to hold it in the Union throughout the war.

THE LINCOLNS IN THE WHITE HOUSE

The Lincoln family now had their first opportunity to settle down in their new quarters in the White House. Mrs. Lincoln was destined to be disappointed in her ambition to become the reigning social queen of the nation's capital. The Southern families who had dominated Washington society withdrew from the city to return to their homes. The Northern ladies who succeeded them had no intention of accepting Mrs. Lincoln as their leader. To them she was a parvenue from the Middle West, unworthy of ranking among the great families of New England and New York. She had not been in Washington since her husband's brief sojourn there as an obscure Congressman, so she had no acquaintanceship with important people in the city. And the fact that several members of her family in Kentucky joined the rebel army made her suspect not only in society circles, but among the plain people as well. She became exceedingly unpopular, and her own imperious manner alienated even those few who had been predisposed to be friendly toward her. Her life in the White House was an unhappy one. The wife of a war President can make a name for herself in history, but she is not likely to become a great social success. Only a woman impervious to public opinion would make the attempt to do so at a time when the best blood of the nation was being poured out in fratricidal strife.

The plain, simple man who had become President naturally paid no attention to his wife's social ambitions. He was busy with affairs of state and the conduct of war. He found relaxation playing with his two young sons who romped through the dignified and historic Executive Mansion as though it were an old stable. The eldest son, Robert, was away at Harvard, so Lincoln depended upon Willie and Tad for companionship. During the darkest moments of the early campaigns he was able to throw off his fits of despondency in their company. He had a natural love for children that was, perhaps, in some way a compensation for his lack of success in dealing with women. He may have been an indifferent lover and an abstracted and neglectful husband, but the only failure that could be charged against him as a father was that he completely spoiled his children. And he spoiled them not only because he was excessively devoted to them; but also because he himself was so restless under restraint that he could not bear seeing his children disciplined. When they played tricks on the grave-faced Cabinet members and army officers who came to visit him, he would never mete out punishment. His behavior in the most formal residence in the land was entirely informal. He brought to the White House the unvarnished manners of the frontier and the small town.

He was criticized even in the North as a buffoon and a vulgarian. But it must be remembered that the mores he offended were the elaborately refined ones that had been imported from Victorian England. When he spoke plain language and acted like a natural human being, the overstuffed gentlemen winced and the Dresden-china ladies swooned. Lincoln's secretary, John Hay, who zealously respected the manners of the best society himself, nevertheless was astute enough to see through Lincoln's surface crudities to the real man underneath. He said of him:

I believe that Lincoln is well understood by the people; but there is a patent-leather, kid-glove set who know no more of him than an owl does of a comet blazing into his blinking eyes. Their estimates of him are in many cases disgraceful exhibitions of ignorance and prejudice. Their effeminate natures shrink instinctively from the contact of a great reality like Lincoln's character. I consider Lincoln republicanism incarnate, with all its faults and all its virtues. As, in spite of some rudeness, republicanism is the sole hope of a sick world, so Lincoln with all his foibles, is the greatest character since Christ.

Young Hay became greatly devoted to the whimsical, unconventional President whom he irreverently refers to in his diary as the Tycoon or the Ancient. He describes Lincoln prowling restlessly through the dark halls of the White House in shirt-tails and slippers to find someone with whom he could share a particularly funny passage from Artemus Ward or

Thomas Hood. Hay was vastly amused at the President's feet, which always seemed to be seeking a level higher than his head; he speaks of how Lincoln would use them to steady a telescope as he inspected shipping on the Potomac, and of how visitors to the White House were sometimes shocked to see a windowsill lined with a row of men's shoe soles—the biggest of which were always proudly pointed out by the servants as belonging to the President himself.

But Hay realized, too, that although the President was sometimes undignified, he was never lacking in true dignity. He could spend time playing with his children and jesting with his friends, but actually he was a terribly serious person whose whole energies were concentrated on winning the War. Only three weeks after the firing on Sumter, Lincoln had already figured out for himself the essential nature of the conflict. Hay recorded this analysis in his diary, reproducing the President's own words:

For my part, I consider the central idea pervading this struggle is the necessity that is upon us, of proving that popular government is not an absurdity. We must settle this question now, whether in a free government the minority have the right to break up the government whenever they choose. If we fail it will go far to prove the incapability of the people to govern themselves. There may be one consideration used in stay of such final judgment, but that is not for us to use in advance.

That is, that there exists in our case, an instance of so vast and far-reaching a disturbing element, which the history of no other free nation will probably ever present. That, however, is not for us to say at present. Taking the government as we found it we will see if the majority can preserve it.

Under the President's energetic leadership a majority of the Northern people came to the defense of the system of popular government. Troops, munitions and money were readily provided. The South, which had nourished the delusion that the Yankees would not fight, now began to realize that she had a first-class war on her hands. The border states wavered between Northern and Southern allegiance, and their wavering weakened the South more than it did the North. The North was in such a powerful position that these few undecided states did not seriously matter, although Lincoln greatly overestimated their importance. There were 22,000,000 people in the states that finally stood with the Union, against fewer than 9,000,000 people in the Confederate states, nearly 4,000,000 of whom were slaves who could hardly be expected to fight to preserve their own bondage. Even more disparate was the proportion of wealth in the North and in the South. An analysis of resources in the two sections at the beginning of the war shows that:

In 1860, the North had produced $167,295,000 worth of flour and meal as compared with the South's $55,849,000. . . . The North had 19,770 miles of railway track; the South, 10,513. . . . The North . . . had 109,000 manufacturing establishments to the South's 31,300. The capital investment in Northern manufactures was $842,000,000 to the South's $167,855,000. The number of workers in Northern manufactures was 1,131,600 to the South's 189,500. The value of the manufactured products turned out in the North was $1,594,486,000 to the South's $291,375,000. . . . The capital stock of the North's banks was put at $292,594,000; of the South's banks, at $129,287,000. The total bank deposits in the North stood at $187,678,000; in the South, at $66,124,000. In the North, money in circulation totaled $119,826,000; in the South, $87,276,000. (*The United States—A Graphic History.* Hacker, Modley and Taylor. New York, 1937.)

As the war went on this disparity increased enormously. For the first year the South stupidly withheld her cotton from the European market, then, as the Northern blockade became more efficient it almost entirely shut off the Southern ports. The North was able to raise a huge purchasing fund through taxation and loans. The South had to resort to inflation early in the War. Because of the depreciation of currency on both sides it is impossible to arrive at any reasonable comparison of war income. All that can be said is that in 1865 the printing-press money issued by the Confederacy had no value at all, whereas the North, which had spent more than three billion dollars in financing the War, still had a currency with an exchange value of at least fifty cents in gold. Even during the lowest tide of Northern defeat, the United States dollar never went below thirty-nine cents; it rose rapidly after the War, reaching par in less than fourteen years. The North emerged from the War stronger and more powerful than ever.

But if the North had population and wealth, the South had the one thing that the North lacked most—able military leaders. The President of the Confederacy, Jefferson Davis, was a professional soldier. The group of generals headed by Robert E. Lee were the pick of the men who had been trained at West Point and in army service. Lincoln's greatest problem during the first years of the War was to find at least one man competent to lead the great Northern army to victory.

General Winfield Scott, seventy-five-year-old veteran of the War of 1812, was the titular head of the little Federal army when the War began. It was obvious that he did not have the energy or the health to see the campaign through. Nor was there any likely successor to him anywhere in sight. The United States, as usual, had been too sure of peace to bother with training adequate leaders for war.

The first active fighting took place in the border states, where a few miniature battles occurred. The western and mountainous part of Virginia, which had no part in the slave economy of the tidewater section, gave early indications of her intentions to stay with the North. Late in June, a young Union commander, George Brinton McClellan, distinguished himself by waging successful warfare against the few rebels remaining in that part of the state. McClellan was a West Point man, a professional soldier who had resigned from the army to engage in railroad work. He left the presidency of an Ohio railroad to become a soldier again. With a dearth of Union leaders, McClellan's minor victories made him seem outstanding. Lincoln watched his career with interest. He needed bright young men to lead his armies.

As the Northern army continued to grow, an expeditionary force was sent from Washington across the river to clear the rebels out of Alexandria and Arlington Heights. One of the leaders of this force, a young colonel from Illinois, E. E. Ellsworth, was killed in an attempt to take down the Confederate flag that had so long been flaunted in the face of the President and the people in Washington. This young soldier's death brought home the reality of war with great personal effect to Lincoln. Ellsworth had accompanied him on the train from Springfield to Washington, and he had become very much attached to the dashing boy commander. He wrote a moving letter of condolence to Ellsworth's parents.

Early in June, the capital of the Confederate States was transferred from Montgomery, Alabama, to Richmond, Virginia. As the Federal armies spread out around Washington and increased in size, the Northern people, whipped up by newspaper comment, began to feel that a quick drive against the new Confederate capital would put down the insurrection and restore peace. The cry became "On to Richmond!" The Confederate Congress was due to assemble there on July 20, and it seemed possible that a well-organized attack might prevent the Rebel Congress from sitting.

The extraordinary session of Congress convened by Presidential proclamation met in Washington on July 4. The seats that had been occupied by Senators and Representatives from Southern states stood vacant as silent reminders of the fact that the nation was now disunited. But dissension and wrangling had gone with the departed Congressmen; the men who remained almost unanimously supported the President's war measures. When he asked for 400,000 more men and $400,000,000 to carry on a War that had as yet been nothing but a series of skirmishes, only five votes were cast in the House against supplying the necessary means.

In the special message addressed to this Congress, Lincoln outlined the first few steps that the Government had taken in order to meet the rebellion against it; he answered the Southern arguments on the right of secession; and he went out of his way to speak to the people of the nation in order to make it clear to them that the War was "essentially a people's contest."

He saw clearly that the issue was basic—one that would serve as precedent in the conduct of democratic governments throughout the world for generations to come. He summed up the essential meaning of the American Civil War in a single paragraph that can stand as the central core of the democratic argument against the slaveholder's rebellion which apologists have tried to explain away by tenuous constitutional reasoning and much sophistry. The words he had spoken in private to John Hay were now made public in a rephrased and tightly developed form:

And this issue embraces more than the fate of these United States. It presents to the whole family of man the question whether a constitutional republic or democracy—a government of the people by the same people—can or cannot maintain its territorial integrity against its own domestic foes. It presents the question whether discontented individuals, too few in numbers to control administration according to organic law in any case, can always, upon the pretenses made in this case, or on any other pretenses, or arbitrarily without any pretense, break up their government, and thus practically put an end to free government upon the earth. It forces us to ask: "Is there, in all republics, this inherent and fatal weakness?" "Must a government, of necessity, be too strong for the liberties of its own people, or too weak to maintain its own existence?"

BULL RUN

As he spoke, preparations were under way for the first major encounter with the Confederate forces. A large body of troops under the command of General Beauregard had been lying near Manassas Junction for two months. Manassas, which lay in a valley watered by a creek named Bull Run, was about thirty miles from the Union camps around Arlington. The two armies had fired occasional shots at each other's pickets, but had never actually approached each other. Under pressure of Northern public opinion, Federal troops were being made ready to march against the Confederates in order to capture the important Manassas railroad junction and to drive on toward Richmond.

On July 16, about twenty-eight thousand men under the command of General McDowell started out to meet the enemy's force of thirty-two thousand. Several days of marching, maneuvering and preliminary encounters took place before the main battle on Sunday, July 21. On that day, Congressmen and Washington people drove out to see their army defeat the rebels. Lincoln waited anxiously in the White House for the outcome of this first major test of arms.

During the afternoon the telegraphic dispatches from the field were very encouraging, although it seemed that the battle might have to continue for another day before victory was assured. The President went for his usual afternoon drive. When he returned, his secretaries told him in great excitement that Seward had been to the White House with news that the Union forces had been routed. Lincoln walked over to the army headquarters, where he was handed a telegram reading: "General McDowell's army in full retreat. . . . The day is lost. Save Washington and the remnants of this army. . . . The routed troops will not re-form."

During the evening the news was confirmed. The President waited up all night, listening to the accounts given him by

Congressmen and other civilians who had fled madly before the retreating soldiers. When morning came, the sky was heavily overcast and a steady rain was falling. The first of the troops, whose inexperience in warfare had cost them the battle, began to stream into Washington. Sympathetic citizens set up coffee-stands, where the unhappy men munched their breakfasts in silence. Their Commander-in-Chief stood at a window in the White House, looking out at the falling rain. He had not erred in asking Congress for 400,000 men. The War was not going to be an easy one.

The defeat at Bull Run* had an immediately disheartening effect upon the North. No one had foreseen that a war was ahead; what had happened in the South was looked upon as a sectional insurrection, widespread in area but localized in a few disaffected states. It was naturally expected that the Federal Government would put down this rebellion by force of arms and restore the nation to its normal state without much trouble. As soon as this first setback occurred some of the Northern people raised the cry for surrender. Greeley, who had wanted to let the Southern states go in peace, wrote to Lincoln in black despair, hinting at the need for an armistice. In a *Tribune* editorial, he blasted away at the Cabinet heads, calling for their dismissal.

Lincoln, however, was determined to carry on the work he had begun. While the troops were still streaming into Washington from the battlefield, he drew up a memorandum of war policy, outlining the steps to be taken to crush Southern resistance. Point by point he put down the things that had to be accomplished in order to press on successfully with the opposition to the rebellion that had grown into a war.

---

* Had the Confederates been clever enough to follow up their victory, they could probably have taken Washington that day. But their green and untried troops were almost as much surprised at victory as the Northerners were at their own defeat. Some of the Confederate soldiers, taking it for granted that the War was over, laid down their arms and started for home.

A few days after the battle, he summoned McClellan to Washington and placed him in charge of organizing a huge army that was to march into the South to overwhelm the insurgent slaveholders. Preparations for a real war were made. Enlistment terms had already been changed from three months to three years. It was realized that the three months' period had been a mistake.

By an unfortunate coincidence, the battle of Bull Run had taken place almost exactly three months after the time many of the first volunteers had enlisted for three months' service. Some of them had refused to go into the battle because their term of enlistment was expiring.

The new army was to be made up of three-year men. Their training was undertaken seriously; months of activity were given over to organization. McClellan was a stickler for drill, for military efficiency and for absolute thoroughness in all details of commissary and support.

Lincoln's difficulties in finding leaders for his troops were just beginning. McDowell had been unsatisfactory; for the moment it seemed that McClellan would be the heaven-sent commander needed by the Union. Meanwhile, the problem of military leadership was creating trouble in the West. Sporadic fighting was going on in Missouri between bands of rebels and Union men. An able commander was needed there to hold the state in line. Lincoln appointed John C. Frémont, the Republican nominee for the Presidency in 1856, to the command of the Department of the West. Not long after Frémont took charge, reports began to filter east that he was incompetent, if not actually corrupt. Military expenditures in his Department swelled to huge proportions, but no sign of action came from his armies. Late in August, Lincoln was surprised to see in the newspapers that Frémont had published a proclamation freeing the slaves of all those persons in Missouri who had taken up arms against the United States. Frémont had consulted with no one about this tremendously important move. It had seemed like a good idea to him at the time, and he had promptly put it into effect, perhaps to win support from the abolitionists for himself. Certainly he had no moral interest in setting the slaves free. He was an opportunist and a shallow-minded malcontent who was interested only in furthering his own career. Without any thought of the far-reaching consequences to the nation, he casually made a move that had only been discussed with bated breath by the President and the members of his Cabinet. What he did was especially embarrassing because it immediately met with great approbation by people who were sincerely interested in emancipation but did not realize that Frémont was acting rashly, with no consideration for the delicate situation in the border states which were still wavering in loyalty.

Lincoln wanted to keep the border states in the Union. Naturally, their people would not tolerate Frémont's highhanded decision to free the slaves. The President wrote a letter to his Western commander, gently chiding him for what he had done, and suggesting that he modify his proclamation to conform to previously enacted legislation for the confiscation of property used for insurrectionary purposes. Frémont replied that if his order were to be modified it must be done so by Presidential command—he was obviously trying to put Lincoln in a position from which he could not extricate himself so far as abolitionist opinion was concerned.

Lincoln patiently sent through the official notice. As soon as it became known that he had officially countermanded Frémont's order of emancipation, he was denounced by the abolitionists. Even his old friend, O. H. Browning, wrote to him from Illinois, criticizing him for what he had done. Lincoln replied to him on September 22, 1861, in an effort to justify his own stand. He made out an airtight argument for his position against emancipation. He was to reverse himself completely hardly more than a year later.

Frémont's ill-considered proclamation gave rise to an issue

that Lincoln would rather not have seen raised—the question of whether the country was fighting a war to preserve the Union or to free the slaves. Lincoln had made up his mind to fight on the Union issue; the abolitionists, however, were just as determined to make the war a holy one for Negro freedom. They were in a minority, but they made up for their lack of numbers by their intensity of effort and moral zeal. Their cause was not allowed to remain a simple ethical crusade. As the War progressed, leadership was taken over from the idealists who regarded their work as the work of God. Men of more practical nature—politicians—stepped in because they saw in the anti-slavery movement a vigorous force that could be directed toward the winning of the War. And those who stood most to gain from the War, the Northern industrialists, quietly put their chips behind these men.

Frémont, who had brought the issue of emancipation into the open, became hopelessly bad as a military commander. McClellan grew in power as his army became stronger. General Scott resigned on October 31; on November 1, McClellan was appointed General in Chief in his place. On November 2, Lincoln removed Frémont from his command. The outcry immediately raised against Lincoln was based on political antagonisms. Frémont was a leading Republican, McClellan was a Democrat. Frémont, in the eyes of many Northerners, stood for the anti-slavery forces; McClellan was a member of the Democratic party which had been the representative of the South and slavery. Lincoln, of course, acted without thought of party, but the country was sensitive about the political affiliations of the men who were to lead its armies.

THE TRENT AFFAIR

Only a week after McClellan's appointment, something happened that made the North forget party issues for the moment. This was the famous *Trent* affair. The Confederate Government attempted to send two commissioners, James M.

Mason and John Slidell, to England and France by way of Havana. On November 8, the day after the British steamer *Trent* had left Cuba with Mason and Slidell on board, a United States man-of-war stopped the ship and seized the two commissioners. News of this event reached the North on November 16, and was received with wild enthusiasm. So far the North had seen nothing but defeat. This was her first small victory.

The triumph was short lived. The President realized that Great Britain would insist that the commissioners had been removed from one of her ships by an act contrary to international law. The commissioners would have to be surrendered, disappointing as this concession would be to the public.

The *Trent* reached England on November 27. Reaction there was immediate and violent, especially among those upper-class people who considered the United States a democratic upstart and a dangerous commercial rival. They promptly set up a clamor for war. Since these were the people who had charge of the British government, they were in a position to see that forcible measures were carried out at once against the United States. Eight thousand soldiers were dispatched to Canada, and an embargo was placed on arms and munitions. A peremptory demand for the release of the commissioners and an apology for their seizure was sent to the British Minister in Washington, with instructions for him to return to England unless the demand was granted within seven days of its delivery.

The sharp tone of the British note naturally was irritating to the Cabinet members who met on Christmas Day to deliberate on a course of action. Nevertheless, the attitude which Lincoln had taken from the beginning finally prevailed, and the Cabinet agreed that the commissioners should be turned over to the British. Seward, in drafting his reply, could not resist the temptation to twist the lion's tail. After consenting to return the prisoners, he said: "Nor have I been tempted at all by suggestions that cases might be found in history where Great Britain refused to yield to other nations, and even to ourselves, claims like that which is now before us."

On January 1, 1862, the much-publicized prisoners were taken from Boston Harbor to Provincetown, where they were safely transferred to a British gunboat. There was an ironic aftermath. One of the transports bringing British troops to Canada found that the St. Lawrence was frozen over. She sailed to Portland, Maine, where permission had to be sought from the United States Government to let the troops travel across Maine to Canada. Permission was cheerfully granted, and the troops who had been sent as a threat to the United States shamefacedly entered the country they had come to invade, while the North grinned at Britain's discomfiture.

The Trent affair, with its implications of a foreign war ended with a comic incident, but the President's troubles with his generals never ceased. McClellan had spent the rest of the summer and the early autumn getting his magnificent army ready, but he seemed to be exceedingly reluctant to make any use of it. Everyone had expected that a drive would be started against the Confederate armies still lying at Manassas, but nothing happened. The public became impatient, the President worried, and as soon as Congress met, criticism of McClellan's inactivity became increasingly severe.

The thirty-four-year-old general was undoubtedly suffering from an over-inflated egotism that made him difficult to handle. His predecessor, General Scott, had resigned because of genuinely bad health, but McClellan's arrogance to the almost helpless old man had hastened his retirement. McClellan not only felt that Scott was a superannuated fool—he showed that he felt it in every speech, letter and deed. But if his attitude toward General Scott was unkind, his behavior toward the President who had selected him as his own personal choice for commander exceeded all bounds of common sense and human decency. Only thirteen days after Lincoln had made

him General in Chief, McClellan revealed himself as a badly
spoiled child who should have been spanked with the flat of
his own sword. Hay tells the story in his diary:

November 13. I wish here to record what I consider a portent
of evil to come. The President, Governor Seward and I, went over
to McClellan's house tonight. The servant at the door said the
General . . . would soon return. We went in, and after we had
waited about an hour, McC. came in and without paying any particular attention to the porter, who told him the President was
waiting to see him, went upstairs, passing the door of the room
where the President and Secretary of State were seated. They waited
about half-an-hour, and sent once more a servant to tell the General
they were there, and the answer coolly came that the General had
gone to bed.

I merely record this unparalleled insolence of epaulettes without
comment. It is the first indication I have yet seen of the threatened
supremacy of the military authorities.

The ever-patient Lincoln swallowed the insult, remarking
calmly to Hay that perhaps it was better during such perilous
times not to make a point of etiquette or personal dignity. He
said later that he would hold McClellan's stirrup, if he would
win him victories. But the pompous young general showed no
signs of moving toward the enemy. Winter came, and McClellan confessed that he was glad to see the snow fall, for it
meant that he could not be forced to make his army get under
way until it was completely ready. In his contention that the
army must be thoroughly trained and supplied before it ventured forth, McClellan was probably right. But the character
traits he had betrayed in his dealings with two old men who
wished him well correctly indicated that he was not the man
to lead it.

While McClellan's delay engaged the North in bitter dispute, Congress, which had adjourned on August 6, met again
for its regular session on December 3. The President, in his
first Annual Message to this Congress, touched only obliquely

on the question of slavery, but went on at some length to expound his ideas on the relationship of capital and labor. Free labor in the North was playing an important part in the War, and Lincoln was eager to win the allegiance of the working class to the Northern cause.

The anti-slavery Radical Republican group in Congress* was disappointed at the President's unwillingness to take a positive stand on the matter of freeing the slaves. This Congressional cabal was growing in power; it had already approached the President in October to try to make him force McClellan's hand to move into battle; it was now no longer content to let matters rest with the President—it initiated the formation of a Congressional committee to inquire into the conduct of the War. Generals were brought before this committee, investigators were sent into the field and a typical American scandal-hunting inquiry was staged.

Because of what happened in the South during Reconstruction days after the War, the Radicals have been treated with undue unfairness in history. They have been called the Vindictives, and every motive from overweening personal ambition to sheer malice has been attributed to them. Like most men, they were neither wholly good nor entirely bad. They were radicals in that they wanted the Republican party to get down to the root of the matter that had caused it to be founded—opposition to slavery. They were vindictive only in that they were implacably set against any compromise with slavery and wanted to punish the South that had gone to war to defend it. Lincoln hated slavery as an abstract thing; these men, like the non-political abolitionists whose cause they took over, hated slavery as a living evil. To them slavery was a force that stood for oppression and nothing else. They saw it in personal

* The members of this group changed somewhat from time to time but the leading spirits were Thaddeus Stevens, Zachariah Chandler, Benjamin F. Wade, Charles Sumner, George W. Julian and two of Lincoln's friends from Illinois, Lyman Trumbull and Owen Lovejoy. Later in the War they were joined by Henry Winter Davis.

terms as a demonic Simon Legree who was lashing the flesh and enchaining the souls of four million fellow creatures.

The Radicals were not without guile, not without dishonesty in their methods. They made use of what political power they could grasp to further their battle against what they considered the greatest menace of their time. Yet in essence they were honest men, as honest, many of them, as Lincoln himself, and a good deal more forthright. Only that curious duality of political interest already mentioned—the alliance of finance capitalism with the progressive anti-slavery forces—made the Radicals a disturbing and sometimes dangerous element in the waging of a war in which the Northern cause was itself dual in nature.

A prime example of this strange alliance of holy zeal and the almighty dollar can be seen in the next incident with which Lincoln had to deal at this time. His Secretary of War, Simon Cameron, who had certainly not been Lincoln's choice for that office, became the target of a widespread protest against war profiteering. Cameron himself almost surely did not profit directly from any of the enormous war contracts being handed out. As he very frankly said, he didn't need the money. Nevertheless, there were scandals, and friends of his were profiting at the Government's expense. In December, when he submitted his annual report, Cameron made a curious move. Induced perhaps by the Radicals, or encouraged by the abolitionists' approval of Frémont's bold gesture of emancipation, Cameron incorporated in his report a recommendation that the Government arm the slaves and incite them to turn against their masters. In order to force the issue, Cameron, without consulting the President, put printed copies of his report in the mails for release to the press. Lincoln quickly ordered the report recalled, and re-worded the recommendation so as to make it relatively harmless. Early in January, Cameron was out of the Cabinet, and was appointed Minister to Russia.

Lincoln replaced Cameron with Stanton, a strange choice under the circumstances, for Stanton, although incorruptible in placing war contracts, was even closer to the Radicals than Cameron had been. He was, however, an able director of affairs; he threw his great energy into the administration of the War Department and made things hum. He kept in active touch with the armies and held an iron hand over the generals. He was friendly toward McClellan when he first took office, but relations between the two men soon became strained.

On January 27, only a few days after Stanton's appointment, the President, under pressure from public opinion and Congress, issued his General War Order Number One which was a public command to the army and navy to move toward the insurgents on February 22. Lincoln had been studying military tactics, reading books on the subject very much as he had studied law, surveying and Euclid. McClellan objected to this order, pointing out that publishing the exact day on which the army was to move permitted the enemy to prepare for the attack. He said that roads would not be in fit condition for the movement of a large army so early in the spring. He also insisted that his own forces were not yet large enough to be used against the Confederates.* In all he managed to persuade Lincoln that an advance on February 22 would be impractical.

During the month of February, Lincoln was plunged into such personal grief that he was in no mood to argue with his recalcitrant general. His son Willie became seriously ill, and then, on February 20, he died. The shock of this death seemed to be the final touch needed to send the already emotionally overburdened man into a period of the deepest gloom. All his old melancholy returned, and with it the twists and idiosyncrasies of his nature. He twice had his dead son's body exhumed so he could look at his face again.

* McClellan seems to have made almost exclusive use of scouts and spies who could not count. Johnston's army at Manassas was only one-third the size of his; it was less well equipped and its men were in poorer condition. Yet McClellan spoke constantly about being outnumbered.

Meanwhile the President's General War Order had been taken more seriously in the West than in the East. Early in February, two strategically situated river forts in Western Tennessee were captured by a hitherto little-known Union commander, Ulysses S. Grant. The winning of these forts was the first Northern victory of any importance. After so many months of defeat and disappointment it helped to make the nation feel that perhaps the tide of secession had turned at last. Spring was close at hand. McClellan's peerless army could be expected to get under way in a few weeks in a campaign that would strike the death blow to the rebellion. Peace would be established before the summer was over. The people of the North, and Lincoln, too, were still under the impression that one great battle would end the War and compel the Confederates to abandon the cause for which they had been fighting.

As spring approached, the Confederate General Johnston realized that his position at Manassas was untenable in the face of McClellan's superior numbers. He slowly began to withdraw his army, and, by March 11, had moved it beyond the Rappahannock River. McClellan, hearing of this, started hotly for the famous Junction. When he arrived there with his army he found the place deserted. He also found that it had never been adequately protected. Dummy guns made from logs commanded many of the earthworks. McClellan marched his army back to Washington again, to find the whole country laughing at him. The President, finally having lost confidence in him, quietly relieved McClellan of his general command, leaving him as commander of the Army of the Potomac only. The ostensible reason for this was that McClellan was about to take the field, where he would not be in a position to supervise the other armies. No one was deceived.

Just before McClellan had made his drive against a phantom army, a naval battle took place that terrified all the seaports of the North. The Confederates had raised one of the vessels sunk at the Norfolk Navy Yard, and had converted her hulk into an armor-sheathed boat with an underwater ram. This strange craft, which had once been the *Merrimac* but which was now named the *Virginia*, slowly steamed out into Hampton Roads on March 8, and methodically proceeded to annihilate the wooden ships of the Northern fleet while their cannonballs bounced harmlessly off her armor. Stanton trembled for the safety of Washington; a delegation of New York businessmen rushed to the capital begging for some kind of protection for their city.

The next day the whole affair was over. An even stranger-looking and much smaller craft, John Ericsson's ironclad *Monitor*, which had just recently been built as an experiment by the North, moved across Hampton Roads with her deck almost awash and only a round gun turret visible. This "cheese-box on a raft," as she was popularly described, just as methodically proceeded to put the *Virginia* (née *Merrimac*) out of business. The North breathed easier, but the naval experts of the world went into hurried consultations. The wooden warship had become obsolete; and every navy had to be rebuilt.

THE FIRST CAMPAIGN AGAINST RICHMOND

As soon as this marine interlude was over, attention again became concentrated on McClellan's long-awaited move toward Richmond. On March 13, the now somewhat tarnished general completed his plan of attack. Instead of moving directly south through Manassas as the President had expected, McClellan determined to make a flank attack by land and water, moving up the Peninsula between the York and the James Rivers. This oblique movement left Washington exposed to the possibility of a direct attack from the Confederate forces lying north of Richmond. In order to forestall this, an adequate army had to be left to defend the capital. Lincoln protested against this whole plan of campaign, but he permitted his objections to be overruled, since he was admittedly inexperienced in military matters.

Early in April, McClellan was near Yorktown with more than a hundred thousand men. The old Revolutionary battleground again heard the tread of marching men; some of the ancient trenches there were dug out and reconditioned—Lincoln's army was beginning its first great campaign where Washington's army had won its final victory. Unfortunately for sentiment, the portent turned out to be meaningless. McClellan spent a month elaborating a siege against Yorktown which was held by a force only one-tenth the size of his own. During the time he was toying with this pretty demonstration of military-school tactics, the Union armies in the West went on to win the fiercely contested battle of Shiloh and to capture the city of New Orleans which was the key to the Mississippi River.

While these military moves against the Confederacy were under way, the President and Congress had been engaged in organizing the first tentative moves toward solving the basic problem of slavery. A bill was passed prohibiting slavery in the territories; another abolished slavery in the District of Columbia with compensation for loss of property. The drift of public opinion was making it evident that the War would necessarily have to make an end to the issue that had torn the country in two. Lincoln, averse as usual to any violent change in the nation's structure, drew up a plan whereby the slaves would be gradually freed and their owners compensated for their property. He submitted this to Congress on March 6, 1862. To emphasize the practicality of his proposal, he pointed out that the expenses incurred in eighty-seven days of war would purchase all the slaves in four border states and the District of Columbia.

Lincoln's scheme for achieving emancipation as painlessly as possible might have been successful if his army had marched resolutely toward Richmond to reinforce his proposal by putting down armed resistance. But McClellan, after putting his siege batteries in place before Yorktown, again found that the elusive Johnston, who had escaped him at 'Manassas, did not wait to be attacked. He withdrew up the Peninsula, leaving McClellan to follow. The Federal fleet sailed up the James to a point eight miles from the city. McClellan slowly advanced with his army during the month of May. He had been expecting additional troops for the intended assault on Richmond, but a clever feint by "Stonewall" Jackson made Lincoln and Stanton believe that Washington was in danger, and the supporting troops were withheld to protect the capital. Much disgruntled, McClellan finally arrived at Fair Oaks, only a few miles from Richmond. On May 31 he was attacked there by Johnston. The Confederate commander was wounded in the ensuing battle and was replaced the next day by Robert E. Lee, who had not yet distinguished himself in the field. He rapidly did so.

McClellan permitted nearly a month to pass while his army lay near the city. Lee took advantage of this respite to strengthen his forces. Then, on June 25, he threw his army of defense into an offensive attack against McClellan's forces. The famous seven days before Richmond began; they ended in McClellan's army being forced to retreat, fighting desperately all the way to the James River.

McClellan fortified his position at Harrison's Landing, where the Federal fleet came to his support. Lee retired to Richmond to rest his army after having driven the invader back. McClellan waited for more men and fresh supplies to renew his attack against Richmond. He refused to admit that the Peninsular campaign was over, but actually it was, and it had been a costly failure for the North.

On July 8, Lincoln visited his defeated army. No one knew what his thoughts were during the river journey to and from Harrison's Landing, but this bitter voyage marks the turning point in his Presidential career. So far he had been dominated by events, molding his policies only after expediency demanded that they be changed. Now all hesitancy and doubt vanished; he became strong and daring. It was strength born of desperation, but it was strength. The man had been in hell for months. He had never looked so worn and haggard as he did at this time. The memory of his son's death was still with him; he had seen Congress and the country go against him; he had been unable to find a competent general to lead his Eastern armies—and he faced the realization that the year-long preparations against Richmond had come to nothing.

McClellan's petulance over the lack of support which he insisted had caused his repulse probably did not help matters in his dealings with the President. Lincoln returned to Washington maturing his plans for action on the way. He moved with unwonted swiftness as soon as he reached the city. He had already made an indirect appeal through the Governors of the states for 300,000 more men and he had summoned General Pope from the West to take charge of the campaign in Virginia. He also called Halleck to come East to be the General in Chief of all the Northern armies. Most important of all, he prepared to meet the issue of slavery squarely for the first time in his career.

The demand for the suppression of the institution that had brought on the War had been rising insistently in the North. Frémont had given the original impetus to this demand with his unauthorized act of military emancipation. On May 9, one of Lincoln's most trusted generals, his own personal friend, David Hunter, had issued a similar proclamation. No charge of political ambition could be made against Hunter; he was an honest and forthright man, and the President knew it. Reluctantly he had countermanded his friend's order, but the very words he had used in doing so indicated that he was beginning to weaken in his opposition to such measures.

On his return to Washington Lincoln called a meeting of the Senators and Representatives of the border states. He had addressed them once before when the Peninsular campaign was just beginning, pleading with them then to accept his plan of compensated emancipation. They had refused it. He gave them this one last chance to accept. They refused again. His mind was made up. The first evidence of his intention came the next day, July 13. In company with Welles and Seward he attended a funeral, the funeral of Stanton's infant son. The occasion, which must have reminded him forcefully of the burial of his own son only five months before, may have had something to do with his breaking his customary silence on matters of future policy. He spoke aloud his thoughts on the subject of military emancipation. Welles reported the occasion in his diary:

He [Lincoln] dwelt earnestly on the gravity, importance and delicacy of the movement, said he had given it much thought and had come to the conclusion that it was a military necessity absolutely essential for the salvation of the Union, that we must free the slaves or be ourselves subdued. . . .

During the next week Lincoln grappled with the problem he had so long been avoiding. Until this time he would have been content to let slavery exist within its own well-established boundaries, hoping that natural evolutionary processes would some day bring it to an end. Now he realized that in order to win the War he had to eradicate the basic cause of the conflict. His chief difficulty was that he still did not want to alienate the people in the border states who were loyal to the Union. He had to find a device that would permit him to free the slaves of the enemies of the Union and at the same time allow its friends to retain their property. He was a politician and he could not afford to antagonize his allies, no matter what their internal policies might be.

On July 22, he entered a Cabinet meeting with his plan completely worked out. He was ready to present it to his advisers, but he was not asking for their approval; he told them frankly that the question was already settled in his own mind and that he would take full responsibility for it. He then read the draft of his proclamation. It declared that on the first of January, 1863, "all persons held as slaves within any state or states wherein the constitutional authority of the United States shall not then have been practically recognized . . . shall then, thenceforward and forever be free."

This carefully phrased wording covered the device needed to hold the border slave states in the Union. The emancipation provision was directed only at the Confederate states—the states that were in rebellion against the Union. Men in those states were to lose their slaves; men in states that had remained loyal were to be permitted to keep their slave property. The proclamation of emancipation was not a philanthropic gesture to benefit the enslaved Negroes—it was a wartime measure intended to weaken the insurgent states.

Lincoln's obviously determined manner overcame any possible opposition on the part of his Cabinet. Seward, however, astutely pointed out that if the proclamation were made public at this moment of disaster when the Richmond campaign had just failed, it would sound like a despairing cry from a bewildered administration. Why not wait for a victory before releasing it?

This suggestion seemed sensible. Lincoln decided to withhold his proclamation until the Northern armies made a sufficient show of success to provide a favorable psychological reception for it. During the time he had to wait for a victory, the abolitionists, not knowing what was in his mind, kept up pressure for emancipation. On August 19, Greeley published his famous letter entitled "The Prayer of Twenty Millions" in which he appealed to the President to make an end of slavery. Lincoln replied to him three days later: "My paramount object is to save the Union, and not either to save or to destroy slavery," he said. "If I could save the Union without freeing any slave, I would do it; and if I could save it by

freeing all the slaves, I would do it; and if I could save it by
freeing some and leaving others alone, I would also do that."
This was his declaration of official policy for the moment.
He tempered it in closing by saying: "I intend no modification of my oft-expressed personal wish that all men could
everywhere be free."

A few weeks later (September 13), a committee of religious denominations waited on the President to supplement
Greeley's plea. In view of the date on which this incident
took place and the events that were to happen hardly more
than a week later, it is curious to see Lincoln still steadfastly
defending the policy that he was ready to abandon as soon
as any kind of victory would permit him to do so. It is almost
as though he were trying to present the other side of the argument. He gives all the practical reasons for not issuing a proclamation of emancipation. He admits candidly that no words
of his would have any effect in the South. But his final words
give the clue to what was passing in his own mind:

Do not misunderstand me because I have mentioned these objections. They indicate the difficulties that have thus far prevented
my action. . . . I have not decided against a proclamation of
liberty to the slaves, but hold the matter under advisement; and I
can assure you that the subject is on my mind, by day and night,
more than any other. Whatever shall appear to be God's will, I
will do.

The military maneuvers that were so intimately tied up with
emancipation were progressing rapidly. A victory was in the
offing, although events leading up to it hardly seemed pro-
pitious. Pope had made a miserable fizzle of his command of
the Army of Virginia. On August 29-30, he had been attacked
by the Confederates on the old battlefield of Manassas and
had seen his forces routed there almost as badly as the green
troops of McDowell had been in the first major encounter of
the War. Lee had driven on around him, heading north to-

ward Maryland. McClellan, who had returned from the Peninsula with his troops, was hastily put in charge of the counter-offensive against Lee. The two armies met in Maryland on September 17, just beyond Harper's Ferry, facing each other across an obscure country creek named Antietam that became famous that day. The battle that was fought on its banks was the bloodiest single day of the War, but it ended in Lee's being driven southward into Virginia.

THE PROCLAMATION OF EMANCIPATION

Antietam was no great and decisive victory, but it would have to do. On September 22, 1862, the President read the final wording of his Proclamation of Emancipation to the Cabinet; two days later it was released to the press. The immediate reaction in the North was rather disappointing. After waiting a few days to determine public opinion, Lincoln wrote to the Vice President, Hannibal Hamlin, on September 28, saying that "while commendation in newspapers and by distinguished individuals is all that a vain man could wish, stocks have declined, and troops come forward more slowly than ever. . . . The North responds to the proclamation sufficiently in breath; but breath alone kills no rebels."

Lack of great enthusiasm over this first movement toward freeing the slaves was not the only burden Lincoln had to bear at this time. He was having trouble with McClellan again. McClellan had forced Lee to withdraw across the Potomac, but he did nothing about going in pursuit of him. On October 1, Lincoln visited his procrastinating commander. He reviewed the troops in and around Harper's Ferry and then went to McClellan's headquarters at Antietam.* Evidently the Presi-

* An incident which took place en route was used against Lincoln to show that he was heartless and unfeeling. His visit occurred sixteen days after the battle, when all the dead and wounded had been removed. While traveling toward McClellan's camp, Lincoln asked his aide and bodyguard, Ward Hill Lamon, to sing one of his sad little songs for him. This story was magnified and distorted by Lincoln's enemies until it became a wild tale of a callous President driving past heaps of corpses while Lamon roared out

dent considered the troops to be in better condition and better supplied than McClellan did. The Western army had just won the battle of Corinth; the Eastern army was completely inactive while its commander complained to Washington about his cavalry mounts and his lack of supplies. On October 13, Lincoln wrote to McClellan criticizing him for his over-cautiousness. McClellan replied, saying that his horses were in no condition to move. Then Lincoln's patience gave way. He telegraphed sharply: "Will you pardon me for asking what the horses of your army have done since the battle of Antietam that fatigues anything?"

This was the beginning of the end. On October 26, McClellan reluctantly started out after Lee, but he was not quick enough to prevent him from crossing the Blue Ridge Mountains and reaching Central Virginia. Lincoln had already made up his mind that if McClellan permitted this to happen he would remove him from his command. On November 5, the fatal order went out, and McClellan's troubled career as the head of the Union army was finished forever.

Burnside was placed in charge of McClellan's army. Under his command it moved down slowly into Virginia to Fredericksburg, where it fought a hopeless battle in the middle of December, charging against Confederates solidly entrenched on the heights beyond that city until the loss of life was so great that the whole North was appalled. The end of 1862 was a period of the deepest gloom and depression throughout the Northern states. The year that had begun so favorably was petering out in defeat, and the Government was in a quandary as to what to do about its military failures. Lincoln was the object of bitter attack, and he must have felt his position keenly. The November elections had gone against the administration; Congress was bitterly critical; a Cabinet crisis threat-

obscene ditties. Two years later, on September 12, 1864, Lincoln wrote out an account of the journey for Lamon to use in correcting the absurd story which was still being told.

ened as Seward and Chase offered to resign because of the disputes over the responsibility for what had happened at Fredericksburg. The public debt had risen enormously; currency inflation had begun, and, worst of all, the troops had not been paid for five months. The Proclamation of Emancipation, which had been issued after a Northern victory, took effect on January 1, 1863, in the lowest ebb of Northern defeat.

When Lincoln addressed his message to Congress on December 1, 1862, he asked that the war measure of emancipation be implemented by the adoption of an amendment to the Constitution embodying his plan for compensation. Two years passed before this was finally accomplished, on January 31, 1865,* and then no provision for compensation was made. When the next amendment (the Fourteenth) was ratified in 1868, it specifically forbade compensation of any kind.

As a military measure, the Proclamation of Emancipation was easily justified, although there was some doubt about its constitutionality. It accomplished several purposes: It acted as a thorn in the side of the Confederacy; it helped win liberal opinion in Europe to the Northern side; and it increased the strength of the Northern armies by adding Negro soldiers to their ranks. Several colored regiments were formed immediately; by the end of the War, 186,000 Negroes had enrolled on the Union side.

At the end of his message to Congress on December 1, 1862, a large part of which is devoted to a discussion of the then forthcoming Proclamation of Emancipation and the supporting legislation required for it, Lincoln gives an indication of what his own inner feelings were in the matter of freeing the slaves. He concludes with the moving words:

Fellow-citizens, we cannot escape history. We of this Congress and this administration will be remembered in spite of ourselves.

---

* Lincoln did not live to see the slaves freed. The final ratification by the states was not completed until December 18, 1865—eight months after his death.

No personal significance or insignificance can spare one or another of us. The fiery trial through which we pass will light us down, in honor or dishonor, to the latest generation. We say we are for the Union. The world will not forget that we say this. We know how to save the Union. The world knows we do know how to save it. We—even we here—hold the power and bear the responsibility. In giving freedom to the slave, we assure freedom to the free—honorable alike in what we give and what we preserve. We shall nobly save or meanly lose the last best hope of earth. Other means may succeed; this could not fail. The way is plain, peaceful, generous, just—a way which, if followed, the world will forever applaud, and God must forever bless.

Lincoln was keenly conscious of the tides of opinion throughout the world. He was in full sympathy with liberal thought and he was eager to have the real nature of the cause for which his country was fighting understood by people everywhere. In England a remarkable division of attitude had occurred. The aristocracy, as has already been indicated, was in almost complete sympathy with the South, but the British working people were in hearty accord with the aims of the North. Even the operators in the Lancashire mills, who were being starved as a result of the cotton shortage caused by the blockade, steadfastly supported the Union cause. The working-men of Manchester addressed a letter to the President at the beginning of the new year 1863, enclosing a resolution of sympathy with the aims of the Northern Government. On January 19, Lincoln answered them, saying that the example set by the Lancashire mill operators was "an instance of sublime Christian heroism which has not been surpassed in any age or in any country." The people of the Northern states, moved by the plight of the English factory hands, subscribed large sums of money for relief and sent shiploads of wheat to Liverpool.

The horizon of the Illinois lawyer who had become President was expanding. He had been occupied successively with

town, county, state and national problems. Now his mind had
to take in those vast and subtly interconnected relationships
which tie together all the peoples of the world. He realized
that he was playing a role in history; he knew that what he did
would be commented on for generations to come; he knew
that what he said would be recorded for all time. A man who
is conscious of his historic destiny thinks and acts in terms
of long-range conduct. Nevertheless, the Lincoln of the White
House was still the Lincoln of New Salem hill and Speed's
store and the circuit-towns of the prairies. He had not forgotten his origins or his training. He was now applying to
greater problems the simple universal things he had learned
during his youth.

Stories of his humanity and his sympathy multiply during
the war years until they merge into a legend that is half truth
and half fiction. Yet however unsubstantiated some of the incidents may be there is no doubt of the underlying truth. And
Abraham Lincoln is remembered by the mass of people, not
for his politician's skill or his historical importance, but for
the way he acted in little personal relationships with the
common people who came to see him for all sorts of reasons.
The entrance hall to the White House was always filled with
them. Indians, Tennessee mountaineers, Negroes, immigrants,
religious men of all denominations, wives and widows, old
friends and neighbors—and just plain citizens—came in an endless stream. He saw them all. Even lunatics came to him in
droves, with all sorts of wild schemes to which he listened
gravely. By treating the insane as though they were sane he
found that he could deal with them easily. Actually, to the
tired and aging man who sat in the White House day after
day listening to the pleas and criticism and curses of his people, they must eventually all have come to seem alike, sane
and insane.

However, the time he spent with his visitors was by no
means wasted. It enabled him to take a public-opinion poll

of his own. His secretaries were often surprised to find that the President, who read so little, knew so much about what was going on in the country. Nothing of what he heard was lost on him. He listened and he remembered. When the time came he acted accordingly.

Familiar as it is, no part of the Lincoln legend is more worthy of serious respect than that which has to do with his pardoning of soldiers. No record was ever kept of the actual number of cases that passed through his hands, but it must, by all accounts, have been large. And, contrary to popular belief, he did not pardon every case that was brought to his attention. He went out of his way to see that justice was done, and he was earnestly averse to permitting a man to be executed for anything except a clear-cut criminal cause. He sought desperately for excuses to pardon, often delaying a case until he could think of a good reason for granting amnesty. He admitted to his more sternly minded colleagues that he was pigeon-hearted. He agreed cheerfully with Stanton and Bates that he was demoralizing the army. But he went right on granting pardons.

GETTYSBURG

The Lincoln of legend and sentiment reaches its height during 1863. 1862 belongs to McClellan; 1864 to Grant; for these were years of complicated military maneuvers. But 1863 was a year in which the two chief military movements came together at the same time in the Union victories at Vicksburg and Gettysburg. And Gettysburg belongs to Lincoln even more than to the men who fought there. Lincoln was never more mistaken than when he said: "The world will little note nor long remember what we say here, but it can never forget what they did here."

The year began inauspiciously enough. Burnside, who had made such a pathetic failure at Fredericksburg, was replaced by Joseph Hooker. Desertions from the army were heavy, and

recruits were almost impossible to get. Hooker, who was known
as "Fighting Joe," managed to reinvigorate the tired and
apathetic soldiers. However, he had his own ideas on national
administration and army policy which were at variance with
Lincoln's beliefs in the free methods of a democracy. When
he appointed Hooker to his command on January 26, 1863,
Lincoln wrote to him saying: "I have heard, in such a way
as to believe it, of your recently saying that both the army and
the government needed a dictator. Of course it was not for
this, but in spite of it, that I have given you the command.
Only those generals who gain successes can set up dictators.
What I now ask of you is military success, and I will risk the
dictatorship."

The general who was celebrated for his fighting abilities and
his favoring of strong-arm methods lasted for just one battle—
Chancellorsville—which was fought early in May on the outskirts of Fredericksburg, and which ended in the loss of 18,000
men and the full retreat of the Union army.

The South had won both Fredericksburg and Chancellorsville, but she needed more than these victories to help her
cause. The inexorable laws of economics were working to defeat her. Food was terribly scarce; there had been a bread riot
in Richmond early in April; inflation was under way, and the
food that could be had brought enormous prices. Butter sold
for $4 a pound; tea for $10 a pound; brown sugar—white was
unobtainable—for $1.50 a pound; eggs for $1.50 a dozen.

Lee, after consulting with Jefferson Davis, decided on a bold
course of action. The Confederacy would carry the war into
the North, invade Pennsylvania, relieve the hard-fought soil
of Virginia, and press forward with a smashing drive against
the Northern cities which had yet not tasted warfare. Early
in June he started his armies on their journey north. Rumors
of Lee's intended invasion reached Washington and measures
were taken to forestall it, but Hooker was too slow. Lee's
army, stretched out in a dangerously long line, passed up the

Shenandoah Valley, crossed the Potomac and Maryland, and entered Pennsylvania. An advance guard pushed north while the main army gathered just beyond the border. Confederate troops seized York and compelled the city to ransom itself with clothing and money. Some of the troops approached within four miles of Harrisburg and the people there could hear the sound of gunfire. The whole North was thrown into consternation. Refugees fled before the marching army; Eastern Governors desperately tried to raise volunteers for defense and pleaded with the authorities at Washington to put McClellan in charge again; citizens purchased arms; Philadelphia and New Jersey prepared themselves against invasion.

The Union army was rushed forward to meet the invader. Lincoln was afraid to trust his dictator-loving general at such a moment of crisis. He sought for some one else. McClellan was out of the question; almost every Northern commander of note had already been tried. At the last moment Lincoln decided upon an unforeseen choice. He picked General George G. Meade, a Corps commander in the Army of the Potomac. Meade had quarreled with the irascible Hooker a few hours before his notification of appointment arrived. "Am I under arrest?" he asked sleepily as he was awakened on the early morning of June 28, to be told that he had been made commander of the Army of the Potomac.

Meade hurried his forces into Pennsylvania. On July 1, the two armies, groping for each other, met almost accidentally at Gettysburg. The most spectacular battle of the war ensued. The widely dispersed forces were quickly concentrated, facing each other on the outskirts of the little town. The Confederates carried the first day, and were still supreme on the second. On the third day of battle, Lee issued orders for a tremendous assault on the Union lines. An artillery duel began at one o'clock in the afternoon. Then fifteen thousand Confederates led by General Pickett moved across the long valley separating the armies. They walked into a concentrated volley of cannon and musketry fire that cut them down like wheat. This was the high-water mark of the Confederacy. Lee's army, broken and defeated, started south the next day. The rain that so often follows a great battle came down in torrents as the Confederate army, transporting its wounded in wagons, headed back to the Shenandoah Valley.

On this same day, July 4, the fortified city of Vicksburg, which had been under siege for months, surrendered to General Grant. The last important Confederate stronghold on the Mississippi was in Federal hands. Lincoln said in picturesque phrase: "The Father of Waters again goes unvexed to the sea."

Had the War been fought by two countries it would probably have ended at this time. But it was a War between two divisions of the same people—determination was equal on both sides. The Confederacy, lacking in ammunition, money, supplies and men for her armies, nevertheless grimly decided to continue what seems to us now a hopeless struggle. It did not seem quite so hopeless then. Gettysburg, which might have been a decisive and final victory, turned out to be only a repulse of the invading Southern army. Lincoln tried to force Meade to follow up his success with a strong attack that would annihilate Lee, but the pursuit was not carried out efficiently. It was Antietam all over again, with Meade playing the part of the dilatory McClellan. Lee reached Central Virginia, where he remained quietly throughout the fall and winter.

Even in the summer of 1863, when the North was in the full flush of victory, many of its own people were doing their best to defeat its cause. Copperheadism was on the increase. Disaffected areas were rife with opposition to the Northern war policy; treason became commonplace. Recruiting had fallen off so badly that men had to be offered large bounties for enlistment. Even this did not help. Men had to be drafted into the army, and the resistance to this measure became so great that in New York City it flared out into open violence only ten days after Gettysburg.

An attack was made on an office where names were being drawn for the draft. The building was burned, and police and soldiers were assaulted. The mob then surged through the city for four days terrorizing the populace, burning a Negro orphan asylum and running down and killing Negroes wherever they could be found. Nearly one thousand people were killed or wounded, and property damage ran into several millions of dollars.

Copperheadism in New York and in certain sections of the Middle West was, of course, not truly representative of Northern opinion. The victories at Gettysburg and Vicksburg did restore the confidence of many Northern people in their own cause, and they had a great influence on the elections held in the fall of 1863. These elections were for state officers, but the results could be taken as an indication of public attitude on the administration's handling of the War. In Illinois the election was regarded as so important that the President was asked to come to Springfield to address a Republican meeting that was to be held there. Lincoln could not leave Washington during such critical days, so he wrote instead a remarkable letter of policy to James C. Conkling, a Springfield lawyer who was his personal friend. In this letter, dated August 26, 1863, Lincoln put forth his views on the War, Emancipation and the Negro. His message was effective in shaping sentiment in favor of the administration which was under heavy attack from both Radical Republicans and Democrats, but what really decided the issue was an almost unnoticed groundswell of public opinion. Intellectuals had stood with the President almost from the first, and even those who had held back at first were now being won over. And the people of the Northern states, by some strange kind of intuitive judgment, were making up their minds that Abraham Lincoln was a good man and an honest one despite everything that was being said about him by his enemies.

Citizens who had visited the President at the White House went to their far-scattered homes to tell their neighbors what "Old Abe" was really like; soldiers carried the word home when they returned on furlough or were sent back from the front wounded; wives and widows of soldiers helped to spread the gospel—all over the country the voice of the people was speaking, but as has often happened, the politicians were too busy listening to the sound of their own voices to hear it. They heard it when the votes were counted. The country went for Lincoln and elected the men who had supported him.

Shortly after the elections, a ceremony was held for the dedication of a national cemetery for the men who had died at Gettysburg. After the battle, the bodies of the dead had been hastily buried in shallow graves. These bodies were now being recovered and were slowly being reinterred in the new cemetery. Various celebrated people were invited to attend the ceremony, the President among them. The chief oration of the day had been assigned to Edward Everett, a noted speaker in the great classic tradition then popular. At the last moment it was decided to ask the President to deliver "a few appropriate remarks" after Everett had finished.

The request for these few appropriate remarks was received at the White House on November 2, hardly more than two weeks before the scheduled date of the dedication ceremony, November 19, 1863.* But it was naturally expected that the President would say only a few words that would need no especial preparation. Everett's speech was the main event of the day, and anything that came after it would necessarily be anti-climactic.

* It is interesting to note that just ten days before the ceremony, the President went to the theater in company with Mrs. Lincoln and his secretaries, Nicolay and Hay, to see *The Marble Heart*, the leading actor in which was John Wilkes Booth.

Lincoln went to Gettysburg by train, but he had no opportunity to work on his speech during the journey. He had already completed the first half in Washington; he added the last few lines in Gettysburg on the morning of the day on which the ceremony was to be held. Shortly before eleven o'clock in the morning he left the town on horseback to go to the new cemetery on its outskirts. An official procession accompanied him across the battlefield which still showed marks of the terrible struggle that had taken place there only four months before. Dead horses were still lying on the field and the sick sweet odor of decay tainted the crisp November air. The graves in front of the speakers' stand were only partly filled; the audience stood scattered among them, and many of its members became impatient and wandered away to see the famous battleground while Everett delivered his two-hour discourse. Everett was late in beginning and he did not finish until two o'clock in the afternoon. By that time the audience was hungry and restless. After Everett's oration, a funeral dirge was sung. Then Ward Lamon stepped forward to introduce the President of the United States.

Most of the people were more eager to see what the President looked like than to hear what he had to say. They applauded him dutifully. The tall angular man on the platform adjusted his spectacles and shuffled the two bits of paper in his hands. A photographer in the crowd leisurely prepared his camera in order to take a picture of the President while he was speaking.

The thin high voice rose over the field of Gettysburg where the dead were lying in their temporary graves. The crowd was still taking the President's measure, paying little attention to his words.

"Fourscore and seven years ago," he began, "our fathers brought forth upon this continent a new nation, conceived in liberty, and dedicated to the proposition that all men are created equal. Now we are engaged in a great civil war, testing

whether that nation, or any nation so conceived, and so dedicated, can long endure. We are met on a great battlefield of
that war. We are met to dedicate a portion of it as the final
resting-place for those who have given their lives that that
nation might live. It is altogether fitting and proper that we
should do this. But in a larger sense we cannot dedicate, we
cannot consecrate, we cannot hallow this ground. The brave
men, living and dead, who struggled here, have consecrated
it far above our power to add or detract."

There was a polite burst of applause, but the President went
on. "The world will little note, nor long remember what we
say here, but it can never forget what they did here. It is for
us, the living, rather to be dedicated here to the unfinished
work that they have thus far so nobly carried on. It is rather
for us to be here dedicated to the great task remaining before
us, that from these honored dead we take increased devotion
to that cause for which they here gave the last full measure of
devotion; that we here highly resolve that these dead shall not
have died in vain; that the nation shall, under God, have a
new birth of freedom; and that government of the people,
by the people, for the people, shall not perish from the
earth."*

And then it was all over. The people who had just begun
to listen were astonished when the President stopped so soon.
The man with the camera was still trying to get his unwieldy
instrument ready. But the speech was finished, and not one
among all those who had heard it realized that he had been
present at the birth of an immortal prose poem. The general
effect was that of disappointment; the President himself
considered his address a failure. Nor did newspaper comment
the next day make him feel any better about it. Many of the
most important journals did not even mention his speech, and

* This version of the speech is taken from the dispatches of the day in an
attempt to reproduce Lincoln's words as they were actually spoken. The
version printed in the Lincoln text differs from it slightly, since Lincoln
made some revisions afterward.

the hostile Democratic papers denounced it as silly and unworthy of the occasion.

Exultation in the North over the midsummer victory at Gettysburg died down even before the men who had fallen there were buried in their final resting place. A Union victory was being won in Tennessee, where battles raged around Chattanooga during the fall until Federal troops finally repulsed the Confederates late in November, leaving the city and the greater part of the state in Union hands. But Western victories never received their due appreciation in the East—to the people of the Atlantic states, where the majority of the population of the North lived, the War was being fought in Virginia, and the importance of the Western campaigns was always seriously underestimated by them.

THE PRESIDENT VS. CONGRESS

As winter came on, military activity slackened, but the political front was as busy as ever. The President had to fight to get his own way in dealing with legislative matters needed to support both accomplished and anticipated military victories. By this time there was no doubt in his mind that the North eventually would win the War. He had to prepare for what would come afterward.

On December 8, he issued a proclamation which offered amnesty to all those who would take a specified oath of allegiance pledging their loyalty to the Union. He made exceptions only of high-ranking officers in the Confederate army or Government and of men who had abandoned Federal office to join the rebel cause. In this same proclamation he also outlined a plan for setting up new state governments in former Confederate territory. This plan provided that as soon as ten percent of any state's previous voting population would take the oath of allegiance, the government established by that portion of the citizens would be recognized as legitimate.

Despite the fact that the common people of the North appreciated the President's efforts to rehabilitate the country, his unpopularity with the press and with Congress increased as the War dragged on. He was attacked not only by Democratic papers but even by various Republican editors who were dominated by factional strife and petty hatreds. In the spring of 1864, when Lincoln called Grant to Washington to become the first Lieutenant General since Washington, the successful Western commander was so infinitely more popular than Lincoln with both Republican and Democratic politicians that he was already being closely watched as a Presidential possibility for the election of 1864. Only the fact that he was badly needed as a military commander put a stop to the movement for making him President.

On March 10, Lincoln gave Grant command of all the Union armies. Grant put Sherman in charge of the Western campaign, and a plan of action was drawn up for a concerted drive against the Confederates. On May 4, the Army of the Potomac crossed the Rapidan to march toward Richmond. At the same time, Sherman started his preparations to advance from Chattanooga into Georgia to attempt the capture of the city of Atlanta. Only Johnston's army stood in his way, and it was so depleted in numbers that it could do no more than keep up a harassing attack as it retreated. Lee, however, was still strong and he rose to meet Grant's challenge immediately. On May 5, he attacked the Army of the Potomac as it was proceeding through the Wilderness area lying west of Fredericksburg. It was unfavorable ground for the Union army, and its losses were extraordinarily heavy during the two-day battle. Nevertheless, Grant stubbornly pressed forward to Spottsylvania, where thousands more of his men died a few days later. Despite his losses, Grant was doggedly determined to carry on his campaign. It was from Spottsylvania, on May 11, that he sent his famous message to Stanton in which he declared: "I propose to fight it out on this line if it takes all summer." He shifted his plan of attack, and in a little more than two weeks he was at Cold Harbor, only a few miles from Richmond, and practically on the same ground where McClellan had met bitter defeat two years before. Again a tremendous assault was made on the Confederate lines, and again it was rolled back with fearful slaughter. Fifty-five thousand Northern soldiers had perished in less than a month in the three battles around Richmond, and the city's defenses were still intact. Grant's whirlwind offensive tactics had failed. The South, starving behind its ring of steel, rejoiced, while the North, still untouched and prosperous, was in despair at the defeat of the terrific drive launched by its greatest fighting general.

As the casualty lists brought home the War to every Northern city and village, discouragement rose and a cry to end the slaughter went up. If Grant could not take Richmond at this terrible price, the city must really be impregnable.

In the midst of all this defeat and disaster, preparations for the Presidential elections of 1864 had to be made. The Radical Republicans were eager to be rid of Lincoln. They favored Chase as the next President, because they believed that he would push the War more vigorously than Lincoln had, and they were convinced that he would deal more firmly with the South, once the War was over. A movement in Chase's behalf was started. As soon as it was made public, he offered to resign from the Cabinet. Lincoln, however, felt that Chase's Presidential ambitions were not incompatible with his duties as Secretary of the Treasury, so he quietly suggested that he remain at his post.

While the Radical Republicans laid their plots to oust Lincoln, another dissident group, which called itself the Radical Democracy, met in convention in Cleveland on May 31 to nominate the already discredited Frémont. This party adopted two ingenious principles in its platform: to restrict the Presidency to a one-term tenure by Constitutional amendment, and to endorse Congress, rather than the President, as the proper body to deal with reconstruction.

Left in a centrist position, the main body of the Republicans who still supported Lincoln decided to make an appeal to men of all parties to join a united front to keep the administration in office during the War. The name "Republican" was changed to "National Unionist." A platform was adopted that pledged no compromise with the rebels; it favored the administration measures already taken against slavery, and recommended passage of the proposed Constitutional amendment intended to eradicate it altogether The National Union convention was held at Baltimore on June 7, only a few days after Grant's defeat at Cold Harbor. The full import of this battle was not yet realized in the North, so the convention was able to nominate Lincoln without much opposition. Andrew Johnson, War Governor of Tennessee, was chosen as his running-mate for the Vice Presidency.

The Democrats, in order to see which way the wind would blow, postponed their convention until August 29. This seemed like a clever move at the time, but as events actually turned out, a more unpropitious date could hardly have been chosen.

On June 12, Grant, whose efforts to overwhelm Richmond in a smashing drive from the north had come to nothing, suddenly changed his whole plan of campaign and marched his army south of Richmond. This time, instead of flinging his men against the Confederate breastworks, he began a formal siege that was to keep him for nearly ten months before Petersburg, which was an important railroad center and the key to Richmond.

This war of attrition had an adverse effect on Lincoln's prospects for re-election. The North was keyed up to expect a victory when Grant took charge; it became impatient when Grant seemed to be stalemated in front of the strongly held redoubts of Petersburg. Sherman was advancing steadily toward Atlanta as Johnston gave ground before him, but he was far away and few communications came from him. The eyes of the nation were on Grant.

Grant was given everything that any general could ask to further his campaign. Even the defending force around Washington was depleted in order to send men to his armies. As a result, the President again had to experience the humiliation of seeing his capital come within a hair's breadth of falling into Confederate hands. A raiding party under the command of Jubal Early swept around to the west and descended upon Washington on July 11 and 12. Early's party was not very large, but it was determined, and it threw a terrible scare into the people in the capital city of the nation. Lincoln visited the fortifications during the height of the firing that was going on in the outskirts. Bullets flew thick around his tall form as he strolled around the little fort. One of the officers who was standing near him was hit, and then the young colonel in charge of the fort insisted that the President retire to a safer place.

The excitement over the attack on the city died down; the long summer days passed without word of success from Grant's army. Everything seemed to be going against Lincoln that summer. July and August were the unhappiest months in his Presidential career. Chase again offered to withdraw from the Cabinet, this time over a relatively trivial matter. Lincoln accepted his resignation—mutual embarrassment had made it impossible for them to work together. A movement for ending the War gained impetus in the North, where people were discouraged by Grant's attrition methods and disheartened by the constant call for more and more men— and no victories anywhere.

Peace negotiations with the Confederates were actually begun. Through Horace Greeley, two Southern commissioners in Canada made vague overtures to Washington for a settlement. Greeley was sent by the President to Niagara

Falls to meet them, but the negotiations collapsed when it became obvious that the commissioners were without authority, and that the South would consider no terms which prevented her from keeping her status as a separate nation. Another attempt at a rapprochement was made when Lincoln allowed two private citizens to go to Richmond to discuss peace with Jefferson Davis. Their efforts also came to nothing. Davis was quoted by them as saying: "This war must go on until the last of the generation falls in his tracks . . . unless you acknowledge our right to self-government." Lincoln was unwilling to concede any such right, too much blood had already been spilled for him to permit the War to be terminated without accomplishing its purpose of re-establishing the Union.

The problems heaped upon Lincoln's head during this summer were enough to have driven a weaker man mad. And war and politics were not the only sources of the troubles that were piling up for him—a private difficulty was being prepared for him in his own home. Mercifully, he never knew what was going on behind the scenes in the White House, but he must have felt the effects of what was happening. His wife, who had been thwarted in her plans for conquering Washington society, was giving expression to her mania for self-aggrandizement by indulging in an extravagant passion for clothes and personal adornment. She had run up a debt of $27,000, and the stores from which she had purchased her finery were pressing her for payment. She was frightened lest her husband discover how much she owed; she thought that if he were re-elected she would somehow be able to pay her bills. So she began a private campaign to make sure that he would win the election. She pulled wires and consorted with all sorts of strange people in an effort to gain another term for her husband and a four-year respite for herself.

Lincoln's troubles had no let up all summer. On August 5, Greeley's *Tribune* printed a document which marked an open break between the Radicals in Congress and the President. This was the Wade-Davis manifesto, named after its authors, Benjamin F. Wade and Henry Winter Davis. The Radicals were on the warpath; they denounced the President for his reconstruction policies. They were already beginning to reach out jealously for control over a South that was not yet conquered.

In February, the Radicals had drawn up a bill which ran counter to the President's Proclamation of Amnesty and Reconstruction in that it required a majority of voters instead of only ten percent; it furthermore provided that the new state constitutions must prohibit slavery. This bill passed the House and the Senate and was presented to the President less than an hour before Congress adjourned on July 4. Lincoln pocketed the bill, refusing either to sign or to veto it, saying that it was of too great importance to be rushed through at the last moment, and also that he doubted the authority of Congress to act on the status of slavery within the states. He, as President, could extend his emergency powers to cover the matter, but Congress had no such authorization under the Constitution.

Four days later, on July 8, Lincoln issued a proclamation in which he explained his position on the Congressional bill. Its adoption, he said, would endanger reconstruction plans already under way in two states; he was also unwilling to make a formal commitment to any one plan of reconstruction at this time. However, he did not rule out all consideration of the bill, for he said that if the people of any state preferred it to his, he was perfectly willing to let them use it.

This concession did not mollify the Radicals. They took counsel, and led by Davis and Wade, issued the manifesto that represented a public attack on the President. The ancient rivalry between Congress and the Chief Executive as to which should have the power to originate legislation had come to a head. Congress was naturally resentful of the unlimited extent of the President's wartime power, and the Radicals seized upon this dissatisfaction as a vantage point from which they could direct a campaign against the President's policies. That they should have done so when the candidate of their own party was standing for re-election was, to say the least, decidedly inopportune.

The reaction against Lincoln within his party now gained ground. Day after day in August was passing without word of anything being accomplished in the War except Farragut's capture of Mobile, the importance of which was not fully realized at the time. Backstage politicians became worried about Lincoln's chances of winning the election. They had blindly shut themselves off from public opinion and were judging the country by the bitterness of discussion taking place in the corridors of the Capitol and in smoke-filled hotel rooms in the big cities. They held a secret meeting at which they discussed ways and means of dealing with the situation. A proposal was made that Lincoln be asked to withdraw, or at least that another convention be held late in September at which it could be decided whether or not another candidate should be put forward. News of this reached Lincoln. The unsteadiness of his political support was further emphasized when some of his closest advisers and personal friends told him frankly that they did not believe he could be re-elected. The Democratic convention was due to be held in Chicago on August 29, and it was already obvious that its nominee for the Presidency would be General McClellan. Republican politicians were convinced that McClellan could beat Lincoln.

On August 23, the President entered a Cabinet meeting with a folded and sealed piece of paper in his hand. He asked each member present to sign his name on the back of it; he then dated the paper and put it away without saying anything further about it. On this day, the nadir of his career as President, Lincoln renounced all thought of himself in an attempt to preserve the Union no matter how the election

went. The memorandum which the Cabinet had been asked
to endorse blindly read:

This morning, as for some days past, it seems exceedingly probable that this administration will not be re-elected. Then it will be
my duty to so co-operate with the President-elect as to save the
Union between the election and the inauguration; as he will have
secured his election on such ground that he cannot possibly save
it afterward.

On November 11, a few days after his election, Lincoln
opened the paper and read it to his Cabinet. He then explained the motives that had led him to write it when his own
prospects had seemed so dark, and when the Democratic
convention had been only six days away:

You will remember that this was written at a time when as yet
we had no adversary, and seemed to have no friends. I then
solemnly resolved on the course of action indicated above. I resolved, in case of the election of General McClellan (being certain
that he would be the candidate), that I would see him and talk
matters over with him. I would say, "General, the election has
demonstrated that you are stronger, have more influence with the
American people than I. Now let us together—you with your influence and I with all the executive power of the Government—try
to save the country. You raise as many troops as you possibly can
for this final trial, and I will devote all my energies to assisting
and finishing the war."

The Cabinet members listened to the President's explanation with surprise. Seward commented ironically: "And the
General would answer you 'Yes, yes'; and the next day when
you saw him again and pressed these views upon him, he
would say, 'Yes, yes'; and so on forever, and would have done
nothing at all."

"At least," Lincoln replied, "I should have done my duty
and have stood clear before my own conscience."

But before this happened, before the election was held, the

President, whose chief worry during that incredibly disastrous
month of August was not for his own but for his country's
welfare, had still to endure the final ordeal—the ordeal of
personal danger and imminent death. One night while he
was riding alone to his summer quarters outside the city, a
shot was fired at him in the darkness. The bullet came so
close that it went through his hat and knocked it off. He
spurred his horse and rode on to his destination where he
made light of what happened to him, so that no word of it
would reach the public. But he had felt death reach out for
him in the darkness, and he knew that the plots against his
life were real. During the next few months they were to
multiply. Men were gathering in secret places to whisper and
plan; soon they were to try to put their plans into effect.

THE PRESIDENTIAL CAMPAIGN OF 1864

The dismal month finally drew to a close. On the twenty-
ninth, the Democrats held their convention at Chicago. The
general who had failed to save the nation on the field of battle
was nominated to save it by political means. A platform
was adopted which declared that four years of warfare had
failed to restore the Union, and that every Constitutional
right of the people had been trampled on in the process. It
recommended that "immediate efforts be made for a cessation of hostilities, with a view to an ultimate convention of
the states, or other peaceable means, to the end that at the
earliest practicable moment, peace may be restored on the
basis of the Federal Union of the states."

When this platform was submitted to McClellan, together
with the nomination, he explicitly repudiated the platform
but accepted the nomination. McClellan realized that he
could not afford to admit that the blood of his soldiers had
been poured out in vain. He knew that his best chance of
election was to stand on his war record, hesitating and unsuccessful as it had been.

The Democratic convention at Chicago ended on August 31 with high hopes for the election of its candidate. These hopes lasted just two days. On September 2, Sherman's army, which had been besieging Atlanta for weeks, finally entered the city. A Northern victory had come at last to clear the air. The first deep wound had been made in the body of the Confederacy, and the rebellious section, which for so long had seemed to be impregnable, was beginning to crack up under external pressure and internal strain. The news of Atlanta's fall was received with such enthusiasm in the North that it blasted the chances of Lincoln's rivals for the Presidency. Frémont withdrew from the campaign, and McClellan's backers began to lose heart.

During September, Grant sent Sheridan into the Shenandoah Valley to attack Early, who had retired there after his raid on Washington. Several engagements took place (one of which served to inspire Thomas Buchanan Read's famous poem on Sheridan's ride from Winchester), and then the Union army proceeded to devastate the smiling valley that had sheltered Confederate forces throughout the War.

Grant and his generals were embarking on a new plan of warfare. They determined to bring fire and destruction to complete the work of the sword. When Sherman took Atlanta, he ordered its people to evacuate the city, and he had his men wreck everything of military value. When he set out from Atlanta in November for his march to the sea, his army left behind it a city abandoned to the flames with the smoke of its burning standing like a vast pillar in the sky.

Nothing that the North did during the whole War infuriated the South so much as these measures taken to destroy property. Human lives and human suffering were forgotten in the outcry raised over the burning and wrecking of inanimate objects. The bodies of the dead are quickly buried out of sight, but the fire-blackened walls of gutted buildings remain for years as stark reminders of terror long past.

This ruthless campaign gave the death-blow to the already weakened Confederacy. By the time the November elections were held, it was obvious, even to the most skeptical Northerner, that the end of the War was really in sight and that the Union armies must prevail.

The politicians had misjudged the people's support of the President, although it is true, of course, that the autumn victories swung an even larger vote to the administration. Twenty-five states participated in the election; twenty-two of them were carried by Lincoln. McClellan received the electoral votes of only New Jersey, Delaware and Kentucky. The popular vote was 2,214,000 for Lincoln and 1,802,000 for McClellan.

On the two nights following his election, Lincoln spoke to the people in answer to serenades of victory. In his speech of November 10, he outlined his own attitude toward the election: "It has long been a grave question whether any government, not too strong for the liberties of its people, can be strong enough to maintain itself in existence in great emergencies. . . . We cannot have free government without elections; and if the rebellion could force us to forego or postpone a national election, it might fairly claim to have already conquered and ruined us. . . . What has occurred in this case must ever recur in similar cases. Human nature will not change. In any future great national trial, compared with the men of this, we shall have as weak and as strong, as silly and as wise, as bad and as good. Let us, therefore, study the incidents of this as philosophy to learn wisdom from, and none of them as wrongs to be avenged."

Once the long-dreaded election was over, the administration could make long-term plans for the future, but its immediate problem was to try to bring the War to a speedy close. Sherman set out from Atlanta on November 15, severing his lines of communication and marching across Georgia, cutting a swath of destruction sixty miles wide as he went. Grant tightened his stranglehold on Petersburg and Richmond. Richmond was now in desperate straits; food prices skyrocketed as money became almost worthless, and criticism of the government was increasing daily. Sherman continued his inexorable advance; on December 21 he captured Savannah and then prepared to head northward through the heart of the Confederacy.

On December 6, Lincoln delivered his annual message to Congress. He reminded that body that although the House had previously refused to pass the amendment to the Constitution abolishing slavery, the election had been a clear-cut call from the voters of the nation for it to do so now. He expressed pessimistic views on dealing with Jefferson Davis for peace—Davis was evidently committed to a last-stand policy. The President indicated, however, that the Southern people might be more willing than their leader to sue for a settlement to end the War. He stood firmly on his emancipation policy and said that he would not be a party to any effort to re-enslave Negroes already set free by it.

On the same day, Lincoln announced his choice for the Chief Justice of the Supreme Court, a position which had been made vacant by the death of the superannuated Taney in October. In making his decision, Lincoln again forgot personal rivalries and selected the man he felt was best fitted to serve. He appointed Salmon P. Chase, whom he regarded as a great lawyer, and he ignored the fact that Chase was a Radical Republican who had sat for three years in the Cabinet offering more opposition to the President than any other member.

The new year brought high hopes to the North. To the South it brought only a dull realization of impending defeat. The Richmond *Sentinel* published a remarkable article admitting the exhaustion of the Confederacy's resources, and suggesting that an alliance be made with England, France or Spain to preserve independence from the North even at the price of allowing a foreign power to gain a foothold on the American continent. As a concession to tender European feelings, the *Sentinel* recommended that slavery in the Southern states be abolished before any alliance was sought. Rebellion had run its course; this was the logical conclusion of the separation-at-any-price policy.

While the theoreticians in Richmond played with such ideas as this, Sherman's army left Savannah on January 14 and pushed steadily northward. By February 18, Columbia, South Carolina's capital, was in his hands, and like Atlanta, it too went up in smoke, although this time Sherman claimed that the fire had been set by the retreating Confederates. Not only Columbia, but the proud city of Charleston had to yield before the advance of Sherman's victorious army. As soon as her railroad communications were cut, Charleston collapsed. She had been holding out for several years against a Federal fleet besieging her harbor. Now the fleet sailed in unresisted, and "the cradle of secession" was in the hands of the Northern invaders.

Before the first month of the new year was out, Congress heeded the President's urgent request to pass the Constitutional amendment abolishing slavery. The vote was taken on January 31 in the presence of an intensely interested public audience which greeted with wild applause the announcement that the required two-thirds majority had been obtained.

THE BEGINNING OF THE END

A few days later, Lincoln, who had so recently spoken against entering into peace negotiations with the Richmond Government, now became a direct party to such a move himself. On February 3, he held a conference with three Confederate commissioners. They came to see him at Hampton Roads on board the *River Queen*, a ship often used by Lincoln when he traveled by water routes. This attempt to effect a reconciliation turned out to be as fruitless as all the others had been. Davis wanted peace and independence; Lincoln insisted on peace and reunion, so the commissioners were powerless and could accomplish no direct result. The conference, however, was probably not without influence upon Lincoln's policies. One of the commissioners was Alexander Stephens, Vice President of the Confederacy, a former Whig and United States Congressman. The South could not have chosen a better person to deal with Lincoln. They had both been in Congress together, and Lincoln had long admired this man who was one of the most beloved figures in the South. Lincoln had corresponded with him when he was President-elect in 1860. They were unalterably opposed to each other on the slavery issue, but they had always gotten on well together, and they talked for a while about old times. Although Lincoln was adamant about reunion, he intimated that he would be liberal in dealing with the Southern states if they would return. He also said that he favored some kind of compensation for the expropriation of slave property, for he believed that the North shared the South's guilt in having permitted slavery to be established in the nation.

During the interview, Lincoln had occasion to remark that he doubted whether it was proper for him as the leader of a nation to deal directly with rebels who were opposing the authority of his government by force of arms. One of the commissioners cited the case of Charles I as precedent. It was an unfortunate example. Lincoln immediately said: "I don't profess to be posted in history—all I distinctly recollect about Charles I is that he lost his head."

When the commissioners were about to leave the ship, Stephens said to Lincoln: "I understand, then, that you regard us as rebels who are liable to be hanged for treason?"

Lincoln nodded solemnly.

"Well, we supposed that would have to be your view," Stephens said with equal solemnity. Then he smiled as he turned to go, and his eyes twinkled as he looked at Lincoln,

"But to tell you the truth, we have none of us been much afraid of being hanged with you as President!"

We have no way of knowing how much the President's contact with his old friend, Alexander Stephens, influenced his policies, but it is interesting to note that on Sunday evening, February 5, only twenty-four hours after his return from the Hampton Roads conference, Lincoln called a special Cabinet meeting. He had evidently spent the day preparing a proposal which incorporated a twofold plan to end the War quickly and to compensate the Southern slaveowners for the loss of their property. The document he read to his Cabinet provided that if the Confederacy would lay down arms by April 1, the United States would pay $400,000,000 to the rebellious states as an indemnity for their loss of slave property. The liberality of such an idea stunned the Cabinet. Pay the enemy for stopping a war that was almost won! There was an embarrassed silence. Hardly any discussion was given to the President's plan. One after another the members of the Cabinet voted against it. Reluctantly the President had to write on the sheets of paper in his hand:

February 5, 1865. Today these papers, which explain themselves, were drawn up and submitted to the Cabinet and unanimously disapproved by them. A. Lincoln.

And then he put the documents away in his files. They were not made public until after his death.

Implicit in this proposal is the trend of purpose that now dominated Lincoln. He was eager to see the War end as quickly as possible, for every day less of fighting meant fewer men killed. He knew, however, that the War could not last very long—the South had been cut in half when the Mississippi was won; it was now being quartered by Sherman's army. But even more important than bringing to a quick end a War that must inevitably end quickly anyway, was the problem of reconciling the two hostile sections. The South had gone to war to defend slavery and had declared her independence in order to maintain the "peculiar institution" that was the mainstay of her economy. The War had completely ruined the South; her economy was wrecked; her manpower depleted. The North, however, had become richer and stronger during the War. Huge factories had been erected; railroads and telegraph lines had been extended; grain acreage had increased enormously in the new West; more and more gold and silver were being mined. Hundreds of thousands of Northern youths had died in the War, but millions of people in Europe were eager to come to America to take their places, and it was obvious that they would settle, not in the war ruined South, but in the thriving factory areas of the North and in the new lands of the West.

To Lincoln the United States was still one nation. He had never recognized the independence of the South, never granted that the seceding states were out of the Union. Now he simply wanted to restore peace and prosperity to the whole country. In order to make reconciliation easy, he was willing to take some of the North's wealth to use for the rehabilitation of the South. More than three billion dollars had been spent by the North to subdue the South—surely the victorious section could afford to give $400,000,000—seven and a half percent of the war expenditure—to the South as a stake with which she could begin a new life. This money was to be an indemnity for the loss of property represented in freeing the slaves. Lincoln's legal training made him feel that expropriation without proper compensation would be unjust.

There was no malice in his mind, no hatred of the men who had taken up arms against the United States. He was willing to do anything that would make the South an integral part of the nation again. He was a kindly and generous person who wanted to buy peace at any price so long as he could re-establish the Union. Unfortunately he was no economist. He arrived at his conclusion by sheer intuitive judgment. As a result, he did not see the fallacy in his argument—that by indemnifying the slaveholders for their loss of property he would be strengthening the very men who had brought on the War. He thought that the provision made in his plan requiring emancipation as part of the bargain would eliminate the slavery that was the root of their power, but he did not realize that if he indemnified them, they would still be the dominant group in the new South that he hoped to see established. If they were permitted to hold their power, the same old cycle would begin all over again, and the South would still be ruled by an oligarchy* instead of by the democratic methods he hoped to establish there. Perhaps the Cabinet sensed this. At any rate they disapproved, and Lincoln's dream was swept into the dustbin of history.

Yet the spirit that pervaded Lincoln's proposal of February 5 was the spirit that was to be expressed in developed form in the famous Second Inaugural Address. To Lincoln, slavery was a hateful and offensive thing—a sin in the sight of the Lord. In the second inaugural he speaks of the War as a heaven-sent retribution for this sin. But evil as he thought slavery was in the abstract, he held no malice against the Southern people who had gone to war to defend it. To him North and South equally shared the guilt of slavery; the retribution was visited upon them both for the trespass against righteousness that they had both committed in allowing it to flourish upon the nation's soil. He wanted them now to forget the years of hatred—the hideous period of fratricidal strife.

* This, of course, is exactly what happened anyway. After the Radical Republican reconstruction measures had run their first course, the former slaveholders re-established their grip on the government of the South by using violent means to gain control—of which the Ku Klux Klan was only one. The North won its chief objective by becoming the dominant force in the government of the nation; the Southern oligarchy won its secondary objective of keeping itself in power in its own section. The real losers in the War were the poor whites and the Negroes. Sharecropping and the exploitation of cheap labor replaced the slave system, and the democratic methods that Lincoln hoped to see extended to the South were postponed for generations.

His last words—the last words he was ever to speak in an official capacity before a great audience—were an apostrophe to peace and a plea for charity toward all those who erred in inflicting human bondage upon their fellow creatures.

The occasion of the delivery of this celebrated speech marked the differences which four years of battle had made. Outwardly the inauguration ceremonies of 1865 may have seemed much the same as they had been four years before. Again precautions had to be taken to protect the life of the President; again there were riflemen on the housetops; again there was a long covered passage leading to the speaker's platform. And the actual ceremonial procedure itself, of course, did not vary. But the great dome of the Capitol, which had been under construction in 1861, was now finished, and from its top the huge bronze statue of Freedom looked down at the scene. There were more subtle differences, too. Instead of the ancient Taney with memories of the infamous Dred Scott decision hanging over him, Lincoln's own appointee, Chief Justice Chase, administered the oath of office. The pathetically small garrison of 1861 was replaced by huge numbers of soldiers whose uniforms were seen everywhere in the city. Among them were the wounded; they were a commonplace sight in Washington. The President, too, had changed. His ordeal had steeled him in dealing with strong men, but it had mellowed him also in dealing with the weak and the defeated. The man who had had to be persuaded in 1861 not to close his inaugural address with a clear-cut offer of peace or a sword was still firm in his belief in the righteousness of his cause:

The Almighty has His own purposes. "Woe unto the world because of offenses! for it must needs be that offenses come; but woe to that man by whom the offense cometh." If we shall suppose that American slavery is one of those offenses which, in the providence of God, must needs come, but which, having continued through His appointed time, He now wills to remove, and

that He gives to both North and South this terrible war, as the
woe due to those by whom the offense came, shall we discern
therein any departure from those divine attributes which the believers in a living God always ascribe to Him? Fondly do we hope—
fervently do we pray—that this mighty scourge of war may speedily
pass away. Yet, if God wills that it continue until all the wealth
piled by the bondsman's two hundred and fifty years of unrequited toil shall be sunk, and until every drop of blood drawn
with the lash shall be paid by another drawn with the sword, as
was said three thousand years ago, so still it must be said, "The
judgments of the Lord are true and righteous altogether."

But his very last words were a plea for peace—peace with
out malice, peace which would "bind up the nation's wounds":

With malice toward none; with charity for all; with firmness in
the right, as God gives us to see the right, let us strive on to finish
the work we are in; to bind up the nation's wounds; to care for
him who shall have borne the battle, and for his widow, and his
orphan—to do all which may achieve and cherish a just and lasting
peace among ourselves, and with all nations.

As he spoke, the sun which had been behind the clouds all
day, came out to shine down on the crowd gathered in front
of the long façade of the Capitol. The people, taking this for a
good omen, cheered the President heartily. The distant guns
thundered a salute to the man who had just entered on his
second term of office, and Abraham Lincoln, fifty-six years
old, tired, and showing the strain of war, entered his carriage
to return to the White House. He then had just six weeks
to live.

PLOTS AND COUNTERPLOTS

While he had been pleading for the renunciation of revenge, an almost unnoticed incident had been taking place
on the edge of the crowd standing on the platform. A man had
tried to force his way nearer to the President. Something
about his actions made one of the guards stop him. There was

a brief scuffle, and the man was then ejected from the Capitol. It seems strange that he was not taken into custody for questioning. If he had been, his arrest would have caused a sensation, for he was a well-known person. He was a member of a family whose name was famous in the theater, and he had made a reputation for his own name, John Wilkes Booth.

Booth was the leader of a band of conspirators who had been engaged for months in an effort to strike at Lincoln. They had unsuccessfully tried abduction, thinking that they could spirit the President away to Richmond to be held for ransom. Booth regarded Lincoln personally responsible for having begun the War and for having waged it until the South was on the verge of ruin. He hoped vaguely that Lincoln's removal would encourage the South to continue fighting, but reason or thought of consequence played little part in his mad scheme; he was the half-insane son of an insane father, Junius Brutus Booth, whose wild idiosyncrasies had been notorious in the theater.

The conspirators were desperately anxious to strike. On March 17, the day before Booth was scheduled to play in Washington at Ford's Theater in *The Apostate*, a last attempt was made to take the President alive while he was riding out of the city to attend an amateur theatrical performance at one of the soldiers' camps. This plot, too, was unsuccessful. Booth became frantic; the War was rapidly drawing to a close. Johnston's army had advanced until it was only 140 miles south of Grant's. Grant was ready to give the word to his men to begin the assault on Petersburg.

Lincoln's sudden decision to leave Washington at this time probably gave him a few more weeks of life. On March 23, he, Mrs. Lincoln and Tad left on the *River Queen* to visit Grant's headquarters at City Point. A message was sent to Sherman to leave his army in charge of his second in command and join the President and General Grant for a conference before the final campaign was begun.

At City Point, while waiting for Sherman to arrive, Lincoln rode out to inspect armies, fortifications and artillery positions. One of these occasions marked a new point of advance in Mary Lincoln's rapidly disintegrating control of herself. She and Mrs. Grant were riding to a review in an army wagon, when one of Grant's aides casually remarked that the troops were evidently getting ready to go into action because all the officer's wives had been sent to the rear. He then incautiously added that General Griffin's wife, a handsome Washington society lady, had been given a special permit by the President to remain at the front. Mrs. Lincoln immediately burst out in jealous fury. "Do you mean to say that she saw the President alone?" she demanded. "Do you know that I never allow the President to see any woman alone?" She insisted that the wagon be stopped at once so that she could get out to demand an explanation from her husband. Fortunately, General Meade, the hero of Gettysburg, came up, and he lied gallantly, saying that Mrs. Griffin had received her permit from the Secretary of War.

The next day there was even more trouble of the same kind. Mrs. Lincoln saw General Ord's wife riding by the side of her husband. She threatened to jump out of the wagon to stop her. Mrs. Grant tried to bring the infuriated woman to her senses but succeeded only in drawing a tirade upon herself. When the wagon came to a halt, Mrs. Lincoln insulted Mrs. Ord to her face, calling her names and reducing her to tears in front of the whole party. At dinner she tried to get the President to remove General Ord from his post. When he refused to do so, she attacked him bitterly in the presence of her embarrassed guests. Lincoln said nothing, but sat unhappy and patiently forbearing while she carried on. Perhaps he suspected that the woman with whom he had lived for twenty-two years was no longer responsible for her actions. He had seen many evidences of her strange behavior, but he was unaware of the one fact that might have given him the final clue to her mental instability—the fact that her desire for expensive clothes had gone beyond all reasonable bounds. The woman who had sought her husband's re-election in order to be able to pay her enormous debts had gone right on acquiring more and more finery and trinkets until she now owed the astounding sum of $70,000.*

It was an ironic touch that Mrs. Lincoln's insane jealousy should have increased at this time until she was driven to make a public display of it, for the husband she was trying to keep away from other women had become an old man whose health was breaking and whose strength was gone. The photographic portraits taken during the War years show with amazing fidelity how his features were aging. Year by year, the War had burned out his life. And the changes being wrought upon him were not only physical ones. The once-ready laughter had almost ceased; the vivid interest in the absurd and ridiculous had dwindled. The Lincoln of 1865 was obviously a man who had met sorrow and been conquered by it. He had seen more than a half million young men from the North and the South march away to their deaths, and the thought of them never left his mind.

It was an old man, dreaming of patching up quarrels between the sons of his family, who went into conference with his generals on the River Queen on March 27. Grant and Sherman knew that victory was theirs for the taking; only the terms of surrender had to be considered.

No one realized better than Lincoln that many people in the North were calling out for blood. "Hang the traitors!"

---

* Mrs. Lincoln's debts were to cause her endless trouble and disgrace. Her husband's death left her in control of a considerable sum of money, but it was not large enough to enable her to pay what she owed and still have enough to live on. She threatened to hold a public auction in order to raise funds. Her debts were finally liquidated by payment in part by herself, and in part by secret donations direct to her creditors from her husband's former political associates. In 1875 she was committed for a short while to an asylum; she was then taken to Springfield, where she died on July 16, 1882, in the house in which she had been married.

was their cry. Exact the full measure of vengeance from the men whose rebellion had brought suffering and death to the whole country! A younger man than Lincoln would almost surely have been more severe in imposing penalties upon the South. But Lincoln was old and tired, and his heart yearned for the days of his youth when he had seen men of the North and South mingle together to make a continental nation out of a wilderness. He wanted only to place the seal of an understanding peace upon his life's work. The only thing that mattered to him was the re-establishment of the Union. That and that alone was the major task he had yet to accomplish, and in order to make reconciliation as easy as possible he wanted to be sure that his two chief generals would offer generous terms to the vanquished.

Exactly what he said to Grant and Sherman in the cabin of the River Queen has never been made clear. Neither of them ever reported the conversation in detail, and it is entirely likely that he asked them not to do so. But what came out of this conference can lead to only one conclusion: that Abraham Lincoln, President of the United States, made full use of his official position to specify the terms of surrender. Both Grant and Sherman offered terms that were almost identical in detail, and that were absolutely identical in the spirit of generosity implicit in them.*

In addition to providing the most favorable terms of surrender possible, Lincoln sounded out his generals to see if the pending battle could in some way be avoided. The Confederates, bottled up within their capital, obviously had no chance of further success. Every drop of blood spilled now seemed horribly unnecessary. Both Grant and Sherman, however, concurred in believing that Lee would not give up without making a last-stand fight. Disappointed in this, Lincoln,

---

* This generosity later proved embarrassing to Sherman. He accepted Johnston's surrender a few days after Lincoln's death and came in for bitter criticism against which he then had no way of defending himself.

nevertheless, spoke with gentle indirection about the fate of the Confederate leaders. If they were captured he was afraid that their execution would be demanded. He hinted that if they were permitted to escape from the country, the issue of what should be done with them would never have to be met.

Sherman returned to his army. Grant gave the word for the assault on the fortifications around Petersburg. Events now moved with fearful swiftness. Grant intensified the pressure on Petersburg. On April 2, Lee telegraphed to Davis that he could no longer hold his lines—the city must be evacuated immediately. The Confederate Government fled to Danville, where it was hoped that Lee could join Johnston to make another stand. Lee's army streamed out of the redoubts around Petersburg. Sheridan started in hot pursuit. A running battle took place that lasted for several days. By April 8 it was all over. Sheridan headed off Lee, and Grant was on the heels of the fleeing army. The next day, at Appomattox Court House, Grant accepted Lee's surrender and gave him the generous terms proposed by Lincoln.

Lee's men were permitted to keep their horses so they could take them home to do the spring plowing; officers and men were simply asked to sign paroles not to take up arms again and to surrender all military equipment except their side-arms. And then the War was ended—not officially and finally, but to all practical purposes.

The Confederates had set Richmond on fire when they abandoned it. A huge conflagration raged there, consuming seven hundred buildings in the heart of the city. On April 3, when the vanguard of the Union army marched in, one of its first tasks was to help put out the fire.

On April 4, Lincoln set out with a small escort to see the city that had been the main goal of his war aims. He sailed up the James River in company with Admiral Porter. When the ship came to a barrier placed by the Confederates in the channel, the Presidential party had to proceed in a small barge. This was landed on the waterfront not far from Libby Prison—a place that had become infamous in the North for the dreadful stories told about the treatment of prisoners of war held there. The prison was deserted, the streets around it silent. The great fire, still burning in some parts of the city, covered the scene with a pall of smoke. When the President stepped ashore, a few Negroes recognized him. In a short time a large crowd of colored people gathered around him, eager to see the man they looked upon as a saint and a messiah. Followed by them, the President walked through the city to the building Davis had used as the Executive Mansion of the Confederacy. Lincoln entered and went to the desk that Davis had so recently vacated; then he sat down in the chair that had belonged to the President of the Confederate States of America. For the first time in his career as President, Lincoln held his position unchallenged.

He returned through the city safely, although there must have been hundreds of men still in hiding there who would have been glad to kill the man they held responsible for their defeat. He returned to City Point and waited for the outcome of the running battle still going on with Lee.

Word came to him that Secretary Seward had been seriously injured in a carriage accident in Washington and was in bed suffering from a fractured jaw and severe shock. Lincoln felt that his presence at the capital was needed; he left City Point on April 8.

The River Queen headed up the Potomac. While it was on its way back to Washington Lincoln held long conversations with his friends, speaking to them about literature and poetry. He read Shakespeare to them, and one incident fastened itself forever on their minds. When Lincoln was reading *Macbeth*, he came to the passage:

> Duncan is in his grave.
> After life's fitful fever he sleeps well;
> Treason has done its worst; nor steel nor poison,

Malice domestic, foreign levy, nothing
Can touch him further.

And then he stopped and read the passage over again as if struck by its significance. Nor was this the only portent he had at this time. He later recounted to Lamon a dream which must have occurred during this period, for his references to dispatches from the front date it. He told the story to Lamon some time prior to April 11, so the dream must have taken place about April 1, while he was at City Point waiting for the news of Grant's assault on the lines of Petersburg.

About ten days ago I retired very late. I had been up waiting for important dispatches from the front. I could not have been long in bed when I fell into a slumber, for I was weary. I soon began to dream. There seemed to be a death-like stillness about me. Then I heard subdued sobs, as if a number of people were weeping. I thought I left my bed and wandered downstairs. There the silence was broken by the same pitiful sobbing, but the mourners were invisible. I went from room to room; no living person was in sight, but the same mournful sounds of distress met me as I passed along. It was light in all the rooms; every object was familiar to me; but where were all the people who were grieving as if their hearts would break? I was puzzled and alarmed. What could be the meaning of all this? Determined to find the cause of a state of things so mysterious and so shocking, I kept on until I arrived at the East Room [of the White House], which I entered. There I met with a sickening surprise. Before me was a catafalque, on which rested a corpse wrapped in funeral vestments. Around it were stationed soldiers who were acting as guards; and there was a throng of people, some gazing mournfully upon the corpse, whose face was covered, others weeping pitifully. "Who is dead in the White House?" I demanded of one of the soldiers. "The President," was his answer; "he was killed by an assassin!" Then came a loud burst of grief from the crowd, which awoke me from my dream. I slept no more that night.

The man who was returning to the White House to meet

the realization of his own death dream entered Washington on April 9, the day of Lee's surrender at Appomattox. The news was received early on the morning of the tenth, and the city, which had just gone through a week of celebration over the fall of Richmond, began another period of wild rejoicing.

VICTORY AND PEACE

News of victory and peace spread across the Northern states, creating an emotional outburst that can be compared only with the spontaneous display of public feeling on Armistice Day, 1918. Lincoln knew that he still faced a struggle with Congress over the problems of a merciful reconstruction for the South, but he must have been glad that no more men were marching to their deaths at his command. Observers all say that he seemed to be imbued with a new energy after his return from City Point. Spring was at hand, and the air was warm and invigorating. The dreadful War years were over, and the President could look forward to peace and the conduct of ordinary affairs.

On the night of April 10, a torchlight procession went to the White House to serenade him. He was unwilling to speak extemporaneously at a time when every word might be taken as a declaration of policy. He good-naturedly asked the crowd to return the next evening, promising to prepare a speech for the occasion. He then suggested that the band play "Dixie," a tune, he said, that could rightfully be considered a contraband of war.

Advance notice that the President would deliver a speech of victory encouraged a large turn-out the next evening. If the people who came to the White House expected a speech of exultation they must have been disappointed, for the President had quite another idea in mind. He spoke chiefly about the provisional state government that had been set up in Louisiana, and he made it clear that he expected to treat the Southern states as if they had never been out of the Union at all; according to him, they had simply been "out of their proper practical relation" to it. He indicated also that he would favor the franchise for those Negroes who were very intelligent or who had served as soldiers. He pleaded that the new state government be sustained; it was not perfect, he admitted, but it was the best that could be obtained under the circumstances.

It was, in many ways, a strange speech to make in response to a serenade of victory. Except for the brief introduction there was no mention of victory in it. Lincoln had already discounted the winning of the War and was pressing on to the winning of the peace. It was evident, also, that he was preparing to take the issue of reconstruction to the public in order to gain support for his anticipated struggle with Congress. But this was his valedictory address. The hostile eyes of conspirators were glaring at him as he spoke.

The next two days passed quickly. April 12 was the fourth anniversary of the day on which the Confederate forts in Charleston harbor had opened fire on Sumter. The War had lasted almost exactly four years. On April 14, which was the anniversary of Sumter's surrender, a public ceremony was held inside the ruined fort. Robert Anderson, the Union officer who had been compelled to haul down his country's flag there four years before, now pulled the halyards that flung the same flag to the sea breezes over Sumter's historic walls.

In Washington, April 14 was a blustery spring day with sunshine and shadow alternating as the hours passed. At eleven o'clock in the morning, a Cabinet meeting was held at which General Grant was present as a guest of honor. The ever-present problem of reconstruction was discussed, and then mention was made of Sherman. Word was expected hourly from him of Johnston's surrender. The President told his Cabinet that he was sure the news would come soon, for he had had a dream which came before almost every great battle of the War—Sumter, Bull Run, Antietam, Gettysburg, Vicksburg, etc. He, the dreamer, had dreamed again, and he explained that in this dream he always stood on the deck of a strange vessel sailing rapidly toward a dark and unknown shore. He felt that his dream was an augury that something eventful was about to happen—it would probably be the news from Sherman, he said.

He had arranged to go to the theater that evening with General and Mrs. Grant, but during the Cabinet meeting a note was received from Mrs. Grant, saying that she had decided to go to New Jersey to visit her children who were at school there. General Grant asked to be excused from the theater party. No other reason was given, but his wife probably did not wish to expose herself again to the embarrassment Mrs. Lincoln had caused her at City Point.

And so it was that the President and Mrs. Lincoln went to Ford's Theater that night with only a young officer and his fiancée for company. Had General Grant been with them it is at least possible that the tragedy due to be staged there might never have occurred. Grant was a tough old campaigner, alert against attack and experienced with the ways of violent men.

The Presidential party entered the theater shortly after eight o'clock. The play was *Our American Cousin*, and the star was Laura Keene, who had already given more than a thousand performances in the leading role. It was a silly comedy at which the President laughed heartily, glad to have an opportunity to forget the problems of the day. During the second act he suddenly felt cold and got up to put his coat around him. And then, during the next act, a door behind him opened so quietly that no one noticed it. A shot rang out, and Abraham Lincoln's consciousness of the living world ceased at that moment. The infuriated Booth cried out his singularly inappropriate phrase "*Sic semper tyrannis*," slashed with a dagger at the young officer in the box and then was gone to keep his own rendezvous with death somewhere in Virginia.

The unconscious President was carried out of the theater in the midst of wild pandemonium. He was taken to a boarding-house across the street, where he was laid on a bed in a hall room. Surgeons worked over him for hours, but it was obvious that he could not live, that he could not even regain consciousness. Mrs. Lincoln, weeping and hysterical, waited all night in the front parlor of the little house. Members of the Cabinet and high government officials came to gather around the President. Everybody suspected that the assassination was part of a concerted rebel attempt to capture the city. At the same moment Lincoln was shot, another conspirator had entered the house where Seward was lying helpless in bed. Seward escaped death, but the infuriated intruder wounded several people who got in his way.

As the night passed, the noise of a city gone mad reached the room where the President lay dying. Mobs surged through the streets; cavalry patrols thundered past. But the people standing around the motionless figure on the bed had ears only for the labored breathing that came and went. Shortly after dawn, the rain began to fall. Gray daylight filtered in through the window. A surgeon, listening to the last faint breathing, closed his watch at seven-twenty-two; he then lifted the wasted hands and folded them across the motionless chest. The life-course that had begun in a Kentucky mountain cabin had run full cycle.

"NIGHT AND DAY JOURNEYS A COFFIN"

At nine-thirty the body of the dead President was carried through the streets of Washington to the White House. As the funeral cortege passed along in the rain, people were taking down the banners of victory to replace them with the dark trappings of mourning. And all through the North the news of the President's death was received with incredulity, with paralyzing shock, and then with rage that was to shake the nation for years to come.

The body was kept in the East Room of the White House until the official funeral was held on Wednesday, April 19. On that day, the procession moved through vast throngs of people to the Capitol, where the body was left to lie in state under the huge dome. All day Thursday thousands of people, white and black, civilians and soldiers, stood patiently in the rain, waiting to pass the flower-decked bier. Then on Friday, the funeral train left Washington bound for Springfield over the same route Lincoln had taken when he had come east as President-elect. An enormous crowd turned out in Baltimore to mourn for the man whose life had once not been safe there. Harrisburg and Philadelphia were visited in turn. The train moved on to New York where an impressive out door ceremony was held. Then it went along the Hudson to Albany, across the state to Buffalo, to Cleveland, Columbus, Indianapolis and Chicago, taking nearly two weeks to complete its journey. Everywhere people came to see it pass. They stood at country crossroads and lined the tracks on the out skirts of the cities. And everywhere the response was the same. Party feuds and political differences were forgotten as the nation came to mourn. This, and not Appomattox, was Lincoln's hour of triumph. In death he had won the love of his people.

On the night of May 2 the funeral train left Chicago and headed southward through the small towns of Illinois. It was raining, but people came to stand along the railroad track. They built bonfires to light the scene, and as the train passed slowly through the greening fields of the prairie country, thousands of silent figures were silhouetted against the dull red flames. All night long the train traveled toward Springfield; it passed Bloomington of the famous "Lost Speech" shortly before dawn; it reached the little town of Atlanta as the sun rose to bring fair weather to the day. It moved on through Lincoln, Elkhart and Williamsville in the early morning hours. It approached Springfield about nine o'clock, running with bell tolling and a long black plume of smoke trailing across the level fields outside the city.

Tens of thousands of people were in Springfield. They had come from prairie villages, from farms and from isolated places scattered far across the state. Among them were men who had known Lincoln on the circuit, people who remembered him from New Salem days, pioneers who could recall the time when an ox-cart had first brought his family to Illinois.

The train steamed slowly along the tracks where country wagons were drawn up to see it pass; it crossed a bridge over the winding brown waters of the Sangamon River; it approached the forest grove in which Springfield had been built; it came to the first houses on the edge of the town; it entered the business center where people were standing on the tops of buildings because the streets were so crowded that it was impossible to get near the railroad station. And then, at ten minutes after nine, it pulled into the Chicago and Alton depot, where regiments of soldiers and the dignitaries of Springfield were waiting to receive it.

Minute guns began their solemn firing. A military band played the slow measures of a funeral dirge. The bells of the city began to toll. But there was a sudden hush of voices around the station as the train came to a stop.

The people of Springfield stood watching in terrible silence as the body of their fellow townsman was taken from the train.

Abraham Lincoln had come home.

CHRONOLOGY

1806 JUNE 12. Thomas Lincoln and Nancy Hanks are married near Beechland, Washington Co., Ky. They then settle in Elizabethtown, Hardin Co.

1807 FEBRUARY 10. Their first child, Sarah Lincoln, is born.

1808 MAY. They move to Sinking Spring Farm near Hodgenville, Ky.

1809 FEBRUARY 12. Abraham Lincoln is born there.

MARCH 4. James Madison is inaugurated President, succeeding Thomas Jefferson.

1811 Some time during this year the Lincoln family moves to a farm on Knob Creek. Lincoln attends the ABC schools in the neighborhood for a short period.

1813 MARCH 4. James Madison is inaugurated for a second term.

1816 DECEMBER (circa). The Lincoln family moves to Southern Indiana and builds an open-faced camp near Gentryville in what is now Spencer Co.

1817 MARCH 4. James Monroe is inaugurated.

1818 OCTOBER 5. Nancy Hanks Lincoln dies.

WINTER. Abraham and his sister Sarah go to school.

DECEMBER 13. Mary Todd, who is to become Abraham Lincoln's wife, is born in Lexington, Ky.

1819 DECEMBER 2. Thomas Lincoln marries a widow, Sarah Bush Johnston, in Elizabethtown, Ky. and takes her and her three children to his home in Indiana.

1820 MARCH 8. The Missouri Compromise is adopted, forbidding slavery in the territories north of 36° 30'.

1821 MARCH 4. James Monroe is inaugurated for a second term.

1825 MARCH 4. John Quincy Adams is inaugurated.

1826 AUGUST 2. Sarah Lincoln, Abraham's elder sister, marries Aaron Grigsby.

1828 JANUARY 20. Sarah Lincoln Grigsby dies in childbirth.

APRIL to JUNE. Abraham Lincoln is hired by James Gentry to make a flatboat trip down the Mississippi to New Orleans.

1829 MARCH 4. Andrew Jackson is inaugurated.

1830 MARCH. The Lincoln family moves from Indiana to Illinois. They settle near Decatur.

1831 JANUARY 1. William Lloyd Garrison issues the first number of *The Liberator*, an anti-slavery newspaper.

MARCH. Lincoln goes down the Sangamon River in a canoe with John Hanks. They land four miles from Springfield, where they build a flatboat for Denton Offut for a voyage to New Orleans. On APRIL 19 the boat is stranded on a milldam at New Salem, but Lincoln succeeds in getting it across and continues toward New Orleans.

JUNE. Lincoln returns from New Orleans by steamboat to St. Louis and walks to Decatur, Ill.

JULY. Lincoln goes to New Salem to become a storekeeper for Denton Offut.

AUGUST 21. A slave insurrection, led by Nat Turner, breaks out in Virginia and is put down after much bloodshed.

1832 JANUARY 6. Garrison founds the New England Anti-Slavery Society, the first in America.

SPRING. Offut's store having failed, Lincoln decides to run for the State Legislature on the Whig ticket and issues his first campaign address on MARCH 9.

APRIL 6. The Indian Chief, Black Hawk, enters Illinois with five hundred warriors.

APRIL 21. Lincoln enrolls in the army for the Black Hawk War, and is elected Captain of his company. He is mustered out on JULY 16 without having seen any actual fighting.

AUGUST 6. Lincoln is defeated in the campaign for the

Legislature, although his own precinct votes 277 to 7 for him.

1832 AUTUMN. In partnership with William Berry, Lincoln takes over the stock of another store.

1833 MARCH 4. Andrew Jackson is inaugurated for a second term.

SPRING. The Lincoln-Berry store fails. Berry dies later (JANUARY 10, 1835), leaving Lincoln saddled with a debt of $1100.

MAY 7. Lincoln is made Postmaster of New Salem, his first Federal office.

1834 SUMMER. Lincoln runs again for the State Legislature and on AUGUST 4 is elected. In DECEMBER he leaves Springfield for Vandalia to take his seat. There he meets Stephen A. Douglas for the first time.

1835 FEBRUARY 13. The session ended, Lincoln returns to New Salem.

It is during this year that the love affair between Lincoln and Ann Rutledge is supposed to have culminated in an engagement. In AUGUST, she becomes ill with fever, and on AUGUST 25, she dies.

1836 MARCH 2. Texas declares its independence of Mexico. On MARCH 6 the Alamo falls. In APRIL, the Mexican Army under Santa Anna is defeated and he is taken prisoner.

JUNE 13. Lincoln announces his candidacy for re-election to the Legislature.

AUGUST 1. Mary Owens first arrives in New Salem and Lincoln begins to court her. On this same day, Lincoln is again elected to the Legislature with the highest votes of all the candidates in Sangamon Co.

SEPTEMBER 9. Lincoln applies for a license to practice law.

DECEMBER 5. The Legislature convenes at Vandalia.

1837 FEBRUARY 28. In a vote in the Legislature, Springfield is chosen as the state capital. Lincoln plays a prominent part in making this move.

MARCH 1. The Supreme Court of Illinois grants Lincoln a certificate of admission to the bar.

MARCH 4. Martin Van Buren is inaugurated.

MARCH 15. The Legislature adjourns, and Lincoln returns to New Salem.

APRIL 12. Lincoln arranges to become the law partner of John T. Stuart.

APRIL 15. Lincoln leaves New Salem and takes up residence in Springfield where he rooms with Joshua Speed.

AUGUST 16. Lincoln writes to Mary Owens giving her an opportunity to end the rather tepid romance between them.

SUMMER. Mary Todd visits Springfield, but Lincoln does not meet her. Lincoln is re-elected to the State Legislature.

NOVEMBER 7. Elijah Lovejoy, abolitionist editor, is killed at Alton, Illinois, by a pro-slavery mob.

1838 JANUARY 27. Lincoln speaks before the Young Men's Lyceum of Springfield on the subject: "The Perpetuation of Our Political Institutions."

1839 JUNE 20. The state officers are officially ordered to move from Vandalia to Springfield—the new state capital.

AUTUMN. Mary Todd returns to Springfield and Lincoln meets her for the first time.

DECEMBER 9. The Legislature begins its initial session at Springfield.

1840 Lincoln plays a prominent part in the Whig political campaign this year. He is elected for the fourth and last time to the State Legislature which convenes on NOVEMBER 23rd.

1840 During this year—probably in the latter part of it—he becomes engaged to Mary Todd.

1841 JANUARY 1. "The fatal first of January." Lincoln breaks off (or attempts to break off) his engagement to Mary Todd. According to Herndon, he was to have been married to her on this day. On this day also, Speed sells his store, and, a few months later moves to Louisville, Ky.

MARCH 4. William Henry Harrison is inaugurated.

APRIL 4. Harrison dies, and John Tyler becomes President.

APRIL 14. The Lincoln-Stuart law partnership is dissolved, and Lincoln becomes a partner of Stephen T. Logan.

AUGUST. Lincoln visits Speed in Louisville.

1842. SPRING and SUMMER. Lincoln has a long and intimate correspondence with Joshua Speed on the general subject of matrimony.

LATE SUMMER. Lincoln again meets Mary Todd and they write a series of letters for the *Sangamon Journal* lampooning a rival Democratic politician, James Shields.

SEPTEMBER 17. Lincoln is challenged to a duel by Shields.

SEPTEMBER 22. Lincoln and Shields go to Alton to fight, but the duel is called off at the last moment.

NOVEMBER 4. Lincoln is married to Mary Todd. They go to live at the Globe Tavern in Springfield.

1843 AUGUST 1. A son, Robert Todd Lincoln, is born to the Lincolns while they are still living at the Globe Tavern. Shortly after this they move to 214 South 4th Street.

1844 MAY. The Lincolns move into their final home at 8th and Jackson Streets, Springfield.

AUTUMN. The Lincoln-Logan partnership is dissolved. William H. Herndon's association with Lincoln begins at this time, although Herndon has not yet been admitted to the bar.

AUTUMN. Lincoln is made a Presidential elector on the Whig ticket for Henry Clay. During the campaign he returns to Indiana to speak and addresses his old friends at Gentryville.

DECEMBER 9. Herndon is admitted to the bar and becomes Lincoln's partner.

1845 MARCH 4. James K. Polk is inaugurated.

DECEMBER 22. Texas is annexed by the United States.

1846 MARCH 10. A second son, Edward Baker, is born to Lincoln.

APRIL 18. Lincoln sends an example of his poetry to Andrew Johnston, a friend who also aspires to write poetry.

MAY 1. The Whig Convention in Petersburg, Illinois, nominates Lincoln for the United States Congress.

MAY 8. Battles take place between United States and Mexican forces at Palo Alto, and, on MAY 9, at Resaca de la Palma.

AUGUST 3. Lincoln is elected to Congress.

AUGUST 8. The Wilmot Proviso, forbidding slavery in any territory acquired from Mexico, is passed in the House.

AUGUST 10. The Wilmot Proviso is held up in the Senate at the end of a session which is permitted to expire without the final passage of the Proviso or of a $2,000,000 war-supplies bill.

SEPTEMBER 6. Lincoln again corresponds with Andrew Johnston, sending him another example of his poetry.

1847 JULY 1. Lincoln leaves Springfield to visit Chicago for the first time. He attends the River and Harbor Convention there on JULY 5-7.

1847 OCTOBER 25. The Lincoln family leaves Springfield for Kentucky en route to Washington.

NOVEMBER 25. The Lincolns leave Lexington to proceed to Washington, where they arrive on DECEMBER 2.

DECEMBER 6. The House of Representatives convenes, and Lincoln is seated for the first time.

DECEMBER 22. Lincoln offers a series of resolutions in the House, asking the President whether the "spot" on which American blood was first spilled in the war with Mexico was on United States or Mexican territory.

1848 JANUARY 12. Lincoln attacks President Polk's war policy during a speech in the House of Representatives.

FEBRUARY 2. A treaty between the United States and Mexico is signed at Guadalupe Hidalgo, ending the Mexican War.

JUNE 7-9. Lincoln attends the Whig National Convention in Philadelphia where he supports Zachary Taylor for the Presidential nomination.

JULY 4. Lincoln is present at the great ceremony of the laying of the cornerstone of the Washington monument.

AUGUST 14. Congress adjourns.

SEPTEMBER 9. Lincoln leaves Washington for a speaking tour in New England in behalf of Zachary Taylor, Whig nominee for President. He visits Worcester, New Bedford, Boston, Lowell, Dorchester, Chelsea, Dedham, Cambridge and Taunton.

SEPTEMBER 22. Lincoln and Seward speak on the same platform at a Whig mass meeting at Tremont Temple, Boston.

SEPTEMBER 23. Lincoln returns to Springfield where he arrives on OCTOBER 10 to find that his constituents are disgusted with his attack on the administration's handling of the Mexican War.

1848 LATE NOVEMBER. Lincoln leaves Springfield for Washington where he arrives on DECEMBER 7.

1849 JANUARY 13. Lincoln attempts to introduce a bill to abolish slavery in the District of Columbia with provision for compensation to owners.

MARCH 4. The House adjourns early on Sunday morning. Lincoln's term as Congressman expires.

MARCH 5. Lincoln attends Zachary Taylor's inauguration and goes to the inaugural ball during the evening.

MARCH 7. The United States Supreme Court admits Lincoln to practice before it. About two weeks later he leaves Washington and returns to Springfield where he arrives on MARCH 31.

MAY 22. A patent is granted to Abraham Lincoln for an invention intended to buoy vessels over shoals.

JUNE 10. In an effort to obtain the appointment to the Commissionership of the General Land Office, Lincoln leaves Springfield and goes to Washington where he arrives on JUNE 19.

JUNE 25. Having failed to obtain the appointment, he returns to Springfield.

SEPTEMBER. Lincoln is offered, and declines, the secretaryship of Oregon.

1850 FEBRUARY 1. Edward, Lincoln's second son, dies after a two weeks' illness.

MARCH 7. Daniel Webster speaks in the Senate in defense of the Compromise of 1850 and is denounced in the North for defending it.

JULY 9. President Taylor dies. On JULY 10, Vice President Millard Fillmore becomes President.

SEPTEMBER 18. The Fugitive Slave Act, which is part of the Compromise of 1850, is approved by the President.

1850 DECEMBER 21. William Wallace, a third son, is born to the Lincolns.

1851 JANUARY 17. Thomas Lincoln, Lincoln's father, dies in Coles County, Illinois.

JUNE. *Uncle Tom's Cabin*, by Harriet Beecher Stowe, begins as a serial in *The National Era*, an abolitionist newspaper in Washington. It runs throughout this year and continues into the spring of 1852.

1852 MARCH 20. *Uncle Tom's Cabin* is published in book form and becomes a sensational success.

JUNE 29. Henry Clay dies.

OCTOBER 24. Daniel Webster dies.

NOVEMBER 10. Lincoln takes Ward Hill Lamon as his law partner for business to be handled in Danville, Ill.

1853 MARCH 4. Franklin Pierce is inaugurated.

APRIL 4. Thomas ("Tad"), Lincoln's fourth son is born.

1854 APRIL 4. Herndon is elected Mayor of Springfield.

MAY 30. The Kansas-Nebraska Act is signed by President Pierce.

AUGUST 9. Lincoln's interest in politics has been re-awakened by the fight over the Kansas-Nebraska bill. He meets Richard Yates, anti-Nebraska Congressman from Illinois, while Yates is on his way home from Washington. Lincoln agrees to campaign for Yates in his fight against the bill.

OCTOBER 4. On the previous day Douglas had spoken in Springfield in defense of the Nebraska Bill. During the afternoon of the fourth Lincoln speaks for three hours in reply to Douglas.

OCTOBER 5. Abolitionists in Springfield using the new name "Republicans" hold a meeting on this day, to which they invite Lincoln. At Herndon's suggestion he avoids alliance with them and leaves town in order to evade the issue.

OCTOBER 16. Douglas speaks again at Peoria, and Lincoln

replies to him during the evening, delivering the address that he had given twelve days before at Springfield, but with some emendations and additions. This is the first of his great speeches.

1854 AUTUMN. Lincoln has an opportunity to become United States Senator because of his position as leader of the anti-Nebraska men in Illinois. He canvasses the members of the Legislature to find out how much support he can get.

1855 FEBRUARY 8. Lincoln is defeated in the race for United States Senator. He throws his votes to an anti-Nebraska Democrat, Lyman Trumbull, who is elected. Lincoln continues to fight against the Kansas-Nebraska Act.

AUGUST 24. Lincoln writes a long letter to Joshua Speed in which he sets forth his own attitude toward slavery and makes clear his political standing.

SEPTEMBER 20-21. Lincoln is employed as associate counsel in a patent suit, McCormick vs. Manny, which is tried at Cincinnati. Edwin M. Stanton, later to be Lincoln's Secretary of War, is senior counsel; he snubs Lincoln, and Lincoln plays no part in the trial.

1856 MAY 21. Lawrence, Kansas, is sacked by a pro-slavery mob.

MAY 22. Preston Brooks attacks Charles Sumner in the Senate, beating him over the head with a cane and severely injuring him.

MAY 29. Lincoln attends the Republican State Convention at Bloomington, Ill. He is nominated as a Presidential elector and makes a speech that brings the crowd to its feet cheering. (The famous "Lost Speech.") This marks Lincoln's first open adherence to the principles of the Republican party.

JUNE 19. The Republican party, in convention at Philadelphia, nominates John C. Frémont for President. In the balloting, Lincoln receives 110 votes for Vice

President, but W. L. Dayton of New Jersey is nominated. During the next few months Lincoln speaks more than fifty times for Frémont.

1856 NOVEMBER 4. Frémont is defeated, and James Buchanan is elected President on the Democratic ticket.

DECEMBER 10. Although the Republicans have lost the election, they feel that they have made many political gains. They hold a banquet at Chicago at which Lincoln speaks.

1857 MARCH 4. James Buchanan is inaugurated.

MARCH 6-7. The Dred Scott decision is made public by the Supreme Court which rules that Negroes can not become citizens and that the Missouri Compromise of 1820 was invalid from its inception.

JUNE 12. Stephen A. Douglas speaks in Springfield on the Dred Scott decision and on Kansas.

JUNE 15. An election is held in Kansas at which delegates to a constitutional convention are to be chosen. The Free State men, fearing duplicity, refuse to participate in the election.

JUNE 26. Lincoln speaks in Springfield in reply to Douglas.

LATE JULY. Lincoln makes a brief trip to New York, the purpose of which is unknown.

OCTOBER 5. The Free State men in Kansas win control of the Legislature. Nevertheless, on OCTOBER 19, the proslavery constitutional convention meets, determined to make Kansas a slave state.

DECEMBER 9. Douglas speaks in the United States Senate, denouncing the Lecompton constitution for Kansas and breaking with Buchanan and the Democratic party.

DECEMBER 21. An election is held in Kansas on the adoption of the Lecompton constitution. Again the Free State men refuse to vote. The election is proved to be based on fraudulent returns. The anti-slavery Kansas Legislature appoints another election day at which the whole constitution may be accepted or rejected.

1858 JANUARY 4. This election is held in Kansas, and the Lecompton constitution is rejected by an overwhelming vote which shows that Kansas is a section predominantly opposed to slavery.

MARCH. Herndon goes East to consult with anti-slavery leaders there.

MAY 7. Lincoln successfully defends Duff Armstrong, son of Hannah Armstrong, an old New Salem friend, in a trial for murder held at Beardstown. He proves his case by the use of an almanac.

JUNE 16. The Illinois Republican Convention, meeting at Springfield, unanimously chooses Lincoln for the United States Senate to replace Douglas. During the evening, Lincoln delivers his celebrated "House Divided" speech.

JULY 9. Douglas speaks in Chicago from the balcony of the Tremont House. Lincoln is present and takes notes of what he says.

JULY 10. Lincoln, speaking at the same place, replies to Douglas.

JULY 17. During the afternoon Douglas speaks at an open air meeting in Springfield. Lincoln replies to him in the evening, speaking in the Hall of Representatives.

JULY 24-31. The Republicans are dissatisfied at the way Lincoln has been following Douglas. They urge him to challenge Douglas to a series of formal debates. This is now arranged.

AUGUST 2. The people of Kansas again refuse the Lecompton constitution together with a free-land bribe. The debates between Lincoln and Douglas are held as follows:

AUGUST 21. At Ottawa.

1858 AUGUST 27. At Freeport.

SEPTEMBER 15. At Jonesboro.

SEPTEMBER 18. At Charleston.

OCTOBER 7. At Galesburg.

OCTOBER 13. At Quincy.

OCTOBER 15. At Alton.

NOVEMBER 2. Election day. The Republicans in Illinois are successful in electing some state officers and in making general gains, but the Democrats still hold a majority in the Legislature, making it almost certain that Douglas will be elected to the Senate.

1859 JANUARY 5. The election is held in the State Legislature at which Douglas is returned to the Senate—a foregone conclusion.

SEPTEMBER 16. Lincoln speaks at Columbus, Ohio.

SEPTEMBER 17. He speaks at Cincinnati.

SEPTEMBER 30. He speaks before the Wisconsin Agricultural Society at Milwaukee.

OCTOBER 16. John Brown captures the Federal arsenal at Harper's Ferry.

OCTOBER 18. John Brown is captured at daybreak and is taken the next day to jail at Charlestown, Virginia.

NOVEMBER 2. John Brown is sentenced to death.

NOVEMBER 30. Lincoln leaves Springfield for a speaking tour in Kansas.

DECEMBER 2. John Brown is hanged.

DECEMBER 8. Lincoln returns to Springfield.

DECEMBER 20. Lincoln writes an autobiographical sketch, intended for use in publicizing him for President, and sends it to Jesse W. Fell of Bloomington, Ill.

1860 FEBRUARY 23. Lincoln leaves Springfield to go to New York where he has been invited to speak.

FEBRUARY 27. During the evening of this day, Lincoln delivers his celebrated speech at Cooper Union.

FEBRUARY 28. He leaves New York and goes on a speaking tour of New England during which he visits his son, Robert, at school in Exeter.

1860 MARCH 11. On this day he goes to hear Henry Ward Beecher preach at his Plymouth Church in Brooklyn. The next day he leaves New York for Springfield, where he arrives on MARCH 14. From this time on he is actively engaged in winning the Republican nomination for the Presidency.

APRIL 23. The Democratic National Convention meets at Charleston, S. C., and splits over sectional differences.

MAY 9. At the Republican State Convention at Decatur, Ill., John Hanks brings in two fence rails which he and Lincoln had split in the Sangamon bottom 30 years before. Lincoln becomes nationally known as "the rail-splitter candidate." The convention instructs its delegates to vote for Lincoln at the Republican National Convention.

MAY 18. The Republican National Convention, meeting in Chicago, nominates Lincoln for President of the United States.

MAY 19. The official nominating committee arrives in Springfield and visits Lincoln at his home.

The Constitutional Union party nominates John Bell of Tennessee.

JUNE 1. (?) Lincoln prepares a lengthy autobiographical sketch which is to be used in writing a campaign biography.

JUNE 18. Douglas is nominated by the Northern Democrats.

JUNE 28. The Southern Democrats nominate John C. Breckinridge of Kentucky.

SUMMER. Lincoln stays at home in Springfield while the hotly contested Presidential campaign is being fought.

OCTOBER 11. News is received in Springfield that the

Republicans have carried the early elections in Ohio, Indiana and Pennsylvania.

1860 OCTOBER 26. Lincoln hears that some of the army officers at Fort Kearney have threatened to desert and take their arms into the South if a Republican President is elected.

NOVEMBER 6. Abraham Lincoln is elected President of the United States.

NOVEMBER 10. The South Carolina Legislature passes a bill calling for a convention on DECEMBER 17 at which the matter of the state's relationship to the national Government is to be taken up.

DECEMBER 4. Buchanan reads his annual message to Congress in which he puts forth his views that the South has no right to secede. However, he takes no action.

DECEMBER 17. The South Carolina convention meets at Columbia. Smallpox is raging there. The convention moves to Charleston, and there, on DECEMBER 20, passes an ordinance of secession, severing that state's connection with the Union.

DECEMBER 20. Thurlow Weed, Seward's political manager, comes to Springfield to sound out Lincoln on compromise with the South. He is told that no compromise on extending slavery will be countenanced by the President-elect.

1861 JANUARY 9. Mississippi secedes.

JANUARY 10. Florida secedes.

JANUARY 11. Alabama secedes.

JANUARY 19. Georgia secedes.

JANUARY 26. Louisiana secedes.

JANUARY 30-31. Lincoln goes to Coles County to visit his stepmother, Sarah Bush Lincoln, who is living near Charleston, Ill.

FEBRUARY 1. Texas secedes.

1861 FEBRUARY 4. Delegates from the first six of these states meet at Montgomery, Alabama, to form the Confederate Government.

FEBRUARY 11. Lincoln leaves Springfield for what is to be the last time. He addresses his friends and fellow citizens at the railroad station just before his train pulls out. He goes on toward Washington, stopping at Indianapolis, Cincinnati, Columbus, Pittsburgh, Cleveland, Buffalo, Albany, New York, Trenton, Philadelphia and Harrisburg.

FEBRUARY 18. Jefferson Davis is inaugurated President of the Confederate States of America.

FEBRUARY 21. At Philadelphia Lincoln is warned that he will be assassinated in Baltimore. He leaves Harrisburg secretly on the night of FEBRUARY 22 and arrives safely in Washington the next morning.

MARCH 4. At noon, Abraham Lincoln is inaugurated President of the United States.

MARCH 15. Lincoln asks advice from his Cabinet on Fort Sumter. Only two of the Cabinet members are in favor of making an attempt to hold the fort.

APRIL 1. Secretary of State Seward sends the President a memorandum entitled "Some Thoughts For The President's Consideration," in which Seward puts forth his own views on what should be done.

APRIL 6. Lincoln orders a relief expedition to sail to Fort Sumter.

APRIL 12. The Confederates fire on Sumter.

APRIL 14. Sumter surrenders.

APRIL 15. Lincoln issues a proclamation calling for 75,-000 volunteers and convening Congress in special session on JULY 4.

APRIL 17. Virginia secedes.

APRIL 18. The arsenal at Harper's Ferry is burned to prevent it from falling into Confederate hands.

1861 APRIL 19. Men from the Sixth Massachusetts Regiment are attacked as they pass through Baltimore on their way to Washington. Lincoln issues a proclamation of naval blockade.

APRIL 20. The Gosport Navy Yard is burned.

APRIL 22. Washington is completely isolated from the North.

APRIL 25. Troops finally get through and come to the relief of Washington.

MAY 6. Arkansas secedes.

MAY 21. North Carolina secedes.

MAY 24. Troops advance into Virginia from Washington and take possession of Alexandria and Arlington Heights. Colonel E. E. Ellsworth is killed during the occupation of Alexandria.

JUNE 3. Stephen A. Douglas dies in Chicago.

JUNE 8. Tennessee votes in favor of secession.

JUNE 16. Western Virginia declares its independence from the rest of the state and decides to stay with the Union.

JUNE 17. A convention is held in Eastern Tennessee to hold that part of the state in the Union.

JULY 4. Congress meets in special session.

JULY 16. McDowell starts out from Arlington to meet the Rebel forces at Manassas.

JULY 21. The Battle of Bull Run. The Union forces are defeated and retreat toward Washington. Lincoln immediately draws up a memorandum of military policy; he also summons George Brinton McClellan to Washington and puts him in charge of organizing a large Federal army.

AUGUST 6. The special session of Congress adjourns.

AUGUST 30. Frémont, in command of the Department of the West, issues a proclamation emancipating the slaves of all those in his territory who have taken arms against the United States.

1861 SEPTEMBER 2. Lincoln urges Frémont to modify his proclamation.

SEPTEMBER 11. Frémont having refused to do so, Lincoln issues an official order for the modification.

OCTOBER 31. General Winfield Scott resigns as head of the army.

NOVEMBER 1. McClellan is appointed General in Chief.

NOVEMBER 2. Lincoln removes Frémont from the command of the West.

NOVEMBER 8. Mason and Slidell are taken in mid-ocean from the British steamer, *Trent*, and brought to the United States.

NOVEMBER 27. The *Trent* reaches England, and the British Government issues an ultimatum to the United States.

DECEMBER 3. Congress meets in regular session, and Lincoln delivers his first annual message.

DECEMBER 25. The Cabinet meets to discuss the *Trent* affair.

1862 JANUARY 1. Mason and Slidell are delivered to a British gunboat in Provincetown Harbor.

JANUARY 13. Cameron resigns as Secretary of War; Stanton is appointed in his place.

JANUARY 27. Lincoln issues his General War Order Number One which commands the army and navy to advance toward the insurgents on FEBRUARY 22.

FEBRUARY 6. Fort Henry, on the Tennessee River, is captured by Federal forces.

FEBRUARY 16. Fort Donelson, on the Cumberland River in Tennessee, is also captured. This, with the capture of Fort Henry, is the first victory for the North.

FEBRUARY 20. Lincoln's son, William Wallace, dies in the White House.

1862 FEBRUARY 22. McClellan has succeeded in persuading Lincoln not to have his armies advance on this day as previously ordered.

MARCH 6. Lincoln submits to Congress a proposal to free the slaves gradually and to compensate their owners for loss of property.

MARCH 8. The ironclad *Merrimac* (renamed the *Virginia*) does great damage to the Federal fleet lying in Hampton Roads.

MARCH 9. The *Monitor* goes into action against the *Merrimac* and puts her out of commission.

MARCH 11. McClellan occupies Manassas only to find that the Confederates have already evacuated it. McClellan is relieved of his general command, and Halleck is put in charge of the Department of the Mississippi.

APRIL. McClellan's Peninsular campaign gets under way.

APRIL 6. The Battle of Shiloh is fought in the western theater of war.

APRIL 7. Island No. 10 is captured by Federal forces in this same campaign.

APRIL 25. After several days of firing on the Mississippi River forts, Farragut runs his fleet past them and captures New Orleans.

MAY 9. General Hunter, in command of the Department of the South, issues a proclamation emancipating the slaves in Georgia, Florida and South Carolina. Lincoln countermands his order on MAY 19.

MAY 31. McClellan, who has proceeded up the Peninsula until he is within a few miles of Richmond, is attacked at Fair Oaks in a battle which lasts for two days.

JUNE. McClellan's army lies almost within sight of Richmond for the first three weeks of this month.

1862 JUNE 25. The beginning of the Seven Days Battle before Richmond in which McClellan's army is repulsed.

JULY 8. Lincoln visits McClellan at Harrison's Landing.

JULY 11. Lincoln, on his return to Washington, appoints General Henry W. Halleck to the command of all the Federal armies.

JULY 13. Lincoln reveals to Welles and Seward that he regards emancipation of the slaves as a military necessity.

JULY 22. He presents to his Cabinet the draft of his Proclamation of Emancipation. Acting on Seward's suggestion, he decides to wait for a Northern victory before making the Proclamation public.

AUGUST 29-30. The Second Battle of Bull Run is fought —and lost—under the command of General Pope.

SEPTEMBER 17. The bloody battle of Antietam, Maryland is won by a Federal army under McClellan's command. Lincoln takes this as a signal of victory and, on SEPTEMBER 22, reads the final wording of the Proclamation of Emancipation to his Cabinet. He then releases it to the press.

OCTOBER 1. Lincoln leaves Washington to visit McClellan at Antietam.

OCTOBER 26. McClellan, after much urging, starts out after Lee's army, but is too late to prevent it from reaching central Virginia again.

NOVEMBER 5. Lincoln issues an order finally relieving McClellan from his command and appointing General Burnside in his place.

DECEMBER 1. Lincoln delivers his annual message to Congress.

DECEMBER 13. The Battle of Fredericksburg, Virginia, is lost by Burnside.

DECEMBER 18. Seward and Chase offer to resign from the Cabinet because of attacks made on them by

Republican Senators over the disaster at Fredericksburg.

1863 JANUARY 25. General Joseph Hooker is given command of the Army of the Potomac, replacing Burnside.

APRIL 1. A bread riot takes place in Richmond.

MAY 2-4. Hooker loses the Battle of Chancellorsville. Shortly after this battle, Lee's army heads north to invade Pennsylvania.

JUNE 28. Hooker is removed and replaced with General George G. Meade.

JULY 1-3. The Battle of Gettysburg. After the failure of Pickett's charge, on the third day, Lee retreats toward the Shenandoah Valley.

JULY 4. Vicksburg, on the Mississippi River, is captured by Grant.

JULY 13-16. Draft riots take place in New York during which hundreds of people are killed or wounded, and several million dollars' worth of property is destroyed.

AUGUST and SEPTEMBER. The Federal fleet makes an unsuccessful attempt to capture Charleston harbor.

SEPTEMBER 19-20. The Battle of Chickamauga, Georgia.

NOVEMBER 19. Lincoln delivers his celebrated address at the National Cemetery at Gettysburg.

NOVEMBER 23-25. Battle of Chattanooga and Missionary Ridge.

DECEMBER 8. Lincoln issues a Proclamation of Amnesty and Reconstruction and delivers his annual message to Congress.

1864 MARCH 10. Lincoln puts Ulysses S. Grant in command of all the Union armies. Grant consults with Sherman for a concerted plan of action against the Confederate forces.

MAY 4. The Army of the Potomac, under Grant's command, crosses the Rapidan and moves toward Richmond.

1864 MAY 5-6. Lee attacks Grant in the Battle of the Wilderness, and Grant sustains heavy losses.
> Sherman sets out toward Atlanta.

> MAY 10-12. Grant presses on and is again attacked by Lee at Spottsylvania Court House.

> MAY 31. Battle of Cold Harbor, Virginia, which continues until JUNE 3. Grant is unable to take Richmond and has lost 55,000 men in less than a month.
> The Radical Democracy holds its national convention in Cleveland and nominates John C. Frémont for President.

> JUNE 7. The National Union Convention meets at Baltimore and on JUNE 8 nominates Abraham Lincoln for President.

> JUNE 12. Grant withdraws from Cold Harbor and proceeds south toward Petersburg.

> JUNE 19. The Kearsarge sinks the Confederate raider Alabama off the coast of Cherbourg, France.

> JUNE 30. Salmon P. Chase, Secretary of the Treasury, resigns.

> JULY 11-12. Jubal Early raids Washington.

> JULY. Two peace moves take place simultaneously—Greeley's with three Confederate commissioners at Niagara Falls, and Jacques and Gilmore's mission to Richmond.

> JULY 30. A huge mine is exploded under the Confederate redoubts at Petersburg, but the Union forces are unsuccessful in the action that follows.

> AUGUST 5. Farragut captures Mobile.
> The Wade-Davis manifesto attacking the President is printed in The New York Tribune.

> AUGUST 23. Lincoln asks his Cabinet to endorse, sight unseen, a secret memorandum which he does not show to them until November 11.

1864 AUGUST 29. The Democratic National Convention meets at Chicago.

AUGUST 31. McClellan is nominated for President on the Democratic ticket.

SEPTEMBER 2. Sherman takes Atlanta.

SEPTEMBER 21. Frémont withdraws from the Presidential race.

SEPTEMBER. The Shenandoah Valley campaign under Sheridan takes place.

OCTOBER 12. Roger B. Taney, Chief Justice of the United States Supreme Court, dies.

NOVEMBER 8. Abraham Lincoln is elected President of the United States for a second term.

NOVEMBER 11. He opens and reads his secret paper of August 23 to the Cabinet. It is a declaration of his intention to co-operate with whoever might be elected so that the Union might be saved.

NOVEMBER 15. Atlanta is set on fire; Sherman starts out across Georgia, marching toward the sea.

DECEMBER 6. Lincoln delivers his annual message to Congress; he appoints Salmon P. Chase Chief Justice of the Supreme Court to replace Taney.

DECEMBER 21. Savannah is captured by Sherman.

1865 JANUARY 14. Sherman's army leaves Savannah and starts north.

JANUARY 31. The House of Representatives passes the Thirteenth Amendment to the Constitution, abolishing slavery in the United States.

FEBRUARY 3. Lincoln holds a conference on board the *River Queen* in Hampton Roads with three Confederate commissioners, one of whom is his old friend, Alexander Stephens. They discuss peace terms, but the interview proves to be fruitless.

FEBRUARY 5. Lincoln calls a special Cabinet meeting

and presents an amazing plan for compensating the slaveholders with $400,000,000 for loss of their slaves. The Cabinet disapproves the proposal.

1865 FEBRUARY 18. Sherman captures Columbia, S. C. Charleston surrenders to the Federal fleet.

MARCH 4. Abraham Lincoln is inaugurated for a second term of office.

MARCH 23. Lincoln leaves on the *River Queen* to visit Grant's headquarters at City Point.

MARCH 27. He enters into a conference with Grant and Sherman to discuss terms of surrender for the Confederates.

MARCH 29. A forward movement of the Army of the Potomac begins, which continues during the next few days.

APRIL 2. Lee notifies Jefferson Davis that Richmond will have to be evacuated. The Confederate government flees on this night to Danville, Va. Richmond is set on fire by the retreating Confederates.

APRIL 3. Federal troops enter Richmond.

APRIL 4. Lincoln visits Richmond, walking through the city almost unattended.

APRIL 5. Seward is injured in a carriage accident. Lincoln decides to return to Washington. He leaves City Point on APRIL 8.

APRIL 9. Lee surrenders to Grant at Appomattox Courthouse, Va.

APRIL 11. Lincoln delivers his last public address, a speech on reconstruction in Louisiana.

APRIL 14. At 10:20 P.M., Lincoln is shot at Ford's Theater by John Wilkes Booth.

APRIL 15. Lincoln dies at 7:22 A.M. His body is removed during the morning to the White House.

APRIL 19. An imposing public funeral is held in Washington, where Lincoln's body is carried from the White House to the Capitol.

1865 APRIL 21. The funeral train carrying Lincoln's body leaves Washington bound for Springfield.

MAY 3. The funeral train reaches Springfield.

THE WRITINGS OF
ABRAHAM LINCOLN

THE WRITINGS OF
ABRAHAM LINCOLN

FROM LINCOLN'S FIRST PUBLIC ADDRESS

Seven months after his arrival in New Salem, and when he was only twenty-three years old, Lincoln became a candidate for the State Legislature. This is his campaign address; it was distributed in the form of a handbill to the people. John McNamar, his rival for the hand of Ann Rutledge, helped him in the writing of it. So did Mentor Graham, the local school teacher who assisted Lincoln in his process of self-education. In the address, Lincoln takes a safe stand on public improvements, avoiding all reference to controversial national issues. He was a Whig and a Henry Clay man in a section predominantly in favor of Andrew Jackson. He lost the election—the only election in which he was defeated by a direct vote of the people.

New Salem, March 9, 1832

To the People of Sangamon County: Having become a candidate for the honorable office of one of your Representatives in the next General Assembly of this State, in accordance with an established custom and the principles of true Republicanism, it becomes my duty to make known to you, the people whom I propose to represent, my sentiments with regard to local affairs.

Time and experience have verified to a demonstration the public utility of internal improvements. That the poorest and most thinly populated countries would be greatly benefited by the opening of good roads and in the clearing of navigable streams within their limits, is what no person will deny. Yet it is folly to undertake works of this or any other kind, without first knowing that we are able to finish them—as half-finished work generally proves to be labor lost.

There cannot justly be any objection to having railroads and canals, any more than to other good things, provided they cost nothing. The only objection is to paying for them; and the objection arises from the want of ability to pay.

With respect to the County of Sangamon, some more easy means of communication than it now possesses, for the purpose of facilitating the task of exporting the surplus products of its fertile soil, and importing necessary articles from abroad, are indispensably necessary. A meeting has been held of the citizens of Jacksonville and the adjacent country for the purpose of deliberating and inquiring into the expediency of constructing a railroad from some eligible point on the Illinois River through the town of Jacksonville, in Morgan County, to the town of Springfield, in Sangamon County. This is, indeed, a very desirable object. No other improvement that reason will justify us in hoping for can equal in utility the railroad. It is a never-failing source of communication between places of business remotely situated from each other. Upon the railroad the regular progress of commercial intercourse is not interrupted by either high or low water, or freezing weather, which are the principal difficulties that render our future hopes of water communication precarious and uncertain.

Yet, however desirable an object the construction of a railroad through our country may be; however high our imaginations may be heated at thoughts of it; there is always a heart-appalling shock accompanying the account of its cost which forces us to shrink from our pleasing anticipations. The probable cost of this contemplated railroad is estimated at $290,000; the bare statement of which, in my opinion, is sufficient to justify the belief that the improvement of the Sangamon River is an object much better suited to our infant resources.

Respecting this view, I think I may say, without the fear of

being contradicted, that its navigation may be rendered completely practicable as high as the mouth of the South Fork, or
probably higher, to vessels of from twenty-five to thirty tons'
burden, for at least one half of all common years, and to vessels
of much greater burden a part of the time. From my peculiar
circumstances, it is probable that for the last twelve months
I have given as particular attention to the stage of the water in
this river as any other person in the country. In the month of
March, 1831, in company with others, I commenced the building of a flatboat on the Sangamon, and finished and took her
out in the course of the spring. Since that time I have been
concerned in the mill at New Salem. These circumstances are
sufficient evidence that I have not been very inattentive to the
stages of the water. The time at which we crossed the milldam
being in the last days of April, the water was lower than it had
been since the breaking of winter in February, or than it was
for several weeks after. The principal difficulties we encoun-
tered . . . were from the drifted timber, which obstructions
all know are not difficult to be removed. . . .

Upon the subject of education, not presuming to dictate
any plan or system respecting it, I can only say that I view it as
the most important subject which we as a people can be engaged in. That every man may receive at least a moderate education, and thereby be enabled to read the histories of his own
and other countries, by which he may duly appreciate the value
of our free institutions, appears to be an object of vital importance, even on this account alone, to say nothing of the advantages and satisfaction to be derived from all being able to read
the Scriptures, and other works both of a religious and moral
nature, for themselves.

For my part, I desire to see the time when education—and
by its means, morality, sobriety, enterprise, and industry—shall
become much more general than at present, and should be
gratified to have it in my power to contribute something to the

advancement of any measure which might have a tendency to accelerate that happy period.

With regard to existing laws, some alterations are thought to be necessary. Many respectable men have suggested that our estray laws, the law respecting the issuing of executions, the road law, and some others, are deficient in their present form, and require alterations. But, considering the great probability that the framers of those laws were wiser than myself, I should prefer not meddling with them, unless they were first attacked by others; in which case I should feel it both a privilege and a duty to take that stand which, in my view, might tend most to the advancement of justice.

But, fellow-citizens, I shall conclude. Considering the great degree of modesty which should always attend youth, it is probable I have already been more presuming than becomes me. However, upon the subjects of which I have treated, I have spoken as I have thought. I may be wrong in regard to any or all of them; but, holding it a sound maxim that it is better only sometimes to be right than at all times to be wrong, so soon as I discover my opinions to be erroneous, I shall be ready to renounce them.

Every man is said to have his peculiar ambition. Whether it be true or not, I can say, for one, that I have no other so great as that of being truly esteemed of my fellow-men, by rendering myself worthy of their esteem. How far I shall succeed in gratifying this ambition is yet to be developed. I am young, and unknown to many of you. I was born, and have ever remained, in the most humble walks of life. I have no wealthy or popular relations or friends to recommend me. My case is thrown exclusively upon the independent voters of the country; and, if elected, they will have conferred a favor upon me for which I shall be unremitting in my labors to compensate. But, if the good people in their wisdom shall see fit to keep me in the background, I have been too familiar with disappointments to be very much chagrined.

ANNOUNCEMENT OF POLITICAL VIEWS

Lincoln had been elected to the Legislature in 1834. Now he was ready to stand for election again. In this letter to the Sangamon Journal, he gives his political views and makes a statement which indicates that he was in favor of woman suffrage—an unusual attitude for any politician to take in 1836.

New Salem, June 13, 1836

To THE EDITOR OF THE *Sangamon Journal*: In your paper of last Saturday I see a communication, over the signature of "Many Voters," in which the candidates who are announced in the *Journal* are called upon to "show their hands." Agreed. Here's mine.

I go for all sharing the privileges of the government who assist in bearing its burdens. Consequently, I go for admitting all whites to the right of suffrage who pay taxes or bear arms (by no means excluding females).

If elected, I shall consider the whole people of Sangamon my constituents, as well those that oppose as those that support me.

While acting as their representative, I shall be governed by their will on all subjects upon which I have the means of knowing what their will is; and upon all others, I shall do what my own judgment teaches me will best advance their interests. . . .

LETTER TO ROBERT ALLEN

Lincoln squelches a whispering campaign. Allen had been a colonel in the Black Hawk War and was now Lincoln's Democratic rival for election to the Legislature. This is Lincoln's reply to Allen's vaguely mentioned charges hinting at corruption of some kind.

He challenges Allen to make his information public, effectually silencing him. Ninian W. Edwards was the husband of Mary Todd's sister Elizabeth. Lincoln, however, had not yet met his future wife.

New Salem, June 21, 1836

DEAR COLONEL: I am told that during my absence last week you passed through this place, and stated publicly that you were in possession of a fact or facts which, if known to the public, would entirely destroy the prospects of N. W. Edwards and myself at the ensuing election; but that, through favor to us, you should forbear to divulge them. No one has needed favors more than I, and, generally, few have been less unwilling to accept them; but in this case favor to me would be injustice to the public, and therefore I must beg your pardon for declining it. That I once had the confidence of the people of Sangamon, is sufficiently evident; and if I have since done anything, either by design or misadventure, which if known would subject me to a forfeiture of that confidence, he that knows of that thing, and conceals it, is a traitor to his country's interest.

I find myself wholly unable to form any conjecture of what fact or facts, real or supposed, you spoke; but my opinion of your veracity will not permit me for a moment to doubt that you at least believed what you said. I am flattered with the personal regard you manifested for me; but I do hope that, on more mature reflection, you will view the public interest as a paramount consideration, and therefore determine to let the worst come. I here assure you that the candid statement of facts on your part, however low it may sink me, shall never break the tie of personal friendship between us. I wish an answer to this, and you are at liberty to publish both, if you choose.

LETTER TO MISS MARY OWENS

Lincoln writes to Mary Owens, to whom he had turned for solace after Ann Rutledge's death. His letter is impersonal and speaks mostly of political events. It is addressed from Vandalia which was then the state capital.

Vandalia, December 13, 1836

MARY: I have been sick ever since my arrival, or I should have written sooner. It is but little difference, however, as I have very little even yet to write. And more, the longer I can avoid the mortification of looking in the postoffice for your letter and not finding it, the better. You see I am mad about that old letter yet. I don't like very well to risk you again. I'll try you once more, anyhow.

The new State House is not yet finished, and consequently the legislature is doing little or nothing. The governor delivered an inflammatory political message, and it is expected there will be some sparring between the parties about it as soon as the two Houses get to business. . . .

Our chance to take the seat of government to Springfield is better than I expected. An internal-improvement convention was held here since we met, which recommended a loan of several millions of dollars, on the faith of the State, to construct railroads. Some of the legislature are for it, and some against it; which has the majority I cannot tell. There is great strife and struggling for the office of the United States Senator here at this time. It is probable we shall ease their pains in a few days. The opposition men have no candidate of their own, and consequently they will smile as complacently at the angry snarl of the contending Van Buren candidates and their respective friends as the Christian does at Satan's rage.

You recollect that I mentioned at the outset of this letter

that I had been unwell. That is the fact, though I believe I am about well now; but that, with other things I cannot account for, have conspired, and have gotten my spirits so low that I feel that I would rather be any place in the world than here. I really cannot endure the thought of staying here ten weeks. Write back as soon as you get this, and, if possible, say something that will please me, for really I have not been pleased since I left you. This letter is so dry and stupid that I am ashamed to send it, but with my present feelings I cannot do any better.

LETTER TO MISS MARY OWENS

Lincoln had been in Springfield for only three weeks when he wrote this letter to Mary Owens. It is a persuasive argument for her not to marry him. The sister he speaks of was a resident of New Salem, at whose home he had first met Mary Owens. New Salem was breaking up; the thought of another family moving away from the village he had so long been associated with brought on his hypochondriasm again.

Springfield, May 7, 1837

Miss Mary S. Owens.

Friend Mary: I have commenced two letters to send you before this, both of which displeased me before I got half done, and so I tore them up. The first I thought was not serious enough, and the second was on the other extreme. I shall send this, turn out as it may.

This thing of living in Springfield is rather a dull business, after all; at least it is to me. I am quite as lonesome here as I ever was anywhere in my life. I have been spoken to by but one woman since I have been here, and should not have been by her if she could have avoided it. I've never been to church yet, and probably shall not be soon. I stay away because I am conscious I should not know how to behave myself.

I am often thinking of what we said about your coming to live at Springfield. I am afraid you would not be satisfied. There is a great deal of flourishing about in carriages here, which it would be your doom to see without sharing it. You would have to be poor, without the means of hiding your poverty. Do you believe you could bear that patiently? Whatever woman may cast her lot with mine, should any ever do so, it is my intention to do all in my power to make her happy and contented; and there is nothing I can imagine that would make me more unhappy than to fail in the effort. I know I should be much happier with you than the way I am, provided I saw no signs of discontent in you. What you have said to me may have been in the way of jest, or I may have misunderstood it. If so, then let it be forgotten; if otherwise, I much wish you would think seriously before you decide. What I have said I will most positively abide by, provided you wish it. My opinion is that you had better not do it. You have not been accustomed to hardship, and it may be more severe than you now imagine. I know you are capable of thinking correctly on any subject, and if you deliberate maturely upon this before you decide, then I am willing to abide your decision.

You must write me a good long letter after you get this. You have nothing else to do, and though it might not seem interesting to you after you had written it, it would be a good deal of company to me in this "busy wilderness." Tell your sister I don't want to hear any more about selling out and moving. That gives me the "hypo" whenever I think of it.

LETTER TO MISS MARY OWENS

The Mary Owens affair had dragged on fruitlessly. In this letter Lincoln gives the lady an opportunity to break it off finally—an opportunity that she evidently took, for their known correspondence ceases at this point.

Springfield, August 16, 1837

FRIEND MARY: You will no doubt think it rather strange that I should write you a letter on the same day on which we parted, and I can only account for it by supposing that seeing you lately makes me think of you more than usual; while at our late meeting we had but few expressions of thoughts. You must know that I cannot see you or think of you with entire indifference; and yet it may be that you are mistaken in regard to what my real feelings toward you are. If I knew you were not, I should not trouble you with this letter. Perhaps any other man would know enough without further information; but I consider it my peculiar right to plead ignorance, and your bounden duty to allow the plea. I want in all cases to do right, and most particularly so in all cases with women. I want at this particular time, more than anything else, to do right with you; and if I knew it would be doing right, as I rather suspect it would, to let you alone, I would do it. And for the purpose of making the matter as plain as possible, I now say that you can now drop the subject, dismiss your thoughts (if you ever had any) from me forever, and leave this letter unanswered, without calling forth one accusing murmur from me. And I will even go further, and say that if it will add anything to your comfort or peace of mind to do so, it is my sincere wish that you should. Do not understand by this that I wish to cut your acquaintance. I mean no such thing. What I do wish is that our further acquaintance shall depend upon yourself. If such

further acquaintance would contribute nothing to your happiness, I am sure it would not to mine. If you feel yourself in
any degree bound to me, I am now willing to release you, provided you wish it; while, on the other hand, I am willing and
even anxious to bind you faster, if I can be convinced that it
will, in any considerable degree, add to your happiness. This,
indeed, is the whole question with me. Nothing would make
me more miserable than to believe you miserable—nothing
more happy than to know you were so.

In what I have now said, I think I cannot be misunderstood,
and to make myself understood is the only object of this letter.

If it suits you best to not answer this, farewell. A long life
and a merry one attend you. But if you conclude to write back,
speak as plainly as I do. There can be neither harm nor danger
in saying to me anything you think, just in the manner you
think it.

ADDRESS BEFORE
THE YOUNG MEN'S LYCEUM OF SPRINGFIELD

*This is Lincoln's earliest speech of any importance which has come
down to us. It was printed in The Sangamon Journal for February
3, 1838. It is remarkably modern in tone; he speaks against mob
violence, warns of the dangers of dictatorship and mourns the
passing of the living memories of the Revolution, since at this time
the men who had fought in it were rapidly dying off. He is skeptical of foreign invasion but fears internal strife.*

January 27, 1838

As a subject for the remarks of the evening, "The perpetuation of our political institutions" is selected.

In the great journal of things happening under the sun, we,
the American people, find our account running under date of
the nineteenth century of the Christian era. We find ourselves

in the peaceful possession of the fairest portion of the earth as regards extent of territory, fertility of soil, and salubrity of climate. We find ourselves under the government of a system of political institutions conducing more essentially to the ends of civil and religious liberty than any of which the history of former times tells us. We, when mounting the stage of existence, found ourselves the legal inheritors of these fundamental blessings. We toiled not in the acquirement or establishment of them; they are a legacy bequeathed us by a once hardy, brave, and patriotic, but now lamented and departed, race of ancestors. Theirs was the task (and nobly they performed it) to possess themselves, and through themselves us, of this goodly land, and to uprear upon its hills and its valleys a political edifice of liberty and equal rights; 'tis ours only to transmit these—the former unprofaned by the foot of an invader, the latter undecayed by the lapse of time and untorn by usurpation—to the latest generation that fate shall permit the world to know. This task of gratitude to our fathers, justice to ourselves, duty to posterity, and love for our species in general, all imperatively require us faithfully to perform.

How then shall we perform it? At what point shall we expect the approach of danger? By what means shall we fortify against it? Shall we expect some transatlantic military giant to step the ocean and crush us at a blow? Never! All the armies of Europe, Asia, and Africa combined, with all the treasure of the earth (our own excepted) in their military chest, with a Bonaparte for a commander, could not by force take a drink from the Ohio or make a track on the Blue Ridge in a trial of a thousand years.

At what point, then, is the approach of danger to be expected? I answer, If it ever reach us it must spring up amongst us; it cannot come from abroad. If destruction be our lot we must ourselves be its author and finisher. As a nation of freemen we must live through all time, or die by suicide.

I hope I am over wary; but if I am not, there is even now

something of ill omen amongst us. I mean the increasing disregard for law which pervades the country—the growing disposition to substitute the wild and furious passions in lieu of the sober judgment of courts, and the worse than savage mobs for the executive ministers of justice. This disposition is awfully fearful in any community; and that it now exists in ours, though grating to our feelings to admit, it would be a violation of truth and an insult to our intelligence to deny. Accounts of outrages committed by mobs form the every-day news of the times. They have pervaded the country from New England to Louisiana; they are neither peculiar to the eternal snows of the former nor the burning suns of the latter; they are not the creature of climate, neither are they confined to the slaveholding or the non-slaveholding States. Alike they spring up among the pleasure-hunting masters of Southern slaves, and the order-loving citizens of the land of steady habits. Whatever then their cause may be, it is common to the whole country.

It would be tedious as well as useless to recount the horrors of all of them. Those happening in the State of Mississippi and at St. Louis are perhaps the most dangerous in example and revolting to humanity. In the Mississippi case they first commenced by hanging the regular gamblers—a set of men certainly not following for a livelihood a very useful or very honest occupation, but one which, so far from being forbidden by the laws, was actually licensed by an act of the Legislature passed but a single year before. Next, Negroes suspected of conspiring to raise an insurrection were caught up and hanged in all parts of the State; then, white men supposed to be leagued with the Negroes; and finally, strangers from neighboring States, going thither on business, were in many instances subjected to the same fate. Thus went on this process of hanging, from gamblers to Negroes, from Negroes to white citizens, and from these to strangers, till dead men were seen literally dangling from the boughs of trees upon every roadside, and in numbers almost sufficient to rival the native Spanish moss of the country as a drapery of the forest.

Turn, then, to that horror-striking scene at St. Louis. A single victim only was sacrificed there. This story is very short, and is perhaps the most highly tragic of anything of its length that has ever been witnessed in real life. A mulatto man by the name of McIntosh was seized in the street, dragged to the suburbs of the city, chained to a tree, and actually burned to death; and all within a single hour from the time he had been a freeman attending to his own business and at peace with the world.

Such are the effects of mob law, and such are the scenes becoming more and more frequent in this land so lately famed for love of law and order, and the stories of which have even now grown too familiar to attract anything more than an idle remark.

But you are perhaps ready to ask, "What has this to do with the perpetuation of our political institutions?" I answer, "It has much to do with it." Its direct consequences are, comparatively speaking, but a small evil, and much of its danger consists in the proneness of our minds to regard its direct as its only consequences. Abstractly considered, the hanging of the gamblers at Vicksburg was of but little consequence. They constitute a portion of population that is worse than useless in any community; and their death, if no pernicious example be set by it, is never matter of reasonable regret with any one. If they were annually swept from the stage of existence by the plague or smallpox, honest men would perhaps be much profited by the operation. Similar, too, is the correct reasoning in regard to the burning of the Negro at St. Louis. He had forfeited his life by the perpetration of an outrageous murder upon one of the most worthy and respectable citizens of the city, and had he not died as he did, he must have died by the sentence of the law in a very short time afterward. As to him alone, it was as well the way it was as it could otherwise have been. But the example in either case was fearful. When men take it in their heads today to hang gamblers or burn murderers, they should recollect that in the confusion usually attending such transactions they will be as likely to hang or burn some one who is neither a gambler nor a murderer as one who is, and that, acting upon the example they set, the mob of tomorrow may, and probably will, hang or burn some of them by the very same mistake. And not only so; the innocent, those who have ever set their faces against violations of law in every shape, alike with the guilty fall victims to the ravages of mob law; and thus it goes up, step by step, till all the walls erected for the defense of the persons and property of individuals are trodden down and disregarded. But all this, even, is not the full extent of the evil. By such examples, by instances of the perpetrators of such acts going unpunished, the lawless in spirit are encouraged to become lawless in practice; and having been used to no restraint but dread of punishment, they thus become absolutely unrestrained. Having ever regarded government as their deadliest bane, they make a jubilee of the suspension of its operations, and pray for nothing so much as its total annihilation. While, on the other hand, good men, men who love tranquillity, who desire to abide by the laws and enjoy their benefits, who would gladly spill their blood in the defense of their country, seeing their property destroyed, their families insulted, and their lives endangered, their persons injured, and seeing nothing in prospect that forebodes a change for the better, become tired of and disgusted with a government that offers them no protection, and are not much averse to a change in which they imagine they have nothing to lose. Thus, then, by the operation of this mobocratic spirit which all must admit is now abroad in the land, the strongest bulwark of any government, and particularly of those constituted like ours, may effectually be broken down and destroyed—I mean the attachment of the people. Whenever this effect shall be produced among us; whenever the vicious portion of population shall be permitted to gather in bands of hundreds and thousands, and burn churches, ravage and rob provision-stores, throw printing-presses into rivers, shoot editors,* and hang and burn obnoxious persons at pleasure and with impunity, depend on it, this government cannot last. By such things the feelings of the best citizens will become more or less alienated from it, and thus it will be left without friends, or with too few, and those few too weak to make their friendship effectual. At such a time, and under such circumstances, men of sufficient talent and ambition will not be wanting to seize the opportunity, strike the blow, and overturn that fair fabric which for the last half century has been the fondest hope of the lovers of freedom throughout the world.

I know the American people are much attached to their government; I know they would suffer much for its sake; I know they would endure evils long and patiently before they would ever think of exchanging it for another—yet, notwithstanding all this, if the laws be continually despised and disregarded, if their rights to be secure in their persons and property are held by no better tenure than the caprice of a mob, the alienation of their affections from the government is the natural consequence; and to that, sooner or later, it must come.

Here, then, is one point at which danger may be expected. The question recurs, "How shall we fortify against it?" The answer is simple. Let every American, every lover of liberty, every well-wisher to his posterity swear by the blood of the Revolution never to violate in the least particular the laws of the country, and never to tolerate their violation by others. As

* Lincoln refers here to the shooting of Elijah Lovejoy, editor of the abolitionist *Alton Observer.* Lovejoy had had three printing presses thrown into the river. He was killed by a pro-slavery mob while trying to defend the fourth one. Owen Lovejoy, brother of Elijah, played an important part in Lincoln's political career. See Lincoln's letter to James Lemen, March 2, 1857, in which he refers to Lovejoy's murder as "the most important single event that ever happened in the new world." The reference to Lovejoy's death, which occurred on November 7, 1837, correctly dates this speech as having been delivered in 1838. Many editions of Lincoln's writings have wrongly dated it January 27, 1837.

the patriots of seventy-six did to the support of the Declaration of Independence, so to the support of the Constitution and laws let every American pledge his life, his property, and his sacred honor—let every man remember that to violate the law is to trample on the blood of his father, and to tear the charter of his own and his children's liberty. Let reverence for the laws be breathed by every American mother to the lisping babe that prattles on her lap; let it be taught in schools, in seminaries, and in colleges; let it be written in primers, spelling-books, and in almanacs; let it be preached from the pulpit, proclaimed in legislative halls, and enforced in courts of justice. And, in short, let it become the political religion of the nation; and let the old and the young, the rich and the poor, the grave and the gay of all sexes and tongues and colors and conditions, sacrifice unceasingly upon its altars.

While ever a state of feeling such as this shall universally or even very generally prevail throughout the nation, vain will be every effort, and fruitless every attempt, to subvert our national freedom.

When I so pressingly urge a strict observance of all the laws, let me not be understood as saying there are no bad laws, or that grievances may not arise for the redress of which no legal provisions have been made. I mean to say no such thing. But I do mean to say that although bad laws, if they exist, should be repealed as soon as possible, still, while they continue in force, for the sake of example they should be religiously observed. So also in unprovided cases. If such arise, let proper legal provisions be made for them with the least possible delay, but till then let them, if not too intolerable, be borne with.

There is no grievance that is a fit object of redress by mob law. In any case that may arise, as, for instance, the promulgation of abolitionism, one of two positions is necessarily true— that is, the thing is right within itself, and therefore deserves the protection of all law and all good citizens, or it is wrong, and therefore proper to be prohibited by legal enactments; and in neither case is the interposition of mob law either necessary, justifiable, or excusable.

But it may be asked, "Why suppose danger to our political institutions? Have we not preserved them for more than fifty years? And why may we not for fifty times as long?"

We hope there is no sufficient reason. We hope all danger may be overcome; but to conclude that no danger may ever arise would itself be extremely dangerous. There are now, and will hereafter be, many causes, dangerous in their tendency, which have not existed heretofore, and which are not too insignificant to merit attention. That our government should have been maintained in its original form, from its establishment until now, is not much to be wondered at. It had many props to support it through that period, which now are decayed and crumbled away. Through that period it was felt by all to be an undecided experiment; now it is understood to be a successful one. Then, all that sought celebrity and fame and distinction expected to find them in the success of that experiment. Their all was staked upon it; their destiny was inseparably linked with it. Their ambition aspired to display before an admiring world a practical demonstration of the truth of a proposition which had hitherto been considered at best no better than problematical—namely, the capability of a people to govern themselves. If they succeeded they were to be immortalized; their names were to be transferred to counties, and cities, and rivers, and mountains; and to be revered and sung, toasted through all time. If they failed, they were to be called knaves, and fools, and fanatics for a fleeting hour; then to sink and be forgotten. They succeeded. The experiment is successful, and thousands have won their deathless names in making it so. But the game is caught; and I believe it is true that with the catching end the pleasures of the chase. This field of glory is harvested, and the crop is already appropriated. But new reapers will arise, and they too will seek a field. It is to deny what the history of the world tells us is true, to suppose that men of ambition and talents will not continue to spring up amongst us. And when they do, they will as naturally seek the gratification of their ruling passion as others have done before them. The question then is: Can that gratification be found in supporting and maintaining an edifice that has been erected by others? Most certainly it cannot. Many great and good men, sufficiently qualified for any task they should undertake, may ever be found whose ambition would aspire to nothing beyond a seat in Congress, a gubernatorial or a presidential chair; but such belong not to the family of the lion, or the tribe of the eagle. What! think you these places would satisfy an Alexander, a Cæsar, or a Napoleon? Never! Towering genius disdains a beaten path. It seeks regions hitherto unexplored. It sees no distinction in adding story to story upon the monuments of fame erected to the memory of others. It denies that it is glory enough to serve under any chief. It scorns to tread in the footsteps of any predecessor, however illustrious. It thirsts and burns for distinction; and if possible, it will have it, whether at the expense of emancipating slaves or enslaving freemen. Is it unreasonable, then, to expect that some man possessed of the loftiest genius, coupled with ambition sufficient to push it to its utmost stretch, will at some time spring up among us? And when such an one does, it will require the people to be united with each other, attached to the government and laws, and generally intelligent, to successfully frustrate his designs.

Distinction will be his paramount object, and although he would as willingly, perhaps more so, acquire it by doing good as harm, yet, that opportunity being past, and nothing left to be done in the way of building up, he would set boldly to the task of pulling down.

Here then is a probable case, highly dangerous, and such an one as could not have well existed heretofore.

Another reason which once was, but which, to the same extent, is now no more, has done much in maintaining our institutions thus far. I mean the powerful influence which the interesting scenes of the Revolution had upon the passions of the people as distinguished from their judgment. By this influence, the jealousy, envy, and avarice incident to our nature, and so common to a state of peace, prosperity, and conscious strength, were for the time in a great measure smothered and rendered inactive, while the deep-rooted principles of hate, and the powerful motive of revenge, instead of being turned against each other, were directed exclusively against the British nation. And thus, from the force of circumstances, the basest principles of our nature were either made to lie dormant, or to become the active agents in the advancement of the noblest of causes—that of establishing and maintaining civil and religious liberty.

But this state of feeling must fade, is fading, had faded, with the circumstances that produced it.

I do not mean to say that the scenes of the Revolution are now or ever will be entirely forgotten, but that, like everything else, they must fade upon the memory of the world, and grow more and more dim by the lapse of time. In history, we hope, they will be read of, and recounted, so long as the Bible shall be read; but even granting that they will, their influence cannot be what it heretofore has been. Even then they cannot be so universally known nor so vividly felt as they were by the generation just gone to rest. At the close of that struggle, nearly every adult male had been a participator in some of its scenes. The consequence was that of those scenes, in the form of a husband, a father, a son, or a brother, a living history was to be found in every family—a history bearing the indubitable testimonies of its own authenticity, in the limbs mangled, in the scars of wounds received, in the midst of the very scenes related—a history, too, that could be read and understood alike by all, the wise and the ignorant, the learned and the unlearned. But those histories are gone. They can be read no more forever. They were a fortress of strength; but what invading foeman could never do, the silent artillery of time has done—the leveling of its walls. They are gone. They were a forest of giant oaks; but the all-resistless hurricane has swept over them, and left only here and there a lonely trunk, despoiled of its verdure, shorn of its foliage, unshading and unshaded, to murmur in a few more gentle breezes, and to combat with its mutilated limbs a few more ruder storms, then to sink and be no more.

They were pillars of the temple of liberty; and now that they have crumbled away that temple must fall unless we, their descendants, supply their places with other pillars, hewn from the solid quarry of sober reason. Passion has helped us, but can do so no more. It will in future be our enemy. Reason—cold, calculating, unimpassioned reason—must furnish all the materials for our future support and defense. . . .

LETTER TO MRS. O. H. BROWNING

In this letter to the wife of Orville H. Browning, whom he had met in Vandalia, Lincoln reviews the whole course of his affair with Mary Owens, much to that lady's disparagement. When Ward Lamon first made this letter public in his Life of Abraham Lincoln in 1872 (while Mary Owens was still alive), he said, "For many reasons the publication of this letter is an extremely painful duty." Nevertheless, it sheds much light on Lincoln's early development and especially on his relations with women.

Springfield, April 1, 1838

DEAR MADAM: Without apologizing for being egotistical, I shall make the history of so much of my life as has elapsed since I saw you the subject of this letter. And, by the way, I now discover that in order to give a full and intelligible account of the things I have done and suffered since I saw you, I shall necessarily have to relate some that happened before.

It was, then, in the autumn of 1836 that a married lady of my acquaintance, and who was a great friend of mine, being about to pay a visit to her father and other relatives residing in Kentucky, proposed to me that on her return she would bring a sister of hers with her on condition that I would engage to become her brother-in-law with all convenient despatch. I, of course, accepted the proposal, for you know I could not have done otherwise had I really been averse to it; but privately between you and me, I was most confoundedly well pleased with the project. I had seen the said sister some three years before, thought her intelligent and agreeable, and saw no good objection to plodding life through hand in hand with her. Time passed on, the lady took her journey and in due time returned, sister in company, sure enough. This astonished me a little, for it appeared to me that her coming so readily showed that she was a trifle too willing, but on reflection it occurred to me that she might have been prevailed on by her married sister to come, without anything concerning me having been mentioned to her, and so I concluded that if no other objection presented itself, I would consent to waive this. All this occurred to me on hearing of her arrival in the neighborhood—for, be it remembered, I had not yet seen her, except about three years previous, as above mentioned. In a few days we had an interview, and, although I had seen her before, she did not look as my imagination had pictured her. I knew she was over-size, but now she appeared a fair match for Falstaff. I knew she was called an "old maid," and I felt no doubt of the truth of at least half of the appellation, but now, when I beheld her, I could not for my life avoid thinking of my mother; and this, not from withered features—for her skin was too full of fat to permit of its contracting into wrinkles—but from her want of teeth, weatherbeaten appearance in general, and from a kind of notion that ran in my head that nothing could have commenced at the size of infancy and reached her present bulk in less than thirty-five or forty years; and, in short, I was not at all pleased with her. But what could I do? I had told her sister that I would take her for better or for worse, and I made a point of honor and conscience in all things to stick to my word, especially if others had been induced to act on it, which in this case I had no doubt they had, for I was now fairly convinced that no other man on earth would have her, and hence the conclusion that they were bent on holding me to my bargain. "Well," thought I, "I have said it, and, be the consequences what they may, it shall not be my fault if I fail to do it." At once I determined to consider her my wife, and this done, all my powers of discovery were put to work in search of perfections in her which might be fairly set off against her defects. I tried to imagine her handsome, which, but for her unfortunate corpulency, was actually true. Exclusive of this, no woman that I have ever seen has a finer face. I also tried to convince myself that the mind was much more to be valued than the person, and in this she was not inferior, as I could discover, to any with whom I had been acquainted.

Shortly after this, without attempting to come to any positive understanding with her, I set out for Vandalia, when and where you first saw me. During my stay there I had letters from her which did not change my opinion of either her intellect or intention, but, on the contrary, confirmed it in both.

All this while, although I was fixed "firm as the surge-repelling rock" in my resolution, I found I was continually repenting the rashness which had led me to make it. Through life I have been in no bondage, either real or imaginary, from the thraldom of which I so much desired to be free. After my return home I saw nothing to change my opinion of her in any particular. She was the same, and so was I. I now spent my time in planning how I might get along in life after my contemplated change in circumstances should have taken place, and how I might procrastinate the evil day for a time, which I really dreaded as much, perhaps more, than an Irishman does the halter.

After all my sufferings upon this deeply interesting subject, here I am, wholly, unexpectedly, completely. out of the "scrape," and I now want to know if you can guess how I got out of it—out, clear, in every sense of the term—no violation of word, honor, or conscience. I don't believe you can guess, and so I might as well tell you at once. As the lawyer says, it was done in the manner following, to-wit: After I had delayed the matter as long as I thought I could in honor do (which, by the way, had brought me round into the last fall), I concluded I might as well bring it to a consummation without further delay, and so I mustered my resolution and made the proposal to her direct; but, shocking to relate, she answered, No. At first I supposed she did it through an affectation of modesty, which I thought but ill became her under the peculiar circumstances of her case, but on my renewal of the charge I found she repelled it with greater firmness than before. I tried it again and again, but with the same success, or rather with the same want of success.

I finally was forced to give it up, at which I very unexpectedly found myself mortified almost beyond endurance. I was mortified, it seemed to me, in a hundred different ways. My vanity was deeply wounded by the reflection that I had so long been too stupid to discover her intentions, and at the same time never doubting that I understood them perfectly; and also that she, whom I had taught myself to believe nobody else would have, had actually rejected me with all my fancied greatness. And, to cap the whole, I then for the first time began to suspect that I was really a little in love with her. But let it all go! I'll try and outlive it. Others have been made fools of by the girls, but this can never with truth be said of me. I most emphatically, in this instance, made a fool of myself. I have now come to the conclusion never again to think of marrying, and for this reason—I can never be satisfied with any one who would be blockhead enough to have me.

A. LINCOLN

LETTER TO JOHN T. STUART

Lincoln reports to his first law partner on the prospects for the political campaign in Sangamon County. He describes also a street fight between the mercurial Stephen A. Douglas and Simeon Francis, editor of the pro-Lincoln Sangamo Journal.

Springfield, March 1, 1840

DEAR STUART: I have never seen the prospects of our party so bright in these parts as they are now. We shall carry this county by a larger majority than we did in 1836, when you ran against May. I do not think my prospects individually are very flattering, for I think it probable I shall not be permitted to be a candidate; but the party ticket will succeed triumphantly. . . .

Yesterday Douglas, having chosen to consider himself insulted by something in the *Journal*, undertook to cane Francis in the street. Francis caught him by the hair and jammed him back against a market-cart, where the matter ended by Francis being pulled away from him. The whole affair was so ludicrous that Francis and everybody else (Douglas excepted) have been laughing about it ever since.

LETTER TO W. G. ANDERSON

Abraham Lincoln gives a lesson on how to win friends and influence people.

Laurenceville, October 31, 1840

W. G. ANDERSON.
DEAR SIR: Your note of yesterday is received. In the difficulty between us of which you speak, you say you think I was the

aggressor. I do not think I was. You say my "words imported insult." I meant them as a fair set-off to your own statements, and not otherwise; and in that light alone I now wish you to understand them. You ask for my present "feelings on the subject." I entertain no unkind feelings to you, and none of any sort upon the subject, except a sincere regret that I permitted myself to get into such an altercation.

TO JOHN T. STUART

This letter was written less than three weeks after "the fatal first of January," when Lincoln broke off his engagement to Mary Todd. He says that he has "been making a most discreditable exhibition . . . of hypochondriasm" and tries to get his friend and physician, Dr. A. G. Henry, appointed to the postmastership of Springfield. Unfortunately, Dr. Henry did not receive the appointment.

Springfield, January 20, 1841

DEAR STUART: I have had no letter from you since you left. No matter for that. What I wish now is to speak of our Post-Office. You know I desired Dr. Henry to have that place when you left; I now desire it more than ever. I have within the last few days, been making a most discreditable exhibition of myself in the way of hypochondriasm and thereby got an impression that Dr. Henry is necessary to my existence. Unless he gets that place he leaves Springfield. You therefore see how much I am interested in the matter.

We shall shortly forward you a petition in his favour signed by all or nearly all the Whig members of the Legislature as well as other whigs. This, together with what you know of the Dr.'s position and merits I sincerely hope will secure him the appointment. My heart is very much set upon it. Pardon me for not writing more; I have not sufficient composure to write a long letter.

LETTER TO JOHN T. STUART

Lincoln again writes to his partner in a mood of complete dejection over "the fatal first of January."

Springfield, Illinois, January 23, 1841

Dear Stuart: Yours of the 3d instant is received, and I proceed to answer it as well as I can, though from the deplorable state of my mind at this time, I fear I shall give you but little satisfaction. . . .

For not giving you a general summary of news, you must pardon me; it is not in my power to do so. I am now the most miserable man living. If what I feel were equally distributed to the whole human family, there would not be one cheerful face on the earth. Whether I shall ever be better, I cannot tell; I awfully forbode I shall not. To remain as I am is impossible; I must die or be better, it appears to me. The matter you speak of on my account you may attend to as you say, unless you shall hear of my condition forbidding it. I say this because I fear I shall be unable to attend to any business here, and a change of scene might help me. If I could be myself, I would rather remain at home with Judge Logan. I can write no more.

LETTER TO JOSHUA F. SPEED

Speed had sold out his store on the same day that Lincoln broke with Mary Todd. He then moved to Louisville, Kentucky. Lincoln writes to him six months later to give him the news from Springfield. He describes at length the "murder" of a man who, after much fuss and bother, was found not to have been murdered at all. A few days after Lincoln wrote this letter, Archibald Fisher, the "murdered" man, appeared in Springfield. Neither he nor the men

*accused of his death ever volunteered an explanation of what had
happened, so the real mystery is still unsolved.*

Springfield, June 19, 1841

DEAR SPEED: We have had the highest state of excitement
here for a week past that our community has ever witnessed;
and although the public feeling is somewhat allayed, the
curious affair which aroused it is very far from being even yet
cleared of mystery. It would take a quire of paper to give you
anything like a full account of it, and I therefore only propose
a brief outline. The chief personages in the drama are Archibald Fisher, supposed to be murdered, and Archibald Trailor,
Henry Trailor, and William Trailor, supposed to have murdered him. The three Trailors are brothers; the first, Arch., as
you know, lives in town; the second, Henry, in Clary's Grove;
and the third, William, in Warren County; and Fisher, the
supposed murdered, being without a family, had made his
home with William. On Saturday evening, being the 29th of
May, Fisher and William came to Henry's in a one-horse
dearborn, and there stayed over Sunday; and on Monday all
three came to Springfield (Henry on horseback), and joined
Archibald at Myers's, the Dutch carpenter. That evening at
supper Fisher was missing, and so next morning some ineffectual search was made for him; and on Tuesday, at one
o'clock P. M. William and Henry started home without him.
In a day or two Henry and one or two of his Clary Grove
neighbors came back for him again, and advertised his disappearance in the papers. The knowledge of the matter thus far
had not been general, and here it dropped entirely, till about
the 10th instant, when Keys received a letter from the postmaster in Warren County, that William had arrived at home,
and was telling a very mysterious and improbable story about
the disappearance of Fisher, which induced the community
there to suppose he had been disposed of unfairly. Keys made
this letter public, which immediately set the whole town and

adjoining county agog. And so it has continued until yesterday. The mass of the people commenced a systematic search
for the dead body, while Wickersham was despatched to arrest
Henry Trailor at the Grove, and Jim Maxcy to Warren to
arrest William. On Monday last, Henry was brought in, and
showed an evident inclination to insinuate that he knew
Fisher to be dead, and that Arch. and William had killed
him. He said he guessed the body could be found in Spring
Creek, between the Beardstown road and Hickox's mill. Away
the people swept like a herd of buffalo, and cut down Hickox's
milldam *nolens volens*, to draw the water out of the pond,
and then went up and down and down and up the creek, fish-
ing and raking, and raking and ducking, and diving for two
days, and, after all, no dead body found.

In the mean time a sort of scuffling-ground had been found
in the brush in the angle, or point, where the road leading
into the woods past the brewery and the one leading in past
the brick-yard meet. From the scuffle-ground was the sign of
something about the size of a man having been dragged to the
edge of the thicket, where it joined the track of some small-
wheeled carriage drawn by one horse, as shown by the road-
tracks. The carriage-track led off toward Spring Creek. Near
this drag-trail Dr. Merryman found two hairs, which, after a
long scientific examination, he pronounced to be triangular
human hair, which term, he says, includes within it the
whiskers, the hair growing under the arms and on other parts
of the body; and he judged that these two were of the whiskers,
because the ends were cut, showing that they had flourished
in the neighborhood of the razor's operations.

On Thursday last Jim Maxcy brought in William Trailor
from Warren. On the same day Arch. was arrested and put in
jail. Yesterday (Friday) William was put upon his examining
trial before May and Lovely. Archibald and Henry were both
present. Lamborn prosecuted, and Logan, Baker, and your
humble servant defended. A great many witnesses were intro-

duced and examined, but I shall only mention those whose testimony seemed most important. The first of these was Captain Ransdell. He swore that when William and Henry left Springfield for home on Tuesday before mentioned, they did not take the direct route—which, you know, leads by the butcher shop—but that they followed the street north until they got opposite, or nearly opposite, May's new house, after which he could not see them from where he stood; and it was afterward proved that in about an hour after they started, they came into the street by the butcher shop from toward the brick-yard. Dr. Merryman and others swore to what is stated about the scuffle-ground, drag-trail, whiskers, and carriage-tracks. Henry was then introduced by the prosecution. He swore that when they started for home, they went out north, as Ransdell stated, and turned down west by the brick-yard into the woods, and there met Archibald; that they proceeded a small distance farther, when he was placed as a sentinel to watch for and announce the approach of any one that might happen that way; that William and Arch. took the dearborn out of the road a small distance to the edge of the thicket, where they stopped, and he saw them lift the body of a man into it; that they then moved off with the carriage in the direction of Hickox's mill, and he loitered about for something like an hour, when William returned with the carriage, but without Arch., and said they had put him in a safe place; that they went somehow—he did not know exactly how—into the road close to the brewery, and proceeded on to Clary's Grove. He also stated that some time during the day William told him that he and Arch. had killed Fisher the evening before; that the way they did it was by him (William) knocking him down with a club, and Arch. then choking him to death.

An old man from Warren, called Dr. Gilmore, was then introduced on the part of the defense. He swore that he had known Fisher for several years; that Fisher had resided at his

house a long time at each of two different spells—once while
he built a barn for him, and once while he was doctored for
some chronic disease; that two or three years ago Fisher had
a serious hurt in his head by the bursting of a gun, since which
he had been subject to continued bad health and occasional
aberration of mind. He also stated that on last Tuesday, being
the same day that Maxcy arrested William Trailor, he (the
doctor) was from home in the early part of the day, and on his
return, about eleven o'clock, found Fisher at his house in bed,
and apparently very unwell; that he asked him how he came
from Springfield; that Fisher said he had come by Peoria, and
also told of several other places he had been at more in the
direction of Peoria, which showed that he at the time of
speaking did not know where he had been wandering about
in a state of derangement. He further stated that in about
two hours he received a note from one of Trailor's friends,
advising him of his arrest, and requesting him to go on to
Springfield as a witness, to testify as to the state of Fisher's
health in former times; that he immediately set off, calling
up two of his neighbors as company, and, riding all evening
and all night, overtook Maxcy and William at Lewiston in
Fulton County; that Maxcy refusing to discharge Trailor upon
his statement, his two neighbors returned and he came on to
Springfield. Some question being made as to whether the doctor's story was not a fabrication, several acquaintances of his
(among whom was the same postmaster who wrote Keys, as
before mentioned) were introduced as sort of compurgators,
who swore that they knew the doctor to be of good character
for truth and veracity, and generally of good character in every
way. Here the testimony ended, and the Trailors were discharged, Arch. and William expressing both in word and
manner their entire confidence that Fisher would be found
alive at the doctor's by Galloway, Mallory, and Myers, who
a day before had been despatched for that purpose; while
Henry still protested that no power on earth could ever show

Fisher alive. Thus stands this curious affair. When the doctor's story was first made public, it was amusing to scan and contemplate the countenances and hear the remarks of those who had been actively in search for the dead body: some looked quizzical, some melancholy, and some furiously angry. Porter, who had been very active, swore he always knew the man was not dead, and that he had not stirred an inch to hunt for him; Langford, who had taken the lead in cutting down Hickox's milldam, and wanted to hang Hickox for objecting, looked most awfully woebegone: he seemed the "victim of unrequited affection," as represented in the comic almanacs we used to laugh over; and Hart, the little drayman that hauled Molly home once, said it was too *damned* bad to have so much trouble, and no hanging after all.

I commenced this letter on yesterday, since which I received yours of the 13th. I stick to my promise to come to Louisville. Nothing new here except what I have written. I have not seen —— since my last trip, and I am going out there as soon as I mail this letter.

LETTER TO MISS MARY SPEED

In August, Lincoln had gone to visit Speed who was living on a farm near Louisville, Kentucky. Lincoln had spent a very pleasant time with the Speed family and he had been a witness to Speed's courtship of Fanny Henning—a courtship that was to have a great influence on Lincoln's own affair with Mary Todd. Speed accompanied Lincoln back to Springfield; shortly after their arrival, Lincoln wrote this letter to Speed's sister Mary. He describes the slaves he had seen on board the river steamer. In 1855, Lincoln was to write to Speed, reminding him of these slaves.

Bloomington, Ill., September 27, 1841

MY FRIEND: Having resolved to write to some of your mother's family, and not having the express permission of any one of them to do so, I have had some little difficulty in determining on which to inflict the task of reading what I now feel must be a most dull and silly letter; but when I remembered that you and I were something of cronies while I was at Farmington, and that while there I was under the necessity of shutting you up in a room to prevent your committing an assault and battery upon me, I instantly decided that you should be the devoted one. I assume that you have not heard from Joshua and myself since we left, because I think it doubtful whether he has written. You remember there was some uneasiness about Joshua's health when we left. That little indisposition of his turned out to be nothing serious, and it was pretty nearly forgotten when we reached Springfield. We got on board the steamboat *Lebanon* in the locks of the canal, about twelve o'clock M. of the day we left, and reached St. Louis the next Monday at 8 P. M. Nothing of interest happened during the passage, except the vexatious delays occasioned by the sand-bars be thought interesting.

By the way, a fine example was presented on board the boat for contemplating the effect of condition upon human happiness. A gentleman had purchased twelve Negroes in different parts of Kentucky, and was taking them to a farm in the South. They were chained six and six together. A small iron clevis was around the left wrist of each, and this was fastened to the main chain by a shorter one, at a convenient distance from the others, so that the Negroes were strung together precisely like so many fish upon a trot-line. In this condition they were being separated forever from the scenes of their childhood, their friends, their fathers and mothers, and brothers and sisters, many of them from their wives and children, and going into perpetual slavery, where the lash of the master is proverbially more ruthless and unrelenting than any other where; and yet amid all these distressing circumstances, as we would think them, they were the most cheerful and apparently happy creatures on board. One whose offense for which he had been sold was an over-fondness for his wife, played the fiddle almost continually, and the others danced, sang, cracked jokes, and played various games with cards from day to day. How true it is that "God tempers the wind to the shorn lamb," or in other words, that he renders the worst of human conditions tolerable, while he permits the best to be nothing better than tolerable.

To return to the narrative. When we reached Springfield, I stayed but one day, when I started on this tedious circuit where I now am. Do you remember my going to the city, while I was in Kentucky, to have a tooth extracted, and making a failure of it? Well, that same old tooth got to paining me so much that about a week since I had it torn out, bringing with it a bit of the jaw-bone, the consequence of which is that my mouth is now so sore that I can neither talk nor eat.

I am literally "subsisting on savory remembrances"—that is, being unable to eat, I am living upon the remembrance of the delicious dishes of peaches and cream we used to have at your house. When we left, Miss Fanny Henning was owing you a visit, as I understood. Has she paid it yet? If she has, are you not convinced that she is one of the sweetest girls in the world? There is but one thing about her, so far as I could perceive, that I would have otherwise than as it is—that is, something of a tendency to melancholy. This, let it be observed, is a misfortune, not a fault.

Give her an assurance of my very highest regard when you see her. Is little Siss Eliza Davis at your house yet? If she is, kiss her "o'er and o'er again" for me.

Tell your mother that I have not got her "present" [a Bible] with me, but I intend to read it regularly when I return home. I doubt not that it is really, as she says, the best cure for the blues, could one but take it according to the truth. Give my respects to all your sisters (including Aunt Emma) and brothers. Tell Mrs. Peay, of whose happy face I shall long retain a pleasant remembrance, that I have been trying to think of a name for her homestead, but as yet cannot satisfy myself with one. I shall be very happy to receive a line from you soon after you receive this, and in case you choose to favor me with one, address it to Charleston, Coles County, Ill., as I shall be there about the time to receive it.

LETTER TO JOSHUA F. SPEED

Joshua Speed was about to leave Springfield to return home, where it was expected that his marriage to Fanny Henning would take place. Speed had evidently caught some of Lincoln's fatal hesitation about entering the married state. Lincoln writes this letter to him so he can take it on his journey. It is intended to re-inspire Speed with the desire to go through with his marriage.

January [3?], 1842

MY DEAR SPEED: Feeling, as you know I do, the deepest solicitude for the success of the enterprise you are engaged in, I adopt this as the last method I can adopt to aid you, in case (which God forbid!) you shall need any aid. I do not place what I am going to say on paper because I can say it better that way than I could by word of mouth, but, were I to say it orally before we part, most likely you would forget it at the very time when it might do you some good. As I think it reasonable that you will feel very badly some time between this and the final consummation of your purpose, it is intended that you shall read this just at such a time. Why I say it is reasonable that you will feel very badly yet, is because of three special causes added to the general one which I shall mention.

The general cause is, that you are naturally of a nervous temperament; and this I say from what I have seen of you personally, and what you have told me concerning your mother at various times, and concerning your brother William at the time his wife died. The first special cause is your exposure to bad weather on your journey, which my experience clearly proves to be very severe on defective nerves. The second is the absence of all business and conversation of friends, which might divert your mind, give it occasional rest from the intensity of thought which will sometimes wear the sweetest idea threadbare and turn it to the bitterness of death. The third is the rapid and near approach of that crisis on which all your thoughts and feelings concentrate.

If from all these causes you shall escape and go through triumphantly, without another "twinge of the soul," I shall be most happily but most egregiously deceived. If, on the contrary, you shall, as I expect you will at some time, be agonized and distressed, let me, who have some reason to speak with judgment on such a subject, beseech you to ascribe it to the causes I have mentioned, and not to some false and ruinous suggestion of the Devil.

"But," you will say, "do not your causes apply to every one engaged in a like undertaking?" By no means. The particular causes, to a greater or less extent perhaps, do apply in all cases; but the general one—nervous debility, which is the key and conductor of all the particular ones, and without which they would be utterly harmless—though it does pertain to you, does not pertain to one in a thousand. It is out of this that the painful difference between you and the mass of the world springs.

I know what the painful point with you is at all times when you are unhappy; it is an apprehension that you do not love her as you should. What nonsense! How came you to court her? Was it because you thought she deserved it, and that you had given her reason to expect it? If it was for that, why did not the same reason make you court Ann Todd, and at least twenty others of whom you can think, and to whom it would apply with greater force than to her? Did you court her for her wealth? Why, you know she had none. But you say you reasoned yourself into it. What do you mean by that? Was it not that you found yourself unable to reason yourself out

of it? Did you not think, and partly form the purpose, of court-
ing her the first time you ever saw her or heard of her? What
had reason to do with it at that early stage? There was nothing
at that time for reason to work upon. Whether she was moral,
amiable, sensible, or even of good character, you did not, nor
could then know, except, perhaps, you might infer the last
from the company you found her in.

All you then did or could know of her was her personal
appearance and deportment; and these, if they impress at all,
impress the heart, and not the head.

Say candidly, were not those heavenly black eyes the whole
basis of all your early reasoning on the subject? After you and
I had once been at the residence, did you not go and take me
all the way to Lexington and back, for no other purpose but
to get to see her again, on our return on that evening to take
a trip for that express object? What earthly consideration
would you take to find her scouting and despising you, and
giving herself up to another? But of this you have no apprehension; and therefore you cannot bring it home to your
feelings.

I shall be so anxious about you that I shall want you to write
by every mail.

LETTER TO JOSHUA F. SPEED

*Speed had written to Lincoln, informing him that Fanny Henning
was very sick and might not recover. Lincoln writes to console him.
Toward the end of the letter, he refers to Sarah Rickard, the seven-
teen-year-old daughter of his landlady with whom he had been
carrying on a not-too-serious courtship in order to forget Mary
Todd.*

Springfield, Illinois, February 3, 1842

Dear Speed: Your letter of the 25th January came to hand
today. You well know that I do not feel my own sorrows much

more keenly than I do yours, when I know of them; and yet I assure you I was not much hurt by what you wrote me of your excessively bad feeling at the time you wrote. Not that I am less capable of sympathizing with you now than ever, not that I am less your friend than ever, but because I hope and believe that your present anxiety and distress about her health and her life must and will forever banish those horrid doubts which I know you sometimes felt as to the truth of your affection for her. If they can once and forever be removed (and I almost feel a presentiment that the Almighty has sent your present affliction expressly for that object), surely nothing can come in their stead to fill their immeasurable measure of misery. The death-scenes of those we love are surely painful enough; but these we are prepared for and expect to see: they happen to all, and all know they must happen. Painful as they are, they are not an unlooked-for sorrow. Should she, as you fear, be destined to an early grave, it is indeed a great consolation to know that she is so well prepared to meet it. Her religion, which you once disliked so much, I will venture you now prize most highly. But I hope your melancholy bodings as to her early death are not well founded. I even hope that ere this reaches you she will have returned with improved and still improving health, and that you will have met her, and forgotten the sorrows of the past in the enjoyments of the present. I would say more if I could, but it seems that I have said enough. It really appears to me that you yourself ought to rejoice, and not sorrow, at this indubitable evidence of your undying affection for her. Why, Speed, if you did not love her, although you might not wish her death, you would most certainly be resigned to it. Perhaps this point is no longer a question with you, and my pertinacious dwelling upon it is a rude intrusion upon your feelings. If so, you must pardon me. You know the hell I have suffered on that point, and how tender I am upon it. You know I do not mean wrong. I have been quite clear of "hypo" since you left; even better than I was along in the fall. I have seen Sarah [Rickard] but once. She seemed very cheerful, and so I said nothing to her about what we spoke of.

Old Uncle Billy Herndon is dead, and it is said this evening that Uncle Ben Ferguson will not live. This, I believe, is all the news, and enough at that unless it were better. Write me immediately on the receipt of this.

LETTER TO JOSHUA F. SPEED

Ten days after the preceding letter, Lincoln writes to Joshua Speed to congratulate him on his marriage—and to offer him some advice on how to forget about it. "Avoid being idle," he says, and this was to be his own formula for escaping from Mary Todd. Then he adds that he "has been quite a man since you left," implying that Speed must have had a difficult time with Lincoln while he had been in Springfield.

Springfield, Illinois, February 13, 1842

DEAR SPEED: Yours of the 1st instant came to hand three or four days ago. When this shall reach you, you will have been Fanny's husband several days. You know my desire to befriend you is everlasting; that I will never cease while I know how to do anything. But you will always hereafter be on ground that I have never occupied, and consequently, if advice were needed, I might advise wrong. I do fondly hope, however, that you will never again need any comfort from abroad. But should I be mistaken in this, should excessive pleasure still be accompanied with a painful counterpart at times, still let me urge you, as I have ever done, to remember, in the depth and even agony of despondency, that very shortly you are to feel well again. I am now fully convinced that you love her as ardently as you are capable of loving. Your ever being happy in her presence, and your intense anxiety about her health, if there were nothing else, would place this beyond all dispute in my mind. I incline to think it probable that your nerves will fail you occasionally for a while; but once you get them firmly guarded now, that trouble is over forever. I think, if I were you, in case my mind were not exactly right, I would avoid being idle. I would immediately engage in some business, or go to making preparations for it, which would be the same thing. If you went through the ceremony calmly, or even with sufficient composure not to excite alarm in any present, you are safe beyond question, and in two or three months, to say the most, will be the happiest of men.

I would desire you to give my particular respects to Fanny; but perhaps you will not wish her to know you have received this, lest she should desire to see it. Make her write me an answer to my last letter to her; at any rate, I would set great value upon a note or letter from her. Write me whenever you have leisure.

P. S. I have been quite a man since you left.

FROM AN ADDRESS TO THE SPRINGFIELD WASHINGTONIAN TEMPERANCE SOCIETY

The temperance movement was making great headway in Illinois during the Forties. Lincoln was asked to make the Washington's birthday address before the local unit of the Washingtonian Temperance Society—an organization composed largely of drunkards who had reformed. A grand parade was held in the streets of Springfield before the address was delivered in the Second Presbyterian Church at noon.

February 22, 1842

ALTHOUGH the temperance cause has been in progress for near twenty years, it is apparent to all that it is just now being crowned with a degree of success hitherto unparalleled.

The list of its friends is daily swelled by the additions of fifties, of hundreds, and of thousands. The cause itself seems suddenly transformed from a cold abstract theory to a living, breathing, active, and powerful chieftain, going forth "conquering and to conquer." The citadels of his great adversary are daily being stormed and dismantled; his temple and his altars, where the rites of his idolatrous worship have long been performed, and where human sacrifices have long been wont to be made, are daily desecrated and deserted. The triumph of the conqueror's fame is sounding from hill to hill, from sea to sea, and from land to land, and calling millions to his standard at a blast.

For this new and splendid success we heartily rejoice. That that success is so much greater now than heretofore is doubtless owing to rational causes; and if we would have it continue, we shall do well to inquire what those causes are.

The warfare heretofore waged against the demon intemperance has somehow or other been erroneous. Either the champions engaged or the tactics they adopted have not been the most proper. These champions for the most part have been preachers, lawyers, and hired agents. Between these and the mass of mankind there is a want of approachability, if the term be admissible, partially, at least, fatal to their success. They are supposed to have no sympathy of feeling or interest with those very persons whom it is their object to convince and persuade.

And again, it is so common and so easy to ascribe motives to men of these classes other than those they profess to act upon. The preacher, it is said, advocates temperance because he is a fanatic, and desires a union of the church and state; the lawyer from his pride and vanity of hearing himself speak; and the hired agent for his salary. But when one who has long been known as a victim of intemperance bursts the fetters that have bound him, and appears before his neighbors "clothed and in his right mind," a redeemed specimen of long-lost humanity, and stands up, with tears of joy trembling in his eyes, to tell of the miseries once endured, now to be endured no more forever; of his once naked and starving children, now clad and fed comfortably; of a wife long weighed down with woe, weeping, and a broken heart, now restored to health, happiness and a renewed affection; and how easily it is all done, once it is resolved to be done; how simple his language!— there is a logic and an eloquence in it that few with human feelings can resist. They cannot say that he desires a union of church and state, for he is not a church member; they cannot say he is vain of hearing himself speak, for his whole demeanor shows he would gladly avoid speaking at all; they cannot say he speaks for pay, for he receives none, and asks for none. Nor can his sincerity in any way be doubted, or his sympathy for those he would persuade to imitate his example be denied.

In my judgment, it is to the battles of this new class of champions that our late success is greatly, perhaps chiefly, owing. But, had the old-school champions themselves been of the most wise selecting, was their system of tactics the most judicious? It seems to me it was not. Too much denunciation against dram-sellers and dram-drinkers was indulged in. This I think was both impolitic and unjust. It was impolitic, because it is not much in the nature of man to be driven to anything; still less to be driven about that which is exclusively his own business; and least of all where such driving is to be submitted to at the expense of pecuniary interest or burning appetite. When the dram-seller and drinker were incessantly told —not in accents of entreaty and persuasion, diffidently addressed by erring man to an erring brother, but in the thundering tones of anathema and denunciation with which the lordly judge often groups together all the crimes of the felon's life, and thrusts them in his face just ere he passes sentence

of death upon him—that they were the authors of all the vice
and misery and crime in the land; that they were the manu-
facturers and material of all the thieves and robbers and murderers that infest the earth; that their houses were the work-
shops of the devil; and that their persons should be shunned
by all the good and virtuous, as moral pestilences—I say, when
they were told all this, and in this way, it is not wonderful that
they were slow, very slow, to acknowledge the truth of such
denunciations, and to join the ranks of their denouncers in a
hue and cry against themselves.

To have expected them to do otherwise than they did—to
have expected them not to meet denunciation with denunciation, crimination with crimination, and anathema with anathema—was to expect a reversal of human nature, which is
God's decree and can never be reversed.

When the conduct of men is designed to be influenced,
persuasion, kind, unassuming persuasion, should ever be
adopted. It is an old and a true maxim "that a drop of honey
catches more flies than a gallon of gall." So with men. If you
would win a man to your cause, first convince him that you
are his sincere friend. Therein is a drop of honey that catches
his heart, which, say what he will, is the great highroad to
his reason, and which, when once gained, you will find but
little trouble in convincing his judgment of the justice of your
cause, if indeed that cause really be a just one. On the contrary, assume to dictate to his judgment, or to command his
action, or to mark him as one to be shunned and despised,
and he will retreat within himself, close all the avenues to his
head and his heart; and though your cause be naked truth
itself, transformed to the heaviest lance, harder than steel,
and sharper than steel can be made, and though you throw it
with more than herculean force and precision, you shall be
no more able to pierce him than to penetrate the hard shell
of a tortoise with a rye straw. Such is man, and so must he be

understood by those who would lead him, even to his own best interests.

*   *   *

Another error, as it seems to me, into which the old reformers fell, was the position that all habitual drunkards were utterly incorrigible, and therefore must be turned adrift and damned without remedy in order that the grace of temperance might abound, to the temperate then, and to all mankind some hundreds of years thereafter. There is in this something so repugnant to humanity, so uncharitable, so cold-blooded and feelingless, that it never did nor ever can enlist the enthusiasm of a popular cause. We could not love the man who taught it—we could not hear him with patience. The heart could not throw open its portals to it, the generous man could not adopt it—it could not mix with his blood. It looked so fiendishly selfish, so like throwing fathers and brothers overboard to lighten the boat for our security, that the noble-minded shrank from the manifest meanness of the thing. And besides this, the benefits of a reformation to be effected by such a system were too remote in point of time to warmly engage many in its behalf. Few can be induced to labor exclusively for posterity; and none will do it enthusiastically. Posterity has done nothing for us; and theorize on it as we may, practically we shall do very little for it, unless we are made to think we are at the same time doing something for ourselves.

What an ignorance of human nature does it exhibit, to ask or expect a whole community to rise up and labor for the temporal happiness of others, after themselves shall be consigned to the dust, a majority of which community take no pains whatever to secure their own eternal welfare at no more distant day? Great distance in either time or space has wonderful power to lull and render quiescent the human mind. Pleasures to be enjoyed, or pains to be endured, after we shall be dead and gone are but little regarded even in our own cases, and much less in the cases of others. Still, in addition to this there is something so ludicrous in promises of good or threats of evil a great way off as to render the whole subject with which they are connected easily turned into ridicule. "Better lay down that spade you are stealing, Paddy; if you don't you'll pay for it at the day of judgment." "Be the powers, if ye'll credit me so long I'll take another jist."

*   *   *

In my judgment such of us as have never fallen victims have been spared more by the absence of appetite than from any mental or moral superiority over those who have. Indeed, I believe if we take habitual drunkards as a class, their heads and their hearts will bear an advantageous comparison with those of any other class. There seems ever to have been a proneness in the brilliant and warm-blooded to fall into this vice—the demon of intemperance ever seems to have delighted in sucking the blood of genius and of generosity. What one of us but can call to mind some relative, more promising in youth than all his fellows, who has fallen a sacrifice to his rapacity? He ever seems to have gone forth like the Egyptian angel of death, commissioned to slay, if not the first, the fairest born of every family. Shall he now be arrested in his desolating career? In that arrest all can give aid that will; and who shall be excused that can and will not? Far around as human breath has ever blown he keeps our fathers, our brothers, our sons, and our friends prostrate in the chains of moral death. To all the living everywhere we cry, "Come sound the moral trump, that these may rise and stand up an exceeding great army." "Come from the four winds, O breath! and breathe upon these slain that they may live." If the relative grandeur of revolutions shall be estimated by the great amount of human misery they alleviate, and the small amount they inflict, then indeed will this be the grandest the world shall ever have seen.

Of our political revolution of '76 we are all justly proud. It has given us a degree of political freedom far exceeding that of any other nation of the earth. In it the world has found a solution of the long-mooted problem as to the capability of man to govern himself. In it was the germ which has vegetated, and still is to grow and expand into the universal liberty of mankind. But, with all these glorious results, past, present, and to come, it had its evils too. It breathed forth famine, swam in blood, and rode in fire; and long, long after, the orphan's cry and the widow's wail continued to break the sad silence that ensued. These were the price, the inevitable price, paid for the blessings it bought.

Turn now to the temperance revolution. In it we shall find a stronger bondage broken, a viler slavery manumitted, a greater tyrant deposed; in it, more of want supplied, more disease healed, more sorrow assuaged. By it no orphans starving, no widows weeping. By it, none wounded in feeling, none injured in interest; even the dram-maker and dram-seller will have glided into other occupations so gradually as never to have felt the change, and will stand ready to join all others in the universal song of gladness. And what a noble ally this to the cause of political freedom; with such an aid its march cannot fail to be on and on, till every son of earth shall drink in rich fruition the sorrow-quenching draughts of perfect liberty. Happy day when—all appetites controlled, all poisons subdued, all matter subjected—mind, all conquering mind, shall live and move, the monarch of the world. Glorious consummation! Hail, fall of fury! Reign of reason, all hail!

And when the victory shall be complete—when there shall be neither a slave nor a drunkard on the earth—how proud the title of that land which may truly claim to be the birthplace and the cradle of both those revolutions that shall have ended in that victory. How nobly distinguished that people who shall have planted and nurtured to maturity both the political and moral freedom of their species. . . .

TWO LETTERS TO JOSHUA F. SPEED

The next two letters must be read together in order to understand them. The first one was written to be shown to Speed's new wife; the second conveys Lincoln's more intimate reactions about the marriage. "If you make a bad bargain, hug it all the tighter," Lincoln quotes as his father's maxim. Before the year was out, he was to be able to apply the maxim to his own marriage.

Springfield, February 25, 1842

DEAR SPEED: Yours of the 16th instant, announcing that Miss Fanny and you are "no more twain, but one flesh," reached me this morning. I have no way of telling you how much happiness I wish you both, though I believe you both can conceive it. I feel somewhat jealous of both of you now: you will be so exclusively concerned for one another, that I shall be forgotten entirely. My acquaintance with Miss Fanny (I call her this, lest you should think I am speaking of your mother) was too short for me to reasonably hope to long be remembered by her; and still I am sure I shall not forget her soon. Try if you cannot remind her of that debt she owes me —and be sure you do not interfere to prevent her paying it.

I regret to learn that you have resolved to not return to Illinois. I shall be very lonesome without you. How miserably things seem to be arranged in this world! If we have no friends, we have no pleasure; and if we have them, we are sure to lose them, and be doubly pained by the loss. I did hope she and you would make your home here; but I own I have no right to insist. You owe obligations to her ten thousand times more sacred than you can owe to others, and in that light let them be respected and observed. It is natural that she should desire to remain with her relatives and friends. As to friends, however, she could not need them anywhere: she would have them in abundance here.

Give my kind remembrance to Mr. Williamson and his family, particularly Miss Elizabeth; also to your mother, brother, and sisters. Ask little Eliza Davis if she will ride to town with me if I come there again. And finally, give Fanny a double reciprocation of all the love she sent me.

(ENCLOSURE)

Springfield, February 25, 1842

DEAR SPEED: I received yours of the 12th written the day you went down to William's place, some days since, but delayed answering it till I should receive the promised one of the 16th, which came last night. I opened the letter with intense anxiety and trepidation; so much so, that, although it turned out better than I expected, I have hardly yet, at a distance of ten hours, become calm.

I tell you, Speed, our forebodings (for which you and I are peculiar) are all the worst sort of nonsense. I fancied, from the time I received your letter of Saturday, that the one of Wednesday was never to come, and yet it *did* come, and what is more, it is perfectly clear, both from its tone and handwriting, that you were much happier, or, if you think the term preferable, less miserable, when you wrote it than when you wrote the last one before. You had so obviously improved at the very time I so much fancied you would have grown worse. You say that something indescribably horrible and alarming still haunts you. You will not say that three months from now, I will venture. When your nerves once get steady now, the whole trouble will be over forever. Nor should you become impatient at their being even very slow in becoming steady. Again you say, you much fear that that Elysium of which you

have dreamed so much is never to be realized. Well, if it shall
not, I dare swear it will not be the fault of her who is now
your wife. I now have no doubt that it is the peculiar misfortune of both you and me to dream dreams of Elysium far exceeding all that anything earthly can realize. Far short of your
dreams as you may be, no woman could do more to realize
them than that same black-eyed Fanny. If you could but contemplate her through my imagination, it would appear ridiculous to you that any one should for a moment think of being
unhappy with her. My old father used to have a saying that
"If you make a bad bargain, hug it all the tighter"; and it occurs to me that if the bargain you have just closed can possibly be called a bad one, it is certainly the most pleasant one
for applying that maxim to which my fancy can by any effort
picture.

I write another letter, inclosing this, which you can show
her, if she desires it. I do this because she would think
strangely, perhaps, should you tell her that you received no
letters from me, or, telling her you do, refuse to let her see
them. I close this, entertaining the confident hope that every
successive letter I shall have from you (which I here pray may
not be few, nor far between) may show you possessing a more
steady hand and cheerful heart than the last preceding it.

LETTER TO JOSHUA F. SPEED

*In this letter Lincoln refers to the "fatal first of January" when he
broke with Mary Todd and speaks of his misery at having made her
unhappy. He also mentions Sarah Rickard, with whom he may or
may not have been in love. It is interesting to note that what he
says about her might well imply that she had been Speed's sweetheart and not Lincoln's.*

Springfield, March 27, 1842

DEAR SPEED: Yours of the 10th instant was received three or four days since. You know I am sincere when I tell you the pleasure its contents gave me was, and is, inexpressible. As to your farm matter, I have no sympathy with you. I have no farm, nor ever expect to have, and consequently have not studied the subject enough to be much interested in it. I can only say that I am glad you are satisfied and pleased with it. But on that other subject, to me of the most intense interest whether in joy or in sorrow, I never had the power to withhold my sympathy from you. It cannot be told how it now thrills me with joy to hear you say you are "far happier than you ever expected to be." That much I know is enough. I know you too well to suppose your expectations were not, at least, sometimes extravagant, and if the reality exceeds them all, I say, Enough, dear Lord. I am not going beyond the truth when I tell you that the short space it took me to read your last letter gave me more pleasure than the total sum of all I have enjoyed since the fatal 1st of January, 1841. Since then it seems to me I should have been entirely happy, but for the never-absent idea that there is one still unhappy whom I have contributed to make so. That still kills my soul. I cannot but reproach myself for even wishing to be happy while she is otherwise. She accompanied a large party on the railroad cars to Jacksonville last Monday, and on her return spoke, so that I heard of it, of having enjoyed the trip exceedingly. God be praised for that.

You know with what sleepless vigilance I have watched you ever since the commencement of your affair; and although I am almost confident it is useless, I cannot forbear once more to say that I think it is even yet possible for your spirits to flag down and leave you miserable. If they should, don't fail to remember that they cannot long remain so. One thing I can tell you which I know you will be glad to hear, and that is that I have seen Sarah and scrutinized her feelings as well as I could, and am fully convinced she is far happier now than she has been for the last fifteen months past.

You will see by the last *Sangamon Journal* that I made a temperance speech on the 22d of February, which I claim that Fanny and you shall read as an act of charity to me; for I cannot learn that anybody else has read it, or is likely to. Fortunately it is not very long, and I shall deem it a sufficient compliance with my request if one of you listens while the other reads it.

*   *   *

The sweet violet you inclosed came safely to hand, but it was so dry, and mashed so flat, that it crumbled to dust at the first attempt to handle it. The juice that mashed out of it stained a place in the letter, which I mean to preserve and cherish for the sake of her who procured it to be sent. My renewed good wishes to her in particular, and generally to all such of your relations who know me.

LETTER TO JOSHUA F. SPEED

Lincoln confides to Speed that he regrets that he has lost his confidence in keeping his own resolutions, referring doubtless to the fact that Speed had told him that he should make up his mind about his engagement with Mary Todd and either stick to it or break it off finally. It was probably about this time that he began seeing her again. He mentions his own superstitiousness. The belief in foreordination that was to dominate his actions had already taken root in his mind.

Springfield, Illinois, July 4, 1842

DEAR SPEED: Yours of the 16th June was received only a day or two since. It was not mailed at Louisville till the 25th. You speak of the great time that has elapsed since I wrote you. Let me explain that. Your letter reached here a day or two after I had started on the circuit. I was gone five or six weeks, so that I got the letters only a few weeks before Butler started to your country. I thought it scarcely worth while to write you the news which he could and would tell you more in detail. On his return he told me you would write me soon, and so I waited for your letter. As to my having been displeased with your advice, surely you know better than that. I know you do, and therefore will not labor to convince you. True, that subject is painful to me; but it is not your silence, or the silence of all the world, that can make me forget it. I acknowledge the correctness of your advice too; but before I resolve to do the one thing or the other, I must gain my confidence in my own ability to keep my resolves when they are made. In that ability you know I once prided myself as the only or chief gem of my character; that gem I lost—how and where you know too well. I have not yet regained it; and until I do, I cannot trust myself in any matter of much importance. I believe now that had you understood my case at the time as well as I understood yours afterward, by the aid you would have given me I should have sailed through clear, but that does not now afford me sufficient confidence to begin that or the like of that again.

You make a kind acknowledgment of your obligations to me for your present happiness. I am pleased with that acknowledgment. But a thousand times more am I pleased to know that you enjoy a degree of happiness worthy of an acknowledgment. The truth is, I am not sure that there was any merit with me in the part I took in your difficulty; I was drawn to it by a fate. If I would I could not have done less than I did. I was always superstitious; I believe God made me one of the instruments of bringing your Fanny and you together, which union I have no doubt he had foreordained. Whatever he designs he will do for me yet. "Stand still, and see the salvation of the Lord" is my text just now. If, as you say, you have told Fanny all, I should have no objection to her seeing this letter, but for its reference to our friend here: let her seeing it depend upon whether she has ever known anything of my affairs; and if she has not, do not let her.

I do not think I can come to Kentucky this season. I am so poor and make so little headway in the world, that I drop back in a month of idleness as much as I gain in a year's sowing. I should like to visit you again. I should like to see that "sis" of yours that was absent when I was there, though I suppose she would run away again if she were to hear I was coming.

My respects and esteem to all your friends there, and, by your permission, my love to your Fanny.

LETTER TO JAMES SHIELDS

This letter marks the beginning of the Lincoln-Shields feud. Shields was the Democratic State Auditor of Public Accounts. He was Irish by birth, experienced as a soldier and he was an expert fencer. Lincoln, with the help of Mary Todd and one of her friends, Julia Jayne, had sent a series of letters supposedly signed by "Rebecca" of the "Lost Townships" to the Whig Sangamon Journal. These letters had made fun of Shields. Lincoln's animus was both political and personal, for he disliked the energetic little Irishman who was an ardent supporter of Stephen A. Douglas.

Tremont, September 17, 1842

JAS. SHIELDS, ESQ.: Your note of today was handed me by General Whitesides. In that note you say you have been informed, through the medium of the editor of *The Journal*, that I am the author of certain articles in that paper which you deem personally abusive of you; and without stopping to inquire whether I really am the author, or to point out what is offensive in them, you demand an unqualified retraction of all that is offensive, and then proceed to hint at consequences.

Now, sir, there is in this so much assumption of facts and so much of menace as to consequences, that I cannot submit to answer that note any further than I have, and to add that the consequences to which I suppose you allude would be matter of as great regret to me as it possibly could to you.

MEMORANDUM OF INSTRUCTIONS TO E. H. MERRYMAN, LINCOLN'S SECOND IN THE LINCOLN-SHIELDS DUEL

Merryman was a young Springfield doctor who was an expert swordsman. He probably did his best to get Lincoln entangled in a situation for which he had no heart. The conditions are very likely Merryman's; the bloodthirsty manner in which the duel was to be fought could hardly have been thought up by the peacefully minded Lincoln. The Missouri side of the Mississippi River opposite Alton was chosen because the Illinois law forbade the fighting of duels. Fortunately for all concerned, some friends interceded, and the duel was called off just as the contestants were ready to go into action.

September 19, 1842

In case Whitesides shall signify a wish to adjust this affair without further difficulty, let him know that if the present papers be withdrawn, and a note from Mr. Shields asking to know if I am the author of the articles of which he complains, and asking that I shall make him gentlemanly satisfaction if I am the author, and this without menace or dictation as to what that satisfaction shall be, a pledge is made that the following answer shall be given:

"I did write the 'Lost Townships' letter which appeared in the *Journal* of the 2d instant, but had no participation in any form in any other article alluding to you. I wrote that wholly for political effect—I had no intention of injuring your personal or private character or standing as a man or a gentleman; and I did not then think, and do not now think, that that article could produce or has produced that effect against you; and had I anticipated such an effect I would have foreborne to write it. And I will add that your conduct toward me, so far as I know, had always been gentlemanly; and that I had no personal pique against you, and no cause for any."

If this should be done, I leave it with you to arrange what shall and what shall not be published. If nothing like this is done, the preliminaries of the fight are to be—

FIRST. *Weapons:* Cavalry broadswords of the largest size, precisely equal in all respects, and such as now used by the cavalry company at Jacksonville.

SECOND. *Position:* A plank ten feet long, and from nine to twelve inches broad, to be firmly fixed on edge, on the ground, as the line between us, which neither is to pass his foot over upon forfeit of his life. Next a line drawn on the ground on either side of said plank and parallel with it, each at the distance of the whole length of the sword and three feet additional from the plank; and the passing of his own such line by either party during the fight shall be deemed a surrender of the contest.

THIRD. *Time:* On Thursday evening at five o'clock, if you can get it so; but in no case to be at a greater distance of time than Friday evening at five o'clock.

FOURTH. *Place:* Within three miles of Alton, on the opposite side of the river, the particular spot to be agreed on by you.

Any preliminary details coming within the above rules you are at liberty to make at your discretion; but you are in no case to swerve from these rules, or to pass beyond their limits.

LETTER TO JOSHUA F. SPEED

*The seconds who had been so eager to push their principals forward
in the Lincoln-Shields duel promptly fell to fighting among themselves. William Butler was Lincoln's friend; Merryman appointed
Lincoln as his second, and the situation then took on all the aspects
of an old-fashioned French farce. This duel also ended without
bloodshed. Much more important than the trivia of the duel, however, is Lincoln's query to Speed: "Are you now in feeling as well
as judgment glad that you are married as you are?" Lincoln was
impatient to know the answer, as he might well be, for just one
month after writing this letter he married Mary Todd.*

Springfield, October [4?], 1842

DEAR SPEED: You have heard of my duel with Shields, and
I have now to inform you that the dueling business still rages
in this city. Day before yesterday Shields challenged Butler,
who accepted, and proposed fighting next morning at sunrise
in Bob Allen's meadow, one hundred yards' distance, with
rifles. To this Whitesides, Shield's second, said "No," because
of the law. Thus ended duel No. 2. Yesterday Whitesides
chose to consider himself insulted by Dr. Merryman, so sent
him a kind of quasi-challenge, inviting him to meet him at the
Planter's House in St. Louis on the next Friday, to settle their
difficulty. Merryman made me his friend, and sent Whitesides
a note, inquiring to know if he meant his note as a challenge,
and if so, that he would, according to the law in such case
made and provided, prescribe the terms of the meeting. Whitesides returned for answer that if Merryman would meet him
at the Planter's House as desired, he would challenge him.
Merryman replied in a note that he denied Whiteside's right
to dictate time and place, but that he (Merryman) would
waive the question of time, and meet him at Louisiana, Mis-

souri. Upon my presenting this note to Whitesides and stating verbally its contents, he declined receiving it, saying he had business in St. Louis, and it was as near as Louisiana. Merryman then directed me to notify Whitesides that he should publish the correspondence between them, with such comments as he thought fit. This I did. Thus it stood at bedtime last night. This morning Whitesides, by his friend Shields, is praying for a new trial, on the ground that he was mistaken in Merryman's proposition to meet him at Louisiana, Missouri, thinking it was the State of Louisiana. This Merryman hoots at, and is preparing his publication; while the town is in a ferment, and a street fight somewhat anticipated.

But I began this letter not for what I have been writing, but to say something on that subject which you know to be of such infinite solicitude to me. The immense sufferings you endured from the first days of September till the middle of February you never tried to conceal from me, and I well understood. You have now been the husband of a lovely woman nearly eight months. That you are happier now than the day you married her I well know, for without you could not be living. But I have your word for it, too, and the returning elasticity of spirits which is manifested in your letters. But I want to ask a close question, "Are you now in feeling as well as judgment glad that you are married as you are?" From anybody but me this would be an impudent question, not to be tolerated; but I know you will pardon it in me. Please answer it quickly, as I am impatient to know. I have sent my love to your Fanny so often, I fear she is getting tired of it. However, I venture to tender it again.

LETTER TO SAMUEL D. MARSHALL

This letter is of no importance except for its last sentence which is filled with poignant significance, for Lincoln wrote it when he had been married just one week.

Springfield, November 11, 1842

DEAR SAM: Yours of the 10th Oct. enclosing five dollars was taken from the office in my absence by Judge Logan who neglected to hand it to me till about a week ago, and just an hour before I took a wife. . . .

I have looked into the Dorman & Lane case, till I believe I understand the facts of it; and I also believe we can reverse it. In the last I may be mistaken, but I think the case at least worth the experiment, and if Dorman will risk the cost, I will do my best for the "biggest kind of a fee" as you say, if we succeed, and nothing if we fail. I have not had a chance to consult Logan since I read your letters, but if the case comes up, I can have the use of him if I need him.

I would advise you to procure the Record and send it up immediately. Attend to the making out of the Record yourself, or most likely, the clerk will not get it all together right.

Nothing new here, except my marrying, which to me, is matter of profound wonder.

LETTER TO RICHARD S. THOMAS

Shortly after his marriage, Lincoln began a long campaign to become a United States Congressman. He had finished his last term in the State Legislature early in 1841—he was compelled to wait until August, 1846, to be elected to Congress. That he wanted very much to go is clearly indicated by this letter.

Springfield, Illinois, February 14, 1843

FRIEND RICHARD: . . . Now if you should hear any one say that Lincoln don't want to go to Congress, I wish you as a personal friend of mine, would tell him you have reason to believe he is mistaken. The truth is, I would like to go very much. Still, circumstances may happen which may prevent my being a candidate.

If there are any who be my friends in such an enterprise, what I now want is that they shall not throw me away just yet.

LETTER TO JOSHUA F. SPEED

Lincoln was disappointed in his ambition to receive the Whig nomination for Congress; the Sangamon County Whigs chose Edward D. Baker as their candidate. Baker was a good friend of Lincoln's. He was a brilliant orator, and he later distinguished himself in politics and on the field of battle in the Mexican War and in the Civil War. He was killed at Ball's Bluff on October 21, 1861. Lincoln named his second son after him. The allusion to a coming child at the end of this letter indicates that Lincoln had promised to name his first born son after Speed. Mrs. Lincoln evidently had something to say in the matter, for the child was named Robert Todd Lincoln after her father.

Springfield, March 24, 1843

DEAR SPEED: We had a meeting of the Whigs of the county here on last Monday to appoint delegates to a district convention; and Baker beat me, and got the delegation instructed to go for him. The meeting, in spite of my attempt to decline it, appointed me one of the delegates; so that in getting Baker the nomination I shall be fixed a good deal like a fellow who is made a groomsman to a man who has cut him out and is marrying his own dear "gal." About the prospects of your having a namesake at our town, can't say exactly yet.

LETTER TO MARTIN M. MORRIS

Morris was a friend of Lincoln's living near New Salem which by this time was in Menard County. Lincoln writes a political letter to him on the coming Congressional nomination. According to Morris, Lincoln was still strong in Menard County because of his former residence at New Salem. Lincoln, although appointed a delegate for Baker, is willing to see if he can still pull the nomination out of the fire. His marriage with Mary Todd with its aristocratic connections is telling against him among the plain country people; so is his reputation for agnosticism. James Short, to whom Lincoln refers, was a New Salem farmer, who had once refunded a debt for Lincoln in order to save his personal property from being seized. It is interesting to note that the Whig nomination for the district was given to neither Baker nor Lincoln, but to John J. Hardin, who was elected to Congress in August, 1843.

Springfield, Illinois, March 26, 1843

FRIEND MORRIS: Your letter of the 23d was received on yesterday morning, and for which (instead of an excuse, which you thought proper to ask) I tender you my sincere thanks. It is truly gratifying to me to learn that while the people of Sangamon have cast me off, my old friends of Menard, who have known me longest and best, stick to me. It would astonish, if not amuse, the older citizens to learn that I (a stranger, friendless, uneducated, penniless boy, working on a flatboat at ten dollars per month) have been put down here as the candidate of pride, wealth, and aristocratic family distinction. Yet so, chiefly, it was. There was, too, the strangest combination of church influence against me. Baker is a Campbellite; and therefore, as I suppose, with few exceptions got all that church. My wife has some relations in the Presbyterian

churches, and some with the Episcopal churches; and therefore, wherever it would tell, I was set down as either the one
or the other, while it was everywhere contended that no Christian ought to go for me, because I belonged to no church, was
suspected of being a deist, and had talked about fighting a
duel. With all these things, Baker, of course, had nothing to
do. Nor do I complain of them. As to his own church going
for him, I think that was right enough, and as to the influences
I have spoken of in the other, though they were very strong,
it would be grossly untrue and unjust to charge that they acted
upon them in a body, or were very near so. I only mean that
those influences levied a tax of a considerable percent upon
my strength throughout the religious controversy. But enough
of this.

You say that in choosing a candidate for Congress you have
an equal right with Sangamon, and in this you are undoubtedly correct. In agreeing to withdraw if the Whigs of Sangamon should go against me, I did not mean that they alone
were worth consulting, but that if she, with her heavy delegation, should be against me, it would be impossible for me to
succeed, and therefore I had as well decline. And in relation
to Menard having rights, permit me fully to recognize them,
and to express the opinion, that if she and Mason act circum-
spectly, they will in the convention be able so far to enforce
their rights as to decide absolutely which one of the candidates
shall be successful. Let me show the reason of this. Hardin, or
some other Morgan candidate, will get Putnam, Marshall,
Woodford, Tazewell, and Logan—making sixteen. Then you
and Mason, having three, can give the victory to either side.

You say you shall instruct your delegates for me, unless I
object. I certainly shall not object. That would be too pleasant
a compliment for me to tread in the dust. And besides, if anything should happen (which, however, is not probable) by
which Baker should be thrown out of the fight, I would be
at liberty to accept the nomination if I could get it. I do, however, feel myself bound not to hinder him in any way from

getting the nomination. I should despise myself were I to attempt it. I think, then, it would be proper for your meeting to appoint three delegates, and to instruct them to go for some one as a first choice, some one else as a second, and perhaps some one as a third; and if in those instructions I were named as the first choice, it would gratify me very much. If you wish to hold the balance of power, it is important for you to attend to and secure the vote of Mason also. You should be sure to have men appointed delegates that you know you can safely confide in. If yourself and James Short were appointed from your county, all would be safe; but whether Jim's woman affair a year ago might not be in the way of his appointment is a question. I don't know whether you know it, but I know him to be as honorable a man as there is in the world. You have my permission, and even request, to show this letter to Short; but to no one else, unless it be a very particular friend, who you know will not speak of it.

LETTER TO JOSHUA F. SPEED

The "coming event" to which Lincoln jestingly refers was the approaching birth of his first child, Robert Todd Lincoln, which was to take place on August 1. Dr. Wallace had married Mary Todd's sister Frances. Ann Todd was Mary's aunt. The Lincolns left their four-dollar-a-week room at the Globe Tavern shortly after their son Robert was born. They moved to a small house on South Fourth Street, where they stayed until May, 1844, when they moved into the house at Eighth and Jackson Streets that was to be their last home in Springfield.

Springfield, May 18, 1843

DEAR SPEED: Yours of the 9th instant is duly received, which I do not meet as a "bore," but as a most welcome visitor. I will answer the business part of it first. . . .

In relation to our Congress matter here, you were right in supposing I would support the nominee. Neither Baker nor I, however, is the man, but Hardin, so far as I can judge from present appearances. We shall have no split or trouble about the matter; all will be harmony. In relation to the "coming events" about which Butler wrote you, I had not heard one word before I got your letter; but I have so much confidence in the judgment of a Butler on such a subject that I incline to think there may be some reality in it. What day does Butler appoint?

By the way, how do "events" of the same sort come on in your family? Are you possessing houses and lands, and oxen and asses, and men-servants and maid-servants, and begetting sons and daughters? We are not keeping house, but boarding at the Globe Tavern, which is very well kept now by a widow lady of the name of Beck. Our room (the same that Dr. Wallace occupied there) and boarding only costs us four dollars a week. Ann Todd was married something more than a year since to a fellow by the name of Campbell, and who, Mary says, is pretty much of a "dunce," though he has a little money and property. They live in Booneville, Missouri, and have not been heard from lately enough for me to say anything about her health. I reckon it will scarcely be in our power to visit Kentucky this year. Besides poverty and the necessity of attending to business, those "coming events," I suspect, would be somewhat in the way. I most heartily wish you and your Fanny would not fail to come. Just let us know the time, and we will have a room provided for you at our house, and all be merry together for a while. Be sure to give my respects to your mother and family; assure her that if ever I come near her, I will not fail to call and see her. Mary joins in sending love to your Fanny and you.

FROM A LETTER TO ROWLAND, SMITH & CO.

This closing to a long letter is interesting for the quaint phrasing that Lincoln uses in a business recommendation.

Springfield, April 24, 1844

As TO the real estate, we can not attend to it as agents, and we therefore recommend that you give the charge of it, to Mr. Isaac S. Button, a trustworthy man, and one whom the Lord made on purpose for such business.

Yours &c

LOGAN & LINCOLN

LETTER TO WILLIAMSON DURLEY

Lincoln makes clear his stand on abolitionism and the question of the annexation of Texas. The position he takes here—to let slavery exist where it was already established, but to prevent its spread into new territory—was to be the attitude he was to hold all his life, until the exigencies of war demanded that the slaves be freed as a military measure.

Springfield, October 3, 1845

WHEN I saw you at home, it was agreed that I should write to you and your brother Madison. Until I then saw you I was not aware of your being what is generally called an Abolitionist, or, as you call yourself, a Liberty man, though I well knew there were many such in your country.

I was glad to hear that you intended to attempt to bring about, at the next election in Putnam, a union of the Whigs proper and such of the Liberty men as are Whigs in principle on all questions save only that of slavery. So far as I can perceive, by such union neither party need yield anything on the point in difference between them. If the Whig Abolitionists of New York had voted with us last fall, Mr. Clay would now be President, Whig principles in the ascendant, and Texas not annexed; whereas, by the division, all that either had at stake in the contest was lost. And, indeed, it was extremely probable, beforehand, that such would be the result. As I always understood, the Liberty men deprecated the annexation of Texas extremely; and this being so, why they should refuse to cast their votes [so] as to prevent it, even to me seemed wonderful. What was their process of reasoning, I can only judge from what a single one of them told me. It was this: "We are not to do evil that good may come." This general proposition is doubtless correct; but did it apply? If by your votes you could have prevented the *extension*, etc., of slavery would it not have been *good*, and not *evil*, so to have used your votes, even though it involved the casting of them for a slave-holder? By the *fruit* the tree is to be known. An *evil* tree cannot bring forth *good* fruit. If the fruit of electing Mr. Clay would have been to prevent the extension of slavery, could the act of electing have been evil?

But I will not argue further. I perhaps ought to say that individually I never was much interested in the Texas question. I never could see much good to come of annexation, inasmuch as they were already a free republican people on our own model. On the other hand, I never could very clearly see how the annexation would augment the evil of slavery. It always seemed to me that slaves would be taken there in about equal numbers, with or without annexation. And if more were taken because of annexation, still there would be just so many the fewer left where they were taken from. It is possibly true, to some extent, that, with annexation, some slaves may be sent to Texas and continued in slavery that otherwise might have been liberated. To whatever extent this may be true, I think annexation an evil. I hold it to be a paramount duty of us in the free States, due to the Union of the States, and perhaps to liberty itself (paradox though it may seem), to let the slavery of the other States alone; while, on the other hand, I hold it to be equally clear that we should never knowingly lend ourselves, directly or indirectly, to prevent that slavery from dying a natural death—to find new places for it to live in, when it can no longer exist in the old. Of course I am not now considering what would be our duty in cases of insurrection among the slaves. To recur to the Texas question, I understand the Liberty men to have viewed annexation as a much greater evil than ever I did; and I would like to convince you, if I could, that they could have prevented it, if they had chosen. . . .

LETTER TO ANDREW JOHNSTON

Andrew Johnston had been in the Illinois House of Representatives with Lincoln in 1839. He, like Lincoln, was an experimenter in verse, and the two men sent each other their poems for criticism. Poe's "The Raven" had been published for the first time in January, 1845, yet its fame had already penetrated into the backwoods country of Illinois. Johnston had written a parody on it. Lincoln's own poem, printed here, is in the melancholy romantic vein popular in the early part of the nineteenth century.

Tremont, April 18, 1846

FRIEND JOHNSTON: Your letter, written some six weeks since, was received in due course, and also the paper with the parody. It is true, as suggested it might be, that I have never seen Poe's "Raven"; and I very well know that a parody is almost entirely dependent for its interest upon the reader's acquaintance with the original. Still there is enough in the polecat, self-considered, to afford one several hearty laughs. I think four or five of the last stanzas are decidedly funny, particularly where Jeremiah "scrubbed and washed, and prayed and fasted."

I have not your letter now before me; but, from memory, I think you ask me who is the author of the piece* I sent you, and that you do so ask as to indicate a slight suspicion that I myself am the author. Beyond all question, I am not the author. I would give all I am worth, and go in debt, to be able to write so fine a piece as I think that is. Neither do I know who is the author. I met it in a straggling form in a newspaper last summer, and I remember to have seen it once before, about fifteen years ago, and this is all I know about it. The piece of poetry of my own which I alluded to, I was led to write under the following circumstances. In the fall of 1844, thinking I might aid some to carry the State of Indiana for Mr. Clay, I went into the neighborhood in that State in which I was raised, where my mother and only sister were buried, and from which I had been absent about fifteen years. That part of the country is, within itself, as unpoetical as any spot of the earth; but still, seeing it and its objects and inhabitants aroused feelings in me which were certainly poetry; though whether my expression of those feelings is poetry is quite an other question. When I got to writing, the change of subjects divided the thing into four little divisions or cantos, the first only of which I send you now and may send the others hereafter.

> My childhood's home I see again,
>   And sadden with the view;
> And still, as memory crowds my brain,
>   There's pleasure in it too.

> O Memory! thou midway world
>   'Twixt earth and paradise,

* This evidently refers to Lincoln's favorite poem, "Mortality" by William Knox, beginning "Oh why should the spirit of mortal be proud?"

Where things decayed and loved ones lost
   In dreamy shadows rise,

And, freed from all that's earthly vile,
   Seem hallowed, pure, and bright,
Like scenes in some enchanted isle
   All bathed in liquid light.

As dusky mountains please the eye
   When twilight chases day,
As bugle-notes that, passing by,
   In distance die away;

As leaving some grand waterfall,
   We, lingering, list its roar—
So memory will hallow all
   We've known, but know no more.

Near twenty years have passed away
   Since here I bid farewell
To woods and fields, and scenes of play,
   And playmates loved so well.

Where many were, but few remain
   Of old familiar things;
But seeing them, to mind again
   The lost and absent brings.

The friends I left that parting day,
   How changed, as time has sped!
Young childhood grown, strong manhood gray,
   And half of all are dead.

I hear the loved survivors tell
   How nought from death could save,
Till every sound appears a knell,
   And every spot a grave.

> I range the fields with pensive tread,
>   And pace the hollow rooms,
> And feel (companion of the dead)
>   I'm living in the tombs.

LETTER TO ANDREW JOHNSTON

Lincoln sends Johnston another poem based on the insanity of a school friend. There is reason to suspect that Lincoln's interest in the insanity of his friend had a subjective basis—that he had feared that he himself might go mad. The terrible fits of melancholy which had come over him in the past had doubtless led him to speculate on that unhappy possibility.

Springfield, September 6, 1846

FRIEND JOHNSTON: You remember when I wrote you from Tremont last spring, sending you a little canto of what I called poetry, I promised to bore you with another some time. I now fulfil the promise. The subject of the present one is an insane man; his name is Matthew Gentry. He is three years older than I, and when we were boys we went to school together. He was rather a bright lad, and the son of the rich man of a very poor neighborhood. At the age of nineteen he unaccountably became furiously mad, from which condition he gradually settled down into harmless insanity. When, as I told you in my other letter, I visited my old home in the fall of 1844, I found him still lingering in this wretched condition. In my poetizing mood, I could not forget the impression his case made upon me. Here is the result:

> But here's an object more of dread
>   Than aught the grave contains—
> A human form with reason fled,
>   While wretched life remains.

When terror spread, and neighbors ran
  Your dangerous strength to bind,
And soon, a howling, crazy man,
  Your limbs were fast confined:

How then you strove and shrieked aloud,
  Your bones and sinews bared;
And fiendish on the gazing crowd
  With burning eyeballs glared;

And begged and swore, and wept and prayed,
  With maniac laughter joined;
How fearful were these signs displayed
  By pangs that killed the mind!

And when at length the drear and long
  Time soothed thy fiercer woes,
How plaintively thy mournful song
  Upon the still night rose!

I've heard it oft as if I dreamed
  Far distant, sweet and lone,
The funeral dirge it ever seemed
  Of reason dead and gone.

To drink its strains I've stole away,
  All stealthily and still,
Ere yet the rising god of day
  Had streaked the eastern hill.

Air held her breath; trees with the spell
  Seemed sorrowing angels round,
Whose swelling tears in dewdrops fell
  Upon the listening ground.

But this is past, and naught remains
  That raised thee o'er the brute;
Thy piercing shrieks and soothing strain
  Are like, forever mute.

Now fare thee well! More thou the cause
　　Than subject now of woe.
All mental pangs by time's kind laws
　　Hast lost the power to know.

O death! thou awe-inspiring prince
　　That keepst the world in fear,
Why dost thou tear more blest ones hence,
　　And leave him lingering here?

If I should ever send another, the subject will be a "Bear-Hunt."

THE BEAR HUNT [1846]

Fortunately the poem to which Lincoln alluded in the last line of his previous letter to Johnston has been preserved. It is probably based on an actual experience which may have taken place during his boyhood in Indiana.

A wild bear chase, didst never see?
　　Then hast thou lived in vain.
Thy richest lump of glorious glee,
　　Lies desert in thy brain.

When first my father settled here,
　　'Twas then the frontier line;
The panther's scream, filled night with fear
　　And bears preyed on the swine.

But wo for Bruin's short lived fun,
　　When rose the squealing cry;
Now man and horse, with dog and gun,
　　For vengeance, at him fly.

A sound of danger strikes his ear;
　　He gives the breeze a snuff;

Away he bounds, with little fear,
    And seeks the tangled rough.

On press his foes, and reach the ground,
    Where's left his half munched meal;
The dogs, in circles, scent around,
    And find his fresh made trail.

With instant cry, away they dash,
    And men as fast pursue;
O'er logs they leap, through water splash,
    And shout the brisk halloo.

Now to elude the eager pack,
    Bear shuns the open ground;
Through matted vines, he shapes his track
    And runs it, round and round.

The tall fleet cur, with deep-mouthed voice,
    Now speeds him, as the wind;
While half-grown pup, and short-legged fice,
    Are yelping far behind.

And fresh recruits are dropping in
    To join the merry corps:
With yelp and yell—a mingled din—
    The woods are in a roar.

And round, and round the chase now goes,
    The world's alive with fun;
Nick Carter's horse, his rider throws,
    And Mose' Hill drops his gun.

Now sorely pressed, bear glances back,
    And lolls his tired tongue;
When is, to force him from his track,
    An ambush on him sprung.

Across the glade he sweeps for flight,
    And fully is in view.
The dogs, new-fired, by the sight,
    Their cry, and speed, renew.

The foremost ones, now reach his rear,
    He turns, they dash away;
And circling now, the wrathful bear,
    They have him full at bay.

At top of speed, the horsemen come,
    All screaming in a row.
"Whoop! Take him Tiger—Seize him Drum"—
    Bang—bang—the rifles go.

And furious now, the dogs he tears,
    And crushes in his ire.
Wheels right and left, and upward rears,
    With eyes of burning fire.

But leaden death is at his heart,
    Vain all the strength he plies,
And, spouting blood from every part,
    He reels, and sinks and dies.

And now a dinsome clamor rose,
    'Bout who should have his skin.
Who first draws blood, each hunter knows,
    This prize must always win.

But who did this, and how to trace
    What's true from what's a lie,
Like lawyers, in a murder case
    They stoutly argufy.

Aforesaid fice, of blustering mood,
    Behind, and quite forgot,
Just now emerging from the wood,
    Arrives upon the spot.

With grinning teeth, and up-turned hair—
  Brim full of spunk and wrath,
He growls, and seizes on dead bear,
  And shakes for life and death.

And swells as if his skin would tear,
  And growls, and shakes again;
And swears, as plain as dog can swear,
  That he has won the skin.

Conceited whelp! we laugh at thee—
  Now mind, that not a few
Of pompous, two-legged dogs there be,
  Conceited quite as you.

LETTER TO JOSHUA F. SPEED

The friendship with Speed is waning, and Lincoln regrets seeing it die. The "true philosophic cause" is probably Mrs. Lincoln's jealousy of Speed combined with the geographical distance that separated the two men. Lincoln had been elected to the United States Congress on August 3 after a bitter campaign against Peter Cartwright, Methodist circuit-riding minister and Illinois pioneer. He had had to wait to see both Hardin and then Baker go to Washington before his own turn finally came. The second son, born on March 10th, is Edward Baker Lincoln, named after Lincoln's friend. This boy died in infancy on February 1, 1850.

Springfield, October 22, 1846

DEAR SPEED: You, no doubt, assign the suspension of our correspondence to the true philosophic cause; though it must be confessed by both of us that this is rather a cold reason for allowing a friendship such as ours to die out by degrees. I propose now that, upon receipt of this, you shall be considered in my debt, and under obligations to pay soon, and that neither shall remain long in arrears hereafter. Are you agreed?

Being elected to Congress, though I am very grateful to our friends for having done it, has not pleased me as much as I expected.

We have another boy, born the 10th of March. He is very much such a child as Bob was at his age, rather of a longer order. Bob is "short and low," and I expect always will be. He talks very plainly—almost as plainly as anybody. He is quite smart enough. I sometimes fear that he is one of the little rare-ripe sort that are smarter at about five than ever after. He has a great deal of that sort of mischief that is the offspring of such animal spirits. Since I began this letter, a messenger came to tell me Bob was lost; but by the time I reached the house his mother had found him and had him whipped, and by now, very likely, he is run away again. Mary has read your letter, and wishes to be remembered to Mrs. Speed and you, in which I most sincerely join her.

LETTER TO ANDREW JOHNSTON

What would have been an important first edition in American literature is projected, but, most unfortunately, it was never carried through. Johnston and Lincoln had planned to publish their own poems. Perhaps some local printer, on second thought, declined to underwrite the venture.

Springfield, February 25, 1847

DEAR JOHNSTON: Yours of the 2d of December was duly delivered to me by Mr. Williams. To say the least, I am not at all displeased with your proposal to publish the poetry, or doggerel, or whatever else it may be called, which I sent you. I consent that it may be done, together with the third canto, which I now send you. Whether the prefatory remarks in my letter shall be published with the verses, I leave entirely to your discretion; but let names be suppressed by all means. I have not sufficient hope of the verses attracting any favorable notice to tempt me to risk being ridiculed for having written them.

FROM NOTES FOR A TARIFF DISCUSSION

This is the first of many speculations made by Lincoln regarding the nature of labor and the relationship of government to it. Labor seems to be the one economic factor in which Lincoln, who was no economist, was really interested. Perhaps the fact that he himself had known from first-hand experience what labor was like made him keenly sensitive to its value. These notes may have been written while Lincoln was en route to Washington to take up his first term as Congressman. He arrived at the capital on December 2, and was seated on December 6.

December 1, 1847[?]

IN THE early days of our race the Almighty said to the first of our race, "In the sweat of thy face shalt thou eat bread"; and since then, if we except the light and the air of heaven, no good thing has been or can be enjoyed by us without having first cost labor. And inasmuch as most good things are produced by labor, it follows that all such things of right belong to those whose labor has produced them. But it has so happened, in all ages of the world, that some have labored, and others have without labor enjoyed a large proportion of the fruits. This is wrong, and should not continue. To secure to each laborer the whole product of his labor, or as nearly as possible, is a worthy object of any good government.

But then a question arises, How can a government best effect this? In our own country, in its present condition, will the protective principle advance or retard this object? Upon this subject the habits of our whole species fall into three great classes—useful labor, useless labor, and idleness. Of these the first only is meritorious, and to it all the products of labor rightfully belong; but the two later, while they exist, are heavy pensioners upon the first, robbing it of a large portion of its just rights. The only remedy for this is to, so far as possible, drive useless labor and idleness out of existence. And, first, as to useless labor. Before making war upon this, we must learn to distinguish it from the useful. It appears to me that all labor done directly and indirectly in carrying articles to the place of consumption, which could have been produced in sufficient abundance, with as little labor, at the place of consumption as at the place they were carried from, is useless labor.

RESOLUTIONS IN THE UNITED STATES
HOUSE OF REPRESENTATIVES

When Lincoln took his seat in Congress, the Mexican War had dragged on for twenty months. The country was sick of it; Whigs and anti-slavery people generally were opposing it. Lincoln was a new and green member of the House; he surprised everybody by getting up and delivering these Resolutions questioning the administration's war policy. Lincoln's query as to the exact location of the spot on which American blood had first been shed, and as to whether that spot was on Mexican or United States territory, was to cause him much trouble. Illinois had been particularly energetic in supporting the war with Mexico; she had sent many troops and important men to lead them. On January 12, 1848 (see below) Lincoln again spoke against the war—and completely alienated his own constituents.

December 22, 1847

WHEREAS, the President of the United States, in his message of May 11, 1846, has declared that "the Mexican Government not only refused to receive him [the envoy of the United States], or to listen to his propositions, but, after a long-continued series of menaces, has at last invaded our territory and shed the blood of our fellow-citizens on our own soil."

And again, in his message of December 8, 1846, that "we had ample cause of war against Mexico long before the breaking out of hostilities; but even then we forebore to take redress into our own hands until Mexico herself became the aggressor, by invading our soil in hostile array, and shedding the blood of our citizens."

And yet again, in his message of December 7, 1847, that "the Mexican Government refused even to hear the terms of adjustment which he [our minister of peace] was authorized to propose, and finally, under wholly unjustifiable pretexts, involved the two countries in war, by invading the territory of the State of Texas, striking the first blow, and shedding the blood of our citizens on our own soil."

And whereas, This House is desirous to obtain a full knowledge of all the facts which go to establish whether the particular spot on which the blood of our citizens was so shed was or was not at that time our own soil; therefore,

Resolved, By the House of Representatives, that the President of the United States be respectfully requested to inform this House—

FIRST. Whether the spot on which the blood of our citizens was shed, as in his message declared, was or was not within the territory of Spain, at least after the treaty of 1819 until the Mexican revolution.

SECOND. Whether that spot is or is not within the territory which was wrested from Spain by the revolutionary Government of Mexico.

THIRD. Whether that spot is or is not within a settlement of people, which settlement has existed ever since long before the Texas revolution, and until its inhabitants fled before the approach of the United States Army.

FOURTH. Whether that settlement is or is not isolated from any and all other settlements by the Gulf and the Rio Grande on the south and west, and by wide uninhabited regions on the north and east.

FIFTH. Whether the people of that settlement, or a majority of them, or any of them, have ever submitted themselves to the government or laws of Texas or of the United States, by consent or by compulsion, either by accepting office, or voting at elections, or paying tax, or serving on juries, or having process served upon them, or in any other way.

SIXTH. Whether the people of that settlement did or did not flee from the approach of the United States Army, leaving unprotected their homes and their growing crops, *before* the blood was shed, as in the message stated; and whether the first blood, so shed, was or was not shed within the inclosure of one of the people who had thus fled from it.

SEVENTH. Whether our citizens, whose blood was shed, as in his message declared, were or were not, at that time, armed officers and soldiers, sent into that settlement by the military order of the President, through the Secretary of War.

EIGHTH. Whether the military force of the United States was or was not so sent into that settlement after General Taylor had more than once intimated to the War Department that, in his opinion, no such movement was necessary to the defense or protection of Texas.

LETTER TO WILLIAM H. HERNDON

In this letter, Lincoln speaks too soon. He discusses, rather coyly, his prospects for re-election. Four days later, his Mexican War speech completely blasted any chance of his being returned to Congress.

Washington, January 8, 1848

DEAR WILLIAM: Your letter of December 27 was received a day or two ago. I am much obliged to you for the trouble you have taken, and promise to take in my little business there. As to speech-making, by way of getting the hang of the House I made a little speech two or three days ago on a post-office question of no general interest. I find speaking here and elsewhere about the same thing. I was about as badly scared, and no worse, as I am when I speak in court. I expect to make one within a week or two, in which I hope to succeed well enough to wish you to see it.

It is very pleasant to learn from you that there are some who desire that I should be re-elected. I most heartily thank them for their kind partiality; and I can say, as Mr. Clay said of the annexation of Texas, that "personally I would not object" to a re-election, although I thought at the time, and still think, it would be quite as well for me to return to the law at the end of a single term. I made the declaration that I would not be a candidate again, more from a wish to deal fairly with others, to keep peace among our friends, and to keep the district from going to the enemy, than for any cause personal to myself; so that, if it should so happen that nobody else wishes to be elected, I could not refuse the people the right of sending me again. But to enter myself as a competitor of others, or to authorize any one so to enter me, is what my word and honor forbid.

I got some letters intimating a probability of so much difficulty amongst our friends as to lose us the district; but I remember such letters were written to Baker when my own case was under consideration, and I trust there is no more ground for such apprehension now than there was then.

FROM A SPEECH IN THE UNITED STATES
HOUSE OF REPRESENTATIVES ON
THE MEXICAN WAR

*The President, to whom Lincoln here refers, was James K. Polk.
Polk was a Democrat, Lincoln was a Whig; Lincoln speaks for his
party here, using arguments which many other Whigs had already
made, nevertheless, this speech ruined him politically in his own
state. The most remarkable statement contained here is Lincoln's
discussion of a people's right to revolution. This right, as here
defined by him, was to be quoted against him, much to his embarrassment, by proponents of secession in 1860.*

January 12, 1848

MR. CHAIRMAN: Some if not all the gentlemen on the other
side of the House who have addressed the committee within
the last two days have spoken rather complainingly, if I have
rightly understood them, of the vote given a week or ten days
ago declaring that the war with Mexico was unnecessarily and
unconstitutionally commenced by the President. I admit that
such a vote should not be given in mere party wantonness, and
that the one given is justly censurable, if it have no other or
better foundation. I am one of those who joined in that vote;
and I did so under my best impression of the truth of the case.
How I got this impression, and how it may possibly be rem-
edied, I will now try to show. When the war began, it was my
opinion that all those who because of knowing too little, or
because of knowing too much, could not conscientiously oppose the conduct of the President in the beginning of it should
nevertheless, as good citizens and patriots, remain silent on
that point, at least till the war should be ended. . . .

The President, in his first war message of May, 1846, declares that the soil was ours on which hostilities were com-

menced by Mexico, and he repeats that declaration almost in the same language in each successive annual message, thus showing that he deems that point a highly essential one. In the importance of that point I entirely agree with the President.

*   *   *

. . . It is a singular fact that if any one should declare the President sent the army into the midst of a settlement of Mexican people who had never submitted, by consent or by force, to the authority of Texas or of the United States, and that there and thereby the first blood of the war was shed, there is not one word in all the President has said which would either admit or deny the declaration. This strange omission it does seem to me could not have occurred but by design. My way of living leads me to be about the courts of justice; and there I have sometimes seen a good lawyer, struggling for his client's neck in a desperate case, employing every artifice to work round, befog, and cover up with many words some point arising in the case which he dared not admit and yet could not deny. Party bias may help to make it appear so, but with all the allowance I can make for such bias, it still does appear to me that just such, and from just such necessity, is the President's struggle in this case. . . .

I propose to state my understanding of the true rule for ascertaining the boundary between Texas and Mexico. It is that wherever Texas was exercising jurisdiction was hers; and wherever Mexico was exercising jurisdiction was hers; and that whatever separated the actual exercise of jurisdiction of the one from that of the other was the true boundary between them. If, as is probably true, Texas was exercising jurisdiction along the western bank of the Nueces, and Mexico was exercising it along the eastern bank of the Rio Grande, then neither river was the boundary; but the uninhabited country between the two was. The extent of our territory in that region depended not on any treaty-fixed boundary (for no treaty had attempted it), but on revolution. Any people anywhere being inclined and having the power have the right to rise up and shake off the existing government, and form a new one that suits them better. This is a most valuable, a most sacred right—a right which we hope and believe is to liberate the world. Nor is this right confined to cases in which the whole people of an existing government may choose to exercise it. Any portion of such people that can may revolutionize and make their own of so much of the territory as they inhabit. More than this, a majority of any portion of such people may revolutionize, putting down a minority, intermingled with or near about them, who may oppose this movement. Such minority was precisely the case of the Tories of our own revolution. It is a quality of revolutions not to go by old lines or old laws; but to break up both, and make new ones.

As to the country now in question, we bought it of France in 1803, and sold it to Spain in 1819, according to the President's statements. After this, all Mexico, including Texas, revolutionized against Spain; still later Texas revolutionized against Mexico. In my view, just so far as she carried her resolution by obtaining the actual, willing or unwilling, submission of the people, so far the country was hers, and no farther. Now, sir, for the purpose of obtaining the very best evidence as to whether Texas had actually carried her revolution to the place where the hostilities of the present war commenced, let the President answer the interrogatories I proposed, as before mentioned, or some other similar ones. Let him answer fully, fairly, and candidly. Let him answer with facts and not with arguments. Let him remember he sits where Washington sat, and so remembering, let him answer as Washington would answer. As a nation should not, and the Almighty will not, be evaded, so let him attempt no evasion—no equivocation. And if, so answering, he can show that the soil was ours where the first blood of the war was shed—that it was not within an inhabited country, or, if within such, that the inhabitants had submitted themselves to the civil authority of Texas or of the United States, and that the same is true of the site of Fort Brown—then I am with him for his justification. In that case I shall be most happy to reverse the vote I gave the other day. I have a selfish motive for desiring that the President may do this—I expect to gain some votes, in connection with the war, which, without his so doing, will be of doubtful propriety in my own judgment, but which will be free from the doubt if he does so. But if he can not or will not do this—if on any pretense or no pretense he shall refuse or omit it—then I shall be fully convinced of what I more than suspect already—that he is deeply conscious of being in the wrong; that he feels the blood of this war, like the blood of Abel, is crying to Heaven against him; that originally having some strong motive—what, I will not stop now to give my opinion concerning—to involve the two countries in a war, and trusting to escape scrutiny by fixing the public gaze upon the exceeding brightness of military glory—that attractive rainbow that arises in showers of blood—that serpent's eye that charms to destroy—he plunged into it, and has swept on and on till, disappointed in his calculation of the ease with which Mexico might be subdued, he now finds himself he knows not where. How like the half-insane mumbling of a fever dream is the whole war part of his late message! At one time telling us that Mexico has nothing whatever that we can get but territory; at another showing us how we can support the war by levying contributions on Mexico. At one time urging the national honor, the security of the future, the prevention of foreign interference, and even the good of Mexico herself as among the objects of the war; at another telling us that "to reject indemnity, by refusing to accept a cession of territory, would be to abandon all our just demands, and to wage the war bearing all its expenses, without a purpose or definite object." So then this national honor, security of the future, and everything but territorial indemnity may be considered the no-purpose and indefinite objects of the war! But,

having it now settled that territorial indemnity is the only
object, we are urged to seize, by legislation here, all that he
was content to take a few months ago, and the whole province
of Lower California to boot, and to still carry on the war—to
take all we are fighting for, and still fight on. Again, the President is resolved under all circumstances to have full territorial
indemnity for the expenses of the war; but he forgets to tell us
how we are to get the excess after those expenses shall have
surpassed the value of the whole of the Mexican territory. So
again, he insists that the separate national existence of Mexico
shall be maintained; but he does not tell us how this can be
done, after we shall have taken all her territory. Lest the questions I have suggested be considered speculative merely, let
me be indulged a moment in trying to show they are not. The
war has gone on some twenty months; for the expenses of
which, together with an inconsiderable old score, the President
now claims about one half of the Mexican territory, and that
by far the better half, so far as concerns our ability to make
anything out of it. It is comparatively uninhabited; so that we
could establish land offices in it, and raise some money in that
way. But the other half is already inhabited, as I understand it,
tolerably densely for the nature of the country, and all its
lands, or all that are valuable, already appropriated as private
property. How then are we to make anything out of these
lands with this encumbrance upon them? or how remove the
encumbrance? I suppose no one would say we should kill the
people, or drive them out, or make slaves of them; or confiscate their property. How, then, can we make much out of
this part of the territory? If the prosecution of the war has in
expenses already equaled the better half of the country, how
long its future prosecution will be in equaling the less valuable half is not a speculative, but a practical, question, pressing
closely upon us. And yet it is a question which the President
seems never to have thought of. As to the mode of terminat-
ing the war and securing peace, the President is equally wan-

dering and indefinite. First, it is to be done by a more vigorous prosecution of the war in the vital parts of the enemy's country; and after apparently talking himself tired on this point, the President drops down into a half-despairing tone, and tells us that "with a people distracted and divided by contending factions, and a government subject to constant changes by successive revolutions, the continued success of our arms may fail to secure a satisfactory peace." Then he suggests the propriety of wheedling the Mexican people to desert the counsels of their own leaders, and, trusting in our protestations, to set up a government from which we can secure a satisfactory peace; telling us that "this may become the only mode of obtaining such a peace." But soon he falls into a doubt of this too; and then drops back onto the already half-abandoned ground of "more vigorous prosecution." All this shows that the President is in nowise satisfied with his own positions. First he takes up one, and in attempting to argue us into it he argues himself out of it, then seizes another and goes through the same process, and then, confused at being able to think of nothing new, he snatches up the old one again, which he has some time before cast off. His mind, taxed beyond its power, is running hither and thither, like some tortured creature on a burning surface, finding no position on which it can settle down and be at ease.

Again, it is a singular omission in this message that it nowhere intimates when the President expects the war to terminate. At its beginning, General Scott was by this same President driven into disfavor, if not disgrace, for intimating that peace could not be conquered in less than three or four months. But now, at the end of about twenty months, during which time our arms have given us the most splendid successes, every department and every part, land and water, officers and privates, regulars and volunteers, doing all that men could do, and hundreds of things which it had ever before been thought men could not do—after all this, this same President gives us a long message, without showing us that as to the end he himself has even an imaginary conception. As I have before said, he knows not where he is. He is a bewildered, confounded, and miserably perplexed man. God grant he may be able to show there is not something about his conscience more painful than all his mental perplexity.

LETTER TO WILLIAM H. HERNDON

George Ashmun had proposed a resolution which declared that the Mexican War was "unnecessarily and unconstitutionally begun by the President of the United States." Lincoln, in company with most Whigs, had voted in support of this resolution. Herndon had written to question the propriety of his doing so. The term, "Locofoco," used here, was applied derisively by Whigs to any Democrat.

Washington, February 1, 1848

DEAR WILLIAM: Your letter of the 19th ultimo was received last night, and for which I am much obliged. The only thing in it that I wish to talk to you at once about is that because of my vote for Ashmun's amendment you fear that you and I disagree about the war. I regret this, not because of any fear we shall remain disagreed after you have read this letter, but because if you misunderstand I fear other good friends may also. That vote affirms that the war was unnecessarily and unconstitutionally commenced by the President; and I will stake my life that if you had been in my place you would have voted just as I did. Would you have voted what you felt and knew to be a lie? I know you would not. Would you have gone out of the House—skulked the vote? I expect not. If you had skulked one vote, you would have had to skulk many more before the end of the session. Richardson's resolutions, introduced before I made any move or gave any vote upon the subject, make the direct question of the justice of the war; so that no man can be silent if he would. You are compelled to speak; and your only alternative is to tell the truth or a lie. I cannot doubt which you would do.

This vote has nothing to do in determining my votes on the questions of supplies. I have always intended, and still intend, to vote supplies; perhaps not in the precise form recommended by the President, but in a better form for all purposes, except Locofoco party purposes. It is in this particular you seem mistaken. The Locos are untiring in their efforts to make the impression that all who vote supplies or take part in the war do of necessity approve the President's conduct in the beginning of it; but the Whigs have from the beginning made and kept the distinction between the two. In the very first act nearly all the Whigs voted against the preamble declaring that war existed by the act of Mexico; and yet nearly all of them voted for the supplies. As to the Whig men who have participated in the war, so far as they have spoken in my hearing, they do not hesitate to pronounce as unjust the President's conduct in the beginning of the war. They do not suppose that such denunciation is directed by undying hatred to him, as *The Register* would have it believed. . . .

I do not mean this letter for the public, but for you. Before it reaches you, you will have seen and read my pamphlet speech, and perhaps been scared anew by it. After you get over your scare, read it over again, sentence by sentence, and tell me honestly what you think of it. I condensed all I could for fear of being cut off by the hour rule, and when I got through I had spoken but forty-five minutes.

LETTER TO WILLIAM H. HERNDON

Lincoln refers here to Alexander Stephens of Georgia, who was later to become Vice President of the Confederacy, and who was to serve as one of the three Confederate commissioners at the historic Hampton Roads conference with Lincoln on February 3, 1865. Stephens was a Southern Whig who was attacking the war policy of Polk and the Democrats.

Washington, February 2, 1848

DEAR WILLIAM: I just take my pen to say that Mr. Stephens, of Georgia, a little, slim, pale-faced, consumptive man, with a voice like Logan's, has just concluded the very best speech of an hour's length I ever heard. My old withered dry eyes are full of tears yet.

LETTER TO WILLIAM H. HERNDON

Lincoln argues with his partner that only Congress, and not the President, has the Constitutional right of making war. The Radical Republicans during the Civil War took exactly this position in opposition to Lincoln, who then held that the emergency warranted him in holding firm rein on the military efforts of the nation. Lincoln, however, always maintained that the Civil War was not war but insurrection, and that he was simply engaged in putting down an internal rebellion.

Washington, February 15, 1848

DEAR WILLIAM: Your letter of the 29th of January was received last night. Being exclusively a constitutional argument, I wish to submit some reflections upon it in the same spirit of kindness that I know actuates you. Let me first state what I understand to be your position. It is that if it shall become necessary to repel invasion, the President may, without violation of the Constitution, cross the line and invade the territory of another country, and that whether such necessity exists in any given case the President is the sole judge.

Before going further consider well whether this is or is not your position. If it is, it is a position that neither the President himself, nor any friend of his, so far as I know, has ever taken. Their only positions are—first, that the soil was ours when the hostilities commenced; and second, that whether it was rightfully ours or not, Congress had annexed it, and the President for that reason was bound to defend it; both of which are as clearly proved to be false in fact as you can prove that your house is mine. The soil was not ours, and Congress did not annex or attempt to annex it. But to return to your position. Allow the President to invade a neighboring nation whenever he shall deem it necessary to repel an invasion, and you allow him to do so whenever he may choose to say he deems it necessary for such purpose, and you allow him to make war at pleasure. Study to see if you can fix any limit to his power in this respect, after having given him so much as you propose. If today he should choose to say he thinks it necessary to invade Canada to prevent the British from invading us, how could you stop him? You may say to him, "I see no probability of the British invading us;" but he will say to you, "Be silent: I see it, if you don't."

The provision of the Constitution giving the war-making power to Congress was dictated, as I understand it, by the following reasons: Kings had always been involving and impoverishing their people in wars, pretending generally, if not always, that the good of the people was the object. This our convention understood to be the most oppressive of all kingly oppressions, and they resolved to so frame the Constitution that no one man should hold the power of bringing this oppression upon us. But your view destroys the whole matter, and places our President where kings have always stood.

LETTER TO DAVID LINCOLN

Congressman McDowell, formerly Governor of Virginia, had given Lincoln the name of another Lincoln in his state. Lincoln now writes to this man to find out whether they are related.

Washington, March 24, 1848

MR. DAVID LINCOLN.

DEAR SIR: Your very worthy representative, Gov. McDowell, has given me your name and address, and as my father was born in Rockingham, from whence his father, Abraham Lincoln, emigrated to Kentucky about the year 1782, I have concluded to address you to ascertain whether we are not of the same family. I shall be much obliged if you will write me, telling me whether you in any way know anything of my grandfather, what relation you are to him, and so on. Also, if you know where your family came from when they settled in Virginia, tracing them back as far as your knowledge extends.

LETTER TO DAVID LINCOLN

The relationship established, Lincoln writes again, giving news of his family in the West. The Lincoln genealogy has recently been traced back to its source in England from where the family came to this country in 1637. Those interested in fine points of Lincoln genealogy will find the subject fully treated in Waldo Lincoln's History of the Lincoln Family.

Washington, April 2, 1848

DEAR SIR: Last evening I was much gratified by receiving and reading your letter of the 30th of March. There is no longer any doubt that your uncle Abraham and my grandfather was the same man. His family did reside in Washington County, Kentucky, just as you say you found them in 1801 or 1802. The oldest son, Uncle Mordecai, near twenty years ago removed from Kentucky to Hancock County, Illinois, where within a year or two afterward he died, and where his surviving children now live. His two sons there now are Abraham and Mordecai; and their post-office is "La Harpe." Uncle Josiah, farther back than my recollection, went from Kentucky to Blue River in Indiana. I have not heard from him in a great many years, and whether he is still living I cannot say. My recollection of what I have heard is that he has several daughters and only one son, Thomas—their post-office is "Coryden, Harrison County, Indiana." My father, Thomas, is still living, in Coles County, Illinois, being in the seventy-first year of his age—his post-office is "Charleston, Coles County, Illinois"—I am his only child. I am now in my fortieth year; and I live in Springfield, Sangamon County, Illinois. This is the outline of my grandfather's family in the West.

I think my father has told me that grandfather had four brothers—Isaac, Jacob, John, and Thomas. Is that correct? And which of them was your father? Are any of them alive? I am quite sure that Isaac resided on Watauga, near a point where Virginia and Tennessee join; and that he has been dead more than twenty, perhaps thirty, years; also that Thomas removed to Kentucky, near Lexington, where he died a good while ago.

What was your grandfather's Christian name? Was he not a Quaker? About what time did he emigrate from Berks County, Pennsylvania, to Virginia? Do you know anything of your family (or rather I may now say our family), farther back than your grandfather?

If it be not too much trouble to you, I shall be much pleased to hear from you again. Be assured I will call on you, should anything ever bring me near you. I shall give your respects to Governor McDowell as you desire.

LETTER TO MARY LINCOLN

Mrs. Lincoln had gone to Lexington, Kentucky, to visit her family there. Lincoln writes to her, admitting that now that she is gone, he is lonely for her. The headaches she suffered from are mentioned here; they may well have had some connection with the mental disorder which finally overcame her. This is a real family letter, showing Lincoln as a devoted father and an affectionate husband. The word "tapila" is probably some household term taken over from the children's private lexicon.

Washington, April 16, 1848

Dear Mary: In this troublesome world, we are never quite satisfied. When you were here, I thought you hindered me some in attending to business; but now, having nothing but business—no vanity—it has grown exceedingly tasteless to me. I hate to sit down and direct documents, and I hate to stay in this old room by myself. You know I told you in last Sunday's letter I was going to make a little speech during the week, but the week has passed away without my getting a chance to do so, and now my interest in the subject has passed away too. Your second and third letters have been received since I wrote before. Dear Eddy thinks father is "gone tapila." Has any further discovery been made as to the breaking into your grandmother's house? If I were she I would not remain there alone. You mention that your Uncle John Parker is likely to be at Lexington. Don't forget to present him my very kindest regards.

I went yesterday to hunt the little plaid stockings as you wished, but found that McKnight has quit business and Allen had not a single pair of the description you give and only one plaid pair of any sort that I thought would fit "Eddy's dear little feet." I have a notion to make another trial tomorrow morning. If I could get them, I have an excellent chance of sending them. Mr. Warrich Tunstall of St. Louis is here. He is to leave early this week and to go by Lexington. He says he knows you, and will call to see you, and he voluntarily asked if I had not some package to send to you.

I wish you to enjoy yourself in every possible way, but is there no danger of wounding the feelings of your good father by being too openly intimate with the Wickliffe family?

Mrs. Broome has not removed yet, but she thinks of doing so tomorrow. All the house or rather all with whom you were on decided good terms send their love to you. The others say nothing. Very soon after you went away I got what I think a very pretty set of shirt-bosom studs—modest little ones, jet set in gold, only costing 50 cents a piece or $1.50 for the whole.

Suppose you do not prefix the "Hon." to the address on your letters to me any more. I like the letters very much but I would rather they should not have that upon them. It is not necessary, as I suppose you have thought, to have them come free.

Are you entirely free from headache? That is good—good considering it is the first spring you have been free from it since we were acquainted. I am afraid you will get so well and fat and young as to be wanting to marry again. Tell Louisa I want her to watch you a little for me. Get weighed and write me how much you weigh.

I did not get rid of the impression of that foolish dream about dear Bobby till I got your letter written the same day. What did he and Eddy think of the little letters father sent them? Don't let the blessed fellows forget father.

A day or two ago Mr. Strong, here in Congress, said to me that Matilda would visit here within two or three weeks. Suppose you write her a letter, and enclose it in one of mine, and if she comes I will deliver it to her, and if she does not. I will send it to her.

Most affectionately,

A. LINCOLN

LETTER TO MARY LINCOLN

Reading between the lines of this letter, one can sense that Mrs. Lincoln's sojourn in Lexington with her family was not simply a social visit—the Lincolns had evidently quarreled. Mary Lincoln is now to be permitted to return to Washington if she will be "a good girl in all things."

Washington, June 12, 1848

MY DEAR WIFE: On my return from Philadelphia yesterday, where in my anxiety I have been led to attend the Whig Convention, I found your last letter. I was so tired and sleepy, having ridden all night, that I could not answer it till today; and now I have to do so in the H.R. The leading matter in your letter is your wish to return to this side of the Mountains—Will you be a *good girl* in all things, if I consent? Then come along, and that as *soon* as possible. Having got the idea in my head, I shall be impatient till I see you. You will not have money enough to bring you, but I presume your uncle will supply you and I will refund him here. By the way you do not mention whether you have received the fifty dollars I sent you. I do not much fear but that you got it; because the want of it would have induced you [to] say something in relation to it. If your uncle is already at Lexington, you might induce him to start in earlier than the first of July; he could stay in Kentucky longer on his return, and so make up for lost time. Since I began this letter, the H.R. has passed a resolution for adjourning on the 17th July, which probably will pass the Senate. I hope this letter will not be disagreeable to you; which, together with the circumstances under which I write, I hope will excuse me for not writing a longer one. Come on just as soon as you can—I want to see you, and our dear *dear* boys very much. Everybody here wants to see our dear Bobby.

Affectionately,

A. LINCOLN

LETTER TO WILLIAM H. HERNDON

Herndon had written that the leadership of the Whigs in Illinois was in the hands of a cabal of older men—a statement which was true. Lincoln urges his partner to go ahead on his own to form young men's political groups. "Old Zach" is Zachary Taylor, the Whig nominee for President.

Washington, June 22, 1848

DEAR WILLIAM: Last night I was attending a sort of caucus of the Whig members, held in relation to the coming presidential election. The whole field of the nation was scanned, and all is high hope and confidence. Illinois is expected to better her condition in this race. . . .

Now, as to the young men. You must not wait to be brought forward by the older men. For instance, do you suppose that I should ever have got into notice if I had waited to be hunted up and pushed forward by older men? You young men get together and form a "Rough and Ready Club," and have regular meetings and speeches. Take in everybody you can get. Harrison Grimsley, L. A. Enos, Lee Kimball, and C. W. Matheny will do to begin the thing; but as you go along gather up all the shrewd, wild boys about town, whether just of age or a little under age—Chris. Logan, Reddick Ridgely, Lewis Zwizler, and hundreds such. Let every one play the part he can play best—some speak, some sing, and all "holler." Your meetings will be of evenings; the older men, and the women, will go to hear you; so that it will not only contribute to the election of "Old Zach," but will be an interesting pastime, and improving to the intellectual faculties of all engaged. Don't fail to do this.

You ask me to send you all the speeches made about "Old Zach," the war, etc. Now this makes me a little impatient. I have regularly sent you the *Congressional Globe* and *Appen-*

dix, and you cannot have examined them, or you would have discovered that they contain every speech made by every man in both Houses of Congress, on every subject, during the session. Can I send any more? Can I send speeches that nobody has made? Thinking it would be most natural that the newspapers would feel interested to give at least some of the speeches to their readers, I at the beginning of the session made arrangements to have one copy of the *Globe* and *Appendix* regularly sent to each Whig paper of the district. And yet, with the exception of my own little speech, which was published in two only of the then five, now four, Whig papers, I do not remember having seen a single speech, or even extract from one, in any single one of those papers. With equal and full means on both sides, I will venture that the *State Register* has thrown before its readers more of Locofoco speeches in a month than all the Whig papers of the district has done of Whig speeches during the session. . . .

LETTER TO MARY LINCOLN

The Lincolns had been married for less than six years when this letter was written, yet two things which were indicative of Mrs. Lincoln's inability to carry her share of the responsibilities of the marriage are already evident. She is running up clothing bills— and she is concealing the fact of their existence from her husband in the stupid hope that they will not be brought to his attention. Also, her manner in dealing with inferiors makes it impossible for her to keep a maid in the house. Her husband takes these lapses calmly—which indicates that he is used to them. The Philadelphia Convention was the Whig National Convention at which Taylor had been nominated as the party candidate for President.

Washington, July 2, 1848

MY DEAR WIFE: Your letter of last Sunday came last night. On that day (Sunday) I wrote the principal part of a letter to you, but did not finish it, or send it till Tuesday, when I had provided a draft for $100 which I sent in it. It is now probable that on that day (Tuesday) you started to Shelbyville; so that when the money reaches Lexington, you will not be there. Before leaving, did you make any provision about letters that might come to Lexington for you? Write me whether you got the draft, if you shall not have already done so, when this reaches you. Give my kindest regards to your uncle John, and all the family. Thinking of them reminds me that I saw your acquaintance, Newton, of Arkansas, at the Philadelphia Convention. We had but a single interview, and that was so brief, and in so great a multitude of strange faces, that I am quite sure I should not recognize him, if I were to meet him again. He was a sort of Trinity, three in one, having the right, in his own person, to cast the three votes of Arkansas. Two or three days ago I sent your uncle John, and a few of our other friends each a copy of the speech I mentioned in my last letter; but I did not send any to you, thinking you would be on the road here, before it would reach you. I send you one now. Last Wednesday, P. H. Hood & Co. dunned me for a little bill of $5.38 cents, and Walter Harper & Co. another for $8.50 cents, for goods which they say you bought. I hesitated to pay them, because my recollection is that you told me when you went away, there was nothing left unpaid. Mention in your next letter whether they are right.

Mrs. Richardson is still here; and what is more, has a baby— so Richardson says, and he ought to know. I believe Mary Hewett has left here and gone to Boston. I met her on the street about fifteen or twenty days ago, and she told me she was going soon. I have seen nothing of her since.

The music in the Capitol grounds on Saturdays, or, rather, the interest in it, is dwindling down to nothing. Yesterday evening the attendance was rather thin. Our two girls, whom you remember seeing first at Canisis, at the exhibition of the Ethiopian Serenaders, and whose peculiarities were the wearing of black fur bonnets, and never being seen in close company with other ladies, were at the music yesterday. One of them was attended by their brother, and the other had a member of Congress in tow. He went home with her; and if I were to guess, I would say, he went away a somewhat altered man—most likely in his pockets, and in some other particular. The fellow looked conscious of guilt, although I believe he was unconscious that everybody around knew who it was that had caught him.

I have had no letter from home, since I wrote you before, except short business letters, which have no interest for you.

By the way, you do not intend to do without a girl, because the one you had has left you? Get another as soon as you can to take charge of the dear codgers. Father expected to see you all sooner; but let it pass; stay as long as you please, and come when you please. Kiss and love the dear rascals.

Affectionately,

A. Lincoln

LETTER TO WILLIAM H. HERNDON

Although he was not yet forty, Lincoln already regards himself as an old man. He writes a fatherly letter of advice to Herndon who was actually only nine years younger than Lincoln.

Washington, July 10, 1848

Dear William: Your letter covering the newspaper slips was received last night. The subject of that letter is exceedingly painful to me; and I cannot but think there is some mistake in your impression of the motives of the old men. I suppose I am now one of the old men; and I declare, on my veracity, which I think is good with you, that nothing could afford me more satisfaction than to learn that you and others of my young friends at home are doing battle in the contest, and endearing themselves to the people, and taking a stand far above any I have ever been able to reach in their admiration. I cannot conceive that other old men feel differently. Of course I cannot demonstrate what I say; but I was young once, and I am sure I was never ungenerously thrust back. I hardly know what to say. The way for a young man to rise is to improve himself every way he can, never suspecting that anybody wishes to hinder him. Allow me to assure you that suspicion and jealousy never did help any man in any situation. There may sometimes be ungenerous attempts to keep a young man down; and they will succeed, too, if he allows his mind to be diverted from its true channel to brood over the attempted injury. Cast about, and see if this feeling has not injured every person you have ever known to fall into it.

Now, in what I have said, I am sure you will suspect nothing but sincere friendship. I would save you from a fatal error. You have been a laborious, studious young man. You are far better informed on almost all subjects than I have been. You cannot fail in any laudable object, unless you allow your mind to be improperly directed. I have somewhat the advantage of you in the world's experience, merely by being older; and it is this that induces me to advise.

LETTER TO WILLIAM H. HERNDON

Lincoln writes to Herndon, almost regretting his didactic letter of the day before. One wonders to what the phrase "Go it while you're young!" refers. The pretty girl alluded to by Lincoln has also had her identity lost in the mists of time.

Washington, July 11, 1848

DEAR WILLIAM: Yours of the 3rd is this moment received; and I hardly need say, it gives unalloyed pleasure. I now almost regret writing the serious, long-faced letter I wrote yesterday; but let the past as nothing be. Go it while you're young!

I write this in the confusion of the H.R., and with several other things to attend to. I will send you about eight different speeches this evening; and as to kissing a pretty girl, I know one very pretty one, but I guess she won't let me kiss her.

FROM A SPEECH IN THE
HOUSE OF REPRESENTATIVES

This is from a long speech (intended to be humorous) in which Lincoln attacked General Lewis Cass who was the Democratic candidate for the Presidency. In this passage he makes fun of Cass's military exploits by comparing them with his own inglorious experiences during the Black Hawk War.

July 27, 1848

BY THE WAY, Mr. Speaker, did you know I am a military hero? Yes, sir; in the days of the Black Hawk war I fought, bled, and came away. Speaking of General Cass's career reminds me of my own. I was not at Stillman's defeat, but I was about as near it as Cass was to Hull's surrender; and, like him, I saw the place very soon afterward. It is quite certain I did not break my sword, for I had none to break; but I bent a musket pretty badly on one occasion. If Cass broke his sword, the idea is he broke it in desperation; I bent the musket by accident. If General Cass went in advance of me in picking huckleberries, I guess I surpassed him in charges upon the wild onions. If he saw any live, fighting Indians, it was more than I did; but I had a good many bloody struggles with the mosquitoes, and although I never fainted from the loss of blood, I can truly say I was often very hungry. Mr. Speaker, if I should ever conclude to doff whatever our Democratic friends may suppose there is of black-cockade federalism about me, and therefore they shall take me up as their candidate for the Presidency, I protest they shall not make fun of me, as they have of General Cass, by attempting to write me into a military hero.

LETTER TO THOMAS LINCOLN

Lincoln's father and the relatives surrounding him were in constant financial difficulty; theirs were the troubles of the poor— the troubles of men who have no money and who are always just one jump ahead of the sheriff. Reluctantly Lincoln sends his father twenty dollars to save his land. He is reluctant, not because of this particular request for money, but because the need and the demand never ceased. Improvidence was encroaching upon him, and Lincoln, who had no reason to be grateful to his father for anything, was annoyed.

Washington, December 24, 1848

My Dear Father: Your letter of the 7th was received night before last. I very cheerfully send you the twenty dollars, which sum you say is necessary to save your land from sale. It is singular that you should have forgotten a judgment against you; and it is more singular that the plaintiff should have let you forget it so long, particularly as I suppose you always had property enough to satisfy a judgment of that amount. Before you pay it, it would be well to be sure you have not paid, or at least that you cannot prove that you have paid it.

Give my love to mother and all the connections. Affectionately your son,

A. Lincoln

LETTER TO JOHN D. JOHNSTON

His foster brother is on his neck for money. Lincoln as tactfully as possible declines to lend him eighty dollars and offers him good solid middle-class advice instead.

December 24, 1848

DEAR JOHNSTON: Your request for eighty dollars I do not think it best to comply with now. At the various times when I have helped you a little you have said to me, "We can get along very well now"; but in a very short time I find you in the same difficulty again. Now, this can only happen by some defect in your conduct. What that defect is, I think I know. You are not lazy, and still you are an idler. I doubt whether, since I saw you, you have done a good whole day's work in any one day. You do not very much dislike to work, and still you do not work much, merely because it does not seem to you that you could get much for it. This habit of uselessly wasting time is the whole difficulty; it is vastly important to you, and still more so to your children, that you should break the habit. It is more important to them, because they have longer to live, and can keep out of an idle habit before they are in it, easier than they can get out after they are in.

You are now in need of some money; and what I propose is, that you shall go to work, "tooth and nail," for somebody who will give you money for it. Let father and your boys take charge of your things at home, prepare for a crop, and make a crop, and you go to work for the best money wages, or in discharge of any debt you owe, that you can get; and, to secure you a fair reward for your labor, I now promise you, that for every dollar you will, between this and the first of May, get for your own labor, either in money or as your own indebtedness, I will then give you one other dollar. By this, if you hire yourself at ten dollars a month, from me you will get ten more, making twenty dollars a month for your work. In this I do not mean you shall go off to St. Louis, or the lead mines, or the gold mines in California, but I mean for you to go at it for the best wages you can get close to home in Coles County. Now, if you will do this, you will be soon out of debt, and, what is better, you will have a habit that will keep you from getting in debt again. But, if I should now clear you out of debt, next year you would be just as deep in as ever. You say you would almost give your place in heaven for seventy or eighty dollars. Then you value your place in heaven very cheap, for I am sure you can, with the offer I make, get the seventy or eighty dollars for four or five months' work. You say if I will furnish you the money you will deed me the land, and, if you don't pay the money back, you will deliver possession. Nonsense! If you can't now live with the land, how will you then live without it? You have always been kind to me, and I do not mean to be unkind to you. On the contrary, if you will but follow my advice, you will find it worth more than eighty times eighty dollars to you.

Affectionately your brother,

A. LINCOLN

LETTER TO C. U. SCHLATER

It is not known who Mr. Schlater was, but he had a sense for autographs that must have been positively psychic. At this time Abraham Lincoln was one of the least promising men in Congress. He knew how undistinguished he was and he makes no bones about saying so.

Washington, January 5, 1849

DEAR SIR: Your note, requesting my "signature with a sentiment" was received, and should have been answered long since, but that it was mislaid. I am not a very sentimental man; and the best sentiment I can think of is, that if you collect the signatures of all persons who are no less distinguished than I, you will have a very undistinguishing mass of names.

APPLICATION FOR A PATENT

Possibly some echo of his experience in getting Offut's flatboat over the dam at New Salem in the spring of 1831 influenced Lincoln in his one attempt at invention. When he returned to Springfield from Congress, the boat he was traveling on was stranded on a shoal. He then invented the device described here. Like most patents it came to nothing. The model is still on exhibition at the Patent Office in Washington.

May 22, 1849[?]

WHAT I claim as my invention, and desire to secure by letters patent, is the combination of expansible buoyant chambers placed at the sides of a vessel with the main shaft or shafts by means of the sliding spars, which pass down through the buoyant chambers and are made fast to their bottoms and the series of ropes and pulleys or their equivalents in such a manner that by turning the main shaft or shafts in one direction the buoyant chambers will be forced downwards into the water, and at the same time expanded and filled with air for buoying up the vessel by the displacement of water, and by turning the shafts in an opposite direction the buoyant chambers will be contracted into a small space and secured against injury.

A. LINCOLN

LETTER TO J. M. CLAYTON

John M. Clayton was Taylor's Secretary of State. He had just come into office on March 4, 1849. Lincoln writes to him to pass on some advice about the way a President should act in order to maintain the respect of his people. He approves Taylor's conduct during the Mexican War when he went against his own council's advice to follow out his own line of action. This letter, which would have been meaningless if Lincoln had remained in obscurity, takes on great significance when interpreted in the light of his own behavior when he became President.

Springfield, Illinois, July 28, 1849

DEAR SIR: It is with some hesitation I presume to address this letter—and yet I wish not only you, but the whole cabinet, and the President too, would consider the subject matter of it. My being among the people while you and they are not, will excuse the apparent presumption. It is understood that the President at first adopted, as a general rule, to throw the responsibility of the appointments upon the respective Departments; and that such rule is adhered to and practised upon. This course I at first thought proper; and, of course, I am not now complaining of it. Still I am disappointed with the effect of it on the public mind. It is fixing for the President the unjust and ruinous character of being a mere man of straw. This must be arrested, or it will damn us all inevitably. It is said Gen. Taylor and his officers held a council of war, at Palo Alto (I believe); and that he then fought the battle against unanimous opinion of those officers. This fact (no matter whether rightfully or wrongfully) gives him more popularity than ten thousand submissions, however really wise and magnanimous those submissions may be.

The appointments need be no better than they have been, but the public must be brought to understand, that they are the *President's* appointments. He must occasionally say, or seem to say, "by the Eternal," "I take the responsibility." Those phrases were the "Samson's locks" of Gen. Jackson, and we dare not disregard the lessons of experience.

LETTER TO J. M. CLAYTON

Lincoln had gone to Washington in June to further his own claim to an appointive position in the Government under the Taylor administration which he had helped to elect. He wanted the Commissionership of the General Land office but it was denied to him; he was considered for the Governorship of Oregon Territory, but was actually offered only the position as Secretary there. Mrs. Lincoln's disinclination to go to the far West, as well as Lincoln's own pride, made him decline the offer. Simeon Francis was the editor of the Illinois Journal, the Whig paper of Springfield. It was his wife who had brought about the reconciliation between Lincoln and Mary Todd.

Springfield, Illinois, September 27, 1849

DEAR SIR: Your letter of the 17th inst., saying you had received no answer to yours informing me of my appointment as Secretary of Oregon, is received, and surprises me very much. I received that letter, accompanied by the commission, in due course of mail, and answered it two days after, declining the office, and warmly recommending Simeon Francis for it. I have also written you several letters since alluding to the same matter, all of which ought to have reached you before the date of your last letter.

LETTER TO JOHN D. JOHNSTON

Johnston was Lincoln's foster brother, the son of his stepmother, Sarah Bush Lincoln, by her previous marriage. As the long series of letters to him indicates, he was improvident and shiftless, constantly appealing to Lincoln for financial assistance. Lincoln here

tries to get him a mail route so he will be able to provide for
himself. The child referred to was Edward Baker Lincoln who had
died on February 1, at the age of four.

Springfield, February 23, 1850

DEAR BROTHER: Your letter about a mail contract was received yesterday. I had made out a bid for you at $120, guaranteed it myself, got our P. M. [Postmaster] here to certify it, and send it on. Your former letter, concerning some man's claim for a pension, was also received. I had the claim examined by those who are practised in such matters, and they decide he cannot get a pension.

As you make no mention of it, I suppose you had not learned that we lost our little boy. He was sick fifteen days, and died in the morning of the first day of this month. It was not our first, but our second child. We miss him very much. Your brother, in haste,

A. LINCOLN

NOTES FOR A LAW LECTURE

It is not known for what purpose Lincoln intended these notes,
but they are good advice to any lawyer and might appropriately
be framed to hang in a law office even today.

July 1, 1850[?]

I AM NOT an accomplished lawyer. I find quite as much material for a lecture in those points wherein I have failed, as in those wherein I have been moderately successful. The leading rule for the lawyer, as for the man of every other calling, is diligence. Leave nothing for tomorrow which can be done today. Never let your correspondence fall behind. Whatever piece of business you have in hand, before stopping, do all the labor pertaining to it which can then be done. When you bring a common-law suit, if you have the facts for doing so, write the declaration at once. If a law point be involved, examine the books, and note the authority you rely on upon the declaration itself, where you are sure to find it when wanted. The same of defenses and pleas. In business not likely to be litigated—ordinary collection cases, foreclosures, partitions, and the like—make all examinations of titles, and note them, and even draft orders and decrees in advance. This course has a triple advantage; it avoids omissions and neglect, saves your labor when once done, performs the labor out of court when you have leisure, rather than in court when you have not. Extemporaneous speaking should be practised and cultivated. It is the lawyer's avenue to the public. However able and faithful he may be in other respects, people are slow to bring him business if he cannot make a speech. And yet there is not a more fatal error to young lawyers than relying too much on speech-making. If any one, upon his rare powers of speaking, shall claim an exemption from the drudgery of the law, his case is a failure in advance.

Discourage litigation. Persuade your neighbors to compromise whenever you can. Point out to them how the nominal winner is often a real loser—in fees, expenses, and waste of time. As a peace-maker the lawyer has a superior opportunity of being a good man. There will still be business enough.

Never stir up litigation. A worse man can scarcely be found than one who does this. Who can be more nearly a fiend than he who habitually overhauls the register of deeds in search of defects in titles, whereon to stir up strife, and put money in his pocket? A moral tone ought to be infused into the profession which should drive such men out of it.

The matter of fees is important, far beyond the mere question of bread and butter involved. Properly attended to, fuller justice is done to both lawyer and client. An exorbitant fee should never be claimed. As a general rule never take your whole fee in advance, nor any more than a small retainer. When fully paid beforehand, you are more than a common mortal if you can feel the same interest in the case, as if something was still in prospect for you, as well as for your client. And when you lack interest in the case the job will very likely lack skill and diligence in the performance. Settle the amount of fee and take a note in advance. Then you will feel that you are working for something, and you are sure to do your work faithfully and well. Never sell a fee note—at least not before the consideration service is performed. It leads to negligence and dishonesty—negligence by losing interest in the case, and dishonesty in refusing to refund when you have allowed the consideration to fail.

There is a vague popular belief that lawyers are necessarily dishonest. I say vague, because when we consider to what extent confidence and honors are reposed in and conferred upon lawyers by the people, it appears improbable that their impression of dishonesty is very distinct and vivid. Yet the impression is common, almost universal. Let no young man choosing the law for a calling for a moment yield to the popular belief— resolve to be honest at all events; and if in your own judgment you cannot be an honest lawyer, resolve to be honest without being a lawyer. Choose some other occupation, rather than one in the choosing of which you do, in advance, consent to be a knave.

LETTER TO JOHN D. JOHNSTON

The problems of life and death engross Lincoln in the midst of his retirement from politics, during this, the most inactive and unhappy period of his life. His father died five days after this letter was written; his wife was in bed with "baby-sickness"—his third son, William Wallace, had been born on December 21. This letter, more than any other, shows Lincoln's lack of affection for his father. It approaches smugness in his advice for the dying man to put his trust in God if it is "his lot to go now." Most significant of all is the phrase: "If we could meet now it is doubtful whether it would not be more painful than pleasant. . . ."

Springfield, January 12, 1851

DEAR BROTHER: On the day before yesterday I received a letter from Harriet, written at Greenup. She says she has just returned from your house, and that father is very low and will hardly recover. She also says you have written me two letters, and that although you do not expect me to come now, you wonder that I do not write.

I received both your letters, and although I have not answered them, it is not because I have forgotten them, or been uninterested about them, but because it appeared to me that I could write nothing which would do any good. You already know I desire that neither father nor mother shall be in want of any comfort, either in health or sickness, while they live; and I feel sure you have not failed to use my name, if necessary, to procure a doctor, or anything else for father in his present sickness. My business is such that I could hardly leave home now, if it was not as it is, that my own wife is sick-a-bed. (It is a case of baby-sickness, and I suppose is not dangerous.) I sincerely hope father may recover his health, but at all events, tell him to remember to call upon and confide in our great and good and merciful Maker, who will not turn away from him in any extremity. He notes the fall of a sparrow, and numbers the hairs of our heads, and He will not forget the dying man who puts his trust in Him. Say to him that if we could meet now it is doubtful whether it would not be more painful than pleasant, but that if it be his lot to go now, he will soon have a joyous meeting with many loved ones gone before, and where the rest of us, through the help of God, hope ere long to join them.

TWO LETTERS TO JOHN D. JOHNSTON

Again Lincoln has to offer his foster brother advice about his affairs; he has to be sterner than ever this time to hold the restless Johnston in line. He adds a postscript addressed to his stepmother, frankly advising her to quit her Charleston home and stay with the husband of Denis Hanks' daughter. He writes again on November 25, still concerned about his stepmother's welfare. It is interesting to note the small amounts of money involved. They are indicative of the scale on which the family lived.

Shelbyville, November 4, 1851

DEAR BROTHER: When I came into Charleston day before yesterday, I learned that you are anxious to sell the land where you live and move to Missouri. I have been thinking of this ever since, and cannot but think such a notion is utterly foolish. What can you do in Missouri better than here? Is the land any richer? Can you there, any more than here, raise corn and wheat and oats without work? Will anybody there, any more than here, do your work for you? If you intend to go to work, there is no better place than right where you are; if you do not intend to go to work, you cannot get along anywhere. Squirming and crawling about from place to place can do no good. You have raised no corn this year; and what you really want is to sell the land, get the money, and spend it. Part with the land you have, and, my life upon it, you will never after own a spot big enough to bury you in. Half you will get for the land you will spend in moving to Missouri, and the other half you will eat, drink, and wear out, and no foot of land will be bought. Now, I feel it my duty to have no hand in such a piece of foolery. I feel that it is so even on your own account, and particularly on mother's account. The eastern forty acres I intend to keep for mother while she lives; if you will not cultivate it, it will rent for enough to support her— at least, it will rent for something. Her dower in the other two forties she can let you have, and no thanks to me. Now, do not misunderstand this letter; I do not write it in any unkindness. I write it in order, if possible, to get you to face the truth, which truth is, you are destitute because you have idled away all your time. Your thousand pretenses for not getting along better are all nonsense; they deceive nobody but yourself. Go to work is the only cure for your case.

A word to mother. Chapman tells me he wants you to go and live with him. If I were you I would try it awhile. If you get tired of it (as I think you will not), you can return to your own home. Chapman feels very kindly to you, and I have no doubt he will make your situation very pleasant. Sincerely your son,

A. LINCOLN

Springfield, November 25, 1851

DEAR BROTHER: Your letter of the 22d is just received. Your proposal about selling the east forty acres of land is all that I want or could claim for *myself*; but I am not satisfied with it on *mother's* account. I want her to have her living, and I feel that it is my duty, to some extent, to see that she is not wronged. She had a right of dower (that is, the use of onethird for life) in the other two forties; but, it seems, she has already let you take that, hook and line. She now has the use of the whole of the east forty, as long as she lives; and if it be sold, of course she is entitled to the interest on *all* the money it brings, as long as she lives; but you propose to sell it for three hundred dollars, take one hundred away with you, and leave her two hundred at 8 percent, making her the *enormous* sum of 16 dollars a year. Now, if you are satisfied with treating her in that way, I am not. It is true, that you are to have that forty for two hundred dollars, *at* mother's death; but you are not to have it *before.* I am confident that land can be made to produce for mother at least $30 a year, and I can not, to oblige any living person, consent that she shall be put on an allowance of sixteen dollars a year.

RESOLUTIONS IN BEHALF OF
HUNGARIAN FREEDOM

The Hungarian Revolution of 1848 had been put down; its leader, Louis Kossuth, was in exile and had come to the United States to appeal for aid for his cause. Lincoln, and the liberals of Springfield, had already expressed their keen interest in the struggle for freedom in Hungary; they had passed resolutions supporting the Hungarian cause in 1849. In this set of resolutions adopted at a meeting in Springfield in 1852, the right to revolution was reaffirmed; not only the cause of Hungarian freedom but that of Ireland was approved, and a final dig at the reactionary nature of the British Government was added. It all sounds curiously modern.

January 9, 1852

Whereas, in the opinion of this meeting, the arrival of Kossuth in our country, in connection with the recent events in Hungary, and with the appeal he is now making in behalf of his country, presents an occasion upon which we, the American people, cannot remain silent, without justifying an interference against our continued devotion to the principles of our free institutions, therefore,

Resolved: 1. That it is the right of any people, sufficiently numerous for national independence, to throw off, to revolutionize, their existing form of government, and to establish such other in its stead as they may choose.

2. That it is the duty of our government to neither foment, nor assist, such revolutions in other governments.

3. That, as we may not legally or warrantably interfere abroad, to aid, so no other government may interfere abroad, to suppress such revolutions; and that we should at once, announce to the world, our determination to insist upon this mutuality of non-intervention, as a sacred principle of the international law.

4. That the late interference of Russia in the Hungarian struggle was, in our opinion, such illegal and unwarrantable interference.

5. That to have resisted Russia in that case, or to resist any power in a like case, would be no violation of our own cherished principles of non-intervention, but, on the contrary, would be ever meritorious, in us, or any independent nation.

6. That whether we will, in fact, interfere in such case, is purely a question of policy, to be decided when the exigencies arise.

7. That we recognize in governor Kossuth of Hungary the most worthy and distinguished representative of the cause of civil and religious liberty on the continent of Europe. A cause for which he and his nation struggled until they were overwhelmed by the armed intervention of a foreign despot, in violation of the more sacred principles of the laws of nature and of nations—principles held dear by the friends of freedom everywhere, and more especially by the people of these United States.

8. That the sympathies of this country, and the benefits of its position, should be exerted in favor of the people of every nation struggling to be free; and whilst we meet to do honor to Kossuth and Hungary, we should not fail to pour out the tribute of our praise and approbation to the patriotic efforts of the Irish, the Germans and the French, who have unsuccessfully fought to establish in their several governments the supremacy of the people.

9. That there is nothing in the past history of the British government, or in its present expressed policy, to encourage the belief that she will aid, in any manner, in the delivery of continental Europe from the rope of despotism; and that her treatment of Ireland, of O'Brien, Mitchell, and other worthy patriots, forces the conclusion that she will join her efforts to the despots of Europe in suppressing every effort of the people to establish free governments, based upon the principles of true religious and civil liberty.

LETTER TO JESSE LINCOLN

This is another genealogical letter. Such correspondence was common in the nineteenth century in America when scattered families first began to become aware of their alliances with other branches descended from the same stock and lost sight of during the pioneer migrations of the earlier period. Uncle Mordecai was the brother of Lincoln's grandfather. He was the young boy who had shot the Indian who was attempting to carry off the child Abraham— Lincoln's grandfather. Mordecai became terribly soured on Indians as a result and was reputed to be willing to shoot them on sight. The Andrew Johnson referred to as Governor of Tennessee was, of course, the same Johnson who became Vice President with Lincoln in 1864.

Springfield, Illinois, April 1, 1854

MY DEAR SIR: On yesterday I had the pleasure of receiving your letter of the 16th of March. From what you say there can be no doubt that you and I are of the same family. The history of your family, as you give it, is precisely what I have always heard, and partly know, of my own. As you have supposed, I am the grandson of your uncle Abraham; and the story of his death by the Indians, and of Uncle Mordecai, then fourteen years old, killing one of the Indians, is the legend more strongly than all others imprinted upon my mind and memory. I am the son of grandfather's youngest son, Thomas. I have often heard my father speak of his uncle Isaac residing at Watauga (I think), near where the then States of Virginia, North Carolina, and Tennessee join—you seem now to be some hundred miles or so west of that. I often saw Uncle Mordecai, and Uncle Josiah but once in my life; but I never resided near either of them. Uncle Mordecai died in 1831 or 2, in Hancock County, Illinois, where he had then recently removed from Kentucky, and where his children had also removed, and still reside, as I understand. Whether Uncle Josiah is dead or living, I cannot tell, not having heard from him for more than twenty years. When I last heard of him he was living on Big Blue River, in Indiana (Harrison Co., I think), and where he had resided ever since before the beginning of my recollection. My father (Thomas) died the 17th of January, 1851, in Coles County, Illinois, where he had resided twenty years. I am his only child. I have resided here, and hereabouts, twenty-three years. I am forty-five years of age, and have a wife and three children, the oldest eleven years. My wife was born and raised at Lexington, Kentucky; and my connection with her has sometimes taken me there, where I have heard the older people of her relations speak of your uncle Thomas and his family. He is dead long ago, and his descendants have gone to some part of Missouri, as I recollect what I was told.

When I was at Washington in 1848, I got up a correspondence with David Lincoln, residing at Sparta, Rockingham County, Virginia, who, like yourself, was a first cousin of my father; but I forget, if he informed me, which of my grandfather's brothers was his father. With Col. Crozier, of whom you speak, I formed quite an intimate acquaintance, for a short one, while at Washington; and when you meet him again I will thank you to present him my respects. Your present governor, Andrew Johnson, was also at Washington while I was;

and he told me of there being people of the name of Lincoln in Carter County, I think. I can no longer claim to be a young man myself; but I infer that, as you are of the same generation as my father, you are some older. I shall be very glad to hear from you again.

SPEECH AT PEORIA, ILLINOIS, IN REPLY TO SENATOR DOUGLAS

Although his preserved correspondence of this period gives little clue to it, Lincoln had been roused from his political apathy by the repeal of the Missouri Compromise implicit in the passage of the Kansas-Nebraska Act on May 30, 1854. Douglas was its chief sponsor; Douglas was an Illinois man; Douglas was the obvious man to attack in making a general attack on this effort to extend the boundaries of slavery. Douglas had spoken in defense of the Nebraska Act at Bloomington, and then at Springfield, on October 4, where Lincoln had replied to him with this speech. He delivered it again at Peoria, amplifying it and extending his arguments. This is the first really great speech of Lincoln's career. The one other speech most nearly like it is his Cooper Union address (February 27, 1860) which also is firmly grounded on a historical survey of the status of slavery in the United States. This Peoria speech is history—history written by one of our greatest statesmen to explain the major issue that dominated his career. A careful reading of it will give the background necessary to understand the many allusions to be made in Lincoln's speeches during the next six years. It can serve as an introduction to his policies, and it should be looked upon as a prelude to the great series of arguments used during the debates with Douglas in 1858. It is reproduced here in its entirety.

October 16, 1854

I DO not rise to speak now, if I can stipulate with the audience to meet me here at half-past six or at seven o'clock. It is now several minutes past five, and Judge Douglas has spoken over three hours. If you hear me at all, I wish you to hear me through. It will take me as long as it has taken him. That will carry us beyond eight o'clock at night. Now, every one of you who can remain that long can just as well get his supper, meet me at seven, and remain an hour or two later. The judge has already informed you that he is to have an hour to reply to me. I doubt not but you have been a little surprised to learn that I have consented to give one of his high reputation and known ability this advantage of me. Indeed, my consenting to it, though reluctant, was not wholly unselfish, for I suspected, if it were understood that the judge was entirely done, you Democrats would leave and not hear me; but by giving him the close, I felt confident you would stay for the fun of hearing him skin me.

At seven o'clock Lincoln began the main body of his speech:

The repeal of the Missouri Compromise, and the propriety of its restoration, constitute the subject of what I am about to say. As I desire to present my own connected view of this subject, my remarks will not be specifically an answer to Judge Douglas; yet, as I proceed, the main points he has presented will arise, and will receive such respectful attention as I may be able to give them. I wish further to say that I do not propose to question the patriotism or to assail the motives of any man or class of men, but rather to confine myself strictly to the naked merits of the question. I also wish to be no less than national in all the positions I may take, and whenever I take ground which others have thought, or may think, narrow, sectional, and dangerous to the Union, I hope to give a reason which will appear sufficient, at least to some, why I think differently.

And as this subject is no other than part and parcel of the larger general question of domestic slavery, I wish to make and to keep the distinction between the existing institution and the extension of it, so broad and so clear that no honest man can misunderstand me, and no dishonest one successfully misrepresent me.

In order to a clear understanding of what the Missouri Compromise is, a short history of the preceding kindred subjects will perhaps be proper.

When we established our independence, we did not own or claim the country to which this compromise applies. Indeed, strictly speaking, the Confederacy then owned no country at all; the States respectively owned the country within their limits, and some of them owned territory beyond their strict State limits. Virginia thus owned the Northwestern Territory—the country out of which the principal part of Ohio, all Indiana, all Illinois, all Michigan, and all Wisconsin have since been formed. She also owned (perhaps within her then limits) what has since been formed into the State of Kentucky. North Carolina thus owned what is now the State of Tennessee; and South Carolina and Georgia owned, in separate parts, what are now Mississippi and Alabama. Connecticut, I think, owned the little remaining part of Ohio, being the same where they now send Giddings to Congress, and beat all creation in making cheese.

These territories, together with the States themselves, constitute all the country over which the Confederacy then claimed any sort of jurisdiction. We were then living under the Articles of Confederation, which were superseded by the Constitution several years afterward. The question of ceding the territories to the General Government was set on foot. Mr. Jefferson, the author of the Declaration of Independence, and otherwise a chief actor in the Revolution; then a delegate in Congress; afterward, twice President; who was, is, and perhaps will continue to be, the most distinguished politician of our history; a Virginian by birth and continued residence, and withal a slaveholder—conceived the idea of taking that occasion to prevent slavery ever going into the Northwestern Territory. He prevailed on the Virginia legislature to adopt his views, and to cede the Territory, making the prohibition of slavery therein a condition of the deed.* Congress accepted the cession with the condition; and the first ordinance (which the acts of Congress were then called) for the government of the Territory provided that slavery should never be permitted therein. This is the famed "Ordinance of '87," so often spoken of.

Thenceforward for sixty-one years, and until, in 1848, the last scrap of this Territory came into the Union as the State of Wisconsin, all parties acted in quiet obedience to this ordinance. It is now what Jefferson foresaw and intended—the happy home of teeming millions of free, white, prosperous people, and no slave among them.

Thus, with the author of the Declaration of Independence, the policy of prohibiting slavery in new territory originated. Thus, away back to the Constitution, in the pure, fresh, free breath of the Revolution, the State of Virginia and the National Congress put that policy into practice. Thus, through more than sixty of the best years of the republic, did that policy steadily work to its great and beneficent end. And thus, in those five States, and in five millions of free, enterprising people, we have before us the rich fruits of this policy.

But now new light breaks upon us. Now Congress declares this ought never to have been, and the like of it must never be again. The sacred right of self-government is grossly violated by it. We even find some men who drew their first breath—and every other breath of their lives—under this very restriction, now live in dread of absolute suffocation if they should be restricted in the "sacred right" of taking slaves to Nebraska. That perfect liberty they sigh for—the liberty of making slaves of other people—Jefferson never thought of, their own fathers

* This was an error which Lincoln later corrected. The prohibition of slavery in ceding the ·Virginia territory was not a condition of the deed.—ED.

never thought of, they never thought of themselves, a year ago. How fortunate for them they did not sooner become sensible of their great misery! Oh, how difficult it is to treat with respect such assaults upon all we have ever really held sacred!

But to return to history. In 1803 we purchased what was then called Louisiana, of France. It included the present States of Louisiana, Arkansas, Missouri, and Iowa; also the Territory of Minnesota, and the present bone of contention, Kansas and Nebraska. Slavery already existed among the French at New Orleans, and to some extent at St. Louis. In 1812 Louisiana came into the Union as a slave state, without controversy. In 1818 or '19, Missouri showed signs of a wish to come in with slavery. This was resisted by Northern members of Congress; and thus began the first great slavery agitation in the nation. This controversy lasted several months, and became very angry and exciting—the House of Representatives voting steadily for the prohibition of slavery in Missouri, and the Senate voting as steadily against it. Threats of the breaking up of the Union were freely made, and the ablest public men of the day became seriously alarmed. At length a compromise was made, in which, as in all compromises, both sides yielded something. It was a law, passed on the 6th of March, 1820, providing that Missouri might come into the Union with slavery, but that in all the remaining part of the territory purchased of France, which lies north of thirty-six degrees and thirty minutes north latitude, slavery should never be permitted. This provision of law is the "Missouri Compromise." In excluding slavery north of the line, the same language is employed as in the ordinance of 1787. It directly applied to Iowa, Minnesota, and to the present bone of contention, Kansas and Nebraska. Whether there should or should not be slavery south of that line, nothing was said in the law. But Arkansas constituted the principal remaining part south of the line; and it has since been admitted as a slave State, without serious controversy. More recently, Iowa, north of the line, came in as

a free State without controversy. Still later, Minnesota, north
of the line, had a territorial organization without controversy.
Texas, principally south of the line, and west of Arkansas,
though originally within the purchase from France, had, in
1819, been traded off to Spain in our treaty for the acquisition
of Florida. It has thus become a part of Mexico. Mexico revolutionized and became independent of Spain. American citizens began settling rapidly with their slaves in the southern
part of Texas. Soon they revolutionized against Mexico, and
established an independent government of their own, adopting
a constitution with slavery, strongly resembling the constitutions of our slaves States. By still another rapid move, Texas,
claiming a boundary much further west than when we parted
with her in 1819, was brought back to the United States, and
admitted into the Union as a slave State.

Then there was little or no settlement in the northern part
of Texas, a considerable portion of which lay north of the
Missouri line; and in the resolutions admitting her into the
Union, the Missouri restriction was expressly extended westward across her territory. This was in 1845, only nine years ago.

Thus originated the Missouri Compromise; and thus has it
been respected down to 1845. And even four years later, in
1849, our distinguished senator, in a public address, held the
following language in relation to it:

The Missouri Compromise has been in practical operation for
about a quarter of a century, and has received the sanction and approbation of men of all parties in every section of the Union. It
has allayed all sectional jealousies and irritations growing out of
this vexed question, and harmonized and tranquilized the whole
country. It has given to Henry Clay, as its prominent champion,
the proud sobriquet of the "Great Pacificator," and by that title,
and for that service, his political friends had repeatedly appealed to
the people to rally under his standard as a presidential candidate,
as the man who had exhibited the patriotism and power to suppress
an unholy and treasonable agitation, and preserve the Union. He

was not aware that any man or any party, from any section of the Union, had ever urged as an objection to Mr. Clay that he was the great champion of the Missouri Compromise. On the contrary, the effort was made by the opponents of Mr. Clay to prove that he was not entitled to the exclusive merit of that great patriotic measure; and that the honor was equally due to others, as well as to him, for securing its adoption—that it had its origin in the hearts of all patriotic men, who desired to preserve and perpetuate the blessings of our glorious Union—an origin akin to that of the Constitution of the United States, conceived in the same spirit of fraternal affection, and calculated to remove forever the only danger which seemed to threaten, at some distant day, to sever the social bond of union. All the evidences of public opinion at that day seemed to indicate that this Compromise had been canonized in the hearts of the American people, as a sacred thing which no ruthless hand would ever be reckless enough to disturb.

I do not read this extract to involve Judge Douglas in an inconsistency. If he afterward thought he had been wrong, it was right for him to change. I bring this forward merely to show the high estimate placed on the Missouri Compromise by all parties up to so late as the year 1849.

But going back a little in point of time. Our war with Mexico broke out in 1846. When Congress was about adjourning that session, President Polk asked them to place two millions of dollars under his control, to be used by him in the recess, if found practicable and expedient, in negotiating a treaty of peace with Mexico, and acquiring some part of her territory. A bill was duly gotten up for the purpose, and was progressing swimmingly in the House of Representatives, when a member by the name of David Wilmot, a Democrat from Pennsylvania, moved as an amendment, "Provided, that in any territory thus acquired there shall never be slavery."

This is the origin of the far-famed Wilmot proviso. It created a great flutter; but it stuck like wax, was voted into the bill, and the bill passed with it through the House. The Senate, however, adjourned without final action on it, and so both appropriation and proviso were lost for the time. The war continued, and at the next session the President renewed his request for the appropriation, enlarging the amount, I think, to three millions. Again came the proviso, and defeated the measure. Congress adjourned again, and the war went on. In December, 1847, the new Congress assembled. I was in the lower House that term. The Wilmot proviso, or the principle of it, was constantly coming up in some shape or other, and I think I may venture to say I voted for it at least forty times during the short time I was there. The Senate, however, held it in check, and it never became a law. In the spring of 1848 a treaty of peace was made with Mexico, by which we obtained that portion of her country which now constitutes the Territories of New Mexico and Utah, and the present State of California. By this treaty the Wilmot proviso was defeated, in so far as it was intended to be a condition of the acquisition of territory. Its friends, however, were still determined to find some way to restrain slavery from getting into the new country. This new acquisition lay directly west of our old purchase from France, and extended west to the Pacific Ocean, and was so situated that if the Missouri line should be extended straight west, the new country would be divided by such extended line, leaving some north and some south of it. On Judge Douglas's motion, a bill, or provision of a bill, passed the Senate to so extend the Missouri line. The proviso men in the House, including myself, voted it down, because, by implication, it gave up the southern part to slavery, while we were bent on having it all free.

In the fall of 1848 the gold-mines were discovered in California. This attracted people to it with unprecedented rapidity, so that on, or soon after, the meeting of the new Congress in December, 1849, she already had a population of nearly a hundred thousand, had called a convention, formed a State Constitution excluding slavery, and was knocking for admission into the Union. The proviso men, of course, were for letting her in, but the Senate, always true to the other side, would not consent to her admission, and there California stood, kept out of the Union because she would not let slavery into her borders. Under all the circumstances, perhaps, this was not wrong. There were other points of dispute connected with the general question of slavery, which equally needed adjustment. The South clamored for a more efficient fugitive-slave law. The North clamored for the abolition of a peculiar species of slave trade in the District of Columbia, in connection with which, in view from the windows of the Capitol, a sort of Negro livery-stable, where droves of Negroes were collected, temporarily kept, and finally taken to Southern markets, precisely like droves of horses, had been openly maintained for fifty years. Utah and New Mexico needed territorial governments; and whether slavery should or should not be prohibited within them was another question. The indefinite western boundary of Texas was to be settled. She was a slave State, and consequently the farther west the slavery men could push her boundary, the more slave country they secured; and the farther east the slavery opponents could thrust the boundary back, the less slave ground was secured. Thus this was just as clearly a slavery question as any of the others.

These points all needed adjustment, and they were held up, perhaps wisely, to make them help adjust one another. The Union now, as in 1820, was thought to be in danger, and devotion to the Union rightfully inclined men to yield somewhat in points, where nothing else could have so inclined them. A compromise was finally effected. The South got their new fugitive-slave law, and the North got California (by far the best part of our acquisition from Mexico) as a free State. The South got a provision that New Mexico and Utah, when admitted as States, may come in with or without slavery as they may then choose; and the North got the slave trade abolished in the District of Columbia. The North got the western boundary of Texas thrown farther back eastward than the

South desired; but, in turn, they gave Texas ten millions of dollars with which to pay her old debts. This is the compromise of 1850.

Preceding the Presidential election of 1852, each of the great political parties, Democrats and Whigs, met in convention and adopted resolutions indorsing the compromise of '50, as a "finality," a final settlement, so far as these parties could make it so, of all slavery agitation. Previous to this, in 1851, the Illinois legislature had indorsed it.

During this long period of time, Nebraska had remained substantially an uninhabited country, but now emigration to and settlement within it began to take place. It is about one-third as large as the present United States, and its importance, so long overlooked, begins to come into view. The restriction of slavery by the Missouri Compromise directly applies to it —in fact was first made, and has since been maintained, expressly for it. In 1853, a bill to give it a territorial government passed the House of Representatives, and, in the hands of Judge Douglas, failed of passing only for want of time. This bill contained no repeal of the Missouri Compromise. Indeed, when it was assailed because it did not contain such repeal, Judge Douglas defended it in its existing form. On January 4, 1854, Judge Douglas introduces a new bill to give Nebraska territorial government. He accompanies this bill with a report, in which last he expressly recommends that the Missouri Compromise shall neither be affirmed nor repealed. Before long the bill is so modified as to make two territories instead of one, calling the southern one Kansas.

Also, about a month after the introduction of the bill, on the judge's own motion it is so amended as to declare the Missouri Compromise inoperative and void; and, substantially, that the people who go and settle there may establish slavery, or exclude it, as they may see fit. In this shape the bill passed both branches of Congress and became a law.*

* It was signed by President Pierce on May 30, 1854.

This is the repeal of the Missouri Compromise. The foregoing history may not be precisely accurate in every particular, but I am sure it is sufficiently so for all the use I shall attempt to make of it, and in it we have before us the chief material enabling us to judge correctly whether the repeal of the Missouri Compromise is right or wrong. I think, and shall try to show, that it is wrong—wrong in its direct effect, letting slavery into Kansas and Nebraska, and wrong in its prospective principle, allowing it to spread to every other part of the wide world where men can be found inclined to take it.

This declared indifference, but, as I must think, covert real zeal, for the spread of slavery, I cannot but hate. I hate it because of the monstrous injustice of slavery itself. I hate it because it deprives our republican example of its just influence in the world; enables the enemies of free institutions with plausibility to taunt us as hypocrites; causes the real friends of freedom to doubt our sincerity; and especially because it forces so many good men among ourselves into an open war with the very fundamental principles of civil liberty, criticizing the Declaration of Independence, and insisting that there is no right principle of action but self-interest.

Before proceeding let me say that I think I have no prejudice against the Southern people. They are just what we would be in their situation. If slavery did not now exist among them, they would not introduce it. If it did now exist among us, we should not instantly give it up. This I believe of the masses North and South. Doubtless there are individuals on both sides who would not hold slaves under any circumstances, and others who would gladly introduce slavery anew if it were out of existence. We know that some Southern men do free their slaves, go North and become tip-top Abolitionists, while some Northern ones go South and become most cruel slave-masters.

When Southern people tell us they are no more responsible for the origin of slavery than we are, I acknowledge the fact.

When it is said that the institution exists, and that it is very difficult to get rid of it in any satisfactory way, I can understand and appreciate the saying. I surely will not blame them for not doing what I should not know how to do myself. If all earthly power were given me, I should not know what to do as to the existing institution. My first impulse would be to free all the slaves, and send them to Liberia, to their own native land. But a moment's reflection would convince me that whatever of high hope (as I think there is) there may be in this in the long run, its sudden execution is impossible. If they were all landed there in a day, they would all perish in the next ten days; and there are not surplus shipping and surplus money enough to carry them there in many times ten days. What then? Free them all, and keep them among us as underlings? Is it quite certain that this betters their condition? I think I would not hold one in slavery at any rate, yet the point is not clear enough for me to denounce people upon. What next? Free them, and make them politically and socially our equals. My own feelings will not admit of this, and if mine would, we well know that those of the great mass of whites will not. Whether this feeling accords with justice and sound judgment is not the sole question, if indeed it is any part of it. A universal feeling, whether well or ill founded, cannot be safely disregarded. We cannot then make them equals. It does seem to me that systems of gradual emancipation might be adopted, but for their tardiness in this I will not undertake to judge our brethren of the South.

When they remind us of their constitutional rights, I acknowledge them—not grudgingly, but fully and fairly; and I would give them any legislation for the reclaiming of their fugitives which should not in its stringency be more likely to carry a free man into slavery than our ordinary criminal laws are to hang an innocent one.

But all this, to my judgment, furnishes no more excuse for permitting slavery to go into our own free territory than it would for reviving the African slave trade by law. The law which forbids the bringing of slaves from Africa, and that which has so long forbidden the taking of them into Nebraska, can hardly be distinguished on any moral principle, and the repeal of the former could find quite as plausible excuses as that of the latter.

The arguments by which the repeal of the Missouri Compromise is sought to be justified are these: First. That the Nebraska country needed a territorial government. Second. That in various ways the public had repudiated that compromise and demanded the repeal, and therefore should not now complain of it. And, lastly, That the repeal establishes a principle which is intrinsically right.

I will attempt an answer to each of them in its turn. First, then. If that country was in need of a territorial organization, could it not have had it as well without as with a repeal? Iowa and Minnesota, to both of which the Missouri restriction applied, had, without its repeal, each in succession, territorial organizations. And even the year before, a bill for Nebraska itself was within an ace of passing without the repealing clause, and this in the hands of the same men who are now the champions of repeal. Why no necessity then for repeal? But still later, when this very bill was first brought in, it contained no repeal. But, say they, because the people had demanded, or rather commanded, the repeal, the repeal was to accompany the organization whenever that should occur.

Now, I deny that the public ever demanded any such thing —ever repudiated the Missouri Compromise, ever commanded its repeal. I deny it, and call for the proof. It is not contended, I believe, that any such command has ever been given in express terms. It is only said that it was done in principle. The support of the Wilmot proviso is the first fact mentioned to prove that the Missouri restriction was repudiated in principle, and the second is the refusal to extend the Missouri line over the country acquired from Mexico. These are near enough

alike to be treated together. The one was to exclude the
chances of slavery from the whole new acquisition by the
lump, and the other was to reject a division of it, by which
one half was to be given up to those chances. Now, whether
this was a repudiation of the Missouri line in principle depends upon whether the Missouri law contained any principle
requiring the line to be extended over the country acquired
from Mexico. I contend it did not. I insist that it contained
no general principle, but that it was, in every sense, specific.
That its terms limit it to the country purchased from France
is undenied and undeniable. It could have no principle beyond
the intention of those who made it. They did not intend to
extend the line to country which they did not own. If they
intended to extend it in the event of acquiring additional
territory, why did they not say so? It was just as easy to say
that "in all the country west of the Mississippi which we
now own, or may hereafter acquire, there shall never be
slavery," as to say what they did say; and they would have said
it if they had meant it. An intention to extend the law is not
only not mentioned in the law, but is not mentioned in any
contemporaneous history. Both the law itself, and the history
of the times, are a blank as to any principle of extension; and
by neither the known rules of construing statutes and contracts, nor by common sense, can such principle be inferred.

Another fact showing the specific character of the Missouri
law—showing that it intended no more than it expressed,
showing that the line was not intended as a universal dividing
line between free and slave territory, present and prospective,
north of which slavery could never go—is the fact that by that
very law Missouri came in as a slave State, north of the line.
If that law contained any prospective principle, the whole law
must be looked to in order to ascertain what the principle
was. And by this rule the South could fairly contend that
inasmuch as they got one slave State north of the line at the
inception of the law, they have the right to have another given

them north of it occasionally, now and then, in the indefinite westward extension of the line. This demonstrates the absurdity of attempting to deduce a prospective principle from the Missouri Compromise line.

When we voted for the Wilmot proviso we were voting to keep slavery out of the whole Mexican acquisition, and little did we think we were thereby voting to let it into Nebraska, lying several hundred miles distant. When we voted against extending the Missouri line, little did we think we were voting to destroy the old line, then of near thirty years' standing.

To argue that we thus repudiated the Missouri Compromise is no less absurd than it would be to argue that because we have so far forborne to acquire Cuba, we have thereby, in principle, repudiated our former acquisitions and determined to throw them out of the Union. No less absurd than it would be to say that because I may have refused to build an addition to my house, I thereby have decided to destroy the existing house! And if I catch you setting fire to my house, you will turn upon me and say I instructed you to do it!

The most conclusive argument, however, that while for the Wilmot proviso, and while voting against the extension of the Missouri line, we never thought of disturbing the original Missouri Compromise, is found in the fact that there was then, and still is, an unorganized tract of fine country, nearly as large as the State of Missouri, lying immediately west of Arkansas and south of the Missouri Compromise line, and that we never attempted to prohibit slavery as to it. I wish particular attention to this: It adjoins the original Missouri Compromise line by its northern boundary, and consequently is part of the country into which by implication slavery was permitted to go by that compromise. There it has lain open ever since, and there it still lies, and yet no effort has been made at any time to wrest it from the South. In all our struggles to prohibit slavery within our Mexican acquisitions, we never so much as lifted a finger to prohibit it as to this tract. Is not this entirely conclusive that at all times we have held the Missouri Compromise as a sacred thing, even when against ourselves as well as when for us?

Senator Douglas sometimes says the Missouri line itself was in principle only an extension of the line of the Ordinance of '87—that is to say, an extension of the Ohio River. I think this is weak enough on its face. I will remark, however, that, as a glance at the map will show, the Missouri line is a long way farther south than the Ohio, and that if our senator in proposing his extension had stuck to the principle of jogging southward, perhaps it might not have been voted down so readily.

But next it is said that the compromises of '50, and the ratification of them by both political parties in '52, established a new principle which required the repeal of the Missouri Compromise. This again I deny. I deny it, and demand the proof. I have already stated fully what the compromises of '50 are. That particular part of those measures from which the virtual repeal of the Missouri Compromise is sought to be inferred (for it is admitted they contain nothing about it in express terms) is the provision in the Utah and New Mexico laws which permits them when they seek admission into the Union as States to come in with or without slavery, as they shall then see fit. Now I insist this provision was made for Utah and New Mexico, and for no other place whatever. It had no more direct reference to Nebraska than it had to the territories of the moon. But, say they, it had reference to Nebraska in principle. Let us see. The North consented to this provision, not because they considered it right in itself, but because they were compensated—paid for it.

They at the same time got California into the Union as a free State. This was far the best part of all they had struggled for by the Wilmot proviso. They also got the area of slavery somewhat narrowed in the settlement of the boundary of

Texas. Also they got the slave trade abolished in the District of Columbia.

For all these desirable objects the North could afford to yield something; and they did yield to the South the Utah and New Mexico provision. I do not mean that the whole North, or even a majority, yielded, when the law passed; but enough yielded, when added to the vote of the South, to carry the measure. Nor can it be pretended that the principle of this arrangement requires us to permit the same provision to be applied to Nebraska, without any equivalent at all. Give us another free State; press the boundary of Texas still further back; and give us another step toward the destruction of slavery in the District, and you present us a similar case. But ask us not to repeat, for nothing, what you paid for in the first instance. If you wish the thing again, pay again. That is the principle of the compromises of '50, if, indeed, they had any principles beyond their specific terms—it was the system of equivalents.

Again, if Congress, at that time, intended that all future Territories, should, when admitted as States, come in with or without slavery, at their own option, why did it not say so? With such a universal provision, all know the bills could not have passed. Did they, then—could they—establish a principle contrary to their own intention? Still further, if they intended to establish the principle that, whenever Congress had control, it should be left to the people to do as they thought fit with slavery, why did they not authorize the people of the District of Columbia, at their option, to abolish slavery within their limits?

I personally know that this has not been left undone because it was unthought of. It was frequently spoken of by members of Congress, and by citizens of Washington, six years ago; and I heard no one express a doubt that a system of gradual emancipation, with compensation to owners, would meet the approbation of a large majority of the white people of the District. But without the action of Congress they could say nothing; and Congress said "No." In the measures of 1850, Congress had the subject of slavery in the District expressly in hand. If they were then establishing the principle of allowing the people to do as they please with slavery, why did they not apply the principle to that people?

Again, it is claimed that by the resolutions of the Illinois legislature, passed in 1851, the repeal of the Missouri Compromise was demanded. This I deny also. Whatever may be worked out by a criticism of the language of those resolutions, the people have never understood them as being any more than an indorsement of the compromises of 1850, and a release of our senators from voting for the Wilmot proviso. The whole people are living witnesses that this only was their view. Finally, it is asked, "If we did not mean to apply the Utah and New Mexico provision to all future territories, what did we mean when we, in 1852, indorsed the compromises of 1850?"

For myself I can answer this question most easily. I meant not to ask a repeal or modification of the fugitive-slave law. I meant not to ask for the abolition of slavery in the District of Columbia. I meant not to resist the admission of Utah and New Mexico, even should they ask to come in as slave States. I meant nothing about additional Territories, because, as I understood, we then had no Territory whose character as to slavery was not already settled. As to Nebraska, I regarded its character as being fixed by the Missouri Compromise for thirty years—as unalterably fixed as that of my own home in Illinois. As to new acquisitions, I said, "Sufficient unto the day is the evil thereof." When we make new acquisitions, we will, as heretofore, try to manage them somehow. That is my answer; that is what I meant and said; and I appeal to the people to say each for himself, whether that is not also the universal meaning of the free States.

And now, in turn, let me ask a few questions. If, by any or all these matters, the repeal of the Missouri Compromise was commanded, why was not the command sooner obeyed? Why was the repeal omitted in the Nebraska bill of 1853? Why was it omitted in the original bill of 1854? Why in the accompanying report was such a repeal characterized as a departure from the course pursued in 1850? and its continued omission recommended?

I am aware Judge Douglas now argues that the subsequent express repeal is no substantial alteration of the bill. This argument seems wonderful to me. It is as if one should argue that white and black are not different. He admits, however, that there is a literal change in the bill, and that he made the change in deference to other senators who would not support the bill without. This proves that those other senators thought the change a substantial one, and that the judge thought their opinions worth deferring to. His own opinions, therefore, seem not to rest on a very firm basis, even in his own mind; and I suppose the world believes, and will continue to believe, that precisely on the substance of that change this whole agitation has arisen.

I conclude, then, that the public never demanded the repeal of the Missouri Compromise.

I now come to consider whether the appeal, with its avowed principles, is intrinsically right. I insist that it is not. Take the particular case. A controversy had arisen between the advocates and opponents of slavery, in relation to its establishment within the country we had purchased of France. The southern, and then best, part of the purchase was already in as a slave State. The controversy was settled by also letting Missouri in as a slave State; but with the agreement that within all the remaining part of the purchase, north of a certain line, there should never be slavery. As to what was to be done with the remaining part south of the line, nothing was said; but perhaps the fair implication was, it should come in with slavery if it should so choose. The southern part, except a portion heretofore mentioned, afterward did come in with slavery, as the State of

Arkansas. All these many years, since 1820, the northern part had remained a wilderness. At length settlements began in it also. In due course Iowa came in as a free State, and Minnesota was given a territorial government, without removing the slavery restriction. Finally, the sole remaining part north of the line—Kansas and Nebraska—was to be organized; and it is proposed, and carried, to blot out the old dividing line of thirty-four years' standing, and to open the whole of that country to the introduction of slavery. Now this, to my mind, is manifestly unjust. After an angry and dangerous controversy, the parties made friends by dividing the bone of contention. The one party first appropriates her own share, beyond all power to be disturbed in the possession of it, and then seizes the share of the other party. It is as if two starving men had divided their only loaf; the one had hastily swallowed his half, and then grabbed the other's half just as he was putting it to his mouth.

Let me here drop the main argument, to notice what I consider rather an inferior matter. It is argued that slavery will not go to Kansas and Nebraska, in any event. This is a palliation, a lullaby. I have some hope that it will not; but let us not be too confident. As to climate, a glance at the map shows that there are five slave States—Delaware, Maryland, Virginia, Kentucky, and Missouri, and also the District of Columbia, all north of the Missouri Compromise line. The census returns of 1850 show that within these there are 867,276 slaves, being more than one-fourth of all the slaves in the nation.

It is not climate then, that will keep slavery out of these Territories. Is there anything in the peculiar nature of the country? Missouri adjoins these Territories by her entire western boundary, and slavery is already within every one of her western counties. I have even heard it said that there are more slaves in proportion to whites in the northwestern county of Missouri, than within any other county in the State. Slavery pressed entirely up to the old western boundary of the State, and when rather recently a part of that boundary at the north-west was moved out a little farther west, slavery followed on quite up to the new line. Now when the restriction is removed, what is to prevent it from going still farther? Climate will not, no peculiarity of the country will, nothing in nature will. Will the disposition of the people prevent it? Those nearest the scene are all in favor of the extension. The Yankees who are opposed to it may be most numerous; but, in military phrase, the battlefield is too far from their base of operations.

But it is said, there now is no law in Nebraska on the subject of slavery, and that, in such case, taking a slave there operates his freedom. That is good book-law, but is not the rule of actual practice. Whatever slavery is it has been first introduced without law. The oldest laws we find concerning it are not laws introducing it, but regulating it as an already existing thing. A white man takes his slave to Nebraska now. Who will inform the Negro that he is free? Who will take him before court to test the question of his freedom? In ignorance of his legal emancipation he is kept chopping, splitting, and plowing. Others are brought, and move on in the same track. At last, if ever the time for voting comes on the question of slavery, the institution already, in fact, exists in the country, and cannot well be removed. The fact of its presence, and the difficulty of its removal, will carry the vote in its favor. Keep it out until a vote is taken, and a vote in favor of it cannot be got in any population of forty thousand on earth, who have been drawn together by the ordinary motives of emigration and settlement. To get slaves into the Territory simultaneously with the whites in the incipient stages of settlement is the precise stake played for and won in this Nebraska measure.

The question is asked us: "If slaves will go in notwithstanding the general principle of law liberates them, why would they not equally go in against positive statute law—go in, even if the Missouri restriction were maintained?" I answer, because it takes a much bolder man to venture in with his property in the latter case than in the former; because the positive congressional enactment is known to and respected by all, or nearly all, whereas the negative principle that no law is free law is not much known except among lawyers. We have some experience of this practical difference. In spite of the ordinance of '87, a few Negroes were brought into Illinois, and held in a state of quasi-slavery, not enough, however, to carry a vote of the people in favor of the institution when they came to form a constitution. But into the adjoining Missouri country, where there was no ordinance of '87—was no restriction, they were carried ten times, nay, a hundred times, as fast, and actually made a slave State. This is fact—naked fact.

Another lullaby argument is that taking slaves to new countries does not increase their number, does not make any one slave who would otherwise be free. There is some truth in this, and I am glad of it; but it is not wholly true. The African slave trade is not yet effectually suppressed; and if we make a reasonable deduction for the white people among us who are foreigners and the descendants of foreigners arriving here since 1808,* we shall find the increase of the black population outrunning that of the white to an extent unaccountable, except by supposing that some of them, too, have been coming from Africa. If this be so, the opening of new countries to the institution increases the demand for and augments the price of slaves, and so does, in fact, make slaves of freemen, by causing them to be brought from Africa and sold into bondage.

But however this may be, we know the opening of new countries to slavery tends to the perpetuation of the institution, and so does keep men in slavery who would otherwise be free. This result we do not feel like favoring, and we are under no legal obligation to suppress our feelings in this respect.

Equal justice to the South, it is said, requires us to consent to the extension of slavery to new countries. That is to say, inasmuch as you do not object to my taking my hog to

* The African slave trade had been forbidden by law in 1808.

Nebraska, therefore I must not object to you taking your slave. Now, I admit that this is perfectly logical, if there is no difference between hogs and Negroes. But while you thus require me to deny the humanity of the Negro, I wish to ask whether you of the South, yourselves, have ever been willing to do as much? It is kindly provided that of all those who come into the world only a small percentage are natural tyrants. That percentage is no larger in the slave States than in the free. The great majority South, as well as North, have human sympathies, of which they can no more divest themselves than they can of their sensibility to physical pain. These sympathies in the bosoms of the Southern people manifest, in many ways, their sense of the wrong of slavery, and their consciousness that, after all, there is humanity in the Negro. If they deny this, let me address them a few plain questions. In 1820 you joined the North, almost unanimously, in declaring the African slave trade piracy, and in annexing to it the punishment of death. Why did you do this? If you did not feel that it was wrong, why did you join in providing that men should be hung for it? The practice was no more than bringing wild Negroes from Africa to such as would buy them. But you never thought of hanging men for catching and selling wild horses, wild buffaloes, or wild bears.

Again, you have among you a sneaking individual of the class of native tyrants known as the "Slave Dealer." He watches your necessities, and crawls up to buy your slave, at a speculating price. If you cannot help it, you sell to him; but if you can help it, you drive him from your door. You despise him utterly. You do not recognize him as a friend, or even as an honest man. Your children must not play with his; they may rollick freely with the little Negroes, but not with the slave dealer's children. If you are obliged to deal with him, you try to get through the job without so much as touching him. It is common with you to join hands with men you meet, but with the slave dealer you avoid the ceremony—instinctively shrinking from the snaky contact. If he grows rich and retires from business, you still remember him, and still keep up the ban of non-intercourse upon him and his family. Now why is this? You do not so treat the man who deals in corn, cotton, or tobacco.

And yet again. There are in the United States and Territories, including the District of Columbia, 433,643 free blacks. At five hundred dollars per head they are worth over two hundred millions of dollars. How comes this vast amount of property to be running about without owners? We do not see free horses or free cattle running at large. How is this? All these free blacks are the descendants of slaves, or have been slaves themselves; and they would be slaves now but for something which has operated on their white owners, inducing them at vast pecuniary sacrifice to liberate them. What is that something? Is there any mistaking it? In all these cases it is your sense of justice and human sympathy continually telling you that the poor Negro has some natural right to himself—that those who deny it and make mere merchandise of him deserve kickings, contempt, and death.

And now why will you ask us to deny the humanity of the slave, and estimate him as only the equal of the hog? Why ask us to do what you will not do yourselves? Why ask us to do for nothing what two hundred millions of dollars could not induce you to do?

But one great argument in support of the repeal of the Missouri Compromise is still to come. That argument is "the sacred right of self-government." It seems our distinguished Senator has found great difficulty in getting his antagonists, even in the Senate, to meet him fairly on this argument. Some poet has said:

Fools rush in where angels fear to tread.

At the hazard of being thought one of the fools of this quotation, I meet that argument—I rush in—I take that bull by the horns. I trust I understand and truly estimate the right of self-government. My faith in the proposition that each man should do precisely as he pleases with all which is exclusively his own lies at the foundation of the sense of justice there is in me. I extend the principle to communities of men as well as to individuals. I so extend it because it is politically wise. as well as naturally just: politically wise in saving us from broils about matters which do not concern us. Here, or at Washington, I would not trouble myself with the oyster laws of Virginia, or the cranberry laws of Indiana. The doctrine of self-government is right—absolutely and eternally right—but it has no just application as here attempted. Or perhaps I should rather say that whether it has such application depends upon whether a Negro is not or is a man. If he is not a man, in that case he who is a man may as a matter of self-government do just what he pleases with him.

But if the Negro is a man, is it not to that extent a total destruction of self-government to say that he too shall not govern himself? When the white man governs himself, that is self-government; but when he governs himself and also governs another man, that is more than self-government—that is despotism. If the Negro is a man, why then my ancient faith teaches me that "all men are created equal," and that there can be no moral right in connection with one man's making a slave of another.

Judge Douglas frequently, with bitter irony and sarcasm, paraphrases our argument by saying: "The white people of Nebraska are good enough to govern themselves, but they are not good enough to govern a few miserable Negroes!"

Well! I doubt not that the people of Nebraska are and will continue to be as good as the average of people elsewhere. I do not say the contrary. What I do say is that no man is good enough to govern another man without that other's consent. I say this is the leading principle, the sheet-anchor of American republicanism. Our Declaration of Independence says:

We hold these truths to be self-evident: That all men are created equal; that they are endowed by their Creator with certain inalienable rights; that among these are life, liberty and the pursuit of happiness. That to secure these rights, governments are instituted among men, DERIVING THEIR JUST POWERS FROM THE CONSENT OF THE GOVERNED.

I have quoted so much at this time merely to show that, according to our ancient faith, the just powers of governments are derived from the consent of the governed. Now the relation of master and slave is *pro tanto* a total violation of this principle. The master not only governs the slave without his consent, but he governs him by a set of rules altogether different from those which he prescribes for himself. Allow all the governed an equal voice in the government, and that, and that only, is self-government.

Let it not be said I am contending for the establishment of political and social equality between the whites and blacks. I have already said the contrary. I am not combating the argument of necessity, arising from the fact that the blacks are already among us; but I am combating what is set up as moral argument for allowing them to be taken where they have never yet been—arguing against the extension of a bad thing, which, where it already exists, we must of necessity manage as we best can.

In support of his application of the doctrine of self-government, Senator Douglas has sought to bring to his aid the opinions and examples of our Revolutionary fathers. I am glad he has done this. I love the sentiments of those old-time men, and shall be most happy to abide by their opinions. He shows us that when it was in contemplation for the colonies to break off from Great Britain, and set up a new government for themselves, several of the States instructed their delegates to go for the measure, provided each State should be allowed to regulate its domestic concerns in its own way. I do not quote; but this is substance. This was right; I see nothing objectionable in it. I also think it probable that it had some reference to the existence of slavery among them. I will not deny that it had. But had it any reference to the carrying of slavery into new countries? That is the question, and we will let the fathers themselves answer it.

This same generation of men, and mostly the same individuals of the generation who declared this principle, who declared independence, who fought the war of the Revolution through, who afterward made the Constitution under which we still live– these same men passed the Ordinance of '87, declaring that slavery should never go to the Northwest Territory. I have no doubt Judge Douglas thinks they were very inconsistent in this. It is a question of discrimination between them and him. But there is not an inch of ground left for his claiming that their opinions, their example, their authority, are on his side in the controversy.

Again, is not Nebraska, while a Territory, a part of us? Do we not own the country? And if we surrender the control of it, do we not surrender the right of self-government? It is part of ourselves. If you say we shall not control it, because it is only part, the same is true of every other part; and when all the parts are gone, what has become of the whole? What is then left of us? What use for the General Government, when there is nothing left for it to govern?

But you say this question should be left to the people of Nebraska, because they are more particularly interested. If this be the rule, you must leave it to each individual to say for himself whether he will have slaves. What better moral right have thirty-one citizens of Nebraska to say that the thirty-second shall not hold slaves than the people of the thirty-one States have to say that slavery shall not go into the thirty-second State at all?

But if it is a sacred right for the people of Nebraska to take and hold slaves there, it is equally their sacred right to buy them where they can buy them cheapest; and that, undoubtedly, will be on the coast of Africa, provided you will consent not to hang them for going there to buy them. You must remove this restriction, too, from the sacred right of self-government. I am aware, you say, that taking slaves from the States to Nebraska does not make slaves of freemen; but the African slave trader can say just as much. He does not catch free Negroes and bring them here. He finds them already slaves in the hands of their black captors, and he honestly buys them at the rate of a red cotton handkerchief a head. This is very cheap, and it is a great abridgment of the sacred right of self-government to hang men for engaging in this profitable trade.

Another important objection to this application of the right of self-government is that it enables the first few to deprive the succeeding many of a free exercise of the right of self-government. The first few may get slavery in, and the subsequent many cannot easily get it out. How common is the remark now in the slave States, "If we were only clear of our slaves, how much better it would be for us." They are actually deprived of the privilege of governing themselves as they would, by the action of a very few in the beginning. The same thing was true of the whole nation at the time our Constitution was formed.

Whether slavery shall go into Nebraska, or other new Territories, is not a matter of exclusive concern to the people who may go there. The whole nation is interested that the best use shall be made of these Territories. We want them for homes of free white people. This they cannot be, to any considerable extent, if slavery shall be planted within them. Slave States are places for poor white people to remove from, not to remove to. New free States are the places for poor people to go to, and better their condition. For this use the nation needs these Territories.

Still further: there are constitutional relations between the slave and free States which are degrading to the latter. We are under legal obligations to catch and return their runaway slaves to them: a sort of dirty, disagreeable job, which, I believe, as a general rule, the slaveholders will not perform for one another. Then again, in the control of the government—the management of the partnership affairs—they have greatly the advantage of us. By the Constitution each State has two senators, each has a number of representatives in proportion to the number of its people, and each has a number of presidential electors equal to the whole number of its senators and representatives together. But in ascertaining the number of the people for this purpose, five slaves are counted as being equal to three whites. The slaves do not vote; they are only counted and so used as to swell the influence of the white people's votes. The practical effect of this is more aptly shown by a comparison of the States of South Carolina and Maine. South Carolina has six representatives, and so has Maine; South Carolina has eight presidential electors, and so has Maine. This is precise equality so far; and of course they are equal in senators, each having two. Thus in the control of the government the two States are equals precisely. But how are they in the number of their white people? Maine has 581,813, while South Carolina has 274,567; Maine has twice as many as South Carolina, and 32,679 over. Thus, each white man in South Carolina is more than the double of any man in Maine. This is all because South Carolina, besides her free people, has 384,984 slaves. The South Carolinian has precisely the same advantage over the white man in every other free State as well as in Maine. He is more than the double of any one of us in this crowd. The same advantage, but not to the same extent, is held by all the citizens of the slave States over those of the free; and it is an absolute truth, without an exception, that there is no voter in any slave State, but who has more legal power in the government than any voter in any free State. There is no instance of exact equality; and the disadvantage is against us the whole chapter through. This principle, in the aggregate, gives the slave States in the present Congress twenty additional representatives, being seven more than the whole majority by which they passed the Nebraska bill.

Now all this is manifestly unfair; yet I do not mention it to complain of it, in so far as it is already settled. It is in the Constitution, and I do not for that cause, or any other cause, propose to destroy, or alter, or disregard the Constitution. I stand to it, fairly, fully, and firmly.

But when I am told I must leave it altogether to other people to say whether new partners are to be bred up and brought into the firm, on the same degrading terms against me, I respectfully demur. I insist that whether I shall be a whole man, or only the half of one, in comparison with others, is a question in which I am somewhat concerned, and one which no other man can have a sacred right of deciding for me. If I am wrong in this—if it really be a sacred right of self-government in the man who shall go to Nebraska to decide whether he will be the equal of me or the double of me, then, after he shall have exercised that right, and thereby shall have reduced me to a still smaller fraction of a man than I already am, I should like for some gentleman, deeply skilled in the mysteries of sacred rights, to provide himself with a microscope, and peep about, and find out, if he can, what has become of my sacred rights. They will surely be too small for detection with the naked eye.

Finally, I insist that if there is anything which it is the duty of the whole people to never intrust to any hands but their own, that thing is the preservation and perpetuity of their own liberties and institutions. And if they shall think, as I do, that the extension of slavery endangers them more than any or all other causes, how recreant to themselves if they submit the question, and with it the fate of their country, to a mere handful of men bent only on self-interest. If this question of slavery extension were an insignificant one—one having no power to do harm—it might be shuffled aside in this way; and being, as it is, the great Behemoth of danger, shall the strong grip of the nation be loosened upon him, to intrust him to the hands of such feeble keepers?

I have done with this mighty argument of self-government. Go, sacred thing! Go in peace.

But Nebraska is urged as a great Union-saving measure. Well, I too go for saving the Union. Much as I hate slavery, I would consent to the extension of it rather than see the Union dissolved, just as I would consent to any great evil to avoid a greater one. But when I go to Union-saving, I must believe, at least, that the means I employ have some adaptation to the end. To my mind, Nebraska has no such adaptation.

It hath no relish of salvation in it.

It is an aggravation, rather, of the only one thing which ever endangers the Union. When it came upon us, all was peace and quiet. The nation was looking to the forming of new bonds of union, and a long course of peace and prosperity seemed to lie before us. In the whole range of possibility, there scarcely appears to me to have been anything out of which the slavery agitation could have been revived, except the very project of repealing the Missouri Compromise. Every inch of territory we owned already had a definite settlement of the slavery question, by which all parties were pledged to abide. Indeed, there was no uninhabited country on the continent which we could acquire, if we except some extreme northern regions which are wholly out of the question.

In this state of affairs the Genius of Discord himself could scarcely have invented a way of again setting us by the ears but by turning back and destroying the peace measures of the past. The counsels of that Genius seem to have prevailed. The Missouri Compromise was repealed; and here we are in the midst of a new slavery agitation, such, I think, as we have never seen before. Who is responsible for this? Is it those who resist the measure, or those who causelessly brought it forward and pressed it through, having reason to know, and in fact knowing, it must and would be so resisted? It could not but be expected by its author that it would be looked upon as a measure for the extension of slavery, aggravated by a gross breach of faith.

Argue as you will and long as you will, this is the naked front and aspect of the measure. And in this aspect it could not but produce agitation. Slavery is founded in the selfishness of man's nature—opposition to it in his love of justice. These principles are an eternal antagonism, and when brought into collision so fiercely as slavery extension brings them, shocks and throes and convulsions must ceaselessly follow. Repeal the Missouri Compromise, repeal all compromises, repeal the Declaration of Independence, repeal all past history, you still cannot repeal human nature. It still will be the abundance of man's heart that slavery extension is wrong, and out of the abundance of his heart his mouth will continue to speak.

The structure, too, of the Nebraska bill is very peculiar. The people are to decide the question of slavery for themselves; but when they are to decide, or how they are to decide, or whether, when the question is once decided, it is to remain so or is to be subject to an indefinite succession of new trials, the law does not say. Is it to be decided by the first dozen settlers who arrive there, or is it to await the arrival of a hundred? Is it to be decided by a vote of the people or a vote of the legislature, or, indeed, by a vote of any sort? To these questions the law gives no answer. There is a mystery about this; for when a member proposed to give the legislature express authority to exclude slavery, it was hooted down by the friends of the bill. This fact is worth remembering. Some Yankees in the East are sending emigrants to Nebraska* to ex-

* An emigrant aid society had been established in New England to give financial assistance to Free State men who were willing to settle in the Kansas-Nebraska Territory.

clude slavery from it; and, so far as I can judge, they expect
the question to be decided by voting in some way or other.
But the Missourians are awake, too. They are within a stone's
throw of the contested ground. They hold meetings and pass
resolutions, in which not the slightest allusion to voting is
made. They resolve that slavery already exists in the Territory;
that more shall go there; that they, remaining in Missouri,
will protect it, and that Abolitionists shall be hung or driven
away. Through all this bowie-knives and six-shooters are seen
plainly enough, but never a glimpse of the ballot-box.

And, really, what is the result of all this? Each party within
having numerous and determined backers without, is it not
probable that the contest will come to blows and bloodshed?
Could there be a more apt invention to bring about collision
and violence on the slavery question than this Nebraska project is? I do not charge or believe that such was intended by
Congress; but if they had literally formed a ring and placed
champions within it to fight out the controversy, the fight
could be no more likely to come off than it is. And if this
fight should begin, is it likely to take a very peaceful, Union-
saving turn? Will not the first drop of blood so shed be the
real knell of the Union?

The Missouri Compromise ought to be restored. For the
sake of the Union, it ought to be restored. We ought to elect
a House of Representatives which will vote its restoration. If
by any means we omit to do this, what follows? Slavery may
or may not be established in Nebraska. But whether it be or
not, we shall have repudiated—discarded from the councils of
the nation—the spirit of compromise; for who, after this, will
ever trust in national compromise? The spirit of mutual concession—that spirit which first gave us the Constitution, and
which has thrice saved the Union—we shall have strangled
and cast from us forever. And what shall we have in lieu of
it? The South flushed with triumph and tempted to excess;
the North, betrayed as they believe, brooding on wrong and

burning for revenge. One side will provoke, the other resent. The one will taunt, the other defy; one agresses, the other re- taliates. Already a few in the North defy all constitutional restraints, resist the execution of the fugitive-slave law, and even menace the institution of slavery in the States where it exists. Already a few in the South claim the constitutional right to take and to hold slaves in the free States—demand the revival of the slave trade—and demand a treaty with Great Britain by which fugitive slaves may be reclaimed from Can- ada. As yet they are but few on either side. It is a grave ques- tion for lovers of the Union, whether the final destruction of the Missouri Compromise, and with it the spirit of all com- promise, will or will not embolden and embitter each of these, and fatally increase the number of both.

But restore the compromise, and what then? We thereby restore the national faith, the national confidence, the national feeling of brotherhood. We thereby reinstate the spirit of con- cession and compromise, that spirit which has never failed us in past perils, and which may be safely trusted for all the future. The South ought to join in doing this. The peace of the nation is as dear to them as to us. In memories of the past and hopes of the future, they share as largely as we. It would be on their part a great act—great in its spirit, and great in its effect. It would be worth to the nation a hundred years' purchase of peace and prosperity. And what of sacrifice would they make? They only surrender to us what they gave us for a consideration long, long ago; what they have not now asked for, struggled or cared for; what has been thrust upon them, not less to their astonishment than to ours.

But it is said we cannot restore it; that though we elect every member of the Lower House, the Senate is still against us. It is quite true that of the senators who passed the Nebraska bill, a majority of the whole Senate will retain their seats in spite of the elections of this and the next year. But if at these elections their several constituencies shall clearly express their will against Nebraska, will these senators disregard their will? Will they neither obey nor make room for those who will?

But even if we fail to technically restore the compromise, it is still a great point to carry a popular vote in favor of the restoration. The moral weight of such a vote cannot be estimated too highly. The authors of Nebraska are not at all satisfied with the destruction of the compromise—an indorsement of this principle they proclaim to be the great object. With them, Nebraska alone is a small matter—to establish a principle for future use is what they particularly desire.

The future use is to be the planting of slavery wherever in the wide world local and unorganized opposition cannot prevent it. Now, if you wish to give them this indorsement, if you wish to establish this principle, do so. I shall regret it, but it is your right. On the contrary, if you are opposed to the principle—intend to give it no such indorsement—let no wheedling, no sophistry, divert you from throwing a direct vote against it.

Some men, mostly Whigs, who condemn the repeal of the Missouri Compromise, nevertheless hesitate to go for its restoration, lest they be thrown in company with the Abolitionists. Will they allow me, as an old Whig, to tell them, good-humoredly, that I think this is very silly? Stand with anybody that stands right. Stand with him while he is right, and part with him when he goes wrong. Stand with the Abolitionist in restoring the Missouri Compromise, and stand against him when he attempts to repeal the fugitive-slave law. In the latter case you stand with the Southern disunionist. What of that? you are still right. In both cases you are right. In both cases you expose the dangerous extremes. In both you stand on middle ground, and hold the ship level and steady. In both you are national, and nothing less than national. This is the good old Whig ground. To desert such ground because of any company, is to be less than a Whig—less than a man—less than an American.

I particularly object to the new position which the avowed principle of this Nebraska law gives to slavery in the body politic. I object to it because it assumes that there can be moral right in the enslaving of one man by another. I object to it as a dangerous dalliance for a free people—a sad evidence that, feeling prosperity, we forget right; that liberty, as a principle, we have ceased to revere. I object to it because the fathers of the republic eschewed and rejected it. The argument of "necessity" was the only argument they ever admitted in favor of slavery; and so far, and so far only, as it carried them did they ever go. They found the institution existing among us, which they could not help, and they cast blame upon the British king for having permitted its introduction. Before the Constitution they prohibited its introduction into the Northwestern Territory, the only country we owned then free from it. At the framing and adoption of the Constitution, they forbore to so much as mention the word "slave" or "slavery" in the whole instrument. In the provision for the recovery of fugitives, the slave is spoken of as a "person held to service or labor." In that prohibiting the abolition of the African slave trade for twenty years, that trade is spoken of as "the migration or importation of such persons as any of the States now existing shall think proper to admit," etc. These are the only provisions alluding to slavery. Thus the thing is hid away in the Constitution, just as an afflicted man hides away a wen or cancer which he dares not cut out at once, lest he bleed to death—with the promise, nevertheless, that the cutting may begin at a certain time. Less than this our fathers could not do, and more they would not do. Necessity drove them so far, and further they would not go. But this is not all. The earliest Congress under the Constitution took the same view of slavery. They hedged and hemmed it in to the narrowest limits of necessity.

In 1794 they prohibited an outgoing slave trade—that is, the taking of slaves from the United States to sell. In 1798 they prohibited the bringing of slaves from Africa into the Mississippi Territory, this Territory then comprising what are now the States of Mississippi and Alabama. This was ten years before they had the authority to do the same thing as to the States existing at the adoption of the Constitution. In 1800 they prohibited American citizens from trading in slaves between foreign countries, as, for instance, from Africa to Brazil. In 1803 they passed a law in aid of one or two slave-State laws, in restraint of the internal slave trade. In 1807, in apparent hot haste, they passed the law, nearly a year in advance to take effect the first day of 1808, the very first day the Constitution would permit—prohibiting the African slave trade by heavy pecuniary and corporal penalties. In 1820, finding these provisions ineffectual, they declared the slave trade piracy, and annexed to it the extreme penalty of death.* While all this was passing in the General Government, five or six of the original slave States had adopted systems of gradual emancipation, by which the institution was rapidly becoming extinct within their limits. Thus we see that the plain, unmistakable spirit of that age toward slavery was hostility to the principle and toleration only by necessity.

But now it is to be transformed into a "sacred right." Nebraska brings it forth, places it on the highroad to extension and perpetuity, and with a pat on its back says to it, "Go, and God speed you." Henceforth it is to be the chief jewel of the nation—the very figurehead of the ship of state. Little by little, but steadily as man's march to the grave, we have been giving up the old for the new faith. Near eighty years ago we began by declaring that all men are created equal; but now from that beginning we have run down to the other declaration, that for some men to enslave others is a "sacred right of self-government." These principles cannot stand together. They are as opposite as God and Mammon; and whoever

* The only man actually put to death under this law was Nathaniel Gordon, who was hanged in 1862 during Lincoln's administration.

holds to the one must despise the other. When Pettit,* in connection with his support of the Nebraska bill, called the Declaration of Independence "a self-evident lie," he only did what consistency and candor require all other Nebraska men to do. Of the forty-odd Nebraska senators who sat present and heard him, no one rebuked him. Nor am I apprised that any Nebraska newspaper, or any Nebraska orator, in the whole nation has ever yet rebuked him. If this had been said among Marion's men, Southerners though they were, what would have become of the man who said it? If this had been said to the men who captured André, the man who said it would probably have been hung sooner than André was. If it had been said in old Independence Hall seventy-eight years ago, the very doorkeeper would have throttled the man and thrust him into the street. Let no one be deceived. The spirit of seventy-six and the spirit of Nebraska are utter antagonisms; and the former is being rapidly displaced by the latter.

Fellow-countrymen, Americans, South as well as North, shall we make no effort to arrest this? Already the liberal party throughout the world express the apprehension "that the one retrograde institution in America is undermining the principles of progress, and fatally violating the noblest political system the world ever saw." This is not the taunt of enemies, but the warning of friends. Is it quite safe to disregard it—to despise it? Is there no danger to liberty itself in discarding the earliest practice and first precept of our ancient faith? In our greedy chase to make profit of the Negro, let us beware lest we "cancel and tear in pieces" even the white man's charter of freedom.

Our republican robe is soiled and trailed in the dust. Let us repurify it. Let us turn and wash it white in the spirit, if not the blood, of the Revolution. Let us turn slavery from its claims of "moral right" back upon its existing legal rights and its argument of "necessity." Let us return it to the position

* John Pettit, Senator from Indiana.

our fathers gave it, and there let it rest in peace. Let us re-adopt the Declaration of Independence, and with it the practices and policy which harmonize with it. Let North and South—let all Americans—let all lovers of liberty everywhere join in the great and good work. If we do this, we shall not only have saved the Union, but we shall have so saved it as to make and to keep it forever worthy of the saving. We shall have so saved it that the succeeding millions of free, happy people, the world over, shall rise up and call us blessed to the latest generations.

At Springfield, twelve days ago, where I had spoken substantially as I have here, Judge Douglas replied to me; and as he is to reply to me here, I shall attempt to anticipate him by noticing some of the points he made there. He commenced by stating I had assumed all the way through that the principle of the Nebraska bill would have the effect of extending slavery. He denied that this was intended, or that this effect would follow.

I will not reopen the argument upon this point. That such was the intention the world believed at the start, and will continue to believe. This was the countenance of the thing, and both friends and enemies instantly recognized it as such. That countenance cannot now be changed by argument. You can as easily argue the color out of the Negro's skin. Like the "bloody hand," you may wash it and wash it, the red witness of guilt still sticks and stares horribly at you.

Next he says that congressional intervention never prevented slavery anywhere; that it did not prevent it in the Northwestern Territory, nor in Illinois; that, in fact, Illinois came into the Union as a slave State; that the principle of the Nebraska bill expelled it from Illinois, from several old States, from everywhere.

Now this is mere quibbling all the way through. If the Ordinance of '87 did not keep slavery out of the Northwest Territory, how happens it that the northwest shore of the Ohio

River is entirely free from it, while the southeast shore, less than a mile distant, along nearly the whole length of the river, is entirely covered with it?

If that ordinance did not keep it out of Illinois, what was it that made the difference between Illinois and Missouri? They lie side by side, the Mississippi River only dividing them while their early settlements were within the same latitude. Between 1810 and 1820, the number of slaves in Missouri increased 7211, while in Illinois in the same ten years they decreased 51. This appears by the census returns. During nearly all of that ten years both were Territories, not States. During this time the ordinance forbade slavery to go into Illinois, and nothing forbade it to go into Missouri. It did go into Missouri, and did not go into Illinois. That is the fact. Can any one doubt as to the reason of it? But he says Illinois came into the Union as a slave State. Silence, perhaps, would be the best answer to this flat contradiction of the known history of the country. What are the facts upon which this bold assertion is based? When we first acquired the country, as far back as 1787, there were some slaves within it held by the French inhabitants of Kaskaskia. The territorial legislation admitted a few Negroes from the slave States as indentured servants. One year after the adoption of the first State constitution, the whole number of them was—what do you think? Just one hundred and seventeen, while the aggregate free population was 55,094—about four hundred and seventy to one. Upon this state of facts the people framed their constitution prohibiting the further introduction of slavery, with a sort of guarantee to the owners of the few indentured servants, giving freedom to their children to be born thereafter, and making no mention whatever of any supposed slave for life. Out of this small matter the judge manufactures his argument that Illinois came into the Union as a slave State. Let the facts be the answer to the argument.

The principles of the Nebraska bill, he says, expelled slavery from Illinois. The principle of that bill first planted it here—that is, it first came because there was no law to prevent it, first came before we owned the country; and finding it here, and having the Ordinance of '87 to prevent its increasing, our people struggled along, and finally got rid of it as best they could.

But the principle of the Nebraska bill abolished slavery in several of the old States. Well, it is true that several of the old States, in the last quarter of the last century, did adopt systems of gradual emancipation by which the institution has finally become extinct within their limits; but it may or may not be true that the principle of the Nebraska bill was the cause that led to the adoption of these measures. It is now more than fifty years since the last of these States adopted its system of emancipation.

If the Nebraska bill is the real author of the benevolent works, it is rather deplorable that it has for so long a time ceased working altogether. Is there not some reason to suspect that it was the principle of the Revolution, and not the principle of the Nebraska bill, that led to emancipation in these old States? Leave it to the people of these old emancipating States, and I am quite certain they will decide that neither that nor any other good thing ever did or ever will come of the Nebraska bill.

In the course of my main argument, Judge Douglas interrupted me to say that the principle of the Nebraska bill was very old; that it originated when God made man, and placed good and evil before him, allowing him to choose for himself, being responsible for the choice he should make. At the time I thought this was merely playful, and I answered it accordingly. But in his reply to me he renewed it as a serious argument. In seriousness, then, the facts of this proposition are not true as stated. God did not place good and evil before man, telling him to make his choice. On the contrary, he did tell him there was one tree of the fruit of which he should not eat, upon pain of certain death. I should scarcely wish so strong a prohibition against slavery in Nebraska.

But this argument strikes me as not a little remarkable in another particular—in its strong resemblance to the old argument for the "divine right of kings." By the latter, the king is to do just as he pleases with his white subjects, being responsible to God alone. By the former, the white man is to do just as he pleases with his black slaves, being responsible to God alone. The two things are precisely alike, and it is but natural that they should find similar arguments to sustain them.*

I had argued that the application of the principle of self-government, as contended for, would require the revival of the African slave trade; that no argument could be made in favor of a man's right to take slaves to Nebraska, which could not be equally well made in favor of his right to bring them from the coast of Africa. The judge replied that the Constitution requires the suppression of the foreign slave trade, but does not require the prohibition of slavery in the Territories. That is a mistake in point of fact. The Constitution does not require the action of Congress in either case, and it does authorize it in both. And so there is still no difference between the cases.

In regard to what I have said of the advantage the slave States have over the free in the matter of representation, the judge replied that we in the free States count five free Negroes as five white people, while in the slave States they count five slaves as three whites only; and that the advantage, at last, was on the side of the free States.

Now, in the slave States they count free Negroes just as we do; and it so happens that, besides their slaves, they have as many free Negroes as we have, and thirty thousand over. Thus their free Negroes more than balance ours; and their advan-

* This is the birth of one of the major themes to be used by Lincoln in his formal debates with Douglas.

tage over us, in consequence of their slaves, still remains as I stated it.

In reply to my argument that the compromise measures of 1850 were a system of equivalents, and that the provisions of no one of them could fairly be carried to other subjects without its corresponding equivalent being carried with it, the judge denied outright that these measures had any connection with or dependence upon each other. This is mere desperation. If they had no connection, why are they always spoken of in connection? Why has he so spoken of them a thousand times? Why has he constantly called them a series of measures? Why does everybody call them a compromise? Why was California kept out of the Union six or seven months,* if it was not because of its connection with the other measures? Webster's leading definition of the verb "to compromise" is "to adjust and settle a difference, by mutual agreement, with concessions of claims by the parties." This conveys precisely the popular understanding of the word "compromise."

We knew, before the judge told us, that these measures passed separately, and in distinct bills, and that no two of them were passed by the votes of precisely the same members. But we also know, and so does he know, that no one of them could have passed both branches of Congress but for the understanding that the others were to pass also. Upon this understanding, each got votes which it could have got in no other way. It is this fact which gives to the measures their true character; and it is the universal knowledge of this fact that has given them the name of "compromises," so expressive of that true character.

I had asked "if, in carrying the Utah and New Mexico laws

* California's application for admission to the Union as a free state was the issue that had brought on the series of compromises in 1850, in which the South was given certain privileges in exchange for letting California be added to the free-state group. Among these privileges was the right of Utah and New Mexico to enter as slave or free states when either was ready to be admitted to the Union.

to Nebraska, you could clear away other objection, how could you leave Nebraska 'perfectly free' to introduce slavery before she forms a constitution during her territorial government, while the Utah and New Mexico laws only authorize it when they form constitutions and are admitted into the Union?" To this Judge Douglas answered that the Utah and New Mexico laws also authorized it before; and to prove this he read from one of their laws, as follows: "That the legislative power of said territory shall extend to all rightful subjects of legislation, consistent with the Constitution of the United States and the provisions of this act."

Now it is perceived from the reading of this that there is nothing express upon this subject, but that the authority is sought to be implied merely for the general provision of "all rightful subjects of legislation." In reply to this I insist, as a legal rule of construction, as well as the plain, popular view of the matter, that the express provisions for Utah and New Mexico coming in with slavery, if they choose, when they shall form constitutions, is an exclusion of all implied authority on the same subject; that Congress, having the subject distinctly in their minds when they made the express provision, they therein expressed their whole meaning on that subject.

The judge rather insinuated that I had found it convenient to forget the Washington territorial law passed in 1853. This was a division of Oregon organizing the northern part as the Territory of Washington. He asserted that by this act the Ordinance of '87, theretofore existing in Oregon, was repealed; that nearly all the members of Congress voted for it, beginning in the House of Representatives with Charles Allen of Massachusetts, and ending with Richard Yates of Illinois; and that he could not understand how those who now oppose the Nebraska bill so voted there, unless it was because it was then too soon after both the great political parties had ratified the compromises of 1850, and the ratification therefore was too fresh to be then repudiated.

Now I had seen the Washington act before, and I have carefully examined it since; and I aver that there is no repeal of the Ordinance of '87, or of any prohibition of slavery, in it. In express terms, there is absolutely nothing in the whole law upon the subject—in fact, nothing to lead a reader to think of the subject. To my judgment it is equally free from everything from which repeal can be legally implied; but however this may be, are men now to be entrapped by a legal implication, extracted from covert language, introduced perhaps for the very purpose of entrapping them? I sincerely wish every man could read this law quite through, carefully watching every sentence and every line for a repeal of the Ordinance of '87, or anything equivalent to it.

Another point on the Washington act. If it was intended to be modeled after the Utah and New Mexico acts, as Judge Douglas insists, why was it not inserted in it, as in them, that Washington was to come in with or without slavery as she may choose at the adoption of her constitution? It has no such provision in it; and I defy the ingenuity of man to give a reason for the omission, other than that it was not intended to follow the Utah and New Mexico laws in regard to the question of slavery.

The Washington act not only differs vitally from the Utah and New Mexico acts, but the Nebraska act differs vitally from both. By the latter act the people are left "perfectly free" to regulate their own domestic concerns, etc.; but in all the former, all their laws are to be submitted to Congress, and if disapproved are to be null. The Washington act goes even further; it absolutely prohibits the territorial legislature, by very strong and guarded language, from establishing banks or borrowing money on the faith of the Territory. Is this the sacred right of self-government we hear vaunted so much? No, sir; the Nebraska bill finds no model in the acts of '50 or the Washington act. It finds no model in any law from Adam till today. As Phillips says of Napoleon, the Nebraska act is grand, gloomy and peculiar, wrapped in the solitude of its own originality, without a model and without a shadow upon the earth.

In the course of his reply Senator Douglas remarked in substance that he had always considered this government was made for the white people and not for the Negroes. Why, in point of mere fact, I think so too. But in this remark of the judge there is a significance which I think is the key to the great mistake (if there is any such mistake) which he has made in this Nebraska measure. It shows that the judge has no very vivid impression that the Negro is human, and consequently had no idea that there can be any moral question in legislating about him. In his view the question of whether a new country shall be slave or free, is a matter of as utter indif·ference as it is whether his neighbor shall plant his farm with tobacco or stock it with horned cattle. Now, whether this view is right or wrong, it is very certain that the great mass of mankind take a totally different view. They consider slavery a great moral wrong, and their feeling against it is not evanescent, but eternal. It lies at the very foundation of their sense of justice, and it cannot be trifled with. It is a great and durable element of popular action, and I think no statesman can safely disregard it.

Our Senator also objects that those who oppose him in this matter do not entirely agree with one another. He reminds me that in my firm adherence to the constitutional rights of the slave States, I differ widely from others who are coöperating with me in opposing the Nebraska bill, and he says it is not quite fair to oppose him in this variety of ways. He should remember that he took us by surprise—astounded us by this measure. We were thunderstruck and stunned, and we reeled and fell in utter confusion. But we rose, each fighting, grasping whatever he could first reach—a scythe, a pitchfork, a chopping-ax, or a butcher's cleaver. We struck in the direction of the sound, and we were rapidly closing in upon him. He must not think to divert us from our purpose by showing us that our drill, our dress, and our weapons are not entirely perfect and uniform. When the storm shall be past he shall find us still Americans, no less devoted to the continued union and prosperity of the country than heretofore.

Finally, the judge invokes against me the memory of Clay and Webster. They were great men, and men of great deeds. But where have I assailed them? For what is it that their life-long enemy shall now make profit by assuming to defend them against me, their life-long friend? I go against the repeal of the Missouri Compromise; did they ever go for it? They went for the compromises of 1850; did I ever go against them? They were greatly devoted to the Union; to the small measure of my ability was I ever less so? Clay and Webster were dead before this question arose; by what authority shall our senator say they would espouse his side of it if alive? Mr. Clay was the leading spirit in making the Missouri Compromise; is it very credible that if now alive he would take the lead in the breaking of it? The truth is that some support from Whigs is now a necessity with the judge, and for this it is that the names of Clay and Webster are invoked. His old friends have deserted him in such numbers as to leave too few to live by. He came to his own, and his own received him not; and lo! he turns unto the Gentiles.

A word now as to the judge's desperate assumption that the compromises of 1850 had no connection with one another; that Illinois came into the Union as a slave State, and some other similar ones. This is no other than a bold denial of the history of the country. If we do not know that the compromises of 1850 were dependent on each other; if we do not know that Illinois came into the Union as a free State—we do not know anything. If we do not know these things, we do not know that we ever had a Revolutionary war or such a chief as Washington. To deny these things is to deny our national axioms—or dogmas, at least—and it puts an end to all argument. If a man will stand up and assert, and repeat and re-assert, that two and two do not make four, I know nothing in the power of argument that can stop him. I think I can answer the judge so long as he sticks to the premises; but when he flies from them, I cannot work any argument into the consistency of a mental gag and actually close his mouth with it. In such a case I can only commend him to the seventy thousand answers just in from Pennsylvania, Ohio, and Indiana.*

LETTER TO E. B. WASHBURNE

Lincoln writes to his friend Elihu B. Washburne to explain the outcome of the Senatorial election which had taken place in the Illinois Legislature on the previous day. Lincoln had hoped to become a United States Senator to succeed the James Shields with whom he had nearly fought a duel in 1842. The letter describes in detail how Lincoln had had to throw his votes to Lyman Trumbull (who was a Democrat, but was opposed to the Nebraska Act) in order to keep Joel Matteson, the moderately pro-Nebraska Democratic candidate and Governor of Illinois, from being elected.

Springfield, February 9, 1855

MY DEAR SIR: The agony is over at last, and the result you doubtless know. I write this only to give you some particulars to explain what might appear difficult of understanding. I began with 44 votes, Shields 41, and Trumbull 5—yet Trumbull was elected. In fact, 47 different members voted for me—getting three new ones on the second ballot, and losing four old ones. How came my 47 to yield to Trumbull's 5? It was Governor Matteson's work. He has been secretly a candidate ever since (before, even) the fall election. All the members round about the canal were Anti-Nebraska but were neverthe-

* In the October elections just held in these states the people had voted heavily against the Kansas-Nebraska Act.

less nearly all Democrats and old personal friends of his. His plan was to privately impress them with the belief that he was as good Anti-Nebraska as any one else—at least could be secured to be so by instructions, which could be easily passed. In this way he got from four to six of that sort of men to really prefer his election to that of any other man—all *sub rosa*, of course. One notable instance of this sort was with Mr. Strunk of Kankakee. At the beginning of the session he came a volunteer to tell me he was for me and would walk a hundred miles to elect me; but lo! it was not long before he leaked it out that he was going for me the first few ballots and then for Governor Matteson.

The Nebraska men, of course, were not for Matteson; but when they found they could elect no avowed Nebraska man, they tardily determined to let him get whomever of our men he could, by whatever means he could, and ask him no questions. In the mean time Osgood, Don Morrison, and Trapp of St. Clair had openly gone over from us. With the united Nebraska force and their recruits, open and covert, it gave Matteson more than enough to elect him. We saw into it plainly ten days ago, but with every possible effort could not head it off. All that remained of the Anti-Nebraska force, excepting Judd, Cook, Palmer, Baker and Allen of Madison, and two or three of the secret Matteson men, would go into caucus, and I could get the nomination of that caucus. But the three senators and one of the two representatives above named "could never vote for a Whig," and this incensed some twenty Whigs to "think" they would never vote for the man of the five. So we stood, and so we went into the fight yesterday— the Nebraska men very confident of the election of Matteson, though denying that he was a candidate, and we very much believing also that they would elect him. But they wanted first to make a show of good faith to Shields by voting for him a few times, and our secret Matteson men also wanted to make a show of good faith by voting with us a few times. So we led off. On the seventh ballot, I think, the signal was given to the Nebraska men to turn to Matteson, which they acted on to a man, with one exception, my old friend Strunk going with them, giving him 44 votes.

Next ballot the remaining Nebraska man and one pretended Anti went over to him, giving him 46. The next still another, giving him 47, wanting only three of an election. In the mean time our friends, with a view of detaining our expected bolters, had been turning from me to Trumbull till he had risen to 35 and I had been reduced to 15. These would never desert me except by my direction; but I became satisfied that if we could prevent Matteson's election one or two ballots more, we could not possibly do so a single ballot after my friends should begin to return to me from Trumbull. So I determined to strike at once, and accordingly advised my remaining friends to go for him, which they did and elected him on the tenth ballot.

Such is the way the thing was done. I think you would have done the same under the circumstances; though Judge Davis, who came down this morning, declares he never would have consented to the forty-seven men being controlled by the five. I regret my defeat moderately, but I am not nervous about it. I could have headed off every combination and been elected, had it not been for Matteson's double game—and his defeat now gives me more pleasure than my own gives me pain. On the whole, it is perhaps as well for our general cause that Trumbull is elected. The Nebraska men confess that they hate it worse than anything that could have happened. It is a great consolation to see them worse whipped than I am. I tell them it is their own fault—that they had abundant opportunity to choose between him and me, which they declined, and instead forced it on me to decide between him and Matteson.

LETTER TO OWEN LOVEJOY

Owen Lovejoy was an outspoken abolitionist, brother of the Elijah Lovejoy who had been murdered by a pro-slavery mob in Alton, Illinois, in 1837. The Know-Nothing party was the one-hundred-percent American party of the day, viciously opposed to all foreigners and Catholics. It had been attacked not only by Lincoln but also by Douglas. Many of the men in the Know-Nothing party were opposed to slavery, but an alliance with them would be embarrassing for a man like Lincoln who believed in liberal principles.

Springfield, August 11, 1855

MY DEAR SIR: Yours of the 7th. was received the day before yesterday. Not even you are more anxious to prevent the extension of slavery than I. And yet the political atmosphere is such, just now, that I fear to do anything, lest I do wrong. Know-Nothingism has not yet entirely tumbled to pieces. Nay, it is even a little encouraged by the late elections in Tennessee, Kentucky and Alabama. Until we can get the elements of this organization there is not sufficient material to successfully combat the Nebraska democracy with. We cannot get them so long as they cling to a hope of success under their own organization; and I fear an open push by us now may offend them and tend to prevent our ever getting them. About us here, they are mostly my old political and personal friends, and I have hoped this organization would die out without the painful necessity of my taking an open stand against them. Of their principles I think little better than I do of those of the slavery extensionists. Indeed I do not perceive how any one professing to be sensitive to the wrongs of the Negro, can join in a league to degrade a class of white men.

I have no objection to "fuse" with any body provided I can fuse on grounds which I think right. And I believe the opponents of slavery extension could now do this if it were not for the K.N.ism. In many speeches last summer I advised those who did me the honor of a hearing to "stand with" any body who stands right, and I am still quite willing to follow my own advice. I lately saw in the _Quincy Whig_ the report of a preamble and resolution made by Mr. Williams, as chairman of a committee, to a public meeting and adopted by the meeting. I saw them but once, and have them not now at command, but so far as I can remember them they occupy the ground I should be willing to "fuse" upon. As to my personal movements this summer and fall, I am quite busy trying to pick up my lost crumbs of last year. I shall be here till September; then with Circuit till the 20th, then to Cincinnati awhile, after a Patent Right case, and back to the Circuit to the end of November. I can be seen here any time this month and at Bloomington at any time from the 10th. to the 17th. of September. As to an extra session of the Legislature, I should know no better how to bring that about than to lift myself over a fence by the straps of my boots.

LETTER TO GEORGE ROBERTSON

Robertson was an elderly Kentuckian who had been in Congress during the passage of the Missouri Compromise in 1820. He was an author and a professor of law. The book to which Lincoln refers was probably an advance copy of Robertson's Scrapbook on Law, Politics, Men and Times. Lincoln writes to him to expound his views on the possibilities of emancipation being accomplished in a peaceful manner—possibilities about which he has by this time become very pessimistic. The last paragraph of this letter foreshadows the famous phrase which Lincoln was to develop in his "House Divided" speech on June 16, 1858.

Springfield, Illinois, August 15, 1855

MY DEAR SIR: The volume you left for me has been received. I am really grateful for the honor of your kind remembrance, as well as for the book. The partial reading I have already given it has afforded me much of both pleasure and instruction. It was new to me that the exact question which led to the Missouri Compromise had arisen before it arose in regard to Missouri, and that you had taken so prominent a part in it. Your short but able and patriotic speech upon that occasion has not been improved upon since by those holding the same views, and, with all the lights you then had, the views you took appear to me as very reasonable.

You are not a friend to slavery in the abstract. In that speech you spoke of "the peaceful extinction of slavery," and used other expressions indicating your belief that the thing was at some time to have an end. Since then we have had thirty-six years of experience; and this experience has demonstrated, I think, that there is no peaceful extinction of slavery in prospect for us. The signal failure of Henry Clay and other good and great men, in 1849, to effect anything in favor of gradual emancipation in Kentucky, together with a thousand other signs, extinguished that hope utterly. On the question of liberty as a principle, we are not what we have been. When we were the political slaves of King George, and wanted to be free, we called the maxim that "all men are created equal" a self-evident truth, but now when we have grown fat, and have lost all dread of being slaves ourselves, we have become so greedy to be masters that we call the same maxim "a self-evident lie." The Fourth of July has not quite dwindled away; it is still a great day—for burning fire-crackers!!!

That spirit which desired the peaceful extinction of slavery has itself become extinct with the occasion and the men of the Revolution. Under the impulse of that occasion, nearly half the States adopted systems of emancipation at once, and it is a significant fact that not a single State has done the like since. So far as peaceful voluntary emancipation is concerned, the condition of the Negro slave in America, scarcely less terrible to the contemplation of a free mind, is now as fixed and hopeless of change for the better, as that of the lost souls of the finally impenitent. The Autocrat of all the Russias will resign his crown and proclaim his subjects free republicans sooner than will our American masters voluntarily give up their slaves.

Our political problem now is, "Can we as a nation continue together permanently—forever—half slave and half free?" The problem is too mighty for me—may God, in his mercy, superintend the solution.

LETTER TO JOSHUA F. SPEED

Lincoln's correspondence with Speed had been long suspended; actually it was dying of inanition, and this letter was to be the last confidential message written to the man who had been Lincoln's confidant since 1837. Speed was theoretically opposed to slavery, but he was a Southerner, affected by the prevailing attitude of the South which had become increasingly bitter toward the anti-slavery agitation which was rising constantly in the North. Lincoln writes to state his own position on the matter; he recalls the shackled slaves he had seen with Speed on their journey from Kentucky to Springfield in 1841. "I bite my lips and keep quiet," he says. Lincoln claims still to be a Whig; he is silent on the charge that he is an abolitionist (which he certainly was not); but he vehemently disavows any connection with the Know-Nothings who were particularly offensive to him. The statement he makes in the next-to-the-last paragraph of this letter has often been quoted.

Springfield, August 24, 1855

DEAR SPEED: You know what a poor correspondent I am. Ever since I received your very agreeable letter of the 22d of

May I have been intending to write you an answer to it. You suggest that in political action, now, you and I would differ. I suppose we would; not quite as much, however, as you may think. You know I dislike slavery, and you fully admit the abstract wrong of it. So far there is no cause of difference. But you say that sooner than yield your legal right to the slave, especially at the bidding of those who are not themselves interested, you would see the Union dissolved. I am not aware that any one is bidding you yield that right; very certainly I am not. I leave that matter entirely to yourself. I also acknowledge your rights and my obligations under the Constitution in regard to your slaves. I confess I hate to see the poor creatures hunted down and caught and carried back to their stripes and unrequited toil; but I bite my lips and keep quiet.

In 1841 you and I had together a tedious low-water trip on a steamboat from Louisville to St. Louis. You may remember, as I well do, that from Louisville to the mouth of the Ohio there were on board ten or a dozen slaves shackled together with irons. That sight was a continued torment to me, and I see something like it every time I touch the Ohio or any other slave border. It is not fair for you to assume that I have no interest in a thing which has, and continually exercises, the power of making me miserable. You ought rather to appreciate how much the great body of the Northern people do crucify their feelings, in order to maintain their loyalty to the Constitution and the Union. I do oppose the extension of slavery because my judgment and feeling so prompt me, and I am under no obligations to the contrary. If for this you and I must differ, differ we must. You say, if you were President, you would send an army and hang the leaders of the Missouri outrages upon the Kansas elections; still, if Kansas fairly votes herself a slave State she must be admitted, or the Union must be dissolved. But how if she votes herself a slave State unfairly, that is, by the very means for which you say you would hang men? Must she still be admitted, or the Union dissolved? That will be the phase of the question when it first becomes a practical one. In your assumption that there may be a fair decision of the slavery question in Kansas, I plainly see you and I would differ about the Nebraska law. I look upon that enactment not as a law, but as a violence from the beginning. It was conceived in violence, is maintained in violence, and is being executed in violence. I say it was conceived in violence, because the destruction of the Missouri Compromise, under the circumstances, was nothing less than violence. It was passed in violence, because it could not have passed at all but for the votes of many members in violence of the known will of their constituents. It is maintained in violence, because the elections since clearly demand its repeal; and the demand is openly disregarded.

You say men ought to be hung for the way they are executing the law; I say the way it is being executed is quite as good as any of its antecedents. It is being executed in the precise way which was intended from the first, else why does no Nebraska man express astonishment or condemnation? Poor Reeder is the only public man who has been silly enough to believe that anything like fairness was ever intended, and he has been bravely undeceived.

That Kansas will form a slave constitution, and with it will ask to be admitted into the Union, I take to be already a settled question, and so settled by the very means you so pointedly condemn. By every principle of law ever held by any court North or South, every Negro taken to Kansas is free; yet, in utter disregard of this—in the spirit of violence merely—that beautiful legislature gravely passes a law to hang any man who shall venture to inform a Negro of his legal rights. This is the subject and real object of the law. If, like Haman, they should hang upon the gallows of their own building, I shall not be among the mourners for their fate. In my humble sphere, I shall advocate the restoration of the Missouri Compromise so

long as Kansas remains a Territory, and when, by all these foul
means, it seeks to come into the Union as a slave State, I shall
oppose it. I am very loath in any case to withhold my assent
to the enjoyment of property acquired or located in good
faith; but I do not admit that good faith in taking a Negro
to Kansas to be held in slavery is a probability with any man.
Any man who has sense enough to be the controller of his
own property has too much sense to misunderstand the outrageous character of the whole Nebraska business.

But I digress. In my opposition to the admission of Kansas
I shall have some company, but we may be beaten. If we are,
I shall not on that account attempt to dissolve the Union. I
think it probable, however, we shall be beaten. Standing as a
unit among yourselves, you can, directly and indirectly, bribe
enough of our men to carry the day, as you could on the open
proposition to establish a monarchy. Get hold of some man
in the North whose position and ability is such that he can
make the support of your measure, whatever it may be, a
Democratic party necessity, and the thing is done. Apropos
of this, let me tell you an anecdote. Douglas introduced the
Nebraska bill in January. In February afterward there was a
called session of the Illinois legislature. Of the one hundred
members composing the two branches of that body, about
seventy were Democrats. These latter held a caucus, in which
the Nebraska bill was talked of, if not formally discussed. It
was thereby discovered that just three, and no more, were in
favor of the measure. In a day or two Douglas's orders came
on to have resolutions passed approving the bill; and they
were passed by large majorities!!! The truth of this is vouched
for by a bolting Democratic member. The masses, too, Democratic as well as Whig, were even nearer unanimous against
it; but, as soon as the party necessity of supporting it became
apparent, the way the Democrats began to see the wisdom and
justice of it was perfectly astonishing.

You say that if Kansas fairly votes herself a free State, as a
Christian you will rejoice at it. All decent slaveholders talk

that way, and I do not doubt their candor. But they never vote that way. Although in a private letter or conversation you will express your preference that Kansas shall be free, you would vote for no man for Congress who would say the same thing publicly. No such man could be elected from any district in a slave State. You think Stringfellow and company ought to be hung; and yet at the next presidential election you will vote for the exact type and representative of Stringfellow. The slave breeders and slave traders are a small, odious, and detested class among you; and yet in politics they dictate the course of all of you, and are as completely your masters as you are the master of your own Negroes.

You inquire where I now stand. That is a disputed point. I think I am a Whig; but others say there are no Whigs, and that I am an Abolitionist. When I was at Washington, I voted for the Wilmot proviso as good as forty times; and I never heard of any one attempting to unwhig me for that. I now do no more than oppose the extension of slavery. I am not a Know-Nothing; that is certain. How could I be? How can any one who abhors the oppression of Negroes be in favor of degrading classes of white people? Our progress in degeneracy appears to me to be pretty rapid. As a nation we began by declaring that "all men are created equal." We now practically read it "all men are created equal, except Negroes." When the Know-Nothings get control, it will read "all men are created equal, except Negroes and foreigners and Catholics." When it comes to this, I shall prefer emigrating to some country where they make no pretense of loving liberty—to Russia, for instance, where despotism can be taken pure, and without the base alloy of hypocrisy.

Mary will probably pass a day or two in Louisville in October. My kindest regards to Mrs. Speed. On the leading subject of this letter, I have more of her sympathy than I have of yours; and yet let me say I am

Your friend forever,

A. Lincoln

LETTER TO ISHAM REAVIS

Lincoln gives advice to a young boy who aspires to be a lawyer.

Springfield, November 5, 1855

MY DEAR SIR: I have just reached home, and found your letter of the 23rd ult. I am from home too much of my time, for a young man to read law with me advantageously. If you are resolutely determined to make a lawyer of yourself, the thing is more than half done already. It is but a small matter whether you read with anybody or not. I did not read with anyone. Get the books, and read and study them till you understand them in their principal features; and that is the main thing. It is of no consequence to be in a large town while you are reading. I read at New Salem, which never had three hundred people living in it. The books, and your capacity for understanding them, are just the same in all places. Mr. Dummer is a very clever man and an excellent lawyer (much better than I, in law-learning); and I have no doubt he will cheerfully tell you what books to read, and also loan you the books.

Always bear in mind that your own resolution to succeed, is more important than any other one thing.

LETTER TO GEORGE P. FLOYD

Lawyer Lincoln doesn't want to be thought a high-priced man. He returns part of a client's fee.

Springfield, Illinois, February 21, 1856

DEAR SIR: I have just received yours of 16th, with check on Flagg & Savage for twenty-five dollars. You must think I am a high-priced man. You are too liberal with your money.

Fifteen dollars is enough for the job. I send you a receipt for fifteen dollars, and return to you a ten-dollar bill.

LETTER TO LYMAN TRUMBULL

The hotly contested Presidential campaign of 1856 is beginning with the new Republican party in the field for the first time. Lincoln favors John McLean, Supreme Court Justice, as the candidate for his party. He believes that McLean would attract former Whig votes. McLean received nearly two hundred votes at the Republican convention held at Philadelphia on June 19—but John C. Frémont was nominated. Lyman Trumbull was the new Senator from Illinois who had defeated Lincoln for the office.

Springfield, June 7, 1856

MY DEAR SIR: The news of Buchanan's nomination came yesterday; and a good many Whigs, of conservative feelings, and slight pro-slavery proclivities, withal, are inclining to go for him, and will do it, unless the Anti-Nebraska nomination shall be such as to divert them. The man to effect that object is Judge McLean; and his nomination would save every Whig, except such as have already gone over hook and line, as Singleton, Morrison, Constable, and others. J. T. Stuart, Anthony Thornton, James M. Davis (the old settler) and others like them, will heartily go for McLean, but will every one go for Buchanan, as against Chase, Banks, Seward, Blair or Frémont? I think they would stand Blair or Frémont for Vice-President —but not more.

Now there is a grave question to be considered. Nine-tenths of the Anti-Nebraska votes have to come from old Whigs. In setting stakes, is it safe to totally disregard them? Can we possibly win, if we do so? So far they have been disregarded. I need not point out the instances.

I think I may trust you to believe I do not say this on my

own personal account. I am *in*, and shall go for any one nominated unless he be "*platformed*" expressly, or impliedly, on
some ground which I may think wrong. Since the nomination
of Bissell we are in good trim in Illinois, save at the point I
have indicated. If we can save pretty nearly all the Whigs, we
shall elect him, I think, by a very large majority.

I address this to you, because your influence in the Anti-
Nebraska nomination will be greater than that of any other
Illinoian.

Let this be confidential.

FROM A SPEECH MADE AT GALENA, ILLINOIS, DURING THE FREMONT CAMPAIGN

*As soon as the Republican party entered the field, charges of
sectionalism were made against it in the South. The cry of disunion began to be raised. In this speech made nearly five years
before the Civil War began, Lincoln warns the South that any
attempt at disunion will be met by armed force.*

July 23, 1856

You further charge us with being disunionists. If you mean
that it is our aim to dissolve the Union, I for myself answer
that it is untrue; for those who act with me I answer that it is
untrue. Have you heard us assert that as our aim? Do you
really believe that such is our aim? Do you find it in our platform, our speeches, our conventions, or anywhere? If not,
withdraw the charge.

But you may say that though it is not our aim, it will be the
result if we succeed, and that we are therefore disunionists in
fact. This is a grave charge you make against us, and we certainly have a right to demand that you specify in what way we
are to dissolve the Union. How are we to effect this?

The only specification offered is volunteered by Mr. Fillmore in his Albany speech. His charge is that if we elect a President and Vice-President both from the free States, it will dissolve the Union. This is open folly. The Constitution provides that the President and Vice-President of the United States shall be of different States; but says nothing as to the latitude and longitude of those States. . . .

No other specification is made, and the only one that could be made is that the restoration of the restriction of 1820,* making the United States territory free territory, would dissolve the Union. Gentlemen, it will require a decided majority to pass such an act. We, the majority, being able constitutionally to do all that we purpose, would have no desire to dissolve the Union. Do you say that such restriction of slavery would be unconstitutional, and that some of the States would not submit to its enforcement? I grant you that an unconstitutional act is not a law; but I do not ask and will not take your construction of the Constitution. The Supreme Court of the United States is the tribunal to decide such a question, and we will submit to its decisions; and if you do also, there will be an end of the matter. Will you? If not, who are the disunionists—you or we? We, the majority, would not strive to dissolve the Union; and if any attempt is made, it must be by you, who so loudly stigmatize us as disunionists. But the Union, in any event, will not be dissolved. We don't want to dissolve it, and if you attempt it we won't let you. With the purse and sword, the army and navy and treasury, in our hands and at our command, you could not do it. This government would be very weak indeed if a majority with a disciplined army and navy and a well-filled treasury could not preserve itself when attacked by an unarmed, undisciplined, unorganized minority. All this talk about the dissolution of the Union is humbug, nothing but folly. We do not want to dissolve the Union; you shall not.

* The Missouri Compromise.

SPEECH AT KALAMAZOO, MICHIGAN

This speech has only recently been discovered and has never before been printed in any collection of Lincoln's writings. It was delivered during the Frémont campaign at an enthusiastically attended Republican concourse. Lincoln spoke from one of five different stands, all of which were kept going at once as separate crowds gathered around the various speakers. This is one of Lincoln's clearest cut arguments against letting slavery spread into the new territories. Lincoln takes especial care to define abolitionism and the relationship of the new Republican party to it.

August 27, 1856

UNDER the Constitution of the United States another Presidential contest approaches us. All over this land—that portion at least, of which I know much—the people are assembling to consider the proper course to be adopted by them. One of the first considerations is to learn what the people differ about. If we ascertain what we differ about, we shall be better able to decide. The question of slavery, at the present day, should be not only the greatest question, but very nearly the sole question. Our opponents, however, prefer that this should not be the case. To get at this question, I will occupy your attention but a single moment. The question is simply this: Shall slavery be spread into the new Territories, or not? This is the naked question. If we should support Frémont successfully in this, it may be charged that we will not be content with restricting slavery in the new Territories. If we should charge that James Buchanan, by his platform, is bound to extend slavery into the Territories, and that he is in favor of its being thus spread, we should be puzzled to prove it. We believe it, nevertheless. By taking the issue as I present it, whether it shall be permitted as an issue is made up between the parties. Each takes his own stand. This is the question: Shall the Government of the United States prohibit slavery in the United States.

We have been in the habit of deploring the fact that slavery exists amongst us. We have ever deplored it. Our forefathers did, and they declared, as we have done in later years, the blame rested on the mother Government of Great Britain. We constantly condemn Great Britain for not preventing slavery from coming amongst us. She would not interfere to prevent it, and so individuals were enabled to introduce the institution without opposition. I have alluded to this, to ask you if this is not exactly the policy of Buchanan and his friends, to place this Government in the attitude then occupied by the Government of Great Britain—placing the nation in the position to authorize the Territories to reproach it, for refusing to allow them to hold slaves. I would like to ask your attention, any gentleman to tell me when the people of Kansas are going to decide. When are they to do it? How are they to do it? I asked that question two years ago—when, and how are they to do it? Not many weeks ago, our new Senator from Illinois, [Lyman Trumbull] asked Douglas how it could be done. Douglas is a great man—at keeping from answering questions he don't want to answer. He would not answer. He said it was a question for the Supreme Court to decide. In the North, his friends argue that the people can decide it at any time. The Southerners say there is no power in the people, whatever. We know that from the time that white people have been allowed in the Territory, they have brought slaves with them. Suppose the people come up to vote as freely, and with as perfect protection as we could do it here. Will they be at liberty to vote their sentiments? If they can, then all that has ever been said about our provincial ancestors is untrue, and they could have done so, also. We know our Southern friends say that the general Government cannot interfere. The people, say they, have no right to interfere.

They could as truly say: "It is amongst us—we cannot get rid of it."

But I am afraid I waste too much time on this point. I take it as an illustration of the principle that slaves are admitted into the Territories. And, while I am speaking of Kansas, how will that operate? Can men vote truly? We will suppose that there are ten men who go into Kansas to settle. Nine of these are opposed to slavery. One has ten slaves. The slaveholder is a good man in other respects; he is a good neighbor, and being a wealthy man, he is enabled to do the others many neighborly kindnesses. They like the man, though they don't like the system by which he holds his fellow men in bondage. And here let me say, that in intellectual and physical structure, our Southern brethren do not differ from us. They are, like us, subject to passions, and it is only their odious institution of slavery, that makes the breach between us. These ten men of whom I was speaking, live together three or four years; they intermarry; their family ties are strengthened. And who wonders that in time, the people learn to look upon slavery with complacency? This is the way in which slavery is planted, and gains so firm a foothold. I think this is a strong card that the Nebraska party have played, and won upon, in this game.

I suppose that this crowd are opposed to the admission of slavery into Kansas, yet it is true that in all crowds there are some who differ from the majority. I want to ask the Buchanan men, who are against the spread of slavery, if there be any present, why not vote for the man who is against it? I understand that Mr. Fillmore's position is precisely like Buchanan's. I understand that, by the Nebraska bill, a door has been opened for the spread of slavery in the Territories. Examine, if you please, and see if they have ever done any such thing as try to shut the door. It is true that Fillmore tickles a few of his friends with the notion that he is not the cause of the door being opened. Well; it brings him into this position: he tries to get both sides, one by denouncing those who opened the door, and the other by hinting that he doesn't care a fig for its being open. If he were President, he would have one side or the other—he would either restrict slavery or not. Of course it would be so. There could be no middle way. You who hate slavery and love freedom, why not, as Fillmore and Buchanan are on the same ground, vote for Frémont? Why not vote for the man who takes your side of the question? "Well," says Buchanier, "it is none of our business." But is it not our business? There are several reasons why I think it is our business. But let us see how it is. Others have urged these reasons before, but they are still of use. By our Constitution we are represented in Congress in proportion to numbers, and in counting the numbers that give us our representatives, three slaves are counted as two people. The State of Maine has six representatives in the lower house of Congress. In strength South Carolina is equal to her. But stop! Maine has *twice as many* white people, and 32,000 to boot! And is that fair? I don't complain of it. This regulation was put in force when the exigencies of the times demanded it, and could not have been avoided. Now, one man in South Carolina is the same as two men here. Maine should have twice as many men in Congress as South Carolina. It is a fact that any man in South Carolina has more influence and power in Congress today than any two now before me. The same thing is true of all slave States, though it may not be in the same proportion. It is a truth that cannot be denied, that in all the free States no white man is the equal of the white man of the slave States. But this is in the Constitution, and we must stand up to it. The question, then is: "Have we no interest as to whether the white man of the North shall be the equal of the white man of the South?" Once when I used this argument in the presence of Douglas, he answered that in the North the black man was counted as a full man, and had an equal vote with the white, while at the South they were counted at but three-fifths. And Douglas, when he had made this reply, doubtless thought he had forever silenced the objection.

Have we no interest in the free Territories of the United States—that they should be kept open for the homes of free white people? As our Northern States are growing more and more in wealth and population, we are continually in want of an outlet, through which it may pass out to enrich our country. In this we have an interest—a deep and abiding interest. There is another thing, and that is the mature knowledge we have—the greatest interest of all. It is the doctrine, that the people are to be driven from the maxims of our free Government, that despises the spirit which for eighty years has celebrated the anniversary of our national independence.

We are a great empire. We are eighty years old. We stand at once the wonder and admiration of the whole world, and we must enquire what it is that has given us so much prosperity, and we shall understand that to give up that one thing, would be to give up all future prosperity. This cause is that every man can make himself. It has been said that such a race of prosperity has been run nowhere else. We find a people on the North-east, who have a different government from ours, being ruled by a Queen. Turning to the South, we see a people who, while they boast of being free, keep their fellow beings in bondage. Compare our free States with either, shall we say here that we have no interest in keeping that principle alive? Shall we say—"Let it be." No—we have an interest in the maintenance of the principles of the Government, and without this interest, it is worth nothing. I have noticed in Southern newspapers, particularly the Richmond *Enquirer*, the Southern view of the free States. They insist that slavery has a right to spread. They defend it upon principle. They insist that their slaves are far better off than Northern freemen. What a mistaken view do these men have of Northern laborers! They think that men are always to remain laborers here—but there is no such class. The man who labored for another last year, this year labors for himself, and next year he will hire others to labor for him. These men don't understand when they think in this manner of Northern free labor. When these reasons can be introduced, tell me not that we have no interest in keeping the Territories free for the settlement of free laborers.

I pass, then, from this question. I think we have an ever growing interest in maintaining the free institutions of our country.

It is said that our party is a sectional party. It has been said in high quarters that if Frémont and Dayton were elected the Union would be dissolved. The South do not think so. I believe it! I believe it! It is a shameful thing that the subject is talked of so much. Did we not have a Southern President and Vice President at one time? And yet the Union has not yet been dissolved. Why, at this very moment, there is a Northern President and Vice President. Pierce and King were elected, and King died without ever taking his seat. The Senate elected a Northern man from their own numbers, to perform the duties of the Vice President. He resigned his seat, however, as soon as he got the job of making a slave State out of Kansas. Was not that a great mistake?

[A voice: "He didn't mean that!"]

Then why didn't he speak what he did mean? Why did not he speak what he ought to have spoken? That was the very thing. He should have spoken manly, and we should then, have known where to have found him. It is said we expect to elect Frémont by Northern votes. Certainly we do not think the South will elect him. But let us ask the question differently. Does not Buchanan expect to be elected by Southern votes? Fillmore, however, will go out of this contest the most national man we have. He has no prospect of having a single vote on either side of Mason and Dixon's line, to trouble his poor soul about. [Laughter and cheers.]

We believe that it is right that slavery should not be tolerated in the new Territories, yet we cannot get support for this doctrine, except in one part of the country. Slavery is looked upon by men in the light of dollars and cents. The estimated worth of the slaves at the South is $1,000,000,000, and in a very few years, if the institution shall be admitted into the territories, they will have increased fifty percent in value.

Our adversaries charge Frémont with being an Abolitionist. When pressed to show proof, they frankly confess that they can show no such thing. They then run off upon the assertion that his supporters are Abolitionists. But this they have never attempted to prove. I know of no word in the language that has been used so much as that one "Abolitionist." Having no definition, it has no meaning unless taken as designating a person who is abolishing something. If that be its significa- tion, the supporters of Frémont are not Abolitionists. In Kansas all who come there are perfectly free to regulate their own social relations. There has never been a man there who was an Abolitionist—for what was there to be abolished? Peo- ple there had perfect freedom to express what they wished on the subject when the Nebraska bill was first passed. Our friends in the South, who support Buchanan, have five dis- union men to one at the North. This disunion is a sectional question. Who is to blame for it? Are we? I don't care how you express it. This Government is sought to be put on a new track. Slavery is to be made a ruling element in our Govern- ment. The question can be avoided in but two ways. By the one, we must submit, and allow slavery to triumph, or, by the other, we must triumph over the black demon. We have chosen the latter manner. If you of the North wish to get rid of this question, you must decide between these two ways—

submit and vote for Buchanan, submit and vote that slavery is a just and good thing, and immediately get rid of the question; or unite with us, and help us to triumph. We would all like to have the question done away with, but we cannot submit.

They tell us that we are in company with men who have long been known as Abolitionists. What care we how many may feel disposed to labor for our cause? Why do not you, Buchanan men, come in and use your influence to make our party respectable? [Laughter.] How is the dissolution of the Union to be consummated? They tell us that the Union is in danger. Who will divide it? Is it those who make the charge? Are they themselves the persons who wish to see this result? A majority will never dissolve the Union. Can a minority do it? When this Nebraska bill was first introduced into Congress, the sense of the Democratic party was outraged. That party has ever prided itself, that it was the friend of individual, universal freedom. It was that principle upon which they carried their measures. When the Kansas scheme was conceived, it was natural that this respect and sense should have been outraged. Now I make this appeal to the Democratic citizens here. Don't you find yourself making arguments in support of these measures, which you never would have made before? Did you ever do it before this Nebraska bill compelled you to do it? If you answer this in the affirmative, see how a whole party have been turned away from their love of liberty! And now, my Democratic friends, come forward. Throw off these things, and come to the rescue of this great principle of equality. Don't interfere with anything in the Constitution.— That must be maintained, for it is the only safeguard of our liberties. And not to Democrats alone do I make this appeal, but to all who love these great and true principles. Come, and keep coming! Strike, and strike again! So sure as God lives, the victory shall be yours.

FROM A SPEECH ON SECTIONALISM MADE
DURING THE FREMONT CAMPAIGN

*The charge of sectionalism, which was to be the dominant note
used against Lincoln during his own Presidential campaign, was
often made during the Frémont-Buchanan canvass. This reply to
the charge was made by Lincoln, probably at Alton, during the
State Fair that was held there.*

October [2?], 1856

THE thing which gives most color to the charge of sectionalism, made against those who oppose the spread of slavery into
free territory, is the fact that they can get no votes in the slave
States, while their opponents get all, or nearly so, in the slave
States, and also a large number in the free States. To state it
in another way, the extensionists can get votes all over the
nation, while the restrictionists can get them only in the free
States.

This being the fact, why is it so? It is not because one side
of the question dividing them is more sectional than the other,
nor because of any difference in the mental or moral structure
of the people North and South. It is because in that question
the people of the South have an immediate palpable and im-
mensely great pecuniary interest, while with the people of the
North it is merely an abstract question of moral right, with
only slight and remote pecuniary interest added.

The slaves of the South, at a moderate estimate, are worth
a thousand millions of dollars. Let it be permanently settled
that this property may extend to new territory without restraint, and it greatly enhances, perhaps quite doubles, its
value at once. This immense palpable pecuniary interest on
the question of extending slavery unites the Southern people
as one man. But it cannot be demonstrated that the North

will gain a dollar by restricting it. Moral principle is all, or nearly all, that unites us of the North. Pity 't is, it is so, but this is a looser bond than pecuniary interest. Right here is the plain cause of their perfect union and our want of it. And see how it works. If a Southern man aspires to be President, they choke him down instantly, in order that the glittering prize of the Presidency may be held up on Southern terms to the greedy eyes of Northern ambition. With this they tempt us and break in upon us.

The Democratic party in 1844 elected a Southern President. Since then they have neither had a Southern candidate for election nor nomination. Their conventions of 1848, 1852 and 1856 have been struggles exclusively among Northern men, each vying to outbid the other for the Southern vote; the South standing calmly by to finally cry "Going, going, gone" to the highest bidder, and at the same time to make its power more distinctly seen, and thereby to secure a still higher bid at the next succeeding struggle.

"Actions speak louder than words" is the maxim, and if true the South now distinctly says to the North, "Give us the measures and you take the men." The total withdrawal of Southern aspirants for the Presidency multiplies the number of Northern ones. These last, in competing with each other, commit themselves to the utmost verge that, through their own greediness, they have the least hope their Northern supporters will bear. Having got committed in a race of competition, necessity drives them into union to sustain themselves. Each at first secures all he can on personal attachments to him and through hopes resting on him personally. Next they unite with one another and with the perfectly banded South, to make the offensive position they have got into "a party measure." This done, large additional numbers are secured.

When the repeal of the Missouri Compromise was first proposed, at the North there was literally "nobody" in favor of it. In February, 1854, our legislature met in called, or extra, session. From them Douglas sought an indorsement of his then pending measure of repeal. In our legislature were about seventy Democrats to thirty Whigs. The former held a caucus, in which it was resolved to give Douglas the desired indorsement. Some of the members of the caucus bolted—would not stand it—and they now divulge the secrets. They say that the caucus fairly confessed that the repeal was wrong, and they pleaded the determination to indorse it solely on the ground that it was necessary to sustain Douglas. Here we have the direct evidence of how the Nebraska bill obtained its strength in Illinois. It was given, not in a sense of right, but in the teeth of a sense of wrong, to sustain Douglas. So Illinois was divided. So New England for Pierce, Michigan for Cass, Pennsylvania for Buchanan, and all for the Democratic party.

And when by such means they have got a large portion of the Northern people into a position contrary to their own honest impulses and sense of right, they have the impudence to turn upon those who do stand firm, and call them sectional. Were it not too serious a matter, this cool impudence would be laughable, to say the least. Recurring to the question, "Shall slavery be allowed to extend into United States territory now legally free?" This is a sectional question—that is to say, it is a question in its nature calculated to divide the American people geographically. Who is to blame for that? Who can help it? Either side can help it; but how? Simply by yielding to the other side; there is no other way; in the whole range of possibility there is no other way. Then, which side shall yield? To this, again, there can be but one answer—the side which is in the wrong. True, we differ as to which side is wrong, and we boldly say, let all who really think slavery ought to be spread into free territory, openly go over against us; there is where they rightfully belong. But why should any go who really think slavery ought not to spread? Do they really think the right ought to yield to the wrong? Are they afraid to stand by the right? Do they fear that the Constitution is too weak to sustain them in the right? Do they really think that by right surrendering to wrong the hopes of our Constitution, our Union, and our liberties can possibly be bettered?

FROM A SPEECH AT A REPUBLICAN BANQUET, CHICAGO

The Republican candidate, Frémont, had been defeated in November, but the Republicans had made substantial gains in local and state elections. They had also polled a large national vote. As a result there was much rejoicing in the new party, and its prospects looked bright. A banquet was given in Chicago at the Tremont House which was attended by three hundred good party men from Northern Illinois—Lincoln among them. At this banquet the phrase "1860!—There's a good time coming, boys!" appeared on the printed program. President Pierce had delivered his last annual message to Congress only a few days before this banquet was held. He was a Northern President who was wholeheartedly devoted to the Southern cause. In response to a toast, Lincoln took the opportunity to attack Pierce's message. He also defines here his idea of the relationship between public opinion and popular government.

December 10, 1856

WE HAVE another annual Presidential message. Like a rejected lover making merry at the wedding of his rival, the President [Pierce] felicitates himself hugely over the late Presidential election. He considers the result a signal triumph of good principles and good men, and a very pointed rebuke of bad ones. He says the people did it. He forgets that the "people," as he complacently calls only those who voted for Buchanan, are in a minority of the whole people by about four hundred thousand votes—one full tenth of all the votes. Remembering this, he might perceive that the "rebuke" may not be quite as durable as he seems to think—that the majority may not choose to remain permanently rebuked by that minority.

The President thinks the great body of us Frémonters, being ardently attached to liberty, in the abstract, were duped by a few wicked and designing men. There is a slight difference of opinion on this. We think he, being ardently attached to the hope of a second term, in the concrete, was duped by men who had liberty every way. He is the cat's-paw. By much dragging of chestnuts from the fire for others to eat, his claws are burnt off to the gristle, and he is thrown aside as unfit for further use. As the fool said of *King Lear*, when his daughters had turned him out of doors, "He's a shelled peascod."

So far as the President charges us "with a desire to change the domestic institutions of existing States," and of "doing everything in our power to deprive the Constitution and the laws of moral authority," for the whole party on belief, and for myself on knowledge, I pronounce the charge an unmixed and unmitigated falsehood.

Our government rests in public opinion. Whoever can change public opinion can change the government practically just so much. Public opinion, on any subject, always has a "central idea," from which all its minor thoughts radiate. That "central idea" in our political public opinion at the beginning was, and until recently has continued to be, "the equality of men." And although it has always submitted patiently to whatever of inequality there seemed to be as matter of actual necessity, its constant working has been a steady progress toward the practical equality of all men. The late Presidential election was a struggle by one party to discard that central idea and to substitute for it the opposite idea that slavery is right in the abstract, the workings of which as a central idea may be the perpetuity of human slavery and its extension to all countries and colors. Less than a year ago the Richmond *Enquirer*, an avowed advocate of slavery, regardless of color, in order to favor his views, invented the phrase "State equality," and now the President, in his message, adopts the *Enquirer's* catch-phrase, telling us the people "have asserted the constitutional equality of each and all of the States of the Union as States." The President flatters himself that the new central idea is completely inaugurated; and so indeed it is, so far as the mere fact of a Presidential election can inaugurate it. To us it is left to know that the majority of the people have not yet declared for it, and to hope that they never will. All of us who did not vote for Mr. Buchanan, taken together, are a majority of four hundred thousand.

But in the late contest we were divided between Frémont and Fillmore. Can we not come together for the future? Let every one who really believes, and is resolved, that free society is not and shall not be a failure, and who can conscientiously declare that in the past contest he has done only what he thought best—let every such one have charity to believe that every other one can say as much. Thus let bygones be bygones; let past differences as nothing be; and with steady eye on the real issue, let us reinaugurate the good old "central ideas" of the republic. We can do it. The human heart is with us; God is with us. We shall again be able not to declare that "all States as States are equal," nor yet that "all citizens as citizens are equal," but to renew the broader, better declaration, including both these and much more, that "all men are created equal."

FROM A SPEECH IN SPRINGFIELD, ILLINOIS

The Dred Scott decision had been made public a few days after Buchanan's inauguration. Douglas had been invited to speak in Springfield on June 12 to defend the decision. Lincoln had been present at this occasion. The crux of Douglas's argument had been that his principle of popular sovereignty was the panacea that would solve all difficulties. So far as the Dred Scott decision was concerned, it was simply the duty of every citizen to submit to any decision that might be made by the highest court of the land. Then, through popular sovereignty, people in the territories would be able to decide for themselves whether free or slave states should be formed in these areas. Douglas, furthermore, stated that if equality were granted the Negro, every slave must be freed, and Negroes would have to be permitted to intermarry with the whites. In the same Hall of Representatives in which Douglas had spoken, Lincoln made his reply. In the speech he delivered that night may be seen the foreshadowing of the arguments he was to use during his formal debates with Douglas in 1858.

The "rebellion in Utah" to which Lincoln alludes was restlessness among the Mormons who had attempted to escape from the jurisdiction of the United States in 1847-48 when they settled in the Great Salt Lake Valley. The treaty of Guadalupe Hidalgo at the end of the Mexican War had again placed them under United States law. They applied for Utah's admission into the Union as a state or territory in 1849, and in 1850 Utah had been admitted as a territory. The Mormons, however, were still insurgent; several outbursts of violence between them and Federal troops took place, and later in 1857 the famous Mountain Meadows massacre occurred.

The election which had just been held in Kansas on June 15 was for delegates to a constitutional convention. The Free State men there, who had been tricked again and again in fraudulent elections at which proslavery supporters from Missouri entered the territory to vote illegally, were suspicious of the proposal to draw up a constitution. They refrained from voting; fewer than one-fourth of the registered voters went to the polls; proslavery delegates met at Lecompton, and the long controversy over the constitution named for that town began.

June 26, 1857

FELLOW-CITIZENS: I am here tonight, partly by the invitation of some of you, and partly by my own inclination. Two weeks ago Judge Douglas spoke here on the several subjects of Kansas, the Dred Scott decision, and Utah. I listened to the speech at the time, and have the report of it since. It was intended to controvert opinions which I think just, and to assail (politically, not personally) those men who, in common with me, entertain those opinions. For this reason I wished then, and still wish, to make some answer to it, which I now take the opportunity of doing.

I begin with Utah. If it prove to be true, as is probable, that the people of Utah are in open rebellion to the United States, then Judge Douglas is in favor of repealing their territorial organization, and attaching them to the adjoining states for judicial purposes. I say, too, if they are in rebellion, they ought to be somehow coerced to obedience; and I am not now prepared to admit or deny that the judge's mode of coercing them is not as good as any. The Republicans can fall in with it without taking back anything they have ever said. To be sure, it would be a considerable backing down by Judge Douglas from his much-vaunted doctrine of self-government for the Territories; but this is only additional proof of what was very plain from the beginning, that that doctrine was a mere deceitful pretense for the benefit of slavery. Those who could not see that much in the Nebraska Act itself, which forced governors, and secretaries, and judges on the people of the Territories without their choice or consent, could not be made to see, though one should rise from the dead.

But in all this, it is very plain the judge evades the only question the Republicans have ever pressed upon the Democracy in regard to Utah. That question the judge well knew to be this: "If the people of Utah shall peacefully form a State constitution tolerating polygamy, will the Democracy admit them into the Union?" There is nothing in the United States Constitution or law against polygamy; and why is it not a part of the judge's "sacred right of self-government" for the people to have it, or rather to keep it, if they choose? These questions, so far as I know, the judge never answers. It might involve the Democracy to answer them either way, and they go unanswered.

As to Kansas. The substance of the judge's speech on Kansas is an effort to put the free-State men in the wrong for not voting at the election of delegates to the constitutional convention. He says: "There is every reason to hope and believe that the law will be fairly interpreted and impartially executed, so as to insure to every *bona fide* inhabitant the free and quiet exercise of the elective franchise."

It appears extraordinary that Judge Douglas should make such a statement. He knows that, by the law, no one can vote who has not been registered; and he knows that the free-State men place their refusal to vote on the ground that but few of them have been registered. It is possible that this is not true, but Judge Douglas knows it is asserted to be true in letters, newspapers, and public speeches, and borne by every mail and blown by every breeze to the eyes and ears of the world. He knows it is boldly declared that the people of many whole counties, and many whole neighborhoods in others, are left unregistered; yet he does not venture to contradict the declaration, or to point out how they can vote without being registered; but he just slips along, not seeming to know there is any such question of fact, and complacently declares: "There is every reason to hope and believe that the law will be fairly and impartially executed, so as to insure to every *bona fide* inhabitant the free and quiet exercise of the elective franchise."

I readily agree that if all had a chance to vote, they ought to have voted. If, on the contrary, as they allege, and Judge Douglas ventures not to particularly contradict, few only of the free-State men had a chance to vote, they were perfectly right in staying from the polls in a body.

By the way, since the judge spoke, the Kansas election has come off. The judge expressed his confidence that all the Democrats in Kansas would do their duty—including "free-State Democrats," of course. The returns received here as yet are very incomplete; but so far as they go, they indicate that only about one-sixth of the registered voters have really voted; and this, too, when not more, perhaps, than one-half of the rightful voters have been registered, thus showing the thing to have been altogether the most exquisite farce ever enacted. I am watching with considerable interest to ascertain what figure "the free-State Democrats" cut in the concern. Of course they voted—all Democrats do their duty—and of course they did not vote for slave-State candidates. We soon shall know how many delegates they elected, how many candidates they had pledged to a free State, and how many votes were cast for them.

Allow me to barely whisper my suspicion that there were no such things in Kansas as "free-State Democrats"—that they were altogether mythical, good only to figure in newspapers and speeches in the free States. If there should prove to be one real living free-State Democrat in Kansas, I suggest that it might be well to catch him, and stuff and preserve his skin as an interesting specimen of that soon-to-be-extinct variety of the genus Democrat.

And now as to the Dred Scott decision. That decision declares two propositions—first, that a Negro cannot sue in the United States courts; and secondly, that Congress cannot prohibit slavery in the Territories. It was made by a divided court

—dividing differently on the different points. Judge Douglas does not discuss the merits of the decision, and in that respect I shall follow his example, believing I could no more improve on McLean and Curtis than he could on Taney.

He denounces all who question the correctness of that decision, as offering violent resistance to it. But who resists it? Who has, in spite of the decision, declared Dred Scott free, and resisted the authority of his master over him?

Judicial decisions have two uses—first, to absolutely determine the case decided; and secondly, to indicate to the public how other similar cases will be decided when they arise. For the latter use, they are called "precedents" and "authorities."

We believe as much as Judge Douglas (perhaps more) in obedience to, and respect for, the judicial department of government. We think its decisions on constitutional questions, when fully settled, should control not only the particular cases decided, but the general policy of the country, subject to be disturbed only by amendments of the Constitution as provided in that instrument itself. More than this would be revolution. But we think the Dred Scott decision is erroneous. We know the court that made it has often overruled its own decisions, and we shall do what we can to have it to overrule this. We offer no resistance to it.

Judicial decisions are of greater or less authority as precedents according to circumstances. That this should be so accords both with common sense and the customary understanding of the legal profession.

If this important decision had been made by the unanimous concurrence of the judges, and without any apparent partisan bias, and in accordance with legal public expectation and with the steady practice of the departments throughout our history, and had been in no part based on assumed historical facts which are not really true; or, if wanting in some of these, it had been before the court more than once, and had there been affirmed and reaffirmed through a course of years, it then might be, perhaps would be, factious, nay, even revolutionary, not to acquiesce in it as a precedent.

But when, as is true, we find it wanting in all these claims to the public confidence, it is not resistance, it is not factious, it is not even disrespectful, to treat it as not having yet quite established a settled doctrine for the country. . . .

I have said, in substance, that the Dred Scott decision was in part based on assumed historical facts which were not really true, and I ought not to leave the subject without giving some reasons for saying this; I therefore give an instance or two, which I think fully sustains me. Chief Justice Taney, in delivering the opinion of the majority of the court, insists at great length that Negroes were no part of the people who made, or for whom was made, the Declaration of Independence, or the Constitution of the United States.

On the contrary, Judge Curtis, in his dissenting opinion, shows that in five of the then thirteen States—to-wit, New Hampshire, Massachusetts, New York, New Jersey, and North Carolina—free Negroes were voters, and in proportion to their numbers had the same part in making the Constitution that the white people had. . . .

Again, Chief Justice Taney says:

It is difficult at this day to realize the state of public opinion, in relation to that unfortunate race, which prevailed in the civilized and enlightened portions of the world at the time of the Declaration of Independence, and when the Constitution of the United States was framed and adopted.

And again, after quoting from the Declaration, he says:

The general words above quoted would seem to include the whole human family, and if they were used in a similar instrument at this day, would be so understood.

In these the Chief Justice does not directly assert, but plainly assumes, as a fact, that the public estimate of the black man is more favorable now than it was in the days of the Revolution.

This assumption is a mistake. In some trifling particulars the condition of that race has been ameliorated; but as a whole, in this country, the change between then and now is decidedly the other way; and their ultimate destiny has never appeared so hopeless as in the last three or four years. In two of the five States—New Jersey and North Carolina—that then gave the free Negro the right of voting, the right has since been taken away, and in a third—New York—it has been greatly abridged; while it has not been extended, so far as I know, to a single additional State, though the number of the States has more than doubled. In those days, as I understand, masters could, at their own pleasure, emancipate their slaves; but since then such legal restraints have been made upon emancipation as to amount almost to prohibition. In those days legislatures held the unquestioned power to abolish slavery in their respective States, but now it is becoming quite fashionable for State constitutions to withhold that power from the legislatures. In those days, by common consent, the spread of the black man's bondage to the new countries was prohibited, but now Congress decides that it will not continue the prohibition, and the Supreme Court decides that it could not if it would. In those days our Declaration of Independence was held sacred by all, and thought to include all; but now, to aid in making the bondage of the Negro universal and eternal, it is assailed and sneered at and construed, and hawked at and torn, till, if its framers could rise from their graves, they could not at all recognize it. All the powers of earth seem rapidly combining against him. Mammon is after him, ambition follows, philosophy follows, and the theology of the day is fast joining the cry. They have him in his prison-house; they have searched his person, and left no prying instrument with him. One after another they have closed the heavy iron doors upon him; and now they have him, as it were, bolted in with a lock of a hundred keys, which can never be unlocked without the concurrence of every key—the keys in the hands of a hundred different men, and they scattered to a hundred different and distant places; and they stand musing as to what invention, in all the dominions of mind and matter, can be produced to make the impossibility of his escape more complete than it is.

It is grossly incorrect to say or assume that the public estimate of the Negro is more favorable now than it was at the origin of the government.

Three years and a half ago, Judge Douglas brought forward his famous Nebraska bill. The country was at once in a blaze. He scorned all opposition, and carried it through Congress. Since then he has seen himself superseded in a presidential nomination by one indorsing the general doctrine of his measure, but at the same time standing clear of the odium of its untimely agitation and its gross breach of national faith; and he has seen that successful rival constitutionally elected, not by the strength of friends, but by the division of adversaries, being in a popular minority of nearly four hundred thousand votes. He has seen his chief aids in his own State, Shields and Richardson, politically speaking, successively tried, convicted, and executed for an offense not their own, but his. And now he sees his own case standing next on the docket for trial.

There is a natural disgust in the minds of nearly all white people at the idea of an indiscriminate amalgamation of the white and black races; and Judge Douglas evidently is basing his chief hope upon the chances of his being able to appropriate the benefit of this disgust to himself. If he can, by much drumming and repeating, fasten the odium of that idea upon his adversaries, he thinks he can struggle through the storm. He therefore clings to this hope, as a drowning man to the last plank. He makes an occasion for lugging it in from the opposition of the Dred Scott decision. He finds the Republicans insisting that the Declaration of Independence includes *all* men, black as well as white, and forthwith he boldly denies that it includes Negroes at all, and proceeds to argue gravely that all who contend it does do so only because they want to

vote, and eat, and sleep, and marry with Negroes! He will have
it that they cannot be consistent else. Now I protest against
the counterfeit logic which concludes that, because I do not
want a black woman for a slave I must necessarily want her
for a wife. I need not have her for either. I can just leave her
alone. In some respects she certainly is not my equal; but in
her natural right to eat the bread she earns with her own hands
without asking leave of any one else, she is my equal, and the
equal of all others.

Chief Justice Taney, in his opinion in the Dred Scott case,
admits that the language of the Declaration is broad enough
to include the whole human family, but he and Judge Douglas argue that the authors of that instrument did not intend to
include Negroes, by the fact that they did not at once actually
place them on an equality with the whites. Now this grave
argument comes to just nothing at all, by the other fact that
they did not at once, or ever afterward, actually place all white
people on an equality with one another. And this is the staple
argument of both the chief justice and the senator for doing
this obvious violence to the plain, unmistakable language of
the Declaration.

I think the authors of that notable instrument intended to
include *all* men, but they did not intend to declare all men
equal *in all respects*. They did not mean to say all were equal
in color, size, intellect, moral developments, or social capacity.
They defined with tolerable distinctness in what respects they
did consider all men created equal—equal with "certain inalienable rights, among which are life, liberty, and the pursuit
of happiness." This they said, and this they meant. They did
not mean to assert the obvious untruth that all were then
actually enjoying that equality, nor yet that they were about to
confer it immediately upon them. In fact, they had no power
to confer such a boon. They meant simply to declare the right,
so that enforcement of it might follow as fast as circumstances
should permit.

They meant to set up a standard maxim for free society, which should be familiar to all, and revered by all; constantly looked to, constantly labored for, and even though never perfectly attained, constantly approximated, and thereby constantly spreading and deepening its influence and augmenting the happiness and value of life to all people of all colors everywhere. The assertion that "all men are created equal" was of no practical use in effecting our separation from Great Britain; and it was placed in the Declaration not for that, but for future use. Its authors meant it to be—as, thank God, it is now proving itself—a stumbling-block to all those who in after times might seek to turn a free people back into the hateful paths of despotism. They knew the proneness of prosperity to breed tyrants, and they meant when such should reappear in this fair land and commence their vocation, they should find left for them at least one hard nut to crack. . . .

I have now briefly expressed my view of the meaning and object of that part of the Declaration of Independence which declares that "all men are created equal."

Now let us hear Judge Douglas's view of the same subject, as I find it in the printed report of his late speech. Here it is:

No man can vindicate the character, motives, and conduct of the signers of the Declaration of Independence, except upon the hypothesis that they referred to the white race alone, and not to the African, when they declared all men to have been created equal; that they were speaking of British subjects on this continent being equal to British subjects born and residing in Great Britain; that they were entitled to the same inalienable rights, and among them were enumerated life, liberty, and the pursuit of happiness. The Declaration was adopted for the purpose of justifying the colonists in the eyes of the civilized world in withdrawing their allegiance from the British crown, and dissolving their connection with the mother country.

My good friends, read that carefully over some leisure hour, and ponder well upon it; see what a mere wreck—mangled ruin—it makes of our once glorious Declaration.

"They were speaking of British subjects on this continent being equal to British subjects born and residing in Great Britain!" Why, according to this, not only Negroes but white people outside of Great Britain and America were not spoken of in that instrument. The English, Irish, and Scotch, along with white Americans, were included, to be sure, but the French, Germans, and other white people of the world are all gone to pot along with the judge's inferior races!

I had thought the Declaration promised something better than the condition of British subjects; but no, it only meant that we should be equal to them in their own oppressed and unequal condition. According to that, it gave no promise that, having kicked off the King and Lords of Great Britain, we should not at once be saddled with a king and lords of our own.

I had thought the Declaration contemplated the progressive improvement in the condition of all men everywhere; but no, it merely "was adopted for the purpose of justifying the colonists in the eyes of the civilized world in withdrawing their allegiance from the British crown, and dissolving their connection with the mother country." Why, that object having been effected some eighty years ago, the Declaration is of no practical use now—mere rubbish—old wadding left to rot on the battlefield after the victory is won.

I understand you are preparing to celebrate the "Fourth," tomorrow week. What for? The doings of that day had no reference to the present; and quite half of you are not even descendants of those who were referred to at that day. But I suppose you will celebrate, and will even go as far as to read the Declaration. Suppose, after you read it once in the old-fashioned way, you read it once more with Judge Douglas's version. It will then run thus: "We hold these truths to be self-evident, that all British subjects who were on this continent eighty-one years ago, were created equal to all British subjects born and then residing in Great Britain."

And now I appeal to all—to Democrats as well as others—are you really willing that the Declaration shall thus be frittered away?—thus left no more, at most, than an interesting memorial of the dead past?—thus shorn of its vitality and practical value, and left without the germ or even the suggestion of the individual rights of man in it?

But Judge Douglas is especially horrified at the thought of the mixing of blood by the white and black races. Agreed for once—a thousand times agreed. There are white men enough to marry all the white women, and black men enough to marry all the black women; and so let them be married. On this point we fully agree with the judge, and when he shall show that his policy is better adapted to prevent amalgamation than ours, we shall drop ours and adopt his. Let us see. In 1850 there were in the United States 405,751 mulattos. Very few of these are the offspring of whites and free blacks; nearly all have sprung from black slaves and white masters. A separation of the races is the only perfect preventive of amalgamation; but as an immediate separation is impossible, the next best thing is to keep them apart where they are not already together. If white and black people never get together in Kansas, they will never mix blood in Kansas. That is at least one self-evident truth. A few free colored persons may get into the free States, in any event; but their number is too insignificant to amount to much in the way of mixing blood. In 1850 there were in the free States 56,649 mulattos; but for the most part they were not born there—they came from the slave States, ready made up. In the same year the slave States had 348,874 mulattos, all of home production. The proportion of free mulattos to free blacks—the only colored classes in the free States—is much greater in the slave than in the free States. It is worthy of note, too, that among the free States those which make the colored man the nearest equal to the white have proportionably the fewest mulattos, the least of amalgamation. In New Hampshire, the State which goes farthest toward equality between the races, there are just 184 mulattos, while there are in Virginia—how many do you think?—79,775, being 23,126 more than in all the free States together.

These statistics show that slavery is the greatest source of amalgamation, and next to it, not the elevation, but the degradation of the free blacks. Yet Judge Douglas dreads the slightest restraints on the spread of slavery, and the slightest human recognition of the Negro, as tending horribly to amalgamation. . . .

The very Dred Scott case affords a strong test as to which party most favors amalgamation, the Republicans or the dear Union-saving Democracy. Dred Scott, his wife, and two daughters were all involved in the suit. We desired the court to have held that they were citizens so far at least as to entitle them to a hearing as to whether they were free or not; and then, also, that they were in fact and in law really free. Could we have had our way, the chances of these black girls ever mixing their blood with that of white people would have been diminished at least to the extent that it could not have been without their consent. But Judge Douglas is delighted to have them decided to be slaves, and not human enough to have a hearing, even if they were free, and thus left subject to the forced concubinage of their masters, and liable to become the mothers of mulattos in spite of themselves: the very state of case that produces nine-tenths of all the mulattos—all the mixing of blood in the nation.

Of course, I state this case as an illustration only, not meaning to say or intimate that the master of Dred Scott and his family, or any more than a percentage of masters generally, are inclined to exercise this particular power which they hold over their female slaves.

I have said that the separation of the races is the only perfect preventive of amalgamation. I have no right to say all the members of the Republican party are in favor of this, nor to say that as a party they are in favor of it. There is nothing in their platform directly on the subject. But I can say a very large proportion of its members are for it, and that the chief plank in their platform—opposition to the spread of slavery—is most favorable to that separation.

Such separation, if ever effected at all, must be effected by colonization; and no political party, as such, is now doing anything directly for colonization. Party operations at present only favor or retard colonization incidentally. The enterprise is a difficult one; but "where there is a will there is a way," and what colonization needs most is a hearty will. Will springs from the two elements of moral sense and self-interest. Let us be brought to believe it is morally right, and at the same time favorable to, or at least not against, our interest to transfer the African to his native clime, and we shall find a way to do it, however great the task may be. The children of Israel, to such numbers as to include four hundred thousand fighting men, went out of Egyptian bondage in a body.

How differently the respective courses of the Democratic and Republican parties incidentally bear on the question of forming a will—a public sentiment—for colonization, is easy to see. The Republicans inculcate, with whatever of ability they can, that the Negro is a man, that his bondage is cruelly wrong, and that the field of his oppression ought not to be enlarged. The Democrats deny his manhood; deny, or dwarf to insignificance, the wrong of his bondage; so far as possible, crush all sympathy for him, and cultivate and excite hatred and disgust against him; compliment themselves as Union-savers for doing so; and call the indefinite outspreading of his bondage "a sacred right of self-government."

The plainest print cannot be read through a gold eagle; and it will be ever hard to find many men who will send a slave to Liberia, and pay his passage, while they can send him to a new country—Kansas, for instance—and sell him for fifteen hundred dollars, and the rise.

LETTER TO HANNAH ARMSTRONG

Hannah Armstrong was the wife of Jack Armstrong, leader of the Clary's Grove boys at New Salem, the man with whom Lincoln had had a famous wrestling match. Hannah's son, Duff, was being held on a murder charge. In this letter Lincoln offers his services for the boy's defense. During the trial, which took place on May 7th, 1858, Lincoln introduced as testimony an almanac which proved that there could not have been enough moonlight at the time specified for the witness to have observed what he claimed to have seen. As a result of Lincoln's strategy, Duff Armstrong went free.

Springfield, Ill., September, 1857

DEAR MRS. ARMSTRONG: I have just heard of your deep affliction, and the arrest of your son for murder. I can hardly believe that he can be capable of the crime alleged against him. It does not seem possible. I am anxious that he should be given a fair trial at any rate; and gratitude for your long-continued kindness to me in adverse circumstances prompts me to offer my humble services gratuitously in his behalf.

It will afford me an opportunity to requite, in a small degree, the favors I received at your hand, and that of your lamented husband, when your roof afforded me a grateful shelter, without money and without price.

SPEECH DELIVERED AT SPRINGFIELD, ILLINOIS, AT THE REPUBLICAN STATE CONVENTION WHICH HAD MADE LINCOLN ITS CANDIDATE FOR UNITED STATES SENATOR

This is the famous "House Divided" speech, so called from the Biblical quotation that Lincoln cites in the first paragraph. The

*Republican State Convention met in the Hall of Representatives
where Lincoln read this speech from manuscript. He had been
made the unanimous choice of the convention to run against
Douglas in the campaign for the United States Senatorship. During
his speech Lincoln insinuates that the Dred Scott decision was
the result of a conspiracy on the part of Douglas, Pierce, Taney
and Buchanan. He points out also that even though Douglas had
since broken with Buchanan over the Lecompton constitution in
Kansas, he was still not to be trusted and certainly not to be looked
upon as a person who might be used as an instrument with which
to break the political power of the slaveholders. With this speech
Lincoln becomes Douglas's official opponent with his party's full
backing.*

June 16, 1858

MR. PRESIDENT AND GENTLEMEN OF THE CONVENTION: If we
could first know where we are, and whither we are tending,
we could better judge what to do, and how to do it. We are
now far into the fifth year since a policy was initiated with the
avowed object and confident promise of putting an end to
slavery agitation. Under the operation of that policy, that agitation has not only not ceased but has constantly augmented.
In my opinion, it will not cease until a crisis shall have been
reached and passed. "A house divided against itself cannot
stand." I believe this government cannot endure permanently
half slave and half free. I do not expect the Union to be dissolved—I do not expect the house to fall—but I do expect it
will cease to be divided. It will become all one thing, or all
the other. Either the opponents of slavery will arrest the further spread of it, and place it where the public mind shall rest
in the belief that it is in the course of ultimate extinction; or
its advocates will push it forward till it shall become alike lawful in all the States, old as well as new, North as well as South.
Have we no tendency to the latter condition?

Let any one who doubts carefully contemplate that now almost complete legal combination—piece of machinery, so to speak—compounded of the Nebraska doctrine and the Dred Scott decision. Let him consider not only what work the machinery is adapted to do, and how well adapted; but also let him study the history of the construction, and trace, if he can, or rather fail, if he can, to trace the evidences of design and concert of action among its chief architects, from the beginning.

The new year of 1854 found slavery excluded from more than half the States by State constitutions, and from most of the national territory by congressional prohibition. Four days later commenced the struggle which ended in repealing that congressional prohibition. This opened all the national territory to slavery, and was the first point gained.

But, so far, Congress only had acted; and an indorsement by the people, real or apparent, was indispensable to save the point already gained and give chance for more.

This necessity had not been overlooked, but had been provided for, as well as might be, in the notable argument of "squatter sovereignty," otherwise called "sacred right of self-government," which latter phrase, though expressive of the only rightful basis of any government, was so perverted in this attempted use of it as to amount to just this: That if any one man choose to enslave another, no third man shall be allowed to object. That argument was incorporated into the Nebraska bill itself, in the language which follows: "It being the true intent and meaning of this act not to legislate slavery into any Territory or State, nor to exclude it therefrom; but to leave the people thereof perfectly free to form and regulate their domestic institutions in their own way, subject only to the Constitution of the United States." Then opened the roar of loose declamation in favor of "squatter sovereignty" and "sacred right of self-government." "But," said opposition members, "let us amend the bill so as to expressly declare that the people of the Territory may exclude slavery." "Not we," said the friends of the measure; and down they voted the amendment.

While the Nebraska bill was passing through Congress, a law case involving the question of a Negro's freedom, by reason of his owner having voluntarily taken him first into a free State and then into a Territory covered by the congressional prohibition, and held him as a slave for a long time in each, was passing through the United States Circuit Court for the District of Missouri; and both Nebraska bill and lawsuit were brought to a decision in the same month of May, 1854. The Negro's name was Dred Scott, which name now designates the decision finally made in the case. Before the then next presidential election, the law case came to and was argued in the Supreme Court of the United States; but the decision of it was deferred until after the election. Still, before the election, Senator Trumbull, on the floor of the Senate, requested the leading advocate of the Nebraska bill to state his opinion whether the people of a Territory can constitutionally exclude slavery from their limits; and the latter answered: "That is a question for the Supreme Court."

The election came. Mr. Buchanan was elected, and the indorsement, such as it was, secured. That was the second point gained. The indorsement, however, fell short of a clear popular majority by nearly four hundred thousand votes, and so, perhaps, was not overwhelmingly reliable and satisfactory. The outgoing President, in his last annual message, as impressively as possible echoed back upon the people the weight and authority of the indorsement. The Supreme Court met again; did not announce their decision, but ordered a reargument. The presidential inauguration came, and still no decision of the court; but the incoming President in his inaugural address fervently exhorted the people to abide by the forthcoming decision, whatever it might be. Then, in a few days, came the decision.

The reputed author* of the Nebraska bill finds an early occasion to make a speech at this capital indorsing the Dred Scott decision, and vehemently denouncing all opposition to it. The new President, too, seizes the early occasion of the Silliman letter to indorse and strongly construe that decision, and to express his astonishment that any different view had ever been entertained!

At length a squabble springs up between the President and the author of the Nebraska bill, on the mere question of fact, whether the Lecompton constitution was or was not, in any just sense, made by the people of Kansas; and in that quarrel the latter declares that all he wants is a fair vote for the people, and that he cares not whether slavery be voted down or voted up. I do not understand his declaration that he cares not whether slavery be voted down or voted up to be intended by him other than as an apt definition- of the policy he would impress upon the public mind—the principle for which he declares he has suffered so much, and is ready to suffer to the end. And well may he cling to that principle. If he has any parental feeling, well may he cling to it. That principle is the only shred left of his original Nebraska doctrine. Under the Dred Scott decision "squatter sovereignty" squatted out of existence, tumbled down like temporary scaffolding—like the mold at the foundry, served through one blast and fell back into loose sand—helped to carry an election, and then was kicked to the winds. His late joint struggle with the Republicans against the Lecompton constitution involves nothing of the original Nebraska doctrine. That struggle was made on a point—the right of a people to make their own constitution—upon which he and the Republicans have never differed.

The several points of the Dred Scott decision, in connection with Senator Douglas's "care not" policy, constitute the piece of machinery in its present state of advancement. This was the third point gained. The working points of that machinery are:

* Stephen A. Douglas.

(1) That no Negro slave, imported as such from Africa, and no descendant of such slave, can ever be a citizen of any State, in the sense of that term as used in the Constitution of the United States. This point is made in order to deprive the Negro in every possible event of the benefit of that provision of the United States Constitution which declares that "the citizens of each State shall be entitled to all the privileges and immunities of citizens in the several States."

(2) That, "subject to the Constitution of the United States," neither Congress nor a territorial legislature can exclude slavery from any United States Territory. This point is made in order that individual men may fill up the Territories with slaves, without danger of losing them as property and thus enhance the chances of permanency to the institution through all the future.

(3) That whether the holding a Negro in actual slavery in a free State makes him free as against the holder, the United States courts will not decide, but will leave to be decided by the courts of any slave State the Negro may be forced into by the master. This point is made not to be pressed immediately, but, if acquiesced in for a while, and apparently indorsed by the people at an election, then to sustain the logical conclusion that what Dred Scott's master might lawfully do with Dred Scott in the free State of Illinois, every other master may lawfully do with any other one or one thousand slaves in Illinois or in any other free State.

Auxiliary to all this, and working hand in hand with it, the Nebraska doctrine, or what is left of it, is to educate and mold public opinion, at least Northern public opinion, not to care whether slavery is voted down or voted up. This shows exactly where we now are, and partially, also, whither we are tending.

It will throw additional light on the latter, to go back and run the mind over the string of historical facts already stated. Several things will now appear less dark and mysterious than they did when they were transpiring. The people were to be left "perfectly free," "subject only to the Constitution." What the Constitution had to do with it outsiders could not then see. Plainly enough now, it was an exactly fitted niche for the Dred Scott decision to afterward come in, and declare the perfect freedom of the people to be just no freedom at all. Why was the amendment expressly declaring the right of the people voted down? Plainly enough now, the adoption of it would have spoiled the niche for the Dred Scott decision. Why was the court decision held up? Why even a senator's individual opinion withheld till after the Presidential election? Plainly enough now, the speaking out then would have damaged the "perfectly free" argument upon which the election was to be carried. Why the outgoing President's [Pierce] felicitation on the indorsement? Why the delay of a reargument? Why the incoming President's [Buchanan] advance exhortation in favor of the decision? These things look like the cautious patting and petting of a spirited horse preparatory to mounting him, when it is dreaded that he may give the rider a fall. And why the hasty after-endorsement of the decision by the President and others?

We cannot absolutely know that all these exact adaptations are the result of preconcert. But when we see a lot of framed timbers, different portions of which we know have been gotten out at different times and places and by different workmen— Stephen, Franklin, Roger, and James,* for instance—and we see these timbers joined together, and see they exactly make the frame of a house or a mill, all the tenons and mortises exactly fitting, and all the lengths and proportions of the different pieces exactly adapted to their respective places, and not a piece too many or too few, not omitting even scaffolding— or, if a single piece be lacking, we see the place in the frame exactly fitted and prepared yet to bring such piece in—in such a case we find it impossible not to believe that Stephen and Franklin and Roger and James all understood one another

* Stephen A. Douglas, Franklin Pierce, Roger B. Taney, James Buchanan.

from the beginning, and all worked upon a common plan or draft drawn up before the first blow was struck.

It should not be overlooked that, by the Nebraska bill, the people of a State as well as Territory were to be left "perfectly free," "subject only to the Constitution." Why mention a State? They were legislating for Territories, and not for or about States. Certainly the people of a State are and ought to be subject to the Constitution of the United States; but why is mention of this lugged into this merely territorial law? Why are the people of a Territory and the people of a State therein lumped together, and their relation to the Constitution therein treated as being precisely the same? While the opinion of the court, by Chief Justice Taney, in the Dred Scott case, and the separate opinions of all the concurring judges, expressly declare that the Constitution of the United States neither permits Congress nor a territorial legislature to exclude slavery from any United States Territory, they all omit to declare whether or not the same Constitution permits a State, or the people of a State, to exclude it. Possibly, this is a mere omission; but who can be quite sure, if McLean or Curtis* had sought to get into the opinion a declaration of unlimited power in the people of a State to exclude slavery from their limits, just as Chase and Mace sought to get such declaration, in behalf of the people of a Territory, into the Nebraska bill—I ask, who can be quite sure that it would not have been voted down in the one case as it had been in the other? The nearest approach to the point of declaring the power of a State over slavery is made by Judge Nelson. He approaches it more than once, using the precise idea, and almost the language too, of the Nebraska act. On one occasion his exact language is: "Except in case where the power is restrained by the Constitution of the United States, the law of the State is supreme over the subject of slavery within its jurisdiction." In what cases the power of the States is so restrained by the United States Con-

* Dissenting justices in the Dred Scott decision.

stitution is left an open question, precisely as the same question as to the restraint on the power of the Territories was left open in the Nebraska act. Put this and that together, and we have another nice little niche, which we may, ere long, see filled with another Supreme Court decision declaring that the Constitution of the United States does not permit a State to exclude slavery from its limits. And this may especially be expected if the doctrine of "care not whether slavery be voted down or voted up" shall gain upon the public mind sufficiently to give promise that such a decision can be maintained when made.

Such a decision is all that slavery now lacks of being alike lawful in all the States. Welcome, or unwelcome, such decision is probably coming, and will soon be upon us, unless the power of the present political dynasty shall be met and overthrown. We shall lie down pleasantly dreaming that the people of Missouri are on the verge of making their State free, and we shall awake to the reality instead that the Supreme Court has made Illinois a slave State. To meet and overthrow the power of that dynasty is the work now before all those who would prevent that consummation. That is what we have to do. How can we best do it?

There are those who denounce us openly to their own friends, and yet whisper [to] us softly that Senator Douglas is the aptest instrument there is with which to effect that object. They wish us to infer all from the fact that he now has a little quarrel with the present head of the dynasty; and that he has regularly voted with us on a single point upon which he and we have never differed. They remind us that he is a great man, and that the largest of us are very small ones. Let this be granted. But "a living dog is better than a dead lion." Judge Douglas, if not a dead lion for this work, is at least a caged and toothless one. How can he oppose the advances of slavery? He don't care anything about it. His avowed mission is impressing the "public heart" to care nothing about it. A leading Douglas Democratic newspaper thinks Douglas's superior talent will be needed to resist the revival of the African slave trade. Does Douglas believe an effort to revive that trade is approaching? He has not said so. Does he really think so? But if it is, how can he resist it? For years he has labored to prove it a sacred right of white men to take Negro slaves into the new Territories. Can he possibly show that it is less a sacred right to buy them where they can be bought cheapest? And unquestionably they can be bought cheaper in Africa than in Virginia. He has done all in his power to reduce the whole question of slavery to one of a mere right of property; and as such, how can he oppose the foreign slave trade? How can he refuse that trade in that "property" shall be "perfectly free," unless he does it as a protection to the home production? And as the home producers will probably not ask the protection, he will be wholly without a ground of opposition.

Senator Douglas holds, we know, that a man may rightfully be wiser today than he was yesterday—that he may rightfully change when he finds himself wrong. But can we, for that reason, run ahead, and infer that he will make any particular change of which he, himself, has given no intimation? Can we safely base our action upon any such vague inference? Now, as ever, I wish not to misrepresent Judge Douglas's position, question his motives, or do aught that can be personally offensive to him. Whenever, if ever, he and we can come together on principle so that our great cause may have assistance from his great ability, I hope to have interposed no adventitious obstacle. But clearly, he is not now with us—he does not pretend to be—he does not promise ever to be.

Our cause, then, must be intrusted to, and conducted by, its own undoubted friends—those whose hands are free, whose hearts are in the work, who do care for the result. Two years ago the Republicans of the nation mustered over thirteen-hundred thousand strong. We did this under the single impulse of resistance to a common danger, with every external circumstance against us. Of strange, discordant, and even hostile elements, we gathered from the four winds, and formed and fought the battle through, under the constant hot fire of a disciplined, proud, and pampered enemy. Did we brave all then to falter now?—now, when that same enemy is wavering, dissevered, and belligerent? The result is not doubtful. We shall not fail—if we stand firm, we shall not fail. Wise counsels may accelerate or mistakes delay it, but, sooner or later, the victory is sure to come.

LETTER TO JOHN L. SCRIPPS

John L. Scripps was a Chicago newspaperman who was later to become Lincoln's first biographer when he wrote a brief campaign biography which was used in 1860. Lincoln writes to Scripps to assure him that nothing in his speech of June 16 was to be interpreted as showing any desire on his part "to interfere with slavery in the states where it exists."

Springfield, June 23, 1858

MY DEAR SIR: Your kind note of yesterday is duly received. I am much flattered by the estimate you place on my late speech; and yet I am much mortified that any part of it should be construed so differently from any thing intended by me. The language, "place it where the public mind shall rest in the belief that it is in course of ultimate extinction," I used deliberately, not dreaming then, nor believing now, that it asserts or intimates any power or purpose, to interfere with slavery in the states where it exists. But to not cavil about language, I declare that whether the clause used by me will bear such construction or not, I never so intended it. I have declared a thousand times, and now repeat that, in my opinion, neither the General Government, nor any other power outside of the slave States, can constitutionally or rightfully interfere with slaves or slavery where it already exists. I believe that whenever the effort to spread slavery into the new Territories, by whatever means, and into the free States themselves, by Supreme Court decisions, shall be fairly headed off, the institution will then be in course of ultimate extinction; and by the language used I meant only this.

I do not intend this for publication; but still you may show it to any one you think fit. I think I shall, as you suggest, take some early occasion to publicly repeat the declaration I have already so often made as before stated.

FROM A SPEECH AT CHICAGO

Douglas had not been allowed to speak when he had tried to address a Chicago crowd in 1854, just after he had engineered the Kansas-Nebraska Act through Congress. Now that he had broken with his own party on a matter of principle—the unacceptability of the Lecompton constitution which the pro-slavery men were attempting to ram down the throats of Kansas citizens—Chicago greeted him enthusiastically. He was a hero again. He spoke on the night of July 9 from the balcony of the Tremont House to a vast crowd gathered in the streets. Behind him, taking down notes, sat Abraham Lincoln, the Republican party's official candidate for Douglas's office, but a man who was still obscure and who had not yet been tried in any major political campaign. Douglas cheerfully admitted that he was attacking the Lecompton constitution, not because it was a thinly disguised measure to help the spread of slavery, but because it was being submitted in an unfair manner to the people so that they did not really have a free choice in the matter. He assailed the principle stated by Lincoln in his "House Divided" speech—the principle which maintained that the nation could not endure half slave and half free. Such a doctrine, Douglas said, would bring about "a war of sections, a war of the North against the South, of the free states against the slave states, a war of extermination to be continued relentlessly until the one *or the other shall be subdued and all the states shall either become free or become slave." Uniformity of this kind had not been intended by the men who had founded the nation; they had allowed for sectional differences of climate and custom. To aim for uniformity was to achieve despotism. The Constitution must be maintained, the decision of the Supreme Court in the Dred Scott case must not be resisted. Douglas then came out unequivocally for white supremacy, saying: "I am opposed to Negro equality. . . . No amalgamation, political or otherwise, with inferior races." Lincoln was called upon to answer his opponent that night, but he refused to do so, and promised to speak the next night at the same place instead. Douglas had repeated many of the arguments used in his address at Springfield on June 12, 1857; Lincoln also repeats many of his own counter-arguments here. The chain of reasoning begins to become standardized, but Lincoln continues to improve upon the wording and the cogency of his arguments from this time on.*

July 10, 1858

JUDGE DOUGLAS made two points upon my recent speech at Springfield. He says they are to be the issues of this campaign. The first one of these points he bases upon the language in a speech which I delivered at Springfield, which I believe I can quote correctly from memory. I said there that "we are now far into the fifth year since a policy was instituted for the avowed object and with the confident promise of putting an end to slavery agitation; under the operation of that policy, that agitation has not only not ceased, but has constantly augmented. I believe it will not cease until a crisis shall have been reached and passed. 'A house divided against itself cannot stand.' I believe this government cannot endure permanently half slave and half free. I do not expect the Union to be dissolved"—I am quoting from my speech—"I do not expect the house to fall, but I do expect it will cease to be

divided. It will become all one thing or all the other. Either
the opponents of slavery will arrest the further spread of it,
and place it where the public mind shall rest in the belief that
it is in the course of ultimate extinction, or its advocates will
push it forward until it shall become alike lawful in all the
States, old as well as new, North as well as South."

That is the paragraph! In this paragraph which I have
quoted in your hearing, and to which I ask the attention of
all, Judge Douglas thinks he discovers great political heresy. I
want your attention particularly to what he has inferred from
it. He says I am in favor of making all the States of this Union
uniform in all their internal regulations; that in all their domestic concerns I am in favor of making them entirely uniform. He draws this inference from the language I have quoted
to you. He says that I am in favor of making war by the North
upon the South for the extinction of slavery; that I am also in
favor of inviting (as he expresses it) the South to a war upon
the North, for the purpose of nationalizing slavery. Now, it is
singular enough, if you will carefully read that passage over,
that I did not say that I was in favor of anything in it. I only
said what I expected would take place. I made a prediction
only—it may have been a foolish one, perhaps. I did not even
say that I desired that slavery should be put in course of ultimate extinction. I do say so now, however, so there need be no
longer any difficulty about that. It may be written down in the
great speech.

Gentlemen, Judge Douglas informed you that this speech of
mine was probably carefully prepared. I admit that it was. I
am not master of language; I have not a fine education; I am
not capable of entering into a disquisition upon dialectics, as I
believe you call it; but I do not believe the language I employed bears any such construction as Judge Douglas puts upon
it. But I don't care about a quibble in regard to words. I know
what I meant, and I will not leave this crowd in doubt, if I can

explain it to them, what I really meant in the use of that paragraph.

I am not, in the first place, unaware that this government has endured eighty-two years half slave and half free. I know that. I am tolerably well acquainted with the history of the country, and I know that it has endured eighty-two years half slave and half free. I believe—and that is what I meant to allude to there—I believe it has endured because during all that time, until the introduction of the Nebraska bill, the public mind did rest all the time in the belief that slavery was in course of ultimate extinction. That was what gave us the rest that we had through that period of eighty-two years; at least, so I believe. I have always hated slavery, I think, as much as any Abolitionist—I have been an old-line Whig—I have always hated it, but I have always been quiet about it until this new era of the introduction of the Nebraska bill began. I always believed that everybody was against it, and that it was in course of ultimate extinction. . . . The great mass of the nation have rested in the belief that slavery was in course of ultimate extinction. They had reason so to believe.

The adoption of the Constitution and its attendant history led the people to believe so, and that such was the belief of the framers of the Constitution itself. Why did those old men, about the time of the adoption of the Constitution, decree that slavery should not go into the new Territory, where it had not already gone? Why declare that within twenty years the African slave trade, by which slaves are supplied, might be cut off by Congress? Why were all these acts—? I might enumerate more of these acts—but enough. What were they but a clear indication that the framers of the Constitution intended and expected the ultimate extinction of that institution? And now, when I say—as I said in my speech that Judge Douglas has quoted from—when I say that I think the opponents of slavery will resist the farther spread of it, and place it where the public mind shall rest in the belief that it is in course of ultimate extinction, I only mean to say that they will place it where the founders of this government originally placed it.

I have said a hundred times, and I have now no inclination to take it back, that I believe there is no right and ought to be no inclination in the people of the free States to enter into the slave States and interfere with the question of slavery at all. I have said that always; Judge Douglas has heard me say it—if not quite a hundred times, at least as good as a hundred times; and when it is said that I am in favor of interfering with slavery where it exists, I know it is unwarranted by anything I have ever intended, and, as I believe, by anything I have ever said. If by any means I have ever used language which could fairly be so construed (as, however, I believe I never have), I now correct it.

So much, then, for the inference that Judge Douglas draws, that I am in favor of setting the sections at war with one another. I know that I never meant any such thing, and I believe that no fair mind can infer any such thing from anything I have ever said.

Now in relation to his inference that I am in favor of a general consolidation of all the local institutions of the various States. I will attend to that for a little while, and try to inquire, if I can, how on earth it could be that any man could draw such an inference from anything I said. I have said very many times in Judge Douglas's hearing that no man believed more than I in the principle of self-government; that it lies at the bottom of all my ideas of just government from beginning to end. I have denied that his use of that term applies properly. But for the thing itself I deny that any man has ever gone ahead of me in his devotion to the principle, whatever he may have done in efficiency in advocating it. I think that I have said it in your hearing—that I believe each individual is naturally entitled to do as he pleases with himself and the fruit of his labor, so far as it in no wise interferes with any other man's rights; that each community, as a State, has a right to do exactly as it pleases with all the concerns within that State that interfere with the right of no other State; and that the General Government, upon principle, has no right to interfere with anything other than that general class of things that does not concern the whole. I have said that at all times. I have said as illustrations that I do not believe in the right of Illinois to interfere with the cranberry laws of Indiana, the oyster laws of Virginia, or the liquor laws of Maine. I have said these things over and over again, and I repeat them here as my sentiments.

How is it, then, that Judge Douglas infers, because I hope to see slavery put where the public mind shall rest in the belief that it is in the course of ultimate extinction, that I am in favor of Illinois going over and interfering with the cranberry laws of Indiana? What can authorize him to draw any such inference? I suppose there might be one thing that at least enabled him to draw such an inference that would not be true with me or many others; that is, because he looks upon all this matter of slavery as an exceedingly little thing—this matter of keeping one-sixth of the population of the whole nation in a state of oppression and tyranny unequaled in the world. He looks upon it as being an exceedingly little thing, only equal to the question of the cranberry laws of Indiana—as something having no moral question in it—as something on a par with the question of whether a man shall pasture his land with cattle or plant it with tobacco—so little and so small a thing that he concludes, if I could desire that anything should be done to bring about the ultimate extinction of that little thing, I must be in favor of bringing about an amalgamation of all the other little things in the Union. Now, it so happens—and there, I presume, is the foundation of this mistake—that the judge thinks thus; and it so happens that there is a vast portion of the American people that do not look upon that matter as being this very little thing. They look upon it as a vast moral evil; they can prove it as such by the writings of those who gave us the blessings of liberty which we enjoy, and that they so looked upon it, and not as an evil merely confining itself to the States where it is situated; and while we agree that, by the Constitution we assented to, in the States where it exists we have no right to interfere with it, because it is in the Constitution, we are by both duty and inclination to stick by that Constitution in all its letter and spirit from beginning to end.

So much, then, as to my disposition—my wish—to have all the State legislatures blotted out, and to have one consolidated government, and a uniformity of domestic regulations in all the States; by which I suppose it is meant, if we raise corn here, we must make sugarcane grow here too, and we must make those which grow North grow in the South. All this I suppose he understands I am in favor of doing. Now, so much for all this nonsense—for I must call it so. The judge can have no issue with me on a question of establishing uniformity in the domestic regulations of the States.

A little now on the other point—the Dred Scott decision. Another of the issues he says that is to be made with me, is upon his devotion to the Dred Scott decision, and my opposition to it.

I have expressed heretofore, and I now repeat, my opposition to the Dred Scott decision; but I should be allowed to state the nature of that opposition, and I ask your indulgence while I do so. What is fairly implied by the term Judge Douglas has used, "resistance to the decision"? I do not resist it. If I wanted to take Dred Scott from his master, I would be interfering with property, and that terrible difficulty that Judge Douglas speaks of, of interfering with property, would arise. But I am doing no such thing as that; all that I am doing is refusing to obey it as a political rule. If I were in Congress, and a vote should come up on a question whether slavery should be prohibited in a new Territory, in spite of the Dred Scott decision, I would vote that it should.

That is what I would do. Judge Douglas said last night that before the decision he might advance his opinion, and it might be contrary to the decision when it was made; but after it was made he would abide by it until it was reversed. Just so! We let this property abide by the decision, but we will try to reverse that decision. We will try to put it where Judge Douglas would not object, for he says he will obey it until it is reversed. Somebody has to reverse that decision, since it is made; and we mean to reverse it, and we mean to do it peaceably.

What are the uses of decisions of courts? They have two uses. As rules of property they have two uses. First—they decide upon the question before the court. They decide in this case that Dred Scott is a slave. Nobody resists that. Not only that, but they say to everybody else that persons standing just as Dred Scott stands are as he is. That is, they say that when a question comes up upon another person, it will be so decided again, unless the court decides in another way, unless the court overrules its decision. Well, we mean to do what we can to have the court decide the other way. That is one thing we mean to try to do.

The sacredness that Judge Douglas throws around this decision is a degree of sacredness that has never been before thrown around any other decision. I have never heard of such a thing. Why, decisions apparently contrary to that decision, or that good lawyers thought were contrary to that decision, have been made by that very court before. It is the first of its kind; it is an astonisher in legal history. It is a new wonder of the world. It is based upon falsehood in the main as to the facts—allegations of facts upon which it stands are not facts at all in many instances—and no decision made on any question—the first instance of a decision made under so many unfavorable circumstances—thus placed, has ever been held by the profession as law, and it has always needed confirmation before the lawyers regarded it as settled law. But Judge Douglas will have it that all hands must take this extraordinary decision, made under these extraordinary circumstances, and give their vote in Congress in accordance with it, yield to it and obey it in every possible sense. . . .

We were often—more than once at least—in the course of Judge Douglas's speech last night reminded that this government was made for white men—that he believed it was made for white men. Well, that is putting it into a shape in which no one wants to deny it; but the judge then goes into his passion for drawing inferences that are not warranted. I protest, now and forever, against that counterfeit logic which presumes that because I do not want a Negro woman for a slave, I do necessarily want her for a wife. My understanding is that I need not have her for either; but, as God made us separate, we can leave one another alone, and do one another much good thereby. There are white men enough to marry all the white women, and enough black men to marry all the black women, and in God's name let them be so married. The judge regales us with the terrible enormities that take place by the mixture of races; that the inferior race bears the superior down. Why, Judge, if we do not let them get together in the Territories, they won't mix there. I should say at least that that is a self-evident truth.

Now, it happens that we meet together once every year, somewhere about the 4th of July, for some reason or other. These 4th of July gatherings I suppose have their uses. If you will indulge me, I will state what I suppose to be some of them.

We are now a mighty nation: we are thirty, or about thirty, millions of people, and we own and inhabit about one-fifteenth part of the dry land of the whole earth. We run our memory back over the pages of history for about eighty-two years, and we discover that we were then a very small people, in point of numbers vastly inferior to what we are now, with a vastly less extent of country, with vastly less of everything we deem desirable among men. We look upon the change as exceedingly advantageous to us and to our posterity, and we fix upon something that happened away back as in some way or other being connected with this rise of prosperity. We find a race of men living in that day whom we claim as our fathers and grandfathers; they were iron men; they fought for the principle that they were contending for; and we understood that by what they then did it has followed that the degree of prosperity which we now enjoy has come to us. We hold this annual celebration to remind ourselves of all the good done in this process of time, of how it was done and who did it, and how we are historically connected with it; and we go from these meetings in better humor with ourselves—we feel more attached the one to the other, and more firmly bound to the country we inhabit. In every way we are better men, in the age, and race, and country in which we live, for these celebrations. But after we have done all this, we have not yet reached the whole. There is something else connected with it. We have, besides these men—descended by blood from our ancestors—among us, perhaps half our people who are not descendants at all of these men; they are men who have come from Europe—German, Irish, French, and Scandinavian—men that have come from Europe themselves, or whose ancestors have come hither and settled here, finding themselves our equal in all things. If they look back through this history to trace their connection with those days by blood, they find they have none; they cannot carry themselves back into that glorious epoch and make themselves feel that they are part of us; but when they look through that old Declaration of Independence, they find that those old men say that "We hold these truths to be self-evident, that all men are created equal," and then they feel that the moral sentiment taught in that day evidences their relation to those men, that it is the father of all moral principle in them, and that they have a right to claim it as though they were blood of the blood, and flesh of the flesh, of the men who wrote that Declaration, and so they are. That is the electric cord in that Declaration that links the hearts of patriotic and liberty-loving men together, that will link those patriotic hearts as long as the love of freedom exists in the minds of men throughout the world.

Now, sirs, for the purpose of squaring things with this idea of "don't care if slavery is voted up or voted down," for sustaining the Dred Scott decision, for holding that the Declaration of Independence did not mean anything at all, we have Judge Douglas giving his exposition of what the Declaration of Independence means, and we have him saying that the people of America are equal to the people of England. According to his construction, you Germans* are not connected with it. Now I ask you, in all soberness, if all these things, if indulged in, if ratified, if confirmed and indorsed, if taught to our children, and repeated to them, do not tend to rub out the sentiment of liberty in the country, and to transform this government into a government of some other form? Those arguments that are made, that the inferior race are to be treated with as much allowance as they are capable of enjoying; that as much is to be done for them as their condition will allow—what are these arguments? They are the arguments that kings have made for enslaving the people in all ages of the world. You will find that all the arguments in favor of kingcraft were of this class; they always bestrode the necks of the people—not that they wanted to do it, but because the people were better off for being ridden. That is their argument, and this argument of the judge is the same old serpent that says: "You work and I eat, you toil and I will enjoy the fruits of it." Turn in whatever way you will—whether it come from the mouth of a king, an excuse for enslaving the people of his country, or from the mouth of men of one race as a

* A German political club had just marched into the crowd.

reason for enslaving the men of another race, it is all the same old serpent, and I hold if that course of argumentation that is made for the purpose of convincing the public mind that we should not care about this should be granted, it does not stop with the Negro. I should like to know—taking this old Declaration of Independence, which declares that all men are equal upon principle, and making exceptions to it—where will it stop? If one man says it does not mean a Negro, why not another say it does not mean some other man? If that Declaration is not the truth, let us get the statute-book in which we find it, and tear it out! Who is so bold as to do it? If it is not true, let us tear it out. [Cries of "No, no!"] Let us stick to it, then; let us stand firmly by it, then.

It may be argued that there are certain conditions that make necessities and impose them upon us, and to the extent that a necessity is imposed upon a man, he must submit to it. I think that was the condition in which we found ourselves when we established this government. We had slaves among us; we could not get our Constitution unless we permitted them to remain in slavery; we could not secure the good we did secure if we grasped for more; but having by necessity submitted to that much, it does not destroy the principle that is the charter of our liberties. Let that charter stand as our standard.

My friend has said to me that I am a poor hand to quote Scripture. I will try it again, however. It is said in one of the admonitions of our Lord, "Be ye [therefore] perfect even as your Father which is in heaven is perfect." The Saviour, I suppose, did not expect that any human creature could be perfect as the Father in heaven; but he said, "As your Father in heaven is perfect, be ye also perfect." He set that up as a standard, and he who did most toward reaching that standard attained the highest degree of moral perfection. So I say in relation to the principle that all men are created equal, let it be as nearly reached as we can. If we cannot give freedom to every creature, let us do nothing that will impose slavery upon any other creature. Let us then turn this government back into the channel in which the framers of the Constitution originally placed it. Let us stand firmly by each other. If we do not do so, we are tending in the contrary direction that our friend Judge Douglas proposes—not intentionally—working in the traces that tend to make this one universal slave nation. He is one that runs in that direction, and as such I resist him.

My friends, I have detained you about as long as I desired to do, and I have only to say, let us discard all this quibbling about this man and the other man, this race and that race and the other race being inferior, and therefore they must be placed in an inferior position. Let us discard all these things, and unite as one people throughout this land, until we shall once more stand up declaring that all men are created equal.

My friends, I could not, without launching off upon some new topic, which would detain you too long, continue tonight. I thank you for this most extensive audience that you have furnished me tonight. I leave you, hoping that the lamp of liberty will burn in your bosoms until there shall no longer be a doubt that all men are created free and equal.

FROM A SPEECH AT SPRINGFIELD, ILLINOIS

On July 16, Douglas had spoken at Bloomington, elaborating upon his Chicago speech. He strengthened his arguments by saying that slavery could not exist in places where the people did not want to let it flourish. No law and no legislative act could put slavery where the people were determined not to have it. Therefore the Dred Scott decision could have no practical effect; therefore popular sovereignty was the ultimate solution for all problems. Lincoln was present when Douglas spoke and declined to answer him at the meeting called in Douglas's behalf. Douglas went on to Springfield the next day to speak in a grove north of the town. He laughed off Lincoln's charges of conspiracy in the Dred Scott decision and repeated his standard arguments. Lincoln replied to him during the evening of the same day, speaking in the Hall of Representatives. This is the last speech Lincoln made before the challenge to the series of formal debates was issued.

July 17, 1858

Senator Douglas is of world-wide renown. All the anxious politicians of his party, or who have been of his party for years past, have been looking upon him as certainly, at no distant day, to be the President of the United States. They have seen in his round, jolly, fruitful face, post-offices, land-offices, marshalships and cabinet appointments, chargéships and foreign missions, bursting and sprouting out in wonderful exuberance, ready to be laid hold of by their greedy hands. And as they have been gazing upon this attractive picture so long, they cannot, in the little distraction that has taken place in the party, bring themselves to give up the charming hope; but with greedier anxiety they rush about him, sustain him, and give him marches, triumphal entries, and receptions beyond what even in the days of his highest prosperity they could have brought about in his favor. On the contrary, nobody has ever expected me to be President. In my poor, lean, lank face nobody has ever seen that any cabbages were sprouting out. These are disadvantages all, taken together, that the Republicans labor under. We have to fight this battle upon principle, and upon principle alone. I am, in a certain sense, made the standard-bearer in behalf of the Republicans. I was made so merely because there had to be some one so placed, I being in no wise preferable to any other one of the twenty-five, perhaps a hundred, we have in the Republican ranks. Then I say I wish it to be distinctly understood and borne in mind, that we have to fight this battle without many—perhaps without any—of the external aids which are brought to bear against us.

So I hope those with whom I am surrounded have principle enough to nerve themselves for the task, and leave nothing undone that can be fairly done to bring about the right result.

*   *   *

Although I have ever been opposed to slavery, so far I rested in the hope and belief that it was in the course of ultimate extinction. For that reason, it had been a minor question with me. I might have been mistaken; but I had believed, and now believe, that the whole public mind, that is, the mind of the great majority, had rested in that belief up to the repeal of the Missouri Compromise. But upon that event, I became convinced that either I had been resting in a delusion, or the institution was being placed on a new basis—a basis for making it perpetual, national, and universal. Subsequent events have greatly confirmed me in that belief. I believe that bill to be the beginning of a conspiracy for that purpose. So believing, I have since then considered that question a paramount one. So believing, I think the public mind will never rest till the power of Congress to restrict the spread of it shall again be acknowledged and exercised on the one hand, or, on the other, all resistance be entirely crushed out. I have expressed that opinion, and I entertain it tonight. It is denied that there is any tendency to the nationalization of slavery in these States.

*   *   *

Now, I wish to know what the judge can charge upon me, with respect to decisions of the Supreme Court, which does not lie in all its length, breadth, and proportions at his own door. The plain truth is simply this: Judge Douglas is for Supreme Court decisions when he likes, and against them when he does not like them. He is for the Dred Scott decision because it tends to nationalize slavery—because it is part of the original combination for that object. It so happens, singularly enough, that I never stood opposed to a decision of the Supreme Court till this. On the contrary, I have no recollection that he was ever particularly in favor of one till this. He never was in favor of any, nor opposed to any, till the present one, which helps to nationalize slavery.

Free men of Sangamon, free men of Illinois, free men everywhere, judge ye between him and me upon this issue!

He says this Dred Scott case is a very small matter at most; that it has no practical effect; that at best, or rather, I suppose, at worst, it is but an abstraction. I submit that the proposition that the thing which determines whether a man is free or a slave is rather concrete than abstract. I think you would conclude that it was if your liberty depended upon it, and so would Judge Douglas if his liberty depended upon it. But suppose it was on the question of spreading slavery over the new Territories that he considers it as being merely an abstract matter, and one of no practical importance. How has the planting of slavery in new countries always been effected? It has now been decided that slavery cannot be kept out of our new Territories by any legal means. In what do our new Territories now differ in this respect from the old colonies when slavery was first planted within them? It was planted as Mr. Clay once declared, and as history proves true, by individual men in spite of the wishes of the people; the mother government refusing to prohibit it, and withholding from the people of the colonies the authority to prohibit it for themselves. Mr. Clay says this was one of the great and just causes of complaint against Great Britain by the colonies, and the best apology we can now make for having the institution amongst us. In that precise condition our Nebraska politicians have at last succeeded in placing our own new Territories; the government will not prohibit slavery within them, nor allow the people to prohibit it.

I defy any man to find any difference between the policy

which originally planted slavery in these colonies and that which now prevails in our new Territories.

*   *   *

One more thing. Last night Judge Douglas tormented himself with horrors about my disposition to make Negroes perfectly equal with white men in social and political relations. He did not stop to show that I have said any such thing, or that it legitimately follows from anything I have said, but he rushes on with his assertions. I adhere to the Declaration of Independence. If Judge Douglas and his friends are not willing to stand by it, let them come up and amend it. Let them make it read that all men are created equal, except Negroes. Let us have it decided whether the Declaration of Independence, in this blessed year of 1858, shall be thus amended. In his construction of the Declaration last year, he said it only meant that Americans in America were equal to Englishmen in England. Then, when I pointed out to him that by that rule he excludes the Germans, the Irish, the Portuguese, and all the other people who have come amongst us since the Revolution, he reconstructs his construction. In his last speech he tells us it meant Europeans.

I press him a little further, and ask if it meant to include the Russians in Asia? or does he mean to exclude the vast population from the principles of our Declaration of Independence? I expect ere long he will introduce another amendment to his definition. He is not at all particular. He is satisfied with anything which does not endanger the nationalizing of Negro-slavery. It may draw white men down, but it must not lift Negroes up. Who shall say, "I am the superior, and you are the inferior?"

My declarations upon this subject of Negro slavery may be misrepresented, but cannot be misunderstood. I have said that I do not understand the Declaration to mean that all men were created equal in all respects. They are not our equal in color; but I suppose that it does mean to declare that all men are equal in some respects; they are equal in their right to "life, liberty, and the pursuit of happiness." Certainly the Negro is not our equal in color—perhaps not in many other respects; still, in the right to put into his mouth the bread that his own hands have earned, he is the equal of every other man, white or black. In pointing out that more has been given you, you cannot be justified in taking away the little which has been given him. All I ask for the Negro is that if you do not like him, let him alone. If God gave him but little, that little let him enjoy.

When our government was established, we had the institution of slavery among us. We were in a certain sense compelled to tolerate its existence. It was a sort of necessity. We had gone through our struggle, and secured our own independence. The framers of the Constitution found the institution of slavery amongst their other institutions at the time. They found that by an effort to eradicate it, they might lose much of what they had already gained. They were obliged to bow to the necessity. They gave power to Congress to abolish the slave trade at the end of twenty years. They also prohibited slavery in the Territories where it did not exist. They did what they could and yielded to necessity for the rest. I also yield to all which follows from that necessity. What I would most desire would be the separation of the white and black races.

One more point on this Springfield speech which Judge Douglas says he has read so carefully. I expressed my belief in the existence of a conspiracy to perpetuate and nationalize slavery. I did not profess to know it, nor do I now. I showed the part Judge Douglas had played in the string of facts, constituting to my mind the proof of that conspiracy. I showed the parts played by others. I charged that the people had been deceived in carrying the last presidential election, by the impression that the people of the Territories might exclude slavery if they chose, when it was known in advance by the conspirators, that the court was to decide that neither Congress nor the people could so exclude slavery. These charges are more distinctly made than anything else in the speech.

Judge Douglas has carefully read and re-read that speech. He has not, so far as I know, contradicted those charges. In the two speeches which I heard he certainly did not. On his own tacit admission I renew that charge. I charge him with having been a party to that conspiracy, and to that deception, for the sole purpose of nationalizing slavery.

LETTER TO STEPHEN A. DOUGLAS

CHALLENGE TO THE JOINT DEBATES

The Republicans were dissatisfied at seeing their candidate trail Douglas around the state, speaking only after he had spoken. Pressure was put on Lincoln to challenge Douglas to a series of debates at which both candidates would have an opportunity to address the same audiences. Lincoln thereupon sent this letter to Douglas. The Republican press immediately printed it so Douglas could not back out without making the fact known to the public. Douglas answered it promptly, saying that all his arrangements had been made; that there had been talk of a third candidate entering the field against him; and that Lincoln should have approached him sooner if he had wished to arrange for a series of debates. Nevertheless, he was willing to meet Lincoln on the platform, and he suggested Freeport, Ottawa, Galesburg, Quincy, Alton, Jonesboro, and Charleston as the places at which the debates should be held.

Chicago, Illinois, July 24, 1858

MY DEAR SIR: Will it be agreeable to you to make an arrangement for you and myself to divide time, and address the same audiences the present canvass? Mr. Judd, who will hand you this, is authorized to receive your answer; and, if agreeable to you, to enter into the terms of such arrangement.

LETTER TO STEPHEN A. DOUGLAS

Lincoln had not received Douglas's letter mentioned in the previous note. He had dined with him on July 28, and curiously enough, neither man mentioned the one thought that must have been uppermost in both their minds. Lincoln came home to find Douglas's letter, to which he now replies.

Springfield, July 29, 1858

DEAR SIR: Yours of the 24th in relation to an arrangement to divide time and address the same audiences is received; and in apology for not sooner replying, allow me to say that when I sat by you at dinner yesterday I was not aware that you had answered my note, nor certainly that my own had been presented to you. An hour after I saw a copy of your answer in the Chicago *Times*, and reaching home, I found the original awaiting me. Protesting that your insinuations of attempted unfairness on my part are unjust, and with the hope that you did not very considerately make them, I proceed to reply. To your statement that "It has been suggested recently that an arrangement had been made to bring out a third candidate for the United States Senate, who, with yourself, should canvass the State in opposition to me," etc., I can only say that such suggestion must have been made by yourself, for certainly none such has been made by or to me, or otherwise, to my knowledge. Surely you did not deliberately conclude, as you insinuate, that I was expecting to draw you into an arrangement of terms, to be agreed on by yourself, by which a third candidate and myself "in concert might be able to take the opening and closing speech in every case."

As to your surprise that I did not sooner make the proposal

to divide time with you, I can only say I made it as soon as I resolved to make it. I did not know but that such proposal would come from you; I waited respectfully to see. It may have been well known to you that you went to Springfield for the purpose of agreeing on the plan of campaign; but it was not so known to me. When your appointments were announced in the papers, extending only to the 21st of August, I for the first time considered it certain that you would make no proposal to me, and then resolved that, if my friends concurred, I would make one to you. As soon thereafter as I could see and consult with friends satisfactorily, I did make the proposal. It did not occur to me that the proposed arrangement could derange your plans after the latest of your appointments already made. After that, there was before the election largely over two months of clear time.

For you to say that we have already spoken at Chicago and Springfield, and that on both occasions I had the concluding speech, is hardly a fair statement. The truth rather is this: At Chicago, July 9, you made a carefully prepared conclusion on my speech of June 16. Twenty-four hours after, I made a hasty conclusion on yours of the 9th. You had six days to prepare, and concluded on me again at Bloomington on the 16th. Twenty-four hours after, I concluded again on you at Springfield. In the mean time, you had made another conclusion on me at Springfield which I did not hear, and of the contents of which I knew nothing when I spoke; so that your speech made in daylight, and mine at night, of the 17th, at Springfield, were both made in perfect independence of each other. The dates of making all these speeches will show, I think, that in the matter of time for preparation the advantage has all been on your side, and that none of the external circumstances have stood to my advantage.

I agreed to an arrangement for us to speak at the seven places you have named, and at your own times, provided you name the times at once, so that I, as well as you, can have to myself the time not covered by the arrangement. As to the other details, I wish perfect reciprocity, and no more. I wish as much time as you, and that conclusions shall alternate. That is all. Your obedient servant,

A. Lincoln

P. S. As matters now stand, I shall be at no more of your exclusive meetings; and for about a week from today a letter from you will reach me at Springfield.

LETTER TO STEPHEN A. DOUGLAS

On July 30, Douglas wrote to Lincoln setting the time for each debate; he cleverly chose for himself the first opening in a series of seven which necessarily gave him four openings to Lincoln's three. Lincoln writes to accept—and complain.

Springfield, July 31, 1858

Dear Sir: Yours of yesterday, naming places, times, and terms for joint discussions between us, was received this morning. Although by the terms, as you propose, you take four openings and closes to my three, I accede, and thus close the arrangement. I direct this to you at Hillsboro, and shall try to have both your letter and this appear in the *Journal* and *Register* of Monday morning.

LETTER TO HENRY ASBURY

Asbury was a Quincy lawyer and a good friend of Lincoln's. While the debates were in the process of being arranged, he had written to Lincoln proposing that he ask Douglas publicly a question that would put him between the horns of a dilemma. Lincoln was to use this question during his debate with Douglas at Freeport on August 27, and Douglas's answer to it ruined his own prospects in the South during the campaign for the Presidency in 1860. Lincoln here foresees the effect that such a question will have on Douglas.

Lincoln was correct in predicting that Douglas would let his chances with the South go in order to win the coming election, but he underestimated Douglas's desires to hold his power in the South. Douglas did not believe that he was as dead there as Lincoln thought he was.

Springfield, July 31, 1858

MY DEAR SIR: Yours of the 28th is received. The points you propose to press upon Douglas he will be very hard to get up to, but I think you labor under a mistake when you say no one cares how he answers. This implies that it is equal with him whether he is injured here or at the South. That is a mistake. He cares nothing for the South; he knows he is already dead there. He only leans Southward more to keep the Buchanan party from growing in Illinois. You shall have hard work to get him directly to the point whether a territorial legislature has or has not the power to exclude slavery. But if you succeed in bringing him to it—though he will be compelled to say it possesses no such power—he will instantly take ground that slavery cannot actually exist in the Territories unless the people desire it, and so give it protection by territorial legislation. If this offends the South, he will let it offend them, as at all events he means to hold on to his chances in Illinois.

FROM LINCOLN'S REPLY IN THE FIRST JOINT DEBATE AT OTTAWA, ILLINOIS

During the first three weeks in August, both Douglas and Lincoln continued actively to speak in various towns throughout Illinois. Lincoln spoke at Beardstown, Havana, Bath, Lewistown and Peoria. People poured into the little town of Ottawa on the afternoon of Friday, August 20, and camped on the outskirts for the night. Early on Saturday morning, the crowd began to assemble in the court-house square where a rough board platform had been erected. No provision was made to seat the audience. Douglas entered the town in a carriage shortly before noon, and was greeted by a salute from two brass cannon. Almost at the same time a seventeen-car train arrived from Chicago bearing Lincoln and the Republican contingent. Rival Democratic and Republican processions became entangled; they stood still while their respective brass bands tried to drown each other out. At two-thirty the speakers came to the platform and were greeted with wild cheering. Douglas was the first to speak. He began with an account of the way in which the old Whig party and the Democratic party had ruled the country peacefully, always managing to arrive at some kind of compromise on difficult issues. Until 1854, he said, when he had introduced the Kansas-Nebraska Act into the Senate, all had gone well. He then charged Lincoln and Trumbull with entering into an arrangement to try to dissolve the old Whig party and the Democratic party in order to make way for an abolition party which was to be disguised under the name Republican. This, of course, was utterly untrue, and Douglas was unfortunate enough to use incorrect evidence to support his stand. He then asked Lincoln a series of questions, hoping to compromise him in the southern part of the state where the people were strongly pro-slavery in their sympathies. He reviewed Lincoln's public record briefly in order to embarrass him with certain of his past attitudes such as his stand during the Mexican War. He branded Lincoln as an abolitionist, and attacked his "House Divided" speech, bringing up his usual charge that it tended to create dissension. After an hour of speaking he gave way to Lincoln. Lincoln had one hour and a half in which to reply; Douglas then had half an hour for his rejoinder.

August 21, 1858

Now, gentlemen, I hate to waste my time on such things, but in regard to that general Abolition tilt that Judge Douglas makes, when he says that I was engaged at that time in selling out and Abolitionizing the Old Whig party, I hope you will permit me to read a part of a printed speech that I made then at Peoria, which will show altogether a different view of the position I took in that contest of 1854. [Voice: "Put on your specs."] Yes, sir, I am obliged to do so. I am no longer a young man.

[Reads the long passage from his Peoria speech of October 16, 1854, regarding his stand on slavery.]

I have reason to know that Judge Douglas knows that I said this. I think he has the answer here to one of the questions he put to me. I do not mean to allow him to catechize me unless he pays back for it in kind. I will not answer questions one after another, unless he reciprocates; but as he has made this inquiry, and I have answered it before, he has got it without my getting anything in return. He has got my answer on the fugitive-slave law.

Now, gentlemen, I don't want to read at any great length, but this is the true complexion of all I have ever said in regard to the institution of slavery and the black race. This is the whole of it, and anything that argues me into his idea of perfect social and political equality with the Negro is but a specious and fantastic arrangement of words, by which a man can prove a horse-chestnut to be a chestnut horse. I will say here, while upon this subject, that I have no purpose, either directly or indirectly, to interfere with the institution of slavery in the States where it exists. I believe I have no lawful right to do so, and I have no inclination to do so. I have no purpose to introduce political and social equality between the white and the black races. There is a physical difference between the two, which, in my judgment, will probably forever forbid their living together upon the footing of perfect equality; and inasmuch as it becomes a necessity that there must be a difference, I, as well as Judge Douglas, am in favor of the race to which I belong having the superior position. I have never said anything to the contrary, but I hold that, notwithstanding all this, there is no reason in the world why the Negro is not entitled to all the natural rights enumerated in the Declaration of Independence—the right to life, liberty, and the pursuit of happiness. I hold that he is as much entitled to these as the white man. I agree with Judge Douglas he is not my equal in many respects—certainly not in color, perhaps not in moral or intellectual endowment. But in the right to eat the bread, without the leave of anybody else, which his own hand earns, he is my equal and the equal of Judge Douglas, and the equal of every living man.

Now I pass on to consider one or two more of these little follies. The judge is woefully at fault about his early friend Lincoln being a "grocery-keeper." I don't know that it would be a great sin if I had been; but he is mistaken. Lincoln never kept a grocery anywhere in the world.* It is true that Lincoln did work the latter part of one winter in a little still-house up at the head of a hollow. And so I think my friend, the judge, is equally at fault when he charges me at the time when I was in Congress of having opposed our soldiers who were fighting in the Mexican War. The judge did not make his charge very distinctly, but I tell you what he can prove, by referring to the record. You remember I was an Old Whig, and whenever the Democratic party tried to get me to vote that the war had been righteously begun by the President, I would not do it. But whenever they asked for any money, or land-warrants, or anything to pay the soldiers there, during all that time, I gave the same vote that Judge Douglas did. You can think as you please as to whether that was consistent. Such is the truth; and the judge has the right to make all he can out of it. But when he, by a general charge, conveys the idea that I withheld supplies from the soldiers who were fighting in the Mexican War, or did anything else to hinder the soldiers, he

* The word "grocery" in those days meant a store where liquor was sold.

is, to say the least, grossly and altogether mistaken, as a consultation of the records will prove to him.

As I have not used up so much of my time as I had supposed, I will dwell a little longer upon one or two of these minor topics upon which the judge has spoken. He has read from my speech in Springfield in which I say that "a house divided against itself cannot stand." Does the judge say it can stand? I don't know whether he does or not. The judge does not seem to be attending to me just now, but I would like to know if it is his opinion that a house divided against itself can stand. If he does, then there is a question of veracity, not between him and me, but between the judge and an authority of a somewhat higher character.

Now, my friends, I ask your attention to this matter for the purpose of saying something seriously. I know that the judge may readily enough agree with me that the maxim which was put forth by the Saviour is true, but he may allege that I misapply it; and the judge has a right to urge that in my application I do misapply it, and then I have a right to show that I do not misapply it. When he undertakes to say that because I think this nation, so far as the question of slavery is concerned, will all become one thing or all the other, I am in favor of bringing about a dead uniformity in the various States in all their institutions, he argues erroneously. The great variety of the local institutions in the States, springing from differences in the soil, differences in the face of the country, and in the climate, are bonds of union. They do not make "a house divided against itself," but they make a house united. If they produce in one section of the country what is called for by the wants of another section, and this other section can supply the wants of the first, they are not matters of discord but bonds of union, true bonds of union. But can this question of slavery be considered as among these varieties in the institutions of the country? I leave it to you to say whether, in the history of our government, this institution of slavery has not always failed to be a bond of union, and, on the contrary, been an apple of discord and an element of division in the house. I ask you to consider whether, so long as the moral constitution of men's minds shall continue to be the same, after this generation and assemblage shall sink into the grave, and another race shall arise with the same moral and intellectual development we have—whether, if that institution is standing in the same irritating position in which it now is, it will not continue an element of division?

If so, then I have a right to say that, in regard to this question, the Union is a house divided against itself; and when the judge reminds me that I have often said to him that the institution of slavery has existed for eighty years in some States, and yet it does not exist in some others, I agree to the fact, and I account for it by looking at the position in which our fathers originally placed it—restricting it from the new Territories where it had not gone, and legislating to cut off its source by the abrogation of the slave trade, thus putting the seal of legislation against its spread. The public mind did rest in the belief that it was in the course of ultimate extinction. But lately, I think—and in this I charge nothing on the judge's motives—lately, I think, that he, and those acting with him, have placed that institution on a new basis, which looks to the perpetuity and nationalization of slavery. And while it is placed upon this new basis, I say, and I have said, that I believe we shall not have peace upon the question until the opponents of slavery arrest the further spread of it, and place it where the public mind shall rest in the belief that it is in the course of ultimate extinction; or, on the other hand, that its advocates will push it forward until it shall become alike lawful in all the States, old as well as new, North as well as South. Now I believe if we could arrest the spread, and place it where Washington and Jefferson and Madison placed it, it would be in the course of ultimate extinction, and the public mind would, as for eighty years past, believe that it was in the course of ultimate extinction. The crisis would be past, and the institution might be let alone for a hundred years—if it should live so long—in the States where it exists, yet it would be going out of existence in the way best for both the black and the white races. [A voice: "Then do you repudiate popular sovereignty?"] Well, then, let us talk about popular sovereignty! What is popular sovereignty? Is it the right of the people to have slavery or not have it, as they see fit, in the Territories? I will state—and I have an able man to watch me—my understanding is that popular sovereignty, as now applied to the question of slavery, does allow the people of a Territory to have slavery if they want to, but does not allow them not to have it if they do not want it. I do not mean that if this vast concourse of people were in a Territory of the United States, any one of them would be obliged to have a slave if he did not want one; but I do say that, as I understand the Dred Scot decision, if any one man wants slaves, all the rest have no way of keeping that one man from holding them.

When I made my speech at Springfield, of which the judge complains, and from which he quotes, I really was not thinking of the things which he ascribes to me at all. I had no thought in the world that I was doing anything to bring about a war between the free and slave States. I had no thought in the world that I was doing anything to bring about a political and social equality of the black and white races. It never occurred to me that I was doing anything or favoring anything to reduce to a dead uniformity all the local institutions of the various States. But I must say, in all fairness to him, if he thinks I am doing something which leads to these bad results, it is none the better that I did not mean it. It is just as fatal to the country, if I have any influence in producing it, whether I intend it or not. But can it be true, that placing this institution upon the original basis—the basis upon which our fathers placed it—can have any tendency to set the Northern and the Southern States at war with one another, or that it can have any tendency to make the people of Vermont raise sugarcane because they raise it in Louisiana, or that it can compel the people of Illinois to cut pine logs on the Grand Prairie, where they will not grow, because they cut pine logs in Maine, where they do grow? The judge says this is a new principle started in regard to this question. Does the judge claim that he is working on the plan of the founders of the government? I think he says in some of his speeches—indeed, I have one here now—that he saw evidence of a policy to allow slavery to be south of a certain line, while north of it it should be excluded, and he saw an indisposition on the part of the country to stand upon that policy, and therefore he set about studying the subject upon original principles, and upon original principles he got up the Nebraska bill! I am fighting it upon these "original principles"—fighting it in the Jeffersonian, Washingtonian, and Madisonian fashion.

Now, my friends, I wish you to attend for a little while to one or two other things in that Springfield speech. My main object was to show, so far as my humble ability was capable of showing to the people of this country, what I believed was the truth—that there was a tendency, if not a conspiracy, among those who have engineered this slavery question for the last four or five years, to make slavery perpetual and universal in this nation. . . .

When my friend, Judge Douglas, came to Chicago on the 9th of July, this speech having been delivered on the 16th of June, he made an harangue there in which he took hold of this speech of mine, showing that he had carefully read it; and while he paid no attention to this matter at all, but complimented me as being a "kind, amiable, and intelligent gentleman," notwithstanding I had said this, he goes on and deduces, or draws out, from my speech this tendency of mine to set the States at war with one another, to make all the institutions uniform, and set the niggers and white people to marry together. Then, as the judge had complimented me with these pleasant titles (I must confess to my weakness), I was a little "taken," for it came from a great man. I was not very much accustomed to flattery, and it came the sweeter to me. I was rather like the Hoosier with the gingerbread, when he said he reckoned he loved it better than any other man, and got less of it. As the judge had so flattered me, I could not make up my mind that he meant to deal unfairly with me; so I went to work to show him that he misunderstood the whole scope of my speech, and that I really never intended to set the people at war with one another. As an illustration, the next time I met him, which was at Springfield, I used this expression, that I claimed no right under the Constitution, nor had I any inclination, to enter into the slave States and interfere with the institutions of slavery. He says upon that: "Lincoln will not enter into the slave States, but will go to the banks of the Ohio, on this side, and shoot over!" He runs on, step by step, in the horse-chestnut style of argument, until in the Springfield speech he says, "Unless he shall be successful in firing his batteries, until he shall have extinguished slavery in all the States, the Union shall be dissolved." Now I don't think that was exactly the way to treat "a kind, amiable, intelligent gentleman." I know if I had asked the judge to show when or where it was I had said, that if I didn't succeed in firing into the slave States until slavery should be extinguished, the Union should be dissolved, he could not have shown it. I understand what he would do. He would say, "I don't mean to quote from you, but this was the result of what you say." But I have the right to ask, and I do ask now, did you not put it in such a form that an ordinary reader or listener would take it as an expression from me?

In a speech at Springfield on the night of the 17th, I thought I might as well attend to my business a little, and I recalled his attention as well as I could to this charge of conspiracy to nationalize slavery. I called his attention to the fact that he had acknowledged in my hearing twice that he had carefully read the speech; and, in the language of the lawyers, as he had twice read the speech, and still had put in no plea or answer, I took a default on him. I insisted that I had a right then to renew that charge of conspiracy.

Ten days afterward I met the judge at Clinton—that is to say, I was on the ground, but not in the discussion—and heard him make a speech. Then he comes in with his plea to this charge, for the first time, and his plea when put in, as well as I can recollect it, amounted to this: that he never had any talk with Judge Taney or the President of the United States with regard to the Dred Scott decision before it was made. I (Lincoln) ought to know that the man who makes a charge without knowing it to be true, falsifies as much as he who knowingly tells a falsehood; and lastly, that he would pronounce the whole thing a falsehood; but he would make no personal application of the charge of falsehood, not because of any regard for the "kind, amiable, intelligent gentleman," but because of his own personal self-respect! I have understood since then (but [*turning to Judge Douglas*] will not hold the judge to it if he is not willing) that he has broken through the "self-respect," and has got to saying the thing out. The judge nods to me that it is so. It is fortunate for me that I can keep as good-humored as I do, when the judge acknowledges that he has been trying to make a question of veracity with me. I know the judge is a great man, while I am only a small man, but I feel that I have got him. I demur to that plea. I waive all objections that it was not filed till after default was taken, and demur to it upon the merits. What if Judge Douglas never did talk with Chief Justice Taney and the President before the Dred Scott decision was made; does it follow that he could not have had as perfect an understanding without talking as with it? I am not disposed to stand upon my legal advantage. I am disposed to take his denial as being like an answer in chancery, that he neither had any knowledge, information, nor belief in the existence of such a conspiracy. I am disposed to take his answer as being as broad as though he had put it in these words. And now, I ask, even if he had done so, have not I a right to prove it on him, and to offer the evidence of more than two witnesses, by whom to prove it; and if the evidence proves the existence of the conspiracy, does his broad answer, denying all knowledge, information, or belief, disturb the fact? It can only show that he was used by conspirators, and was not a leader of them.

Now, in regard to his reminding me of the moral rule that persons who tell what they do not know to be true, falsify as much as those who knowingly tell falsehoods. I remember the rule, and it must be borne in mind that in what I have read to you, I do not say that I know such a conspiracy to exist. To that I reply, I believe it. If the judge says that I do not believe it, then he says what he does not know, and falls within his own rule that he who asserts a thing which he does not know to be true, falsifies as much as he who knowingly tells a falsehood. . . .

When the judge spoke at Clinton, he came very near making a charge of falsehood against me. He used, as I found it printed in a newspaper, which, I remember was very nearly like the real speech, the following language:

I did not answer the charge [of conspiracy] before for the reason that I did not suppose there was a man in America with a heart so corrupt as to believe such a charge could be true. I have too much respect for Mr. Lincoln to suppose he is serious in making the charge.

I confess this is rather a curious view, that out of respect for me he should consider I was making what I deemed rather a grave charge in fun. I confess it strikes me rather strangely. But I let it pass. As the judge did not for a moment believe that there was a man in America whose heart was so "corrupt" as to make such a charge, and as he places me among the "men in America" who have hearts base enough to make such a charge, I hope he will excuse me if I hunt out another charge very like this; and if it should turn out that in hunting I should find that other, and it should turn out to be Judge Douglas himself who made it, I hope he will reconsider this question of the deep corruption of heart he has thought fit to ascribe to me. . . .

Although on these questions I would like to talk twice as long as I have, I could not enter upon another head and discuss it properly without running over my time. I ask the attention of the people here assembled and elsewhere, to the course that Judge Douglas is pursuing every day as bearing upon this question of making slavery national. Not going back to the records, but taking the speeches he makes, the speeches he made yesterday and day before, and makes constantly all over the country I ask your attention to them.

In the first place, what is necessary to make the institution national? Not war. There is no danger that the people of Kentucky will shoulder their muskets, and, with a young nigger stuck on every bayonet, march into Illinois and force them upon us. There is no danger of our going over there and making war upon them. Then what is necessary for the nationalization of slavery? It is simply the next Dred Scott decision. It is merely for the Supreme Court to decide that no State under the Constitution can exclude it, just as they have already decided that under the Constitution neither Congress nor the territorial legislature can do it. When that is decided and acquiesced in, the whole thing is done. This being true, and this being the way, as I think, that slavery is to be made national, let us consider what Judge Douglas is doing every day to that end. In the first place, let us see what influence he is exerting on public sentiment.

In this and like communities, public sentiment is everything. With public sentiment, nothing can fail; without it, nothing can succeed. Consequently he who molds public sentiment goes deeper than he who enacts statutes or pronounces decisions. He makes statutes and decisions possible or impossible to be executed. This must be borne in mind, as also the additional fact that Judge Douglas is a man of vast influence, so great that it is enough for many men. to profess to believe anything when they once find out that Judge Douglas professes to believe it. Consider also the attitude he occupies at the head of a large party—a party which he claims has a majority of all the voters in the country.

This man sticks to a decision which forbids the people of a Territory to exclude slavery, and he does so not because he says it is right in itself—he does not give any opinion on that—but because it has been decided by the court, and, being decided by the court, he is, and you are, bound to take it in your political action as law—not that he judges at all of its merits, but because a decision of the court is to him a "Thus saith the Lord." He places it on that ground alone, and you will bear in mind that thus committing himself unreservedly to this decision, commits him to the next one just as firmly as to this. He did not commit himself on account of the merit or demerit of the decision, but it is a "Thus saith the Lord." The next decision, as much as this, will be a "Thus saith the Lord." There is nothing that can divert or turn him away from this decision.

*   *   *

Henry Clay, my beau ideal of a statesman, the man for whom I fought all my humble life—Henry Clay once said of a class of men who would repress all tendencies to liberty and ultimate emancipation, that they must, if they would do this, go back to the era of our independence, and muzzle the cannon which thunders its annual joyous return; they must blow out the moral lights around us; they must penetrate the human soul, and eradicate there the love of liberty; and then, and not till then, could they perpetuate slavery in this country! To my thinking, Judge Douglas is, by his example and vast influence, doing that very thing in this community when he says that the Negro has nothing in the Declaration of Independence. Henry Clay plainly understood the contrary. Judge Douglas is going back to the era of our Revolution, and to the extent of his ability muzzling the cannon which thunders its annual joyous return. When he invites any people, willing to have slavery, to establish it, he is blowing out the moral lights around us. When he says he "cares not whether slavery is voted down or voted up"—that it is a sacred right of self-government—he is, in my judgment, penetrating the human soul and eradicating the light of reason and the love of liberty in this American people.

And now I will only say that when, by all these means and appliances, Judge Douglas shall succeed in bringing public sentiment to an exact accordance with his own views—when these vast assemblages shall echo back all these sentiments—when they shall come to repeat his views and to avow his principles, and to say all that he says on these mighty questions—then it needs only the formality of the second Dred Scott decision, which he indorses in advance, to make slavery alike lawful in all the States—old as well as new, North as well as South.

FROM LINCOLN'S OPENING SPEECH
AT THE SECOND JOINT DEBATE
AT FREEPORT, ILLINOIS

Douglas's use of incorrect evidence at the Ottawa debate caused him trouble. He had been given a newspaper clipping which was represented to him as a reproduction of a strong abolitionist stand taken at the Springfield Republican convention in 1854 and supposedly indorsed by Lincoln. Actually the resolutions were from an entirely different meeting. The Republican press immediately charged Douglas with forgery. He was in hot water and he knew it, but his next incautious action made even more trouble for him. He telegraphed to a friend, U. F. Linder of Charleston, to come and help him out. A copy of the telegram, which read: "The hellhounds are on my track. For God's sake, Linder, come and help me fight them," was sold to the Republican papers who published it with great glee. Douglas's enemies howled with delight, and Linder was dubbed "For-God's-sake-Linder" for the rest of his life. The two candidates went on to Freeport which, like Ottawa, was also in the northern part of the state. Lincoln was criticized for not answering the questions Douglas had put to him at Ottawa. He was now prepared not only to answer them but to pose some of his own, the second of which was the famous question that ruined Douglas in the South. Lincoln rode in a prairie schooner to the place where the debate was to be held; Douglas, seeing this parody of his own ceremonial method of arriving in a coach, insisted on walking. The crowd was a large one, larger even than the one at Ottawa, and it was almost entirely with Lincoln from the beginning. Lincoln here has the opening speech.

August 27, 1858

I HAVE supposed myself, since the organization of the Republican party at Bloomington, in May, 1856, bound as a party man by the platforms of the party then and since. If in any interrogatories which I shall answer I go beyond the scope of what is within these platforms, it will be perceived that no one is responsible but myself. Having said this much, I will take up the judge's interrogatories as I find them printed in the Chicago Times, and answer them seriatim. In order that there may be no mistake about it, I have copied the interrogatories in writing, and also my answers to them. The first one of these interrogatories is in these words:

QUESTION 1. "I desire to know whether Lincoln today stands as he did in 1854, in favor of the unconditional repeal of the fugitive-slave law?"

ANSWER: I do not now, nor ever did, stand in favor of the unconditional repeal of the fugitive-slave law.

Q. 2. "I desire him to answer whether he stands pledged today as he did in 1854, against the admission of any more slave States into the Union, even if the people want them?"

A. I do not now, nor ever did, stand pledged against the admission of any more slave States into the Union.

Q. 3. "I want to know whether he stands pledged against the admission of a new State into the Union with such a constitution as the people of that State may see fit to make?"

A. I do not stand pledged against the admission of a new State into the Union with such a constitution as the people of that State may see fit to make.

Q. 4. "I want to know whether he stands today pledged to the abolition of slavery in the District of Columbia?"

A. I do not stand today pledged to the abolition of slavery in the District of Columbia.

Q. 5. "I desire him to answer whether he stands pledged to the prohibition of the slave trade between the different States?"

A. I do not stand pledged to the prohibition of the slave trade between the different States.

Q. 6. "I desire to know whether he stands pledged to prohibit slavery in all the Territories of the United States, North as well as South of the Missouri Compromise line?"

A. I am impliedly, if not expressly, pledged to a belief in the right and duty of Congress to prohibit slavery in all the United States Territories.

Q. 7. "I desire him to answer whether he is opposed to the acquisition of any new territory unless slavery is first prohibited therein?"

A. I am not generally opposed to honest acquisition of territory; and, in any given case, I would or would not oppose such acquisition, accordingly as I might think such acquisition would or would not aggravate the slavery question among ourselves.

Now, my friends, it will be perceived upon an examination of these questions and answers, that so far I have only answered that I was not pledged to this, that, or the other. The judge has not framed his interrogatories to ask me anything more than this, and I have answered in strict accordance with the interrogatories, and have answered truly that I am not pledged at all upon any of the points to which I have answered. But I am not disposed to hang upon the exact form of his interrogatory. I am really disposed to take up at least some of these questions, and state what I really think upon them.

As to the first one, in regard to the fugitive-slave law, I have never hesitated to say, and I do not now hesitate to say, that I think, under the Constitution of the United States, the people of the Southern States are entitled to a congressional fugitive-slave law. Having said that, I have had nothing to say in regard to the existing fugitive-slaw law, further than that I think it should have been framed so as to be free from some of the objections that pertain to it, without lessening its efficiency. And inasmuch as we are not now in an agitation in regard to an alteration or modification of that law, I would not be the man to introduce it as a new subject of agitation upon the general question of slavery.

In regard to the other question, of whether I am pledged to the admission of any more slave States into the Union, I state to you very frankly that I would be exceedingly sorry ever to be put in a position of having to pass upon that question. I should be exceedingly glad to know that there would never be another slave State admitted into the Union; but I must add, that if slavery shall be kept out of the Territories during the territorial existence of any one given Territory, and then the people shall, having a fair chance and a clear field, when they come to adopt the Constitution, do such an extraordinary thing as to adopt a slave constitution, uninfluenced by the actual presence of the institution among them, I see no alternative, if we own the country, but to admit them into the Union.

The third interrogatory is answered by the answer to the second, it being, as I conceive, the same as the second.

The fourth one is in regard to the abolition of slavery in the District of Columbia. In relation to that, I have my mind very distinctly made up. I should be exceedingly glad to see slavery abolished in the District of Columbia. I believe that Congress possesses the constitutional power to abolish it. Yet as a member of Congress, I should not with my present views be in favor of endeavoring to abolish slavery in the District of Columbia unless it would be upon these conditions: First, that the abolition should be gradual; second, that it should be on a vote of the majority of qualified voters in the District; and third, that compensation should be made to unwilling owners. With these three conditions, I confess I would be exceedingly glad to see Congress abolish slavery in the District of Columbia, and, in the language of Henry Clay, "sweep from our capital that foul blot upon our nation."

In regard to the fifth interrogatory, I must say here that as to the question of the abolition of the slave trade between the different States, I can truly answer, as I have, that I am pledged to nothing about it. It is a subject to which I have not given that mature consideration that would make me feel authorized to state a position so as to hold myself entirely bound by it. In other words, that question has never been prominently enough before me to induce me to investigate whether we really have the constitutional power to do it. I could investigate it if I had sufficient time to bring myself to a conclusion upon that subject, but I have not done so, and I say so frankly to you here and to Judge Douglas. I must say, however, that if I should be of opinion that Congress does possess the constitutional power to abolish the slave trade among the different States, I should still not be in favor of the exercise of that power unless upon some conservative principle as I conceive it, akin to what I have said in relation to the abolition of slavery in the District of Columbia.

My answer as to whether I desire that slavery should be prohibited in all the Territories of the United States is full and explicit within itself, and cannot be made clearer by any comments of mine.

So I suppose in regard to the question whether I am opposed to the acquisition of any more territory unless slavery is first prohibited therein, my answer is such that I could add nothing by way of illustration, or making myself better understood, than the answer which I have placed in writing.

Now in all this the judge has me, and he has me on the record. I suppose he had flattered himself that I was really entertaining one set of opinions for one place and another set for another place—that I was afraid to say at one place what I uttered at another. What I am saying here I suppose I say to a vast audience as strongly tending to Abolitionism as any audience in the State of Illinois, and I believe I am saying that which, if it would be offensive to any persons and render them enemies to myself, would be offensive to persons in this audience.

I now proceed to propound to the judge the interrogatories so far as I have framed them. I will bring forward a new installment when I get them ready. I will bring them forward now, only reaching to number four.

The first one is:

Question 1. If the people of Kansas shall, by means entirely unobjectionable in all other respects, adopt a State constitution, and ask admission into the Union under it, before they have the requisite number of inhabitants according to the English bill—some ninety-three thousand—will you vote to admit them?

Q. 2. Can the people of a United States Territory, in any lawful way, against the wish of any citizen of the United States, exclude slavery from its limits prior to the formation of a State constitution?

Q. 3. If the Supreme Court of the United States shall decide that States cannot exclude slavery from their limits, are you in favor of acquiescing in, adopting, and following such decision as a rule of political action?

Q. 4. Are you in favor of acquiring additional territory, in disregard of how such acquisition may affect the nation on the slavery question?

*   *   *

I have been in the habit of charging as a matter of belief on my part, that, in the introduction of the Nebraska bill into Congress, there was a conspiracy to make slavery perpetual and national. I have arranged from time to time the evidence which establishes and proves the truth of this charge. I recurred to this charge at Ottawa. I shall not now have time to dwell upon it at very great length; but inasmuch as Judge Douglas in his reply of half an hour made some points upon me in relation to it, I propose noticing a few of them.

The judge insists that, in the first speech I made, in which I very distinctly made that charge, he thought for a good while I was in fun—that I was playful—that I was not sincere about it—and that he only grew angry and somewhat excited when he found that I insisted upon it as a matter of earnestness. He says he characterized it as a falsehood as far as I implicated his moral character in that transaction. Well, I did not know, till he presented that view, that I had implicated his moral character. He is very much in the habit, when he argues me up into a position I never thought of occupying, of very cozily saying he has no doubt Lincoln is "conscientious" in saying so. He should remember that I did not know but what he was altogether "conscientious" in that matter.

I can conceive it possible for men to conspire to do a good thing, and I really find nothing in Judge Douglas's course of arguments that is contrary to or inconsistent with his belief of a conspiracy to nationalize and spread slavery as being a good and blessed thing, and so I hope he will understand that I do not at all question but that in all this matter he is entirely "conscientious." . . .

I pass one or two points I have because my time will very soon expire, but I must be allowed to say that Judge Douglas recurs again, as he did upon one or two other occasions, to the enormity of Lincoln—an insignificant individual like Lincoln—upon his *ipse dixit* charging a conspiracy upon a large number of members of Congress, the Supreme Court, and two Presidents, to nationalize slavery. I want to say that, in the first place, I have made no charge of this sort upon my *ipse dixit*. I have only arrayed the evidence tending to prove it, and presented it to the understanding of others, saying what I think it proves, but giving you the means of judging whether it proves it or not. . . .

FROM LINCOLN'S REJOINDER
IN THE SECOND JOINT DEBATE
AT FREEPORT, ILLINOIS

Douglas, in his reply, expressed his gratitude to Lincoln for answering the questions he had put to him, and then proceeded to answer Lincoln's questions. As Lincoln had predicted, he said in response to the second question—the trick question—that the people in a territory could exclude slavery before drawing up a state constitution. The temper of the crowd was against Douglas, and he several times lost his temper during his speech. He kept calling the audience "Black Republicans" and every time he used the term there was a protest. He charged Lincoln with being unwilling to take a definite stand on the matter of admitting more slave states to the Union. Lincoln here makes his reply to the charge.

August 27, 1858

THE judge complains that I did not fully answer his questions. If I have the sense to comprehend and answer those questions, I have done so fairly. If it can be pointed out to me how I can more fully and fairly answer him, I will do it—but I aver I have not the sense to see how it is to be done. He says I do not declare I would in any event.vote for the admission of a slave State into the Union. If I have been fairly reported, he will see that I did give an explicit answer to his interroga-tories. I did not merely say that I would dislike to be put to the test; but I said clearly, if I were put to the test, and a Territory from which slavery had been excluded should present herself with a State constitution sanctioning slavery—a most extraordinary thing and wholly unlikely to happen—I did not see how I could avoid voting for her admission. But he refuses to understand that I said so, and he wants this audience to understand that I did not say so. Yet it will be so reported in the printed speech that he cannot help seeing it.

He says if I should vote for the admission of a slave State I would be voting for a dissolution of the Union, because I hold that the Union can not permanently exist half slave and half free. I repeat that I do not believe this government can endure permanently half slave and half free, yet I do not admit, nor does it at all follow, that the admission of a single slave State will permanently fix the character and establish this as a uni-versal slave nation.

FROM A SPEECH AT EDWARDSVILLE, ILLINOIS

During the period between debates both candidates went right on speaking to audiences all over the state. Most of these addresses made in very small towns have been lost, but a fragment of the one made by Lincoln at Edwardsville has been preserved. This speech has been dated September 13 in previous editions of Lincoln works, but he was in Edwardsville for only one day—the eleventh.

September 11, 1858

WHEN . . . you have succeeded in dehumanizing the Negro; when you have put him down and made it impossible for him to be but as the beasts of the field; when you have extinguished his soul in this world and placed him where the ray of hope is blown out as in the darkness of the damned, are you quite sure that the demon you have roused will not turn and rend you? What constitutes the bulwark of our own liberty and independence? It is not our frowning battlements, our bristling sea coasts, our army and our navy. These are not our reliance against tyranny. All of those may be turned against us without making us weaker for the struggle. Our reliance is in the love of liberty which God has planted in us. Our defence is in the spirit which prized liberty as the heritage of all men, in all lands everywhere. Destroy this spirit and you have planted the seeds of despotism at your own doors. Familiarize yourselves with the chains of bondage and you prepare your own limbs to wear them. Accustomed to trample on the rights of others, you have lost the genius of your own independence and become the fit subjects of the first cunning tyrant who rises among you.

FROM LINCOLN'S REPLY IN THE THIRD JOINT DEBATE AT JONESBORO, ILLINOIS

Jonesboro is in the extreme southern part of Illinois, in the section called "Egypt." Douglas had been eager to bring his opponent to this part of the state because he knew that the pro-slavery audience would be antagonistic to Lincoln for his alleged abolitionist sentiments. The smallest crowd in all the debates gathered here. Douglas had the opening speech; he repeated the substance of his speech at Ottawa, shading it darker, however, to suit the tastes of his pro-slavery audience. He played on the anti-Negro prejudices of the crowd, winning their approval and preparing them to listen antagonistically to what Lincoln would have to say. In his reply, Lincoln, not to be outdone, seizes upon Douglas's answer to his second Freeport question and hammers its significance home to the crowd. He then goes on to ask another embarrassing question. Douglas's byplay on Lincoln having to be carried off the platform at Ottawa was based on the fact that his Republican admirers had carried him away on their shoulders at the end of the debate.

September 15, 1858

LADIES AND GENTLEMEN: There is very much in the principles that Judge Douglas has here enunciated that I most cordially approve, and over which I shall have no controversy with him. In so far as he has insisted that all the States have the right to do exactly as they please about all their domestic relations, including that of slavery, I agree entirely with him. He places me wrong in spite of all I can tell him, though I repeat it again and again, insisting that I have made no difference with him upon this subject. I have made a great many speeches, some of which have been printed, and it will be utterly impossible for him to find anything that I have ever put in print contrary to what I now say upon this subject. I hold myself under constitutional obligations to allow the people in all the States, without interference, direct or indirect, to do exactly as they please, and I deny that I have any inclination to interfere with them, even if there were no such constitutional obligation. I can only say again that I am placed improperly—altogether improperly, in spite of all I can say—

when it is insisted that I entertain any other view or purpose in regard to that matter.

*   *   *

At Freeport I answered several interrogatories that had been propounded to me by Judge Douglas at the Ottawa meeting. The judge has yet not seen fit to find any fault with the position that I took in regard to those seven interrogatories, which were certainly broad enough, in all conscience, to cover the entire ground. In my answers, which have been printed, and all have had the opportunity of seeing, I take the ground that those who elect me must expect that I will do nothing which will not be in accordance with those answers. I have some right to assert that Judge Douglas has no fault to find with them. But he chooses to still try to thrust me upon different ground without paying any attention to my answers, the obtaining of which from me cost him so much trouble and concern. At the same time, I propounded four interrogatories to him, claiming it as a right that he should answer as many interrogatories for me as I did for him, and I would reserve myself for a future installment when I got them ready. The judge, in answering me upon this occasion, put in what I suppose he intends as answers to all four of my interrogatories. The first one of these interrogatories I have before me, and it is in these words:

QUESTION 1. If the people of Kansas shall, by means entirely unobjectionable in all other respects, adopt a State constitution, and ask admission into the Union under it, before they have the requisite number of inhabitants according to the English bill—some ninety-three thousand—will you vote to admit them?

As I read the judge's answer in the newspaper, and as I remember it as propounded at the time, he does not give any answer which is equivalent to yes or no—I will or I won't. He answers at very considerable length, rather quarreling with me for asking the question, and insisting that Judge Trumbull had done something that I ought to say something about; and finally getting out such statements as induce me to infer that he means to be understood he will, in that supposed case, vote for the admission of Kansas. I only bring this forward now for the purpose of saying that, if he chooses to put a different construction upon his answer, he may do it. But if he does not, I shall from this time forward assume that he will vote for the admission of Kansas in disregard of the English bill. He has the right to remove any misunderstanding I may have. I only mention it now that I may hereafter assume this to be the true construction of his answer, if he does not now choose to correct me.

The second interrogatory that I propounded to him was this:

QUESTION 2. Can the people of a United States Territory, in any lawful way, against the wish of any citizen of the United States, exclude slavery from its limits prior to the formation of a State constitution?

To this Judge Douglas answered that they can lawfully exclude slavery from the Territory prior to the formation of a constitution. He goes on to tell us how it can be done. As I understand him, he holds that it can be done by the territorial legislature refusing to make any enactments for the protection of slavery in the Territory, and especially by adopting unfriendly legislation to it. For the sake of clearness, I state it again: that they can exclude slavery from the Territory—first, by withholding what he assumes to be an indispensable assistance to it in the way of legislation; and, second, by unfriendly legislation. If I rightly understand him, I wish to ask your attention for a while to his position.

In the first place, the Supreme Court of the United States has decided that any congressional prohibition of slavery in the Territories is unconstitutional—they have reached this proposition as a conclusion from their former proposition, that the Constitution of the United States expressly recognizes property in slaves; and from that other constitutional provision, that no person shall be deprived of property without due process of law. Hence they reach the conclusion that as the Constitution of the United States expressly recognizes property in slaves, and prohibits any person from being deprived of property without due process of law, to pass an act of Congress by which a man who owned a slave on one side of a line would be deprived of him if he took him on the other side is depriving him of that property without due process of law. That I understand to be the decision of the Supreme Court. I understand also that Judge Douglas adheres most firmly to that decision; and the difficulty is, how it is possible for any power to exclude slavery from the Territory unless in violation of that decision? That is the difficulty. . . .

I hold that the proposition that slavery cannot enter a new country without police regulations is historically false. It is not true at all. I hold that the history of this country shows that the institution of slavery was originally planted upon this continent without these "police regulations" which the judge now thinks necessary for the actual establishment of it. Not only so, but is there not another fact—how came this Dred Scott decision to be made? It was made upon the case of a Negro being taken and actually held in slavery in Minnesota Territory, claiming his freedom because the act of Congress prohibited his being so held there. Will the judge pretend that Dred Scott was not held there without police regulations? There is at least one matter of record as to his having been held in slavery in the Territory, not only without police regulations, but in the teeth of congressional legislation supposed to be valid at the time. This shows that there is vigor enough in slavery to plant itself in a new country even against unfriendly legislation. It takes not only law but the enforcement of law to keep it out. That is the history of this country upon the subject.

*   *   *

At the end of what I have said here I propose to give the judge my fifth interrogatory, which he may take and answer at his leisure. My fifth interrogatory is this:

If the slaveholding citizens of a United States Territory should need and demand congressional legislation for the protection of their slave property in such Territory, would you, as a member of Congress, vote for or against such legislation? . . .

I am aware that in some of the speeches Judge Douglas has made, he has spoken as if he did not know or think that the Supreme Court had decided that a territorial legislature cannot exclude slavery. Precisely what the judge would say upon the subject—whether he would say definitely that he does not understand they have so decided, or whether he would say he does understand that the court have so decided, I do not know; but I know that in his speech at Springfield he spoke of it as a thing they had not decided yet; and in his answer to me at Freeport, he spoke of it again, so far as I can comprehend it, as a thing that had not yet been decided. Now I hold that if the judge does entertain that view, I think that he is not mistaken in so far as it can be said that the court has not decided anything save the mere question of jurisdiction. I know the legal arguments that can be made—that after a court has decided that it cannot take jurisdiction in a case, it then has decided all that is before it, and that is the end of it. A plausible argument can be made in favor of that proposition, but I know that Judge Douglas has said in one of his speeches that the court went forward, like honest men as they were, and decided all the points in the case. If any points are really extrajudicially decided because not neces-

sarily before them, then this one as to the power of the territorial legislature to exclude slavery is one of them, as also the
one that the Missouri Compromise was null and void. They
are both extrajudicial, or neither is, according as the court
held that they had no jurisdiction in the case between the
parties, because of want of capacity of one party to maintain
a suit in that court. I want, if I have sufficient time, to show
that the court did pass its opinion, but that is the only thing
actually done in the case. If they did not decide, they showed
what they were ready to decide whenever the matter was
before them. What is that opinion? After having argued that
Congress had no power to pass a law excluding slavery from
a United States Territory, they then used language to this
effect: That inasmuch as Congress itself could not exercise
such a power, it followed as a matter of course that it could
not authorize a territorial government to exercise it, for the
territorial legislature can do no more than Congress could
do. Thus it expressed its opinion emphatically against the
power of a territorial legislature to exclude slavery, leaving
us in just as little doubt on that point as upon any other
point they really decided.

Now, fellow-citizens, my time is nearly out. I find a report of a speech made by Judge Douglas at Joliet, . . . in
which Judge Douglas says:

You know at Ottawa I read this platform, and asked him if he
concurred in each and all of the principles set forth in it. He would
not answer these questions. At last I said frankly, "I wish you to
answer them, because when I get them up here where the color of
your principles is a little darker than in Egypt, I intend to trot you
down to Jonesboro." The very notice that I was going to take him
down to Egypt made him tremble in the knees so that he had to
be carried from the platform. He laid up seven days, and in the
meantime held a consultation with his political physicians; they
had Lovejoy and Farnsworth and all the leaders of the Abolition
party. They consulted it all over, and at last Lincoln came to the

conclusion that he would answer; so he came to Freeport last Friday.

Now that statement altogether furnishes a subject for philosophical contemplation. I have been treating it in that way, and I have really come to the conclusion that I can explain it in no other way than by believing the judge is crazy. If he was in his right mind, I cannot conceive how he would have risked disgusting the four or five thousand of his own friends who stood there and knew, as to my having been carried from the platform, that there was not a word of truth in it.

JUDGE DOUGLAS: Didn't they carry you off?

MR. LINCOLN: There; that question illustrates the character of this man Douglas exactly. He smiles now and says, "Didn't they carry you off?" But he said then, "He had to be carried off"; and he said it to convince the country that he had so completely broken me down by his speech that I had to be carried away. Now he seeks to dodge it, and asks, "Didn't they carry you off?" Yes, they did. But, Judge Douglas, why didn't you tell the truth? I would like to know why you didn't tell the truth about it. And then again, "He laid up seven days." He puts this in print for the people of the country to read as a serious document. I think if he had been in his sober senses he would not have risked that barefacedness in the presence of thousands of his own friends, who knew that I made speeches within six of the seven days at Henry, Marshall County; Augusta, Hancock County; and Macomb, McDonough County, including all the necessary travel to meet him again at Freeport at the end of the six days. Now, I say, there is no charitable way to look at that statement, except to conclude that he is actually crazy.

There is another thing in that statement that alarmed me very greatly as he states it—that he was going to "trot me down to Egypt." Thereby he would have you to infer that I would not come to Egypt unless he forced me—that I could

not be got here, unless he, giant-like, had hauled me down
here. That statement he makes, too, in the teeth of the knowledge that I made the stipulation to come down here, and that
he himself had been very reluctant to enter into the stipulation. More than all this, Judge Douglas, when he made that
statement, must have been crazy, and wholly out of his sober
senses, or else he would have known that, when he got me
down here, that promise—that windy promise—of his powers
to annihilate me wouldn't amount to anything. Now, how little do I look like being carried away trembling? Let the judge
go on, and after he is done with his half hour, I want you all,
if I can't go home myself, to let me stay and rot here; and
if anything happens to the judge, if I cannot carry him to
the hotel and put him to bed, let me stay here and rot. I
say, then, there is something extraordinary in this statement.
I ask you if you know any other living man who would make
such a statement?

Did the judge talk of trotting me down to Egypt to scare
me to death? Why, I know this people better than he does.
I was raised just a little east of here. I am a part of this people. But the judge was raised further north, and perhaps he
has some horrid idea of what this people might be induced to
do. But really I have talked about this matter perhaps longer
than I ought, for it is no great thing, and yet the smallest are
often the most difficult things to deal with. The judge has
set about seriously trying to make the impression that when
we meet at different places I am literally in his clutches—
that I am a poor, helpless, decrepit mouse, and that I can do
nothing at all. This is one of the ways he has taken to create
that impression. I don't know any other way to meet it,
except this. I don't want to quarrel with him—to call him a
liar—but when I come square up to him I don't know what
else to call him, if I must tell the truth out. I want to be at
peace, and reserve all my fighting powers for necessary occasions. My time, now, is very nearly out, and I give up the trifle

that is left to the judge to let him set my knees trembling
again—if he can.

FROM LINCOLN'S OPENING SPEECH
AT THE FOURTH JOINT DEBATE
AT CHARLESTON, ILLINOIS

*Charleston is in the eastern part of Illinois near the Indiana border.
People came there from Indiana to hear Lincoln speak. His family
had passed through the town when they had first entered Illinois,
and some Charleston people had made a huge pictorial banner
showing Lincoln with his family's pioneer wagon. The section was
filled with old-time Whigs, so Lincoln felt very much at home.
He had the opening speech, and he starts out by telling an
anecdote of what had happened to him at his hotel in Charleston
when a gentleman came to ask him if he really believed in Negro
equality. The rest of his speech was devoted largely to a consideration of an attack made by Trumbull on Douglas, in 1856. This
attack has been deleted here because it was only of emphemeral
interest.*

September 18, 1858

WHILE I was at the hotel today, an elderly gentleman called
upon me to know whether I was really in favor of producing
a perfect equality between the Negroes and white people.
While I had not proposed to myself on this occasion to say
much on that subject, yet as the question was asked me I
thought I would occupy perhaps five minutes in saying something in regard to it. I will say then that I am not, nor ever
have been, in favor of bringing about in any way the social
and political equality of the white and black races—that I am
not, nor ever have been, in favor of making voters or jurors
of Negroes, nor of qualifying them to hold office, nor to intermarry with white people; and I will say in addition to this

that there is a physical difference between the white and black races which I believe will forever forbid the two races living together on terms of social and political equality. And inasmuch as they cannot so live, while they do remain together there must be the position of superior and inferior, and I as much as any other man am in favor of having the superior position assigned to the white race. I say upon this occasion I do not perceive that because the white man is to have the superior position the Negro should be denied everything. I do not understand that because I do not want a Negro woman for a slave I must necessarily want her for a wife. My understanding is that I can just let her alone. I am now in my fiftieth year, and I certainly never have had a black woman for either a slave or a wife. So it seems to me quite possible for us to get along without making either slaves or wives of Negroes. I will add to this that I have never seen, to my knowledge, a man, woman, or child who was in favor of producing a perfect equality, social and political, between Negroes and white men. . . . I will also add to the remarks I have made (for I am not going to enter at large upon this subject), that I have never had the least apprehension that I or my friends would marry Negroes if there was no law to keep them from it; but as Judge Douglas and his friends seem to be in great apprehension that they might, if there was no law to keep them from it, I give him the most solemn pledge that I will to the very last stand by the law of this State, which forbids the marrying of white people with Negroes. I will add one further word, which is this: that I do not understand that there is any place where an alteration of the social and political relations of the Negro and the white man can be made except in the State legislature—not in the Congress of the United States; and as I do not really apprehend the approach of any such thing myself, and as Judge Douglas seems to be in constant horror that some such danger is rapidly approaching, I propose, as the best means to prevent it, that the judge be kept at home and placed in the State legislature to fight the measure.

FROM LINCOLN'S REJOINDER IN THE FOURTH JOINT DEBATE AT CHARLESTON, ILLINOIS

Douglas had given most of his time to meeting the Trumbull charges brought up by Lincoln; he also answered Lincoln's charges of conspiracy in the Dred Scott decision. He then said that the Republican party changed its principles to fit the sentiments of each section to which it tried to appeal. "Their principles in the north are jet-black; in the center they are . . . a decent mulatto; and in lower Egypt they are almost white." He ended by re-affirming that he believed that the government had been founded "on the white basis," that the country should certainly be able to endure half slave and half free as it had always done.

September 18, 1858

JUDGE DOUGLAS has said to you that he has not been able to get from me an answer to the question whether I am in favor of Negro citizenship. So far as I know, the judge never asked me the question before. He shall have no occasion to ever ask it again, for I tell him very frankly that I am not in favor of Negro citizenship. This furnishes me an occasion for saying a few words upon the subject. I mentioned in a certain speech of mine, which has been printed, that the Supreme Court had decided that a Negro could not possibly be made a citizen, and without saying what was my ground of complaint in regard to that, or whether I had any ground of complaint, Judge Douglas has from that thing manufactured nearly everything that he ever says about my disposition to produce an equality between the Negroes and the white people. If any one will read my speech, he will find I mentioned that as one of the points decided in the course of the Supreme Court opinions, but I did not state what objection I had to it. But Judge Douglas tells the people what my objection was when I did not tell them myself. Now my opinion is that the different States have the power to make a Negro a citizen under the Constitution of the United States, if they choose. The Dred Scott decision decides that they have not that power. If the State of Illinois had that power, I should be opposed to the exercise of it. That is all I have to say about it.

Judge Douglas has told me that he heard my speeches north and my speeches south—that he had heard me at Ottawa and and at Freeport in the north, and recently at Jonesboro in the south, and there was a very different cast of sentiment in the speeches made at the different points. I will not charge upon Judge Douglas that he wilfully misrepresents me, but I call upon every fair-minded man to take these speeches and read them, and I dare him to point out any difference between my speeches north and south. While I am here perhaps I ought to say a word, if I have the time, in regard to the latter portion of the judge's speech, which was a sort of declamation in reference to my having said I entertained the belief that this government would not endure half slave and half free. I have said so, and I did not say it without what seemed to me to be good reasons. It perhaps would require more time than I have now to set forth these reasons in detail; but let me ask you a few questions. Have we ever had any peace on this slavery question? When are we to have peace upon it if it is kept in the position it now occupies? How are we ever to have peace upon it? That is an important question. To be sure, if we will all stop and allow Judge Douglas and his friends to march on in their present career until they plant the institution all over the nation, here and wherever else our flag waves, and we acquiesce in it, there will be peace. But let me ask Judge Douglas how he is going to get the people to do that? They have been wrangling over this question for at least forty years. This was the cause of the agitation resulting in the Missouri Compromise; this produced the troubles at the annexation of Texas, in the acquisition of the territory acquired in the Mexican war. Again, this was the trouble which was quieted by the compromise of 1850, when it was settled "forever," as both the great political parties declared in their national conventions. That "forever" turned out to be just four years, when Judge Douglas himself reopened it.

When is it likely to come to an end? He introduced the Nebraska bill in 1854 to put another end to the slavery agitation. He promised that it would finish it all up immediately, and he has never made a speech since until he got into a quarrel with the President about the Lecompton constitution, in which he has not declared that we are just at the end of the slavery agitation. But in one speech, I think last winter, he did say that he didn't quite see when the end of the slavery agitation would come. Now he tells us again that it is all over, and the people of Kansas have voted down the Lecompton constitution. How is it over? That was only one of the attempts at putting an end to the slavery agitation—one of these "final settlements." Is Kansas in the Union? Has she formed a constitution that she is likely to come in under? Is not the slavery agitation still an open question in that Territory? Has the voting down of that constitution put an end to all the trouble? Is that more likely to settle it than every one of these previous attempts to settle the slavery agitation? Now, at this day in the history of the world we can no more foretell where the end of this slavery agitation will be than we can see the end of the world itself. The Nebraska-Kansas bill was introduced four years and a half ago, and if the agitation is ever to come to an end, we may say we are four years and a half nearer the end. So, too, we can say we are four years and a half nearer the end of the world; and we can just as clearly see the end of the world as we can see the end of this agitation. The Kansas settlement did not conclude it. If Kansas should sink today, and leave a great vacant space in the earth's surface, this vexed question would still be among us. I say, then, there is no way of putting an end to the slavery agitation amongst us but to put it back upon the basis where our fathers placed it, no way but to keep it out of our new Territories —to restrict it forever to the old States where it now exists. Then the public mind will rest in the belief that it is in the course of ultimate extinction. That is one way of putting an end to the slavery agitation.

The other way is for us to surrender and let Judge Douglas and his friends have their way and plant slavery over all the States—cease speaking of it as in any way a wrong—regard slavery as one of the common matters of property, and speak of Negroes as we do of our horses and cattle. But while it drives on in its state of progress as it is now driving, and as it has driven for the last five years, I have ventured the opinion, and I say today, that we will have no end to the slavery agitation until it takes one turn or the other. I do not mean that when it takes a turn toward ultimate extinction it will be in a day, nor in a year, nor in two years. I do not suppose that in the most peaceful way ultimate extinction would occur in less than a hundred years at least; but that it will occur in the best way for both races, in God's own good time, I have no doubt. . . .

NOTES FOR SPEECHES

During his debates with Douglas, Lincoln was in the habit of jotting down random ideas which might be worked up into arguments to be used on the platform. Here are some of his ideas in their embryonic form—the raw material from which his speeches were made.

(Written about October 1, 1858)

SUPPOSE it is true that the Negro is inferior to the white in the gifts of nature; is it not the exact reverse of justice that the white should for that reason take from the Negro any part of the little which he has had given him? "Give to him that is needy" is the Christian rule of charity; but "Take from him that is needy" is the rule of slavery.

Pro-slavery Theology

The sum of pro-slavery theology seems to be this: "Slavery is not universally right, nor yet universally wrong; it is better for some people to be slaves; and, in such cases, it is the will of God that they be such."

Certainly there is no contending against the will of God; but still there is some difficulty in ascertaining and applying it to particular cases. For instance, we will suppose the Rev. Dr. Ross* has a slave named Sambo, and the question is, "Is it the will of God that Sambo shall remain a slave, or be set free?" The Almighty gives no audible answer to the question, and his revelation, the Bible, gives none—or at most none but such as admits of a squabble as to its meaning; no one thinks of asking Sambo's opinion on it.

So at last it comes to this, that Dr. Ross is to decide the question; and while he considers it, he sits in the shade, with gloves on his hands, and subsists on the bread that Sambo is earning in the burning sun. If he decides that God wills Sambo to continue a slave, he thereby retains his own comfortable position; but if he decides that God wills Sambo to be free, he thereby has to walk out of the shade, throw off his gloves, and delve for his own bread. Will Dr. Ross be actuated by the perfect impartiality which has ever been considered most favorable to correct decisions?

*   *   *

Allow me now, in my own way, to state with what aims and objects I did enter upon this campaign. I claim no extraordi-

* The Rev. Dr. Frederick A. Ross was a Presbyterian minister who, in 1856, had attacked abolitionist agitation as atheistic and anarchical.

nary exemption from personal ambition. That I like prefer-
ment as well as the average of men may be admitted. But I
protest I have not entered upon this hard contest solely, or
even chiefly, for a mere personal object. I clearly see, as I
think, a powerful plot to make slavery universal and perpetual
in this nation. The effort to carry that plot through will be
persistent and long continued, extending far beyond the senatorial term for which Judge Douglas and I are just now struggling. I enter upon the contest to contribute my humble and
temporary mite in opposition to that effort.

At the Republican State convention at Springfield I made a
speech. That speech has been considered the opening of the
canvass on my part. In it I arrange a string of incontestable
facts which, I think, prove the existence of a conspiracy to
nationalize slavery. The evidence was circumstantial only; but
nevertheless it seemed inconsistent with every hypothesis, save
that of the existence of such conspiracy. I believe the facts can
be explained today on no other hypothesis. Judge Douglas
can so explain them if any one can. From warp to woof his
handiwork is everywhere woven in.

At New York he finds this speech of mine, and devises his
plan of assault upon it. At Chicago he develops that plan.
Passing over, unnoticed, the obvious purport of the whole
speech, he cooks up two or three issues upon points not discussed by me at all, and then authoritatively announces that
these are to be the issues of the campaign. Next evening I
answer, assuring him that he misunderstands me—that he
takes issues which I have not tendered. In good faith I try to
set him right. If he really has misunderstood my meaning, I
give him language that can no longer be misunderstood. He
will have none of it. At Bloomington, six days later, he speaks
again, and perverts me even worse than before. He seems to
have grown confident and jubilant, in the belief that he has
entirely diverted me from my purpose of fixing a conspiracy
upon him and his co-workers. Next day he speaks again at

Springfield, pursuing the same course, with increased confidence and recklessness of assertion. At night of that day I speak again. I tell him that as he has carefully read my speech making the charge of conspiracy, and has twice spoken of the speech without noticing the charge, upon his own tacit admission I renew the charge against him. I call him, and take a default upon him. At Clifton, ten days after, he comes in with a plea. The substance of that plea is that he never passed a word with Chief Justice Taney as to what his decision was to be in the Dred Scott case, that I ought to know that he who affirms what he does not know to be true falsifies as much as he who affirms what he does know to be false; and that he would pronounce the whole charge of conspiracy a falsehood, were it not for his own self-respect!

Now I demur to this plea. Waiving objection that it was not filed till after default, I demur to it on the merits. I say it does not meet the case. What if he did not pass a word with Chief Justice Taney? Could he not have as distinct an understanding, and play his part just as well, without directly passing a word with Taney, as with it? But suppose we construe this part of the plea more broadly than he puts it himself—suppose we construe it, as in an answer in chancery, to be a denial of all knowledge, information, or belief of such conspiracy. Still I have the right to prove the conspiracy, even against his answer; and there is much more than the evidence of two witnesses to prove it by. Grant that he has no knowledge, information, or belief of such conspiracy, and what of it? That does not disturb the facts in evidence. It only makes him the dupe, instead of a principal, of conspirators.

What if a man may not affirm a proposition without knowing it to be true? I have not affirmed that a conspiracy does exist. I have only stated the evidence, and affirmed my belief in its existence. If Judge Douglas shall assert that I do not believe what I say, then he affirms what he cannot know to be true, and falls within the condemnation of his own rule.

Would it not be much better for him to meet the evidence, and show, if he can, that I have no good reason to believe the charge? Would not this be far more satisfactory than merely vociferating an intimation that he may be provoked to call somebody a liar?

*   *   *

Judge Douglas is a man of large influence. His bare opinion goes far to fix the opinions of others. Besides this, thousands hang their hopes upon forcing their opinions to agree with his. It is a party necessity with them to say they agree with him, and there is danger they will repeat the saying till they really come to believe it. Others dread, and shrink from, his denunciations, his sarcasms, and his ingenious misrepresentations. The susceptible young hear lessons from him, such as their fathers never heard when they were young.

If, by all these means, he shall succeed in molding public sentiment to a perfect accordance with his own; in bringing all men to indorse all court decisions, without caring to know whether they are right or wrong; in bringing all tongues to as perfect a silence as his own, as to there being any wrong in slavery; in bringing all to declare, with him, that they care not whether slavery be voted down or voted up; that if any people want slaves they have a right to have them; that Negroes are not men; have no part in the Declaration of Independence; that there is no moral question about slavery; that liberty and slavery are perfectly consistent—indeed, necessary accompaniments; that for a strong man to declare himself the superior of a weak one, and thereupon enslave the weak one, is the very essence of liberty, the most sacred right of self-government; when, I say, public sentiment shall be brought to all this, in the name of Heaven what barrier will be left against slavery being made lawful everywhere? Can you find one word of his opposed to it? Can you not find many strongly favoring it? If for his life, for his eternal salvation, he was solely striving for that end, could he find any means so well adapted to reach the end?

If our Presidential election, by a mere plurality, and of doubtful significance, brought one Supreme Court decision that no power can exclude slavery from a Territory, how much more shall a public sentiment, in exact accordance with the sentiments of Judge Douglas, bring another that no power can exclude it from a State?

And then, the Negro being doomed, and damned, and forgotten, to everlasting bondage, is the white man quite certain that the tyrant demon will not turn upon him too?

*   *   *

Welcome or unwelcome, agreeable or disagreeable, whether this shall be an entire slave nation is the issue before us. Every incident—every little shifting of scenes or of actors—only clears away the intervening trash, compacts and consolidates the opposing hosts, and brings them more and more distinctly face to face. The conflict will be a severe one; and it will be fought through by those who do care for the result, and not by those who do not care—by those who are for, and those who are against, a legalized national slavery. The combined charge of Nebraskaism and Dred-Scottism must be repulsed and rolled back. The deceitful cloak of "self-government," wherewith "the sum of all villainies" seeks to protect and adorn itself, must be torn from its hateful carcass. That burlesque upon judicial decisions, and slander and profanation upon the honored names and sacred history of republican America, must be overruled and expunged from the books of authority.

To give the victory to the right, not bloody bullets, but peaceful ballots only are necessary. Thanks to our good old Constitution, and organization under it, these alone are necessary. It only needs that every right thinking man shall go to the polls, and without fear or prejudice vote as he thinks.

FROM LINCOLN'S REPLY IN THE FIFTH JOINT DEBATE AT GALESBURG, ILLINOIS

The weather was becoming colder; heavy rains had been falling, and a stiff wind was blowing when the two candidates met in Galesburg. The debate there was held on the campus of Knox College, against the east wall of the Old Main Hall which was decorated with a banner reading: "Knox College for Lincoln." This part of the state was strongly Republican, and the laboring men enthusiastically supported Lincoln. One of the signs displayed at the debate read: "Small-fisted farmers, mud-sills of society, greasy mechanics for A. Lincoln." Douglas had the opening speech. He began by outlining the course of events in Kansas; he then went on to say again that Lincoln was changing his tactics to suit his audience and implied that what Lincoln had said in "Egypt" was very different from what he would say now. The audience was entirely hostile, and every time Douglas tried to make a point against Lincoln, someone in the crowd would howl approval of what Lincoln had said or done. Despite the attitude of his listeners Douglas insisted on maintaining that slavery should be let alone— that it was a natural part of the economy of the country and must be permitted to stay so. He concluded with a plea that the Northern states mind their own business and work for peace by leaving the Southern states alone. For the first time in the debates, Lincoln now introduces the theme of slavery being a moral wrong.

October 7, 1858

THE judge has alluded to the Declaration of Independence, and insisted that Negroes are not included in that Declaration; and that it is a slander upon the framers of that instrument to suppose that Negroes were meant therein; and he asks you: Is it possible to believe that Mr. Jefferson, who penned the immortal paper, could have supposed himself applying the language of that instrument to the Negro race, and yet held a portion of that race in slavery? Would he not at once have freed them? I only have to remark upon this part of the judge's speech (and that, too, very briefly, for I shall not detain myself, or you, upon that point for any great length of time), that I believe the entire records of the world, from the date of the Declaration of Independence up to within three years ago, may be searched in vain for one single affirmation, from one single man, that the Negro was not included in the Declaration of Independence; I think I may defy Judge Douglas to show that he ever said so, that Washington ever said so, that any president ever said so, that any member of Congress ever said so, or that any living man upon the whole earth ever said so, until the necessities of the present policy of the Democratic party, in regard to slavery, had to invent that affirmation. And I will remind Judge Douglas and this audience that while Mr. Jefferson was the owner of slaves, as undoubtedly he was, in speaking upon this very subject, he used the strong language that "he trembled for his country when he remembered that God was just"; and I will offer the highest premium in my power to Judge Douglas if he will show that he, in all his life, ever uttered a sentiment at all akin to that of Jefferson.

*   *   *

The judge has also detained us awhile in regard to the distinction between his party and our party. His he assumes to be a national party—ours a sectional one. He does this in asking the question whether this country has any interest in the maintenance of the Republican party? He assumes that our party is altogether sectional—that the party to which he adheres is national; and the argument is that no party can be a rightful party—can be based upon rightful principles—unless it can announce its principles everywhere. I presume that Judge Douglas could not go into Russia and announce the doctrine of our national Democracy; he could not denounce the doctrine of kings and emperors and monarchies in Russia; and it may be true of this country, that in some places we may not be able to proclaim a doctrine as clearly true as the truth of Democracy, because there is a section so directly opposed to it that they will not tolerate us in doing so. Is it the true test of the soundness of a doctrine, that in some places people won't let you proclaim it? Is that the way to test the truth of any doctrine? . . .

Judge Douglas and I have made perhaps forty speeches apiece, and we have now for the fifth time met face to face in debate, and up to this day I have not found either Judge Douglas or any friend of his taking hold of the Republican platform or laying his finger upon anything in it that is wrong. I ask you all to recollect that. Judge Douglas turns away from the platform of principles to the fact that he can find people somewhere who will not allow us to announce those principles. If he had great confidence that our principles were wrong, he would take hold of them and demonstrate them to be wrong. But he does not do so. The only evidence he has of their being wrong is in the fact that there are people who won't allow us to preach them. I ask again is that the way to test the soundness of a doctrine?

I ask his attention also to the fact that by the rule of nationality he is himself fast becoming sectional. I ask his attention to the fact that his speeches would not go as current now south of the Ohio River as they have formerly gone there. I ask his attention to the fact that he felicitates himself today that all the Democrats of the free States are agreeing with him, while he omits to tell us that the Democrats of any slave State agree with him. If he has not thought of this, I commend to his consideration the evidence in his own declaration, on this day, of his becoming sectional too. I see it rapidly approaching. Whatever may be the result of this ephemeral contest between Judge Douglas and myself, I see the day rapidly approaching when his pill of sectionalism, which he has been thrusting down the throats of Republicans for years past, will be crowded down his own throat.

* * *

The judge tells us, in proceeding, that he is opposed to making any odious distinctions between free and slave States. I am altogether unaware that the Republicans are in favor of making any odious distinctions between the free and slave States. But there still is a difference, I think, between Judge Douglas and the Republicans in this. I suppose that the real difference between Judge Douglas and his friends and the Republicans, on the contrary, is that the judge is not in favor of making any difference between slavery and liberty—that he is in favor of eradicating, of pressing out of view, the questions of preference in this country for free or slave institutions; and consequently every sentiment he utters discards the idea that there is any wrong in slavery. Everything that emanates from him or his coadjutors in their course of policy carefully excludes the thought that there is anything wrong in slavery. All their arguments, if you will consider them, will be seen to exclude the thought that there is anything whatever wrong in slavery. If you will take the judge's speeches, and select the short and pointed sentences expressed by him—as his declaration that he "don't care whether slavery is voted up or down"—you will see at once that this is perfectly logical, if you do not admit that slavery is wrong. If you do admit that it is wrong, Judge Douglas cannot logically say he don't care whether a wrong is voted up or voted down. Judge Douglas declares that if any community wants slavery they have a right to have it. He can say that logically, if he says that there is no wrong in slavery; but if you admit that there is a wrong in it, he cannot logically say that anybody has a right to do wrong. He insists that, upon the score of equality, the owners of slaves and owners of property—of horses and every other sort of property—should be alike, and hold them alike in a new Territory. That is perfectly logical, if the two species of property are alike, and are equally founded in right. But if you admit that one of them is wrong, you cannot institute any equality between right and wrong. And from this difference of sentiment—the belief on the part of one that the institution is wrong, and a policy springing from that belief which looks to the arrest of the enlargement of that wrong; and this other sentiment, that it is no wrong, and a policy sprung from that sentiment which will tolerate no idea of preventing that wrong from growing larger, and looks to there never being an end of it through all the existence of things—arises the real difference between Judge Douglas and his friends on the one hand, and the Republicans on the other. Now, I confess myself as belonging to that class in the country who contemplate slavery as a moral, social, and political evil, having due regard for its actual existence amongst us, and the difficulties of getting rid of it in any satisfactory way, and to all the constitutional obligations which have been thrown about it; but who, nevertheless, desire a policy that looks to the prevention of it as a wrong, and looks hopefully to the time when as a wrong it may come to an end.

FROM LINCOLN'S OPENING SPEECH AT THE SIXTH JOINT DEBATE AT QUINCY, ILLINOIS

Quincy was the largest town of all those in which the debates were held. It was an important commercial center, and a place in which Lincoln had many friends. The Republicans of the town marched to the meeting place with a tall pole on the top of which was a live raccoon—the symbol of the old Whig party whose members they hoped to attract. The Democrats counter-attacked by carrying a pole with a dead raccoon swinging by the tail. Lincoln had the opening speech. In an effort to show that his sentiments had not changed from section to section, Lincoln first reviewed some of the statements he had made during the course of the debates, reading out verbatim many passages from his speeches. He reiterated his belief that slavery was morally wrong. He points out here the significance of the drama the audience was seeing played before it.

October 13, 1858

I was aware, when it was first agreed that Judge Douglas and I were to have these seven joint discussions, that they were the successive acts of a drama—perhaps I should say, to be enacted not merely in the face of audiences like this, but in the face of the nation, and to some extent, by my relation to him, and not from anything in myself, in the face of the world; and I am anxious that they should be conducted with dignity and in the good temper which would be befitting the vast audience before which it was conducted. But when Judge Douglas got home from Washington and made his first speech in Chicago, the evening afterward I made some sort of a reply to it. His second speech was made at Bloomington, in which he commented upon my speech at Chicago, and said that I had used language ingeniously contrived to conceal my intentions, or words to that effect. Now I understand that this is an imputation upon my veracity and my candor. . . . Judge Douglas may not understand that he implicated my truthfulness and my honor when he said I was doing one thing and pretending another; and I misunderstood him if he thought he was treating me in a dignified way, as a man of honor and truth, as he now claims he was disposed to treat me. Even after that time, at Galesburg, when he brings forward an extract from a speech made at Chicago, and an extract from a speech made at Charleston, to prove that I was trying to play a double part—that I was trying to cheat the public, and get votes upon one set of principles at one place and upon another set of principles at another place—I do not understand but what he impeaches my honor, my veracity, and my candor; and because he does this, I do not understand that I am bound, if I see a truthful ground for it, to keep my hands off of him. As soon as I learned that Judge Douglas was disposed to treat me in this way, I signified in one of my speeches that I should be driven to draw upon whatever of humble resources I might have—to adopt a new course with him. I was not entirely sure that I should be able to hold my own with him, but I at least had the purpose made to do as well as I could upon him; and now I say that I will not be the first to cry "Hold!" I think it originated with the judge, and when he quits, I probably will. But I shall not ask any favors at all. He asks me, or he asks the audience, if I wish to push this matter to the point of personal difficulty. I tell him, No. He did not make a mistake, in one of his early speeches, when he called me an "amiable" man, though perhaps he did when he called me an "intelligent" man. It really hurts me very much to suppose that I have wronged anybody on earth. I again tell him, No! I very much prefer, when this canvass shall be over, however it may result, that we at least part without any bitter recollections of personal difficulties.

FROM LINCOLN'S REPLY IN THE SEVENTH AND LAST JOINT DEBATE AT ALTON, ILLINOIS

Lincoln and Douglas both took a river steamer and sailed down the Mississippi from Quincy to Alton, arriving at Alton at five o'clock in the morning of the fifteenth. This, the last joint debate, was held in the town square in front of the City Hall which overlooked the Mississippi. The crowd was not large, and there were many Democrats in it. Douglas had the opening and closing speeches. He reviewed the course of the arguments used during the previous debates, and then launched into an attack on the Buchanan administration, accusing it of favoring the Republican candidate in order to strike back at him. He said that if a President were to be permitted to dictate to Congress only despotism could result. It is interesting to hear Douglas make the charges of Presidential abuse of power, for these same charges were to be hurled against Lincoln by the members of his Congress. Lincoln, of course, was delighted at the opening Douglas's denunciation of his own party gave him, and he begins his reply using this theme as his initial point of attack. This Alton speech represents Lincoln's arguments against Douglas in their most highly developed form; it is for that reason given here almost in its entirety.

October 15, 1858

I HAVE been somewhat, in my own mind, complimented by a large portion of Judge Douglas's speech—I mean that portion which he devotes to the controversy between himself and the present administration. This is the seventh time Judge Douglas and myself have met in these joint discussions, and he has been gradually improving in regard to his war with the administration. At Quincy, day before yesterday, he was a little more severe upon the administration than I had heard him upon any occasion, and I took pains to compliment him for it. I then told him to "give it to them with all the power he had"; and as some of them were present, I told them I would be very much obliged if they would give it to him in about the same way. I take it that he has now vastly improved upon the attack he made then upon the administration. I flatter myself he has really taken my advice on this subject. All I can say now is to re-commend to him and to them what I then commenced—to prosecute the war against one another in the most vigorous manner. I say to them again, "Go it, husband; go it, bear!"

There is one other thing I will mention before I leave this branch of the discussion—although I do not consider it much of my business, anyway. I refer to that part of the judge's remarks where he undertakes to involve Mr. Buchanan in an inconsistency. He reads something from Mr. Buchanan, from which he undertakes to involve him in an inconsistency; and he gets something of a cheer for having done so. I would only remind the judge that while he is very valiantly fighting for the Nebraska bill and the repeal of the Missouri Compromise, it has been but a little while since he was the valiant advocate of the Missouri Compromise. I want to know if Buchanan has not as much right to be inconsistent as Douglas has? Has Douglas the exclusive right in this country of being on all sides of all questions? Is nobody allowed that high privilege but himself? Is he to have an entire monopoly on that subject?

So far as Judge Douglas addressed his speech to me, or so far as it was about me, it is my business to pay some attention to it. I have heard the judge state two or three times what he has stated today—that in a speech which I made at Springfield, Illinois, I had in a very especial manner complained that the Supreme Court in the Dred Scott case had decided that a Negro could never be a citizen of the United States. I have omitted, by some accident, heretofore to analyze this statement, and it is required of me to notice it now. In point of fact it is untrue. I never have complained especially of the Dred Scott decision, because it held that a Negro could not be a citizen, and the judge is always wrong when he says I ever did so complain of it. I have the speech here, and I will thank him or any of his friends to show where I said that a Negro should be a citizen, and complained especially of the Dred Scott decision because it declared he could not be one. I have done no such thing, and Judge Douglas so persistently insisting that I have done so has strongly impressed me with the belief of a predetermination on his part to misrepresent me. He could not get his foundation for insisting that I was in favor of this Negro equality anywhere else as well as he could by assuming that untrue proposition. Let me tell this audience what is true in regard to that matter; and the means by which they may correct me if I do not tell them truly is by a recurrence to the speech itself. I spoke of the Dred Scott decision in my Springfield speech, and I was then endeavoring to prove that the Dred Scott decision was a portion of a system or scheme to make slavery national in this country. I pointed out what things had been decided by the court. I mentioned as a fact that they had decided that a Negro could not be a citizen—that they had done so, as I supposed, to deprive the Negro, under all circumstances, of the remotest possibility of ever becoming a citizen and claiming the rights of a citizen of the United States under a certain clause of the Constitution. I stated that, without making any complaint of it at all. I then went on and stated the other points decided in the case—namely, that the bringing of a Negro into the State of Illinois, and holding him in slavery for two years here, was a matter in regard to which they would not decide whether it would make him free or not; that they decided the further point that taking him into a United States Territory where slavery was prohibited by act of Congress, did not make him free, because that act of Congress, as they held, was unconstitutional. I mentioned these three things as making up the points decided in that case. I mentioned them in a lump taken in connection with the introduction of the Nebraska bill, and the amendment of Chase, offered at the time, declaratory of the right of the people of the Territories to exclude slavery, which was voted down by the friends of the bill. I mentioned all these things together, as evidence tending to prove a combination and conspiracy to make the institution of slavery national. In that connection and in that way I mentioned the decision on the point that a Negro could not be a citizen, and in no other connection.

Out of this, Judge Douglas builds up his beautiful fabrication—of my purpose to introduce a perfect social and political equality between the white and the black races. His assertion that I made an "especial objection" (that is his exact language) to the decision on this account, is untrue in point of fact.

Now, while I am upon this subject, and as Henry Clay has

been alluded to, I desire to place myself, in connection with Mr. Clay, as nearly right before this people as may be. I am quite aware what the judge's object is here by all these allusions. He knows that we are before an audience having strong sympathies southward by relationship, place of birth, and so on. He desires to place me in an extremely Abolition attitude. He read upon a former occasion, and alludes without reading today, to a portion of a speech which I delivered in Chicago. In his quotations from that speech, as he has made them upon former occasions, the extracts were taken in such a way as, I suppose, brings them within the definition of what is called garbling—taking portions of a speech which, when taken by themselves, do not present the entire sense of the speaker as expressed at the time.

*   *   *

At Galesburg the other day, I said, in answer to Judge Douglas, that three years ago there never had been a man, so far as I knew or believed, in the whole world, who had said that the Declaration of Independence did not include Negroes in the term "all men." I reassert it today. I assert that Judge Douglas and all his friends may search the whole records of the country, and it will be a matter of great astonishment to me if they shall be able to find that one human being three years ago had ever uttered the astounding sentiment that the term "all men" in the Declaration did not include the Negro. Do not let me be misunderstood. I know that more than three years ago there were men who, finding this assertion constantly in the way of their schemes to bring about the ascendancy and perpetuation of slavery, denied the truth of it. I know that Mr. Calhoun and all the politicians of his school denied the truth of the Declaration. I know that it ran along in the mouth of some Southern men for a period of years, ending at last in that shameful though rather forcible declaration of Pettit of Indiana, upon the floor of the United States Senate, that the

Declaration of Independence was in that respect "a self-evident lie," rather than a self-evident truth. But I say, with a perfect knowledge of all this hawking at the Declaration without directly attacking it, that three years ago there never had lived a man who had ventured to assail it in the sneaking way of pretending to believe it and then asserting it did not include the Negro. I believe the first man who ever said it was Chief Justice Taney in the Dred Scott case, and the next to him was our friend, Stephen A. Douglas. And now it has become the catchword of the entire party. I would like to call upon his friends everywhere, to consider how they have come in so short a time to view this matter in a way so entirely different from their former belief; to ask whether they are not being borne along by an irresistible current—whither, they know not.

In answer to my proposition at Galesburg last week, I see that some man in Chicago has got up a letter addressed to the Chicago *Times*, to show, as he professes, that somebody had said so before; and he signs himself "An Old-Line Whig," if I remember correctly. In the first place I would say he was not an old-line Whig. I am somewhat acquainted with the old-line Whigs. I was with the old-line Whigs from the origin to the end of that party; I became pretty well acquainted with them, and I know they always had some sense, whatever else you could ascribe to them. I know there never was one who had not more sense than to try to show by the evidence he produces that some man had, prior to the time I named, said that Negroes were not included in the term "all men" in the Declaration of Independence. What is the evidence he produces? I will bring forward his evidence, and let you see what he offers by way of showing that somebody more than three years ago had said Negroes were not included in the Declaration. He brings forward part of a speech from Henry Clay— the part of the speech of Henry Clay which I used to bring forward to prove precisely the contrary. I guess we are surrounded to some extent today by the old friends of Mr. Clay, and they will be glad to hear anything from that authority. While he was in Indiana a man presented a petition to liberate his Negroes, and he (Mr. Clay) made a speech in answer to it, which I suppose he carefully wrote himself and caused to be published. I have before me an extract from that speech which constitutes the evidence this pretended "Old-Line Whig" at Chicago brought forward to show that Mr. Clay didn't suppose the Negro was included in the Declaration of Independence. Hear what Mr. Clay said:

And what is the foundation of this appeal to me in Indiana, to liberate the slaves under my care in Kentucky? It is a general declaration in the act announcing to the world the independence of the thirteen American colonies, that all men are created equal. Now, as an abstract principle, there is no doubt of the truth of that declaration; and it is desirable, in the original construction of society, and in organized societies, to keep it in view as a great fundamental principle. But then I apprehend that in no society that ever did exist, or ever shall be formed, was or can the equality asserted among the members of the human race be practically enforced and carried out. There are portions, large portions—women, minors, insane, culprits, transient sojourners—that will always probably remain subject to the government of another portion of the community.

That declaration, whatever may be the extent of its import, was made by the delegations of the thirteen States. In most of them slavery existed, and had long existed, and was established by law. It was introduced and forced upon the colonies by the paramount law of England. Do you believe that in making that declaration the States that concurred in it intended that it should be tortured into a virtual emancipation of all the slaves within their respective limits? Would Virginia and other Southern States have ever united in a declaration which was to be interpreted into an abolition of slavery among them? Did any one of the thirteen colonies entertain such a design or expectation? To impute such a secret and unavowed purpose would be to charge a political fraud upon the noblest band of patriots that ever assembled in council—a fraud upon the confederacy of the Revolution—a fraud upon the union of those States whose constitution not only recognized the lawfulness of slavery, but permitted the importation of slaves from Africa until the year 1808.

This is the entire quotation brought forward to prove that somebody previous to three years ago had said the Negro was not included in the term "all men" in the Declaration. How does it do so? In what way has it a tendency to prove that? Mr. Clay says it is true as an abstract principle that all men are created equal, but that we cannot practically apply it in all cases. He illustrates this by bringing forward the cases of females, minors, and insane persons, with whom it cannot be enforced; but he says that it is true as an abstract principle in the organization of society, as well as in organized society, and it should be kept in view as a fundamental principle. Let me read a few words more before I add some comments of my own. Mr. Clay says a little further on:

I desire no concealment of my opinions in regard to the institution of slavery. I look upon it as a great evil, and deeply lament that we have derived it from the parent government, and from our ancestors. I wish every slave in the United States was in the country of his ancestors. But here they are, and the question is, how can they be best dealt with? If a state of nature existed, and we were about to lay the foundations of society, no man would be more strongly opposed than I should be, to incorporating the institution of slavery among its elements.

Now, here in this same book—in this same speech—in this same extract brought forward to prove that Mr. Clay held that the Negro was not included in the Declaration of Independence—we find no such statement on his part, but instead the declaration that it is a great fundamental truth, which should be constantly kept in view in the organization of society and in societies already organized. But if I say a word about it; if I attempt, as Mr. Clay said all good men ought to do, to keep it in view; if, in this "organized society," I ask to have the public eye turned upon it; if I ask, in relation to the organization of new Territories, that the public eye should be turned upon it—forthwith I am vilified as you hear me today. What have I done that I have not the license of Henry Clay's illustrious example here in doing? Have I done aught that I have not his authority for, while maintaining that in organizing new Territories and societies, this fundamental principle should be regarded, and in organized society holding it up to the public view and recognizing what he recognized as the great principle of free government?

And when this new principle—this new proposition that no human being ever thought of three years ago—is brought forward, I combat it as having an evil tendency, if not an evil design. I combat it as having a tendency to dehumanize the Negro—to take away from him the right of ever striving to be a man. I combat it as being one of the thousand things constantly done in these days to prepare the public mind to make property, and nothing but property, of the Negro in all the States in this Union. . . .

The principle upon which I have insisted in this canvass, is in relation to laying the foundations of new societies. I have never sought to apply these principles to the old States for the purpose of abolishing slavery in those States. It is nothing but a miserable perversion of what I have said, to assume that I have declared Missouri, or any other slave State, shall emancipate her slaves. I have proposed no such thing. But when Mr. Clay says that in laying the foundations of societies in our Territories where it does not exist, he would be opposed to the introduction of slavery as an element, I insist that we have his warrant—his license for insisting upon the exclusion of that element which he declared in such strong and emphatic language was most hateful to him.

Judge Douglas has again referred to a Springfield speech

in which I said, "A house divided against itself cannot stand." . . .

That extract, and the sentiments expressed in it, have been extremely offensive to Judge Douglas. He has warred upon them as Satan wars upon the Bible. His perversions upon it are endless. Here now are my views upon it in brief.

I said we were now far into the fifth year since a policy was initiated with the avowed object and confident promise of putting an end to the slavery agitation. Is it not so? When that Nebraska bill was brought forward four years ago last January, was it not for the "avowed object" of putting an end to the slavery agitation? We were to have no more agitation in Congress; it was all to be banished to the Territories. . . . We were for a little while quiet on the troublesome thing, and that very allaying-plaster of Judge Douglas's stirred it up again. But was it not undertaken or initiated with the "confident promise" of putting an end to the slavery agitation? Surely it was. In every speech you heard Judge Douglas make, until he got into this "imbroglio," as they call it, with the administration about the Lecompton constitution, every speech on that Nebraska bill was full of his felicitations that we were just at the end of the slavery agitation. The last tip of the last joint of the old serpent's tail was just drawing out of view. But has it proved so? I have asserted that under that policy that agitation "has not only not ceased, but has constantly augmented." When was there ever a greater agitation in Congress than last winter? When was it as great in the country as today?

There was a collateral object in the introduction of that Nebraska policy which was to clothe the people of the Territories with a superior degree of self-government, beyond what they had ever had before. The first object and the main one of conferring upon the people a higher degree of self-government, is a question of fact to be determined by you in answer to a single question. Have you ever heard or known of a people anywhere on earth who had as little to do as, in the first instance of its use, the people of Kansas had with this same right of self-government? In its main policy and in its collateral object, it has been nothing but a living, creeping lie from the time of its introduction till today.

I have intimated that I thought the agitation would not cease until a crisis should have been reached and passed. I have stated in what way I thought it would be reached and passed. I have said that it might go one way or the other. We might, by arresting the further spread of it, and placing it where the fathers originally placed it, put it where the public mind should rest in the belief that it was in the course of ultimate extinction. Thus the agitation may cease. It may be pushed forward until it shall become alike lawful in all the States, old as well as new, North as well as South. I have said, and I repeat, my wish is that the further spread of it may be arrested, and that it may be placed where the public mind shall rest in the belief that it is in the course of ultimate extinction. I have expressed that as my wish. I entertain the opinion, upon evidence sufficient to my mind, that the fathers of this government placed that institution where the public mind did rest in the belief that it was in the course of ultimate extinction. Let me ask why they made provision that the source of slavery—the African slave trade—should be cut off at the end of twenty years? Why did they make provision that in all the new territory we owned at that time, slavery should be forever inhibited? Why stop its spread in one direction and cut off its source in another, if they did not look to its being placed in the course of ultimate extinction?

Again, the institution of slavery is only mentioned in the Constitution of the United States two or three times, and in neither of these cases does the word "slavery" or "Negro race" occur; but covert language is used each time, and for a purpose full of significance. What is the language in regard to the prohibition of the African slave trade? It runs in about this way: "The migration or importation of such persons as any of the States now existing shall think proper to admit, shall not be prohibited by the Congress prior to the year 1808."

The next allusion in the Constitution to the question of slavery and the black race, is on the subject of the basis of representation, and there the language used is: "Representatives and direct taxes shall be apportioned among the several States which may be included within this Union, according to their respective numbers, which shall be determined by adding to the whole number of free persons, including those bound to service for a term of years, and excluding Indians not taxed, three-fifths of all other persons."

It says "persons," not slaves, not Negroes; but this "three-fifths" can be applied to no other class among us than the Negroes.

Lastly, in the provision for the reclamation of fugitive slaves, it is said: "No person held to service or labor in one State, under the laws thereof, escaping into another, shall in consequence of any law or regulation therein be discharged from such service or labor, but shall be delivered up, on claim of the party to whom such service or labor may be due." There, again, there is no mention of the word "Negro," or of slavery. In all three of these places, being the only allusion to slavery in the instrument, covert language is used. Language is used not suggesting that slavery existed or that the black race were among us. And I understand the contemporaneous history of those times to be that covert language was used with a purpose, and that purpose was that in our Constitution, which it was hoped, and is still hoped, will endure forever—when it should be read by intelligent and patriotic men, after the institution of slavery had passed from among us—there should be nothing on the face of the great charter of liberty suggesting that such a thing as Negro slavery had ever existed among us.

This is part of the evidence that the fathers of the government expected and intended the institution of slavery to come to an end. They expected and intended that it should be in the course of ultimate extinction. And when I say that I desire to see the further spread of it arrested, I only say I desire to see that done which the fathers have first done. When I say I desire to see it placed where the public mind will rest in the belief that it is in the course of ultimate extinction, I only say I desire to see it placed where they placed it. It is not true that our fathers, as Judge Douglas assumes, made this government part slave and part free. Understand the sense in which he puts it. He assumes that slavery is a rightful thing within itself —was introduced by the framers of the Constitution.

The exact truth is that they found the institution existing among us, and they left it as they found it. But in making the government they left this institution with many clear marks of disapprobation upon it. They found slavery among them, and they left it among them because of the difficulty—the absolute impossibility—of its immediate removal. And when Judge Douglas asks me why we cannot let it remain part slave and part free, as the fathers of the government made it, he asks a question based upon an assumption which is itself a falsehood; and I turn upon him and ask him the question, when the policy that the fathers of the government had adopted in relation to this element among us was the best policy in the world—the only wise policy, the only policy that we can ever safely continue upon, that will ever give us peace, unless this dangerous element masters us all and becomes a national institution—I turn upon him and ask him why he could not leave it alone. I turn and ask him why he was driven to the necessity of introducing a new policy in regard to it. He has himself said he introduced a new policy. He said so in his speech on the 22d of March of the present year, 1858. I ask him why he could not let it remain where our fathers placed it. I ask, too, of Judge Douglas and his friends, why we shall not again place this institution upon the basis on which the fathers left it? I ask you, when he infers that I am in favor of setting the free and the slave States at war, when the institution was placed in that attitude by those who made the Constitution, did they make any war? If we had no war out of it when thus placed, wherein is the ground of belief that we shall have war out of it if we return to that policy? Have we had any peace upon this matter springing from any other basis? I maintain that we have not. I have proposed nothing more than a return to the policy of the fathers.

I confess, when I propose a certain measure of policy, it is not enough for me that I do not intend anything evil in the result, but it is incumbent on me to show that it has not a tendency to that result. I have met Judge Douglas in that point of view. I have not only made the declaration that I do not mean to produce a conflict between the States, but I have tried to show by fair reasoning, and I think I have shown to the minds of fair men, that I propose nothing but what has a most peaceful tendency. The quotation that I happened to make in that Springfield speech, that "a house divided against itself cannot stand," and which has proved so offensive to the judge, was part and parcel of the same thing. He tries to show that variety in the domestic institutions of the different States is necessary and indispensable. I do not dispute it. I have no controversy with Judge Douglas about that. I shall very readily agree with him that it would be foolish for us to insist upon having a cranberry law here, in Illinois, where we have no cranberries, because they have a cranberry law in Indiana, where they have cranberries. I should insist that it would be exceedingly wrong in us to deny to Virginia the right to enact oyster laws, where they have oysters, because we want no such laws here. I understand, I hope, quite as well as Judge Douglas, or anybody else, that the variety in the soil and climate and face of the country, and consequent variety in the industrial pursuits and productions of a country, require systems of laws conforming to this variety in the natural features of the country. I understand quite as well as Judge Douglas, that if we here raise a barrel of flour more than we want, and the Louisianians raise a barrel of sugar more than they want, it is of mutual advantage to exchange. That produces commerce, brings us together, and makes us better friends. We like one another the more for it. And I understand as well as Judge Douglas, or anybody else, that these mutual accommodations are the cements which bind together the different parts of this Union; that instead of being a thing to "divide the house"—figuratively expressing the Union—they tend to sustain it; they are the props of the house tending always to hold it up.

But when I have admitted all this, I ask if there is any parallel between these things and this institution of slavery? I do not see that there is any parallel at all between them. Consider it. When have we had any difficulty or quarrel amongst ourselves about the cranberry laws of Indiana, or the oyster laws of Virginia, or the pine-lumber laws of Maine, or the fact that Louisiana produces sugar, and Illinois flour? When have we had any quarrels over these things? When have we had perfect peace in regard to this thing which I say is an element of discord in this Union? We have sometimes had peace, but when was it? It was when the institution of slavery remained quiet where it was. We have had difficulty and turmoil whenever it has made a struggle to spread itself where it was not. I ask, then, if experience does not speak in thunder-tones, telling us that the policy which has given peace to the country heretofore, being returned to, gives the greatest promise of peace again. You may say, and Judge Douglas has intimated the same thing, that all this difficulty in regard to the institution of slavery is the mere agitation of office-seekers and ambitious northern politicians. He thinks we want to get "his place," I suppose. I agree that there are office-seekers among us. The Bible says somewhere that we are desperately selfish. I think we would have discovered that fact without the Bible. I do not claim that I am any less so than the average of men, but I do claim that I am not more selfish than Judge Douglas.

But is it true that all the difficulty and agitation we have in regard to this institution of slavery springs from office-seeking —from the mere ambition of politicians? Is that the truth? How many times have we had danger from this question? Go back to the day of the Missouri Compromise. Go back to the nullification question, at the bottom of which lay this same slavery question. Go back to the time of the annexation of Texas. Go back to the troubles that led to the compromise of 1850. You will find that every time, with the single exception of the nullification question, they sprang from an endeavor to spread this institution. There never was a party in the history of this country, and there probably never will be, of sufficient strength to disturb the general peace of the country. Parties themselves may be divided and quarrel on minor questions, yet it extends not beyond the parties themselves. But does not this question make a disturbance outside of political circles? Does it not enter into the churches and rend them asunder? What divided the great Methodist Church into two parts, North and South? What has raised this constant disturbance in every Presbyterian general assembly that meets? What disturbed the Unitarian Church in this very city two years ago? What has jarred and shaken the great American Tract Society recently— not yet splitting it, but sure to divide it in the end? Is it not this same mighty, deepseated power that somehow operates on the minds of men, exciting and stirring them up in every avenue of society—in politics, in religion, in literature, in morals, in all the manifold relations of life? Is this the work of politicians? Is that irresistible power, which for fifty years has shaken the government and agitated the people, to be stilled and subdued by pretending that it is an exceedingly simple thing, and we ought not to talk about it? If you will get everybody else to stop talking about it, I assure you I will quit before they have half done so. But where is the philosophy or statesmanship which assumes that you can quiet that disturbing element in our society which has disturbed us for more

than half a century, which has been the only serious danger
that has threatened our institutions—I say, where is the philosophy or the statemanship based on the assumption that we are
to quit talking about it, and that the public mind is all at
once to cease being agitated by it? Yet this is the policy here
in the North that Douglas is advocating—that we are to care
nothing about it! I ask you if it is not a false philosophy? Is it
not a false statesmanship that undertakes to build up a system of policy upon the basis of caring nothing about the very
thing that everybody does care the most about—a thing which
all experience has shown we care a very great deal about?

The judge alludes very often in the course of his remarks to
the exclusive right which the States have to decide the whole
thing for themselves. I agree with him very readily that the
different States have that right. He is but fighting a man of
straw when he assumes that I am contending against the rights
of the States to do as they please about it. Our controversy
with him is in regard to the new Territories. We agree that
when the States come in as States they have the right and the
power as citizens of the free States, or in our federal capacity
as members of the Federal Union through the General Government, to disturb slavery in the States where it exists. We profess
constantly that we have no more inclination than belief in
the power of the government to disturb it; yet we are driven
constantly to defend ourselves from the assumption that we
are warring upon the rights of the States. What I insist upon
is, that the new Territories shall be kept free from it while in
the territorial condition. Judge Douglas assumes that we have
no interest in them—that we have no right whatever to interfere. I think we have some interest. I think that as white men
we have. Do we wish for an outlet for our surplus population,
if I may so express myself? Do we not feel an interest in getting
to that outlet with such institutions as we would like to have
prevail there? If you go to the Territory opposed to slavery,
and another man comes upon the same ground with his slave,

upon the assumption that the things are equal, it turns out that he has the equal right all his way, and you have no part of it your way. If he goes in and makes it a slave Territory, and by consequence a slave State, is it not time that those who desire to have it a free State were on equal ground? Let me suggest it in a different way. How many Democrats are there about here ["A thousand"] who have left slave States and come into the free State of Illinois to get rid of the institution of slavery? [Another voice: "A thousand and one."] I reckon there are a thousand and one. I will ask you, if the policy you are now advocating had prevailed when this country was in a territorial condition, where would you have gone to get rid of it? Where would you have found your free State or Territory to go to? And when hereafter, for any cause, the people in this place shall desire to find new homes, if they wish to be rid of the institution, where will they find the place to go to?

Now, irrespective of the moral aspect of this question as to whether there is a right or wrong in enslaving a Negro, I am still in favor of our new Territories being in such a condition that white men may find a home—may find some spot where they can better their condition—where they can settle upon new soil, and better their condition in life. I am in favor of this not merely (I must say it here as I have elsewhere) for our own people who are born amongst us, but as an outlet for free white people everywhere, the world over—in which Hans, and Baptiste, and Patrick, and all other men from all the world, may find new homes and better their condition in life.

I have stated upon former occasions, and I may as well state again, what I understand to be the real issue of this controversy between Judge Douglas and myself. On the point of my wanting to make war between the free and the slave States, there has been no issue between us. So, too, when he assumes that I am in favor of introducing a perfect social and political equality between the white and black races. These are false issues, upon which Judge Douglas has tried to force the controversy.

There is no foundation in truth for the charge that I maintain either of these propositions. The real issue in this controversy —the one pressing upon every mind—is the sentiment on the part of one class that looks upon the institution of slavery as a wrong, and of another class that does not look upon it as a wrong. The sentiment that contemplates the institution of slavery in this country as a wrong is the sentiment of the Republican party. It is the sentiment around which all their actions, all their arguments, circle; from which all their propositions radiate. They look upon it as being a moral, social, and political wrong; and while they contemplate it as such, they nevertheless have due regard for its actual existence among us, and the difficulties of getting rid of it in any satisfactory way, and to all the constitutional obligations thrown about it. Yet having a due regard for these, they desire a policy in regard to it that looks to its not creating any more danger. They insist that it, as far as may be, be treated as a wrong, and one of the methods of treating it as a wrong is to make provision that it shall grow no larger. They also desire a policy that looks to a peaceful end of slavery some time, as being a wrong. These are the views they entertain in regard to it, as I understand them; and all their sentiments, all their arguments and propositions, are brought within this range. I have said, and I repeat it here, that if there be a man amongst us who does not think that the institution of slavery is wrong in any one of the aspects of which I have spoken, he is misplaced, and ought not to be with us. And if there be a man amongst us who is so impatient of it as a wrong as to disregard its actual presence among us and the difficulty of getting rid of it suddenly in a satisfactory way, and to disregard the constitutional obligations thrown about it, that man is misplaced if he is on our platform. We disclaim sympathy with him in practical action. He is not placed properly with us.

On this subject of treating it as a wrong, and limiting its spread, let me say a word. Has anything ever threatened the existence of this Union save and except this very institution of slavery? What is it that we hold most dear amongst us? Our own liberty and prosperity. What has ever threatened our liberty and prosperity save and except this institution of slavery? If this is true, how do you propose to improve the condition of things by enlarging slavery—by spreading it out and making it bigger? You may have a wen or cancer upon your person, and not be able to cut it out lest you bleed to death; but surely it is no way to cure it, to engraft it and spread it over your whole body. That is no proper way of treating what you regard as a wrong. You see this peaceful way of dealing with it as a wrong—restricting the spread of it, and not allowing it to go into new countries where it has not already existed. That is the peaceful way, the old-fashioned way, the way in which the fathers themselves set us the example.

On the other hand, I have said there is a sentiment which treats it as not being wrong. That is the Democratic sentiment of this day. I do not mean to say that every man who stands within that range positively asserts that it is right. That class will include all who positively assert that it is right, and all who, like Judge Douglas, treat it as indifferent, and do not say it is either right or wrong. These two classes of men fall within the general class of those who do not look upon it as a wrong. And if there be among you anybody who supposes that he, as a Democrat, can consider himself "as much opposed to slavery as anybody," I would like to reason with him. You never treat it as a wrong. What other thing that you consider as a wrong do you deal with as you deal with that? Perhaps you say it is wrong, but your leader never does, and you quarrel with anybody who says it is wrong. Although you pretend to say so yourself, you can find no fit place to deal with it as a wrong. You must not say anything about it in the free States, because it is not here. You must not say anything about it in the slave States, because it is there. You must not say anything about it in the pulpit, because that is religion, and has nothing to do with it. You must not say anything about it in politics, because that will disturb the security of "my place." There is no place to talk about it as being a wrong, although you say yourself it is a wrong. But finally you will screw yourself up to the belief that if the people of the slave States should adopt a system of gradual emancipation on the slavery question, you would be in favor of it. You would be in favor of it! You say that is getting it in the right place, and you would be glad to see it succeed. But you are deceiving yourself. You all know that Frank Blair and Gratz Brown, down there in St. Louis, undertook to introduce that system in Missouri. They fought as valiantly as they could for the system of gradual emancipation which you pretend you would be glad to see succeed. Now I will bring you to the test. After a hard fight, they were beaten; and when the news came over here, you threw up your hats and hurrahed for Democracy. More than that, take all the argument made in favor of the system you have proposed, and it carefully excludes the idea that there is anything wrong in the institution of slavery. The arguments to sustain that policy carefully exclude it. Even here today you heard Judge Douglas quarrel with me because I uttered a wish that it might some time come to an end. Although Henry Clay could say he wished every slave in the United States was in the country of his ancestors, I am denounced by those pretending to respect Henry Clay, for uttering a wish that it might some time, in some peaceful way, come to an end.

The Democratic policy in regard to that institution will not tolerate the merest breath, the slightest hint, of the least degree of wrong about it. Try it by some of Judge Douglas's arguments. He says he "don't care whether it is voted up or voted down" in the Territories. I do not care myself, in dealing with that expression, whether it is intended to be expressive of his individual sentiments on the subject, or only of the national policy he desires to have established. It is alike valuable for my purpose. Any man can say that who does not see anything wrong in slavery, but no man can logically say it who does see a wrong in it; because no man can logically say he don't care whether a wrong is voted up or voted down. He may say he don't care whether an indifferent thing is voted up or down, but he must logically have a choice between a right thing and a wrong thing. He contends that whatever community wants slaves has a right to have them. So they have if it is not a wrong. But if it is a wrong, he cannot say people have a right to do wrong.

He says that, upon the score of equality, slaves should be allowed to go into a new Territory like other property. This is strictly logical if there is no difference between it and other property. If it and other property are equal, his argument is entirely logical. But if you insist that one is wrong and the other right, there is no use to institute a comparison between right and wrong. You may turn over everything in the Democratic policy from beginning to end, whether in the shape it takes on the statute-book, in the shape it takes in the Dred Scott decision, in the shape it takes in conversation, or the shape it takes in short maxim-like arguments—it everywhere carefully excludes the idea that there is anything wrong in it.

That is the real issue. That is the issue that will continue in this country when these poor tongues of Judge Douglas and myself shall be silent. It is the eternal struggle between these two principles—right and wrong—throughout the world. They are the two principles that have stood face to face from the beginning of time; and will ever continue to struggle. The one is the common right of humanity, and the other the divine right of kings. It is the same principle in whatever shape it develops itself. It is the same spirit that says, "You toil and work and earn bread, and I'll eat it." No matter in what shape it comes, whether from the mouth of a king who seeks to bestride the people of his own nation and live by the fruit of their labor, or from one race of men as an apology for enslaving another race, it is the same tyrannical principle. I was glad to express my gratitude at Quincy, and I reëxpress it here to Judge Douglas—that he looks to no end of the institution of slavery. That will help the people to see where the struggle really is. It will hereafter place with us all men who really do wish the wrong may have an end. And whenever we can get rid of the fog which obscures the real question—when we can get Judge Douglas and his friends to avow a policy looking to its perpetuation—we can get out from among them that class of men and bring them to the side of those who treat it as a wrong. Then there will soon be an end of it, and that end will be its "ultimate extinction." Whenever the issue can be distinctly made, and all extraneous matter thrown out, so that men can fairly see the real difference between the parties, this controversy will soon be settled, and it will be done peaceably too. There will be no war, no violence. It will be placed again where the wisest and best men of the world placed it.

*   *   *

I suppose most of us (I know it of myself) believe that the people of the Southern States are entitled to a congressional fugitive-slave law; that it is a right fixed in the Constitution. But it cannot be made available to them without congressional legislation. In the judge's language, it is a "barren right" which needs legislation before it can become efficient and valuable to the persons to whom it is guaranteed. And, as the right is constitutional, I agree that the legislation shall be granted to it. Not that we like the institution of slavery; we profess to have no taste for running and catching Negroes—at least, I profess no taste for that job at all. Why then do I yield support to a fugitive-slave law? Because I do not understand that the Constitution, which guarantees that right, can be supported without it. And if I believed that the right to hold a slave in a Territory was equally fixed in the Constitution with the right to reclaim fugitives, I should be bound to give it the legislation necessary to support it. I say that no man can deny his obligation to give the necessary legislation to support slavery in a Territory, who believes it is a constitutional right to have it there. No man can, who does not give the Abolitionists an argument to deny the obligation enjoined by the Constitution to enact a fugitive-slave law. Try it now. It is the strongest Abolition argument ever made. I say, if that Dred Scott decision is correct, then the right to hold slaves in a Territory is equally a constitutional right with the right of a slaveholder to have his runaway returned. No one can show the distinction between them. The one is express, so that we cannot deny it; the other is construed to be in the Constitution, so that he who believes the decision to be correct believes in the right. And the man who argues that by unfriendly legislation, in spite of that constitutional right, slavery may be driven from the Territories, cannot avoid furnishing an argument by which Abolitionists may deny the obligation to return fugitives, and claim the power to pass laws unfriendly to the right of the slaveholder to reclaim his fugitive.

I do not know how such an argument may strike a popular assembly like this, but I defy anybody to go before a body of men whose minds are educated to estimating evidence and reasoning, and show that there is an iota of difference between the constitutional right to reclaim a fugitive, and the constitutional right to hold a slave, in a Territory, provided this Dred Scott decision is correct. I defy any man to make an argument that will justify unfriendly legislation to deprive a slaveholder of his right to hold his slave in a Territory, that will not equally, in all its length, breadth, and thickness, furnish an argument for nullifying the fugitive-slave law. Why, there is not such an Abolitionist in the nation as Douglas, after all.

LETTER TO EDWARD LUSK

Again and again, whispered charges were made that Lincoln had favored the Know-Nothing party. Such charges always annoyed him, and he went out of his way to refute them.

Springfield, October 30, 1858

DEAR SIR: I understand the story is still being told and insisted upon that I have been a Know-Nothing. I repeat what I stated in a public speech at Meredosia, that I am not, nor ever have been, connected with the party called the Know-Nothing party, or party calling themselves the American party. Certainly no man of truth, and I believe no man of good character for truth, can be found to say on his own knowledge that I ever was connected with that party.

CONCLUSION OF A SPEECH AT SPRINGFIELD

On this day a huge Republican rally, the last of the campaign, was held in Springfield. Lincoln addressed the crowd during the afternoon, and had difficulty in speaking to an audience that was more interested in celebrating for celebration's sake than in hearing him speak. He had spent months of effort, traveled hundreds of miles and spoken scores of times in the Senatorial campaign; the debates with Douglas were finished; the excitement of battle was over— he had only to look forward to the results of the election. The election was only three days away, and these are Lincoln's final words to a public audience before the defeat that was to overtake him at the polls.

October 30, 1858

MY FRIENDS, today closes the discussions of this canvass. The planting and the culture are over; and there remains but the preparation, and the harvest.

I stand here surrounded by friends—some *political*, *all personal* friends, I trust. May I be indulged, in this closing scene, to say a few words of myself. I have borne a laborious, and, in some respects to myself, a painful part in the contest. Through all, I have neither assailed, nor wrestled with any part of the constitution. The legal right of the Southern people to reclaim their fugitives I have constantly admitted. The legal right of Congress to interfere with their institution in the states, I have constantly denied. In resisting the spread of slavery to new territory, and with that, what appears to me to be a tendency to subvert the first principle of free government itself my whole effort has consisted. To the best of my judgment I have labored *for*, and not *against* the Union. As I have not felt, so I have not expressed any harsh sentiment towards our Southern brethren. I have constantly declared, as I really believed, the only difference between them and us, is the difference of circumstances.

I have meant to assail the motives of no party, or individual; and if I have, in any instance (of which I am not conscious) departed from my purpose, I regret it.

I have said that in some respects the contest has been painful to me. Myself, and those with whom I act have been constantly accused of a purpose to destroy the Union; and bespattered with every imaginable odious epithet; and some who were friends, as it were but yesterday have made themselves most active in this. I have cultivated patience, and made no attempt at a retort.

Ambition has been ascribed to me. God knows how sincerely I prayed from the first that this field of ambition might not be opened. I claim no insensibility to political honors; but today could the Missouri restriction be restored, and the whole slavery question be replaced on the old ground of "toleration" by *necessity* where it exists, with unyielding hostility to the spread of it, on principle, I would, in consideration, gladly agree, that Judge Douglas should never be out, and I never in, an office, so long as we both or either, live.

LETTER TO N. B. JUDD

Nothing is so painful as to have to pay the expenses of a campaign that has been a failure. Lincoln was not elected, but two weeks after election day, N. B. Judd, chairman of the Republican State Central Committee, was on his heels for a contribution toward paying the expenses of his canvass. Lincoln had spent months of hard work in the political field to the neglect of his law practice; he was short of funds—nevertheless he pledges more money to cover the expenses incurred by the party.

Springfield, November 16, 1858

DEAR SIR: Yours of the 15th is just received. I wrote you the same day. As to the pecuniary matter, I am willing to pay according to my ability; but I am the poorest hand living to get others to pay.

I have been on expenses so long without earning anything that I am absolutely without money now for even household purposes. Still, if you can put in two hundred and fifty dollars for me toward discharging the debt of the committee, I will allow it when you and I settle the private matter between us.

This, with what I have already paid, and with an outstanding note of mine, will exceed my subscription of five hundred dollars. This, too, is exclusive of my ordinary expenses during the campaign, all of which being added to my loss of time and business, bears pretty heavily upon one no better off in [this] world's goods than I; but as I had the post of honor, it is not for me to be over nice. You are feeling badly—"And this too shall pass away," never fear.

LETTER TO HENRY ASBURY

Lincoln writes to the man who had suggested to him the famous second question of the Freeport debate. He predicts that "another explosion will soon.come."

Springfield, November 19, 1858

DEAR SIR: Yours of the 13th was received some days ago. The fight must go on. The cause of civil liberty must not be surrendered at the end of one or even one hundred defeats. Douglas had the ingenuity to be supported in the late contest both as the best means to break down and to uphold the slave interest. No ingenuity can keep these antagonistic elements in harmony long. Another explosion will soon come.

FROM A LETTER TO A. G. HENRY

This is the Doctor Henry for whom Lincoln tried to get a Postmastership in 1841, when he wanted to keep a friendly physician near him because of the state of his mind after his break with Mary Todd. Part of this letter has been destroyed.

Springfield, November 19, 1858

As A general rule, out of Sangamon as well as in it, much of the plain old Democracy is with us, while nearly all the old exclusive silk-stocking Whiggery is against us. I don't mean nearly all the Old Whig party, but nearly all of the nice exclusive sort. And why not? There has been nothing in politics since the Revolution so congenial to their nature as the present position of the great Democratic party.

I am glad I made the late race. It gave me a hearing on

the great and durable question of the age, which I could have had in no other way; and though I now sink out of view, and shall be forgotten, I believe I have made some marks which will tell for the cause of civil liberty long after I am gone.

LETTER TO DR. B. CLARKE LUNDY

Again Lincoln writes to state his position on the results of his struggle with Douglas. This letter is an almost exact paraphrase of his letter to Asbury on November 19.

Springfield, November 26, 1858

My DEAR SIR: Your kind letter with enclosure is received, and for which I thank you. It being my own judgment that the fight must go on, it affords me great pleasure to learn that our friends are nowhere dispirited.

There will be another "blow up" in the democracy. Douglas managed to be supported both as the best instrument to *break down,* and to *up-hold* the slave power. No ingenuity can keep this deception—this double position—up a great while.

LETTER TO ALEXANDER SYMPSON

Lincoln writes an optimistic letter to an old friend and political supporter to forecast that "we shall beat them in the long run."

Springfield, December 12, 1858

My DEAR SIR: I expect the result of the election went hard with you. So it did with me, too, perhaps not quite so hard as you may have supposed. I have an abiding faith that we shall beat them in the long run. Step by step the objects of the leaders will become too plain for the people to stand them. I write merely to let you know that I am neither dead nor dying. Please give my respects to your good family, and all inquiring friends.

LETTER TO THOMAS J. PICKETT

Pickett was a newspaper editor in Rock Island, Ill., who had invited Lincoln to deliver a lecture on "Inventions and Discoveries" in that city. In the last sentence Lincoln says that he does not consider himself fit for the Presidency. Two years later, less one day, he was inaugurated.

Springfield, March 5, 1859

My Dear Sir: Yours of the 2nd inst. inviting me to deliver my lecture on "Inventions" in Rock Island, is at hand and I regret to be unable, from press of business to comply therewith.

In regard to the other matter you speak of, I beg that you will not give it a further mention. Seriously, I do not think I am fit for the Presidency.

LETTER TO H. L. PIERCE AND OTHERS

Lincoln was again invited to lecture, this time in Boston. Again he declined. He had been asked to speak in honor of Thomas Jefferson. He writes here a careful letter on Jefferson that was doubtless intended to be read at the Boston meeting. In it he makes the point that the Republicans, and not the Democrats, had become the spiritual heirs of Jefferson. He also shows how political parties, over a course of time, can switch their points of views so completely that they take each other's former position.

Springfield, Ill., April 6, 1859

GENTLEMEN: Your kind note inviting me to attend a festival in Boston, on the 28th instant, in honor of the birthday of Thomas Jefferson, was duly received. My engagements are such that I cannot attend.

Bearing in mind that about seventy years ago two great political parties were first formed in this country, that Thomas Jefferson was the head of one of them and Boston the headquarters of the other, it is both curious and interesting that those supposed to descend politically from the party opposed to Jefferson should now be celebrating his birthday in their own original seat of empire, while those claiming political descent from him have nearly ceased to breathe his name everywhere.

Remembering, too, that the Jefferson party was formed upon its supposed superior devotion to the personal rights of men, holding the rights of property to be secondary only, and greatly inferior, and assuming that the so-called Democracy of today are the Jefferson, and their opponents the anti-Jefferson, partly, it will be equally interesting to note how completely the two have changed hands as to the principle upon which they were originally supposed to be divided. The Democracy of today hold the liberty of one man to be absolutely nothing, when in conflict with another man's right of property; Republicans, on the contrary, are for both the man and the dollar, but in case of conflict the man before the dollar.

I remember being once much amused at seeing two partially intoxicated men engaged in a fight with their great-coats on, which fight, after a long and rather harmless contest, ended in each having fought himself out of his own coat and into that of the other. If the two leading parties of this day are really identical with the two in the days of Jefferson and Adams, they have performed the same feat as the two drunken men.

But, soberly, it is now no child's play to save the principles of Jefferson from total overthrow in this nation. One would state with great confidence that he could convince any sane child that the simpler propositions of Euclid are true; but nevertheless he would fail, utterly, with one who should deny the definitions and axioms. The principles of Jefferson are the definitions and axioms of free society. And yet they are denied and evaded, with no small show of success. One dashingly calls them "glittering generalities." Another bluntly calls them "self-evident lies." And others insidiously argue that they apply to "superior races." These expressions, differing in form, are identical in object and effect—the supplanting [of] the principles of free government, and restoring those of classification, caste, and legitimacy. They would delight a convocation of crowned heads plotting against the people. They are the vanguard, the miners and sappers of returning despotism. We must repulse them, or they will subjugate us. This is a world of compensation; and he who would be no slave must consent to have no slave. Those who deny freedom to others deserve it not for themselves, and, under a just God, cannot long retain it. All honor to Jefferson—to the man, who, in the concrete pressure of a struggle for national independence by a single people, had the coolness, forecast, and capacity to introduce into a merely revolutionary document an abstract truth, applicable to all men and all times, and so to embalm it there that today and in all coming days it shall be a rebuke and a stumbling-block to the very harbingers of reappearing tyranny and oppression.

LETTER TO SALMON PORTLAND CHASE

Lincoln writes to the man who was to become his Secretary of the Treasury and his most outspoken opponent in his own Cabinet. Chase, at this time, was the Republican leader of Ohio. The Fugitive Slave Law was the most bitterly opposed law in the North.

Abolitionists were eager to get rid of it; most of them openly flouted it. Few people in the North would defend it. Conservatives like Lincoln, however, were willing to let it stand in order to preserve peace.

Springfield, Ill., June 9, 1859

DEAR SIR: Please pardon the liberty I take in addressing you, as I now do. It appears by the papers that the late Republican State convention of Ohio adopted a Platform, of which the following is one plank, "A repeal of the atrocious Fugitive Slave Law."

This is already damaging us here. I have no doubt that if that plank be even *introduced* into the next Republican National convention, it will explode it. Once introduced, its supporters and its opponents will quarrel irreconcilably. The latter believe the U. S. Constitution declares that a fugitive slave *"shall be delivered up"*; and they look upon the above plank as dictated by the spirit which declares a fugitive slave *"shall not be delivered up."*

I enter upon no argument one way or the other; but I assure you the cause of Republicanism is hopeless in Illinois, if it be in any way made responsible for that plank. I hope you can, and will, contribute something to relieve us from it.

LETTER TO SALMON PORTLAND CHASE

Lincoln gives Chase a Constitutional interpretation of the Fugitive Slave Law, although Lincoln says that his only object is to warn Chase against bringing this subject into the party platform, for it is political dynamite.

Springfield, Ill., June 20, 1859

MY DEAR SIR: Yours of the 13th Inst. is received. You say you would be glad to have my views. Although I think Congress has constitutional authority to enact a Fugitive Slave law, I have never elaborated an opinion upon the subject. My view has been, and is, simply this. The U. S. Constitution says the fugitive slave "*shall be delivered up*" but it does not expressly say who shall deliver him up. Whatever the Constitution says "shall be done" and has omitted saying who shall do it, the government established by that Constitution, *ex vi termini*, is vested with the power of doing; and Congress is, by the Constitution, expressly empowered to make all laws which shall be necessary and proper for carrying into execution all powers vested by the Constitution in the government of the United States. This would be my view, on a simple reading of the Constitution; and it is greatly strengthened by the historical fact that the Constitution was adopted, in great part, in order to get a government which could execute its own behests, in contradistinction to that under the Articles of Confederation, which depended in many respects, upon the States, for its execution; and the other fact that one of the earliest congresses, under the Constitution, did enact a Fugitive Slave law.

But I did not write you on this subject, with any view of discussing the constitutional question. My only object was to impress you with what I believe is true, that the introduction of a proposition for repeal of the Fugitive Slave law, into the next Republican National convention, will explode the convention and the party. Having turned your attention to the point, I wish to do no more.

FROM A SPEECH AT COLUMBUS, OHIO

Lincoln goes to Ohio to take the stump in behalf of the Republicans in their campaign there. Speaking at Columbus, he touches on the threatened revival of the African slave trade that was beginning to disturb the country, but he devotes most of his speech to an attack on Douglas's doctrine of popular sovereignty. The refer-

ence to "crocodiles" was inspired by a remark Douglas had made
to the effect that when there was a struggle between a white man
and a Negro he was always for the white man; when there was a
struggle between a Negro and a crocodile, he would be for the
Negro.

September 16, 1859

THE American people, on the first day of January, 1854, found
the African slave trade prohibited by a law of Congress. In a
majority of the States of this Union, they found African slavery, or any other sort of slavery, prohibited by State constitutions. They also found a law existing, supposed to be valid,
by which slavery was excluded from almost all the territory
the United States then owned. This was the condition of the
country, with reference to the institution of slavery, on the
first of January, 1854. A few days after that, a bill was introduced into Congress, which ran through its regular course in
the two branches of the national legislature, and finally passed
into a law in the month of May, by which the act of Congress
prohibiting slavery from going into the Territories of the
United States was repealed. In connection with the law itself,
and, in fact, in the terms of the law, the then existing prohibition was not only repealed, but there was a declaration of a
purpose on the part of Congress never thereafter to exercise
any power that they might have, real or supposed, to prohibit
the extension or spread of slavery. This was a very great
change; for the law thus repealed was of more than thirty
years' standing. Following rapidly upon the heels of this action
of Congress, a decision of the Supreme Court is made, by
which it is declared that Congress, if it desires to prohibit the
spread of slavery into the Territories, has no constitutional
power to do so. Not only so, but that decision lays down the
principles, which, if pushed to their logical conclusion—I say

pushed to their logical conclusion—would decide that the constitutions of free States, forbidding slavery, are themselves unconstitutional. Mark me, I do not say the judges said this, and let no man say I affirm the judges used these words; but I only say it is my opinion that what they did say, if pressed to its logical conclusion, will inevitably result thus.

Looking at these things, the Republican party, as I understand its principles and policy, believes that there is great danger of the institution of slavery being spread out and extended, until it is ultimately made alike lawful in all the States of this Union; so believing, to prevent that incidental and ultimate consummation is the original and chief purpose of the Republican organization. I say "chief purpose" of the Republican organization; for it is certainly true that if the national house shall fall into the hands of the Republicans, they will have to attend to all the other matters of national housekeeping as well as this. The chief and real purpose of the Republican party is eminently conservative. It proposes nothing save and except to restore this government to its original tone in regard to this element of slavery, and there to maintain it, looking for no further change in reference to it than that which the original framers of the government themselves expected and looked forward to.

The chief danger to this purpose of the Republican party is not just now the revival of the African slave trade, or the passage of a congressional slave code, or the declaring of a second Dred Scott decision, making slavery lawful in all the States. These are not pressing us just now. They are not quite ready yet. The authors of these measures know that we are too strong for them; but they will be upon us in due time, and we will be grappling with them hand to hand, if they are not now headed off. They are not now the chief danger to the purpose of the Republican organization; but the most imminent danger that now threatens that purpose is that insidious

Douglas popular sovereignty. This is the miner and sapper. While it does not propose to revive the African slave trade, nor to pass a slave code, nor to make a second Dred Scott decision, it is preparing us for the onslaught and charge of these ultimate enemies when they shall be ready to come on, and the word of command for them to advance shall be given. I say this Douglas popular sovereignty—for there is a broad distinction, as I now understand it, between that article and a genuine popular sovereignty.

I believe there is a genuine popular sovereignty. I think a definition of genuine popular sovereignty, in the abstract, would be about this: That each man shall do precisely as he pleases with himself, and with all those things which exclusively concern him. Applied to government, this principle would be, that a general government shall do all those things which pertain to it, and all the local governments shall do precisely as they please in respect to those matters which exclusively concern them. I understand that this government of the United States, under which we live, is based upon this principle; and I am misunderstood if it is supposed that I have any war to make upon that principle.

Now, what is Judge Douglas's popular sovereignty? It is, as a principle, no other than that if one man chooses to make a slave of another man, neither that other man nor anybody else has a right to object. Applied in government, as he seeks to apply it, it is this: If, in a new Territory into which a few people are beginning to enter for the purpose of making their homes, they choose to either exclude slavery from their limits or to establish it there, however one or the other may affect the persons to be enslaved, or the infinitely greater number of persons who are afterward to inhabit that Territory, or the other members of the families of communities, of which they are but an incipient member, or the general head of the family of States as parent of all—however their action may affect one or the other of these, there is no power or right to interfere. That is Douglas's popular sovereignty applied.

*   *   *

. . . This insidious Douglas popular sovereignty is the measure that now threatens the purpose of the Republican party to prevent slavery from being nationalized in the United States. I propose to ask your attention for a little while to some propositions in affirmance of that statement. Take it just as it stands, and apply it as a principle; extend and apply that principle elsewhere, and consider where it will lead you. I now put this proposition, that Judge Douglas's popular sovereignty applied will reopen the African slave trade; and I will demonstrate it by any variety of ways in which you can turn the subject or look at it.

The judge says that the people of the Territories have the right, by his principle, to have slaves if they want them. Then I say that the people in Georgia have the right to buy slaves in Africa if they want them, and I defy any man on earth to show any distinction between the two things—to show that the one is either more wicked or more unlawful; to show, on original principles, that one is better or worse than the other; or to show by the Constitution that one differs a whit from the other. He will tell me, doubtless, that there is no constitutional provision against people taking slaves into the new Territories, and I tell him that there is equally no constitutional provision against buying slaves in Africa. He will tell you that a people in the exercise of popular sovereignty ought to do as they please about that thing, and have slaves if they want them; and I tell you that the people of Georgia are as much entitled to popular sovereignty, and to buy slaves in Africa, if they want them, as the people of the Territory are to have slaves if they want them. I ask any man, dealing honestly with himself, to point out a distinction.

I have recently seen a letter of Judge Douglas's, in which,

without stating that to be the object, he doubtless endeavors to make a distinction between the two. He says he is unalterably opposed to the repeal of the laws against the African slave trade. And why? He then seeks to give a reason that would not apply to his popular sovereignty in the Territories. What is that reason? "The abolition of the African slave trade is a compromise of the Constitution." I deny it. There is no truth in the proposition that the abolition of the African slave trade is a compromise of the Constitution. No man can put his finger on anything in the Constitution, or on the line of history, which shows it. It is a mere barren assertion, made simply for the purpose of getting up a distinction between the revival of the African slave trade and his "great principle."

At the time the Constitution of the United States was adopted it was expected that the slave trade would be abolished. I should assert, and insist upon that, if Judge Douglas denied it. But I know that it was equally expected that slavery would be excluded from the Territories, and I can show by history that in regard to these two things public opinion was exactly alike, while in regard to positive action, there was more done in the ordinance of '87 to resist the spread of slavery than was ever done to abolish the foreign slave trade. Lest I be misunderstood, I say again that at the time of the formation of the Constitution, public expectation was that the slave trade would be abolished, but no more so than that the spread of slavery in the Territories should be restrained. They stand alike, except that in the ordinance of '87 there was a mark left by public opinion, showing that it was more committed against the spread of slavery in the Territories than against the foreign slave trade.

Compromise! What word of compromise was there about it? Why, the public sense was then in favor of the abolition of the slave trade; but there was at the time a very great commercial interest involved in it, and extensive capital in that branch of trade. There were doubtless the incipient stages of improvement in the South in the way of farming, dependent on the slave trade, and they made a proposition to Congress to abolish the trade after allowing it twenty years, a sufficient time for the capital and commerce engaged in it to be transferred to other channels. They made no provision that it should be abolished in twenty years; I do not doubt that they expected it would be; but they made no bargain about it. The public sentiment left no doubt in the minds of any that it would be done away. I repeat, there is nothing in the history of those times in favor of that matter being a compromise of the Constitution. It was the public expectation at the time, manifested in a thousand ways, that the spread of slavery should also be restricted.

Then I say if this principle is established, that there is no wrong in slavery, and whoever wants it has a right to have it; that it is a matter of dollars and cents; a sort of question as to how they shall deal with brutes; that between us and the Negro here there is no sort of question, but that at the South the question is between the Negro and the crocodile; that it is a mere matter of policy; that there is a perfect right, according to interest, to do just as you please—when this is done, where this doctrine prevails, the miners and sappers will have formed public opinion for the slave trade. They will be ready for Jeff Davis and Stephens, and other leaders of that company, to sound the bugle for the revival of the slave trade, for the second Dred Scott decision, for the flood of slavery to be poured over the free States, while we shall be here tied down and helpless, and run over like sheep.

It is to be a part and parcel of this same idea to say to men who want to adhere to the Democratic party, who have always belonged to that party, and are only looking about for some excuse to stick to it, but nevertheless hate slavery, that Douglas's popular sovereignty is as good a way as any to oppose slavery. They allow themselves to be persuaded easily, in accordance with their previous dispositions, into this belief, that it is about as good a way of opposing slavery as any, and we can do that without straining our old party ties or breaking up old political associations. We can do so without being called Negro-worshippers. We can do that without being subjected to the gibes and sneers that are so readily thrown out in place of argument where no argument can be found. So let us stick to this popular sovereignty—this insidious popular sovereignty. Now let me call your attention to one thing that has really happened, which shows this gradual and steady debauching of public opinion, this course of preparation for the revival of the slave trade, for the territorial slave code, and the new Dred Scott decision that is to carry slavery into the free States. Did you ever, five years ago, hear of anybody in the world saying that the Negro had no share in the Declaration of National Independence; that it did not mean Negroes at all, and when "all men" were spoken of Negroes were not included?

I am satisfied that five years ago that proposition was not put upon paper by any living being anywhere. I have been unable at any time to find a man in an audience who would declare that he had ever known anybody saying so five years ago. But last year there was not a "Douglas popular sovereignty" man in Illinois who did not say it. Is there one in Ohio who declares his firm belief that the Declaration of Independence did not mean Negroes at all? I do not know how this is; I have not been here much; but I presume you are very much alike everywhere. Then I suppose that all now express the belief that the Declaration of Independence never did mean Negroes. I call upon one of them to say that he said it five years ago.

If you think that now, and did not think it then, the next thing that strikes me is to remark that there has been a change wrought in you, and a very significant change it is, being no less than changing the Negro, in your estimation, from the rank of a man to that of a brute. They are taking him down,

and placing him, when spoken of, among reptiles and crocodiles, as Judge Douglas himself expresses it.

Is not this change wrought in your minds a very important
change? Public opinion in this country is everything. In a
nation like ours this popular sovereignty and squatter sovereignty have already wrought a change in the public mind to
the extent I have stated. There is no man in this crowd who
can contradict it.

Now, if you are opposed to slavery honestly, as much as
anybody, I ask you to note that fact, and the like of which is
to follow, to be plastered on, layer after layer, until very soon
you are prepared to deal with the Negro everywhere as with
the brute. If public sentiment has not been debauched already
to this point, a new turn of the screw in that direction is all
that is wanting; and this is constantly being done by the
teachers of this insidious popular sovereignty. You need but
one or two turns further until your minds, now ripening under
these teachings, will be ready for all these things, and you will
receive and support, or submit to, the slave trade revived with
all its horrors, a slave code enforced in our Territories, and a
new Dred Scott decision to bring slavery up into the very
heart of the free North. This, I must say, is but carrying out
those words prophetically spoken by Mr. Clay many, many
years ago—I believe more than thirty years—when he told an
audience that if they would repress all tendencies to liberty
and ultimate emancipation, they must go back to the era of
our independence and muzzle the cannon which thundered
its annual joyous return on the Fourth of July; they must
blow out the moral lights around us; they must penetrate the
human soul, and eradicate the love of liberty; but until they
did these things, and others eloquently enumerated by him,
they could not repress all tendencies to ultimate emancipation.

I ask attention to the fact that in a preëminent degree these
popular sovereigns are at this work: blowing out the moral
lights around us; teaching that the Negro is no longer a man,

but a brute; that the Declaration has nothing to do with him; that he ranks with the crocodile and the reptile; that man, with body and soul, is a matter of dollars and cents. I suggest to this portion of the Ohio Republicans, or Democrats, if there be any present, the serious consideration of this fact, that there is now going on among you a steady process of debauching public opinion on this subject. With this, my friends, I bid you adieu.

FROM A SPEECH AT CINCINNATI

On the day after his Columbus speech, Lincoln spoke at Cincinnati. Douglas had been there before him, so Lincoln's speech sounds like an echo of the year-old debates. But even as he spoke, a new and disturbing element was being prepared that was to force the issue to a climax—John Brown was in Chambersburg, Pennsylvania, shipping arms and ammunition to a farm on the outskirts of Harper's Ferry.

September 17, 1859

I should not wonder if there are some Kentuckians about this audience; we are close to Kentucky; and whether that be so or not, we are on elevated ground, and by speaking distinctly I should not wonder if some of the Kentuckians would hear me on the other side of the river. For that reason I propose to address a portion of what I have to say to the Kentuckians.

I say, then, in the first place, to the Kentuckians, that I am what they call, as I understand it, a "Black Republican." I think slavery is wrong, morally and politically. I desire that it should be no further spread in these United States, and I should not object if it should gradually terminate in the whole Union. While I say this for myself, I say to you Kentuckians that I understand you differ radically with me upon this proposition; that you believe slavery is a good thing; that slavery is right; that it ought to be extended and perpetuated in this Union. Now, there being this broad difference between us, I do not pretend, in addressing myself to you Kentuckians, to attempt proselyting you; that would be a vain effort. I do not enter upon it. I only propose to try to show you that you ought to nominate for the next presidency, at Charleston, my distinguished friend, Judge Douglas. In all that there is no real difference between you and him; I understand he is as sincerely for you, and more wisely for you, than you are for yourselves. I will try to demonstrate that proposition. Understand now, I say that I believe he is as sincerely for you, and more wisely for you, than you are for yourselves.

What do you want more than anything else to make successful your views of slavery—to advance the outspread of it, and to secure and perpetuate the nationality of it? What do you want more than anything else? What is needed absolutely? What is indispensable to you? Why, if I may be allowed to answer the question, it is to retain a hold upon the North—it is to retain support and strength from the free States. If you can get this support and strength from the free States, you can succeed. If you do not get this support and this strength from the free States, you are in the minority, and you are beaten at once.

If that proposition be admitted—and it is undeniable—then the next thing I say to you is, that Douglas of all the men in this nation is the only man that affords you any hold upon the free States; that no other man can give you any strength in the free States. This being so, if you doubt the other branch of the proposition, whether he is for you—whether he is really for you, as I have expressed it—I propose asking your attention for a while to a few facts.

The issue between you and me, understand, is that I think slavery is wrong, and ought not to be outspread, and you think it is right, and ought to be extended and perpetuated. I now proceed to try to show to you that Douglas is as sincerely for you, and more wisely for you, than you are for yourselves.

In the first place, we know that in a government like this, a government of the people, where the voice of all the men of the country, substantially, enters into the administration of the government, what lies at the bottom of all of it is public opinion. I lay down the proposition that Judge Douglas is not only the man that promises you in advance a hold upon the North, and support in the North, but that he constantly molds public opinion to your ends; that in every possible way he can, he molds the public opinion of the North to your ends; and if there are a few things in which he seems to be against you—a few things which he says that appear to be against you, and a few that he forbears to say which you would like to have him say—you ought to remember that the saying of the one, or the forbearing to say the other, would lose his hold upon the North, and, by consequence, would lose his capacity to serve you.

Upon this subject of molding public opinion, I call your attention to the fact—for a well-established fact it is—that the judge never says your institution of slavery is wrong; he never says it is right, to be sure, but he never says it is wrong. There is not a public man in the United States, I believe, with the exception of Senator Douglas, who has not, at some time in his life, declared his opinion whether the thing is right or wrong; but Senator Douglas never declares it is wrong. He leaves himself at perfect liberty to do all in your favor which he would be hindered from doing if he were to declare the thing to be wrong. On the contrary, he takes all the chances that he has for inveigling the sentiment of the North, opposed to slavery, into your support, by never saying it is right. This you ought to set down to his credit. You ought to give him full credit for this much, little though it be in comparison to the whole which he does for you.

Some other things I will ask your attention to. He said

upon the floor of the United States Senate, and he has repeated it, as I understand, a great many times, that he does not care whether slavery is "voted up or voted down." This again shows you, or ought to show you, if you would reason upon it, that he does not believe it to be wrong; for a man may say, when he sees nothing wrong in a thing, that he does not care whether it be voted up or voted down; but no man can logically say that he cares not whether a thing goes up or goes down which appears to him to be wrong. You therefore have a demonstration in this, that to Judge Douglas's mind your favorite institution, which you desire to have spread out and made perpetual, is no wrong.

Another thing he tells you, in a speech made at Memphis, in Tennessee, shortly after the canvass in Illinois, last year. He there distinctly told the people that there was a "line drawn by the Almighty across this continent, on the one side of which the soil must always be cultivated by slaves"; that he did not pretend to know exactly where that line was, but that there was such a line. I want to ask your attention to that proposition again—that there is one portion of this continent where the Almighty has designed the soil shall always be cultivated by slaves; that its being cultivated by slaves at that place is right; that it has the direct sympathy and authority of the Almighty. Whenever you can get these Northern audiences to adopt the opinion that slavery is right on the other side of the Ohio; whenever you can get them, in pursuance of Douglas's views, to adopt that sentiment, they will very readily make the other argument, which is perfectly logical, that that which is right on that side of the Ohio cannot be wrong on this, and that if you have that property on that side of the Ohio, under the seal and stamp of the Almighty, when by any means it escapes over here, it is wrong to have constitutions and laws "to devil" you about it. So Douglas is molding the public opinion of the North, first to say that the thing is right in your State over the Ohio River, and hence to say that that which is right there is not wrong here, and that all laws and constitutions here, recognizing it as being wrong, are themselves wrong, and ought to be repealed and abrogated. He will tell you, men of Ohio, that if you choose here to have laws against slavery, it is in conformity to the idea that your climate is not suited to it; that your climate is not suited to slave labor, and therefore you have constitutions and laws against it.

*   *   *

I often hear it intimated that you mean to divide the Union whenever a Republican or anything like it is elected President of the United States. [A voice: "That is so."] "That is so," one of them says; I wonder if he is a Kentuckian? [A voice: "He is a Douglas man."] Well, then, I want to know what you are going to do with your half of it? Are you going to split the Ohio down through, and push your half off a piece? Or are you going to keep it right alongside of us outrageous fellows? Or are you going to build up a wall some way between your country and ours, by which that movable property of yours can't come over here any more, to the danger of your losing it? Do you think you can better yourselves on that subject by leaving us here under no obligation whatever to return those specimens of your movable property that come hither? You have divided the Union because we would not do right with you, as you think, upon that subject; when we cease to be under obligations to do anything for you, how much better off do you think you will be? Will you make war upon us and kill us all? Why, gentlemen, I think you are as gallant and as brave men as live; that you can fight as bravely in a good cause, man for man, as any other people living; that you have shown yourselves capable of this upon various occasions; but man for man, you are not better than we are, and there are not so many of you as there are of us. You will never make much of a hand at whipping us. If we were fewer in numbers than you, I think that you could whip us; if we were equal it would likely be a drawn battle; but being inferior in numbers, you will make nothing by attempting to master us.

But perhaps I have addressed myself as long, or longer, to the Kentuckians than I ought to have done, inasmuch as I have said that whatever course you take, we intend in the end to beat you. I propose to address a few remarks to our friends, by way of discussing with them the best means of keeping that promise that I have in good faith made.

*   *   *

Labor is the great source from which nearly all, if not all, human comforts and necessities are drawn. There is a difference in opinion about the elements of labor in society. Some men assume that there is a necessary connection between capital and labor, and that connection draws within the whole of the labor of the community. They assume that nobody works unless capital excites them to work. They begin next to consider what is the best way. They say there are but two ways—one is to hire men and to allure them to labor by their consent; the other is to buy the men and drive them to it, and that is slavery. Having assumed that, they proceed to discuss the question of whether the laborers themselves are better off in the condition of slaves or of hired laborers, and they usually decide that they are better off in the condition of slaves.

In the first place, I say that the whole thing is a mistake. That there is a certain relation between capital and labor, I admit. That it does exist, and rightfully exists, I think is true. That men who are industrious and sober and honest in the pursuit of their own interests should after a while accumulate capital, and after that should be allowed to enjoy it in peace, and also if they should choose, when they have accumulated it, to use it to save themselves from actual labor, and hire other people to labor for them, is right. In doing so, they do not wrong the man they employ, for they find men who have not their own land to work upon, or shops to work in, and who are benefited by working for others—hired laborers, receiving their capital for it. Thus a few men that own capital hire a few others, and these establish the relation of capital and labor rightfully—a relation of which I make no complaint. But I insist that that relation, after all, does not embrace more than one-eighth of the labor of the country.

I have taken upon myself, in the name of some of you, to say that we expect upon these principles to ultimately beat them. In order to do so, I think we want and must have a national policy in regard to the institution of slavery that acknowledges and deals with that institution as being wrong. Whoever desires the prevention of the spread of slavery and the nationalization of that institution, yields all when he yields to any policy that either recognizes slavery as being right, or as being an indifferent thing. Nothing will make you successful but setting up a policy which shall treat the thing as being wrong. When I say this, I do not mean to say that this General Government is charged with the duty of redressing or preventing all the wrongs in the world; but I do think that it is charged with preventing and redressing all wrongs which are wrongs to itself. This government is expressly charged with the duty of providing for the general welfare. We believe that the spreading out and perpetuity of the institution of slavery impairs the general welfare. We believe—nay, we know—that that is the only thing that has ever threatened the perpetuity of the Union itself. The only thing which has ever menaced the destruction of the government under which we live, is this very thing. To repress this thing, we think, is providing for the general welfare. Our friends in Kentucky differ from us. We need not make our argument for them; but we who think it is wrong in all its relations, or in some of them at least, must decide as to our own actions, and our own course, upon our own judgment.

I say that we must not interfere with the institution of slavery in the States where it exists, because the Constitution forbids it, and the general welfare does not require us to do so. We must not withhold an efficient Fugitive Slave law, because the Constitution requires us, as I understand it, not to withhold such a law. But we must prevent the outspreading of the institution, because neither the Constitution nor general welfare requires us to extend it. We must prevent the revival of the African slave trade, and the enacting by Congress of a territorial slave code. We must prevent each of these things being done by either congresses or courts. The people of these United States are the rightful masters of both congresses and courts, not to overthrow the Constitution, but to overthrow the men who pervert the Constitution.

After saying this much, let me say a little on the other side. There are plenty of men in the slave States that are altogether good enough for me to be either President or Vice President, provided they will profess their sympathy with our purpose, and will place themselves on such ground that our men, upon principle, can vote for them. There are scores of them—good men in their character for intelligence, and talent, and integrity. If such an one will place himself upon the right ground, I am for his occupying one place upon the next Republican or Opposition ticket. I will heartily go for him. But unless he does so place himself, I think it is a matter of perfect nonsense to attempt to bring about a union upon any other basis; that if a union be made, the elements will scatter so that there can be no success for such a ticket, nor anything like success. The good old maxims of the Bible are applicable, and truly applicable, to human affairs, and in this, as in other things, we may say here that he who is not for us is against us; he who gathereth not with us scattereth. I should be glad to have some of the many good, and able, and noble men of the South to place themselves where we can confer upon them the high honor of an election upon one or the other end of our ticket. It would do my soul good to do that thing. It would enable us to teach them that, inasmuch as we select one of their own number to carry out our principles, we are free from the charge that we mean more than we say.

FROM AN ADDRESS BEFORE THE WISCONSIN STATE AGRICULTURAL SOCIETY, MILWAUKEE

In this address, Lincoln puts forth in its most developed form his theory of the relationship between capital and labor. He also relates one of his favorite parables, the story of an Eastern monarch who wanted a phrase that would be true under any and all circumstances. The sense of impermanence and the implicit death-longing in the phrase "And this, too, shall pass away" are characteristic of Lincoln.

September 30, 1859

THE world is agreed that labor is the source from which human wants are mainly supplied. There is no dispute upon this point. From this point, however, men immediately diverge. Much disputation is maintained as to the best way of applying and controlling the labor element. By some it is assumed that labor is available only in connection with capital—that nobody labors, unless somebody else owning capital, somehow, by the use of it, induces him to do it. Having assumed this, they proceed to consider whether it is best that capital shall hire laborers, and thus induce them to work by their own consent, or buy them, and drive them to it, without their consent. Having proceeded so far, they naturally conclude that all laborers are naturally either hired laborers or slaves. They further assume that whoever is once a hired laborer, is fatally fixed in that condition for life; and thence again, that his condition is as bad as, or worse than, that of a slave. This is

the "mud-sill" theory.* But another class of reasoners hold
the opinion that there is no such relation between capital and
labor as assumed; that there is no such thing as a free man
being fatally fixed for life in the condition of a hired laborer;
that both these assumptions are false, and all inferences from
them groundless. They hold that labor is prior to, and independent of, capital; that, in fact, capital is the fruit of labor,
and could never have existed if labor had not first existed;
that labor can exist without capital, but that capital could
never have existed without labor. Hence they hold that labor
is the superior—greatly the superior—of capital.

They do not deny that there is, and probably always will
be, a relation between labor and capital. The error, as they
hold, is in assuming that the whole labor of the world exists
within that relation. A few men own capital; and that few
avoid labor themselves, and with their capital hire or buy another few to labor for them. A large majority belong to neither
class—neither work for others, nor have others working for
them. Even in all our slave States except South Carolina, a
majority of the whole people of all colors are neither slaves
nor masters. In these free States, a large majority are neither
hirers nor hired. Men, with their families—wives, sons and
daughters—work for themselves, on their farms, in their houses,
and in their shops, taking the whole product to themselves,
and asking no favors of capital on the one hand, nor of hire-
lings or slaves on the other. It is not forgotten that a considerable number of persons mingle their own labor with capital—
that is, labor with their own hands and also buy slaves or hire
free men to labor for them; but this is only a mixed, and not

* Senator Hammond of South Carolina had referred in a speech to a building he had erected on swampy ground using "mud-sills" sunk by his slaves.
This was the kind of work that made slavery necessary, he said, rough work
directed by men of intelligence. He said further that the "hireling system"
of the North did the same thing. This aroused much resentment. At the
Galesburg debate with Douglas, Lincoln's followers had brought in a banner
with the words: "Small-fisted farmers, mud-sills of society, greasy mechanics,
for A. Lincoln."

a distinct, class. No principle stated is disturbed by the existence of this mixed class. Again, as has already been said, the
opponents of the "mud-sill" theory insist that there is not, of
necessity, any such thing as the free hired laborer being fixed
to that condition for life. There is demonstration for saying
this. Many independent men in this assembly doubtless a few
years ago were hired laborers. And their case is almost, if not
quite, the general rule.

The prudent, penniless beginner in the world labors for
wages awhile, saves a surplus with which to buy tools or land
for himself, then labors on his own account another while,
and at length hires another new beginner to help him. This,
say its advocates, is free labor—the just, and generous, and
prosperous system, which opens the way for all, gives hope to
all, and energy, and progress, and improvement of condition
to all. If any continue through life in the condition of the
hired laborer, it is not the fault of the system, but because of
either a dependent nature which prefers it, or improvidence,
folly, or singular misfortune. I have said this much about the
elements of labor generally, as introductory to the consideration of a new phase which that element is in process of assuming. The old general rule was that educated people did not
perform manual labor. They managed to eat their bread, leaving the toil of producing it to the uneducated. This was not
an insupportable evil to the working bees, so long as the class
of drones remained very small. But now, especially in these
free States, nearly all are educated—quite too nearly all to
leave the labor of the uneducated in any wise adequate to the
support of the whole. It follows from this that henceforth
educated people must labor. Otherwise, education itself would
become a positive and intolerable evil. No country can sustain in idleness more than a small percentage of its numbers.
The great majority must labor at something productive. From
these premises the problem springs, "How can labor and education be the most satisfactorily combined?"

By the "mud-sill" theory it is assumed that labor and education are incompatible, and any practical combination of them impossible. According to that theory, a blind horse upon a tread-mill is a perfect illustration of what a laborer should be—all the better for being blind, that he could not kick understandingly. According to that theory, the education of laborers is not only useless but pernicious and dangerous. In fact, it is, in some sort, deemed a misfortune that laborers should have heads at all. Those same heads are regarded as explosive materials, only to be safely kept in damp places, as far as possible from that peculiar sort of fire which ignites them. A Yankee who could invent a strong-handed man without a head would receive the everlasting gratitude of the "mud-sill" advocates.

But free labor says, "No." Free labor argues that as the Author of man makes every individual with one head and one pair of hands, it was probably intended that heads and hands should co-operate as friends, and that that particular head should direct and control that pair of hands. As each man has one mouth to be fed, and one pair of hands to furnish food, it was probably intended that that particular pair of hands should feed that particular mouth—that each head is the natural guardian, director, and protector of the hands and mouth inseparably connected with it; and that being so, every head should be cultivated and improved by whatever will add to its capacity for performing its charge. In one word, free labor insists on universal education.

I have so far stated the opposite theories of "mud-sill" and "free labor," without declaring any preference of my own between them. On an occasion like this, I ought not to declare any. I suppose, however, I shall not be mistaken in assuming as a fact that the people of Wisconsin prefer free labor, with its natural companion, education.

*   *   *

The thought recurs that education—cultivated thought—can best be combined with agricultural labor, or any labor, on the principle of thorough work; that careless, half-performed, slovenly work makes no place for such combination; and thorough work, again, renders sufficient the smallest quantity of ground to each man; and this, again, conforms to what must occur in a world less inclined to wars and more devoted to the arts of peace than heretofore. Population must increase rapidly, more rapidly than in former times, and ere long the most valuable of all arts will be the art of deriving a comfortable subsistence from the smallest area of soil. No community whose every member possesses this art, can ever be the victim of oppression in any of its forms. Such community will be alike independent of crowned kings, money kings, and land kings.

But, according to your program, the awarding of premiums awaits the closing of this address. Considering the deep interest necessarily pertaining to that performance, it would be no wonder if I am already heard with some impatience. I will detain you but a moment longer. Some of you will be successful, and such will need but little philosophy to take them home in cheerful spirits; others will be disappointed, and will be in a less happy mood. To such let it be said: "Lay it not too much to heart." Let them adopt the maxim: "Better luck next time," and then by renewed exertion make that better luck for themselves.

And by the successful and unsuccessful let it be remembered that while occasions like the present bring their sober and durable benefits, the exultations and mortifications of them are but temporary; that the victor will soon be vanquished if he relax in his exertion; and that the vanquished this year may be victor the next, in spite of all competition.

It is said an Eastern monarch once charged his wise men to invent him a sentence to be ever in view, and which should be true and appropriate in all times and situations. They presented him the words: "And this, too, shall pass away." How much it expresses! How chastening in the hour of pride! How consoling in the depths of affliction! "And this, too, shall pass away." And yet, let us hope, it is not quite true. Let us hope, rather, that by the best cultivation of the physical world beneath and around us, and the best intellectual and moral world within us, we shall secure an individual, social, and political prosperity and happiness, whose course shall be onward and upward, and which, while the earth endures, shall not pass away.

LETTER TO J. W. FELL

Between Lincoln's address at Milwaukee and this letter to J. W. Fell, a whole act in the drama of America had been played. John Brown had made his attempt to capture Harper's Ferry; he had failed, been captured, tried, convicted and hanged. The entire nation had been tremendously disturbed by what had happened, but Lincoln said practically nothing on the subject during the time it was happening, although he had been in Kansas on a speaking tour early in December, and Kansas was the scene of many of John Brown's first struggles against slavery. At the time he wrote this letter, the Presidential election of 1860 was actively being prepared for in political circles. Lincoln had been approached by Fell for some information about himself; he writes to give this brief autobiographical sketch which should be compared with the more elaborate one he wrote later (June 1, 1860).

Springfield, December 20, 1859

My Dear Sir: Herewith is a little sketch, as you requested. There is not much of it, for the reason, I suppose, that there is not much of me. If anything be made out of it, I wish it to be modest, and not to go beyond the material. If it were thought necessary to incorporate anything from any of my speeches, I suppose there would be no objection. Of course it must not appear to have been written by myself.

I was born February 12, 1809, in Hardin County, Kentucky. My parents were both born in Virginia, of undistinguished families—second families, perhaps I should say. My mother, who died in my tenth year, was of a family of the name of Hanks, some of whom now reside in Adams, and others in Macon County, Illinois. My paternal grandfather, Abraham Lincoln, emigrated from Rockingham County, Virginia, to Kentucky about 1781 or 1782, where a year or two later* he was killed by the Indians, not in battle, but by stealth, when he was laboring to open a farm in the forest. His ancestors, who were Quakers, went to Virginia from Berks County, Pennsylvania. An effort to identify them with the New England family of the same name ended in nothing more definite than a similarity of Christian names in both families, such as Enoch, Levi, Mordecai, Solomon, Abraham, and the like.†

My father, at the death of his father, was but six years of age, and he grew up literally without education. He removed from Kentucky to what is now Spencer County, Indiana, in my eighth year. We reached our new home about the time the State came into the Union. It was a wild region, with many bears and other wild animals still in the woods. There I grew up. There were some schools, so called, but no qualification was ever required of a teacher beyond "readin', writin', and cipherin' " to the rule of three. If a straggler supposed to understand Latin happen to sojourn in the neighborhood, he was looked upon as a wizard. There was absolutely nothing to excite ambition for education. Of course, when I came of age I did not know much. Still, somehow, I could read, write,

* Modern research indicates that he was probably killed in the spring of 1786.
† The connection has been definitely established by more recent genealogical research.

and cipher to the rule of three, but that was all. I have not been to school since. The little advance I now have upon this store of education, I have picked up from time to time under the pressure of necessity.

I was raised to farm work, which I continued till I was twenty-two. At twenty-one I came to Illinois, Macon County. Then I got to New Salem, at that time in Sangamon, now in Menard County, where I remained a year as a sort of clerk in a store. Then came the Black Hawk War; and I was elected a captain of volunteers, a success which gave me more pleasure than any I have had since. I went the campaign, was elated, ran for the legislature the same year (1832), and was beaten—the only time I ever have been beaten by the people. The next and three succeeding biennial elections I was elected to the legislature. I was not a candidate afterward. During this legislative period I had studied law, and removed to Springfield to practise it. In 1846 I was once elected to the lower House of Congress. Was not a candidate for re-election. From 1849 to 1854, both inclusive, practised law more assiduously than ever before. Always a Whig in politics; and generally on the Whig electoral tickets, making active canvasses. I was losing interest in politics when the repeal of the Missouri Compromise aroused me again. What I have done since then is pretty well known.

If any personal description of me is thought desirable, it may be said I am, in height, six feet four inches, nearly; lean in flesh, weighing on an average one hundred and eighty pounds; dark complexion, with coarse black hair and gray eyes. No other marks or brands recollected.

LETTER TO A. JONAS

Abraham Jonas, an English-born Jew living in Quincy, Illinois, was a good friend of Lincoln, as is evidenced by this letter. The book to which Lincoln refers is a collection of his debates with Douglas, published in Columbus, Ohio, under the title Political Debates Between Hon. Abraham Lincoln and Hon. Stephen A. Douglas in the Celebrated Campaign of 1858 in Illinois.

Springfield, Feb. 4, 1860

Hon. A. Jonas

MY DEAR SIR: Yours of the 3rd inquiring how you can get a copy of the debates now being published in Ohio is received. As you are one of my most valued friends, and have complimented me by the expression of a wish for the book, I propose doing myself the honor of presenting you with one, as soon as I can. By the arrangement our Ohio friends have made with the publishers, I am to have one hundred copies gratis. When I shall receive them I will send you one by express. I understand they will not be out before March and I probably shall be absent about that time, so that you must not be disappointed if you do not receive yours before about the middle of the month.

ADDRESS AT COOPER INSTITUTE, NEW YORK

This speech was one of the greatest efforts of Lincoln's career—a keystone in the edifice of his writings and his attitudes toward the life-long struggle in which he was engaged. It was his first important and widely publicized appearance before an Eastern audience. He chose his words carefully, using as a starting point Douglas's statement that the founders of the nation had known what they were doing about slavery when they had created the American Government. The first part of the speech is an elaborate historical survey, much in the nature of the Peoria address of October 16, 1854; the second part deals with issues that were before the country in 1860. He pleads with the Southern people for a better understanding; he repudiates John Brown; he tries to free the central core of his party from the charge that some of its more radical abolitionist members had made use of Helper's book, The Impending Crisis of the South, as an argument to serve their cause. Helper was a Southerner of poor-white origin who had written a book to show that slavery was a bad thing for the white people of the South. His book had precipitated a quarrel at the opening of Congress in December. It had gained enormously from this publicity, and at the time Lincoln spoke at Cooper Union, it had become the national best seller of the day. Lincoln goes out of his way during his address to state the conservative point of view represented by men like himself in the Republican party. Nevertheless, the patience and the nerves of the people of the North had become so irritated by the South's attitude that Lincoln himself, even in making a conservative speech, expresses some of this irritation. He closes with an appeal to the people of the North to stand fast and not to let themselves be frightened out of their belief in the rightness of their own cause. The audience before which he spoke was a very distinguished one, although a snowstorm had cut down attendance to fifteen hundred. William Cullen Bryant introduced the speaker, whose new suit of clothes had become badly creased from packing. A member of the committee in charge of the arrangements wrote of him: "His form and manner were indeed very odd, and we thought him the most unprepossessing public man we had ever met." Yet at the conclusion of the address, Noah Brooks, writing for the Tribune, said: "No man ever made such an impression on his first appeal to a New York audience."

February 27, 1860

MR. PRESIDENT AND FELLOW-CITIZENS OF NEW YORK: The facts with which I shall deal this evening are mainly old and familiar; nor is there anything new in the general use I shall make of them. If there shall be any novelty, it will be in the mode of presenting the facts, and the inferences and observations following that presentation. In his speech last autumn at Columbus, Ohio, as reported in The New-York Times, Senator Douglas said:

Our fathers, when they framed the government under which we live, understood this question just as well, and even better, than we do now.

I fully indorse this, and I adopt it as a text for this discourse. I so adopt it because it furnishes a precise and an agreed starting-point for a discussion between Republicans and that wing of the Democracy headed by Senator Douglas. It simply leaves the inquiry: What was the understanding those fathers had of the question mentioned?

What is the frame of government under which we live? The answer must be, "The Constitution of the United States." That Constitution consists of the original, framed in 1787, and under which the present government first went into operation, and twelve subsequently framed amendments, the first ten of which were framed in 1789.

Who were our fathers that framed the Constitution? I

suppose the "thirty-nine" who signed the original instrument may be fairly called our fathers who framed that part of the present government. It is almost exactly true to say they framed it, and it is altogether true to say they fairly represented the opinion and sentiment of the whole nation at that time. Their names, being familiar to nearly all, and accessible to quite all, need not now be repeated.

I take these "thirty-nine," for the present, as being "our fathers who framed the government under which we live." What is the question which, according to the text, those fathers understood "just as well, and even better, than we do now"?

It is this: Does the proper division of local from Federal authority, or anything in the Constitution, forbid our Federal Government to control as to slavery in our Federal Territories?

Upon this, Senator Douglas holds the affirmative, and Republicans the negative. This affirmation and denial form an issue; and this issue—this question—is precisely what the text declares our fathers understood "better than we." Let us now inquire whether the "thirty-nine," or any of them, ever acted upon this question; and if they did, how they acted upon it— how they expressed that better understanding. In 1784, three years before the Constitution, the United States then owning the Northwestern Territory, and no other, the Congress of the Confederation had before them the question of prohibiting slavery in that Territory; and four of the "thirty-nine" who afterward framed the Constitution were in that Congress, and voted on that question. Of these, Roger Sherman, Thomas Mifflin, and Hugh Williamson voted for the prohibition, thus showing that, in their understanding, no line dividing local from Federal authority, nor anything else, properly forbade the Federal Government to control as to slavery in Federal territory. The other of the four, James McHenry, voted against the prohibition, showing that for some cause he thought it improper to vote for it.

In 1787, still before the Constitution, but while the convention was in session framing it, and while the Northwestern Territory still was the only Territory owned by the United States, the same question of prohibiting slavery in the Territory again came before the Congress of the Confederation; and two more of the "thirty-nine" who afterward signed the Constitution were in that Congress, and voted on the question. They were William Blount and William Few; and they both voted for the prohibition—thus showing that in their understanding no line dividing local from Federal authority, nor anything else, properly forbade the Federal Government to control as to slavery in Federal territory. This time the prohibition became a law, being part of what is now well known as the ordinance of '87.

The question of Federal control of slavery in the Territories seems not to have been directly before the convention which framed the original Constitution; and hence it is not recorded that the "thirty-nine," or any of them, while engaged on that instrument, expressed any opinion on that precise question.

In 1789, by the first Congress which sat under the Constitution, an act was passed to enforce the ordinance of '87, including the prohibition of slavery in the Northwestern Territory. The bill for this act was reported by one of the "thirty-nine" —Thomas Fitzsimmons, then a member of the House of Representatives from Pennsylvania. It went through all its stages without a word of opposition, and finally passed both branches without ayes and nays, which is equivalent to a unanimous passage. In this Congress there were sixteen of the thirty-nine fathers who framed the original Constitution. They were John Langdon, Nicholas Gilman, Wm. S. Johnson, Roger Sherman, Robert Morris, Thos. Fitzsimmons, William Few, Abraham Baldwin, Rufus King, William Paterson, George Clymer,

Richard Bassett, George Read, Pierce Butler, Daniel Carroll and James Madison.

This shows that, in their understanding, no line dividing local from Federal authority, nor anything in the Constitution, properly forbade Congress to prohibit slavery in the Federal territory; else both their fidelity to correct principle, and their oath to support the Constitution, would have constrained them to oppose the prohibition.

Again, George Washington, another of the "thirty-nine," was then President of the United States and as such approved and signed the bill, thus completing its validity as a law, and thus showing that, in his understanding, no line dividing local from Federal authority, nor anything in the Constitution, forbade the Federal Government to control as to slavery in Federal territory.

No great while after the adoption of the original Constitution, North Carolina ceded to the Federal Government the country now constituting the State of Tennessee; and a few years later Georgia ceded that which now constitutes the States of Mississippi and Alabama. In both deeds of cession it was made a condition by the ceding States that the Federal Government should not prohibit slavery in the ceded country. Besides this, slavery was then actually in the ceded country. Under these circumstances, Congress, on taking charge of these countries, did not absolutely prohibit slavery within them. But they did interfere with it—take control of it—even there, to a certain extent. In 1798 Congress organized the Territory of Mississippi. In the act of organization they prohibited the bringing of slaves into the Territory from any place without the United States, by fine, and giving freedom to slaves so brought. This act passed both branches of Congress without yeas and nays. In that Congress were three of the "thirty-nine" who framed the original Constitution. They were John Langdon, George Read, and Abraham Baldwin. They all probably voted for it. Certainly they would have

placed their opposition to it upon record if, in their understanding, any line dividing local from Federal authority, or
anything in the Constitution, properly forbade the Federal
Government to control as to slavery in Federal territory.

In 1803 the Federal Government purchased the Louisiana
country. Our former territorial acquisitions came from certain
of our own States; but this Louisiana country was acquired
from a foreign nation. In 1804 Congress gave a territorial organization to that part of it which now constitutes the State
of Louisiana. New Orleans, lying within that part, was an old
and comparatively large city. There were other considerable
towns and settlements, and slavery was extensively and thoroughly intermingled with the people. Congress did not, in the
Territorial Act, prohibit slavery; but they did interfere with
it—take control of it—in a more marked and extensive way
than they did in the case of Mississippi. The substance of the
provision therein made in relation to slaves was:

1st. That no slave should be imported into the Territory
from foreign parts.

2d. That no slave should be carried into it who had been
imported into the United States since the first day of May,
1798.

3d. That no slave should be carried into it, except by the
owner, and for his own use as a settler; the penalty in all the
cases being a fine upon the violator of the law, and freedom to
the slave.

This act also was passed without ayes or nays. In the Congress which passed it there were two of the "thirty-nine." They
were Abraham Baldwin and Jonathan Dayton. As stated in the
case of Mississippi, it is probable they both voted for it. They
would not have allowed it to pass without recording their opposition to it if, in their understanding, it violated either the
line properly dividing local from Federal authority, or any provision of the Constitution.

In 1819–20 came and passed the Missouri question. Many

votes were taken, by yeas and nays, in both branches of Congress, upon the various phases of the general question. Two of the "thirty-nine"—Rufus King and Charles Pinckney—were members of that Congress. Mr. King steadily voted for slavery prohibition and against all compromises, while Mr. Pinckney as steadily voted against slavery prohibition and against all compromises. By this, Mr. King showed that, in his understanding, no line dividing local from Federal authority, nor anything in the Constitution, was violated by Congress prohibiting slavery in Federal territory; while Mr. Pinckney, by his votes, showed that, in his understanding, there was some sufficient reason for opposing such prohibition in that case.

The cases I have mentioned are the only acts of the "thirty-nine," or of any of them, upon the direct issue, which I have been able to discover.

To enumerate the persons who thus acted as being four in 1784, two in 1787, seventeen in 1789, three in 1798, two in 1804, and two in 1819–20, there would be thirty of them. But this would be counting John Langdon, Roger Sherman, William Few, Rufus King, and George Read each twice, and Abraham Baldwin three times. The true number of those of the "thirty-nine" whom I have shown to have acted upon the question which, by the text, they understood better than we, is twenty-three, leaving sixteen not shown to have acted upon it in any way.

Here, then, we have twenty-three out of our thirty-nine fathers "who framed the government under which we live," who have, upon their official responsibility and their corporal oaths, acted upon the very question which the text affirms they "understood just as well, and even better, than we do now"; and twenty-one of them—a clear majority of the whole "thirty-nine"—so acting upon it as to make them guilty of gross political impropriety and wilful perjury if, in their understanding, any proper division between local and Federal authority, or anything in the Constitution they had made themselves, and sworn to support, forbade the Federal Government to control as to slavery in the Federal Territories. Thus the twenty-one acted; and, as actions speak louder than words, so actions under such responsibility speak still louder.

Two of the twenty-three voted against congressional prohibition of slavery in the Federal Territories, in the instances in which they acted upon the question. But for what reasons they so voted is not known. They may have done so because they thought a proper division of local from Federal authority, or some provision or principle of the Constitution, stood in the way; or they may, without any such question, have voted against the prohibition on what appeared to them to be sufficient grounds of expediency. No one who has sworn to support the Constitution can conscientiously vote for what he understands to be an unconstitutional measure, however expedient he may think it; but one may and ought to vote against a measure which he deems constitutional if, at the same time, he deems it inexpedient. It, therefore, would be unsafe to set down even the two who voted against the prohibition as having done so because, in their understanding, any proper division of local from Federal authority, or anything in the Constitution, forbade the Federal Government to control as to slavery in Federal territory.

The remaining sixteen of the "thirty-nine," so far as I have discovered, have left no record of their understanding upon the direct question of Federal control of slavery in the Federal Territories. But there is much reason to believe that their understanding upon that question would not have appeared different from that of their twenty-three compeers, had it been manifested at all.

For the purpose of adhering rigidly to the text, I have purposely omitted whatever understanding may have been manifested by any person, however distinguished, other than the thirty-nine fathers who framed the original Constitution; and, for the same reason, I have also omitted whatever understanding may have been manifested by any of the "thirty-nine" even on any other phase of the general question of slavery. If we should look into their acts and declarations on those other phases, as the foreign slave trade, and the morality and policy of slavery generally, it would appear to us that on the direct question of Federal control of slavery in Federal Territories, the sixteen, if they had acted at all, would probably have acted just as the twenty-three did. Among that sixteen were several of the most noted antislavery men of those times—as Dr. Franklin, Alexander Hamilton, and Gouverneur Morris—while there was not one now known to have been otherwise, unless it may be John Rutledge, of South Carolina.

The sum of the whole is that of our thirty-nine fathers who framed the original Constitution, twenty-one—a clear majority of the whole—certainly understood that no proper division of local from Federal authority, nor any part of the Constitution, forbade the Federal Government to control slavery in the Federal Territories; while all the rest had probably the same understanding. Such, unquestionably, was the understanding of our fathers who framed the original Constitution; and the text affirms that they understood the question "better than we."

But, so far, I have been considering the understanding of the question manifested by the framers of the original Constitution. In and by the original instrument, a mode was provided for amending it; and, as I have already stated, the present frame of "the government under which we live" consists of that original, and twelve amendatory articles framed and adopted since. Those who now insist that Federal control of slavery in Federal Territories violates the Constitution, point us to the provisions which they suppose it thus violates; and, as I understand, they all fix upon provisions in these amendatory articles, and not in the original instrument. The Supreme Court, in the Dred Scott case, plant themselves upon the Fifth Amendment, which provides that no person shall be deprived of "life, liberty, or property without due process of law"; while Senator Douglas and his peculiar adherents plant themselves upon the Tenth Amendment, providing that "the powers not delegated to the United States by the Constitution" "are reserved to the States respectively, or to the people."

Now, it so happens that these amendments were framed by the first Congress which sat under the Constitution—the identical Congress which passed the act, already mentioned, enforcing the prohibition of slavery in the Northwestern Territory. Not only was it the same Congress, but they were the identical, same individual men who, at the same session, and at the same time within the session, had under consideration, and in progress toward maturity, these constitutional amendments, and this act prohibiting slavery in all the territory the nation then owned. The constitutional amendments were introduced before, and passed after, the act enforcing the ordinance of '87; so that, during the whole pendency of the act to enforce the ordinance, the constitutional amendments were also pending.

The seventy-six members of that Congress, including sixteen of the framers of the original Constitution, as before stated, were preëminently our fathers who framed that part of "the government under which we live" which is now claimed as forbidding the Federal Government to control slavery in the Federal Territories.

Is it not a little presumptuous in any one at this day to affirm that the two things which that Congress deliberately framed, and carried to maturity at the same time, are absolutely inconsistent with each other? And does not such affirmation become impudently absurd when coupled with the other affirmation, from the same mouth, that those who did the two things alleged to be inconsistent, understood whether they really were inconsistent better than we—better than he who affirms that they are inconsistent?

It is surely safe to assume that the thirty-nine framers of the original Constitution, and the seventy-six members of the Congress which framed the amendments thereto, taken together, do certainly include those who may be fairly called "our fathers who framed the government under which we live." And so assuming, I defy any man to show that any one of them ever, in his whole life, declared that, in his understanding, any proper division of local from Federal authority, or any part of the Constitution, forbade the Federal Government to control as to slavery in the Federal Territories. I go a step further. I defy any one to show that any living man in the whole world ever did, prior to the beginning of the present century (and I might almost say prior to the beginning of the last half of the present century), declare that, in his understanding, any proper division of local from Federal authority, or any part of the Constitution, forbade the Federal Government to control as to slavery in the Federal Territories. To those who now so declare I give not only "our fathers who framed the government under which we live," but with them all other living men within the century in which it was framed, among whom to search, and they shall not be able to find the evidence of a single man agreeing with them.

Now, and here, let me guard a little against being misunderstood. I do not mean to say we are bound to follow implicitly in whatever our fathers did. To do so would be to discard all the lights of current experience—to reject all progress, all improvement. What I do say is that if we would supplant the opinions and policy of our fathers in any case, we should do so upon evidence so conclusive, and argument so clear, that even their great authority, fairly considered and weighed, cannot stand; and most surely not in a case whereof we ourselves declare they understood the question better than we.

If any man at this day sincerely believes that a proper division of local from Federal authority, or any part of the Constitution, forbids the Federal Government to control as to slavery in the Federal Territories, he is right to say so, and to enforce his position by all truthful evidence and fair argument which he can. But he has no right to mislead others, who have less access to history, and less leisure to study it, into the false belief that "our fathers who framed the government under which we live" were of the same opinion—thus substituting falsehood and deception for truthful evidence and fair argument. If any man at this day sincerely believes "our fathers who framed the government under which we live" used and applied principles, in other cases, which ought to have led them to understand that a proper division of local from Federal authority, or some part of the Constitution, forbids the Federal Government to control as to slavery in the Federal Territories, he is right to say so. But he should, at the same time, brave the responsibility of declaring that, in his opinion, he understands their principles better than they did themselves, and especially should he not shirk that responsibility by asserting that they "understood the question just as well, and even better, than we do now."

But enough! Let all who believe that "our fathers who framed the government under which we live understood this question just as well, and even better, than we do now," speak as they spoke, and act as they acted upon it. This is all Republicans ask—all Republicans desire—in relation to slavery. As those fathers marked it, so let it be again marked, as an evil not to be extended, but to be tolerated and protected only because of and so far as its actual presence among us makes that toleration and protection a necessity. Let all the guaranties those fathers gave it be not grudgingly, but fully and fairly, maintained. For this Republicans contend, and with this, so far as I know or believe, they will be content.

And now, if they would listen—as I suppose they will not—I would address a few words to the Southern people.

I would say to them: You consider yourselves a reasonable and a just people; and I consider that in the general qualities of reason and justice you are not inferior to any other people.

Still, when you speak of us Republicans, you do so only to denounce us as reptiles, or, at the best, as no better than outlaws. You will grant a hearing to pirates or murderers, but nothing like it to "Black Republicans." In all your contentions with one another, each of you deems an unconditional condemnation of "Black Republicanism" as the first thing to be attended to. Indeed, such condemnation of us seems to be an indispensable prerequisite—license, so to speak—among you to be admitted or permitted to speak at all. Now can you or not be prevailed upon to pause and to consider whether this is quite just to us, or even to yourselves? Bring forward your charges and specifications, and then be patient long enough to hear us deny or justify.

You say we are sectional. We deny it. That makes an issue; and the burden of proof is upon you. You produce your proof; and what is it? Why, that our party has no existence in your section—gets no votes in your section. The fact is substantially true; but does it prove the issue? If it does, then in case we should, without change of principle, begin to get votes in your section, we should thereby cease to be sectional. You cannot escape this conclusion; and yet, are you willing to abide by it? If you are, you will probably soon find that we have ceased to be sectional, for we shall get votes in your section this very year. You will then begin to discover, as the truth plainly is, that your proof does not touch the issue. The fact that we get no votes in your section is a fact of your making, and not of ours. And if there be fault in that fact, that fault is primarily yours, and remains so until you show that we repel you by some wrong principle or practice. If we do repel you by any wrong principle or practice, the fault is ours; but this brings you to where you ought to have started—to a discussion of the right or wrong of our principle. If our principle, put in practice, would wrong your section for the benefit of ours, or for any other object, then our principle, and we with it, are sectional, and are justly opposed and denounced as such. Meet us, then, on the question of whether our principle, put in practice, would wrong your section; and so meet us as if it were possible that something may be said on our side. Do you accept the challenge? No! Then you really believe that the principle which "our fathers who framed the government under which we live" thought so clearly right as to adopt it, and indorse it again and again, upon their official oaths, is in fact so clearly wrong as to demand your condemnation without a moment's consideration.

Some of you delight to flaunt in our faces the warning against sectional parties given by Washington in his Farewell Address. Less than eight years before Washington gave that warning, he had, as President of the United States, approved and signed an act of Congress enforcing the prohibition of slavery in the Northwestern Territory, which act embodied the policy of the government upon that subject up to and at the very moment he penned that warning; and about one year after he penned it, he wrote Lafayette that he considered that prohibition a wise measure, expressing in the same connection his hope that we should at some time have a confederacy of free States.

Bearing this in mind, and seeing that sectionalism has since arisen upon this same subject, is that warning a weapon in your hands against us, or in our hands against you? Could Washington himself speak, would he cast the blame of that sectionalism upon us, who sustain his policy, or upon you, who repudiate it? We respect that warning of Washington, and we commend it to you, together with his example pointing to the right application of it.

But you say you are conservative—eminently conservative— while we are revolutionary, destructive, or something of the sort. What is conservatism? Is it not adherence to the old and tried, against the new and untried? We stick to, contend for, the identical old policy on the point in controversy which was adopted by "our fathers who framed the government under which we live"; while you with one accord reject, and scout, and spit upon that old policy, and insist upon substituting something new. True, you disagree among yourselves as to what that substitute shall be. You are divided on new propositions and plans, but you are unanimous in rejecting and denouncing the old policy of the fathers. Some of you are for reviving the foreign slave trade; some for a congressional slave code for the Territories; some for Congress forbidding the Territories to prohibit slavery within their limits; some for maintaining slavery in the Territories through the judiciary; some for the "gur-reat pur-rinciple" that "if one man would enslave another, no third man should object," fantastically called "popular sovereignty"; but never a man among you is in favor of Federal prohibition of slavery in Federal Territories, according to the practice of "our fathers who framed the government under which we live." Not one of all your various plans can show a precedent or an advocate in the century within which our government originated. Consider, then, whether your claim of conservatism for yourselves, and your charge of destructiveness against us, are based on the most clear and stable foundations.

Again, you say we have made the slavery question more prominent than it formerly was. We deny it. We admit that it is more prominent, but we deny that we made it so. It was not we, but you, who discarded the old policy of the fathers. We resisted, and still resist, your innovation; and thence comes the greater prominence of the question. Would you have that question reduced to its former proportions? Go back to that old policy. What has been will be again, under the same conditions. If you would have the peace of the old times, readopt the precepts and policy of the old times.

You charge that we stir up insurrections among your slaves. We deny it; and what is your proof? Harper's Ferry! John Brown!! John Brown was no Republican; and you have failed to implicate a single Republican in his Harper's Ferry enterprise. If any member of our party is guilty in that matter, you know it, or you do not know it. If you do know it, you are inexcusable for not designating the man and proving the fact. If you do not know it, you are inexcusable for asserting it, and especially for persisting in the assertion after you have tried and failed to make the proof. You need not be told that persisting in a charge which one does not know to be true, is simply malicious slander.

Some of you admit that no Republican designedly aided or encouraged the Harper's Ferry affair, but still insist that our doctrines and declarations necessarily lead to such results. We do not believe it. We know we hold no doctrine, and make no declaration, which were not held to and made by "our fathers who framed the government under which we live." You never dealt fairly by us in relation to this affair. When it occurred, some important State elections were near at hand, and you were in evident glee with the belief that, by charging the blame upon us, you could get an advantage of us in those elections. The elections came, and your expectations were not quite fulfilled. Every Republican man knew that, as to himself at least, your charge was a slander, and he was not much inclined by it to cast his vote in your favor. Republican doctrines and declarations are accompanied with a continual protest against any interference whatever with your slaves, or with you about your slaves. Surely, this does not encourage them to revolt. True, we do, in common with "our fathers who framed the government under which we live," declare our belief that slavery is wrong; but the slaves do not hear us declare even this. For anything we say or do, the slaves would scarcely know there is a Republican party. I believe they would not, in fact, generally know it but for your misrepresentations of us in their hearing. In your political contests among yourselves, each faction charges the other with sympathy with Black Republicanism; and then, to give point to the charge, defines Black

Republicanism to simply be insurrection, blood, and thunder among the slaves.

Slave insurrections are no more common now than they were before the Republican party was organized. What induced the Southampton insurrection, twenty-eight years ago, in which at least three times as many lives were lost as at Harper's Ferry? You can scarcely stretch your very elastic fancy to the conclusion that Southampton was "got up by Black Republicanism." In the present state of things in the United States, I do not think a general, or even a very extensive, slave insurrection is possible. The indispensable concert of action cannot be attained. The slaves have no means of rapid communication; nor can incendiary freemen, black or white, supply it. The explosive materials are everywhere in parcels; but there neither are, nor can be supplied, the indispensable connecting trains.

Much is said by Southern people about the affection of slaves for their masters and mistresses; and a part of it, at least, is true. A plot for an uprising could scarcely be devised and communicated to twenty individuals before some one of them, to save the life of a favorite master or mistress, would divulge it. This is the rule; and the slave revolution in Hayti was not an exception to it, but a case occurring under peculiar circumstances. The gunpowder plot of British history, though not connected with slaves, was more in point. In that case, only about twenty were admitted to the secret; and yet one of them, in his anxiety to save a friend, betrayed the plot to that friend, and, by consequence, averted the calamity. Occasional poisonings from the kitchen, and open or stealthy assassinations in the field, and local revolts extending to a score or so, will continue to occur as the natural results of slavery; but no general insurrection of slaves, as I think, can happen in this country for a long time. Whoever much fears, or much hopes, for such an event, will be alike disappointed.

In the language of Mr. Jefferson, uttered many years ago,

"It is still in our power to direct the process of emancipation and deportation peaceably, and in such slow degrees, as that the evil will wear off insensibly; and their places be, *pari passu*, filled up by free white laborers. If, on the contrary, it is left to force itself on, human nature must shudder at the prospect held up."

Mr. Jefferson did not mean to say, nor do I, that the power of emancipation is in the Federal Government. He spoke of Virginia; and, as to the power of emancipation, I speak of the slaveholding States only. The Federal Government, however, as we insist, has the power of restraining the extension of the institution—the power to insure that a slave insurrection shall never occur on any American soil which is now free from slavery.

John Brown's effort was peculiar. It was not a slave insurrection. It was an attempt by white men to get up a revolt among slaves, in which the slaves refused to participate. In fact, it was so absurd that the slaves, with all their ignorance, saw plainly enough it could not succeed. That affair, in its philosophy, corresponds with the many attempts, related in history, at the assassination of kings and emperors. An enthusiast broods over the oppression of a people till he fancies himself commissioned by Heaven to liberate them. He ventures the attempt, which ends in little else than his own execution. Orsini's attempt on Louis Napoleon, and John Brown's attempt at Harper's Ferry, were, in their philosophy, precisely the same. The eagerness to cast blame on old England in the one case, and on New England in the other, does not disprove the sameness of the two things.

And how much would it avail you, if you could, by the use of John Brown, Helper's book,* and the like, break up the Republican organization? Human action can be modified to some extent, but human nature cannot be changed. There is a judgment and a feeling against slavery in this nation, which

* Hinton Rowan Helper's *The Impending Crisis of the South.*

cast at least a million and a half of votes. You cannot destroy that judgment and feeling—that sentiment—by breaking up the political organization which rallies around it. You can scarcely scatter and disperse an army which has been formed into order in the face of your heaviest fire; but if you could, how much would you gain by forcing the sentiment which created it out of the peaceful channel of the ballot-box into some other channel? What would that other channel probably be? Would the number of John Browns be lessened or enlarged by the operation?

But you will break up the Union rather than submit to a denial of your constitutional rights.

That has a somewhat reckless sound; but it would be palliated, if not fully justified, were we proposing, by the mere force of numbers, to deprive you of some right plainly written down in the Constitution. But we are proposing no such thing.

When you make these declarations you have a specific and well-understood allusion to an assumed constitutional right of yours to take slaves into the Federal Territories, and to hold them there as property. But no such right is specifically written in the Constitution. That instrument is literally silent about any such right. We, on the contrary, deny that such a right has any existence in the Constitution, even by implication.

Your purpose, then, plainly stated, is that you will destroy the government, unless you be allowed to construe and force the Constitution as you please, on all points in dispute between you and us. You will rule or ruin in all events.

This, plainly stated, is your language. Perhaps you will say the Supreme Court has decided the disputed constitutional question in your favor.* Not quite so. But waiving the lawyer's distinction between dictum and decision, the court has decided the question for you in a sort of way. The court has substantially said, it is your constitutional right to take slaves into the Federal Territories, and to hold them there as property. When

---

* In the Dred Scott decision.

I say the decision was made in a sort of way, I mean it was made in a divided court, by a bare majority of the judges, and they not quite agreeing with one another in the reasons for making it; that it is so made as that its avowed supporters disagree with one another about its meaning, and that it was mainly based upon a mistaken statement of fact—the statement in the opinion that "the right of property in a slave is distinctly and expressly affirmed in the Constitution."

An inspection of the Constitution will show that the right of property in a slave is not "distinctly and expressly affirmed" in it. Bear in mind, the judges do not pledge their judicial opinion that such right is impliedly affirmed in the Constitution; but they pledge their veracity that it is "distinctly and expressly" affirmed there—"distinctly," that is, not mingled with anything else—"expressly," that is, in words meaning just that, without the aid of any inference, and susceptible of no other meaning.

If they had only pledged their judicial opinion that such right is affirmed in the instrument by implication, it would be open to others to show that neither the word "slave" nor "slavery" is to be found in the Constitution, nor the word "property" even, in any connection with language alluding to the things slave, or slavery; and that wherever in that instrument the slave is alluded to, he is called a "person"; and wherever his master's legal right in relation to him is alluded to, it is spoken of as "service or labor which may be due"—as a debt payable in service or labor. Also it would be open to show, by contemporaneous history, that this mode of alluding to slaves and slavery, instead of speaking of them, was employed on purpose to exclude from the Constitution the idea that there could be property in man.

To show all this is easy and certain.

When this obvious mistake of the judges shall be brought to their notice, is it not reasonable to expect that they will withdraw the mistaken statement, and reconsider the conclusion based upon it?

And then it is to be remembered that "our fathers who framed the government under which we live"—the men who made the Constitution—decided this same constitutional question in our favor long ago: decided it without division among themselves when making the decision; without division among themselves about the meaning of it after it was made, and, so far as any evidence is left, without basing it upon any mistaken statement of facts.

Under all these circumstances, do you really feel yourselves justified to break up this government unless such a court decision as yours is shall be at once submitted to as a conclusive and final rule of political action? But you will not abide the election of a Republican president! In that supposed event, you say, you will destroy the Union; and then, you say, the great crime of having destroyed it will be upon us! That is cool. A highwayman holds a pistol to my ear, and mutters through his teeth, "Stand and deliver, or I shall kill you, and then you will be a murderer!"

To be sure, what the robber demanded of me—my money—was my own; and I had a clear right to keep it; but it was no more my own than my vote is my own; and the threat of death to me, to extort my money, and the threat of destruction to the Union, to extort my vote, can scarcely be distinguished in principle.

A few words now to Republicans. It is exceedingly desirable that all parts of this great Confederacy shall be at peace, and in harmony one with another. Let us Republicans do our part to have it so. Even though much provoked, let us do nothing through passion and ill temper. Even though the Southern people will not so much as listen to us, let us calmly consider their demands, and yield to them if, in our deliberate view of our duty, we possibly can. Judging by all they say and do, and by the subject and nature of their controversy with us, let us determine, if we can, what will satisfy them.

Will they be satisfied if the Territories be unconditionally surrendered to them? We know they will not. In all their present complaints against us, the Territories are scarcely mentioned. Invasions and insurrections are the rage now. Will it satisfy them if, in the future, we have nothing to do with invasions and insurrections? We know it will not. We so know, because we know we never had anything to do with invasions and insurrections; and yet this total abstaining does not exempt us from the charge and the denunciation.

The question recurs, What will satisfy them? Simply this: we must not only let them alone, but we must somehow convince them that we do let them alone. This, we know by experience, is no easy task. We have been so trying to convince them from the very beginning of our organization, but with no success. In all our platforms and speeches we have constantly protested our purpose to let them alone; but this has had no tendency to convince them. Alike unavailing to convince them is the fact that they have never detected a man of us in any attempt to disturb them.

These natural and apparently adequate means all failing, what will convince them? This, and this only: cease to call slavery wrong, and join them in calling it right. And this must be done thoroughly—done in acts as well as in words. Silence will not be tolerated—we must place ourselves avowedly with them. Senator Douglas's new sedition law must be enacted and enforced, suppressing all declarations that slavery is wrong, whether made in politics, in presses, in pulpits, or in private. We must arrest and return their fugitive slaves with greedy pleasure. We must pull down our Free-State constitutions. The whole atmosphere must be disinfected from all taint of opposition to slavery, before they will cease to believe that all their troubles proceed from us.

I am quite aware they do not state their case precisely in

this way. Most of them would probably say to us, "Let us alone; do nothing to us, and say what you please about slavery." But we do let them alone—have never disturbed them—so that, after all, it is what we say which dissatisfies them. They will continue to accuse us of doing, until we cease saying.

I am also aware they have not as yet in terms demanded the overthrow of our Free-State constitutions. Yet those constitutions declare the wrong of slavery with more solemn emphasis than do all other sayings against it; and when all these other sayings shall have been silenced, the overthrow of these constitutions will be demanded, and nothing be left to resist the demand. It is nothing to the contrary that they do not demand the whole of this just now. Demanding what they do, and for the reason they do, they can voluntarily stop nowhere short of this consummation. Holding, as they do, that slavery is morally right and socially elevating, they cannot cease to demand a full national recognition of it as a legal right and a social blessing.

Nor can we justifiably withhold this on any ground save our conviction that slavery is wrong. If slavery is right, all words, acts, laws, and constitutions against it are themselves wrong, and should be silenced and swept away. If it is right, we cannot justly object to its nationality—its universality; if it is wrong, they cannot justly insist upon its extension—its enlargement. All they ask we could readily grant, if we thought slavery right; all we ask they could as readily grant, if they thought it wrong. Their thinking it right and our thinking it wrong is the precise fact upon which depends the whole controversy. Thinking it right, as they do, they are not to blame for desiring its full recognition as being right; but thinking it wrong, as we do, can we yield to them? Can we cast our votes with their view, and against our own? In view of our moral, social, and political responsibilities, can we do this?

Wrong as we think slavery is, we can yet afford to let it alone where it is, because that much is due to the necessity arising from its actual presence in the nation; but can we, while our votes will prevent it, allow it to spread into the national Territories, and to overrun us here in these free States? If our sense of duty forbids this, then let us stand by our duty fearlessly and effectively. Let us be diverted by none of those sophistical contrivances wherewith we are so industriously plied and belabored—contrivances such as groping for some middle ground between the right and the wrong: vain as the search for a man who should be neither a living man nor a dead man; such as a policy of "don't care" on a question about which all true men do care; such as Union appeals beseeching true Union men to yield to Disunionists, reversing the divine rule, and calling, not the sinners, but the righteous to repentance; such as invocations to Washington, imploring men to unsay what Washington said and undo what Washington did.

Neither let us be slandered from our duty by false accusations against us, nor frightened from it by menaces of destruction to the government, nor of dungeons to ourselves. Let us have faith that right makes might, and in that faith let us to the end dare to do our duty as we understand it.

FROM A SPEECH AT NEW HAVEN, CONN.

After his address at Cooper Union, Lincoln went on through New England to make a speaking tour there. At New Haven he delivered his celebrated statement approving of labor's right to strike.

March 6, 1860

ANOTHER specimen of this bushwhacking—that "shoe strike." Now be it understood that I do not pretend to know all about the matter. I am merely going to speculate a little about some of its phases, and at the outset I am glad to see that a system of labor prevails in New England under which laborers can strike when they want to, where they are not obliged to work under all circumstances, and are not tied down and obliged to labor whether you pay them or not! I like the system which lets a man quit when he wants to, and wish it might prevail everywhere. One of the reasons why I am opposed to slavery is just here. What is the true condition of the laborer? I take it that it is best for all to leave each man free to acquire property as fast as he can. Some will get wealthy. I don't believe in a law to prevent a man from getting rich; it would do more harm than good. So while we do not propose any war upon capital, we do wish to allow the humblest man an equal chance to get rich with everybody else. When one starts poor, as most do in the race of life, free society is such that he knows he can better his condition; he knows that there is no fixed condition of labor for his whole life. I am not ashamed to confess that twenty-five years ago I was a hired laborer, mauling rails, at work on a flatboat—just what might happen to any poor man's son. I want every man to have a chance—and I believe a black man is entitled to it—in which he can better his condition—when he may look forward and hope to be a hired laborer this year and the next, work for himself afterward, and finally to hire men to work for him. That is the true system. Up here in New England you have a soil that scarcely sprouts black-eyed beans, and yet where will you find wealthy men so wealthy, and poverty so rarely in extremity? There is not another such place on earth! I desire that if you get too thick here, and find it hard to better your condition on this soil, you may have a chance to strike and go somewhere else, where you may not be degraded, nor have your family corrupted by forced rivalry with Negro slaves. . . .

FROM A LETTER TO MARK W. DELAHAY

Delahay was a lawyer and a professional politician whom Lincoln had known in Illinois. He had gone to Kansas to live, and there Lincoln had met him again in December, 1859, while on a speaking tour. In this strange letter, Lincoln, after avowing that it is wrong to "enter the ring on the money basis," offers to furnish one hun-

dred dollars to Delahay to pay his expenses to the Republican Convention at Chicago so he could try to swing Kansas for Lincoln. The aftermath of this is interesting: Delahay was not appointed a delegate; Lincoln then offered him money to go as a ringside booster; after he became President, Lincoln made him Surveyor-General of Kansas and Nebraska; in 1863 he made him United States District Judge for Kansas—all this against the warnings of his friends that Delahay was corrupt, a drunkard and an incompetent person. In 1864, Delahay hastily resigned from his judgeship just as impeachment proceedings were being brought against him. Why Lincoln backed this man again and again has never been explained. The strange relationship is one of the unsolved mysteries of Lincoln's life.

Springfield, Ill., March 16, 1860

Dear Delahay: I have just returned from the East. . . . I sincerely wish you could be elected one of the first Senators from Kansas; but how to help you I do not know. If it were permissible for me to interfere, I am not personally acquainted with a single member of your Legislature. If my known friendship for you could be of any advantage, that friendship was abundantly manifested by me last December while in Kansas. . . .

As to your kind wishes for myself, allow me to say I can not enter the ring on the money basis—first, because, in the main, it is wrong; and secondly, I have not, and can not get, the money. I say, in the main, the use of money is wrong; but for certain objects, in a political contest, the use of some, is both right and indispensable. With me as with yourself, this long struggle has been one of great pecuniary loss. I now distinctly say this: If you shall be appointed a delegate to Chicago, I will furnish one hundred dollars to bear the expenses of the trip.

LETTER TO E. STAFFORD

Lincoln writes again on the money situation. He has not got, and could not raise, ten thousand dollars.

Springfield, Illinois, March 17, 1860

DEAR SIR: Reaching home on the 14th instant, I found yours of the 1st. Thanking you very sincerely for your kind purposes toward me, I am compelled to say the money part of the arrangement you propose is, with me, an impossibility. I could not raise ten thousand dollars if it would save me from the fate of John Brown. Nor have my friends, so far as I know, yet reached the point of staking any money on my chances of success. I wish I could tell you better things, but it is even so.

LETTER TO SAMUEL GALLOWAY

The prospective Republican Presidential nominee candidly appraises his own chances for election—if nominated.

Chicago, March 24, 1860

MY DEAR SIR: I am here attending a trial in court. Before leaving home I received your kind letter of the 15th. Of course I am gratified to know I have friends in Ohio who are disposed to give me the highest evidence of their friendship and confidence. Mr. Parrott, of the legislature, had written me to the same effect. If I have any chance, it consists mainly in the fact that the whole opposition would vote for me, if nominated. (I don't mean to include the pro-slavery opposition of the South, of course.) My name is new in the field, and I suppose I am not the first choice of a very great many. Our policy, then, is to give no offense to others—leave them in a mood to come to us if they shall be compelled to give up their first love. This, too, is dealing justly with all, and leaving us in a mood to support heartily whoever shall be nominated. . . .

LETTER TO C. F. McNEIL

Lincoln had been in Chicago attending court; he returned to find that he had been criticized in a newspaper article for accepting pay for delivering his Cooper Union address. He writes to a friend to explain.

Springfield, April 6, 1860

Dear Sir: Reaching home yesterday, I found yours of the 23d March, inclosing a slip from *The Middleport Press*. It is not true that I ever charged anything for a political speech in my life; but this much is true: Last October I was requested by letter to deliver some sort of speech in Mr. Beecher's church, in Brooklyn—two hundred dollars being offered in the first letter. I wrote that I could do it in February, provided they would take a political speech if I could find time to get up no other. They agreed; and subsequently I informed them the speech would have to be a political one. When I reached New York, I for the first time learned that the place was changed to "Cooper Institute."

I made the speech, and left for New Hampshire, where I have a son at school, neither asking for pay, nor having any offered me. Three days after, a check for two hundred dollars was sent to me at New Hampshire; and I took it, and did not know it was wrong. My understanding now is—though I knew nothing of it at the time—that they did charge for admittance to the Cooper Institute, and that they took in more than twice two hundred dollars.

I have made this explanation to you as a friend; but I wish

no explanation made to our enemies. What they want is a squabble and a fuss, and that they can have if we explain; and they cannot have it if we don't.

When I returned through New York from New England, I was told by the gentlemen who sent me the check that a drunken vagabond in the club, having learned something about the two hundred dollars, made the exhibition out of which the *Herald* manufactured the article quoted by the *Press* of your town.

My judgment is, and therefore my request is, that you give no denial and no explanation.

REPLY TO THE COMMITTEE SENT TO NOTIFY LINCOLN OF HIS NOMINATION FOR PRESIDENT

The incredible had happened. The obscure native son of Illinois had received the Republican nomination for President at the Chicago convention on May 18. On the next day, the official nominating committee arrived in Springfield to tell Lincoln what he already knew. They visited him at his home, calling on him during the evening, while a great crowd waited in the street, and bonfires were lighted to celebrate the event. This is Lincoln's verbal reply to the committee.

Springfield, Illinois, May 21, 1860

MR. CHAIRMAN AND GENTLEMEN OF THE COMMITTEE: I tender to you, and through you to the Republican National Convention, and all the people represented in it, my profoundest thanks for the high honor done me, which you now formally announce.

Deeply and even painfully sensible of the great responsibility which is inseparable from this high honor—a responsibility which I could almost wish had fallen upon some one of the far more eminent men and experienced statesmen whose distinguished names were before the convention—I shall, by your leave, consider more fully the resolutions of the convention, denominated the platform, and without any unnecessary or unreasonable delay respond to you, Mr. Chairman, in writing, not doubting that the platform will be found satisfactory, and the nomination gratefully accepted.

And now I will not longer defer the pleasure of taking you, and each of you, by the hand.

LETTER TO GEORGE ASHMUN AND THE REPUBLICAN NATIONAL CONVENTION

Lincoln writes his official letter of acceptance, addressing it to George Ashmun, president of the Chicago convention, a man to whom he was later to address the last bit of writing he ever penned (April 14, 1865).

Springfield, Illinois, May 23, 1860

Sir: I accept the nomination tendered me by the convention over which you presided, and of which I am formally apprised in the letter of yourself and others, acting as a committee of the convention for that purpose.

The declaration of principles and sentiments which accompanies your letter meets my approval; and it shall be my care not to violate or disregard it in any part.

Imploring the assistance of Divine Providence, and with due regard to the views and feelings of all who were represented in the convention—to the rights of all the States and Territories and people of the nation; to the inviolability of the Constitution; and the perpetual union, harmony, and prosperity of all—I am most happy to co-operate for the practical success of the principles declared by the convention.

LETTER TO SAMUEL HAYCRAFT

Now that Lincoln had become famous through his nomination to the Presidency, all sorts of people began writing to him about all sorts of things. Haycraft was the clerk of the court at Elizabethtown, Kentucky, and a man interested in preserving records of local history. Lincoln gives him some genealogical facts and begins a correspondence that was soon to cause him much trouble (see June 4, August 16 and August 23, 1860).

Springfield, Illinois, May 28, 1860

DEAR SIR: In the main you are right about my history. My father was Thomas Lincoln, and Mrs. Sally Johnston was his second wife. You are mistaken about my mother. Her maiden name was Nancy Hanks. I was not born at Elizabethtown, but my mother's first child, a daughter, two years older than myself, and now long since deceased, was. I was born February 12, 1809, near where Hogginsville [Hodgenville] now is, then in Hardin County. I do not think I ever saw you, though I very well know who you are—so well that I recognized your handwriting, on opening your letter, before I saw the signature. My recollection is that Ben Helm was first clerk, that you succeeded him, that Jack Thomas and William Farleigh graduated in the same office, and that your handwritings were all very similar. Am I right?

My father has been dead near ten years; but my step-mother, (Mrs. Johnston) is still living.

I am really very glad of your letter, and shall be pleased to receive another at any time.

AUTOBIOGRAPHICAL SKETCH
WRITTEN FOR USE IN PREPARING
A CAMPAIGN BIOGRAPHY

Demands for biographical information about the Republican nominee were increasing; campaign biographies had to be written, and more facts about Lincoln's life were needed. He writes here in the third person to give the necessary structure of personal data for such works. (See also letter to Samuel Galloway, June 19, 1860.)

June 1, 1860 (circa)

ABRAHAM LINCOLN was born February 12, 1809, then in Hardin, now in the more recently formed county of La Rue, Kentucky. His father, Thomas, and grandfather, Abraham, were born in Rockingham County, Virginia, whither their ancestors had come from Berks County, Pennsylvania. His lineage has been traced no farther back than this. The family were originally Quakers, though in later times they have fallen away from the peculiar habits of that people. The grandfather, Abraham, had four brothers—Isaac, Jacob, John, and Thomas. So far as known, the descendants of Jacob and John are still in Virginia. Isaac went to a place near where Virginia, North Carolina, and Tennessee join; and his descendants are in that region. Thomas came to Kentucky, and after many years died there, whence his descendants went to Missouri. Abraham, grandfather of the subject of this sketch, came to Kentucky, and was killed by Indians about the year 1784.* He left a widow, three sons, and two daughters. The eldest son, Mordecai, remained in Kentucky till late in life, when he removed to Hancock County, Illinois, where soon after he died, and where several of his descendants still remain. The second son, Josiah, removed at an early day to a place on Blue River, now

* 1786.

within Hancock County, Indiana, but no recent information of him or his family has been obtained. The eldest sister, Mary, married Ralph Crume, and some of her descendants are now known to be in Breckenridge County, Kentucky. The second sister, Nancy, married William Brumfield, and her family are not known to have left Kentucky, but there is no recent information from them. Thomas, the youngest son, and father of the present subject, by the early death of his father, and very narrow circumstances of his mother, even in childhood was a wandering labouring-boy, and grew up literally without education. He never did more in the way of writing than to bunglingly write his own name. Before he was grown he passed one year as a hired hand with his uncle Isaac on Watauga, a branch of the Holston River. Getting back into Kentucky, and having reached his twenty-eighth year, he married Nancy Hanks—mother of the present subject—in the year 1806. She also was born in Virginia, and relatives of hers of the name of Hanks, and of other names, now reside in Coles, in Macon, and in Adams counties, Illinois, and also in Iowa. The present subject has no brother or sister of the whole or half blood. He had a sister, older than himself, who was grown and married, but died many years ago, leaving no child; also a brother, younger than himself, who died in infancy. Before leaving Kentucky, he and his sister were sent, for short periods, to ABC schools, the first kept by Zachariah Riney, and the second by Caleb Hazel.

At this time his father resided on Knob Creek, on the road from Bardstown, Kentucky, to Nashville, Tennessee, at a point three or three and a half miles south or southwest of Atherton's Ferry, on the Rolling Fork. From this place he removed to what is now Spencer County, Indiana, in the autumn of 1816, Abraham then being in his eighth year. This removal was partly on account of slavery, but chiefly on account of the difficulty in land titles in Kentucky. He settled in an unbroken forest, and the clearing away of surplus wood was the great task ahead. Abraham, though very young, was large of his age, and had an ax put into his hands at once; and from that till within his twenty-third year he was almost constantly handling that most useful instrument—less, of course, in plowing and harvesting seasons. At this place Abraham took an early start as a hunter, which was never much improved afterward. A few days before the completion of his eighth year, in the absence of his father, a flock of wild turkeys approached the new log cabin, and Abraham with a rifle-gun, standing inside, shot through a crack and killed one of them. He has never since pulled a trigger on any larger game. In the autumn of 1818 his mother died; and a year afterward his father married Mrs. Sally Johnston, at Elizabethtown, Kentucky, a widow with three children of her first marriage. She proved a good and kind mother to Abraham, and is still living in Coles County, Illinois. There were no children of this second marriage. His father's residence continued at the same place in Indiana till 1830. While here Abraham went to ABC schools by littles, kept successively by Andrew Crawford, [William] Sweeney, and Azel W. Dorsey. He does not remember any other. The family of Mr. Dorsey now resides in Schuyler County, Illinois. Abraham now thinks that the aggregate of all his schooling did not amount to one year. He was never in a college or academy as a student, and never inside of a college or academy building till since he had a law license. What he has in the way of education he has picked up. After he was twenty-three and had separated from his father, he studied English grammar—imperfectly, of course, but so as to speak and write as well as he now does. He studied and nearly mastered the six books of Euclid since he was a member of Congress. He regrets his want of education, and does what he can to supply the want. In his tenth year he was kicked by a horse, and apparently killed for a time. When he was nineteen, still residing in Indiana, he made his first trip upon a flatboat to New Orleans. He was a hired hand merely, and he and a son of the owner, without other assistance, made the trip. The nature of part of the "cargo-load," as it was called, made it necessary for them to linger and trade along the sugar coast; and one night they were attacked by seven Negroes with intent to kill and rob them. They were hurt some in the melée, but succeeded in driving the Negroes from the boat, and then "cut cable," "weighed anchor," and left.

March 1, 1830, Abraham, having just completed his twenty-first year, his father and family, with the families of the two daughters and sons-in-law of his stepmother, left the old homestead in Indiana and came to Illinois. Their mode of conveyance was wagons drawn by ox-teams, and Abraham drove one of the teams. They reached the county of Macon, and stopped there some time within the same month of March. His father and family settled a new place on the north side of the Sangamon River, at the junction of the timberland and prairie, about ten miles westerly from Decatur. Here they built a log cabin, into which they removed, and made sufficient of rails to fence ten acres of ground, fenced and broke the ground, and raised a crop of sown corn upon it the same year. These are, or are supposed to be, the rails about which so much is being said just now,* though these are far from being the first or only rails ever made by Abraham.

The sons-in-law were temporarily settled in other places in the county. In the autumn all hands were greatly afflicted with ague and fever, to which they had not been used, and by which they were greatly discouraged, so much so that they determined on leaving the county. They remained, however, through the succeeding winter, which was the winter of the very celebrated "deep snow" of Illinois. During that winter Abraham, together with his stepmother's son, John D. Johnston, and John Hanks, yet residing in Macon County, hired

* At the Republican State Convention in Decatur on May 9, John Hanks had brought in two fence rails that Lincoln had split in 1830. They bore a placard reading: "Abraham Lincoln, The Rail Candidate for President in 1860."

themselves to Denton Offutt to take a flatboat from Beardstown, Illinois, to New Orleans; and for that purpose were to
join him—Offutt—at Springfield, Illinois, so soon as the snow
should go off. When it did go off, which was about the first
of March, 1831, the county was so flooded as to make traveling by land impracticable; to obviate which difficulty they purchased a large canoe, and came down the Sangamon River in
it. This is the time and the manner of Abraham's first entrance into Sangamon County. They found Offutt at Springfield, but learned from him that he had failed in getting a boat
at Beardstown. This led to their hiring themselves to him for
twelve dollars per month each, and getting the timber out of
the trees and building a boat at Old Sangamon town on the
Sangamon River, seven miles northwest of Springfield, which
boat they took to New Orleans, substantially upon the old
contract.

During this boat-enterprise acquaintance with Offutt, who
was previously an entire stranger, he conceived a liking for
Abraham, and believing he could turn him to account, he contracted with him to act as clerk for him, on his return from
New Orleans, in charge of a store and mill at New Salem, then
in Sangamon, now in Menard County. Hanks had not gone
to New Orleans, but having a family, and being likely to be
detained from home longer than at first expected, had turned
back from St. Louis. He is the same John Hanks who now
engineers the "rail enterprise" at Decatur, and is a first cousin
to Abraham's mother. Abraham's father, with his own family
and others mentioned, had, in pursuance of their intention,
removed from Macon to Coles County. John D. Johnston, the
stepmother's son, went to them, and Abraham stopped indefinitely and for the first time, as it were, by himself at New
Salem, before mentioned. This was in July, 1831. Here he
rapidly made acquaintances and friends. In less than a year
Offutt's business was failing—had almost failed—when the
Black Hawk war of 1832 broke out. Abraham joined a volun-

teer company, and, to his own surprise, was elected captain of it. He says he has not since had any success in life which gave him so much satisfaction. He went to the campaign, served near three months, met the ordinary hardships of such an expedition, but was in no battle. He now owns, in Iowa, the land upon which his own warrants for the service were located. Returning from the campaign, and encouraged by his great popularity among his immediate neighbors, he the same year ran for the legislature, and was beaten—his own precinct, however, casting its votes 277 for and 7 against him—and that, too, while he was an avowed Clay man, and the precinct the autumn afterward giving a majority of 115 to General Jackson over Mr. Clay. This was the only time Abraham was ever beaten on a direct vote of the people.

He was now without means and out of business, but was anxious to remain with his friends who had treated him with so much generosity, especially as he had nothing elsewhere to go to. He studied what he should do—thought of learning the blacksmith trade—thought of trying to study law—rather thought he could not succeed at that without a better education. Before long, strangely enough, a man offered to sell, and did sell, to Abraham and another as poor as himself, an old stock of goods, upon credit. They opened as merchants; and he says that was *the* store. Of course they did nothing but get deeper and deeper in debt. He was appointed postmaster at New Salem—the office being too insignificant to make his politics an objection. The store winked out. The surveyor of Sangamon offered to depute to Abraham that portion of his work which was within his part of the county. He accepted, procured a compass and chain, studied Flint and Gibson a little, and went at it. This procured bread, and kept soul and body together. The election of 1834 came, and he was then elected to the legislature by the highest vote cast for any candidate. Major John T. Stuart, then in full practice of the law, was also elected. During the canvass, in a private conversation he encouraged Abraham [to] study law. After the election he borrowed books of Stuart, took them home with him, and went at it in good earnest. He studied with nobody. He still mixed in the surveying to pay board and clothing bills. When the legislature met, the law-books were dropped, but were taken up again at the end of the session. He was re-elected in 1836, 1838, and 1840. In the autumn of 1836 he obtained a law license, and on April 15, 1837, removed to Springfield, and commenced the practice—his old friend Stuart taking him into partnership. March 3, 1837, by a protest entered upon the *Illinois House Journal* of that date, at pages 817 and 818, Abraham, with Dan Stone, another representative of Sangamon, briefly defined his position on the slavery question; and so far as it goes, it was then the same that it is now. The protest is as follows:

Resolutions upon the subject of domestic slavery having passed both branches of the General Assembly at its present session, the undersigned hereby protest against the passage of the same.

They believe that the institution of slavery is founded on both injustice and bad policy, but that the promulgation of Abolition doctrines tends rather to increase than abate its evils.

They believe that the Congress of the United States has no power under the Constitution to interfere with the institution of slavery in the different States.

They believe that the Congress of the United States has the power, under the Constitution, to abolish slavery in the District of Columbia, but that the power ought not to be exercised unless at the request of the people of the District.

The difference between these opinions and those contained in the above resolutions is their reason for entering this protest.

DAN STONE,

A. LINCOLN,

Representatives from the County of Sangamon.

In 1838 and 1840, Mr. Lincoln's party voted for him as Speaker, but being in the minority he was not elected. After

1840 he declined a reëlection to the legislature. He was on the Harrison electoral ticket in 1840, and on that of Clay in 1844, and spent much time and labor in both those canvasses. In November, 1842, he was married to Mary, daughter of Robert S. Todd, of Lexington, Kentucky. They have three living children, all sons, one born in 1843, one in 1850, and one in 1853. They lost one, who was born in 1846.

In 1846 he was elected to the lower House of Congress, and served one term only, commencing in December, 1847, and ending with the inauguration of General Taylor, in March, 1849. All the battles of the Mexican war had been fought before Mr. Lincoln took his seat in Congress, but the American army was still in Mexico, and the treaty of peace was not fully and formally ratified till the June afterward. Much has been said of his course in Congress in regard to this war. A careful examination of the *Journal* and *Congressional Globe* shows that he voted for all the supply measures that came up, and for all the measures in any way favorable to the officers, soldiers, and their families, who conducted the war through: with the exception that some of these measures passed without yeas and nays, leaving no record as to how particular men voted. The *Journal* and *Globe* also show him voting that the war was unnecessarily and unconstitutionally begun by the President of the United States. This is the language of Mr. Ashmun's amendment, for which Mr. Lincoln and nearly or quite all other Whigs of the House of Representatives voted.

Mr. Lincoln's reasons for the opinion expressed by this vote were briefly that the President had sent General Taylor into an inhabited part of the country belonging to Mexico, and not to the United States, and thereby had provoked the first act of hostility, in fact the commencement of the war; that the place, being the country bordering on the east bank of the Rio Grande, was inhabited by native Mexicans, born there under the Mexican government, and had never submitted to, nor been conquered by, Texas or the United States, nor transferred to either by treaty; that although Texas claimed the Rio Grande as her boundary, Mexico had never recognized it, and neither Texas nor the United States had ever enforced it; that there was a broad desert between that and the country over which Texas had actual control; that the country where hostilities commenced, having once belonged to Mexico, must remain so until it was somehow legally transferred, which had never been done.

Mr. Lincoln thought the act of sending an armed force among the Mexicans was unnecessary, inasmuch as Mexico was in no way molesting or menacing the United States or the people thereof; and that it was unconstitutional, because the power of levying war is vested in Congress, and not in the President. He thought the principal motive for the act was to divert public attention from the surrender of "Fifty-four, forty, or fight" to Great Britain, on the Oregon boundary question.

Mr. Lincoln was not a candidate for reëlection. This was determined upon and declared before he went to Washington, in accordance with an understanding among Whig friends, by which Colonel Hardin and Colonel Baker had each previously served a single term in this same district.

In 1848, during his term in Congress, he advocated General Taylor's nomination for the presidency, in opposition to all others, and also took an active part for his election after his nomination, speaking a few times in Maryland, near Washington, several times in Massachusetts, and canvassing quite fully his own district in Illinois, which was followed by a majority in the district of over 1,500 for General Taylor.

Upon his return from Congress he went to the practice of the law with greater earnestness than ever before. In 1852 he was upon the Scott electoral ticket, and did something in the way of canvassing, but owing to the hopelessness of the cause in Illinois he did less than in previous presidential canvasses.

In 1854 his profession had almost superseded the thought of politics in his mind, when the repeal of the Missouri Compromise aroused him as he had never been before.

In the autumn of that year he took the stump with no broader practical aim or object than to secure, if possible, the reëlection of Hon. Richard Yates to Congress. His speeches at once attracted a more marked attention than they had ever before done. As the canvass proceeded he was drawn to different parts of the State outside of Mr. Yates's district. He did not abandon the law, but gave his attention by turns to that and politics. The State agricultural fair was at Springfield that year, and Douglas was announced to speak there.

In the canvass of 1856 Mr. Lincoln made over fifty speeches, no one of which, so far as he remembers, was put in print. One of them was made at Galena, but Mr. Lincoln has no recollection of any part of it being printed; nor does he remember whether in that speech he said anything about a Supreme Court decision. He may have spoken upon that subject, and some of the newspapers may have reported him as saying what is now ascribed to him; but he thinks he could not have expressed himself as represented.

LETTER TO F. A. WOOD

Lincoln's fame was growing—here is tangible evidence of it. This is only one of many such requests sent to the Republican nominee at this time.

Springfield, Illinois, June 1, 1860

DEAR SIR: Yours of May 24th is received. You say you are not a Lincoln man; "but still would like to have Mr. L's autograph." Well, here it is.

Yours with respect

A. LINCOLN

LETTER TO SAMUEL HAYCRAFT

(Private)

Again Lincoln writes to the clerk of the court in Elizabethtown, Kentucky, to give him more biographical and family information, but in this letter Lincoln is incautious enough to say that he was afraid he might be lynched if he visited Kentucky. This was one of those careless slips that every public figure makes at least once and has cause to regret. Word of this reached the newspapers—they immediately seized upon it and used it against Lincoln.

Springfield, Illinois, June 4, 1860

DEAR SIR: Your second letter, dated May 31st, is received. You suggest that a visit to the place of my nativity might be pleasant to me. Indeed it would. But would it be safe? Would not the people lynch me?

The place on Knob Creek, mentioned by Mr. Read, I remember very well; but I was not born there. As my parents have told me, I was born on Nolin, very much nearer Hodgen's Mill than the Knob Creek place is. My earliest recollection, however, is of the Knob Creek place. Like you, I belonged to the Whig party from its origin to its close. I never belonged to the American party organization*; nor ever to a party called a Union party, though I hope I neither am, nor ever have been, less devoted to the Union than yourself or any other patriotic man.

It may not be altogether without interest to let you know that my wife is a daughter of the late Robert S. Todd, of Lexington, Ky., and that a half-sister of hers is the wife of Ben Hardin Helm, born and raised at your town, but residing at Louisville now, as I believe.

* The Know-Nothings.

LETTER TO SAMUEL GALLOWAY

(Especially confidential)

Book publishers rushed through hastily compiled biographies of Lincoln to be used for campaign purposes. Among these was one by William Dean Howells, which was announced for publication in June, but was delayed. The publishers, much to Lincoln's annoyance, indicated that he had authorized its writing, which, of course, he had not done. He writes here to Galloway to explain the whole matter. Howells' book was finally issued on July 26; during the summer Lincoln corrected a copy of it. A reprint of this corrected copy has recently been issued by The Abraham Lincoln Association of Springfield, Ill.

Springfield, Illinois, June 19, 1860

My Dear Sir: Your very kind letter of the 15th is received. Messrs. Follet, Foster & Co.'s *Life* of me is *not* by my authority; and I have scarcely been so much astounded by anything, as their public announcement that it is authorized by me. They have fallen into some strange misunderstanding. I certainly knew they contemplated publishing a biography, and I certainly did not object to their doing so, upon *their own responsibility*. I even took pains to facilitate them. But, at the same time, I made myself tiresome, if not hoarse, with repeating to Mr. Howard, their only agent seen by me, my protest that I *authorized nothing*—would be *responsible for nothing*. How they could so misunderstand me, passes comprehension. As a matter, *wholly my own*, I would authorize no biography, without *time* and *opportunity* to carefully examine and consider every word of it; and, in this case, in the nature of things, I can have no such time and opportunity. But, in my present position, when, by the lessons of the past, and the united voice of all discreet friends, I can neither write nor speak a word for the public, how dare I to send forth, by my authority, a volume of hundreds of pages, for adversaries to make points upon without end? Were I to do so, the Convention would have a right to re-assemble, and substitute another name for mine.

For these reasons, I would not look at the proof sheets. I am determined to maintain the position of truly saying I never saw the proof sheets, or any part of their work, before its publication.

Now, do not mistake me. I feel great kindness for Messrs. F., F. & Co.—do not think they have intentionally done wrong. There may be nothing wrong in their proposed book. I sincerely hope there will not. I barely suggest that you, or any of the friends there, on the party account, look it over, and exclude what you may think would embarrass the party, bearing in mind, at all times, that *I authorize nothing—will be responsible for nothing.*

LETTER TO A. G. HENRY

Dr. A. G. Henry, Lincoln's friend and former personal physician, had left Springfield and gone to Oregon to live. Lincoln now writes him there, giving him his interpretation of the political set-up against him. The son alluded to as being in his tenth year was Willie Lincoln.

Springfield, Illinois, July 4, 1860

My Dear Doctor: Your very agreeable letter of May 15th was received three days ago. We are just now receiving the first sprinkling of your Oregon election returns—not enough, I think, to indicate the result. We should be too happy if both Logan and Baker should triumph.

Long before this you have learned who was nominated at

Chicago. We know not what a day may bring forth, but today it looks as if the Chicago ticket will be elected. I think the chances were more than equal that we could have beaten the Democracy united. Divided as it is, its chance appears indeed very slim. But great is Democracy in resources; and it may yet give its fortunes a turn. It is under great temptation to do something; but what can it do which was not thought of, and found impracticable, at Charleston and Baltimore? The signs now are that Douglas and Breckinridge will each have a ticket in every State. They are driven to this to keep up their bombastic claims of nationality, and to avoid the charge of sectionalism which they have so much lavished upon us.

It is an amusing fact, after all Douglas has said about nationality and sectionalism, that I had more votes from the southern section at Chicago than he had at Baltimore. In fact, there was more of the southern section represented at Chicago than in the Douglas rump concern at Baltimore!

Our boy, in his tenth year (the baby when you left), has just had a hard and tedious spell of scarlet fever, and he is not yet beyond all danger. I have a headache and a sore throat upon me now, inducing me to suspect that I have an inferior type of the same thing.

Our eldest boy, Bob, has been away from us nearly a year at school, and will enter Harvard University this month. He promises very well, considering we never controlled him much. Write again when you receive this. Mary joins in sending our kindest regards to Mrs. H., yourself, and all the family.

LETTER TO HANNIBAL HAMLIN

Lincoln writes to introduce himself to the man who had been nominated as Vice President on the same ticket with him. They first met in Chicago after their election in November.

Springfield, Illinois, July 18, 1860

My Dear Sir: It appears to me that you and I ought to be acquainted, and accordingly I write this as a sort of introduction of myself to you. You first entered the Senate during the single term I was a member of the House of Representatives, but I have no recollection that we were introduced. I shall be pleased to receive a line from you.

The prospect of Republican success now appears very flattering, so far as I can perceive. Do you see anything to the contrary?

LETTER TO A. JONAS

(Confidential)

Abraham Jonas, an English-born Jew living in Quincy, Ill., was one of Lincoln's best friends. He writes to him to deny that he had ever had any connection with the Know-Nothings who were violently opposed to all foreigners, Jews and Catholics. Lincoln wishes the whole matter to remain quiet since many of the Know-Nothings (who also called themselves "the Americans") had joined the Republican party, and he was afraid of losing their support.

Springfield, Illinois, July 21, 1860

My Dear Sir: Yours of the 20th is received. I suppose as good or even better men than I may have been in American or Know-Nothing lodges; but, in point of fact, I never was in one at Quincy or elsewhere. I was never in Quincy but one day and two nights while Know-Nothing lodges were in existence, and you were with me that day and both those nights. I had never been there before in my life, and never afterward, till the joint debate with Douglas in 1858. It was in 1854 when I spoke in some hall there, and after the speaking, you, with others, took me to an oyster-saloon, passed an hour there, and you walked with me to, and parted with me at, the Quincy House, quite late at night. I left by stage for Naples before daylight in the morning, having come in by the same route after dark the evening previous to the speaking, when I found you waiting at the Quincy House to meet me. A few days after I was there, Richardson, as I understood, started this same story about my having been in a Know-Nothing lodge. When I heard of the charge as I did soon after, I taxed my recollection for some incident which could have suggested it; and I remembered that on parting with you the last night, I went to the office of the hotel to take my stage-passage for the morning, was told that no stage-office for that line was kept there, and that I must see the driver before retiring, to insure his calling for me in the morning; and a servant was sent with me to find the driver, who, after taking me a square or two, stopped me, and stepped perhaps a dozen steps farther, and in my hearing called to some one, who answered him, apparently from the upper part of a building, and promised to call with the stage for me at the Quincy House. I returned, and went to bed, and before day the stage called and took me. This is all.

That I never was in a Know-Nothing lodge in Quincy, I should expect could be easily proved by respectable men who were always in the lodges and never saw me there. An affidavit of one or two such would put the matter at rest.

And now a word of caution. Our adversaries think they can gain a point if they could force me to openly deny the charge, by which some degree of offense would be given to the Americans. For this reason it must not publicly appear that I am paying any attention to the charge.

LETTER TO SAMUEL HAYCRAFT

There is reason to believe that Lincoln himself had been incautious enough to tell a newspaper correspondent that he had said he was afraid he would be lynched if he went to Kentucky. The New York Herald seized upon the item and gave it wide publicity—much to Lincoln's embarrassment. Lincoln writes to Haycraft to cover himself lest the news be spread in Kentucky.

Springfield, Illinois, August 16, 1860

MY DEAR SIR: A correspondent of the *New York Herald*, who was here a week ago, writing to that paper, represents me as saying I had been invited to visit Kentucky, but that I suspected it was a trap to inveigle me into Kentucky in order to do violence to me. This is wholly a mistake. I said no such thing. I do not remember, but possibly I did mention my correspondence with you. But very certainly I was not guilty of stating, or insinuating, a suspicion of any intended violence, deception or other wrong, against me, by you or any other Kentuckian. Thinking the *Herald* correspondence might fall under your eye, I think it due to myself to enter my protest against the correctness of this part of it. I scarcely think the correspondent was malicious, but rather that he misunderstood what was said.

LETTER TO SAMUEL HAYCRAFT

Lincoln writes to explain that Haycraft was in no way to blame for what had happened.

Springfield, Illinois, August 23, 1860

MY DEAR SIR: Yours of the 19th just received. I now fear I may have given you some uneasiness by my last letter. I did not mean to intimate that I had, to any extent, been involved or embarrassed by you; nor yet to draw from you anything to relieve myself from difficulty. My only object was to assure you that I had not, as represented by the *Herald* correspondent, charged you with an attempt to inveigle me into Kentucky to do me violence. I believe no such thing of you or of Kentuckians generally; and I dislike to be represented to them as slandering them in that way.

LETTER TO JOHN HANKS

John Hanks was a relative of Lincoln's mother. He had been with Lincoln in Indiana, had helped him build a boat for Offut in 1831, and at the Decatur convention on May 9, 1860, had brought in the rail fences that had made Lincoln famous as the "Rail-splitter Candidate." Lincoln writes to him to answer a query about the family.

Springfield, Illinois, August 24, 1860

My Dear Sir: Yours of the 23rd is received. My recollection is that I never lived in the same neighborhood with Charles Hanks till I came to Macon county, Illinois, after I was twenty-one years of age. As I understand, he and I were born in different counties of Kentucky, and never saw each other in that State; that while I was a very small boy my father moved to Indiana, and your father with his family remained in Kentucky for many years. At length you, a young man grown, came to our neighborhood, and were at our house, off and on, a great deal for three, four, or five years; and during the time, your father, with his whole family, except William, Charles, and William Miller, who had married one of your sisters, came to the same neighborhood in Indiana, and remained a year or two, and then went to Illinois. William, Charles, and William Miller, had moved directly from Kentucky to Illinois, not even passing through our neighborhood in Indiana. Once, a year or two before I came to Illinois,

Charles, with some others, had been back to Kentucky, and returning to Illinois, passed through our neighborhood in Indiana. He stopped, I think, but one day (certainly not as much as three); and this was the first time I ever saw him in my life, and the *only* time, till I came to Illinois, as before stated. The year I passed in Macon County I was with him a good deal—mostly on his own place, where I helped him at breaking prairie, with a joint team of his and ours, which in turn, broke some on the new place we were improving.

This is, as I remember it. Don't let this letter be made public by any means.

LETTER TO ANSON G. CHESTER

(Private)

In the rough-and-tumble politics of the sixties it was not unusual to invent and even to forge documents that would discredit an opponent. Lincoln nails the lie to one of these—a forgery which stated that he had once slandered Thomas Jefferson.

Springfield, Illinois, September 5, 1860

My Dear Sir: Yours of the 1st is received. The extract upon a newspaper slip which you sent, and which I herewith return, is a base forgery, so far as its authorship is imputed to me. I never said anything like it, at any time or place. I do not recognize it as anything I have ever seen before, emanating from any source. I wish my name not to be used; but my friends will be entirely safe in denouncing the thing as a forgery, so far as it is ascribed to me.

(The Clipping)

Lincoln on Jefferson.—The Macomb (Ill.) *Eagle* rakes up the following extract from a speech made by Mr. Lincoln in 1844:

"Mr. Jefferson is a statesman whose praises are never out of the mouth of the democratic party. Let us attend to this uncompromising friend of freedom, whose name is continually invoked against the Whig party. The character of Jefferson was repulsive. Continually puling about liberty, equality, and the degrading curse of slavery, he brought his own children to the hammer, and made money of his debaucheries. Even at his death he did not manumit his numerous offspring, but left them, soul and body, to degradation, and the cart whip. A daughter of this vaunted champion of democracy was sold some years ago at public auction in New Orleans, and purchased by a society of gentlemen, who wished to testify by her liberation their admiration of the statesman who

'Dreampt of freedom in a slave's embrace.'

"This single line I have quoted gives more insight to the character of the man than whole volumes of panegyric. It will outlive his epitaph, write it who may."

LETTER TO NATHANIEL GRIGSBY

Nathaniel Grigsby was the brother of Aaron, whom Lincoln's sister had married in 1826. She died in childbirth shortly afterwards. Part of the Grigsby family had moved to Missouri, and Lincoln writes to Nathaniel there.

Springfield, Illinois, September 20, 1860

MY DEAR SIR: Your letter of July 19th was received only a few days ago having been mailed by your brother at Gentryville, Ind., on the 12th of the month. A few days ago, Gov. Wood of Quincy told me he saw you, and that you said you had written me. I had not then received your letter.

Of our three families who removed from Indiana together, my father, Squire Hall, and John D. Johnston, are dead, and all the rest of us are yet living, of course the younger ones are grown up, marriages contracted and new ones born. I have three boys now, the oldest of which is seventeen years of age.

There is now a Republican electoral ticket in Missouri, so that you can vote for me if your neighbors will let you. I would advise you not to get into any trouble about it. Give my kindest regards to your brother Charlie. Within the present year I have had two letters from John Gorden, who is living somewhere in Missouri, I forget exactly where, and he says his father and mother are still living near him.

LETTER TO MRS. M. J. GREEN

Lincoln admits that he had never had much to do with ladies—not even to write to them.

Springfield, Illinois, September 22, 1860

MY DEAR MADAM: Your kind congratulatory letter, of August, was received in due course, and should have been answered sooner. The truth is I have never corresponded much with ladies; and hence I postpone writing letters to them, as a business which I do not understand. I can only say now I thank you for the good opinion you express of me, fearing, at the same time, I may not be able to maintain it through life.

LETTER TO MISS GRACE BEDELL

(Private)

A little girl in Westfield, New York, had written to the President-elect to suggest that he let his whiskers grow so as to appear more dignified for his new position. He writes to tell her about his family, and he queries the whiskers suggestion. When the train bearing him to Washington as President-elect stopped for a moment at Westfield, Lincoln asked for Grace Bedell. She was brought to the train and there was kissed by the newly whiskered man.

Springfield, Illinois, October 19, 1860

MY DEAR LITTLE MISS: Your very agreeable letter of the 15th is received. I regret the necessity of saying I have no daughter. I have three sons—one seventeen, one nine, and one seven years of age. They, with their mother, constitute my whole family. As to the whiskers, having never worn any, do you not think people would call it a piece of silly affectation if I were to begin it now?

LETTER TO MAJOR DAVID HUNTER

(*Private and confidential*)

As election day approached, it became more and more evident that the South was determined to resist forcibly the election of a Republican President. For months Southern sympathizers in important Federal offices had been shipping arms and war material from Northern armories and arsenals to Southern ones. Threats of secession were made openly and, as is indicated in this letter, army officers of Southern birth were announcing their intention to desert. Lincoln here writes to Hunter asking for confirmation of such rumors.

Springfield, Illinois, October 26, 1860

MY DEAR SIR: Your very kind letter of the 20th was duly received, for which please accept my thanks. I have another letter, from a writer unknown to me, saying the officers of the army at Fort Kearny have determined, in case of Republican success at the approaching Presidential election, to take themselves, and the arms at that point, South, for the purpose of resistance to the government. While I think there are many chances to one that this is a humbug, it occurs to me that any real movement of this sort in the army would leak out and become known to you. In such case, if it would not be un-professional or dishonorable (of which you are to be judge), I shall be much obliged if you will apprise me of it.

LETTER TO GEORGE D. PRENTICE

(Private and confidential)

Lincoln writes to George D. Prentice, editor of the Louisville Journal, to assure him that his conservative views had been expressed again and again in the Republican platform and in his debates with Douglas which had been printed in book form. On the original of this letter an endorsement in Lincoln's handwriting appears on the back: "(Confidential). The within letter was written on the day of its date, and on reflection withheld till now. It expresses the views I still entertain."

Springfield, Illinois, October 29, 1860

MY DEAR SIR: Yours of the 26th is just received. Your suggestion that I in a certain event shall write a letter setting forth my conservative views and intentions is certainly a very worthy one. But would it do any good? If I were to labor a month I could not express my conservative views and intentions more clearly and strongly than they are expressed in our platform and in my many speeches already in print and before the public. And yet even you, who do occasionally speak of me in terms of personal kindness, give no prominence to these oft-repeated expressions of conservative views and intentions, but busy yourself with appeals to all conservative men to vote for Douglas—to vote any way which can possibly defeat me—thus impressing your readers that you think I am the very worst man living. If what I have already said has failed to convince you, no repetition of it would convince you. The writing of your letter, now before me, gives assurance that you would publish such a letter from me as you suggest; but, till now, what reason had I to suppose the *Louisville Journal*, even, would publish a repetition of that which is already at its command, and which it does not press upon the public attention?

And now, my friend—for such I esteem you personally—do not misunderstand me. I have not decided that I will not do substantially what you suggest. I will not forbear from doing so merely on punctilio and pluck. If I do finally abstain, it will be because of apprehension that it would do harm. For the good men of the South—and I regard the majority of them as such—I have no objection to repeat seventy and seven times. But I have bad men to deal with, both North and South; men who are eager for something new upon which to base new misrepresentations; men who would like to frighten me, or at least to fix upon me the character of timidity and cowardice. They would seize upon almost any letter I could write as being an "awful coming down." I intend keeping my eye upon these gentlemen, and to not unnecessarily put any weapons in their hands.

LETTER TO HANNIBAL HAMLIN

(Confidential)

On November 6, Abraham Lincoln had been elected President of the United States, and on the same ticket with him, Hannibal Hamlin had been elected Vice President. The two men had never met. Lincoln writes to arrange an interview with Hamlin in Chicago.

Springfield, Illinois, November 8, 1860

My Dear Sir: I am anxious for a personal interview with you at as early a day as possible. Can you, without much inconvenience, meet me at Chicago? If you can, please name as early a day as you conveniently can, and telegraph me, unless there be sufficient time before the day named to communicate by mail.

LETTER TO TRUMAN SMITH

Lincoln was determined to make no statements of policy during the dangerous period between his election and his inauguration. He explains here his reasons for maintaining this attitude. The financial depression to which he refers was caused by the fact that trade between the North and the South had come to a standstill.

(Private and confidential)

Springfield, Illinois, November 10, 1860

My Dear Sir: This is intended as a strictly private letter to you. . . . It is with the most profound appreciation of your motive, and highest respect for your judgment, too, that I feel constrained, for the present at least, to make no declaration for the public.

First. I could say nothing which I have not already said, and which is in print, and open for the inspection of all. To press a repetition of this upon those who have listened, is useless; to press it upon those who have refused to listen, and still refuse, would be wanting in self-respect, and would have an appearance of sycophancy and timidity which would excite the contempt of good men and encourage bad ones to clamor the more loudly.

I am not insensible to any commercial or financial depression that may exist, but nothing is to be gained by fawning around the "respectable scoundrels" who got it up. Let them go to work and repair the mischief of their own making, and then perhaps they will be less greedy to do the like again.

LETTER TO JOSHUA SPEED

After a long silence, Lincoln renews his correspondence with his old friend Joshua Speed, and writes to suggest that Speed meet him in Chicago where he was going to confer with Hannibal Hamlin.

Springfield, Illinois, November 19, 1860

DEAR SPEED: Yours of the 14th is received. I shall be at Chicago Thursday the 22nd. Inst, and one or two succeeding days. Could you not meet me there?

Mary thinks of going with me; and therefore I suggest that Mrs. S. accompany you.

Please let this be private, as I prefer a very great crowd should not gather at Chicago.

Respects to Mrs. S.

Your friend, as ever,

A. LINCOLN

LETTERS TO W. H. SEWARD

These two letters, one of which is a formal message informing Seward that he is to be appointed Secretary of State, and the other an informal letter graciously assuring Seward of the sincerity of Lincoln's intentions, were not sent directly to Seward. Lincoln cautiously forwarded them to Hannibal Hamlin with a covering note which said: "Consult with Judge Trumbull; and if you and he see no reason to the contrary, deliver the letter to Governor Seward at once. If you see reason to the contrary, write me at once."

Springfield, Illinois, December 8, 1860

MY DEAR SIR: With your permission I shall at the proper time nominate you to the Senate for confirmation as Secretary of State for the United States. Please let me hear from you at your own earliest convenience.

(Private and confidential)

Springfield, Illinois, December 8, 1860

My Dear Sir: In addition to the accompanying and more formal note inviting you to take charge of the State Department, I deem it proper to address you this. Rumors have got into the newspapers to the effect that the department named above would be tendered you as a compliment, and with the expectation that you would decline it. I beg you to be assured that I have said nothing to justify these rumors. On the contrary, it has been my purpose, from the day of the nomination at Chicago, to assign you, by your leave, this place in the administration. I have delayed so long to communicate that purpose in deference to what appeared to me a proper caution in the case. Nothing has been developed to change my view in the premises; and I now offer you the place in the hope that you will accept it, and with the belief that your position in the public eye, your integrity, ability, learning, and great experience, all combine to render it an appointment preëminently fit to be made.

One word more. In regard to the patronage sought with so much eagerness and jealousy, I have prescribed for myself the maxim, "Justice to all"; and I earnestly beseech your coöperation in keeping the maxim good.

LETTER TO LYMAN TRUMBULL

(Private and confidential)

Talk of arriving at a last-minute compromise with the South reached its height during December, 1860. The President-elect, however, was firmly determined to allow no compromise on the matter of extending slavery from the states in which it already existed to new territories. He writes here to Trumbull to state his position and points out the still-present danger of popular sovereignty being used as an opening wedge to extend slavery.

Springfield, Illinois, December 10, 1860

MY DEAR SIR: Let there be no compromise on the question of extending slavery. If there be, all our labor is lost, and, ere long, must be done again. The dangerous ground—that into which some of our friends have a hankering to run—is Pop. Sov. Have none of it. Stand firm. The tug has to come, and better now than any time hereafter.

LETTER TO E. B. WASHBURNE

In a brief letter which comes directly to the point, Lincoln writes to E. B. Washburne, Illinois Congressman, to tell him to stand firm on the matter of compromise. Eli Thayer was a Massachusetts abolitionist who had organized the Emigrant Aid Society to send anti-slavery settlers into Kansas. In 1860 he was working with Horace Greeley to establish what he called "real popular sovereignty."

(Private and confidential)

Springfield, Illinois, December 13, 1860

MY DEAR SIR: Yours of the 10th is received. Prevent, as far as possible, any of our friends from demoralizing themselves and our cause by entertaining propositions for compromise of any sort on "slavery extension." There is no possible compromise upon it but which puts us under again, and leaves all our work to do over again. Whether it be a Missouri line or Eli Thayer's popular sovereignty, it is all the same. Let either be done, and immediately filibustering and extending slavery recommences. On that point hold firm, as with a chain of steel.

LETTER TO JOHN A. GILMER

Lincoln had been desperately seeking a prominent Southerner to serve in his Cabinet. He had seriously considered John A. Gilmer, Congressman from North Carolina, as his Secretary of the Treasury. He writes to him to explain his own position on slavery in the most conciliatory terms possible.

(Strictly confidential)

Springfield, Illinois, December 15, 1860

MY DEAR SIR: Yours of the 10th is received. I am greatly disinclined to write a letter on the subject embraced in yours; and I would not do so, even privately as I do, were it not that I fear you might misconstrue my silence. Is it desired that I shall shift the ground upon which I have been elected? I cannot do it. You need only to acquaint yourself with that ground, and press it on the attention of the South. It is all in print and easy of access.

May I be pardoned if I ask whether even you have ever attempted to procure the reading of the Republican platform, or my speeches, by the Southern people? If not, what reason have I to expect that any additional production of mine would meet a better fate? It would make me appear as if I repented for the crime of having been elected, and was anxious to apologize and beg forgiveness. To so represent me would be the principal use made of any letter I might now thrust upon the public. My old record cannot be so used; and that is precisely the reason that some new declaration is so much sought.

Now, my dear sir, be assured that I am not questioning your candor; I am only pointing out that while a new letter would hurt the cause which I think a just one, you can quite as well effect every patriotic object with the old record. Carefully read pages 18, 19, 74, 75, 88, 89, and 267 of the volume of joint debates between Senator Douglas and myself, with the Republican platform adopted at Chicago, and all your questions will be substantially answered. I have no thought of recommending the abolition of slavery in the District of Columbia, nor the slave trade among the slave States, even on the conditions indicated; and if I were to make such recommendation, it is quite clear Congress would not follow it.

As to employing slaves in arsenals and dockyards, it is a thing I never thought of in my recollection, till I saw your letter; and I may say of it precisely as I have said of the two points above.

As to the use of patronage in the slave States, where there are few or no Republicans, I do not expect to inquire for the politics of the appointee, or whether he does or not own slaves. I intend in that matter to accommodate the people in the several localities, if they themselves will allow me to accommodate them. In one word, I never have been, am not now, and probably never shall be in a mood of harassing the people either North or South.

On the territorial question I am inflexible, as you see my position in the book.* On that there is a difference between you and us; and it is the only substantial difference. You think slavery is right and ought to be extended; we think it is wrong and ought to be restricted. For this neither has any just occasion to be angry with the other.

As to the State laws, mentioned in your sixth question, I really know very little of them. I never have read one. If any

* The book containing the Lincoln-Douglas debates.

of them are in conflict with the fugitive-slave clause, or any other part of the Constitution, I certainly shall be glad of their repeal; but I could hardly be justified, as a citizen of Illinois, or as President of the United States, to recommend the repeal of a statute of Vermont or South Carolina.

LETTER TO THURLOW WEED

Thurlow Weed was Seward's political adviser and boss of the New York Republican machine. Lincoln writes to him to explain his own attitude on the matter of compromise. Weed arrived in Springfield on December 20 to discuss compromise in detail. On December 20, news of South Carolina's secession reached Springfield. Nevertheless, Lincoln stood firm against any compromise that would permit slavery to be extended into new territory.

Springfield, Illinois, December 17, 1860

MY DEAR SIR: Yours of the 11th was received two days ago. Should the convocation of governors of which you speak seem desirous to know my views on the present aspect of things tell them you judge from my speeches that I will be inflexible on the territorial question; that I probably think either the Missouri line exended, or Douglas's and Eli Thayer's popular sovereignty, would lose us everything we gain by the election; that filibustering for all south of us and making slave States of it would follow, in spite of us, in either case; also that I probably think all opposition, real and apparent, to the fugitive-slave clause of the Constitution ought to be withdrawn.

I believe you can pretend to find but little, if anything, in my speeches about secession. But my opinion is, that no State can in any way lawfully get out of the Union without the consent of the others; and that it is the duty of the President and other government functionaries to run the machine as it is.

LETTER TO LYMAN TRUMBULL

When Weed left Springfield he took with him three resolutions on compromise which Lincoln had put down in his own handwriting. These resolutions, unfortunately, have been either lost or destroyed. Lincoln writes to Trumbull to inform him about his conference with Weed.

(Confidential)

Springfield, Illinois, December 21, 1860

MY DEAR SIR: Thurlow Weed was with me nearly all day yesterday, and left last night with three short resolutions which I drew up, and which, or the substance of which, I think, would do much good if introduced and unanimously supported by our friends. They do not touch the territorial question. Mr. Weed goes to Washington with them; and says that he will first of all confer with you and Mr. Hamlin. I think it would be best for Mr. Seward to introduce them, and Mr. Weed will let him know that I think so. Show this to Mr. Hamlin, but beyond him do not let my name be known in the matter.

LETTER TO ALEXANDER H. STEPHENS

Lincoln writes to Alexander Stephens of Georgia who had been in Congress with him in 1848-49, and with whom he had, at that time, become very friendly. His letter, in essence, is the same as the one he wrote to Gilmer on December 15. Although Stephens in 1860 was still supporting the Union cause, as soon as the War was declared, he became Vice President of the Confederacy. On the day Lincoln wrote this letter, a rumor reached Springfield that Buchanan had given orders to surrender Fort Sumter if it was attacked. *Lincoln is reported to have said of this, "If that is true they ought to hang him!"*

(*For your own eye only*)

Springfield, Illinois, December 22, 1860

MY DEAR SIR: Your obliging answer to my short note is just received, and for which please accept my thanks. I fully appreciate the present peril the country is in, and the weight of responsibility on me. Do the people of the South really entertain fears that a Republican administration would, directly or indirectly, interfere with the slaves, or with them about the slaves? If they do, I wish to assure you, as once a friend, and still, I hope, not an enemy, that there is no cause for such fears. The South would be in no more danger in this respect than it was in the days of Washington. I suppose, however, this does not meet the case. You think slavery is right and ought to be extended, while we think it is wrong and ought to be restricted. That, I suppose, is the rub. It certainly is the only substantial difference between us.

LETTER TO GENERAL DUFF GREEN

Duff Green was an elderly Kentucky politician who had been associated with Jackson during the nullification controversy. He had come to Springfield to get a letter from Lincoln giving his stand on a proposed amendment to the Constitution which would legalize slavery forever. Lincoln did not give him a letter but sent the letter printed here to Trumbull in Washington to pass on to Green or not, as he saw fit. Lincoln took the second clause of this letter directly from the Republican platform. Trumbull evidently felt that it would be inexpedient to pass the letter on to Green, so it was never published.

Springfield, Illinois, December 28, 1860

MY DEAR SIR: I do not desire any amendment of the Constitution. Recognizing, however, that questions of such amendment rightfully belong to the American people, I should not feel justified nor inclined to withhold from them, if I could, a fair opportunity of expressing their will thereon through either of the modes prescribed in the instrument.

In addition I declare that the maintenance inviolate of the rights of the States, and especially the right of each State to order and control its own domestic institutions according to its own judgment exclusively, is essential to that balance of powers on which the perfection and endurance of our political fabric depend; and I denounce the lawless invasion by armed force of the soil of any State or Territory, no matter under what pretext, as the gravest of crimes.

I am greatly averse to writing anything for the public at this time; and I consent to the publication of this only upon the condition that six of the twelve United States Senators for the States of Georgia, Alabama, Mississippi, Louisiana, Florida, and Texas shall sign their names to what is written on this sheet below my name, and allow the whole to be published together.

Yours truly,
A. LINCOLN

We recommend to the people of the States we represent respectively, to suspend all action for dismemberment of the Union, at least until some act deemed to be violative of our rights shall be done by the incoming administration.

LETTER TO W. H. SEWARD

Although Abraham Lincoln had clearly been elected President of the United States, according to the country's laws his election was not official until the electoral vote had been counted by the

President of the Senate in the presence of both Houses of Congress. This ceremony, which is ordinarily only a ceremony and nothing more, in his case offered great possibilities for trouble, as he explains in this letter to Seward. As the letter indicates, he was also still uncertain of the composition of his Cabinet, still trying to get some representation from the South. On this very day he wrote to Cameron trying to get out of his promise to take him into the Cabinet.

(Private)

Springfield, Illinois, January 3, 1861

MY DEAR SIR: Yours without signature was received last night. I have been considering your suggestions as to my reaching Washington somewhat earlier than is usual. It seems to me the inauguration is not the most dangerous point for us. Our adversaries have us now clearly at disadvantage. On the second Wednesday of February, when the votes should be officially counted, if the two Houses refuse to meet at all, or meet without a quorum of each, where shall we be? I do not think that this counting is constitutionally essential to the election; but how are we to proceed in absence of it?

In view of this, I think it best for me not to attempt appearing in Washington till the result of that ceremony is known. It certainly would be of some advantage if you could know who are to be at the heads of the War and Navy departments; but until I can ascertain definitely whether I can get any suitable men from the South, and who, and how many, I cannot well decide. . . .

LETTER TO JAMES T. HALE

In this, and in the next letter to Seward, Lincoln makes clear his belief that the acquisition of new territory was the real cause of the *dispute over slavery, since the slaveholders would unceasingly try to extend their power to such new territory as fast as it was acquired.*

(Confidential)

Springfield, Illinois, January 11, 1861

MY DEAR SIR: Yours of the 6th is received. I answer it only because I fear you would misconstrue my silence. What is our present condition? We have just carried an election on principles fairly stated to the people. Now we are told in advance the Government shall be broken up unless we surrender to those we have beaten, before we take the offices. In this they are either attempting to play upon us or they are in dead earnest. Either way, if we surrender, it is the end of us and of the Government. They will repeat the experiment upon us *ad libitum*. A year will not pass till we shall have to take Cuba as a condition upon which they will stay in the Union. They now have the Constitution under which we have lived over seventy years, and acts of Congress of their own framing, with no prospect of their being changed; and they can never have a more shallow pretext for breaking up the Government, or extorting a compromise, than now. There is in my judgment but one compromise which would really settle the slavery question, and that would be a prohibition against acquiring any more territory.

FROM A LETTER TO W. H. SEWARD

As soon as Lincoln returned to Springfield from his visit to his stepmother, Sarah Bush Lincoln, he wrote to Seward, again stating his position on the matter of not permitting slavery to be extended. The letters of this period make clear why Lincoln set himself inflexibly against any further compromise with the South.

(Private and confidential)

Springfield, Illinois, February 1, 1861

MY DEAR SIR: . . . I say now . . . as I have all the while said, that on the territorial question—that is, the question of extending slavery under the national auspices—I am inflexible. I am for no compromise which assists or permits the extension of the institution on soil owned by the nation. And any trick by which the nation is to acquire territory, and then allow some local authority to spread slavery over it, is as obnoxious as any other. I take it that to effect some such result as this, and to put us again on the highroad to a slave empire, is the object of all these proposed compromises. I am against it. As to fugitive slaves, District of Columbia, slave trade among the slave States, and whatever springs of necessity from the fact that the institution is amongst us, I care but little, so that what is done be comely and not altogether outrageous. Nor do I care much about New Mexico, if further extension were hedged against.

FAREWELL ADDRESS AT SPRINGFIELD, ILLINOIS

This famous and brief address was spoken from the platform of the observation car of the train that was to take Lincoln to Washington. The time was shortly before eight o'clock in the morning; the place, the Great Western station in Springfield; the setting, a gray winter day with the rain falling.

February 11, 1861

MY FRIENDS: No one, not in my situation, can appreciate my feeling of sadness at this parting. To this place, and the kindness of these people, I owe everything. Here I have lived a quarter of a century, and have passed from a young to an old man. Here my children have been born, and one is buried. I now leave, not knowing when or whether ever I may return, with a task before me greater than that which rested upon Washington. Without the assistance of that Divine Being who ever attended him, I cannot succeed. With that assistance, I cannot fail. Trusting in Him who can go with me, and remain with you, and be everywhere for good, let us confidently hope that all will yet be well. To His care commending you, as I hope in your prayers you will commend me, I bid you an affectionate farewell.

FROM AN ADDRESS TO THE GERMANS AT CINCINNATI, OHIO

Mrs. Lincoln and Lincoln's sons had joined the Presidential train at Indianapolis. The train went on to Cincinnati, where it arrived during the afternoon. Cincinnati, then as now, had a large German population. Lincoln's attitude toward foreign-born citizens is most clearly brought out in this address.

February 12, 1861

. . . I AGREE with you, Mr. Chairman, that the workingmen are the basis of all governments, for the plain reason that they are the more numerous, and as you added that those were the sentiments of the gentlemen present, representing not only the working-class, but citizens of other callings than those of the mechanic, I am happy to concur with you in these sentiments, not only of the native-born citizens, but also of the Germans and foreigners from other countries.

Mr. Chairman, I hold that while man exists it is his duty to improve not only his own condition, but to assist in ameliorating mankind; and therefore, without entering upon the details of the question, I will simply say that I am for those means which will give the greatest good to the greatest number. . . .

In regard to the Germans and foreigners, I esteem them no better than other people, nor any worse. It is not my nature, when I see a people borne down by the weight of their shackles—the oppression of tyranny—to make their life more bitter by heaping upon them greater burdens; but rather would I do all in my power to raise the yoke than to add anything that would tend to crush them.

Inasmuch as our country is extensive and new, and the countries of Europe are densely populated, if there are any abroad who desire to make this the land of their adoption, it is not in my heart to throw aught in their way to prevent them from coming to the United States.

FROM AN ADDRESS AT PITTSBURGH

From Cincinnati, the Presidential train had gone on to Columbus, and then to Pittsburgh, where it arrived during the evening of February 14 in a heavy rain. In the course of this address, Lincoln unfortunately said, "There is no crisis but an artificial one"—a statement that alienated even his own supporters.

February 15, 1861

. . . THE condition of the country is an extraordinary one, and fills the mind of every patriot with anxiety. It is my intention to give this subject all the consideration I possibly can before specially deciding in regard to it, so that when I do speak it may be as nearly right as possible. When I do speak I hope I may say nothing in opposition to the spirit of the Constitution, contrary to the integrity of the Union, or which will prove inimical to the liberties of the people, or to the peace of the whole country. And, furthermore, when the time arrives for me to speak on this great subject, I hope I may say nothing to disappoint the people generally throughout the country, especially if the expectation has been based upon anything which I may have heretofore said. Notwithstanding the troubles across the river [*points across the Monongahela, toward Western Virginia*], there is no crisis but an artificial one. What is there now to warrant the condition of affairs presented by our friends over the river? Take even their own view of the questions involved, and there is nothing to justify the course they are pursuing. I repeat, then, there is no crisis, excepting such a one as may be gotten up at any time by turbulent men aided by designing politicians. My advice to them, under such circumstances, is to keep cool. If the great American people only keep their temper on both sides of the line, the troubles will come to an end, and the question which now distracts the country will be settled, just as surely as all other difficulties of a like character which have originated in this government have been adjusted. Let the people on both sides keep their self-possession, and just as other clouds have cleared away in due time, so will this great nation continue to prosper as heretofore. . . .

FROM AN ADDRESS AT CLEVELAND, OHIO

The train reached Cleveland at 4:30 in the afternoon, and the President-elect was taken to the Weddell House where he delivered a brief address. Again he alludes to the crisis as an artificial one.

February 15, 1861

FELLOW-CITIZENS OF CLEVELAND AND OHIO: We have come here upon a very inclement afternoon. We have marched for two miles through the rain and the mud.

The large numbers that have turned out under these circumstances testify that you are in earnest about something, and what is that something? I would not have you suppose that I think this extreme earnestness is about me. I should be exceedingly sorry to see such devotion if that were the case. But I know it is paid to something worth more than any one man, or any thousand or ten thousand men. You have assembled to testify your devotion to the Constitution, to the Union, and the laws, to the perpetual liberty of the people of this country. It is, fellow-citizens, for the whole American people, and not for one single man alone, to advance the great cause of the Union and the Constitution. And in a country like this, where every man bears on his face the marks of intelligence, where every man's clothing, if I may so speak, shows signs of comfort, and every dwelling signs of happiness and contentment, where schools and churches abound on every side, the Union can never be in danger. I would, if I could, instil some degree of patriotism and confidence into the political mind in relation to this matter.

Frequent allusion is made to the excitement at present existing in our national politics, and it is as well that I should also allude to it here. I think that there is no occasion for any excitement. I think the crisis, as it is called, is altogether an artificial one. In all parts of the nation there are differences of opinion on politics; there are differences of opinion even here. You did not all vote for the person who now addresses you, although quite enough of you did for all practical purposes, to be sure.

What they do who seek to destroy the Union is altogether artificial. What is happening to hurt them? Have they not all their rights now as they ever have had? Do not they have their fugitive slaves returned now as ever? Have they not the same Constitution that they have lived under for seventy-odd years? Have they not a position as citizens of this common country, and have we any power to change that position? [Cries of "No!"] What then is the matter with them? Why all this excitement? Why all these complaints? As I said before, this crisis is altogether artificial. It has no foundation in fact. It can't be argued up, and it can't be argued down. Let it alone, and it will go down of itself. . . .

ADDRESS AT HUDSON, NEW YORK

On February 18th, Lincoln had received word that Jefferson Davis had been inaugurated as President of the Confederate States of America. At the train's stop at Hudson, N. Y. he had nothing that he wanted to say publicly. He tries as tactfully as possible to get out of making a speech.

February 19, 1861

FELLOW-CITIZENS: I see that you have provided a platform, but I shall have to decline standing on it. The superintendent tells me I have not time during our brief stay to leave the train. I had to decline standing on some very handsome platforms prepared for me yesterday. But I say to you, as I said to them, you must not on this account draw the inference that I have any intention to desert any platform I have a legitimate right to stand on. I do not appear before you for the purpose of making a speech. I come only to see you, and to give you the opportunity to see me; and I say to you, as I have before said to crowds where there were so many handsome ladies as there are here, I think I have decidedly the best of the bargain. I have only, therefore, to thank you most cordially for this kind reception, and bid you all farewell.

ADDRESS AT NEW YORK CITY

Lincoln arrived in New York City at three o'clock in the afternoon. New York was a Democratic stronghold, and its reception to the President-elect was lacking in enthusiasm. He was taken to the Astor House, and there, in a room in which Webster and Clay had once spoken, he again had to address a crowd and say nothing of any consequence.

February 19, 1861

MR. CHAIRMAN AND GENTLEMEN: I am rather an old man to avail myself of such an excuse as I am now about to do. Yet the truth is so distinct, and presses itself so distinctly upon me, that I cannot well avoid it—and that is, that I did not understand when I was brought into this room that I was to be brought here to make a speech. It was not intimated to me that I was brought into the room where Daniel Webster and Henry Clay had made speeches, and where one in my position might be expected to do something like those men or say something worthy of myself or my audience. I therefore beg you to make allowance for the circumstances in which I have been by surprise brought before you. Now I have been in the habit of thinking and sometimes speaking upon political questions that have for some years past agitated the country; and, if I were disposed to do so, and we could take up some one of the issues, as the lawyers call them, and I were called upon to make an argument about it to the best of my ability, I could do so without much preparation. But that is not what you desire to have done here tonight.

I have been occupying a position, since the Presidential election, of silence, of avoiding public speaking, of avoiding public writing. I have been doing so because I thought, upon full consideration, that was the proper course for me to take. I am brought before you now, and required to make a speech, when you all approve more than anything else of the fact that I have been keeping silence. And now it seems to me that the response you give to that remark ought to justify me in closing just here. I have not kept silence since the Presidential election from any party wantonness, or from any indifference to the anxiety that pervades the minds of men about the aspect of the political affairs of this country. I have kept silence for the reason that I supposed it was peculiarly proper that I should do so until the time came when, according to the custom of the country, I could speak officially.

I still suppose that, while the political drama being enacted in this country, at this time, is rapidly shifting its scenes—forbidding an anticipation with any degree of certainty, today, of what we shall see tomorrow—it is peculiarly fitting that I should see it all, up to the last minute, before I should take ground that I might be disposed (by the shifting of the scenes afterward) also to shift. I have said several times upon this journey, and I now repeat it to you, that when the time does come, I shall then take the ground that I think is right—right for the North, for the South, for the East, for the West, for the whole country. And in doing so, I hope to feel no necessity pressing upon me to say anything in conflict with the Constitution; in conflict with the continued union of these States, in conflict with the perpetuation of the liberties of this people, or anything in conflict with anything whatever that I have ever given you reason to expect from me.

FROM AN ADDRESS
TO THE NEW JERSEY ASSEMBLY

After leaving New York in the morning, the Presidential train stopped for a few minutes in Jersey City and Newark; it reached Trenton at noon. There Lincoln addressed the Senate, and afterward, the Assembly. It was during this speech that he indicated to the public for the first time that he might have to meet a difficult situation seriously. He says: "It may be necessary to put the foot down firmly." New Jersey was predominantly Democratic; it had voted against Lincoln in the Presidential election.

February 21, 1861

You, Mr. Speaker, have well said that this is a time when the bravest and wisest look with doubt and awe upon the aspect presented by our national affairs. Under these circumstances you will readily see why I should not speak in detail of the course I shall deem it best to pursue. It is proper that I should avail myself of all the information and all the time at my command, in order that when the time arrives in which I must speak officially, I shall be able to take the ground which I deem best and safest, and from which I may have no occasion to swerve. I shall endeavor to take the ground I deem most just to the North, the East, the West, the South, and the whole country. I take it, I hope, in good temper, certainly with no malice toward any section. I shall do all that may be in my power to promote a peaceful settlement of all our difficulties. The man does not live who is more devoted to peace than I am, none who would do more to preserve it, but it may be necessary to put the foot down firmly. [Cheers.] And if I do my duty and do right, you will sustain me, will you not? [Cheers, and cries of "Yes, yes; we will!"] Received as I am by the members of a legislature the majority of whom do not agree with me in political sentiments, I trust that I may have their assistance in piloting the ship of state through this voyage, surrounded by perils as it is; for if it should suffer wreck now, there will be no pilot ever needed for another voyage.

SPEECH AT INDEPENDENCE HALL, PHILADELPHIA

Lincoln had reached Philadelphia on the evening of February 21. Upon his arrival there he had been informed of the Baltimore plot against his life. In this speech at Independence Hall, he says: "If this country cannot be saved without giving up this principle (that all should have an equal chance) . . . I would rather be assassinated on this spot than surrender."

February 22, 1861

MR. CUYLER: I am filled with deep emotion at finding myself standing in this place, where were collected together the wisdom, the patriotism, the devotion to principle, from which sprang the institutions under which we live. You have kindly suggested to me that in my hands is the task of restoring peace to our distracted country. I can say in return, sir, that all the political sentiments I entertain have been drawn, so far as I have been able to draw them, from the sentiments which originated in and were given to the world from this hall. I have never had a feeling, politically, that did not spring from the sentiments embodied in the Declaration of Independence. I have often pondered over the dangers which were incurred by the men who assembled here and framed and adopted that Declaration. I have pondered over the toils that were endured by the officers and soldiers of the army who achieved that independence. I have often inquired of myself what great principle or idea it was that kept this Confederacy so long together. It was not the mere matter of separation of the colonies from the motherland, but that sentiment in the Declaration of Independence which gave liberty not alone to the people of this country, but hope to all the world, for all future time. It was that which gave promise that in due time the weights would be lifted from the shoulders of all men, and that all should have an equal chance. This is the sentiment embodied in the Declaration of Independence. Now, my friends, can this country be saved on that basis? If it can, I will consider myself one of the happiest men in the world if I can help to save it. If it cannot be saved upon that principle, it will be truly awful. But if this country cannot be saved without giving up that principle, I was about to say I would rather be assassinated on this spot than surrender it. Now, in my view of the persent aspect of affairs, there is no need of bloodshed and war. There is no necessity for it. I am not in favor of such a course; and I may say in advance that there will be no bloodshed unless it is forced upon the government. The government will not use force, unless force is used against it.

My friends, this is wholly an unprepared speech. I did not expect to be called on to say a word when I came here. I supposed I was merely to do something toward raising a flag. I may, therefore, have said something indiscreet. [Cries of "No, no."] But I have said nothing but what I am willing to live by, and, if it be the pleasure of Almighty God, to die by.

FROM AN ADDRESS AT HARRISBURG

At Harrisburg, Lincoln witnessed a display of military maneuvers. He then replied to Governor Curtin's speech of welcome with this address. At six o'clock in the evening, he left a dinner given in his honor, took a train that was waiting outside the city for him, and traveled incognito to Washington, where he arrived at six o'clock on the morning of February 23.

February 22, 1861

REFERENCE has been made . . . to the distraction of the public mind at this time and to the great task that is before me in entering upon the administration of the General Government. . . . I feel that, under God, in the strength of the arms and wisdom of the heads of these masses, after all, must be my support. As I have often had occasion to say, I repeat to you—I am quite sure I do not deceive myself when I tell you I bring to the work an honest heart; I dare not tell you that I bring a head sufficient for it. If my own strength should fail, I shall at least fall back upon these masses, who, I think, under any circumstances will not fail.

Allusion has been made to the peaceful principles upon which this great commonwealth was originally settled. Allow me to add my meed of praise to those peaceful principles. I hope no one of the Friends who originally settled here, or who lived here since that time, or who live here now, has been or is a more devoted lover of peace, harmony, and concord than my humble self.

While I have been proud to see today the finest military array, I think, that I have ever seen, allow me to say, in regard to those men, that they give hope of what may be done when war is inevitable. But, at the same time, allow me to express the hope that in the shedding of blood their services may never be needed, especially in the shedding of fraternal blood. It shall be my endeavor to preserve the peace of this country so far as it can possibly be done consistently with the maintenance of the institutions of the country. With my consent, or without my great displeasure, this country shall never witness the shedding of one drop of blood in fraternal strife.

FIRST INAUGURAL ADDRESS

To a divided country, in which every citizen was waiting to hear the announcement of policy of the new President, Abraham Lincoln made this address, speaking from a platform on the steps of the unfinished Capitol in Washington. The speech itself was a carefully composed document which Lincoln had begun to write in Springfield and had revised in Washington after consultation with Stephen A. Douglas and William H. Seward. The ending in particular had been changed in order to make a last-minute appeal to the South.

March 4, 1861

Fellow-citizens of the United States: In compliance with a custom as old as the government itself, I appear before you to address you briefly, and to take in your presence the oath prescribed by the Constitution of the United States to be taken by the President "before he enters on the execution of his office."

I do not consider it necessary at present for me to discuss those matters of administration about which there is no special anxiety or excitement.

Apprehension seems to exist among the people of the Southern States that by the accession of a Republican administration their property and their peace and personal security are to be endangered. There has never been any reasonable cause for such apprehension. Indeed, the most ample evidence to the contrary has all the while existed and been open to their inspection. It is found in nearly all the published speeches of him who now addresses you. I do but quote from one of those speeches when I declare that "I have no purpose, directly or indirectly, to interfere with the institution of slavery in the States where it exists. I believe I have no lawful right to do so, and I have no inclination to do so." Those who nominated and elected me did so with full knowledge that I had made this and many similar declarations, and had never recanted them.

And, more than this, they placed in the platform for my acceptance, and as a law to themselves and to me, the clear and emphatic resolution which I now read:

RESOLVED, That the maintenance inviolate of the rights of the States, and especially the right of each State to order and control its own domestic institutions according to its own judgment exclusively, is essential to that balance of power on which the perfection and endurance of our political fabric depend, and we denounce the lawless invasion by armed force of the soil of any State or Territory, no matter under what pretext, as among the gravest of crimes.

I now reiterate these sentiments; and, in doing so, I only press upon the public attention the most conclusive evidence of which the case is susceptible, that the property, peace, and security of no section are to be in any wise endangered by the now incoming administration. I add, too, that all the protection which, consistently with the Constitution and the laws, can be given, will be cheerfully given to all the States when lawfully demanded, for whatever cause—as cheerfully to one section as to another.

There is much controversy about the delivering up of fugitives from service or labor. The clause I now read is as plainly written in the Constitution as any other of its provisions:

No person held to service or labor in one State, under the laws thereof, escaping into another, shall in consequence of any law or regulation therein be discharged from such service or labor, but shall be delivered up on claim of the party to whom such service or labor may be due.

It is scarcely questioned that this provision was intended by those who made it for the reclaiming of what we call fugitive slaves; and the intention of the lawgiver is the law. All members of Congress swear their support to the whole Constitution—to this provision as much as to any other. To the proposition then, that slaves whose cases come within the terms of this clause "shall be delivered up," their oaths are unanimous. Now, if they would make the effort in good temper, could they not with nearly equal unanimity frame and pass a law by means of which to keep good that unanimous oath?

There is some difference of opinion whether this clause should be enforced by national or by State authority; but surely that difference is not a very material one. If the slave is to be surrendered, it can be of but little consequence to him or to others by which authority it is done. And should any one in any case be content that his oath shall go unkept on a merely unsubstantial controversy as to how it shall be kept?

Again, in any law upon this subject, ought not all the safeguards of liberty known in civilized and humane jurisprudence to be introduced, so that a free man be not, in any case, surrendered as a slave? And might it not be well at the same time to provide by law for the enforcement of that clause in the Constitution which guarantees that "the citizens of each State shall be entitled to all privileges and immunities of citizens in the several States"?

I take the official oath today with no mental reservations, and with no purpose to construe the Constitution or laws by any hypercritical rules. And while I do not choose now to specify particular acts of Congress as proper to be enforced, I do suggest that it will be much safer for all, both in official and private stations, to conform to and abide by all those acts which stand unrepealed, than to violate any of them, trusting to find impunity in having them held to be unconstitutional.

It is seventy-two years since the first inauguration of a President under our National Constitution. During that period fifteen different and greatly distinguished citizens have, in succession, administered the executive branch of the government. They have conducted it through many perils, and generally with great success. Yet, with all this scope of precedent, I now enter upon the same task for the brief constitutional term of four years under great and peculiar difficulty. A disruption of the Federal Union, heretofore only menaced, is now formidably attempted.

I hold that, in contemplation of universal law and of the Constitution, the Union of these States is perpetual. Perpetuity is implied, if not expressed, in the fundamental law of all national governments. It is safe to assert that no government proper ever had a provision in its organic law for its own termination.

Continue to execute all the express provisions of our National Constitution, and the Union will endure forever—it being impossible to destroy it except by some action not provided for in the instrument itself.

Again, if the United States be not a government proper, but

an association of States in the nature of contract merely, can it, as a contract, be peaceably unmade by less than all the parties who made it? One party to a contract may violate it—break it, so to speak; but does it not require all to lawfully rescind it?

Descending from these general principles, we find the proposition that, in legal contemplation, the Union is perpetual confirmed by the history of the Union itself. The Union is much older than the Constitution. It was formed, in fact, by the Articles of Association in 1774. It was matured and continued by the Declaration of Independence in 1776. It was further matured, and the faith of all the then thirteen States expressly plighted and engaged that it should be perpetual, by the Articles of Confederation in 1778. And, finally, in 1787 one of the declared objects for ordaining and establishing the Constitution was "to form a more perfect Union."

But if the destruction of the Union by one or by a party only of the States be lawfully possible, the Union is less perfect than before the Constitution, having lost the vital element of perpetuity.

It follows from these views that no State upon its own mere motion can lawfully get out of the Union; that resolves and ordinances to that effect are legally void; and that acts of violence, within any State or States, against the authority of the United States, are insurrectionary or revolutionary, according to circumstances.

I therefore consider that, in view of the Constitution and the laws, the Union is unbroken; and to the extent of my ability I shall take care, as the Constitution itself expressly enjoins upon me, that the laws of the Union be faithfully executed in all the States. Doing this I deem to be only a simple duty on my part; and I shall perform it so far as practicable, unless my rightful masters, the American people, shall withhold the requisite means, or in some authoritative manner direct the contrary. I trust this will not be regarded as a menace, but only as the declared purpose of the Union that it will constitutionally defend and maintain itself.

In doing this there needs to be no bloodshed or violence; and there shall be none, unless it be forced upon the national authority. The power confided to me will be used to hold, occupy, and possess the property and places belonging to the government, and to collect the duties and imposts; but beyond what may be necessary for these objects, there will be no invasion, no using of force against or among the people anywhere. Where hostility to the United States, in any interior locality, shall be so great and universal as to prevent competent resident citizens from holding the Federal offices, there will be no attempt to force obnoxious strangers among the people for that object. While the strict legal right may exist in the government to enforce the exercise of these offices, the attempt to do so would be so irritating, and so nearly impracticable withal, that I deem it better to forego for the time the uses of such offices.

The mails, unless repelled, will continue to be furnished in all parts of the Union. So far as possible, the people everywhere shall have that sense of perfect security which is most favorable to calm thought and reflection. The course here indicated will be followed unless current events and experience shall show a modification or change to be proper, and in every case and exigency my best discretion will be exercised according to circumstances actually existing, and with a view and a hope of a peaceful solution of the national troubles and the restoration of fraternal sympathies and affections.

That there are persons in one section or another who seek to destroy the Union at all events, and are glad of any pretext to do it, I will neither affirm nor deny; but if there be such, I need address no word to them. To those, however, who really love the Union may I not speak?

Before entering upon so grave a matter as the destruction of our national fabric, with all its benefits, its memories, and its hopes, would it not be wise to ascertain precisely why we do it? Will you hazard so desperate a step while there is any possibility that any portion of the ills you fly from have no real existence? Will you, while the certain ills you fly to are greater than all the real ones you fly from—will you risk the commission of so fearful a mistake?

All profess to be content in the Union if all constitutional rights can be maintained. Is it true, then, that any right, plainly written in the Constitution, has been denied? I think not. Happily the human mind is so constituted that no party can reach to the audacity of doing this. Think, if you can, of a single instance in which a plainly written provision of the Constitution has ever been denied. If by the mere force of numbers a majority should deprive a minority of any clearly written constitutional right, it might, in a moral point of view, justify revolution—certainly would if such a right were a vital one. But such is not our case. All the vital rights of minorities and of individuals are so plainly assured to them by affirmations and negations, guarantees and prohibitions, in the Constitution, that controversies never arise concerning them. But no organic law can ever be framed with a provision specifically applicable to every question which may occur in practical administration. No foresight can anticipate, nor any document of reasonable length contain, express provisions for all possible questions. Shall fugitives from labor be surrendered by national or by State authority? The Constitution does not expressly say. May Congress prohibit slavery in the Territories? The Constitution does not expressly say. Must Congress protect slavery in the Territories? The Constitution does not expressly say.

From questions of this class spring all our constitutional controversies, and we divide upon them into majorities and minorities. If the minority will not acquiesce, the majority must, or the government must cease. There is no other alternative; for continuing the government is acquiescence on one side or the other.

If a minority in such case will secede rather than acquiesce, they make a precedent which in turn will divide and ruin them; for a minority of their own will secede from them whenever a majority refuses to be controlled by such minority. For instance, why may not any portion of a new confederacy a year or two hence arbitrarily secede again, precisely as portions of the present Union now claim to secede from it? All who cherish disunion sentiments are now being educated to the exact temper of doing this.

Is there such perfect identity of interests among the States to compose a new Union, as to produce harmony only, and prevent renewed secession?

Plainly, the central idea of secession is the essence of anarchy. A majority held in restraint by constitutional checks and limitations, and always changing easily with deliberate changes of popular opinions and sentiments, is the only true sovereign of a free people. Whoever rejects it does, of necessity, fly to anarchy or to despotism. Unanimity is impossible; the rule of a minority, as a permanent arrangement, is wholly inadmissible; so that, rejecting the majority principle, anarchy or despotism in some form is all that is left.

I do not forget the position, assumed by some, that constitutional questions are to be decided by the Supreme Court; nor do I deny that such decisions must be binding, in any case, upon the parties to a suit, as to the object of that suit, while they are also entitled to very high respect and consideration in all parallel cases by all other departments of the government. And while it is obviously possible that such decision may be erroneous in any given case, still the evil effect following it, being limited to that particular case, with the chance that it may be overruled and never become a precedent for other cases, can better be borne than could the evils of a different practice.

At the same time, the candid citizen must confess that if the policy of the government, upon vital questions affecting the whole people, is to be irrevocably fixed by decisions of the Supreme Court, the instant they are made, in ordinary litigation between parties in personal actions, the people will have ceased to be their own rulers, having to that extent practically resigned their government into the hands of that eminent tribunal. Nor is there in this view any assault upon the court or the judges. It is a duty from which they may not shrink to decide cases properly brought before them, and it is no fault of theirs if others seek to turn their decisions to political purposes.

One section of our country believes slavery is right, and ought to be extended, while the other believes it is wrong, and ought not to be extended. This is the only substantial dispute. The fugitive-slave clause of the Constitution, and the law for the suppression of the foreign slave trade, are each as well enforced, perhaps, as any law can ever be in a community where the moral sense of the people imperfectly supports the law itself. The great body of the people abide by the dry legal obligation in both cases, and a few break over in each. This, I think, cannot be perfectly cured; and it would be worse in both cases after the separation of the sections than before. The foreign slave trade, now imperfectly suppressed, would be ultimately revived, without restriction, in one section, while fugitive slaves, now only partially surrendered, would not be surrendered at all by the other.

Physically speaking, we cannot separate. We cannot remove our respective sections from each other, nor build an impassable wall between them. A husband and wife may be divorced, and go out of the presence and beyond the reach of each other; but the different parts of our country cannot do this. They cannot but remain face to face, and intercourse, either amicable or hostile, must continue between them. Is it possible, then, to make that intercourse more advantageous or more satisfactory after separation than before? Can aliens make treaties easier than friends can make laws? Can treaties be more faithfully enforced between aliens than laws can among friends? Suppose you go to war, you cannot fight always; and when, after much loss on both sides, and no gain on either, you cease fighting, the identical old questions as to terms of intercourse are again upon you.

This country, with its institutions, belongs to the people who inhabit it. Whenever they shall grow weary of the existing government, they can exercise their constitutional right of amending it, or their revolutionary right to dismember or overthrow it. I cannot be ignorant of the fact that many worthy and patriotic citizens are desirous of having the National Constitution amended. While I make no recommendation of amendments, I fully recognize the rightful authority of the people over the whole subject, to be exercised in either of the modes prescribed in the instrument itself; and I should, under existing circumstances, favor rather than oppose a fair opportunity being afforded the people to act upon it. I will venture to add that to me the convention mode seems preferable, in that it allows amendments to originate with the people themselves, instead of only permitting them to take or reject propositions originated by others not specially chosen for the purpose, and which might not be precisely such as they would wish to either accept or refuse. I understand a proposed amendment to the Constitution—which amendment, however, I have not seen—has passed Congress, to the effect that the Federal Government shall never interfere with the domestic institutions of the States, including that of persons held to service. To avoid misconstruction of what I have said, I depart from my purpose not to speak of particular amendments so far as to say that, holding such a provision to now be implied constitutional law, I have no objection to its being made express and irrevocable.

The chief magistrate derives all his authority from the peo-

ple, and they have conferred none upon him to fix terms for
the separation of the States. The people themselves can do
this also if they choose; but the executive, as such, has nothing to do with it. His duty is to administer the present government, as it came to his hands, and to transmit it, unimpaired
by him, to his successor.

Why should there not be a patient confidence in the ultimate justice of the people? Is there any better or equal hope
in the world? In our present differences is either party without faith of being in the right? If the Almighty Ruler of
Nations, with his eternal truth and justice, be on your side
of the North, or on yours of the South, that truth and that
justice will surely prevail by the judgment of this great tribunal of the American people.

By the frame of the government under which we live, this
same people have wisely given their public servants but little
power for mischief; and have, with equal wisdom, provided
for the return of that little to their own hands at very short
intervals. While the people retain their virtue and vigilance,
no administration, by any extreme of wickedness or folly, can
very seriously injure the government in the short space of
four years.

My countrymen, one and all, think calmly and well upon
this whole subject. Nothing valuable can be lost by taking
time. If there be an object to hurry any of you in hot haste
to a step which you would never take deliberately, that object
will be frustrated by taking time; but no good object can be
frustrated by it. Such of you as are now dissatisfied, still have
the old Constitution unimpaired, and, on the sensitive point,
the laws of your own framing under it; while the new administration will have no immediate power, if it would, to change
either. If it were admitted that you who are dissatisfied hold
the right side in the dispute, there still is no single good reason
for precipitate action. Intelligence, patriotism, Christianity,
and a firm reliance on Him who has never yet forsaken this

favored land, are still competent to adjust in the best way all our present difficulty.

In your hands, my dissatisfied fellow-countrymen, and not in mine, is the momentous issue of civil war. The government will not assail you. You can have no conflict without being yourselves the aggressors. You have no oath registered in heaven to destroy the government, while I shall have the most solemn one to "preserve, protect, and defend it."

I am loath to close. We are not enemies, but friends. We must not be enemies. Though passion may have strained, it must not break our bonds of affection. The mystic chords of memory, stretching from every battlefield and patriot grave to every living heart and hearth-stone all over this broad land, will yet swell the chorus of the Union when again touched, as surely they will be, by the better angels of our nature.

NOTE TO EACH OF THE CABINET MEMBERS ASKING FOR OPINIONS ON FORT SUMTER

The first problem faced by the Lincoln administration on coming into office was what to do with Fort Sumter, which either had to be provisioned or surrendered to the Confederates in South Carolina. In reply to this note, all but two of Lincoln's Cabinet members felt that it would be useless to try to hold the fort.

Executive Mansion, March 15, 1861

My Dear Sir: Assuming it to be possible to now provision Fort Sumter, under all the circumstances is it wise to attempt it? Please give me your opinion in writing on this question.

REPLY TO SECRETARY SEWARD'S MEMORANDUM

On April 1, Lincoln received from his Secretary of State, William H. Seward, a memorandum which stated that the month-old ad-

ministration was without either a domestic or a foreign policy. Seward suggested that the question before the public be changed from one of slavery, or about slavery, to a question of union or dis-union, which, as he said, would be a change "from what would be regarded as a party question to one of patriotism or union." He also suggested that the difficulties over Sumter be terminated —although he did not say how—and that all the other Southern forts be maintained. In addition to these ideas, he hinted that a foreign war would serve to reunite the dissatisfied sections. He then subtly implied that if the President wished it, he would be glad to undertake these duties himself, although he sought neither "to evade nor assume responsibility." Lincoln realized that he must deal immediately with his Secretary of State and make him understand that he, and not Seward, was President. In this reply to Seward's memorandum he explains as tactfully as possible his own position in the matter; he nevertheless makes Seward realize who is President.

Executive Mansion, April 1, 1861

MY DEAR SIR: Since parting with you I have been considering your paper dated this day, and entitled "Some Thoughts for the President's Consideration." The first proposition in it is, "*First*, We are at the end of a month's administration, and yet without a policy either domestic or foreign."

At the beginning of that month, in the inaugural, I said: "The power confided to me will be used to hold, occupy, and possess the property and places belonging to the government, and to collect the duties and imposts." This had your distinct approval at the time; and, taken in connection with the order I immediately gave General Scott, directing him to employ every means in his power to strengthen and hold the forts, comprises the exact domestic policy you now urge, with the single exception that it does not propose to abandon Fort Sumter.

Again, I do not perceive how the reinforcement of Fort Sumter would be done on a slavery or a party issue, while that of Fort Pickens would be on a more national and patriotic one.

The news received yesterday in regard to St. Domingo certainly brings a new item within the range of our foreign policy; but up to that time we have been preparing circulars and instructions to ministers and the like, all in perfect harmony, without even a suggestion that we had no foreign policy.

Upon your closing propositions—that "whatever policy we adopt, there must be an energetic prosecution of it.

"For this purpose it must be somebody's business to pursue and direct it incessantly.

"Either the President must do it himself, and be all the while active in it, or

"Devolve it on some member of his Cabinet. Once adopted, debates on it must end, and all agree and abide"—I remark that if this must be done, I must do it. When a general line of policy is adopted, I apprehend there is no danger of its being changed without good reason, or continuing to be a subject of unnecessary debate; still, upon points arising in its progress I wish, and suppose I am entitled to have, the advice of all the Cabinet.

PROCLAMATION CALLING 75,000 MILITIA, AND CONVENING CONGRESS IN EXTRA SESSION

The relief expedition to Sumter had sailed. Before it could come to the relief of the beleaguered fort, the Confederates fired on Sumter on April 12. The tiny garrison was forced to surrender on April 14. On that same day (a Sunday), Lincoln wrote out this proclamation calling for volunteers and convening Congress in special session. It was published on Monday, April 15.

April 15, 1861

WHEREAS the laws of the United States have been for some time past and now are opposed, and the execution thereof obstructed, in the States of South Carolina, Georgia, Alabama, Florida, Mississippi, Louisiana, and Texas, by combinations too powerful to be suppressed by the ordinary course of judicial proceedings, or by the powers vested in the marshals by law:

Now, therefore, I, Abraham Lincoln, President of the United States, in virtue of the power in me vested by the Constitution and the laws, have thought fit to call forth, and hereby do call forth, the militia of the several States of the Union, to the aggregate number of seventy-five thousand, in order to suppress said combinations, and to cause the laws to be duly executed. . . .

I deem it proper to say that the first service assigned to the forces hereby called forth will probably be to repossess the forts, places, and property which have been seized from the Union; and in every event the utmost care will be observed, consistently with the objects aforesaid, to avoid any devastation, and destruction of or interference with property, or any disturbance of peaceful citizens in any part of the country. And I hereby command the persons composing the combinations aforesaid to disperse and retire peacefully to their respective abodes within twenty days from date.

Deeming that the present condition of public affairs presents an extraordinary occasion, I do hereby, in virtue of the power in me vested by the Constitution, convene both Houses of Congress. Senators and Representatives are therefore summoned to assemble at their respective chambers, at twelve o'clock noon, on Thursday, the fourth day of July next, then and there to consider and determine such measures as, in their wisdom, the public safety and interest may seem to demand.

PROCLAMATION OF BLOCKADE

The North realized immediately that the one best way to paralyze Southern commerce, which was largely based on exports of raw material to Europe, was to blockade the Southern ports. Unfortunately, there were 3600 miles of coastline in the Confederate states, and the North had only a limited number of ships with which to blockade the ports. Still more unfortunately, on the day after this blockade was issued, the Gosport Navy Yard at Norfolk, Virginia, was burned, and the Federal fleet was still further reduced. Nevertheless, it was the eventual success of this blockade which forced the South to her knees as she was slowly reduced to financial chaos and starvation.

April 19, 1861

WHEREAS an insurrection against the government of the United States has broken out in the States of South Carolina, Georgia, Alabama, Florida, Mississippi, Louisiana, and Texas, and the laws of the United States for the collection of the revenue cannot be effectually executed therein conformably to that provision of the Constitution which requires duties to be uniform throughout the United States:

And whereas a combination of persons engaged in such insurrection have threatened to grant pretended letters of marque to authorize the bearers thereof to commit assaults on the lives, vessels, and property of good citizens of the country lawfully engaged in commerce on the high seas, and in waters of the United States . . .

Now, therefore, I, Abraham Lincoln, President of the United States, with a view to the same purposes before mentioned, and to the protection of the public peace, and the lives and property of quiet and orderly citizens pursuing their lawful occupations, until Congress shall have assembled and deliberated on the said unlawful proceedings, or until the same shall have ceased, have further deemed it advisable to set on foot a blockade of the ports within the States aforesaid, in pursuance of the laws of the United States, and of the law of nations in such case provided. For this purpose a competent force will be posted so as to prevent entrance and exit of vessels from the ports aforesaid. If, therefore, with a view to violate such blockade, a vessel shall approach or shall attempt to leave either of the said ports, she will be duly warned by the commander of one of the blockading vessels, who will indorse on her register the fact and date of such warning, and if the same vessel shall again attempt to enter or leave the blockaded port, she will be captured and sent to the nearest convenient port, for such proceedings against her and her cargo, as prize, as may be deemed advisable.

And I hereby proclaim and declare that if any person, under the pretended authority of the said States, or under any other pretense, shall molest a vessel of the United States, or the persons or cargo on board of her, such person will be held amenable to the laws of the United States for the prevention and punishment of piracy.

LETTER TO REVERDY JOHNSON

(Confidential)

Reverdy Johnson was a noted Maryland lawyer and politician, a former Whig who had become a Democrat in 1856, a man who supported the Union cause during the War, but who always had a great affection for the South. Lincoln writes to him on a day on which Washington was completely isolated from the North and in immediate fear of invasion from Virginia, which had seceded from the Union on April 17. He explains why troops were being brought through Maryland to come to the defense of Washington.

Executive Mansion, April 24, 1861

My Dear Sir: Your note of this morning is just received. I forbore to answer yours of the 22d because of my aversion (which I thought you understood) to getting on paper and furnishing new grounds for misunderstanding. I do say the sole purpose of bringing troops here is to defend this capital. I do say I have no purpose to invade Virginia with them or any other troops, as I understand the word invasion. But, suppose Virginia sends her troops, or admits others through her borders, to assail this capital, am I not to repel them even to the crossing of the Potomac, if I can? Suppose Virginia erects, or permits to be erected, batteries on the opposite shore to bombard the city, are we to stand still and see it done? In a word, if Virginia strikes us, are we not to strike back, and as effectively as we can? Again, are we not to hold Fort Monroe (for instance) if we can? I have no objection to declare a thousand times that I have no purpose to invade Virginia or any other State, but I do not mean to let them invade us without striking back.

LETTER TO COLONEL ELLSWORTH'S PARENTS

This is one of the most celebrated of all Lincoln's letters, a letter of condolence that ranks second only to the more celebrated letter to Mrs. Bixby (November 21, 1864). Ellsworth had read law in Lincoln's office in Springfield. He was a born soldier, and he had organized a picturesque company of volunteers who had toured the country in 1860 giving demonstrations of precision drilling. Ellsworth had accompanied Lincoln on the Presidential train to Washington, and Lincoln had become very much attached to him. On May 24, Ellsworth had led a regiment of men recruited from the New York Fire Department across the Potomac to Alexandria, Virginia. In attempting to take down a Confederate flag flying from the roof of the Marshall House there, Ellsworth had been shot and killed by the hotel proprietor. His body was removed to the White House, where it lay in state in the East Room. He was the first commissioned officer to be killed in the Civil War.

Washington D. C., May 25, 1861

MY DEAR SIR AND MADAM: In the untimely loss of your noble son, our affliction here is scarcely less than your own. So much of promised usefulness to one's country, and of bright hopes for one's self and friends, have rarely been so suddenly dashed as in his fall. In size, in years, and in youthful appearance a boy only, his power to command men was surpassingly great. This power, combined with a fine intellect, an indomitable energy, and a taste altogether military, constituted in him, as seemed to me, the best natural talent in that department I ever knew.

And yet he was singularly modest and deferential in social intercourse. My acquaintance with him began less than two years ago; yet through the latter half of the intervening period it was as intimate as the disparity of our ages and my engrossing engagements would permit. To me he appeared to have no indulgences or pastimes; and I never heard him utter a profane or an intemperate word. What was conclusive of his good heart, he never forgot his parents. The honors he labored for so laudably, and for which in the sad end he so gallantly gave his life, he meant for them no less than for himself.

In the hope that it may be no intrusion upon the sacredness of your sorrow, I have ventured to address you this tribute to the memory of my young friend and your brave and early fallen child.

May God give you that consolation which is beyond all earthly power.

FROM THE MESSAGE TO CONGRESS
IN SPECIAL SESSION

On July 4, Congress assembled for the special session called by the President's proclamation of April 15. It was a strange session, with the seats of the Southern Congressmen remaining vacant, and a whole country waiting to hear the President's War policies. This message gives a brief summary of how the War began, and of Lincoln's attitude toward the meaning of the great struggle that was just getting under way.

July 4, 1861

FELLOW-CITIZENS OF THE SENATE AND HOUSE OF REPRESENTATIVES: Having been convened on an extraordinary occasion, as authorized by the Constitution, your attention is not called to any ordinary subject of legislation.

At the beginning of the present presidential term, four months ago, the functions of the Federal Government were found to be generally suspended within the several States of South Carolina, Georgia, Alabama, Mississippi, Louisiana, and Florida, excepting only those of the Post-Office Department.

Within these States, all the forts, arsenals, dockyards, custom-houses, and the like, including the movable and stationary property in and about them, had been seized, and were held in open hostility to this government, excepting only Forts Pickens, Taylor, and Jefferson, on and near the Florida coast, and Fort Sumter, in Charleston Harbor, South Carolina. The forts thus seized had been put in improved condition, new ones had been built, and armed forces had been organized and were organizing, all avowedly with the same hostile purpose.

The forts remaining in the possession of the Federal Government in and near these States were either besieged or menaced by warlike preparations, and especially Fort Sumter was nearly surrounded by well-protected hostile batteries, with guns equal in quality to the best of its own, and outnumbering the latter as perhaps ten to one. A disproportionate share of the Federal muskets and rifles had somehow found their way into these States, and had been seized to be used against the government. Accumulations of the public revenue lying within them had been seized for the same object. The navy was scattered in distant seas, leaving but a very small part of it within the immediate reach of the government. Officers of the Federal Army and Navy had resigned in great numbers, and of those resigning a large proportion had taken up arms against the government. Simultaneously, and in connection with all this, the purpose to sever the Federal Union was openly avowed. In accordance with this purpose, an ordinance had been adopted in each of these States, declaring the States respectively to be separated from the National Union. A formula for instituting a combined government of these States had been promulgated; and this illegal organization, in the character of confederate States, was already invoking recognition, aid, and intervention from foreign powers.

Finding this condition of things, and believing it to be an imperative duty upon the incoming executive to prevent, if possible, the consummation of such attempt to destroy the Federal Union, a choice of means to that end became indispensable. This choice was made and was declared in the inaugural address. The policy chosen looked to the exhaustion of all peaceful measures before a resort to any stronger ones. It sought only to hold the public places and property not already wrested from the government, and to collect the revenue, relying for the rest on time, discussion, and the ballot-box. It promised a continuance of the mails, at government expense, to the very people who were resisting the government; and it gave repeated pledges against any disturbance to any of the people, or any of their rights. Of all that which a President might constitutionally and justifiably do in such a case, everything was foreborne without which it was believed possible to keep the government on foot.

. . . The assault upon and reduction of Fort Sumter was in no sense a matter of self-defense on the part of the assailants. They well knew that the garrison in the fort could by no possibility commit aggression upon them. They knew —they were expressly notified—that the giving of bread to the few brave and hungry men of the garrison was all which would on that occasion be attempted, unless themselves, by resisting so much, should provoke more. They knew that this government desired to keep the garrison in the fort, not to assail them, but merely to maintain visible possession, and thus to preserve the Union from actual and immediate dissolution—trusting, as hereinbefore stated, to time, discussion, and the ballot-box for final adjustment; and they assailed and reduced the fort for precisely the reverse object—to drive out the visible authority of the Federal Union, and thus force it to immediate dissolution. That this was their object the executive well understood; and having said to them in the inaugural address, "You can have no conflict without being yourselves the aggressors," he took pains not only to keep this declaration good, but also to keep the case so free from the power of ingenious sophistry that the world should not be able to misunderstand it. By the affair at Fort Sumter, with its surrounding circumstances, that point was reached. Then and thereby the assailants of the government began the conflict of arms, without a gun in sight or in expectancy to return their fire, save only the few in the fort sent to that harbor years before for their own protection, and still ready to give that protection in whatever was lawful. In this act, discarding all else, they have forced upon the country the distinct issue, "immediate dissolution or blood."

And this issue embraces more than the fate of these United States. It presents to the whole family of man the question whether a constitutional republic or democracy—a government of the people by the same people—can or cannot maintain its territorial integrity against its own domestic foes. It presents the question whether discontented individuals, too few in numbers to control administration according to organic law in any case, can always, upon the pretenses made in this case, or on any other pretenses, or arbitrarily without any pretense, break up their government, and thus practically put an end to free government upon the earth. It forces us to ask: "Is there, in all republics, this inherent and fatal weakness?" "Must a government, of necessity, be too strong for the liberties of its own people, or too weak to maintain its own existence?"

So viewing the issue, no choice was left but to call out the war power of the government; and so to resist force employed for its destruction, by force for its preservation.

*   *   *

It is now recommended that you give the legal means for making this contest a short and decisive one: that you place at the control of the government for the work at least four hundred thousand men and $400,000,000. That number of men is about one-tenth of those of proper ages within the regions where, apparently, all are willing to engage; and the sum is less than a twenty-third part of the money value owned by the men who seem ready to devote the whole. A debt of $600,000,000 now is a less sum per head than was the debt of our Revolution when we came out of that struggle; and the money value in the country now bears even a greater proportion to what it was then than does the population. Surely each man has as strong a motive now to preserve our liberties as each had then to establish them.

A right result at this time will be worth more to the world than ten times the men and ten times the money. The evidence reaching us from the country leaves no doubt that the material for the work is abundant, and that it needs only the hand of legislation to give it legal sanction, and the hand of the executive to give it practical shape and efficiency. One of the greatest perplexities of the government is to avoid receiving troops faster than it can provide for them. In a word, the people will save their government if the government itself will do its part only indifferently well.

It might seem, at first thought, to be of little difference whether the present movement at the South be called "secession" or "rebellion." The movers, however, well understand the difference. At the beginning they knew they could never raise their treason to any respectable magnitude by any name which implies violation of law. They knew their people possessed as much of moral sense, as much of devotion to law and order, and as much pride in and reverence for the history and government of their common country as any other civilized and patriotic people. They knew they could make no advancement directly in the teeth of these strong and noble sentiments. Accordingly, they commenced by an insidious debauching of the public mind. They invented an ingenious sophism which, if conceded, was followed by perfectly logical steps, through all the incidents, to the complete destruction of the Union. The sophism itself is that any State of the Union may consistently with the National Constitution, and therefore lawfully and peacefully, withdraw from the Union without the consent of the Union or of any other State. The little disguise that the supposed right is to be exercised only for just cause, themselves to be the sole judges of its justice, is too thin to merit any notice.

With rebellion thus sugar-coated they have been drugging the public mind of their section for more than thirty years, and until at length they have brought many good men to a willingness to take up arms against the government the day after some assemblage of men have enacted the farcical pretense of taking their State out of the Union, who could have been brought to no such thing the day before.

This sophism derives much, perhaps the whole, of its currency from the assumption that there is some omnipotent and sacred supremacy pertaining to a State—to each State of our Federal Union. Our States have neither more nor less power than that reserved to them in the Union by the Constitution—no one of them ever having been a State out of the Union. The original ones passed into the Union even before they cast off their British colonial dependence; and the new ones each came into the Union directly from a condition of dependence, excepting Texas. And even Texas, in its temporary independence, was never designated a State. The new ones only took the designation of States on coming into the Union, while that name was first adopted for the old ones in and by the Declaration of Independence. Therein the "United Colonies" were declared to be "free and independent States"; but even then the object plainly was not to declare their independence of one another or of the Union, but directly the contrary, as their mutual pledge and their mutual action before, at the time, and afterward, abundantly show. The express plighting of faith by each and all of the original thirteen in the Articles of Confederation, two years later, that the Union shall be perpetual, is most conclusive. Having never been States either in substance or in name outside of the Union, whence this magical omnipotence of "State Rights," asserting a claim of power to lawfully destroy the Union itself? Much is said about the "sovereignty" of the States; but the word even is not in the National Constitution, nor, as is believed, in any of the State constitutions. What is "sovereignty" in the political sense of the term? Would it be far wrong to define it "a political community without a political superior"? Tested by this, no one of our States except Texas ever was a sovereignty. And even Texas gave up the character on coming into the Union; by which act she acknowledged the Constitution of the United States, and the laws and treaties of the United States made in pursuance of the Constitution, to be for her the supreme law of the land. The States have their status in the Union, and they have no other legal status. If they break from this, they can only do so against law and by revolution. The Union, and not themselves separately, procured their independence and their liberty. By conquest or purchase the Union gave each of them whatever of independence or liberty it has. The Union is older than any of the States, and, in fact, it created them as States. Originally some dependent colonies made the Union, and, in turn, the Union threw off their old dependence for them, and made them States, such as they are. Not one of them ever had a State constitution independent of the Union. Of course, it is not forgotten that all the new States framed their constitutions before they entered the Union—nevertheless, dependent upon and preparatory to coming into the Union.

Unquestionably the States have the powers and rights reserved to them in and by the National Constitution; but among these surely are not included all conceivable powers, however mischievous or destructive, but, at most, such only as were known in the world at the time as governmental powers; and certainly a power to destroy the government itself had never been known as a governmental, as a merely administrative power. This relative matter of national power and State rights, as a principle, is no other than the principle of generality and locality. Whatever concerns the whole should be confided to the whole—to the General Government; while whatever concerns only the State should be left exclusively to the State. This is all there is of original principle about it. Whether the National Constitution in defining boundaries between the two has applied the principle with exact accuracy, is not to be questioned. We are all bound by that defining, without question.

What is now combated is the position that secession is consistent with the Constitution—is lawful and peaceful. It is not contended that there is any express law for it; and nothing should ever be implied as law which leads to unjust or absurd consequences. The nation purchased with money the countries out of which several of these States were formed. Is it just that they shall go off without leave and without refunding? The nation paid very large sums (in the aggregate, I believe, nearly a hundred millions) to relieve Florida of the aboriginal tribes. Is it just that she shall now be off without consent or without making any return? The nation is now in debt for money applied to the benefit of these so-called seceding States in common with the rest. Is it just either that creditors shall go unpaid or the remaining States pay the whole? A part of the present national debt was contracted to pay the old debts of Texas. Is it just that she shall leave and pay no part of this herself?

Again, if one State may secede, so may another; and when all shall have seceded, none is left to pay the debts. Is this quite just to creditors? Did we notify them of this sage view of ours when we borrowed their money?

If we now recognize this doctrine by allowing the seceders to go in peace, it is difficult to see what we can do if others choose to go or to extort terms upon which they will promise to remain.

The seceders insist that our Constitution admits of secession. They have assumed to make a national constitution of their own, in which of necessity they have either discarded or retained the right of secession as they insist it exists in ours. If they have discarded it, they thereby admit that on principle it ought not to be in ours. If they have retained it by their own construction of ours, they show that to be consistent they must secede from one another whenever they shall find it the easiest way of settling their debts, or effecting any other selfish or unjust object. The principle itself is one of disintegration, and upon which no government can possibly endure.

If all the States save one should assert the power to drive that one out of the Union, it is presumed the whole class of seceder politicians would at once deny the power and denounce the act as the greatest outrage upon State rights. But suppose that precisely the same act, instead of being called "driving the one out," should be called "the seceding of the others from that one," it would be exactly what the seceders claim to do, unless, indeed, they make the point that the one, because it is a minority, may rightfully do what the others, because they are a majority, may not rightfully do. These politicians are subtle and profound on the rights of minorities. They are not partial to that power which made the Constitution and speaks from the preamble called itself "We, the People."

It may well be questioned whether there is to-day a majority of the legally qualified voters of any State, except perhaps South Carolina, in favor of disunion. There is much reason to believe that the Union men are the majority in many, if not in every other one, of the so-called seceded States. The contrary has not been demonstrated in any one of them. It is ventured to affirm this even of Virginia and Tennessee; for the result of an election held in military camps, where the bayonets are all on one side of the question voted upon, can scarcely be considered as demonstrating popular sentiment. At such an election, all that large class who are at once for the Union and against coercion would be coerced to vote against the Union.

It may be affirmed without extravagance that the free institutions we enjoy have developed the powers and improved the condition of our whole people beyond any example in the world. Of this we now have a striking and an impressive illustration. So large an army as the government has now on foot was never before known, without a soldier in it but who has taken his place there of his own free choice. But more than this, there are many single regiments whose members, one and another, possess full practical knowledge of all the arts, sciences, professions, and whatever else, whether useful or elegant, is known in the world; and there is scarcely one from which there could not be selected a President, a Cabinet, a Congress, and perhaps a court, abundantly competent to administer the government itself. Nor do I say this is not true also in the army of our late friends, now adversaries in this contest; but if it is, so much better the reason why the government which has conferred such benefits on both them and us should not be broken up. Whoever in any section proposes to abandon such a government would do well to consider in deference to what principle it is that he does it—what better he is likely to get in its stead—whether the substitute will give, or be intended to give, so much of good to the people? There are some foreshadowings on this subject. Our adversaries have adopted some declarations of independence in which, unlike the good old one, penned by Jefferson, they omit the words "all men are created equal." Why? They have adopted a temporary national constitution, in the preamble of which, unlike our good old one, signed by Washington, they omit "We, the People," and substitute, "We, the deputies of the sovereign and independent States." Why? Why this deliberate pressing out of view the rights of men and the authority of the people?

This is essentially a people's contest. On the side of the Union it is a struggle for maintaining in the world that form and substance of government whose leading object is to elevate the condition of men—to lift artificial weights from all shoulders; to clear the paths of laudable pursuit for all; to afford all an unfettered start, and a fair chance in the race of life. Yielding to partial and temporary departures, from necessity, this is the leading object of the government for whose existence we contend.

I am most happy to believe that the plain people understand and appreciate this. It is worthy of note that while in this, the government's hour of trial, large numbers of those in the army and navy who have been favored with the offices have resigned and proved false to the hand which had pampered them, not one common soldier or common sailor is known to have deserted his flag.

Great honor is due to those officers who remained true, despite the example of their treacherous associates; but the greatest honor, and most important fact of all, is the unanimous firmness of the common soldiers and common sailors. To the last man, so far as known, they have successfully resisted the traitorous efforts of those whose commands, but an hour before, they obeyed as absolute law. This is the patriotic instinct of the plain people. They understand, without an argument, that the destroying of the government which was made by Washington means no good to them.

Our popular government has often been called an experiment. Two points in it our people have already settled—the successful establishing and the successful administering of it. One still remains—its successful maintenance against a formidable internal attempt to overthrow it. It is now for them to demonstrate to the world that those who can fairly carry an election can also suppress a rebellion; that ballots are the rightful and peaceful successors of bullets; and that when ballots have fairly and constitutionally decided, there can be no successful appeal back to bullets; that there can be no successful appeal, except to ballots themselves, at succeeding elections. Such will be a great lesson of peace: teaching men that what they cannot take by an election, neither can they take it by a war; teaching all the folly of being the beginners of a war.

Lest there be some uneasiness in the minds of candid men as to what is to be the course of the government toward the Southern States after the rebellion shall have been suppressed, the executive deems it proper to say it will be his purpose then, as ever, to be guided by the Constitution and the laws;

and that he probably will have no different understanding of the powers and duties of the Federal Government relatively to the rights of the States and the people, under the Constitution, than that expressed in the inaugural address.

He desires to preserve the government, that it may be administered for all as it was administered by the men who made it. Loyal citizens everywhere have the right to claim this of their government, and the government has no right to withhold or neglect it. It is not perceived that in giving it there is any coercion, any conquest, or any subjugation, in any just sense of those terms.

The Constitution provides, and all the States have accepted the provision, that "the United States shall guarantee to every State in this Union a republican form of government." But if a State may lawfully go out of the Union, having done so, it may also discard the republican form of government; so that to prevent its going out is an indispensable means to the end of maintaining the guarantee mentioned; and when an end is lawful and obligatory, the indispensable means to it are also lawful and obligatory.

It was with the deepest regret that the executive found the duty of employing the war power in defense of the government forced upon him. He could but perform this duty or surrender the existence of the government. No compromise by public servants could, in this case, be a cure; not that compromises are not often proper, but that no popular government can long survive a marked precedent that those who carry an election can only save the government from immediate destruction by giving up the main point upon which the people gave the election. The people themselves, and not their servants, can safely reverse their own deliberate decisions.

As a private citizen the executive could not have consented that these institutions shall perish; much less could he, in betrayal of so vast and so sacred a trust as the free people have confided to him. He felt that he had no moral right to shrink, nor even to count the chances of his own life in what might follow. In full view of his great responsibility he has, so far, done what he has deemed his duty. You will now, according to your own judgment, perform yours.

He sincerely hopes that your views and your actions may so accord with his, as to assure all faithful citizens who have been disturbed in their rights of a certain and speedy restoration to them, under the Constitution and the laws.

And having thus chosen our course, without guile and with pure purpose, let us renew our trust in God, and go forward without fear and with manly hearts.

MEMORANDA OF MILITARY POLICY

(Written after the defeat at Bull Run)

The Battle of Bull Run had been fought and lost on July 21. All night long, and throughout the next day, the defeated troops had poured into Washington. Lincoln had stayed up all night to hear first-hand accounts of the battle. On the next night he jotted down this outline of military policy. On July 23, he copied out carefully what he had written, and on July 27, added two more items.

July 23, 1861

1. LET the plan for making the blockade effective be pushed forward with all possible dispatch.

2. Let the volunteer forces at Fort Monroe and vicinity under General Butler be constantly drilled, disciplined, and instructed without more for the present.

3. Let Baltimore be held as now, with a gentle but firm and certain hand.

4. Let the force now under Patterson or Banks be strengthened and made secure in its position.

5. Let the forces in Western Virginia act till further orders according to instructions or orders from General McClellan.

6. [Let] General Frémont push forward his organization and operations in the West as rapidly as possible, giving rather special attention to Missouri.

7. Let the forces late before Manassas, except the three-months men, be reorganized as rapidly as possible in their camps here and about Arlington.

8. Let the three-months forces who decline to enter the longer service be discharged as rapidly as circumstances will permit.

9. Let the new volunteer forces be brought forward as fast as possible, and especially into the camps on the two sides of the river here.

(Added on July 27, 1861)

When the foregoing shall have been substantially attended to:

1. Let Manassas Junction (or some point on one or other of the railroads near it) and Strasburg be seized and permanently held, with an open line from Washington to Manassas, and an open line from Harper's Ferry to Strasburg—the military men to find the way of doing these.

2. This done, a joint movement from Cairo on Memphis, and from Cincinnati on East Tennessee.

LETTER TO GENERAL JOHN C. FRÉMONT

John C. Frémont had been the Presidential candidate during the campaign of 1856. He was picturesque and colorful; more picturesque, however, than competent. Lincoln had placed him in command in Missouri—a border state that was being torn apart by its Confederate and Union allegiances. Frémont bungled the campaign in Missouri, and charges of corruption in army contracts in that section became a public scandal. On August 30, Frémont had issued a proclamation emancipating the slaves belonging to all those people in his territory who had taken up arms against the United States Government. The first word Lincoln had had of his commander's ill-advised attempt at emancipation was when he read an account of it in a newspaper. He writes here a gentle letter to Frémont, suggesting that he modify his proclamation.

Washington, D. C., September 2, 1861

MY DEAR SIR: Two points in your proclamation of August 30 give me some anxiety:

FIRST. Should you shoot a man, according to the proclamation, the Confederates would very certainly shoot our best men in their hands in retaliation; and so, man for man, indefinitely. It is, therefore, my order that you allow no man to be shot under the proclamation without first having my approbation or consent.

SECOND. I think there is a great danger that the closing paragraph, in relation to the confiscation of property and the liberating slaves of traitorous owners, will alarm our Southern Union friends and turn them against us; perhaps ruin our rather fair prospect for Kentucky. Allow me, therefore, to ask that you will, as of your own motion, modify that paragraph so as to conform to the first and fourth sections of the act of Congress entitled, "An act to confiscate property used for insurrectionary purposes," approved August 6, 1861, and a copy of which act I herewith send you.

This letter is written in a spirit of caution, and not of censure. I send it by special messenger, in order that it may certainly and speedily reach you.

ORDER TO GENERAL FRÉMONT

Frémont refused to take Lincoln's suggestion that he modify his proclamation of emancipation and bluntly told Lincoln that if the *proclamation were to be modified, it would have to be done by Presidential command. Lincoln here issues the official order, modifying the proclamation.*

Washington, September 11, 1861

SIR: Yours of the 8th, in answer to mine of the 2d instant, is just received. Assuming·that you, upon the ground, could better judge of the necessities of your position than I could at this distance, on seeing your proclamation of August 30 I perceived no general objection to it. The particular clause, however, in relation to the confiscation of property and the liberation of slaves appeared to me to be objectionable in its nonconformity to the act of Congress passed the 6th of last August upon the same subjects; and hence I wrote you, expressing my wish that that clause should be modified accordingly. Your answer, just received, expresses the preference on your part that I should make an open order for the modification, which I very cheerfully do. It is therefore ordered that the said clause of said proclamation be so modified, held, and construed as to conform to, and not to transcend, the provisions on the same subject contained in the act of Congress entitled, "An act to confiscate property used for insurrectionary purposes," approved August 6, 1861, and that said act be published at length with this order.

Your obedient servant,

A. LINCOLN

LETTER TO O. H. BROWNING

Frémont's attempt to liberate the slaves in the section under his command had been received with great approbation by the abolitionists. Lincoln's order countermanding Frémont's proclamation was widely criticized by them. Browning, a lawyer of Quincy, Illinois, was a close personal friend of Lincoln's. He wrote to the

President questioning what he had done; Lincoln here replies to
him giving him the reasons for his action in the Frémont matter.

(*Private and confidential*)

Executive Mansion, September 22, 1861

My DEAR SIR: Yours of the 17th is just received; and coming
from you, I confess it astonishes me. That you should object
to my adhering to a law which you had assisted in making
and presenting to me less than a month before is odd enough.
But this is a very small part. General Frémont's proclamation as to confiscation of property and the liberation of slaves
is purely political and not within the range of military law or
necessity. If a commanding general finds a necessity to seize
the farm of a private owner for a pasture, an encampment, or
a fortification, he has the right to do so, and to so hold it as
long as the necessity lasts; and this is within military law,
because within military necessity. But to say the farm shall
no longer belong to the owner, or his heirs forever, and this
as well when the farm is not needed for military purposes as
when it is, is purely political, without the savor of military
law about it. And the same is true of slaves. If the general
needs them, he can seize them and use them; but when the
need is past, it is not for him to fix their permanent future
condition. That must be settled according to laws made by
law-makers, and not by military proclamations. The proclamation in the point in question is simply "dictatorship." It
assumes that the general may do anything he pleases—confiscate the lands and free the slaves of loyal people, as well
as of disloyal ones. And going the whole figure, I have no
doubt, would be more popular with some thoughtless people
than that which has been done! But I cannot assume this
reckless position, nor allow others to assume it on my responsibility.

You speak of it as being the only means of saving the government. On the contrary, it is itself the surrender of the government. Can it be pretended that it is any longer the Government of the United States—any government of constitution and laws—wherein a general or a president may make permanent rules of property by proclamation? I do not say Congress might not with propriety pass a law on the point, just such as General Frémont proclaimed. I do not say I might not, as a member of Congress, vote for it. What I object to is, that I, as President, shall expressly or impliedly seize and exercise the permanent legislative functions of the government.

So much as to principle. Now as to policy. No doubt the thing was popular in some quarters, and would have been more so if it had been a general declaration of emancipation. The Kentucky legislature would not budge till that proclamation was modified; and General Anderson telegraphed me that on news of General Frémont having actually issued deeds of manumission, a whole company of our volunteers threw down their arms and disbanded. I was so assured as to think it probable that the very arms we had furnished Kentucky would be turned against us. I think to lose Kentucky is nearly the same as to lose the whole game. Kentucky gone, we cannot hold Missouri, nor, as I think, Maryland. These all against us, and the job on our hands is too large for us. We would as well consent to separation at once, including the surrender of this capital. On the contrary, if you will give up your restlessness for new positions, and back me manfully on the grounds upon which you and other kind friends gave me the election and have approved in my public documents, we shall go through triumphantly. You must not understand I took my course on the proclamation because of Kentucky. I took the same ground in a private letter to General Frémont before I heard from Kentucky.

You think I am inconsistent because I did not also forbid

General Frémont to shoot men under the proclamation. I understand that part to be within military law, but I also think, and so privately wrote General Frémont, that it is impolitic in this, that our adversaries have the power, and will certainly exercise it, to shoot as many of our men as we shoot of theirs. I did not say this in the public letter, because it is a subject I prefer not to discuss in the hearing of our enemies.

NOTE TO MAJOR RAMSEY

This is one of Lincoln's characteristic notes in which the personality of the man comes through the ordinarily cut-and-dried wording of such documents.

Executive Mansion, October 17, 1861

MY DEAR SIR: The lady bearer of this says she has two sons who want to work. Set them at it if possible. Wanting to work is so rare a want that it should be encouraged.

ORDER RETIRING GENERAL SCOTT AND APPOINTING GENERAL McCLELLAN HIS SUCCESSOR

General Winfield Scott was seventy-five years old in 1861 and in bad physical condition—so bad in fact that he was confined to bed most of the time; his heavy body had to be hoisted up into a sitting position by an elaborate harness. He was obviously in no state to command the Federal armies during an important war. Lincoln had brought McClellan to Washington a few days after the Battle of Bull Run. McClellan had treated his elder superior officer with contempt, and relations between the two men had become in-

creasingly strained. *Lincoln here regretfully retires Scott, with Scott's own consent, and appoints McClellan in his stead.*

Executive Mansion, Washington, November 1, 1861

ON THE 1st day of November, A.D., 1861, upon his own application to the President of the United States, Brevet Lieutenant-General Winfield Scott is ordered to be placed, and hereby is placed, upon the list of retired officers of the army of the United States, without reduction in his current pay, subsistence, or allowances.

The American people will hear with sadness and deep emotion that General Scott has withdrawn from the active control of the army, while the President and a unanimous Cabinet express their own and the nation's sympathy in his personal affliction, and their profound sense of the important public services rendered by him to his country during his long and brilliant career, among which will ever be gratefully distinguished his faithful devotion to the Constitution, the Union, and the flag when assailed by parricidal rebellion.

A. LINCOLN

The President is pleased to direct that Major-General George B. McClellan assume the command of the army of the United States. . . .

FROM THE ANNUAL MESSAGE
TO CONGRESS

The special session of Congress called by President Lincoln for July 4 had adjourned on August 6. Congress met in regular session on December 3, and Lincoln here delivers his first annual message. It was delivered against a background of excited public discussion of the Trent Affair. It is interesting to note that Lincoln here de-

parts, for the first time, from the custom used in the earlier July message of mentioning himself only as "he" or "the Executive." He now uses the pronoun "I." In this message he again presents his theories on the relationship between capital and labor.

December 3, 1861

FELLOW-CITIZENS OF THE SENATE AND HOUSE OF REPRESENTATIVES: In the midst of unprecedented political troubles we have cause of great gratitude to God for unusual good health and most abundant harvests.

You will not be surprised to learn that, in the peculiar exigencies of the times, our intercourse with foreign nations has been attended with profound solicitude, chiefly turning upon our own domestic affairs.

A disloyal portion of the American people have, during the whole year, been engaged in an attempt to divide and destroy the Union. A nation which endures factious domestic division is exposed to disrespect abroad; and one party, if not both, is sure, sooner or later, to invoke foreign intervention. Nations thus tempted to interfere are not always able to resist the counsels of seeming expediency and ungenerous ambition, although measures adopted under such influences seldom fail to be unfortunate and injurious to those adopting them.

The disloyal citizens of the United States who have offered the ruin of our country in return for the aid and comfort which they have invoked abroad, have received less patronage and encouragement than they probably expected. If it were just to suppose, as the insurgents have seemed to assume, that foreign nations in this case, discarding all moral, social, and treaty obligations, would act solely and selfishly for the most speedy restoration of commerce, including, especially, the acquisition of cotton, those nations appear as yet not to have seen their way to their object more directly or clearly through the destruction than through the preservation of the Union.

If we could dare to believe that foreign nations are actuated by no higher principle than this, I am quite sure a sound argument could be made to show them that they can reach their aim more readily and easily by aiding to crush this rebellion than by giving encouragement to it.

The principal lever relied on by the insurgents for exciting foreign nations to hostility against us, as already intimated, is the embarrassment of commerce. Those nations, however, not improbably saw from the first that it was the Union which made as well our foreign as our domestic commerce. They can scarcely have failed to perceive that the effort for disunion produces the existing difficulty; and that one strong nation promises more durable peace and a more extensive, valuable, and reliable commerce than can the same nation broken in hostile fragments.

It is not my purpose to review our discussions with foreign states, because, whatever might be their wishes or dispositions, the integrity of our country and the stability of our government mainly depend, not upon them, but on the loyalty, virtue, patriotism, and intelligence of the American people. The correspondence itself, with the usual reservations, is herewith submitted.

I venture to hope it will appear that we have practised prudence and liberality toward foreign powers, averting causes of irritation, and with firmness maintaining our own rights and honor.

*   *   *

The war continues. In considering the policy to be adopted for suppressing the insurrection, I have been anxious and careful that the inevitable conflict for this purpose shall not degenerate into a violent and remorseless revolutionary struggle. I have, therefore, in every case thought it proper to keep the integrity of the Union prominent as the primary object of the contest on our part, leaving all questions which are not

of vital military importance to the more deliberate action of
the legislature. . . .

The last ray of hope for preserving the Union peaceably
expired at the assault upon Fort Sumter; and a general review of what has occurred since may not be unprofitable.
What was painfully uncertain then is much better defined
and more distinct now; and the progress of events is plainly
in the right direction. The insurgents confidently claimed a
strong support from north of Mason and Dixon's line; and
the friends of the Union were not free from apprehension on
the point. This, however, was soon settled definitely, and on
the right side. South of the line, noble little Delaware led
off right from the first. Maryland was made to seem against
the Union. Our soldiers were assaulted, bridges were burned,
and railroads torn up within her limits, and we were many
days, at one time, without the ability to bring a single regiment over her soil to the capital. Now her bridges and railroads are repaired and open to the government; she already
gives seven regiments to the cause of the Union and none to
the enemy; and her people, at a regular election, have sustained the Union by a larger majority and a larger aggregate
vote than they ever before gave to any candidate or any question. Kentucky, too, for some time in doubt, is now decidedly,
and, I think, unchangeably, ranged on the side of the Union.
Missouri is comparatively quiet, and, I believe, cannot again
be overrun by the insurrectionists. These three States of Maryland, Kentucky, and Missouri, neither of which would promise a single soldier at first, have now an aggregate of not less
than forty thousand in the field for the Union, while of their
citizens certainly not more than a third of that number, and
they of doubtful whereabouts and doubtful existence, are in
arms against it. After a somewhat bloody struggle of months,
winter closes on the Union people of western Virginia, leaving them masters of their own country.

An insurgent force of about 1500, for months dominating

the narrow peninsular region constituting the counties of Accomac and Northampton, and known as the eastern shore of Virginia, together with some contiguous parts of Maryland, have laid down their arms, and the people there have renewed their allegiance to and accepted the protection of the old flag. This leaves no armed insurrectionist north of the Potomac or east of the Chesapeake.

Also we have obtained a footing at each of the isolated points, on the southern coast, of Hatteras, Port Royal, Tybee Island, near Savannah, and Ship Island; and we likewise have some general accounts of popular movements in behalf of the Union in North Carolina and Tennessee.

These things demonstrate that the cause of the Union is advancing steadily and certainly southward. . . .

It continues to develop that the insurrection is largely, if not exclusively, a war upon the first principle of popular government—the rights of the people. Conclusive evidence of this is found in the most grave and maturely considered public documents as well as in the general tone of the insurgents. In those documents we find the abridgment of the existing right of suffrage and the denial to the people of all right to participate in the selection of public officers except the legislative, boldly advocated, with labored arguments to prove that large control of the people in government is the source of all political evil. Monarchy itself is sometimes hinted at as a possible refuge from the power of the people.

In my present position I could scarcely be justified were I to omit raising a warning voice against this approach of returning despotism.

It is not needed nor fitting here that a general argument should be made in favor of popular institutions; but there is one point, with its connections, not so hackneyed as most others, to which I ask a brief attention. It is the effort to place capital on an equal footing with, if not above, labor, in the structure of government. It is assumed that labor is available only in connection with capital; that nobody labors unless somebody else, owning capital, somehow by the use of it induces him to labor. This assumed, it is next considered whether it is best that capital shall hire laborers, and thus induce them to work by their own consent, or buy them, and drive them to it without their consent. Having proceeded thus far, it is naturally concluded that all laborers are either hired laborers or what we call slaves. And, further, it is assumed that whoever is once a hired laborer is fixed in that condition for life.

Now, there is no such relation between capital and labor as assumed, nor is there any such thing as a free man being fixed for life in the condition of a hired laborer. Both these assumptions are false, and all inferences from them are groundless.

Labor is prior to, and independent of, capital. Capital is only the fruit of labor, and could never have existed if labor had not first existed. Labor is the superior of capital, and deserves much the higher consideration. Capital has its rights, which are as worthy of protection as any other rights. Nor is it denied that there is, and probably always will be, a relation between labor and capital producing mutual benefits. The error is in assuming that the whole labor of the community exists within that relation. A few men own capital, and that few avoid labor themselves, and with their capital hire or buy another few to labor for them. A large majority belong to neither class—neither work for others nor have others working for them. In most of the Southern States a majority of the whole people, of all colors, are neither slaves nor masters; while in the Northern a large majority are neither hirers nor hired. Men with their families—wives, sons, and daughters—work for themselves, on their farms, in their houses, and in their shops taking the whole product to themselves, and asking no favors of capital on the one hand, nor of hired laborers or slaves on the other. It is not forgotten that a considerable number of persons mingle their own labor with capital—that is, they labor with their own hands and also buy or hire others to labor for them; but this is only a mixed and not a distinct class. No principle stated is disturbed by the existence of this mixed class.

Again, as has already been said, there is not, of necessity, any such thing as the free hired laborer being fixed to that condition for life. Many independent men everywhere in these States, a few years back in their lives, were hired laborers. The prudent, penniless beginner in the world labors for wages awhile, saves a surplus with which to buy tools or land for himself, then labors on his own account another while, and at length hires another new beginner to help him. This is the just and generous and prosperous system which opens the way to all—gives hope to all, and consequent energy and progress and improvement of condition to all. No men living are more worthy to be trusted than those who toil up from poverty—none less inclined to take or touch aught which they have not honestly earned. Let them beware of surrendering a political power which they already possess, and which, if surrendered, will surely be used to close the door of advancement against such as they, and to fix new disabilities and burdens upon them, till all of liberty shall be lost.

From the first taking of our national census to the last are seventy years; and we find our population at the end of the period eight times as great as it was at the beginning. The increase of those other things which men deem desirable has been even greater. We thus have, at one view, what the popular principle, applied to government, through the machinery of the States and the Union, has produced in a given time; and also what, if firmly maintained, it promises for the future. There are already among us those who, if the Union be preserved, will live to see it contain 250,000,000. The struggle of today is not altogether for today—it is for a vast future also. With a reliance on Providence all the more firm and earnest, let us proceed in the great task which events have devolved upon us.

LETTER TO MAJOR-GENERAL HUNTER

*David Hunter had accompanied Lincoln on the Presidential train
to Washington. Lincoln had sent him to Missouri after his difficulties with Frémont, and then to Kansas. Hunter felt that the
Kansas command was a very unimportant one. He wrote to Lincoln, telling him so in no uncertain terms. Lincoln replies to his
dissatisfied general with his usual graciousness and tact.*

Executive Mansion, December 31, 1861

DEAR SIR: Yours of the 23d is received, and I am constrained
to say it is difficult to answer so ugly a letter in good temper.
I am, as you intimate, losing much of the great confidence I
placed in you, not from any act or omission of yours touching
the public service, up to the time you were sent to Leavenworth, but from the flood of grumbling despatches and letters
I have seen from you since. I knew you were being ordered to
Leavenworth at the time it was done; and I aver that with as
tender a regard for your honor and your sensibilities as I had
for my own, it never occurred to me that you were being
"humiliated, insulted and disgraced!" nor have I, up to this
day, heard an intimation that you have been wronged, coming
from any one but yourself. No one has blamed you for the
retrograde movement from Springfield, nor for the information
you gave General Cameron; and this you could readily understand, if it were not for your unwarranted assumption that
the ordering you to Leavenworth must necessarily have been
done as a *punishment* for some *fault*. I thought then, and think
yet, the position assigned to you is as responsible, and as honorable, as that assigned to Buell—I know that General McClellan
expected more important results from it. My impression is that
at the time you were assigned to the new Western Department, it had not been determined to replace General Sherman

in Kentucky; but of this I am not certain, because the idea that a command in Kentucky was very desirable, and one in the farther West undesirable, had never occurred to me. You constantly speak of being placed in command of only 3,000. Now tell me, is this not mere impatience? Have you not known all the while that you are to command four or five times that many?

I have been, and am sincerely your friend; and if, as such, I dare to make a suggestion, I would say you are adopting the best possible way to ruin yourself. "Act well your part, there all the honor lies." He who does *something* at the head of one Regiment, will eclipse him who does *nothing* at the head of a hundred.

GENERAL WAR ORDER NO. ONE

McClellan's army was being assembled, equipped and drilled. Meanwhile the Government and the people were dissatisfied at seeing no action. Lincoln issues this General War Order so as to compel McClellan and his other commanders to move against the Confederate forces. The order was never carried out. McClellan successfully persuaded him that it would be inadvisable to do so, and by the time February 22 (the day for the general movement) had come, Lincoln was in the midst of grief over the loss of his son, Willie, who had died on February 20.

Executive Mansion, January 27, 1862

ORDERED, That the 22d day of February, 1862, be the day for a general movement of all the land and naval forces of the United States against the insurgent forces. That especially the army at and about Fortress Monroe; the Army of the Potomac; the Army of Western Virginia; the army near Munfordville, Kentucky; the army and flotilla at Cairo, and a naval force in the Gulf of Mexico, be ready to move on that day.

That all other forces, both land and naval, with their respective commanders, obey existing orders for the time, and be ready to obey additional orders when duly given.

That the heads of departments, and especially the Secretaries of War and of the Navy, with all their subordinates, and the General-in-Chief, with all other commanders and subordinates of land and naval forces, will severally be held to their strict and full responsibilities for prompt execution of this order.

LETTER TO GENERAL G. B. McCLELLAN

McClellan and Lincoln differed radically on the plan of campaign to be used against Richmond. Lincoln wanted the army to march due south and make a direct attack; McClellan wanted to attack by land and water, moving toward Richmond by a flanking approach up the Peninsula between the York and the James Rivers. Lincoln presents here, with the clarity of a lawyer's brief, his argument for his own plan.

Executive Mansion, February 3, 1862

My Dear Sir: You and I have distinct and different plans for a movement of the Army of the Potomac—yours to be down the Chesapeake, up the Rappahannock to Urbana, and across land to the terminus of the railroad on the York River; mine to move directly to a point on the railroad southwest of Manassas.

If you will give me satisfactory answers to the following questions, I shall gladly yield my plan to yours.

First. Does not your plan involve a greatly larger expenditure of time and money than mine?

Second. Wherein is a victory more certain by your plan than mine?

Third. Wherein is a victory more valuable by your plan than mine?

FOURTH. In fact, would it not be less valuable in this, that it would break no great line of the enemy's communications, while mine would?

FIFTH. In case of disaster, would not a retreat be more difficult by your plan than mine?

RESPITE AND CONFIRMATION OF SENTENCE FOR NATHANIEL GORDON

During the summer of 1860, Captain Nathaniel Gordon of Portland, Maine, had taken his ship, the Erie, to Africa, where he had exchanged a cargo of liquor for a cargo of eight hundred and ninety slaves. All but one hundred and seventy-two of these were children who were safe to carry since there was no danger of resistance from them. His ship was overtaken by the U. S. Mohican near Cuba. The Negroes were sent to the free colony in Liberia, while Gordon was taken to New York for trial. His ship was seized and sold at auction, and he himself was sentenced to be hanged. His friends interceded with the President for a commutation of sentence, but in this case the ordinarily soft-hearted Lincoln was adamant; he simply granted a short respite so Gordon might prepare himself for death. There were threats that a rescuing mob would storm the New York City jail on the day he was hanged. He was led into the jailyard under a heavy guard from the Navy Yard shortly before noon on the day appointed for his death. He almost collapsed on the gallows, but the sentence was carried through, and the slaver was hanged.

February 4, 1862

WHEREAS it appears that . . . Nathaniel Gordon was indicted and convicted for being engaged in the slave trade, and was . . . sentenced to be put to death by hanging by the neck on Friday the 7th day of February, A. D. 1862;

And whereas a large number of respectable citizens have earnestly besought me to commute the said sentence of the said Nathaniel Gordon to a term of imprisonment for life, which application I have felt it to be my duty to refuse;

And whereas it has seemed to me probable that the unsuccessful application made for the commutation of his sentence may have prevented the said Nathaniel Gordon from making the necessary preparation for the awful change which awaits him:

Now, therefore, be it known that I, Abraham Lincoln, President of the United States of America, have granted and do hereby grant unto him, the said Nathaniel Gordon, a respite of the above-recited sentence until Friday, the 21st day of February, A. D. 1862, between the hours of twelve o'clock at noon and three o'clock in the afternoon of the said day, when the said sentence shall be executed.

In granting this respite it becomes my painful duty to admonish the prisoner that, relinquishing all expectation of pardon by human authority, he refer himself alone to the mercy of the common God and Father of all men.

FROM A MESSAGE TO CONGRESS RECOMMENDING COMPENSATED EMANCIPATION

The legally trained Lincoln regarded it as unfair to free slaves that represented property without providing some kind of compensation for their owners. In this message to Congress he presents a plan whereby a state desiring to free its slaves would be given financial compensation by the United States Government.

March 6, 1862

FELLOW-CITIZENS OF THE SENATE AND HOUSE OF REPRESENTATIVES: I recommend the adoption of a joint resolution by your honorable bodies, which shall be substantially as follows:

RESOLVED, That the United States ought to co-operate with any

State which may adopt gradual abolishment of slavery, giving to such State pecuniary aid, to be used by such State, in its discretion, to compensate for the inconveniences, public and private, produced by such change of system.

If the proposition contained in the resolution does not meet the approval of Congress and the country, there is the end; but if it does command such approval, I deem it of importance that the States and people immediately interested should be at once distinctly notified of the fact, so that they may begin to consider whether to accept or reject it. The Federal Government would find its highest interest in such a measure, as one of the most efficient means of self-preservation. The leaders of the existing insurrection entertain the hope that this government will ultimately be forced to acknowledge the independence of some part of the disaffected region, and that all the slave States north of such part will then say, "The Union for which we have struggled being already gone, we now choose to go with the Southern section." To deprive them of this hope substantially ends the rebellion; and the initiation of emancipation completely deprives them of it as to all the States initiating it. The point is not that all the States tolerating slavery would very soon, if at all, initiate emancipation; but that while the offer is equally made to all, the more Northern shall, by such initiation, make it certain to the more Southern that in no event will the former ever join the latter in their proposed confederacy. I say "initiation" because, in my judgment, gradual and not sudden emancipation is better for all. In the mere financial or pecuniary view, any member of Congress, with the census tables and treasury reports before him, can readily see for himself how very soon the current expenditures of this war would purchase, at fair valuation, all the slaves in any named State. Such a proposition on the part of the General Government sets up no claim of a right by Federal authority to interfere with slavery within State limits, referring, as it does, the absolute control of the subject in each case to the State and its people immediately interested. It is proposed as a matter of perfectly free choice with them. . . .

LETTER TO JAMES A. McDOUGALL

Lincoln explains how his plan for gradual emancipation with compensation compared in cost with the expense of the War.

Executive Mansion, March 14, 1862

MY DEAR SIR: As to the expensiveness of the plan of gradual emancipation with compensation, proposed in the late message, please allow me one or two brief suggestions.

Less than one-half-day's cost of this war would pay for all the slaves in Delaware at four hundred dollars per head.

Thus, all the slaves in Delaware
by the census of 1860, are....   1,798
                             400
                           ———

Cost of the slaves............ $719,200
One day's cost of the war......$2,000,000

Again, less than eighty-seven days' cost of this war would, at the same price, pay for all in Delaware, Maryland, District of Columbia, Kentucky, and Missouri.

Thus, slaves in	Delaware...........	1,798
″ ″	Maryland...........	87,188
″ ″	District of Columbia.	3,181
″ ″	Kentucky...........	225,490
″ ″	Missouri...........	114,965
		———
		432,622
		400
		———

Cost of slaves.................$173,048,800
Eighty-seven days' cost of the war $174,000,000

Do you doubt that taking the initiatory steps on the part of those States and this District would shorten the war more than eighty-seven days, and thus be an actual saving of expense?

A word as to the time and manner of incurring the expense. Suppose, for instance, a State devises and adopts a system by which the institution absolutely ceases therein by a named day—say January 1, 1882. Then let the sum to be paid to such a State by the United States be ascertained by taking from the census of 1860 the number of slaves within the State, and multiplying that number by four hundred—the United States to pay such sums to the State in twenty equal annual installments, in six percent bonds of the United States.

The sum thus given, as to time and manner, I think, would not be half as onerous as would be an equal sum raised now for the indefinite prosecution of the war; but of this you can judge as well as I. I inclose a census table for your convenience.

LETTER TO GENERAL G. B. McCLELLAN

In April, 1862, McClellan's Peninsular campaign was just getting under way. The Battle of Shiloh had been fought in the West; the country was impatiently awaiting action from McClellan who seemed to be moving with intolerable slowness. Lincoln had long disagreed with McClellan about his plan of campaign, and there had been further disagreement about the number of troops that should be left for the defense of Washington.

Washington, April 9, 1862

MY DEAR SIR: Your dispatches, complaining that you are not properly sustained, while they do not offend me, do pain me very much. . . .

After you left I ascertained that less than 20,000 unorganized men, without a single field-battery, were all you designed to be left for the defense of Washington and Manassas

Junction, and part of this even was to go to General Hooker's old position; General Banks's corps, once designed for Manassas Junction, was divided and tied up on the line of Winchester and Strasburg, and could not leave it without again exposing the upper Potomac and the Baltimore and Ohio Railroad. This presented (or would present, when McDowell and Sumner should be gone) a great temptation to the enemy to turn back from the Rappahannock and sack Washington. My explicit order that Washington should, by the judgment of all the commanders of corps, be left entirely secure, had been neglected. It was precisely this that drove me to detain McDowell.

I do not forget that I was satisfied with your arrangement to leave Banks at Manassas Junction; but when that arrangement was broken up and nothing was substituted for it, of course I was not satisfied. I was constrained to substitute something for it myself.

And now allow me to ask, do you really think I should permit the line from Richmond via Manassas Junction to this city to be entirely open, except what resistance could be presented by less than 20,000 unorganized troops? This is a question which the country will not allow me to evade.

There is a curious mystery about the number of the troops now with you. When I telegraphed you on the 6th, saying you had over 100,000 with you, I had just obtained from the Secretary of War a statement, taken as he said from your own returns, making 108,000 then with you and en route to you. You now say you will have but 85,000 when all en route to you shall have reached you. How can this discrepancy of 23,000 be accounted for?

As to General Wool's command, I understand it is doing for you precisely what a like number of your own would have to do if that command was away. I suppose the whole force which has gone forward to you is with you by this time; and if so, I think it is the precise time for you to strike a blow. By delay the enemy will relatively gain upon you—that is, he will gain faster by fortifications and reinforcements than you can by reinforcements alone.

And once more let me tell you it is indispensable to you that you strike a blow. I am powerless to help this. You will do me the justice to remember I always insisted that going down the bay in search of a field, instead of fighting at or near Manassas, was only shifting and not surmounting a difficulty; that we would find the same enemy and the same or equal intrenchments at either place. The country will not fail to note—is noting now—that the present hesitation to move upon an intrenched enemy is but the story of Manassas repeated.

I beg to assure you that I have never written you or spoken to you in greater kindness of feeling than now, nor with a fuller purpose to sustain you, so far as in my most anxious judgment I consistently can; but you must act.

LETTER TO GENERAL G. B. McCLELLAN

McClellan's Peninsular campaign was still proceeding very slowly with more talk and wrangling than actual fighting. Lincoln again writes a fatherly letter of advice to his young commander.

Fort Monroe, Virginia, May 9, 1862

My Dear Sir: I have just assisted the Secretary of War in framing part of a dispatch to you relating to army corps, which dispatch of course will have reached you before this will.

I wish to say a few words to you privately on this subject. I ordered the army corps organization not only on the unanimous opinion of the twelve generals whom you had selected and assigned as generals of division, but also on the unanimous opinion of every military man I could get an opinion from (and every modern military book), yourself only excepted. Of course I did not on my own judgment pretend to understand the subject. I now think it indispensable for you to know how your struggle against it is received in quarters which we cannot entirely disregard. It is looked upon as merely an effort to pamper one or two pets and to persecute and degrade their supposed rivals. I have had no word from Sumner, Heintzelman, or Keyes. The commanders of these corps are of course the three highest officers with you, but I am constantly told that you have no consultation or communication with them; that you consult and communicate with nobody but General Fitz-John Porter and perhaps General Franklin. I do not say these complaints are true or just, but at all events it is proper you should know of their existence. Do the commanders of corps disobey your orders in anything?

When you relieved General Hamilton of his command the other day, you thereby lost the confidence of at least one of your best friends in the Senate. And here let me say, not as applicable to you personally, that Senators and Representatives speak of me in their places as they please without question, and that officers of the army must cease addressing insulting letters to them for taking no greater liberty with them.

But to return. Are you strong enough—are you strong enough, even with my help—to set your foot upon the necks of Sumner, Heintzelman, and Keyes all at once? This is a practical and very serious question for you.

The success of your army and the cause of the country are the same, and of course I only desire the good of the cause.

FROM THE PROCLAMATION REVOKING GENERAL HUNTER'S ORDER OF MILITARY EMANCIPATION

On May 9, General Hunter, in command of the Department of the South, had issued a proclamation emancipating the slaves in

Georgia, Florida and South Carolina. This was exactly the same kind of difficulty that Lincoln had had with Frémont during the autumn of 1861. Again he had to countermand his commander's order; he here does so.

May 19, 1862

WHEREAS there appears in the public prints what purports to be a proclamation of Major-General Hunter [freeing the slaves in Georgia, Florida, and South Carolina]:

And whereas the same is producing some excitement and misunderstanding: therefore,

I, Abraham Lincoln, President of the United States, proclaim and declare that the Government of the United States had no knowledge, information, or belief of an intention on the part of General Hunter to issue such a proclamation; nor has it yet any authentic information that the document is genuine. And further, that neither General Hunter, nor any other commander or person, has been authorized by the Government of the United States to make a proclamation declaring the slaves of any State free; and that the supposed proclamation now in question, whether genuine or false, is altogether void so far as respects such a declaration.

I further make known that, whether it be competent for me, as Commander-in-Chief of the army and navy, to declare the slaves of any State or States free, and whether, at any time, in any case, it shall have become a necessity indispensable to the maintenance of the government to exercise such supposed power, are questions which, under my responsibility, I reserve to myself, and which I cannot feel justified in leaving to the decision of commanders in the field. . . .

To the people of [the Southern] States I now earnestly appeal. I do not argue—I beseech you to make arguments for yourselves. You cannot, if you would, be blind to the signs of the times. I beg of you a calm and enlarged consideration of them, ranging, if it may be, far above personal and partisan politics. This proposal makes common cause for a common object, casting no reproaches upon any. It acts not the Pharisee. The change it contemplates would come gently as the dews of heaven, not rending or wrecking anything. Will you not embrace it? So much good has not been done, by one effort, in all past time, as in the providence of God it is now your high privilege to do. May the vast future not have to lament that you have neglected it.

LETTER TO E. M. STANTON, SECRETARY OF WAR

This is one of many such letters that Lincoln found time to write in the midst of his multifarious duties as President.

June, 1862

DEAR SIR: The bearer of this, William J. Post, a member of the 140th Pennsylvania Regiment, wants to go to his home in Washington, Pa. As you can see, he is nothing but a boy, has been sick in the hospital, but I believe he is made of the right kind of stuff. Please see to his release and that he gets transportation home.

TELEGRAM TO GENERAL G. B. McCLELLAN

The Seven Days Battle before Richmond had begun on June 25. McClellan had appealed desperately to Lincoln for more reinforcements which had not been forthcoming. Lincoln again emphasizes to McClellan the necessity for keeping Washington protected against the enemy.

War Department, June 28, 1862

MAJOR-GENERAL McCLELLAN: Save your army, at all events. Will send reinforcements as fast as we can. Of course they cannot reach you today, tomorrow, or next day. I have not said you were ungenerous for saying you needed reinforcements. I thought you were ungenerous in assuming that I did not send them as fast as I could. I feel any misfortune to you and your army quite as keenly as you feel it yourself. If you have had a drawn battle, or a repulse, it is the price we pay for the enemy not being in Washington. We protected Washington, and the enemy concentrated on you. Had we stripped Washington, he would have been upon us before the troops could have gotten to you. Less than a week ago you notified us that reinforcements were leaving Richmond to come in front of us. It is the nature of the case, and neither you nor the government is to blame. Please tell at once the present condition and aspect of things.

TELEGRAM TO GENERAL G. B. McCLELLAN

The Seven Days Battle was still in progress, and McClellan was still appealing for men. Lincoln telegraphs to his general who was fighting a losing battle.

War Department, Washington, July 1, 1862

MAJOR-GENERAL GEORGE B. McCLELLAN: It is impossible to reinforce you for your present emergency. If we had a million of men, we could not get them to you in time. We have not the men to send. If you are not strong enough to face the enemy, you must find a place of security, and wait, rest, and repair. Maintain your ground if you can, but save the army at all events, even if you fall back to Fort Monroe. We still have strength enough in the country, and will bring it out.

LETTER TO GENERAL G. B. McCLELLAN

The Seven Days Battle had been fought, and McClellan's army had met with defeat. McClellan was hoping to attack again. Four days after writing this letter, Lincoln went to visit McClellan at Harrison's Landing and there realized that he would have to appoint a new man to the chief command. On July 11, he placed Halleck in charge of all the Federal armies, although he left McClellan in command of the Army of the Potomac.

War Department, Washington, July 4, 1862

I UNDERSTAND your position as stated in your letter and by General Marcy. To reinforce you so as to enable you to resume the offensive within a month, or even six weeks, is impossible. In addition to that arrived and now arriving from the Potomac (about 10,000 men, I suppose, and about 10,000 I hope you will have from Burnside very soon, and about 5,000 from Hunter a little later), I do not see how I can send you another man within a month. Under these circumstances the defensive for the present must be your only care. Save the army— first, where you are, if you can; secondly, by removal, if you must. You, on the ground, must be the judge as to which you will attempt, and of the means for effecting it. I but give it as my opinion that with the aid of the gunboats and the reinforcements mentioned above, you can hold your present position—provided, and so long as, you can keep the James River open below you. If you are not tolerably confident you can keep the James River open, you had better remove as soon as possible. I do not remember that you have expressed any apprehension as to the danger of having your communication cut on the river below you, yet I do not suppose it can have escaped your attention.

P. S. If at any time you feel able to take the offensive, you are not restrained from doing so.

A. L.

EMANCIPATION PROCLAMATION AS FIRST SUBMITTED TO THE CABINET, JULY 22, 1862

After the failure of the Peninsular campaign and the appointment of Halleck to the general command, Lincoln was in the mood for vigorous action. On July 13, while attending a funeral for Stanton's son, he intimated to Welles and Seward that he at last regarded the emancipation of the slaves as a military necessity. Nine days later he read this first draft of his Emancipation Proclamation to his Cabinet. It was at this meeting that Seward suggested that if the proclamation were issued at this moment of defeat, it would sound like a despairing cry from a bewildered administration. Lincoln agreed to wait for a more favorable moment to release it to the public. The wording of the proclamation was thought out carefully by Lincoln who brought his legally trained mind to bear upon the problem. He could not afford to antagonize the border states, consequently this military measure sets free slaves only in those areas then in rebellion against the United States Government.

In pursuance of the sixth section of the act of Congress entitled "An act to suppress insurrection and to punish treason and rebellion, to seize and confiscate property of rebels, and for other purposes," approved July 17, 1862, and which act and the joint resolution explanatory thereof are herewith published, I, Abraham Lincoln, President of the United States, do hereby proclaim to and warn all persons within the contemplation of said sixth section to cease participating in, aiding, countenancing, or abetting the existing rebellion, or any rebellion, against the Government of the United States, and to return to their proper allegiance to the United States, on pain of the forfeitures and seizures as within and by said sixth section provided.

And I hereby make known that it is my purpose, upon the next meeting of Congress, to again recommend the adoption of a practical measure for tendering pecuniary aid to the free choice or rejection of any and all States which may then be recognizing and practically sustaining the authority of the United States, and which may then have voluntarily adopted, or thereafter may voluntarily adopt, gradual abolishment of slavery within such State or States; that the object is to practically restore, thenceforward to be maintained, the constitutional relation between the General Government and each and all the States wherein that relation is now suspended or disturbed; and that for this object the war, as it has been, will be prosecuted. And as a fit and necessary military measure for effecting this object, I, as Commander-in-Chief of the Army and Navy of the United States, do order and declare that on the first day of January, in the year of our Lord one thousand eight hundred and sixty-three, all persons held as slaves within any State or States wherein the constitutional authority of the United States shall not then be practically recognized, submitted to, and maintained, shall then, thenceforward, and forever be free.

LETTER TO CUTHBERT BULLITT

After New Orleans was captured by Farragut's fleet, Louisiana rapidly passed into Federal hands. Durant was a New Orleans lawyer and politician who was pro-Union in his sympathies. He had written to Bullitt to explain the situation in Louisiana, and Bullitt had shown his letter to Lincoln. Lincoln here writes a forthright message in which he analyzes his own feelings toward those who stood for the Union but did not come forward firmly to express their own loyalty.

(Private)

Washington, D. C., July 28, 1862

SIR: The copy of a letter addressed to yourself by Mr. Thomas J. Durant has been shown to me. The writer appears to be an able, a dispassionate, and an entirely sincere man. The first part of the letter is devoted to an effort to show that the secession ordinance of Louisiana was adopted against the will of a majority of the people. This is probably true, and in that fact may be found some instruction. Why did they allow the ordinance to go into effect? Why did they not assert themselves? Why stand passive and allow themselves to be trodden down by a minority? Why did they not hold popular meetings and have a convention of their own to express and enforce the true sentiment of the State? If preorganization was against them then, why not do this now that the United States Army is present to protect them? The paralysis— the dead palsy—of the government in this whole struggle is, that this class of men will do nothing for the government, nothing for themselves, except demanding that the government shall not strike its open enemies lest they be struck by accident!

Mr. Durant complains that in various ways the relation of master and slave is disturbed by the presence of our army, and he considers it particularly vexatious that this, in part, is done under cover of an act of Congress, while constitutional guaranties are suspended on the plea of military necessity. The truth is, that what is done and omitted about slaves is done and omitted on the same military necessity. It is a military necessity to have men and money; and we can get neither in sufficient numbers or amounts if we keep from or drive from our lines slaves coming to them. Mr. Durant cannot be ignorant of the pressure in this direction, nor of my efforts to hold it within bounds till he and such as he shall have time to help themselves.

I am not posted to speak understandingly on all the police regulations of which Mr. Durant complains. If experience shows any one of them to be wrong, let them be set right. I think I can perceive in the freedom of trade which Mr. Durant urges that he would relieve both friends and enemies from the pressure of the blockade. By this he would serve the enemy more effectively than the enemy is able to serve himself. I do not say or believe that to serve the enemy is the purpose of Mr. Durant, or that he is conscious of any purpose other than national and patriotic ones. Still, if there were a class of men who, having no choice of sides in the contest, were anxious only to have quiet and comfort for themselves while it rages, and to fall in with the victorious side at the end of it without loss to themselves, their advice as to the mode of conducting the contest would be precisely such as his is. He speaks of no duty—apparently thinks of none—resting upon Union men. He even thinks it injurious to the Union cause that they should be restrained in trade and passage without taking sides. They are to touch neither a sail nor a pump, but to be merely passengers—deadheads at that—to be carried snug and dry throughout the storm, and safely landed right side up. Nay, more: even a mutineer is to go untouched, lest these sacred passengers receive an accidental wound. Of course the rebellion will never be suppressed in Louisiana if the professed Union men there will neither help to do it nor permit the government to do it without their help. Now, I think the true remedy is very different from what is suggested by Mr. Durant. It does not lie in rounding the rough angles of the war, but in removing the necessity for the war. The people of Louisiana who wish protection to person and property have but to reach forth their hands and take it. Let them in good faith reinaugurate the national authority, and set up a State government conforming thereto under the Constitution. They know how to do it, and can have the protection of the army while doing it. The army will be withdrawn so soon as such State government can dispense with its presence; and the people of the

State can then, upon the old constitutional terms, govern themselves to their own liking. This is very simple and easy.

If they will not do this—if they prefer to hazard all for the sake of destroying the government, it is for them to consider whether it is probable I will surrender the government to save them from losing all. If they decline what I suggest, you scarcely need to ask what I will do. What would you do in my position? Would you drop the war where it is? Or would you prosecute it in future with elder-stalk squirts charged with rose-water? Would you deal lighter blows rather than heavier ones? Would you give up the contest, leaving any available means unapplied? I am in no boastful mood. I shall not do more than I can, and I shall do all I can, to save the government, which is my sworn duty as well as my personal inclination. I shall do nothing in malice. What I deal with is too vast for malicious dealing.

LETTER TO AUGUST BELMONT

August Belmont, the well-known New York financier, was the American agent for the Rothschilds. Politically, he was a Democrat and had been a delegate to the Democratic Convention in 1860 to support Stephen A. Douglas. Again Lincoln writes to explain his attitude toward the situation in Louisiana.

July 31, 1862

DEAR SIR: You send to Mr. W—— an extract from a letter written at New Orleans the 9th instant, which is shown to me. You do not give the writer's name; but plainly he is a man of ability, and probably of some note. He says: "The time has arrived when Mr. Lincoln must take a decisive course. Trying to please everybody, he will satisfy nobody. A vacillating policy in matters of importance is the very worst. Now is the time, if ever, for honest men who love their country to rally to its support. Why will not the North say officially that it wishes for the restoration of the Union as it was?"

And so, it seems, this is the point on which the writer thinks I have no policy. Why will he not read and understand what I have said?

The substance of the very declaration he desires is in the inaugural, in each of the two regular messages to Congress, and in many, if not all, the minor documents issued by the Executive since the inauguration.

Broken eggs cannot be mended; but Louisiana has nothing to do now but to take her place in the Union as it was, barring the already broken eggs. The sooner she does so, the smaller will be the amount of that which will be past mending. This government cannot much longer play a game in which it stakes all, and its enemies stake nothing. Those enemies must understand that they cannot experiment for ten years trying to destroy the government, and if they fail still come back into the Union unhurt. If they expect in any contingency to ever have the Union as it was, I join with the writer in saying, "Now is the time."

How much better it would have been for the writer to have gone at this, under the protection of the army at New Orleans, than to have sat down in a closet writing complaining letters northward!

FROM A LETTER TO COUNT A. DE GASPARIN

The Count de Gasparin, a French nobleman, had written a book published in translation during 1861 under the title of The Uprising of a Great People. *In this book De Gasparin had demonstrated his belief that slavery was the chief cause of the War. De Gasparin had appealed to European countries to favor the cause of the North and had upheld Lincoln as a great leader of the liberal tradition. Lincoln here writes to him in Switzerland to make clear*

the standing of a private soldier in the United States Army, and
also to give the reasons why the North, with her superiority of
men and resources, was as yet unable to win a decisive victory over
the South.

Executive Mansion, Washington, August 4, 1862

DEAR SIR: With us every soldier is a man of character, and
must be treated with more consideration than is customary in
Europe. Hence our great army, for slighter causes than could
have prevailed there, has dwindled rapidly, bringing the necessity for a new call earlier than was anticipated. We shall easily
obtain the new levy, however. Be not alarmed if you shall learn
that we shall have resorted to a draft for part of this. It seems
strange even to me, but it is true, that the government is now
pressed to this course by a popular demand. Thousands who
wish not to personally enter the service, are nevertheless anxious to pay and send substitutes, provided they can have assurance that unwilling persons, similarly situated, will be compelled to do likewise. Besides this, volunteers mostly choose to
enter newly forming regiments, while drafted men can be sent
to fill up the old ones, wherein man for man they are quite
doubly as valuable.

You ask, "Why is it that the North with her great armies
so often is found with inferiority of numbers face to face with
the armies of the South?" While I painfully know the fact, a
military man—which I am not—would better answer the question. The fact, I know, has not been overlooked; and I suppose
the cause of its continuance lies mainly in the other facts that
the enemy holds the interior and we the exterior lines; and that
we operate where the people convey information to the enemy,
while he operates where they convey none to us. . . .

You are quite right as to the importance to us, for its bearing upon Europe, that we should achieve military successes,
and the same is true for us at home as well as abroad. Yet it

seems unreasonable that a series of successes, extending through half a year, and clearing more than 100,000 square miles of country, should help us so little, while a single half-defeat should hurt us so much. But let us be patient.

I am very happy to know that my course has not conflicted with your judgment of propriety and policy. I can only say that I have acted upon my best convictions, without selfishness or malice, and that by the help of God I shall continue to do so.

FROM AN ADDRESS AT WASHINGTON

When McClellan first came to Washington he had met with Stanton's favor, but relations between the two men had soon become strained. The Peninsular campaign had failed, and McClellan's army was being removed to its original quarters near Washington. The country was torn apart by discussion as to who was responsible for the failure of the campaign. In this speech Lincoln makes a public answer to all the whispered charges.

August 6, 1862

FELLOW-CITIZENS: There has been a very widespread attempt to have a quarrel between General McClellan and the Secretary of War [Edwin M. Stanton]. Now, I occupy a position that enables me to observe that these two gentlemen are not nearly so deep in the quarrel as some pretending to be their friends. General McClellan's attitude is such that, in the very selfishness of his nature, he cannot but wish to be successful, and I hope he will; and the Secretary of War is in precisely the same situation. If the military commanders in the field cannot be successful, not only the Secretary of War, but myself—for the time being the master of them both—cannot but be failures. I know General McClellan wishes to be successful, and I know he does not wish it any more than the Secretary of

War for him, and both of them together no more than I wish it. Sometimes we have a dispute about how many men General McClellan has had, and those who would disparage him say that he has had a very large number, and those who would disparage the Secretary of War insist that General McClellan has had a very small number. The basis for this is, there is always a wide difference, and on this occasion perhaps a wider one than usual, between the grand total on McClellan's rolls and the men actually fit for duty; and those who would disparage him talk of the grand total on paper, and those who would disparage the Secretary of War talk of those at present fit for duty. General McClellan has sometimes asked for things that the Secretary of War did not give him. General McClellan is not to blame for asking for what he wanted and needed, and the Secretary of War is not to blame for not giving when he had none to give. And I say here, as far as I know, the Secretary of War has withheld no one thing at any time in my power to give him. I have no accusation against him. I believe he is a brave and able man, and I stand here, as justice requires me to do, to take upon myself what has been charged on the Secretary of War, as withholding from him.

LETTER TO JOHN M. CLAY

Henry Clay had been the idol of Lincoln's youth. His son sent the President a snuff-box which Clay had used. Lincoln writes a personal letter to thank him for the gift.

Executive Mansion, August 9, 1862

My Dear Sir: The snuffbox you sent, with the accompanying note, was received yesterday. Thanks for this memento of your great and patriotic father. Thanks also for the assurance that, in these days of dereliction, you remain true to his principles. In the concurrent sentiment of your venerable mother, so long the partner of his bosom and his honors, and lingering now where he was but for the call to rejoin him where he is, I recognize his voice, speaking, as it ever spoke, for the Union, the Constitution, and the freedom of mankind.

FROM AN ADDRESS ON COLONIZATION TO A NEGRO DEPUTATION AT WASHINGTON

A committee of Negroes came to the White House at Lincoln's invitation and were addressed by the President. This was the first time in American history that a President of the United States had addressed an exclusively Negro audience. Lincoln was in favor of colonization, of trying to find for the Negroes some place where they would really be welcomed. New Granada had indicated that it would be willing to receive them and he speaks here to persuade them to go there. The arrangement with New Granada fell through, and, in fact, the Negroes themselves did not want to emigrate.

August 14, 1862

Your race is suffering, in my judgment, the greatest wrong inflicted on any people. But even when you cease to be slaves, you are yet far removed from being placed on an equality with the white race. You are cut off from many of the advantages which the other race enjoys. The aspiration of men is to enjoy equality with the best when free, but on this broad continent not a single man of your race is made the equal of a single man of ours. Go where you are treated the best, and the ban is still upon you. I do not propose to discuss this, but to present it as a fact with which we have to deal. I cannot alter it if I would. It is a fact about which we all think and feel alike, I and you. We look to our condition. Owing to the existence of the two races on this continent, I need not recount to you the effects upon white men, growing out of the institution of slavery.

I believe in its general evil effects on the white race. See our present condition—the country engaged in war—our white men cutting one another's throats—none knowing how far it will extend—and then consider what we know to be the truth. But for your race among us there could not be war, although many men engaged on either side do not care for you one way or the other. Nevertheless, I repeat, without the institution of slavery, and the colored race as a basis, the war could not have an existence. It is better for us both, therefore, to be separated. I know that there are free men among you who, even if they could better their condition, are not as much inclined to go out of the country as those who, being slaves, could obtain their freedom on this condition. I suppose one of the principal difficulties in the way of colonization is that the free colored man cannot see that his comfort would be advanced by it. You may believe that you can live in Washington, or elsewhere in the United States, the remainder of your life as easily, perhaps more so, than you can in any foreign country; and hence you may come to the conclusion that you have nothing to do with the idea of going to a foreign country.

This is (I speak in no unkind sense) an extremely selfish view of the case. You ought to do something to help those who are not so fortunate as yourselves. There is an unwillingness on the part of our people, harsh as it may be, for you free colored people to remain with us. Now, if you could give a start to the white people, you would open a wide door for many to be made free. If we deal with those who are not free at the beginning, and whose intellects are clouded by slavery, we have very poor material to start with. If intelligent colored men, such as are before me, would move in this matter, much might be accomplished. It is exceedingly important that we have men at the beginning capable of thinking as white men, and not those who have been systematically oppressed. There is much to encourage you. For the sake of your race you should sacrifice something of your present comfort for the purpose of being as grand in that respect as the white people. It is a cheering thought throughout life, that something can be done to ameliorate the condition of those who have been subject to the hard usages of the world. It is difficult to make a man miserable while he feels he is worthy of himself and claims kindred to the great God who made him. . . .

The colony of Liberia has been in existence a long time. In a certain sense it is a success. . . . The question is, if the colored people are persuaded to go anywhere, why not there?

One reason for unwillingness to do so is that some of you would rather remain within reach of the country of your nativity. I do not know how much attachment you may have toward our race. It does not strike me that you have the greatest reason to love them. But still you are attached to them, at all events.

The place I am thinking about for a colony is in Central America. . . . The country is a very excellent one for any people, and with great natural resources and advantages, and especially because of the similarity of climate with your native soil, thus being suited to your physical condition. The particular place I have in view is to be a great highway from the Atlantic or Caribbean Sea to the Pacific Ocean, and this particular place has all the advantages for a colony. . . .

The practical thing I want to ascertain is, whether I can get a number of able-bodied men, with their wives and children, who are willing to go when I present evidence of encouragement and protection. Could I get a hundred tolerably intelligent men, with their wives and children, and able to "cut their own fodder," so to speak? Can I have fifty? If I could find twenty-five able-bodied men, with a mixture of women and children—good things in the family relation, I think—I could make a successful commencement. I want you to let me know whether this can be done or not. This is the practical part of my wish to see you. These are subjects of very great importance —worthy of a month's study, instead of a speech delivered in an hour. I ask you, then, to consider seriously, not pertaining to yourselves merely, nor for your race and ours for the present time, but as one of the things, if successfully managed, for the good of mankind—not confined to the present generation, but as

> From age to age descends the lay
> To millions yet to be,
> Till far its echoes roll away
> Into eternity.

LETTER TO HORACE GREELEY

Lincoln had already made up his mind to emancipate the slaves as a military measure. On July 22, he had read the first draft of his Proclamation of Emancipation to his Cabinet, but he was still keeping it secret, waiting for a victory before releasing it to the public. On August 19, Horace Greeley had published an emotional appeal to the President in the New York Tribune, *entitled "The Prayer of Twenty Millions." Lincoln replies to Greeley, explaining exactly how he stands on slavery at this time.*

Executive Mansion, Washington, August 22, 1862

DEAR SIR: I have just read yours of the 19th, addressed to myself through the New York *Tribune*. If there be in it any statements or assumptions of fact which I may know to be erroneous, I do not now and here, controvert them. If there be in it any inferences which I may believe to be falsely drawn, I do not, now and here, argue against them. If there be perceptible in it an impatient and dictatorial tone, I waive it in deference to an old friend whose heart I have always supposed to be right.

As to the policy I "seem to be pursuing," as you say, I have not meant to leave any one in doubt.

I would save the Union. I would save it the shortest way under the Constitution. The sooner the national authority can be restored, the nearer the Union will be "the Union as it was." If there be those who would not save the Union unless they could at the same time save slavery, I do not agree with them. If there be those who would not save the Union unless they could at the same time destroy slavery, I do not agree with them. My paramount object in this struggle is to save the Union, and is not either to save or to destroy slavery. If I could save the Union without freeing any slave, I would do it; and if I could save it by freeing all the slaves, I would do it; and if I could save it by freeing some and leaving others alone, I would also do that. What I do about slavery and the colored race, I do because I believe it helps to save the Union; and what I forbear, I forbear because I do not believe it would help to save the Union. I shall do less whenever I shall believe what I am doing hurts the cause, and I shall do more whenever I shall believe doing more will help the cause. I shall try to correct errors when shown to be errors, and I shall adopt new views so fast as they shall appear to be true views.

I have here stated my purpose according to my view of official duty; and I intend no modification of my oft-expressed personal wish that all men everywhere could be free.

REPLY TO A COMMITTEE OF RELIGIOUS DENOM-INATIONS, ASKING THE PRESIDENT TO ISSUE A PROCLAMATION OF EMANCIPATION

Pressure on Lincoln was kept up during the summer of 1862 to force him to commit himself to a policy of emancipation. He speaks here to a deputation of ministers and presents the case against emancipation as ably as though he were actually committed to such a stand. *The day after he spoke, the Battle of South Mountain in Maryland took place as a prelude to the bloody Battle of Antietam on September 17 which was to be Lincoln's signal of victory—the signal that he could at last make the Proclamation of Emancipation public.*

September 13, 1862

THE subject presented in the memorial is one upon which I have thought much for weeks past, and I may even say for months. I am approached with the most opposite opinions and advice, and that by religious men who are equally certain that they represent the divine will. I am sure that either the one or the other class is mistaken in that belief, and perhaps in some respects both. I hope it will not be irreverent for me to say that if it is probable that God would reveal his will to others on a point so connected with my duty, it might be supposed he would reveal it directly to me; for, unless I am more deceived in myself than I often am, it is my earnest desire to know the will of Providence in this matter. And if I can learn what it is, I will do it.

These are not, however, the days of miracles, and I suppose it will be granted that I am not to expect a direct revelation. I must study the plain physical facts of the case, ascertain what is possible, and learn what appears to be wise and right.

The subject is difficult, and good men do not agree. For instance, the other day four gentlemen of standing and intelligence from New York called as a delegation on business connected with the war; but, before leaving, two of them earnestly beset me to proclaim general emancipation, upon which the other two at once attacked them. You know also that the last session of Congress had a decided majority of anti-slavery men, yet they could not unite on this policy. And the same is true of the religious people. Why, the rebel soldiers are praying with a great deal more earnestness, I fear, than our own troops, and expecting God to favor their side . . .

What good would a proclamation of emancipation from me do, especially as we are now situated? I do not want to issue a document that the whole world will see must necessarily be inoperative, like the Pope's bull against the comet. Would my word free the slaves, when I cannot even enforce the Constitution in the rebel States? Is there a single court, or magistrate, or individual that would be influenced by it there? And what reason is there to think it would have any greater effect upon the slaves than the late law of Congress, which I approved, and which offers protection and freedom to the slaves of rebel masters who come within our lines? Yet I cannot learn that that law has caused a single slave to come over to us. And suppose they could be induced by a proclamation of freedom from me to throw themselves upon us, what should we do with them? How can we feed and care for such a multitude? General Butler wrote me a few days since that he was issuing more rations to the slaves who have rushed to him than to all the white troops under his command. They eat, and that is all; though it is true General Butler is feeding the whites also by the thousand, for it nearly amounts to a famine there. If, now, the pressure of the war should call off our forces from New Orleans to defend some other point, what is to prevent the masters from reducing the blacks to slavery again? For I am told that whenever the rebels take any black prisoners, free or slave, they immediately auction them off. They did so with those they took from a boat that was aground in the Tennessee River a few days ago. And then I am very ungenerously attacked for it! For instance, when, after the late battles at and near Bull Run, an expedition went out from Washington under a flag of truce to bury the dead and bring in the wounded, and the rebels seized the blacks who went along to help, and sent them into slavery, Horace Greeley said in his paper that the government would probably do nothing about it. What could I do?

Now, then, tell me, if you please, what possible result or good would follow the issuing of such a proclamation as you desire? Understand, I raise no objections against it on legal or constitutional grounds; for, as Commander-in-Chief of the Army and Navy, in time of war I suppose I have a right to take any measure which may best subdue the enemy; nor do I urge objections of a moral nature, in view of possible consequences of insurrection and massacre at the South.

I view this matter as a practical war measure, to be decided on according to the advantages or disadvantages it may offer to the suppression of the rebellion.

I admit that slavery is the root of the rebellion, or at least its *sine qua non*. The ambition of politicians may have instigated them to act, but they would have been impotent without slavery as their instrument. I will also concede that emancipation would help us in Europe, and convince them that we are incited by something more than ambition. I grant, further, that it would help somewhat at the North, though not so much, I fear, as you and those you represent imagine. Still some additional strength would be added in that way to the war, and then, unquestionably, it would weaken the rebels by drawing off their laborers, which is of great importance; but I am not so sure we could do much with the blacks. If we were to arm them, I fear that in a few weeks the arms would be in the hands of the rebels; and, indeed, thus far we have not had arms enough to equip our white troops. I will mention another thing, though it meet only your scorn and contempt. There are fifty thousand bayonets in the Union armies from the border slave States. It would be a serious matter if, in consequence of a proclamation such as you desire, they should go over to the rebels. I do not think they all would—not so many, indeed, as a year ago, or six months ago—not so many today as yesterday. Every day increases their Union feeling. They are also getting their pride enlisted, and want to beat the rebels.

Let me say one thing more: I think you should admit that we already have an important principle to rally and unite the people, in the fact that constitutional government is at stake. This is a fundamental idea going down about as deep as anything. Do not misunderstand me because I have mentioned these objections. They indicate the difficulties that have thus far prevented my action in some such way as you desire. I have not decided against a proclamation of liberty to the slaves, but hold the matter under advisement; and I can assure you that the subject is on my mind, by day and night, more than any other. Whatever shall appear to be God's will, I will do. I trust that in the freedom with which I have canvassed your views I have not in any respect injured your feelings.

PRELIMINARY EMANCIPATION PROCLAMATION

The Battle of Antietam had been fought and won on September 17. Lincoln entered a Cabinet meeting on September 22 and began the session by reading a chapter from Artemus Ward entitled "High-Handed Outrage at Utica." Then he went on to the serious business of the day and read this draft of the Emancipation Proclamation.

September 22, 1862

I, ABRAHAM LINCOLN, President of the United States of America, and Commander-in-Chief of the Army and Navy thereof, do hereby proclaim and declare that hereafter, as heretofore, the war will be prosecuted for the object of practically restoring the constitutional relation between the United States and each of the States, and the people thereof, in which States that relation is or may be suspended or disturbed.

That it is my purpose, upon the next meeting of Congress, to again recommend the adoption of a practical measure tendering pecuniary aid to the free acceptance or rejection of all slave States, so called, the people whereof may not then be in rebellion against the United States, and which States may then have voluntarily adopted, or thereafter may voluntarily adopt, immediate or gradual abolishment of slavery within their respective limits; and that the effort to colonize persons of African descent with their consent upon this continent or elsewhere, with the previously obtained consent of the governments existing there, will be continued.

That on the first day of January, in the year of our Lord one thousand eight hundred and sixty-three, all persons held as slaves within any State or designated part of a State the people whereof shall then be in rebellion against the United States, shall be then, thenceforward, and forever free; and the Executive Government of the United States, including the military and naval authority thereof, will recognize and maintain the freedom of such persons, and will do no act or acts to repress such persons, or any of them, in any efforts they may make for their actual freedom.

That the Executive will, on the first day of January aforesaid, by proclamation designate the States and parts of States, if any, in which the people thereof, respectively shall then be in rebellion against the United States; and the fact that any State or the people thereof, shall on that day be in good faith represented in the Congress of the United States by members chosen thereto at elections wherein a majority of the qualified voters of such State shall have participated, shall, in the absence of strong countervailing testimony, be deemed conclusive evidence that such State, and the people thereof, are not then in rebellion against the United States.

That attention is hereby called to an act of Congress entitled "An act to make an additional article of war," approved

March 13, 1862, and which act is in the words and figure following:

Be it enacted by the Senate and House of Representatives of the United States of America in Congress assembled, That hereafter the following shall be promulgated as an additional article of war, for the government of the army of the United States, and shall be obeyed and observed as such:

ARTICLE—. All officers or persons in the military or naval service of the United States are prohibited from employing any of the forces under their respective commands for the purpose of returning fugitives from service or labor who may have escaped from any persons to whom such service or labor is claimed to be due; and any officer who shall be found guilty by a court martial of violating this article shall be dismissed from the service.

SEC. 2. And be it further enacted, That this act shall take effect from and after its passage.

Also to the ninth and tenth sections of an act entitled "An act to suppress insurrection, to punish treason and rebellion, to seize and confiscate property of rebels, and for other purposes," approved July 17, 1862, and which sections are in the words and figures following:

SEC. 9. And be it further enacted, That all slaves of persons who shall hereafter be engaged in rebellion against the Government of the United States, or who shall in any way give aid or comfort thereto, escaping from such persons and taking refuge within the lines of the army; and all slaves captured from such persons or deserted by them, and coming under the control of the Government of the United States; and all slaves of such persons found on [or] being within any place occupied by rebel forces and afterwards occupied by the forces of the United States, shall be deemed captives of war, and shall be forever free of their servitude, and not again held as slaves.

SEC. 10. And be it further enacted, That no slave escaping into any State, Territory, or the District of Columbia, from any other State, shall be delivered up, or in any way impeded, or hindered of his liberty except for crime, or some offense against the laws, unless the person claiming said fugitive shall first make oath that the person to whom the labor or service of such fugitive is alleged to be due is his lawful owner, and has not borne arms against the United States in the present rebellion, nor in any way given aid and comfort thereto; and no person engaged in the military or naval service of the United States shall, under any pretense whatever, assume to decide on the validity of the claim of any person to the service or labor of any other person, or surrender up any such person to the claimant, on pain of being dismissed from the service.

And I do hereby enjoin upon and order all persons engaged in the military and naval service of the United States to observe, obey, and enforce, within their respective spheres of service, the act and sections above recited.

And the Executive will in due time recommend that all citizens of the United States who shall have remained loyal thereto throughout the rebellion shall (upon the restoration of the constitutional relation between the United States and their respective States and people, if that relation shall have been suspended or disturbed) be compensated for all losses by acts of the United States, including the loss of slaves.

In witness whereof, I have hereunto set my hand and caused the seal of the United States to be affixed.

Done at the city of Washington, this twenty-second day of September, in the year of our Lord, one thousand [L. S.] eight hundred and sixty-two, and of the independence of the United States the eighty-seventh.

By the President:

ABRAHAM LINCOLN
WILLIAM H. SEWARD, Secretary of State.

LETTER TO HANNIBAL HAMLIN

Lincoln writes to his Vice President to keep him informed about the public reception of the Emancipation Proclamation. As the

letter indicates, the reception was less enthusiastic than the Presi-
dent had expected.

(*Strictly private*)

Executive Mansion, Washington, September 28, 1862

MY DEAR SIR: Your kind letter of the 25th is just received. It
is known to some that while I hope something from the proclamation, my expectations are not as sanguine as are those of
some friends. The time for its effect southward has not come;
but northward the effect should be instantaneous.

It is six days old, and while commendation in newspapers
and by distinguished individuals is all that a vain man could
wish, the stocks have declined, and troops come forward more
slowly than ever. This, looked soberly in the face, is not very
satisfactory. We have fewer troops in the field at the end of
six days than we had at the beginning—the attrition among the
old outnumbering the addition by the new. The North responds to the proclamation sufficiently in breath; but breath
alone kills no rebels.

I wish I could write more cheerfully; nor do I thank you the
less for the kindness of your letter.

REPLY TO AN ADDRESS
BY MRS. ELIZA P. GURNEY

Mrs. Gurney was an elderly Quaker who came to the White House
to thank the President for issuing the Emancipation Proclamation.
This is his reply to her address.

September [28?], 1862

I AM glad of this interview, and glad to know that I have your
sympathy and prayers. We are indeed going through a great
trial—a fiery trial. In the very responsible position in which I

happen to be placed, being a humble instrument in the hands of our Heavenly Father, as I am, and as we all are, to work out his great purposes, I have desired that all my works and acts may be according to his will, and that it might be so, I have sought his aid; but if, after endeavoring to do my best in the light which he affords me, I find my efforts fail, I must believe that for some purpose unknown to me, he wills it otherwise. If I had had my way, this war would never have been commenced. If I had been allowed my way, this war would have been ended before this; but we find it still continues, and we must believe that he permits it for some wise purpose of his own, mysterious and unknown to us; and though with our limited understandings we may not be able to comprehend it, yet we cannot but believe that he who made the world still governs it.

MEDITATION ON THE DIVINE WILL

Although Lincoln had been an agnostic in his youth, the fierce tribulations of the War lent an increasingly religious cast to his mind. He wrote out this brief meditation with no thought of publication. John Hay made a copy of it so that it was preserved.

September [30?], 1862

THE will of God prevails. In great contests each party claims to act in accordance with the will of God. Both may be, and one must be, wrong. God cannot be for and against the same thing at the same time. In the present civil war it is quite possible that God's purpose is something different from the purpose of either party; and yet the human instrumentalities, working just as they do, are of the best adaptation to effect his purpose. I am almost ready to say that this is probably true; that God wills this contest, and wills that it shall not end yet. By his mere great power on the minds of the now contestants, he could have either saved or destroyed the Union without a human contest. Yet the contest began. And, having begun, he could give the final victory to either side any day. Yet the contest proceeds.

LETTER TO GENERAL G. B. McCLELLAN

After Antietam, Lincoln and the people of the North expected that McClellan would follow up his victory with a hard-pressed pursuit of Lee. McClellan, however, remained at his headquarters at Antietam. Lincoln went there to visit him during the first days of October. After the President's return to Washington, McClellan still showed no signs of moving. Lincoln writes to him analyzing Lee's situation and pointing out to McClellan that he is in a dominant position, and that the next move is up to him.

Executive Mansion, Washington, D. C., October 13, 1862

MY DEAR SIR: You remember my speaking to you of what I called your over-cautiousness. Are you not over-cautious when you assume that you cannot do what the enemy is constantly doing? Should you not claim to be at least his equal in prowess, and act upon the claim? As I understand, you telegraphed General Halleck that you cannot subsist your army at Winchester unless the railroad from Harper's Ferry to that point be put in working order. But the enemy does now subsist his army at Winchester, at a distance nearly twice as great from railroad transportation as you would have to do without the railroad last named. He now wagons from Culpeper Court House, which is just about twice as far as you would have to do from Harper's Ferry. He is certainly not more than half as well provided with wagons as you are. I certainly should be pleased for you to have the advantage of the railroad from Harper's Ferry to Winchester, but it wastes all the remainder of autumn to give it to you, and in fact ignores the question of time, which cannot and must not be ignored. Again, one of the standard maxims of war, as you know, is to "operate upon the enemy's communications as much as possible without exposing your own." You seem to act as if this applies against you, but cannot apply in your favor. Change positions with the enemy, and think you not he would break your communication with Richmond within the next twenty-four hours? You dread his going into Pennsylvania; but if he does so in full force, he gives up his communications to you absolutely, and you have nothing to do but to follow and ruin him. If he does so with less than full force, fall upon and beat what is left behind all the easier. Exclusive of the water-line, you are now nearer Richmond than the enemy is by the route that you can and he must take. Why can you not reach there before him, unless you admit that he is more than your equal on a march? His route is the arc of a circle, while yours is the chord. The roads are as good on yours as on his. You know I desired, but did not order, you to cross the Potomac below, instead of above, the Shenandoah and Blue Ridge. My idea was that this would at once menace the enemy's communications, which I would seize if he would permit.

If he should move northward, I would follow him closely, holding his communications. If he should prevent our seizing his communications and move toward Richmond, I would press closely to him, fight him if a favorable opportunity should present, and at least try to beat him to Richmond on the inside track. I say "try"; if we never try, we shall never succeed. If he makes a stand at Winchester, moving neither north nor south, I would fight him there, on the idea that if we cannot beat him when he bears the wastage of coming to us, we never can when we bear the wastage of going to him. This proposition is a simple truth, and is too important to be lost sight of for a moment. In coming to us he tenders us an advantage which we should not waive. We should not so operate as to merely drive him away. As we must beat him somewhere or fail finally, we can do it, if at all, easier near to us than far away. If we cannot beat the enemy where he now is, we never can, he again being within the intrenchments of Richmond. . . .

For a great part of the way you would be practically between the enemy and both Washington and Richmond, enabling us to spare you the greatest number of troops from here. When at length running for Richmond ahead of him enables him to move this way, if he does so, turn and attack him in rear. But I think he should be engaged long before such point is reached. It is all easy if our troops march as well as the enemy, and it is unmanly to say they cannot do it. This letter is in no sense an order.

TELEGRAM TO GENERAL G. B. McCLELLAN

McClellan did not take Lincoln's suggestion that he march against Lee. Instead he kept complaining to the military authorities that he did not have enough horses for his men and that those he did have were in bad condition. For the first time in his dealings with McClellan, Lincoln loses his patience and sends him this sharply worded telegram.

War Department, Washington City, October 24, 1862

MAJOR-GENERAL McCLELLAN: I have just read your dispatch about sore-tongued and fatigued horses. Will you pardon me for asking what the horses of your army have done since the battle of Antietam that fatigues anything?

TELEGRAM TO GENERAL G. B. McCLELLAN

Almost immediately Lincoln regretted his display of impatience toward McClellan. He communicates with him again, using more tactful words. Nevertheless, he had made up his mind that if

McClellan permitted Lee to cross the Blue Ridge Mountains and reach central Virginia, he would remove him from his command.

Executive Mansion, Washington, October 27, 1862

MAJOR-GENERAL McCLELLAN: Yours of yesterday received. Most certainly I intend no injustice to any, and if I have done any I deeply regret it. To be told, after more than five weeks' total inaction of the army, and during which period we sent to the army every fresh horse we possibly could, amounting in the whole to 7,918, that the cavalry horses were too much fatigued to move, presents a very cheerless, almost hopeless, prospect for the future, and it may have forced something of impatience in my dispatch. If not recruited and rested then, when could they ever be? I suppose the river is rising, and I am glad to believe you are crossing.

ORDER RELIEVING GENERAL G. B. McCLELLAN

Lee crossed the Blue Ridge Mountains, and Lincoln kept his promise with himself. This order terminates McClellan's career as a leading commander in the Union Army.

Executive Mansion, Washington, November 5, 1862

BY DIRECTION of the President, it is ordered that Major-General McClellan be relieved from the command of the Army of the Potomac, and that Major-General Burnside take the command of that army. Also that Major-General Hunter take command of the corps in said army which is now commanded by General Burnside. That Major-General Fitz-John Porter be relieved from command of the corps he now commands in said army, and that Major-General Hooker take command of said corps. . . .

FROM A LETTER TO GENERAL CARL SCHURZ

Carl Schurz was one of the many Germans who had been forced to leave his native land after the Revolution of 1848. He had played a leading part in bringing the German population into the Republican party ever since it had been founded. Lincoln had appointed him Minister to Spain, but he had resigned in December, 1861, to become a brigadier general in a volunteer corps. Lincoln writes to him to discuss the local and state elections which had gone against the Republicans. He also speaks frankly about the part played by the loyal Democrats during the War.

(Private and confidential)

Executive Mansion, Washington, November 10, 1862

MY DEAR SIR: Yours of the 8th was, today, read to me by Mrs. S[churz]. We have lost the elections; and it is natural that each of us will believe, and say, it has been because his peculiar views was not made sufficiently prominent. I think I know what it was, but I may be mistaken. Three main causes told the whole story. 1. The Democrats were left in a majority by our friends going to the war. 2. The Democrats observed this and determined to re-instate themselves in power, and 3. Our newspapers, by vilifying and disparaging the administration, furnished them all the weapons to do it with. Certainly, the ill-success of the war had much to do with this. . . .

The plain facts, as they appear to me, are these: The administration came into power, very largely in a minority of the popular vote. Notwithstanding this, it distributed to its party friends as nearly all the civil patronage as any administration ever did. The war came. The administration could not even start in this, without assistance outside of its party. It was mere nonsense to suppose a minority could put down a majority in rebellion. Mr. Schurz (now Gen. Schurz) was about here then and I do not recollect that he then considered all who were not Republicans, were enemies of the government, and that none of them must be appointed to military positions. He will correct me if I am mistaken. It so happened that very few of our friends had a military education or were of the profession of arms. It would have been a question whether the war should be conducted on military knowledge, or on political affinity, only that our own friends (I think Mr. Schurz included) seemed to think that such a question was inadmissible. Accordingly I have scarcely appointed a Democrat to a command, who was not urged by many Republicans and opposed by none. It was so as to McClellan. He was first brought forward by the Republican Governor of Ohio, and claimed, and contended for at the same time by the Republican Governor of Pennsylvania. I received recommendations from the Republican delegations in Congress, and I believe every one of them recommended a majority of Democrats. But, after all many Republicans were appointed; and I mean no disparagement to them when I say I do not see that their superiority of success has been so marked as to throw great suspicion on the good faith of those who are not Republicans.

FROM A LETTER TO GENERAL CARL SCHURZ

Most of Lincoln's correspondence during the War period is coolly objective, nearly always impersonal and often official in tone. His letters to Carl Schurz take on an intimate quality seldom seen in his writing at this time.

Executive Mansion, Washington, November 24, 1862

MY DEAR SIR: I have just received and read your letter of the 20th. The purport of it is that we lost the late elections and the administration is failing because the war is unsuccessful, and that I must not flatter myself that I am not justly to blame for it. I certainly know that if the war fails, the administration fails, and that I will be blamed for it, whether I deserve it or not. And I ought to be blamed if I could do better. You think I could do better; therefore you blame me already. I think I could not do better; therefore I blame you for blaming me. I understand you now to be willing to accept the help of men who are not Republicans, provided they have "heart in it." Agreed. I want no others. But who is to be the judge of hearts, or of "heart in it"? If I must discard my own judgment and take yours, I must also take that of others; and by the time I should reject all I should be advised to reject, I should have none left, Republicans or others—not even yourself. For be assured, my dear sir, there are men who have "heart in it" that think you are performing your part as poorly as you think I am performing mine. I certainly have been dissatisfied with the slowness of Buell and McClellan; but before I relieved them I had great fears I should not find successors to them who would do better; and I am sorry to add that I have seen little since to relieve those fears.

I do not clearly see the prospect of any more rapid movements. I fear we shall at last find out that the difficulty is in our case rather than in particular generals. I wish to disparage no one—certainly not those who sympathize with me; but I must say I need success more than I need sympathy, and that I have not seen the so much greater evidence of getting success from my sympathizers than from those who are denounced as the contrary. . . .

In answer to your question, "Has it not been publicly stated in the newspapers, and apparently proved as a fact, that from the commencement of the war the enemy was continually supplied with information by some of the confidential subordinates of as important an officer as Adjutant-General Thomas?" I must say "No," as far as my knowledge extends. And I add that if you can give any tangible evidence upon the subject, I will thank you to come to this city and do so.

FROM THE ANNUAL MESSAGE TO CONGRESS

Of the four annual messages that Lincoln addressed to Congress, this one is by far the most interesting and the most inspired. It was addressed largely to the people of the border states and to the people of the South. It presents Lincoln's favorite scheme for emancipation with compensation; it shows him making an amusing error in trying to forecast what the population of the United States would be in 1930; and it ends with one of the most moving passages in all his writings.

December 1, 1862

FELLOW-CITIZENS OF THE SENATE AND HOUSE OF REPRESENTATIVES: Since your last annual assembling another year of health and bountiful harvest has passed; and while it has not pleased the Almighty to bless us with a return of peace, we can but press on, guided by the best light he gives us, trusting that in his own good time and wise way all will yet be well.

*   *   *

A nation may be said to consist of its territory, its people, and its laws. The territory is the only part which is of certain durability. "One generation passeth away, and another generation cometh, but the earth abideth forever." It is of the first importance to duly consider and estimate this ever-enduring part. That portion of the earth's surface which is owned and inhabited by the people of the United States is well adapted to be the home of one national family, and it is not well adapted for two or more. Its vast extent and its variety of climate and productions are of advantage in this age for one people, whatever they might have been in former ages. Steam, telegraphs, and

intelligence have brought these to be an advantageous combination for one united people. . . .

There is no line, straight or crooked, suitable for a national
boundary upon which to divide. Trace through, from east to
west, upon the line between the free and slave country, and
we shall find a little more than one-third of its length are
rivers, easy to be crossed, and populated, or soon to be populated, thickly upon both sides; while nearly all its remaining
length are merely surveyors' lines, over which people may walk
back and forth without any consciousness of their presence.
No part of this line can be made any more difficult to pass by
writing it down on paper or parchment as a national boundary.
The fact of separation, if it comes, gives up on the part of the
seceding section the fugitive-slave clause along with all other
constitutional obligations upon the section seceded from,
while I should expect no treaty stipulation would be ever made
to take its place. . . .

Our national strife springs not from our permanent part, not
from the land we inhabit, not from our national homestead.
There is no possible severing of this but would multiply, and
not mitigate, evils among us. In all its adaptations and aptitudes
it demands union and abhors separation. In fact, it would ere
long force reunion, however much of blood and treasure the
separation might have cost.

Our strife pertains to ourselves—to the passing generations
of men; and it can without convulsion be hushed forever with
the passing of one generation.

In this view I recommend the adoption of the following resolution and articles amendatory to the Constitution of the
United States:

Resolved by the Senate and House of Representatives of the
United States of America in Congress assembled (two-thirds of
both houses concurring), That the following articles be proposed
to the legislatures (or conventions) of the several States as amend-

ments to the Constitution of the United States, all or any of which articles when ratified by three-fourths of the said legislatures (or conventions) to be valid as part or parts of the said Constitution, viz.:

ARTICLE [1]

Every state wherein slavery now exists which shall abolish the same therein at any time or times before the first day of January in the year of our Lord one thousand and nine hundred, shall receive compensation from the United States as follows, to wit:

The President of the United States shall deliver to every such State bonds of the United States . . . for each slave shown to have been therein by the eighth census of the United States. . . . Any State having received bonds as aforesaid, and afterward reintroducing or tolerating slavery therein, shall refund to the United States the bonds so received, or the value thereof, and all interest paid thereon.

ARTICLE [2]

All slaves who shall have enjoyed actual freedom by the chances of the war at any time before the end of the rebellion, shall be forever free; but all owners of such who shall not have been disloyal shall be compensated for them at the same rates as are provided for States adopting abolishment of slavery, but in such way that no slave shall be twice accounted for.

ARTICLE [3]

Congress may appropriate money and otherwise provide for colonizing free colored persons, with their own consent, at any place or places without the United States.

I beg indulgence to discuss these proposed articles at some length. Without slavery the rebellion could never have existed; without slavery it could not continue.

Among the friends of the Union there is great diversity of sentiment and of policy in regard to slavery and the African race amongst us. Some would perpetuate slavery; some would abolish it suddenly and without compensation; some would abolish it gradually, and with compensation; some would remove the freed people from us, and some would retain them with us; and there are yet other minor diversities. Because of these diversities we waste much strength in struggles among ourselves. By mutual concession we should harmonize and act together. This would be compromise; but it would be compromise among the friends, and not with the enemies of the Union. These articles are intended to embody a plan of such mutual concessions. If the plan shall be adopted, it is assumed that emancipation will follow at least in several of the States.

As to the first article, the main points are: first, the emancipation; secondly, the length of time for consummating it—thirty-seven years; and, thirdly, the compensation.

The emancipation will be unsatisfactory to the advocates of perpetual slavery; but the length of time should greatly mitigate their dissatisfaction. The time spares both races from the evils of sudden derangement—in fact, from the necessity of any derangement; while most of those whose habitual course of thought will be disturbed by the measure will have passed away before its consummation. They will never see it. Another class will hail the prospect of emancipation, but will deprecate the length of time. They will feel that it gives too little to the now living slaves. But it really gives them much. It saves them from the vagrant destitution which must largely attend immediate emancipation in localities where their numbers are very great; and it gives the inspiring assurance that their posterity shall be free forever. The plan leaves to each State choosing to act under it to abolish slavery now, or at the end of the century, or at any intermediate time, or by degrees extending over the whole or any part of the period; and it obliges no two States to proceed alike. It also provides for compensation, and generally the mode of making it. This, it would seem, must further mitigate the dissatisfaction of those who favor perpetual slavery, and especially of those who are to receive the compensation. Doubtless some of those who are to pay, and not to receive, will object. Yet the measure is both just and economical. In a certain sense the liberation of slaves is the destruction of property—property acquired by descent or by purchase, the same as any other property. It is no less true for having been often said, that the people of the South are not more responsible for the original introduction of this property than are the people of the North; and when it is remembered how unhesitatingly we all use cotton and sugar and share the profits of dealing in them, it may not be quite safe to say that the South has been more responsible than the North for its continuance. If, then, for a common object this property is to be sacrificed, is it not just that it be done at a common charge?

And if, with less money, or money more easily paid, we can preserve the benefits of the Union by this means than we can by the war alone, is it not also economical to do it? Let us consider it then. Let us ascertain the sum we have expended in the war since compensated emancipation was proposed last March, and consider whether, if that measure had been promptly accepted by even some of the slave States, the same sum would not have done more to close the war than has been otherwise done. If so, the measure would save money, and in that view would be a prudent and economical measure. Certainly it is not so easy to pay something as it is to pay nothing; but it is easier to pay a large sum than it is to pay a larger one. And it is easier to pay any sum when we are able, than it is to pay it before we are able. The war requires large sums, and requires them at once. The aggregate sum necessary for compensated emancipation of course would be large. But it would require no ready cash, nor the bonds even, any faster than the emancipation progresses. This might not, and probably would not, close before the end of the thirty-seven years. At that time we shall probably have 100,000,000 of people to share the burden, instead of 31,000,000 as now. And not only so, but the increase of our population may be expected to continue for a long time after that period as rapidly as before, because our territory will not have become full. I do not state this inconsiderately. At the same ratio of increase which we have maintained, on an average, from our first national census of 1790 until that of 1860, we should in 1900 have a population of 103,208,415. And why may we not continue that ratio far beyond that period? Our abundant room—our broad national homestead—is our ample resource. . . .

We have 2,963,000 square miles. Europe has 3,800,000, with a population averaging 73 1-3 persons to the square mile. Why may not our country, at the same time, average as many? Is it less fertile? Has it more waste surface, by mountains, rivers, lakes, deserts, or other causes? Is it inferior to Europe in any natural advantage? If, then, we are at some time to be as populous as Europe, how soon? As to when this may be, we can judge by the past and the present; as to when it will be, if ever, depends much on whether we maintain the Union. . . .

Taking the nation in the aggregate, we find its population and ratio of increase for the several decennial periods to be as follows:

1790.	3,929,827			
1800.	5,305,937	35.02%	ratio of increase
1810.	7,239,814	36.45%	" " "
1820.	9,638,131	33.13%	" " "
1830.	12,866,020	33.49%	" " "
1840.	17,069,453	32.67%	" " "
1850.	23,191,876	35.87%	" " "
1860.	31,443,790	35.58%	" " "

This shows an average decennial increase of 34.60 percent in population through the seventy years from our first to our last census yet taken. It is seen that the ratio of increase at no one of these seven periods is either two percent below or two percent above the average, thus showing how inflexible, and consequently how reliable the law of increase in our case is. Assuming that it will continue, gives the following results:

1870	42,323,341
1880	56,967,216
1890	76,677,872
1900	103,208,415
1910	138,918,526
1920	186,984,335
1930	251,680,914

These figures show that our country may be as populous as Europe now is at some point between 1920 and 1930—say about 1925—our territory, at 73 1-3 persons to the square mile, being of capacity to contain 217,186,000.

And we will reach this, too, if we do not ourselves relinquish the chance by the folly and evils of disunion, or by long and exhausting war springing from the only great element of national discord among us. While it cannot be foreseen exactly how much one huge example of secession, breeding lesser ones indefinitely, would retard population, civilization, and prosperity, no one can doubt that the extent of it would be very great and injurious. . . .

As to the second article, I think it would be impracticable to return to bondage the class of persons therein contemplated. Some of them doubtless, in the property sense, belong to loyal owners; and hence provision is made in this article for compensating such.

The third article relates to the future of the freed people. It does not oblige, but merely authorizes, Congress to aid in colonizing such as may consent. This ought not to be regarded as objectionable, on the one hand or on the other, inasmuch as it comes to nothing unless by the mutual consent of the people to be deported, and the American voters through their representatives in Congress. I cannot make it better known than it already is, that I strongly favor colonization. And yet I wish to say there is an objection urged against free colored persons remaining in the country which is largely imaginary, if not sometimes malicious.

It is insisted that their presence would injure and displace white labor and white laborers. If there ever could be a proper time for mere catch arguments, that time surely is not now. In times like the present, men should utter nothing for which they would not willingly be responsible through time and in eternity. Is it true, then, that colored people can displace any more white labor by being free than by remaining slaves? If they stay in their old places, they jostle no white laborers; if they leave their old places, they leave them open to white laborers. Logically, there is neither more nor less of it. Emancipation, even without deportation, would probably enhance the wages of white labor, and very surely would not reduce them. Thus, the customary amount of labor would still have to be performed; the freed people would surely not do more than their old proportion of it, and very probably for a time would do less, leaving an increased part to white laborers, bringing their labor into greater demand, and consequently enhancing the wages of it. With deportation, even to a limited extent, enhanced wages to white labor is mathematically certain. Labor is like any other commodity in the market—increase the demand for it, and you increase the price of it. Reduce the supply of black labor by colonizing the black labor out of the country, and by precisely so much you increase the demand for, and wages of, white labor.

But it is dreaded that the freed people will swarm forth and cover the whole land? Are they not already in the land? Will liberation make them any more numerous? Equally distributed among the whites of the whole country, and there would be but one colored to seven whites. Could the one in any way greatly disturb the seven? There are many communities now having more than one free colored person to seven whites, and this without any apparent consciousness of evil from it. . . .

The plan consisting of these articles is recommended, not but that a restoration of the national authority would be accepted without its adoption.

Nor will the war, nor proceedings under the proclamation of September 22, 1862, be stayed because of the recommendation of this plan. Its timely adoption, I doubt not, would bring restoration, and thereby stay both.

And, notwithstanding this plan, the recommendation that Congress provide by law for compensating any State which may adopt emancipation before this plan shall have been acted upon, is hereby earnestly renewed. Such would be only an advance part of the plan, and the same arguments apply to both.

This plan is recommended as a means, not in exclusion of, but additional to, all others for restoring and preserving the national authority throughout the Union. The subject is presented exclusively in its economical aspect. The plan would, I am confident, secure peace more speedily, and maintain it more permanently, than can be done by force alone; while all it would cost, considering amounts, and manner of payment, and times of payment, would be easier paid than will be the additional cost of the war if we rely solely upon force. It is much—very much—that it would cost no blood at all.

The plan is proposed as permanent constitutional law. It cannot become such without the concurrence of, first two-thirds of Congress and, afterward, three-fourths of the States. The requisite three-fourths of the States will necessarily include seven of the slave States. Their concurrence, if obtained, will give assurance of their severally adopting emancipation at no very distant day upon the new constitutional terms. This assurance would end the struggle now, and save the Union forever.

I do not forget the gravity which should characterize a paper addressed to the Congress of the nation by the Chief Magistrate of the nation. Nor do I forget that some of you are my seniors, nor that many of you have more experience than I in the conduct of public affairs. Yet I trust that in view of the great responsibility resting upon me, you will perceive no want of respect to yourselves in any undue earnestness I may seem to display.

Is it doubted, then, that the plan I propose, if adopted, would shorten the war, and thus lessen its expenditure of money and of blood? Is it doubted that it would restore the national authority and national prosperity, and perpetuate both indefinitely? Is it doubted that we here—Congress and Executive—can secure its adoption? Will not the good people respond to a united and earnest appeal from us? Can we, can they, by any other means so certainly or so speedily assure these vital objects? We can succeed only by concert. It is not "Can any of us imagine better?" but, "Can we all do better?" Object whatsoever is possible, still the question occurs, "Can we do better?" The dogmas of the quiet past are inadequate to the stormy present. The occasion is piled high with difficulty, and we must rise with the occasion. As our case is new, so we must think anew and act anew. We must disenthrall ourselves, and then we shall save our country.

Fellow-citizens, we cannot escape history. We of this Congress and this administration will be remembered in spite of ourselves. No personal significance or insignificance can spare one or another of us. The fiery trial through which we pass will light us down, in honor or dishonor, to the latest generation. We say we are for the Union. The world will not forget that we say this. We know how to save the Union. The world knows we do know how to save it. We—even we here—hold the power and bear the responsibility. In giving freedom to the slave, we assure freedom to the free—honorable alike in what we give and what we preserve. We shall nobly save or meanly lose the last, best hope of earth. Other means may succeed; this could not fail. The way is plain, peaceful, generous, just—

a way which, if followed, the world will forever applaud, and God must forever bless.

FINAL EMANCIPATION PROCLAMATION

As planned on September 22, 1862, January 1, 1863 was the day on which the Emancipation Proclamation was to go into effect. Its wording had undergone a series of changes; it appears here in its final form.

January 1, 1863

WHEREAS, on the twenty-second day of September, in the year of our Lord one thousand eight hundred and sixty-two, a proclamation was issued by the President of the United States, containing, among other things, the following, to wit:

That on the first day of January, in the year of our Lord one thousand eight hundred and sixty-three, all persons held as slaves within any State, or designated part of a State, the people whereof shall then be in rebellion against the United States, shall be then, thenceforward, and forever free; and the Executive Government of the United States, including the military and naval authority thereof, will recognize and maintain the freedom of such persons, and will do no act or acts to repress such persons, or any of them, in any efforts they may make for their actual freedom.

That the Executive will, on the first day of January aforesaid, by proclamation, designate the States and parts of States, if any, in which the people thereof respectively shall then be in rebellion against the United States; and the fact that any State, or the people thereof, shall on that day be in good faith represented in the Congress of the United States by members chosen thereto at elections wherein a majority of the qualified voters of such State shall have participated, shall in the absence of strong countervailing testimony be deemed conclusive evidence that such State and the people thereof are not then in rebellion against the United States.

Now, therefore, I, Abraham Lincoln, President of the United States, by virtue of the power in me vested as Commander-in-Chief of the Army and Navy of the United States, in time of actual armed rebellion against the authority and government of the United States, and as a fit and necessary war measure for suppressing said rebellion, do, on this first day of January, in the year of our Lord one thousand eight hundred and sixty-three, and in accordance with my purpose so to do, publicly proclaimed for the full period of 100 days from the day first above mentioned, order and designate as the States and parts of States wherein the people thereof, respectively, are this day in rebellion against the United States, the following, to wit:

Arkansas, Texas, Louisiana (except the parishes of St. Bernard, Plaquemines, Jefferson, St. John, St. Charles, St. James, Ascension, Assumption, Terre Bonne, Lafourche, St. Mary, St. Martin, and Orleans, including the city of New Orleans), Mississippi, Alabama, Florida, Georgia, South Carolina, North Carolina, and Virginia (except the forty-eight counties designated as West Virginia, and also the counties of Berkeley, Accomac, Northampton, Elizabeth City, York, Princess Anne, and Norfolk, including the cities of Norfolk and Portsmouth), and which excepted parts are for the present left precisely as if this proclamation were not issued.

And by virtue of the power and for the purpose aforesaid, I do order and declare that all persons held as slaves within said designated States and parts of States are, and henceforward shall be, free; and that the Executive Government of the United States, including the military and naval authorities thereof, will recognize and maintain the freedom of said persons.

And I hereby enjoin upon the people so declared to be free to abstain from all violence, unless in necessary self-defense; and I recommend to them that, in all cases where allowed, they labor faithfully for reasonable wages.

And I further declare and make known that such persons of suitable condition will be received into the armed service of the United States to garrison forts, positions, stations, and other places, and to man vessels of all sorts in said service.

And upon this act, sincerely believed to be an act of justice, warranted by the Constitution upon military necessity, I invoke the considerate judgment of mankind and the gracious favor of Almighty God.

In witness whereof, I have hereunto set my hand and caused the seal of the United States to be affixed.

Done at the city of Washington, this first day of January, in the year of our Lord one thousand eight [L. S.] hundred and sixty-three, and of the independence of the United States of America the eighty-seventh.

By the President:

ABRAHAM LINCOLN

WILLIAM H. SEWARD, Secretary of State.

LETTER TO THE WORKINGMEN OF MANCHESTER, ENGLAND

The shortage of cotton caused by blockading the Southern ports had created a cotton famine in England and had brought the mill operators of Lancashire to a point of starvation. Nevertheless, these English workingmen appreciated the fact that the Northern armies were fighting for human freedom and they upheld the Northern cause.

Executive Mansion, Washington, January 19, 1863

TO THE WORKINGMEN OF MANCHESTER: I have the honor to acknowledge the receipt of the address and resolutions which you sent me on the eve of the new year. . . .

I know and deeply deplore the sufferings which the work-

ingmen at Manchester, and in all Europe, are called to endure
in this crisis. It has been often and studiously represented that
the attempt to overthrow this government, which was built
upon the foundation of human rights, and to substitute for it
one which should rest exclusively on the basis of human slavery, was likely to obtain the favor of Europe. Through the
action of our disloyal citizens, the workingmen of Europe have
been subjected to severe trials, for the purpose of forcing their
sanction to that attempt. Under the circumstances, I cannot
but regard your decisive utterances upon the question as an
instance of sublime Christian heroism which has not been surpassed in any age or in any country. It is indeed an energetic
and reinspiring assurance of the inherent power of truth, and
of the ultimate and universal triumph of justice, humanity
and freedom. I do not doubt that the sentiments you have
expressed will be sustained by your great nation; and, on the
other hand, I have no hesitation in assuring you that they will
excite admiration, esteem and the most reciprocal feelings of
friendship among the American people. I hail this interchange
of sentiment, therefore, as an augury that whatever else may
happen, whatever misfortune may befall your country or my
own, the peace and friendship which now exist between the
two nations will be, as it shall be my desire to make them,
perpetual.

LETTER TO GENERAL J. HOOKER

*When Lincoln removed McClellan on November 5, 1862, he ap-
pointed Burnside in his place. Burnside lasted for only one battle—
Fredericksburg. Lincoln then removed him and placed "Fighting
Joe" Hooker in command. Hooker has been described as "brave,
handsome, vain, insubordinate, plausible, untrustworthy." As this
letter indicates, Lincoln did not trust him too greatly.*

(Private)

Executive Mansion, Washington, D. C., January 26, 1863

GENERAL: I have placed you at the head of the Army of the Potomac. Of course I have done this upon what appear to me to be sufficient reasons, and yet I think it best for you to know that there are some things in regard to which I am not quite satisfied with you. I believe you to be a brave and skilful soldier, which of course I like. I also believe you do not mix politics with your pofession, in which you are right. You have confidence in yourself, which is a valuable if not an indispensable quality. You are ambitious, which, within reasonable bounds, does good rather than harm; but I think that during General Burnside's command of the army you have taken counsel of your ambition and thwarted him as much as you could, in which you did a great wrong to the country and to a most meritorious and honorable brother officer. I have heard, in such a way as to believe it, of your recently saying that both the army and the government needed a dictator. Of course it was not for this, but in spite of it, that I have given you the command. Only those generals who gain successes can set up dictators. What I now ask of you is military success, and I will risk the dictatorship. The government will support you to the utmost of its ability, which is neither more nor less than it has done and will do for all commanders. I much fear that the spirit which you have aided to infuse into the army, of criticising their commander and withholding confidence from him, will now turn upon you. I shall assist you as far as I can to put it down. Neither you nor Napoleon, if he were alive again, could get any good out of an army while such a spirit prevails in it; and now beware of rashness. Beware of rashness, but with energy and sleepless vigilance go forward and give us victories.

LETTER TO HENRY WINTER DAVIS

Henry Winter Davis was a Maryland abolitionist, antagonistic to the Blair faction in the President's Cabinet and a forthright but intolerant person. He was campaigning for Congress at this time, and in order to help him, Lincoln wrote him this letter, putting down in writing what he had said to him verbally on the day before. Davis was elected and he then promptly turned against the President, becoming leader of the Radical Republican organization in the House. (See also note on Proclamation Concerning Reconstruction, July 8, 1864.)

Executive Mansion, March 18, 1863

MY DEAR SIR: There will be in the new House of Representatives, as there were in the old, some members openly opposing the war, some supporting it unconditionally, and some supporting it with "buts," and "ifs," and "ands." They will divide on the organization of the House—on the election of a Speaker. As you ask my opinion, I give it, that the supporters of the war should send no man to Congress who will not pledge himself to go into caucus with the unconditional supporters of the war, and to abide the action of such caucus and vote for the person therein nominated for Speaker. Let the friends of the government first save the government, and then administer it to their own liking.

P. S. This is not for publication, but to prevent misunderstanding of what I verbally said to you yesterday.

LETTER TO GOVERNOR ANDREW JOHNSON
(Private)

Lincoln writes to the Military Governor of Tennessee, the man who was to be Vice President with him in 1864 and President after his death. Immediately after the Emancipation Proclamation was issued, plans were made to form Negro regiments. Lincoln writes to encourage Johnson to use the Negroes in the armies in Tennessee.

Executive Mansion, March 26, 1863

MY DEAR SIR: I am told you have at least thought of raising a Negro military force. In my opinion the country now needs no specific thing so much as some man of your ability and position to go to this work. When I speak of your position, I mean that of an eminent citizen of a slave State and himself a slaveholder. The colored population is the great available and yet unavailed force for restoring the Union. The bare sight of fifty thousand armed and drilled black soldiers upon the banks of the Mississippi would end the rebellion at once; and who doubts that we can present that sight if we but take hold in earnest? If you have been thinking of it, please do not dismiss the thought.

PROCLAMATION FOR A NATIONAL FAST-DAY

This is another example of Lincoln's religious bent of mind which increased as the War progressed. (Cf. "Meditation on the Divine Will," September 30, 1862.)

March 30, 1863

WHEREAS, the Senate of the United States, devoutly recognizing the supreme authority and just government of Almighty God in all the affairs of men and of nations, has by a resolution requested the President to designate and set apart a day for national prayer and humiliation:

And whereas, it is the duty of nations as well as of men to own their dependence upon the overruling power of God; to confess their sins and transgressions in humble sorrow, yet with assured hope that genuine repentance will lead to mercy and pardon; and to recognize the sublime truth, announced in the Holy Scriptures and proven by all history, that those nations only are blessed whose God is the Lord:

And insomuch as we know that by his divine law, nations, like individuals, are subjected to punishments and chastisements in this world, may we not justly fear that the awful calamity of civil war which now desolates the land may be but a punishment inflicted upon us for our presumptuous sins, to the needful end of our national reformation as a whole people? We have been the recipients of the choicest bounties of Heaven. We have been preserved, these many years, in peace and prosperity. We have grown in numbers, wealth, and power as no other nation has ever grown; but we have forgotten God. We have forgotten the gracious hand which preserved us in peace, and multiplied and enriched and strengthened us; and we have vainly imagined, in the deceitfulness of our hearts, that all these blessings were produced by some superior wisdom and virtue of our own. Intoxicated with unbroken success, we have become too self-sufficient to feel the necessity of redeeming and preserving grace, too proud to pray to the God that made us:

It behooves us, then, to humble ourselves before the offended Power, to confess our national sins, and to pray for clemency and forgiveness:

Now, therefore, in compliance with the request, and fully concurring in the views, of the Senate, I do by this my proclamation designate and set apart Thursday the 30th day of April, 1863, as a day of national humiliation, fasting, and prayer. And I do hereby request all the people to abstain on that day from their ordinary secular pursuits, and to unite at their several places of public worship and their respective homes in keeping the day holy to the Lord, and devoted to the humble discharge of the religious duties proper to that solemn occasion. All this being done in sincerity and truth, let us then rest humbly in the hope authorized by the divine teachings, that the united cry of the nation will be heard on high, and answered with blessings no less than the pardon of our national sins, and the restoration of our now divided and suffering country to its former happy condition of unity and peace.

TELEGRAM TO GENERAL J. HOOKER

Early in May, Hooker had lost the Battle of Chancellorsville. Lee's army had started to head north for the invasion of Pennsylvania that was to culminate in the Battle of Gettysburg. When Lincoln wrote this letter, Lee's army was on the march. The President here gives some advice to the dictator-loving general who was to be removed before Gettysburg was fought.

Washington, June 5, 1863

Yours of today was received an hour ago. So much of professional military skill is requisite to answer it, that I have turned the task over to General Halleck. He promises to perform it with his utmost care. I have but one idea which I think worth suggesting to you, and that is, in case you find Lee coming to the north of the Rappahannock, I would by no means cross to the south of it. If he should leave a rear force at Fredericksburg, tempting you to fall upon it, it would fight in intrenchments and have you at disadvantage, and so, man for man, worst you at that point, while his main force would in some way be getting an advantage of you northward. In one word, I would not take any risk of being entangled upon the river, like an ox jumped half over a fence and liable to be torn by dogs from the rear without a fair chance to gore one way or kick the other. If Lee would come to my side of the river, I would keep on the same side, and fight him or act on the defense, according as might be my estimate of his strength relatively to my own. But these are mere suggestions which I desire to be controlled by the judgment of yourself and General Halleck.

TELEGRAM TO MRS. LINCOLN

Dreams played an important part in Lincoln's life. Here is direct evidence of how they influenced his mind.

Executive Mansion, Washington, D. C., June 9, 1863

Mrs. Lincoln, Philadelphia, Pa.: Think you had better put Tad's pistol away. I had an ugly dream about him.

FROM A LETTER TO ERASTUS CORNING AND OTHERS

Erastus Corning was a millionaire, a railroad magnate and the head of an iron foundry. He, in company with the members of the resolutions committee of the Albany Democratic convention, had openly criticized Lincoln for having had Clement L. Vallandigham of Ohio arrested. Vallandigham was the most notorious of all the Copperheads, a man whose strange exploits in obstructing the Government make one of the most fantastic episodes of the Civil War. He had been arrested in May for openly defying a military order prohibiting treasonous statements. Lincoln writes to Corning and his committee, although this letter was intended for publication and was released simultaneously to the newspapers. It is one of Lincoln's most important war documents, containing, as it does, his defense of his Government's abrogation of certain civil rights during a great emergency.

Executive Mansion, June 12, 1863

Gentlemen: Your letter of May 19, inclosing the resolutions of a public meeting held at Albany, New York, on the 16th of the same month, was received several days ago.

The resolutions, as I understand them, are resolvable into two propositions—first, the expression of a purpose to sustain the cause of the Union, to secure peace through victory, and to support the administration in every constitutional and lawful measure to suppress the rebellion; and, secondly, a declaration of censure upon the administration for supposed unconstitutional action, such as the making of military arrests. And from the two propositions a third is deduced, which is that the gentlemen composing the meeting are resolved on doing their part to maintain our common government and country, despite the folly or wickedness, as they may conceive, of any administration. This position is eminently patriotic and as such I thank the meeting, and congratulate the nation for it. My own purpose is the same; so that the meeting and myself have a common object, and can have no difference, except in the choice of means or measures for effecting that object.

And here I ought to close this paper, and would close it, if there were no apprehension that more injurious consequences than any merely personal to myself might follow the censures systematically cast upon me for doing what, in my view of duty, I could not forbear. The resolutions promise to support me in every constitutional and lawful measure to suppress the rebellion; and I have not knowingly employed, nor shall knowingly employ, any other. But the meeting, by their resolutions, assert and argue that certain military arrests and proceedings following them, for which I am ultimately responsible are unconstitutional. I think they are not. The resolutions quote from the Constitution the definition of treason, and also the limiting safeguards and guarantees therein provided for the citizen on trials for treason, and on his being held to answer for capital or otherwise infamous crimes, and in criminal prosecutions his right to a speedy and public trial by an impartial jury. They proceed to resolve "that these safeguards of the rights of the citizen against the pretensions of arbitrary power were intended more especially for his protection in times of civil commotion." And, apparently to demonstrate the proposition, the resolutions proceed: "They were secured substantially to the English people after years of protracted civil war, and were adopted into our Constitution at the close of the revolution." Would not the demonstration have been better if it could have been truly said that these safeguards had been adopted and applied during the civil wars and during our revolution, instead of after the one and at the close of the other? I, too, am devotedly for them after civil war and before civil war, and at all times, "except when, in cases of rebellion or invasion, the public safety may require" their suspension. The resolutions proceed to tell us that these safeguards "have stood the test of seventy-six years of trial under our republican system under circumstances which show that while they constitute the foundation of all free government, they are the elements of the enduring stability of the republic." No one denies that they have so stood the test up to the beginning of the present rebellion . . . nor does any one question that they will stand the same test much longer after the rebellion closes. But these provisions of the Constitution have no application to the case we have in hand, because the arrests complained of were not made for treason—that is, not for the treason defined in the Constitution, and upon the conviction of which the punishment is death—nor yet were they made to hold persons to answer for any capital or otherwise infamous crimes; nor were the proceedings following, in any constitutional or legal sense, "criminal prosecutions." The arrests were made on totally different grounds, and the proceedings following accorded with the grounds of the arrests. Let us consider the real case with which we are dealing, and apply to it the parts of the Constitution plainly made for such cases.

Prior to my installation here it had been inculcated that any State had a lawful right to secede from the national Union, and that it would be expedient to exercise the right whenever the devotees of the doctrine should fail to elect a president to their own liking. I was elected contrary to their liking; and, accordingly, so far as it was legally possible, they had taken seven States out of the Union, had seized many of the United States forts, and had fired upon the United States flag, all before I was inaugurated, and, of course, before I had done any official act whatever. The rebellion thus begun soon ran into the present civil war; and, in certain respects, it began on very unequal terms between the parties. The insurgents had been preparing for it more than thirty years, while the government had taken no steps to resist them. The former had carefully considered all the means which could be turned to their account. It undoubtedly was a well-pondered reliance with them that in their own unrestricted effort to destroy Union, Constitution and law, all together, the government would, in great degree, be restrained by the same Constitution and law from arresting their progress. Their sympathizers pervaded all departments of the government and nearly all communities of the people. From this material, under cover of "liberty of speech," "liberty of the press," and "*habeas corpus*," they hoped to keep on foot amongst us a most efficient corps of spies, informers, suppliers and aiders and abettors of their cause in a thousand ways. They knew that in times such as they were inaugurating, by the Constitution itself the "*habeas corpus*" might be suspended; but they also knew they had friends who would make a question as to who was to suspend it; meanwhile their spies and others might remain at large to help on their cause. Or if, as has happened, the Executive should suspend the writ without ruinous waste of time, instances of arresting innocent persons might occur, as are always likely to occur in such cases; and then a clamor could be raised in regard to this, which might be at least of some service to the insurgent cause. It needed no very keen perception to discover this part of the enemy's program, so soon as by open hostilities their machinery was fairly put in motion.

Yet, thoroughly imbued with a reverence for the guaranteed rights of individuals, I was slow to adopt the strong measures which by degrees I have been forced to regard as being within the exceptions of the Constitution, and as indispensable to the public safety. Nothing is better known to history than that courts of justice are utterly incompetent to such cases. Civil courts are organized chiefly for trials of individuals, or, at most, a few individuals acting in concert—and this in quiet times, and on charges of crimes well defined in the law. Even in times of peace, bands of horse-thieves and robbers frequently grow too numerous and powerful for the ordinary courts of justice. But what comparison, in numbers, have such bands ever borne to the insurgent sympathizers even in many of the loyal States? Again, a jury too frequently has at least one member more ready to hang the panel than to hang the traitor. And yet again, he who dissuades one man from volunteering, or induces one soldier to desert, weakens the Union cause as much as he who kills a Union soldier in battle. Yet this dissuasion or inducement may be so conducted as to be no defined crime of which any civil court would take cognizance.

Ours is a case of rebellion—so called by the resolutions before me—in fact, a clear, flagrant, and gigantic case of rebellion; and the provision of the Constitution that "the privilege of the writ of *habeas corpus* shall not be suspended unless when, in cases of rebellion or invasion, the public safety may require it," is the provision which specially applies to our present case. This provision plainly attests the understanding of those who made the Constitution that ordinary courts of justice are inadequate to "cases of rebellion"—attests their purpose that, in such cases, men may be held in custody whom the courts, acting on ordinary rules, would discharge. *Habeas corpus* does not discharge men who are proved to be guilty of defined crime; and its suspension is allowed by the Constitution on purpose that men may be arrested and held who can not be proved to be guilty of defined crime, "when, in cases of rebellion or invasion, the public safety may require it."

This is precisely our present case—a case of rebellion wherein the public safety does require the suspension. Indeed, arrests by process of courts and arrests in cases of rebellion do not proceed altogether upon the same basis. The former is directed at the small percentage of ordinary and continuous perpetration of crime, while the latter is directed at sudden and extensive uprisings against the government, which, at most, will succeed or fail in no great length of time In the latter case arrests are made not so much for what has been done, as for what probably would be done. The latter is more for the preventive and less for the vindictive than the former. In such cases the purposes of men are much more easily understood than in cases of ordinary crime. The man who stands by and says nothing when the peril of his government is discussed, cannot be misunderstood. If not hindered, he is sure to help the enemy; much more if he talks ambiguously— talks for his country with "buts," and "ifs" and "ands." Of how little value the constitutional provision I have quoted will be rendered if arrests shall never be made until defined crimes shall have been committed, may be illustrated by a few notable examples: General John C. Breckinridge, General Robert E. Lee, General Joseph E. Johnston, General John B. Magruder, General William B. Preston, General Simon B. Buckner, and Commodore Franklin Buchanan, now occupying the very highest places in the rebel war service, were all within the power of the government since the rebellion began, and were nearly as well known to be traitors then as now. Unquestionably if we had seized and held them, the insurgent cause would be much weaker. But no one of them had then committed any crime defined in the law. Every one of them, if arrested, would have been discharged on *habeas corpus* were the writ allowed to operate. In view of these and similar cases,

I think the time not unlikely to come when I shall be blamed for having made too few arrests rather than too many.

By the third resolution the meeting indicate their opinion that military arrests may be constitutional in localities where rebellion actually exists, but that such arrests are unconstitutional in localities where rebellion or insurrection does not actually exist. They insist that such arrests shall not be made "outside of the lines of necessary military occupation and the scenes of insurrection." Inasmuch, however, as the Constitution itself makes no such distinction, I am unable to believe that there is any such constitutional distinction. I concede that the class of arrests complained of can be constitutional only when, in cases of rebellion or invasion, the public safety may require them; and I insist that in such cases they are constitutional wherever the public safety does require them, as well in places to which they may prevent the rebellion extending, as in those where it may be already prevailing; as well where they may restrain mischievous interference with the raising and supplying of armies to suppress the rebellion, as where the rebellion may actually be; as well where they may restrain the enticing men out of the army, as where they would prevent mutiny in the army; equally constitutional at all places where they will conduce to the public safety, as against the dangers of rebellion or invasion. . . .

I understand the meeting whose resolutions I am considering to be in favor of suppressing the rebellion by military force —by armies. Long experience has shown that armies cannot be maintained unless desertion shall be punished by the severe penalty of death. The case requires, and the law and the Constitution sanction, this punishment. Must I shoot a simple-minded soldier boy who deserts, while I must not touch a hair of a wily agitator who induces him to desert? This is none the less injurious when effected by getting a father, or brother, or friend into a public meeting, and there working upon his feelings till he is persuaded to write the soldier boy that he is fighting in a bad cause, for a wicked administration of a contemptible government, too weak to arrest and punish him if he shall desert. I think that, in such a case, to silence the agitator and save the boy is not only constitutional, but withal a great mercy.

If I be wrong on this question of constitutional power, my error lies in believing that certain proceedings are constitutional when, in cases of rebellion or invasion, the public safety requires them, which would not be constitutional when, in absence of rebellion or invasion, the public safety does not require them: in other words, that the Constitution is not in its application in all respects the same in cases of rebellion or invasion involving the public safety, as it is in times of profound peace and public security. The Constitution itself makes the distinction, and I can no more be persuaded that the government can constitutionally take no strong measures in time of rebellion, because it can be shown that the same could not be lawfully taken in time of peace, than I can be persuaded that a particular drug is not good medicine for a sick man because it can be shown to not be good food for a well one. Nor am I able to appreciate the danger apprehended by the meeting, that the American people will by means of military arrests during the rebellion lose the right of public discussion, the liberty of speech and the press, the law of evidence, trial by jury, and *habeas corpus* throughout the indefinite peaceful future which I trust lies before them, any more than I am able to believe that a man could contract so strong an appetite for emetics during temporary illness as to persist in feeding upon them during the remainder of his healthful life. . . .

I further say that, as the war progresses, it appears to me, opinion and action, which were in great confusion at first, take shape and fall into more regular channels, so that the necessity for strong dealing with them gradually decreases. I have every reason to desire that it should cease altogether, and far from the least is my regard for the opinions and wishes of those who, like the meeting at Albany, declare their purpose to sustain the government in every constitutional and lawful measure to suppress the rebellion. Still, I must continue to do so much as may seem to be required by the public safety.

RESPONSE TO A SERENADE

Gettysburg had been fought on July 1, 2 and 3; Vicksburg on July 4. These were both Union victories, and the people of Washington had come to the White House to serenade the President. Several phrases first stated here reappear in more carefully worded form in the famous Gettysburg address.

July 7, 1863

FELLOW CITIZENS: I am very glad indeed to see you tonight, and yet I will not say I thank you for this call; but I do most sincerely thank Almighty God for the occasion on which you have called. How long ago is it?—eighty-odd years since, on the Fourth of July, for the first time in the history of the world, a nation, by its representatives, assembled and declared, as a self-evident truth, "that all men are created equal." That was the birthday of the United States of America. Since then the Fourth of July has had several very peculiar recognitions. The two men most distinguished in the framing and support of the Declaration were Thomas Jefferson and John Adams—the one having penned it, and the other sustained it the most forcibly in debate—the only two of the fifty-five who signed it that were elected Presidents of the United States. Precisely fifty years* after they put their hands to the paper, it pleased Almighty God to take both from this stage of action. This was indeed an extraordinary and remarkable event in our his-

* Jefferson and Adams both died on July 4, 1826.

tory. Another President, five years after, was called from this stage of existence on the same day and month of the year;* and now on this last Fourth of July just passed, when we have a gigantic rebellion, at the bottom of which is an effort to overthrow the principle that all men are created equal, we have the surrender of a most powerful position and army on that very day. And not only so, but in a succession of battles in Pennsylvania, near to us, through three days, so rapidly fought that they might be called one great battle, on the first, second, and third of the month of July; and on the fourth the cohorts of those who opposed the Declaration that all men are created equal "turned tail" and ran. Gentlemen, this is a glorious theme, and the occasion for a speech, but I am not prepared to make one worthy of the occasion. I would like to speak in terms of praise due to the many brave officers and soldiers who have fought in the cause of the Union and liberties of their country from the beginning of the war. These are trying occasions, not only in success, but for the want of success. I dislike to mention the name of one single officer, lest I might do wrong to those I might forget. Recent events bring up glorious names, and particularly prominent ones; but these I will not mention. Having said this much, I will now take the music.

LETTER TO GENERAL GRANT

Lincoln writes to thank Grant for his victory at Vicksburg, Mississippi. The fortified city of Vicksburg, overlooking the Mississippi river from a high bluff, had been under attack for months. Grant, who had been in disfavor with the high command, finally resolved to run his batteries down the river past the rifled guns of the forts in an effort to land in a new position from which he could take the city from the rear. Even after Grant had shut off Vicksburg from the rest of the world, the city had resisted siege from May 19

* James Monroe, who died on July 4, 1831.

to July 4, when its garrison of 37,000 was compelled by starvation to surrender.

Executive Mansion, July 13, 1863

My Dear General: I do not remember that you and I ever met personally. I write this now as a grateful acknowledgment for the almost inestimable service you have done the country. I wish to say a word further. When you first reached the vicinity of Vicksburg, I thought you should do what you finally did —march the troops across the neck, run the batteries with the transports, and thus go below; and I never had any faith, except a general hope that you knew better than I, that the Yazoo Pass expedition and the like could succeed. When you got below and took Port Gibson, Grand Gulf, and vicinity, I thought you should go down the river and join General Banks, and when you turned northward, east of the Big Black, I feared it was a mistake. I now wish to make the personal acknowledgment that you were right and I was wrong.

DRAFT OF LETTER TO GENERAL G. G. MEADE

Lincoln had removed Hooker on the eve of the Battle of Gettysburg and replaced him with Meade. Meade had won the battle, but had failed to pursue Lee when Lee had headed south for the Shenandoah Valley. It is interesting to note that although Lincoln wrote out this letter very carefully, he never sent it to Meade.

Executive Mansion, July 14, 1863

I have just seen your dispatch to General Halleck, asking to be relieved of your command because of a supposed censure of mine. I am very, very grateful to you for the magnificent success you gave the cause of the country at Gettysburg; and I am sorry now to be the author of the slightest pain to you. But I was in such deep distress myself that I could not restrain some expression of it. I have been oppressed nearly ever since the battles of Gettysburg by what appeared to be evidences that yourself and General Couch and General Smith were not seeking a collision with the enemy, but were trying to get him across the river without another battle. What these evidences were, if you please, I hope to tell you at some time when we shall both feel better. The case, summarily stated, is this: You fought and beat the enemy at Gettysburg and, of course, to say the least, his loss was as great as yours. He retreated, and you did not, as it seemed to me, pressingly pursue him; but a flood in the river detained him till, by slow degrees, you were again upon him. You had at least twenty thousand veteran troops directly with you, and as many more raw ones within supporting distance, all in addition to those who fought with you at Gettysburg, while it was not possible that he had received a single recruit, and yet you stood and let the flood run down, bridges be built, and the enemy move away at his leisure without attacking him. And Couch and Smith! The latter left Carlisle in time, upon all ordinary calculation, to have aided you in the last battle at Gettysburg, but he did not arrive. At the end of more than ten days, I believe twelve, under constant urging, he reached Hagerstown from Carlisle, which is not an inch over fifty-five miles, if so much, and Couch's movement was very little different.

Again, my dear general, I do not believe you appreciate the magnitude of the misfortune involved in Lee's escape. He was within your easy grasp, and to have closed upon him would, in connection with our other late successes, have ended the war. As it is, the war will be prolonged indefinitely. If you could not safely attack Lee last Monday, how can you possibly do so south of the river, when you can take with you very few more than two thirds of the force you then had in hand?

It would be unreasonable to expect, and I do not expect

[that], you can now effect much. Your golden opportunity is gone, and I am distressed immeasurably because of it.

I beg you will not consider this a prosecution or persecution of yourself. As you had learned that I was dissatisfied, I have thought it best to kindly tell you why.

[*Indorsement on the Envelope*]
To General Meade, never sent or signed.

LETTER TO GENERAL O. O. HOWARD

After having suppressed his letter to General Meade because he thought that its too-critical attitude would offend that officer, Lincoln takes this opportunity to express the same ideas more gently in a letter to Howard, one of Meade's corps commanders, in full knowledge that Howard would show his letter to Meade. Howard not only showed the letter to Meade but gave it to him, and Meade sent it on to his wife.

Executive Mansion, July 21, 1863

MY DEAR GENERAL HOWARD: Your letter of the 18th is received. I was deeply mortified by the escape of Lee across the Potomac, because the substantial destruction of his army would have ended the war, and because I believed such destruction was perfectly easy—believed that General Meade and his noble army had expended all the skill, and toil, and blood, up to the ripe harvest, and then let the crop go to waste.

Perhaps my mortification was heightened because I had always believed—making my belief a hobby, possibly—that the main rebel army going north of the Potomac could never return, if well attended to; and because I was so greatly flattered in this belief by the operations at Gettysburg. A few days having passed, I am now profoundly grateful for what was done, without criticism for what was not done.

General Meade has my confidence as a brave and skillful officer and a true man.

FROM A LETTER TO
GOVERNOR HORATIO SEYMOUR

Only a few days after Gettysburg, from July 13 to July 16, terrible draft riots had taken place in New York City. Governor Seymour of New York wrote to Lincoln asking him to suspend the draft. Seymour was a Democrat who, in company with Fernando Wood, Democratic Mayor of New York City, had opposed the administration in every way possible. This is Lincoln's answer to Seymour, setting forth the President's ideas on the legality of the draft laws.

Executive Mansion, August 7, 1863

GOVERNOR HORATIO SEYMOUR: Your communication of the third instant has been received and attentively considered.

I cannot consent to suspend the draft in New York, as you request, because, among other reasons, time is too important. . . .

I do not object to abide a decision of the United States Supreme Court, or of the judges thereof, on the constitutionality of the draft law. In fact, I should be willing to facilitate the obtaining of it, but I cannot consent to lose the time while it is being obtained. We are contending with an enemy, who, as I understand, drives every ablebodied man he can reach into his ranks, very much as a butcher drives bullocks into a slaughter-pen. No time is wasted, no argument is used. This produces an army which will soon turn upon our now victorious soldiers, already in the field, if they shall not be sustained by recruits as they should be. It produces an army with a rapidity not to be matched on our side, if we first waste time to re-experiment with the volunteer system already deemed by Congress, and palpably, in fact, so far exhausted as to be, inadequate, and then more time to obtain a court decision as to whether a law is constitutional which requires a part of those not now in the service to go to the aid of those who are already in it, and still more time to determine with absolute certainty that we get those who are to go in the precisely legal proportion to those who are not to go. My purpose is to be in my action just and constitutional, and yet practical, in performing the important duty with which I am charged, of maintaining the unity and the free principles of our common country.

LETTER TO MRS. LINCOLN

In summertime, the Lincoln family customarily moved from the White House to the Soldiers' Home which was about three miles north of the city. Tad kept a pair of goats as pets there; one of them is reported lost. Crittenden, whose death is mentioned here, was John J. Crittenden, Kentucky statesman and author of the Crittenden Compromise of 1860. Brutus Clay, also of Kentucky, was the brother of Cassius Clay, outspoken Southern abolitionist who had been appointed by Lincoln as Minister to Russia. Charles A. Wickliffe, Kentucky politician, had stayed with the Union, but he was a wealthy man whose contempt for laboring people had earned him the title of "The Duke."

Executive Mansion, August 8, 1863

My Dear Wife: All as well as usual, and no particular trouble anyway. I put the money into the Treasury at five percent, with the privilege of withdrawing it any time upon thirty days' notice. I suppose you are glad to learn this. Tell dear Tad poor "Nanny Goat" is lost, and Mrs. Cuthbert and I are in distress about it. The day you left, Nanny was found resting herself and chewing her little cud on the middle of Tad's bed; but now she's gone! The gardener kept complaining that she destroyed the flowers, till it was concluded to bring her down to the White House. This was done, and the second day she had disappeared and has not been heard of since. This is the last we know of poor "Nanny." The weather continues dry and excessively warm here. Nothing very important occurring. The election in Kentucky has gone very strongly right. Old Mr. Wickliffe got ugly, as you know: ran for governor, and is terribly beaten. Upon Mr. Crittenden's death, Brutus Clay, Cassius's brother, was put on the track for Congress, and is largely elected. Mr. Menzies, who, as we thought, behaved very badly last session of Congress, is largely beaten in the district opposite Cincinnati, by Green Clay Smith, Cassius Clay's nephew. But enough.

Affectionately,

A. LINCOLN

OPINION OF THE DRAFT

(Never issued)

The draft laws, resistance to which had caused the riots in New York in July, were still agitating the country. Lincoln prepared this elaborate argument which was intended to convince those Northern Democrats who were basically loyal to the Union; after writing it he decided that it would be politically more advisable not to release it, so he put it away, and it was not published until Nicolay and Hay printed it in 1889.

August [15?], 1863

IT IS at all times proper that misunderstanding between the public and the public servant should be avoided; and this is far more important now than in times of peace and tranquillity. I therefore address you without searching for a precedent upon which to do so. Some of you are sincerely devoted to the republican institutions and territorial integrity of our country, and yet are opposed to what is called the draft, or conscription.

At the beginning of the war, and ever since, a variety of motives, pressing, some in one direction and some in the other, would be presented to the mind of each man physically fit for a soldier, upon the combined effect of which motives he would, or would not, voluntarily enter the service. Among these motives would be patriotism, political bias, ambition, personal courage, love of adventure, want of employment, and convenience, or the opposites of some of these. We already have, and have had in the service, as appears, substantially all that can be obtained upon this voluntary weighing of motives. And yet we must somehow obtain more, or relinquish the original object of the contest, together with all the blood and treasure already expended in the effort to secure it. To meet this necessity the law for the draft has been enacted. You who do not wish to be soldiers do not like this law. This is natural; nor does it imply want of patriotism. Nothing can be so just and necessary as to make us like it if it is disagreeable to us. We are prone, too, to find false arguments with which to excuse ourselves for opposing such disagreeable things. In this case, those who desire the rebellion to succeed, and others who seek reward in a different way, are very active in accommodating us with this class of arguments. They tell us the law is unconstitutional. It is the first instance, I believe, in which the power of Congress to do a thing has ever been questioned in a case when the power is given by the Constitution in express terms. Whether a power can be implied when it is not expressed has often been the subject of controversy; but this is the first case in which the degree of effrontery has been ventured upon of denying a power which is plainly and distinctly written down in the Constitution. The Constitution declares that "The Congress shall have power . . . to raise and support armies; but no appropriation of money to that use shall be for a longer term than two years." The whole scope of the conscription act is "to raise and support armies." There is nothing else in it. It makes no appropriation of money, and hence the money clause just quoted is not touched by it.

The case simply is, the Constitution provides that the Congress shall have power to raise and support armies; and by this act the Congress has exercised the power to raise and support armies. This is the whole of it. It is a law made in literal pursuance of this part of the United States Constitution; and another part of the same Constitution declares that "this Constitution, and the laws made in pursuance thereof, . . . shall be the supreme law of the land, and the judges in every State shall be bound thereby, anything in the constitution or laws of any State to the contrary notwithstanding." Do you admit that the power is given to raise and support armies, and yet insist that by this act Congress has not exercised the power in a constitutional mode?—has not done the thing in the right way? Who is to judge of this? The Constitution gives Congress the power, but it does not prescribe the mode, or expressly declare who shall prescribe it. In such case Congress must prescribe the mode, or relinquish the power. There is no alternative. Congress could not exercise the power to do the thing if it had not the power of providing a way to do it, when no way is provided by the Constitution for doing it. In fact, Congress would not have the power to raise and support armies, if even by the Constitution it were left to the option of any other or others to give or withhold the only mode of doing it. If the Constitution had prescribed a mode, Congress could and must follow that mode; but, as it is, the mode necessarily goes to Congress, with the power expressly given. The power is given fully, completely, unconditionally. It is not a power to raise armies if State authorities consent; nor if the men to compose the armies are entirely willing; but it is a power to raise and support armies given to Congress by the Constitution, without an "if."

It is clear that a constitutional law may not be expedient or proper. Such would be a law to raise armies when no armies were needed. But this is not such. The republican institutions and territorial integrity of our country cannot be maintained without the further raising and supporting of armies. There can be no army without men. Men can be had only voluntarily, or involuntarily. We have ceased to obtain them voluntarily, and to obtain them involuntarily is the draft—the conscription. If you dispute the fact, and declare that men can still be had voluntarily in sufficient numbers, prove the assertion by yourselves volunteering in such numbers, and I shall gladly give up the draft. Or, if not sufficient number, but any one of you will volunteer, he for his single self will escape all the horrors of the draft, and will thereby do only what each one of at least a million of his manly brethren have already done. Their toil and blood have been given as much for you as for themselves. Shall it all be lost rather than that you, too, will bear your part?

I do not say that all who would avoid serving in the war are unpatriotic; but I do think every patriot should willingly take his chance under a law made with great care, in order to secure entire fairness. . . .

Much complaint is made of that provision of the conscription law which allows a drafted man to substitute three hundred dollars for himself; while, as I believe, none is made of that provision which allows him to substitute another man for himself. Nor is the three hundred dollar provision objected to for unconstitutionality; but for inequality, for favoring the rich against the poor. The substitution of men is the provision, if any, which favors the rich to the exclusion of the poor. But this, being a provision in accordance with an old and well-known practice in the raising of armies, is not objected to. There would have been great objection if that provision had been omitted. And yet, being in, the money provision really modifies the inequality which the other introduces. It allows men to escape the service who are too poor to escape but for it. Without the money provision, competition among the more wealthy might, and probably would, raise the price of substitutes above three hundred dollars, thus leaving the man who could raise only three hundred dollars no escape from personal service. True, by the law as it is, the man who cannot raise so much as three hundred dollars, nor obtain a personal substitute for less, cannot escape; but he can come quite as near escaping as he could if the money provision were not in the law To put it another way: is an unobjectionable law which allows only the man to escape who can pay a thousand dollars made objectionable by adding a provision that any one may escape who can pay the smaller sum of three hundred dollars? This is the exact difference at this point between the present law and all former draft laws. It is true that by this law a somewhat larger number will escape than could under a law allowing personal substitutes only; but each additional man thus escaping will be a poorer man than could have escaped by the law in the other form. The money provision enlarges the class of exempts from actual service simply by admitting poorer men into it. How then can the money provision be a wrong to the poor man? The inequality complained of pertains in greater degree to the substitution of men, and is really modified and lessened by the money provision. The inequality could only be perfectly cured by sweeping both provisions away. This, being a great innovation, would probably leave the law more distasteful than it now is.

The principle of the draft, which simply is involuntary or enforced service, is not new. It has been practised in all ages of the world. It was well-known to the framers of our Constitution as one of the modes of raising armies, at the time they placed in that instrument the provision that "the Congress shall have power to raise and support armies." It had been used just before in establishing our independence, and it was also used under the Constitution in 1812. Wherein is the peculiar hardship now? Shall we shrink from the necessary

means to maintain our free government, which our grandfathers employed to establish it and our own fathers have already employed once to maintain it? Are we degenerate? Has
the manhood of our race run out?

LETTER TO JAMES H. HACKETT

Lincoln was fond of the theater and especially fond of Shakespeare.
He had seen James H. Hackett as Falstaff, a part in which Hackett
had made a great reputation for himself. The actor had sent a
copy of his book Notes and Comments on Shakespeare *to the*
President. Lincoln writes to thank Hackett and to comment on
Shakespeare. Hackett, without realizing that he would be pro-
viding fuel for political fires, unthinkingly permitted this letter to
be published. The opposition newspapers gleefully attacked Lincoln
as a Shakespearean critic. (See also letter to Hackett, November
2, 1863.)

Executive Mansion, August 17, 1863

My Dear Sir: Months ago I should have acknowledged the
receipt of your book and accompanying kind note; and I now
have to beg your pardon for not having done so.

For one of my age I have seen very little of the drama.
The first presentation of *Falstaff* I ever saw was yours here,
last winter or spring. Perhaps the best compliment I can pay
is to say, as I truly can, I am very anxious to see it again.
Some of Shakespeare's plays I have never read; while others
I have gone over perhaps as frequently as any unprofessional
reader. Among the latter are *Lear, Richard III, Henry VIII,*
Hamlet, and especially *Macbeth.* I think nothing equals Macbeth. It is wonderful.

Unlike you gentlemen of the profession, I think the solil-
oquy in *Hamlet* commencing "Oh, my offense is rank," surpasses that commencing "To be or not to be." But pardon this

small attempt at criticism. I should like to hear you pronounce the opening speech of Richard III. Will you not soon visit Washington again? If you do, please call and let me make your personal acquaintance.

LETTER TO JAMES C. CONKLING

A mass meeting of loyal Union men was to be held in Springfield, Ill., and Lincoln had been invited to go there to address this important political gathering. At first he had seriously considered leaving Washington to do so but he then realized that the press of national affairs made this impossible. He wrote, instead, this long and important letter which was intended to be read at the meeting and to be published throughout the nation. It was written during the high tide of Northern victory, and it did much to win the people to Lincoln. It was widely commented on by newspapers, not only in America, but also abroad.

Executive Mansion, August 26, 1863

MY DEAR SIR: Your letter inviting me to attend a mass-meeting of unconditional Union men, to be held at the capital of Illinois on the 3d day of September has been received. It would be very agreeable to me to thus meet my old friends at my own home, but I cannot just now be absent from here so long as a visit there would require. . . .

There are those who are dissatisfied with me. To such I would say: You desire peace, and you blame me that we do not have it. But how can we attain it? There are but three conceivable ways: First, to suppress the rebellion by force of arms. This I am trying to do. Are you for it? If you are, so far we are agreed. If you are not for it, a second way is to give up the Union. I am against this. Are you for it? If you are, you should say so plainly. If you are not for force, nor yet for dissolution, there only remains some imaginable compromise.

I do not believe any compromise embracing the maintenance
of the Union is now possible. All I learn leads to a directly
opposite belief. The strength of the rebellion is its military,
its army. That army dominates all the country and all the
people within its range. Any offer of terms made by any man
or men within that range, in opposition to that army, is simply nothing for the present, because such man or men have
no power whatever to enforce their side of a compromise, if
one were made with them.

To illustrate: Suppose refugees from the South and peace
men of the North get together in convention, and frame and
proclaim a compromise embracing a restoration of the Union.
In what way can that compromise be used to keep Lee's army
out of Pennsylvania? Meade's army can keep Lee's army out
of Pennsylvania, and, I think, can ultimately drive it out of
existence. But no paper compromise to which the controllers
of Lee's army are not agreed can at all affect that army. In an
effort at such compromise we should waste time which the
enemy would improve to our disadvantage; and that would be
all. A compromise, to be effective, must be made either with
those who control the rebel army, or with the people first liberated from the domination of that army by the success of our
own army. Now, allow me to assure you that no word or intimation from that rebel army, or from any of the men controlling it, in relation to any peace compromise, has ever come
to my knowledge or belief. All charges and insinuations to
the contrary are deceptive and groundless. And I promise you
that if any such proposition shall hereafter come, it shall not
be rejected and kept a secret from you. I freely acknowledge
myself the servant of the people, according to the bond of
service—the United States Constitution—and that, as such, I
am responsible to them.

But to be plain. You are dissatisfied with me about the
Negro. Quite likely there is a difference of opinion between

you and myself upon that subject. I certainly wish that all men could be free, while I suppose you do not. Yet, I have neither adopted nor proposed any measure which is not consistent with even your view, provided you are for the Union. I suggested compensated emancipation, to which you replied you wished not to be taxed to buy Negroes. But I had not asked you to be taxed to buy Negroes, except in such way as to save you from greater taxation to save the Union exclusively by other means.

You dislike the Emancipation Proclamation, and perhaps would have it retracted. You say it is unconstitutional. I think differently. I think the Constitution invests its Commander-in-Chief with the law of war in time of war. The most that can be said—if so much—is that slaves are property. Is there —has there ever been—any question that by the law of war, property, both of enemies and friends, may be taken when needed? And is it not needed whenever taking it helps us, or hurts the enemy? Armies, the world over, destroy enemies' property when they cannot use it; and even destroy their own to keep it from the enemy. Civilized belligerents do all in their power to help themselves or hurt the enemy, except a few things regarded as barbarous or cruel. Among the exceptions are the massacre of vanquished foes and non-combatants, male and female.

But the proclamation, as law, either is valid or is not valid. If it is not valid, it needs no retraction. If it is valid, it cannot be retracted any more than the dead can be brought to life. Some of you profess to think its retraction would operate favorably for the Union. Why better after the retraction than before the issue? There was more than a year and a half of trial to suppress the rebellion before the proclamation issued; the last one hundred days of which passed under an explicit notice that it was coming, unless averted by those in revolt returning to their allegiance. The war has certainly progressed as favorably for us since the issue of the proclamation as before.

I know, as fully as one can know the opinions of others, that some of the commanders of our armies in the field, who have given us our most important successes, believe the emancipation policy and the use of the colored troops constitute the heaviest blow yet dealt to the rebellion, and that at least one of these important successes could not have been achieved when it was but for the aid of black soldiers. Among the commanders holding these views are some who have never had any affinity with what is called Abolitionism, or with Republican party politics, but who hold them purely as military opinions. I submit these opinions as being entitled to some weight against the objections often urged that emancipation and arming the blacks are unwise as military measures, and were not adopted as such in good faith.

You say you will not fight to free Negroes. Some of them seem willing to fight for you; but no matter. Fight you, then, exclusively, to save the Union. I issued the proclamation on purpose to aid you in saving the Union. Whenever you shall have conquered all resistance to the Union, if I shall urge you to continue fighting, it will be an apt time then for you to declare you will not fight to free Negroes.

I thought that in your struggle for the Union, to whatever extent the Negroes should cease helping the enemy, to that extent it weakened the enemy in his resistance to you. Do you think differently? I thought that whatever Negroes can be got to do as soldiers, leaves just so much less for white soldiers to do in saving the Union. Does it appear otherwise to you? But Negroes, like other people, act upon motives. Why should they do anything for us if we will do nothing for them? If they stake their lives for us they must be prompted by the strongest motive, even the promise of freedom. And the promise, being made, must be kept.

The signs look better. The Father of Waters again goes

unvexed to the sea. Thanks to the great Northwest for it. Nor yet wholly to them. Three hundred miles up they met New England, Empire, Keystone, and Jersey, hewing their way right and left. The sunny South, too, in more colors than one, also lent a hand. On the spot, their part of the history was jotted down in black and white. The job was a great national one, and let none be banned who bore an honorable part in it. And while those who have cleared the great river may well be proud, even that is not all. It is hard to say that anything has been more bravely and well done than at Antietam, Murfrees boro', Gettysburg, and on many fields of lesser note. Nor must Uncle Sam's web-feet be forgotten. At all the watery margins they have been present. Not only on the deep sea, the broad bay, and the rapid river, but also up the narrow, muddy bayou, and wherever the ground was a little damp, they have been and made their tracks. Thanks to all: for the great republic— for the principle it lives by and keeps alive—for man's vast future—thanks to all.

Peace does not appear so distant as it did. I hope it will come soon, and come to stay; and so come as to be worth the keeping in all future time. It will then have been proved that among free men there can be no successful appeal from the ballot to the bullet, and that they who take such appeal are sure to lose their case and pay the cost. And then there will be some black men who can remember that with silent tongue, and clenched teeth, and steady eye, and well-poised bayonet, they have helped mankind on to this great consummation, while I fear there will be some white ones unable to forget that with malignant heart and deceitful speech they strove to hinder it.

Still, let us not be over-sanguine of a speedy final triumph. Let us be quite sober. Let us diligently apply the means, never doubting that a just God, in his own good time, will give us the rightful result.

TELEGRAM TO MRS. HANNAH ARMSTRONG

The implications of this brief telegram reach far back to the days of Lincoln's youth. He had wrestled with Jack Armstrong at New Salem. Jack Armstrong was the leader of the Clary's Grove Boys, and Lincoln had won his loyalty by his physical prowess. Hannah Armstrong was Jack's widow. Lincoln had freed her son, William Duff, in the well-known almanac murder trial on May 7, 1858. Four of her sons had enlisted in the army, one of them had died, and one of them had been wounded. Hannah persuaded a friend in Petersburg, Ill., a village near the abandoned site of New Salem, to write to the President asking him to release William Duff from the army.

Executive Mansion, Washington, September 18, 1863

MRS. HANNAH ARMSTRONG, PETERSBURG, ILL.: I have just ordered the discharge of your boy William as you say, now at Louisville, Ky.

LETTER TO GENERAL H. W. HALLECK

Confederate and Union troops were contesting for the possession of Chattanooga, Tennessee. The first day of the Battle of Chickamauga was raging when Lincoln sent this letter to Halleck. There had been much talk of sending reinforcements from Meade's army to go to the defense of Chattanooga. Meade had been following Lee's army ever since the Battle of Gettysburg early in July but had not come to grips with him since that time. Lincoln writes to Halleck to survey the situation.

Executive Mansion, September 19, 1863

BY GENERAL MEADE's dispatch to you of yesterday it appears that he desires your views and those of the government as to whether he shall advance upon the enemy. I am not prepared to order, or even advise, an advance in this case, wherein I know so little of particulars, and wherein he, in the field, thinks the risk is so great, and the promise of advantage so small.

And yet the case presents matters for very serious consideration in another aspect. These two armies confront each other across a small river, substantially midway between the two capitals, each defending its own capital, and menacing the other. General Meade estimates the enemy's infantry in front of him at not less than 40,000. Suppose we add fifty percent to this for cavalry, artillery, and extra-duty men stretching as far as Richmond, making the whole force of the enemy 60,000.

General Meade, as shown by the returns, has with him, and between him and Washington, of the same classes of well men, over 90,000. Neither can bring the whole of his men into a battle; but each can bring as large a percentage in as the other. For a battle, then, General Meade has three men to General Lee's two. Yet, it having been determined that choosing ground and standing on the defensive gives so great advantage that the three cannot safely attack the two, the three are left simply standing on the defensive also.

If the enemy's 60,000 are sufficient to keep our 90,000 away from Richmond, why, by the same rule, may not 40,000 of ours keep their 60,000 away from Washington, leaving us 50,000 to put to some other use? Having practically come to the mere defensive, it seems to be no economy at all to employ twice as many men for that object as are needed. With no object, certainly, to mislead myself, I can perceive no fault in this statement, unless we admit we are not the equal of the enemy, man for man. I hope you will consider it.

To avoid misunderstanding, let me say that to attempt to fight the enemy slowly back into his intrenchments at Richmond, and then to capture him, is an idea I have been trying to repudiate for quite a year.

My judgment is so clear against it that I would scarcely allow the attempt to be made if the general in command should desire to make it. My last attempt upon Richmond was to get McClellan, when he was nearer there than the enemy was, to run in ahead of him. Since then I have constantly desired the Army of the Potomac to make Lee's army, and not Richmond, its objective point. If our army cannot fall upon the enemy and hurt him where he is, it is plain to me it can gain nothing by attempting to follow him over a succession of intrenched lines into a fortified city.

PROCLAMATION FOR THANKSGIVING

The President of the United States issues a proclamation designating the last Thursday of November—November 26, 1863—as a day of general thanksgiving.

October 3, 1863

THE year that is drawing toward its close has been filled with the blessings of fruitful fields and healthful skies. To these bounties, which are so constantly enjoyed that we are prone to forget the source from which they come, others have been added, which are of so extraordinary a nature that they cannot fail to penetrate and soften the heart which is habitually insensible to the ever-watchful providence of Almighty God. In the midst of a civil war of unequal magnitude and severity, which has sometimes seemed to foreign states to invite and provoke their aggressions, peace has been preserved with all nations, order has been maintained, the laws have been respected and obeyed, and harmony has prevailed everywhere, except in the theater of military conflict; while that theater has been greatly contracted by the advancing armies and navies of the Union.

Needful diversions of wealth and of strength from the fields of peaceful industry to the national defense have not arrested the plow, the shuttle, or the ship; the ax has enlarged the borders of our settlements, and the mines, as well of iron and coal as of the precious metals, have yielded even more abundantly than heretofore. Population has steadily increased, notwithstanding the waste that has been made in the camp, the siege and the battlefield, and the country, rejoicing in the consciousness of augmented strength and vigor, is permitted to expect continuance of years with large increase of freedom.

No human counsel hath devised, nor hath any mortal hand worked out these great things. They are the gracious gifts of the most high God, who, while dealing with us in anger for our sins, hath nevertheless remembered mercy.

It has seemed to me fit and proper that they should be solemnly, reverently, and gratefully acknowledged as with one heart and one voice by the whole American people. I do, therefore, invite my fellow citizens in every part of the United States, and also those who are at sea and those who are sojourning in foreign lands, to set apart and observe the last Thursday of November next as a day of thanksgiving and praise to our beneficent Father who dwelleth in the heavens. And I recommend to them that, while offering up the ascriptions justly due to him for such singular deliverances and blessings, they do also, with humble penitence for our national perverseness and disobedience, commend to his tender care all those who have become widows, orphans, mourners, or sufferers in the lamentable civil strife in which we are unavoidably engaged, and fervently implore the interposition of the almighty hand to heal the wounds of the nation, and to restore it, as soon as may be consistent with the Divine purposes, to the full enjoyment of peace, harmony, tranquillity, and union.

LETTER TO JAMES H. HACKETT

(Private)

Hackett had released Lincoln's letter of August 17 to the press. He had written to the President in an effort to apologize for his error in making the letter public, and Lincoln writes to him here a pathetic paragraph forgiving him for what he had done. The episode had a still unhappier aftermath. When Hackett later visited the President at the White House, he took advantage of the occasion to ask to be appointed to a government office. Noah Brooks reported Lincoln as saying that "it seemed to be impossible for him to have any close relations with people in Washington without finding that the acquaintance thus formed generally ended with an application for office."

Washington, D. C., November 2, 1863

My Dear Sir: Yours of October 22 is received, as also was in due course that of October 3. I look forward with pleasure to the fulfilment of the promise made in the former.

Give yourself no uneasiness on the subject mentioned in that of the 22d.

My note to you I certainly did not expect to see in print; yet I have not been much shocked by the newspaper comments upon it. Those comments constitute a fair specimen of what has occurred to me through life. I have endured a great deal of ridicule without much malice; and have received a great deal of kindness, not quite free from ridicule. I am used to it.

NOTE TO SECRETARY E. M. STANTON

Lincoln had known Dr. Jacob R. Freese in Illinois. He writes this colorful note about him to Stanton, peremptorily instructing his

Secretary of War to make Freese a colonel. Somehow Stanton must have wriggled out of the situation, because Freese, a year later, was editing a newspaper in New Jersey.

Executive Mansion, November 11, 1863

Dear Sir: I personally wish Jacob Freese, of New Jersey, to be appointed colonel for a colored regiment, and this regardless of whether he can tell the exact shade of Julius Cæsar's hair.

ADDRESS AT THE DEDICATION OF
THE GETTYSBURG NATIONAL CEMETERY

Lincoln went to Gettysburg on November 18, leaving behind him his son, Tad, sick in bed in Washington. The special Presidential train arrived in Gettysburg in the early evening, and Lincoln spent the night at the home of Judge David Wills. When serenaders called on him, he said to them: "In my position, it is sometimes important that I should not say foolish things. It very often happens that the only way to help it, is to say nothing at all. Believing that is my present condition this evening, I must beg of you to excuse me from addressing you further." At eleven o'clock the next morning, the President rode on horseback in a procession to the new battle cemetery just outside the town. Edward Everett, the chief orator of the day, was late in arriving; the ceremony was held up until he came. Everett spoke for two hours. The Baltimore Glee Club then sang a brief dirge. Ward Lamon introduced the President, who rose to deliver this speech, which of all his speeches, has become the most celebrated. It is interesting to compare the exact wording of this address as given here in the form in which Lincoln later revised it, with the text shown on page 158 of this volume in a version that reproduces Lincoln's words as they were probably spoken on the field at Gettysburg that day. Whole books have been written on the address and its background. It has been analyzed from every point of view, and its possible origins have been traced. One of the most important origins is Lincoln's own speech on the night of July 7, 1863, when he replied to a serenade in celebration of the victories at Gettysburg and Vicksburg. Another is a sermon by Theodore Parker, abolitionist minister, who spoke in Boston on July 4, 1858, and on that occasion, in a sermon entitled, "The Effect of Slavery on the American People," said: "Democracy is direct self-government, over all the people, for all the people, and by all the people." Parker corresponded regularly with Herndon, and there can be little doubt that Lincoln had seen this phrase of his. He may very well have forgotten it, but it was probably stored away somewhere in his subconscious mind to rise to the surface and be made use of here. The Gettysburg Address has often been compared to the "Funeral Oration" of Pericles, one of the masterpieces of oratory of the ancient world. Colonel Clark E. Carr has made the following interesting analysis of the structure of this well-organized speech in a passage reproduced in William E. Barton's The Life of Abraham Lincoln, Vol. II, p. 224: "It includes all the essential parts of a formal oration. There is an exordium of five short and clear sentences introducing the theme and defining clearly the approach to the discussion. There is an argument of four sentences, and the climax is reached in the last of these. Then there is the dignified peroration in one long sentence." Carr also points out that of the two hundred and sixty-seven words, only thirty-two are of Latin derivation (some are repeated); all the rest are of Anglo-Saxon origin. The first draft this speech, which was written on two sheets of paper, one and the other in pencil, and also the second draft which held in his hands while delivering it, are now in the Congress.

November 19, 1863

FOURSCORE and seven years ago our fathers brought forth on this continent a new nation, conceived in liberty, and dedicated to the proposition that all men are created equal.

Now we are engaged in a great civil war, testing whether that nation, or any nation so conceived and so dedicated, can long endure. We are met on a great battlefield of that war. We have come to dedicate a portion of that field as a final resting-place for those who here gave their lives that that nation might live. It is altogether fitting and proper that we should do this.

But, in a larger sense, we cannot dedicate—we cannot consecrate—we cannot hallow—this ground. The brave men, living and dead, who struggled here, have consecrated it far above our poor power to add or detract. The world will little note nor long remember what we say here, but it can never forget what they did here. It is for us, the living, rather, to be dedicated here to the unfinished work which they who fought here have thus far so nobly advanced. It is rather for us to be here dedicated to the great task remaining before us—that from these honored dead we take increased devotion to that cause for which they gave the last full measure of devotion; that we here highly resolve that these dead shall not have died in vain; that this nation, under God, shall have a new birth of freedom; and that government of the people, by the people, for the people, shall not perish from the earth.

LETTER TO EDWARD EVERETT

Everett h
"I should itten to Lincoln to say of his Gettysburg speech:
the central l if I could flatter myself that I came as near to
minutes." Ev the occasion in two hours as you did in two
                l sent a printed copy of his own speech to

Lincoln before the ceremony at the battlefield, so Lincoln had had an opportunity to become familiar with his text.

Executive Mansion, Washington, D. C.,
November 20, 1863

MY DEAR SIR: Your kind note of today is received. In our respective parts yesterday, you could not have been excused to make a short address, nor I a long one. I am pleased to know that, in your judgment, the little I did say was not entirely a failure.

Of course I knew Mr. Everett would not fail, and yet, while the whole discourse was eminently satisfactory, and will be of great value, there were passages in it which transcended my expectations. . . .

The point made against the theory of the General Government being only an agency whose principals are the States, was new to me, and, as I think, is one of the best arguments for the national supremacy. The tribute to our noble women for their angel ministering to the suffering soldiers surpasses in its way, as do the subjects of it, whatever has gone before.

Our sick boy, for whom you kindly inquire, we hope is past the worst.

PROCLAMATION OF AMNESTY AND RECONSTRUCTION

By the end of 1863, Lincoln felt certain that the ⌐ would would be eventually win the War and that the seceding way for this, brought back into the Union. In order to prepa⌐don to those he drew up this proclamation which provide⌐ United States. who would take a specified oath of allegian⌐ to by Lincoln in This oath of December 8 was often late⌐ the oath and be issuing instructions that certain pri⌐

discharged. *He also outlines here a plan for the reconstruction of the government of those states which had left the Union but which might be willing to come back to it. This plan, which required only one-tenth of the voters who had been registered in 1860 to act in setting up a new state government, met with the violent opposition of the Radical Republicans in Congress (see Proclamation Concerning Reconstruction, July 8, 1864).*

December 8, 1863

WHEREAS, in and by the Constitution of the United States, it is provided that the President "shall have power to grant reprieves and pardons for offenses against the United States, except in cases of impeachment"; and

Whereas a rebellion now exists whereby the loyal State governments of several States have for a long time been subverted, and many persons have committed, and are now guilty of, treason against the United States; and

Whereas, with reference to said rebellion and treason, laws have been enacted by Congress, declaring forfeitures and confiscation of property and liberation of slaves, all upon terms and conditions therein stated, and also declaring that the President was thereby authorized at any time thereafter, by proclamation, to extend to persons who may have participated in the existing rebellion, in any State or part thereof, pardon and amnesty, with such exceptions and at such times and on such conditions as he may deem expedient for the public welfare; and

Whereas the Congressional declaration for limited and conditional ... tion of thin accords with well-established judicial exposition of ...oning power; and

Whereas ... the United ... reference to said rebellion, the President of ... visions in reg...as issued several proclamations, with provisions in reg... e liberation of slaves; and

Whereas it is now desired by some persons heretofore engaged in said rebellion to resume their allegiance to the United States, and to reinaugurate loyal State governments within and for their respective States; therefore

I, Abraham Lincoln, President of the United States, do proclaim, declare, and make known to all persons who have, directly or by implication, participated in the existing rebellion, except as hereinafter excepted, that a full pardon is hereby granted to them and each of them, with restoration of all rights of property, except as to slaves, and in property cases where rights of third parties shall have intervened, and upon the condition that every such person shall take and subscribe an oath, and thenceforward keep and maintain said oath inviolate; and which oath shall be registered for permanent preservation, and shall be of the tenor and effect following, to-wit:

I, —————, do solemnly swear, in presence of almighty God, that I will henceforth faithfully support, protect, and defend the Constitution of the United States, and the union of the States thereunder; and that I will, in like manner, abide by and faithfully support all acts of Congress passed during the existing rebellion with reference to slaves, so long and so far as not repealed, modified, or held void by Congress, or by decision of the Supreme Court; and that I will, in like manner, abide by and faithfully support all proclamations of the President made during the existing rebellion having reference to slaves, so long and so far as not modified or declared void by decision of the Supreme Court. So help me God.

The persons exempted from the benefits of the foregoing provisions are all who are, or shall have been, civil or diplomatic officers or agents of the so-called Confederate Government; all who have left judicial stations under the United States to aid the rebellion; all who are or shall have been military or naval officers of said so-called Confederate Government above the rank of colonel in the army or of lieutenant in the navy; all who left seats in the United States Congress to aid the rebellion; all who resigned commissions in the Army or Navy of the United States and afterward aided the rebellion; and all who have engaged in any way in treating colored persons, or white persons in charge of such, otherwise than lawfully as prisoners of war, and which persons may have been found in the United States service as soldiers, seamen, or in any other capacity.

And I do further proclaim, declare, and make known that whenever, in any of the States of Arkansas, Texas, Louisiana, Mississippi, Tennessee, Alabama, Georgia, Florida, South Carolina, and North Carolina, a number of persons, not less than one-tenth in number of the votes cast in such State at the presidential election of the year of our Lord one thousand eight hundred and sixty, each having taken the oath aforesaid and not having since violated it, and being a qualified voter by the election law of the State existing immediately before the so-called act of secession, and excluding all others, shall reestablish a State government which shall be republican, and in no wise contravening said oath, such shall be recognized as the true government of the State, and the State shall receive thereunder the benefits of the constitutional provision which declares that "the United States shall guarantee to every State in this Union a republican form of government, and shall protect each of them against invasion; and, on application of the legislature, or the executive (when the legislature cannot be convened), against domestic violence."

And I do further proclaim, declare, and make known, that any provision which may be adopted by such State government in relation to the freed people of such State, which shall recognize and declare their permanent freedom, provide for their education, and which may yet be consistent as a temporary arrangement with their present condition as a laboring, landless, and homeless class, will not be objected to by the national executive.

And it is suggested as not improper that, in constructing a

loyal State government in any State, the name of the State, the boundary, the subdivisions, the constitution, and the general code of laws, as before the rebellion, be maintained, subject only to the modifications made necessary by the conditions hereinbefore stated, and such others, if any, not contravening said conditions, and which may be deemed expedient by those framing the new State government.

To avoid misunderstanding, it may be proper to say that this proclamation, so far as it relates to State governments, has no reference to States wherein loyal State governments have all the while been maintained.

And, for the same reason, it may be proper to further say, that whether members sent to Congress from any State shall be admitted to seats, constitutionally rests exclusively with the respective houses, and not to any extent with the executive. And still further, that this proclamation is intended to present the people of the States wherein the national authority has been suspended, and loyal State governments have been subverted, a mode in and by which the national authority and loyal State governments may be re-established within said States, or in any of them; and while the mode presented is the best the executive can suggest, with his present impressions, it must not be understood that no other possible mode would be acceptable.

FROM THE ANNUAL MESSAGE TO CONGRESS

As is customary, the President of the United States here reviews the events of the year for the benefit of Congress. A prominent part of this message was the presentation to Congress of the Proclamation of Amnesty and Reconstruction.

December 8, 1863

FELLOW-CITIZENS OF THE SENATE AND HOUSE OF REPRESENTA-TIVES: Another year of health, and of sufficiently abundant harvests, has passed. For these, and especially for the improved condition of our national affairs, our renewed and profoundest gratitude to God is due.

We remain in peace and friendship with foreign powers.

The efforts of disloyal citizens of the United States to involve us in foreign wars, to aid an inexcusable insurrection, have been unavailing. Her Britannic Majesty's government, as was justly expected, have exercised their authority to prevent the departure of new hostile expeditions from British ports. The Emperor of France has, by a like proceeding, promptly vindicated the neutrality which he proclaimed at the beginning of the contest. Questions of great intricacy and importance have arisen out of the blockade, and other belligerent operations, between the government and several of the maritime powers, but they have been discussed, and, as far as was possible, accommodated, in a spirit of frankness, justice, and mutual good-will. It is especially gratifying that our prize courts, by the impartiality of their adjudications, have commanded the respect and confidence of maritime powers.

The supplemental treaty between the United States and Great Britain for the suppression of the African slave trade, made on the 17th day of February last, has been duly ratified and carried into execution. It is believed that, so far as American ports and American citizens are concerned, that inhuman and odious traffic has been brought to an end.

*   *   *

When Congress assembled a year ago the war had already lasted nearly twenty months, and there had been many conflicts on both land and sea with varying results. The rebellion had been pressed back into reduced limits; yet the tone of public feeling and opinion, at home and abroad, was not satisfactory. With other signs, the popular elections, then just past, indicated uneasiness among ourselves while, amid much that was cold and menacing, the kindest words coming from

Europe were uttered in accents of pity that we were too blind
to surrender a hopeless cause. Our commerce was suffering
greatly by a few armed vessels built upon, and furnished from,
foreign shores, and we were threatened with such additions
from the same quarter as would sweep our trade from the sea
and raise our blockade. We had failed to elicit from European
governments anything hopeful upon this subject. The preliminary emancipation proclamation, issued in September, was
running its assigned period to the beginning of the new year.
A month later the final proclamation came, including the announcement that colored men of suitable condition would be
received into the war service. The policy of emancipation, and
of employing black soldiers, gave to the future a new aspect,
about which hope, and fear, and doubt contended in uncertain
conflict. According to our political system, as a matter of civil
administration, the General Government had no lawful power
to effect emancipation in any State, and for a long time it had
been hoped that the rebellion could be suppressed without
resorting to it as a military measure. It was all the while
deemed possible that the necessity for it might come, and that
if it should, the crisis of the contest would then be presented.
It came, and, as was anticipated, it was followed by dark and
doubtful ways. Eleven months having now passed, we are permitted to take another review. The rebel borders are pressed
still further back, and, by the complete opening of the Mississippi, the country dominated by the rebellion is divided into
distinct parts, with no practical communication between them.
Tennessee and Arkansas have been substantially cleared of
insurgent control, and influential citizens in each, owners of
slaves and advocates of slavery at the beginning of the rebellion, now declare openly for emancipation in their respective
States. Of those States not included in the Emancipation
Proclamation, Maryland and Missouri, neither of which three
years ago would tolerate any restraint upon the extension of

slavery into new Territories, only dispute now as to the best mode of removing it within their own limits.

Of those who were slaves at the beginning of the rebellion, full one hundred thousand are now in the United States military service, about one half of which number actually bear arms in the ranks; thus giving the double advantage of taking so much labor from the insurgent cause, and supplying the places which otherwise must be filled with so many white men. So far as tested, it is difficult to say they are not as good soldiers as any. No servile insurrection, or tendency to violence or cruelty, has marked the measures of emancipation and arming the blacks. These measures have been much discussed in foreign countries, and contemporary with such discussion the tone of public sentiment there is much improved. At home the same measures have been fully discussed, supported, criticized, and denounced and the annual elections following are highly encouraging to those whose official duty it is to bear the country through this great trial. Thus we have the new reckoning. The crisis which threatened to divide the friends of the Union is past.

Looking now to the present and future, and with reference to a resumption of the national authority within the States wherein that authority has been suspended, I have thought fit to issue a proclamation, a copy of which is herewith transmitted. On examination of this proclamation it will appear, as is believed, that nothing is attempted beyond what is amply justified by the Constitution. True, the form of an oath is given, but no man is coerced to take it. The man is only promised a pardon in case he voluntarily takes the oath. The Constitution authorizes the executive to grant or withhold the pardon at his own absolute discretion; and this includes the power to grant on terms, as is fully established by judicial and other authorities.

It is also proffered that if, in any of the States named, a State government shall be, in the mode prescribed, set up, such government shall be recognized and guaranteed by the United States, and that under it the State shall, on the Constitutional conditions, be protected against invasion and domestic violence. The constitutional obligation of the United States to guarantee to every State in the Union a republican form of government, and to protect the State in the cases stated, is explicit and full. But why tender the benefits of this provision only to a State government set up in this particular way? This section of the Constitution contemplates a case wherein the element within a State favorable to republican government in the Union may be too feeble for an opposite and hostile element external to, or even within, the State; and such are precisely the cases with which we are now dealing.

An attempt to guarantee and protect a revived State government, constructed in whole, or in preponderating part, from the very element against whose hostility and violence it is to be protected, is simply absurd. There must be a test by which to separate the opposing elements, so as to build only from the sound; and that test is a sufficiently liberal one which accepts as sound whoever will make a sworn recantation of his former unsoundness.

But if it be proper to require, as a test of admission to the political body, an oath of allegiance to the Constitution of the United States, and to the Union under it, why also to the laws and proclamations in regard to slavery? Those laws and proclamations were enacted and put forth for the purpose of aiding in the suppression of the rebellion. To give them their fullest effect, there had to be a pledge for their maintenance. In my judgment they have aided, and will further aid, the cause for which they were intended. To now abandon them would be not only to relinquish a lever of power, but would also be a cruel and an astounding breach of faith. I may add, at this point, that while I remain in my present position I shall not attempt to retract or modify the Emancipation Proclamation; nor shall I return to slavery any person who is free by the terms of that proclamation, or by any of the acts of Congress. For these and other reasons it is thought best that support of these measures shall be included in the oath; and it is believed the executive may lawfully claim it in return for pardon and restoration of forfeited rights, which he has clear Constitutional power to withhold altogether, or grant upon the terms which he shall deem wisest for the public interest. It should be observed, also, that this part of the oath is subject to the modifying and abrogating power of legislation and supreme judicial decision.

The proposed acquiescence of the national executive in any reasonable temporary State arrangement for the freed people is made with the view of possibly modifying the confusion and destitution which must at best attend all classes by a total revolution of labor throughout whole States. It is hoped that the already deeply afflicted people in those States may be somewhat more ready to give up the cause of their affliction, if, to this extent, this vital matter be left to themselves; while no power of the national executive to prevent an abuse is abridged by the proposition.

The suggestion in the proclamation as to maintaining the political framework of the States on what is called reconstruction is made in the hope that it may do good without danger of harm. It will save labor, and avoid great confusion.

But why any proclamation now upon this subject? This question is beset with the conflicting views that the step might be delayed too long or be taken too soon. In some States the elements for resumption seem ready for action, but remain inactive apparently for want of a rallying-point—a plan of action. Why shall A adopt the plan of B, rather than B that of A? And if A and B should agree, how can they know but that the General Government here will reject their plan? By the proclamation a plan is presented which may be accepted by them as a rallying-point, and which they are assured in advance will not be rejected here. This may bring them to act sooner than they otherwise would.

The objection to a premature presentation of a plan by the national Executive consists in the danger of committals on points which could be more safely left to further developments. Care has been taken to so shape the document as to avoid embarrassments from this source. Saying that, on certain terms, certain classes will be pardoned, with rights restored, it is not said that other classes, or other terms will never be included. Saying that reconstruction will be accepted if presented in a specified way, it is not said it will never be accepted in any other way.

The movements, by State action, for emancipation in several of the States not included in the Emancipation Proclamation, are matters of profound gratulation. And while I do not repeat in detail what I have heretofore so earnestly urged upon this subject, my general views and feelings remain unchanged; and I trust that Congress will omit no fair opportunity of aiding these important steps to a great consummation.

In the midst of other cares, however important, we must not lose sight of the fact that the war power is still our main reliance. To that power alone can we look, yet for a time, to give confidence to the people in the contested regions that the insurgent power will not again overrun them. Until that confidence shall be established, little can be done anywhere for what is called reconstruction. Hence our chiefest care must still be directed to the army and navy, who have thus far borne their harder part so nobly and well. And it may be esteemed fortunate that in giving the greatest efficiency to these indispensable arms, we do also honorably recognize the gallant men, from commander to sentinel, who compose them, and to whom, more than to others, the world must stand indebted for the home of freedom disenthralled, regenerated, enlarged, and perpetuated.

LETTER TO GENERAL DANIEL E. SICKLES

Sickles was one of the more picturesque generals of the Civil War, a man who had gained a certain notoriety for himself in 1859 when he had killed Philip Barton Key for misconduct with his wife. Sickles had lost a leg at Gettysburg and at this time had just recovered from the wound. Lincoln sent him on the confidential mission described in this letter.

Executive Mansion, February 15, 1864

MAJOR-GENERAL SICKLES: I wish you to make a tour for me (principally for observation and information) by way of Cairo and New Orleans, and returning by the gulf and ocean.

All military and naval officers are to facilitate you with suitable transportation, and by conferring with you, and imparting, so far as they can, the information herein indicated; but you are not to command any of them. You will call at Memphis, Helena, Vicksburg, New Orleans, Pensacola, Key West, Charleston Harbor, and such intermediate points as you may think important.

Please ascertain at each place what is being done, if any thing, for reconstruction; how the amnesty proclamation works—if at all; what practical hitches, if any, there are about it; whether deserters come in from the enemy, what number has come in at each point since the amnesty, and whether the ratio of their arrival is any greater since than before the amnesty; what deserters report generally, and particularly whether, and to what extent, the amnesty is known within the rebel lines. Also learn what you can as to the colored people; how they get along as soldiers, as laborers in our service, on leased plantations, and as hired laborers with their old masters, if there be such cases. Also learn what you can as to the colored people within the rebel lines. Also get any other information you may consider interesting, and from time to time, send me what you may deem important to be known here at once, and be ready to make a general report on your return.

LETTER TO SECRETARY STANTON

Private Isaac P. Baird had been sentenced to the guardhouse for some minor offence. Lincoln writes here to Stanton, instructing him to permit the boy to enlist for a new term so he might receive his pay.

Executive Mansion, March 1, 1864

MY DEAR SIR: A poor widow, by the name of Baird, has a son in the army, that for some offense has been sentenced to serve a long time without pay, or at most with very little pay. I do not like this punishment of withholding pay—it falls so very hard upon poor families. After he had been serving in this way for several months, at the tearful appeal of the poor mother, I made a direction that he be allowed to enlist for a new term, on the same conditions as others. She now comes, and says she cannot get it acted upon. Please do it.

LETTER TO GOVERNOR MICHAEL HAHN

After Farragut had captured New Orleans in 1862, Michael Hahn, Louisiana politician, had taken an oath of allegiance to the United States Government and had gone to Congress the following year. He was inaugurated Governor of Louisiana early in March, 1864. Lincoln writes to him to give him advice about maintaining the new state government then being set up in Louisiana. Lincoln's suggestions about Negro voters, first expressed here, were again brought out in the last public speech he ever made—that of April 11, 1865.

(Private)

Executive Mansion, March 13, 1864

My Dear Sir: I congratulate you on having fixed your name in history as the first free-State governor of Louisiana. Now you are about to have a convention, which, among other things, will probably define the elective franchise. I barely suggest for your private consideration, whether some of the colored people may not be let in—as, for instance, the very intelligent, and especially those who have fought gallantly in our ranks. They would probably help, in some trying time to come, to keep the jewel of liberty within the family of freedom. But this is only a suggestion, not to the public, but to you alone.

DRAFT OF LETTER TO SECRETARY STANTON

Civil war, even more than a war between nations, causes untold misery to those who are caught in its meshes. Lincoln pleads with the martinet who was his Secretary of War, for a more merciful treatment of the victims.

Executive Mansion, March 18, 1864

My Dear Sir: I am so pressed in regard to prisoners of war in our custody, whose homes are within our lines, and who wish to not be exchanged, but to take the oath and be discharged, that I hope you will pardon me for again calling up the subject. My impression is that we will not ever force the exchange of any of this class; that, taking the oath and being discharged, none of them will again go to the rebellion; but the rebellion again coming to them, a considerable percentage of them, probably not a majority, would rejoin it; that, by a cautious discrimination, the number so discharged would not be large enough to do any considerable mischief in any event, will relieve distress in at least some meritorious cases, and would give me some relief from an intolerable pressure. I shall be glad, therefore, to have your cheerful assent to the discharge of those whose names I may send, which I will only do with circumspection.

In using the strong hand, as now compelled to do, the government has a difficult duty to perform. At the very best it will by turns do both too little and too much. It can properly have no motive of revenge, no purpose to punish merely for punishment's sake. While we must by all available means prevent the overthrow of the government, we should avoid planting and cultivating too many thorns in the bosom of society. These general remarks apply to several classes of cases, on each of which I wish to say a word.

First. The dismissal of officers when neither incompetency, nor intentional wrong, nor real injury to the service, is imputed. In such cases it is both cruel and impolitic to crush the man and make him and his friends permanent enemies to the administration if not to the government itself. . . .

Another class consists of those who are known or strongly suspected to be in sympathy with the rebellion. An instance of this is the family of Southern, who killed a recruiting officer last autumn in Maryland. He fled, and his family are driven from their home without a shelter or crumb, except when got by burdening our friends more than our enemies. Southern had no justification to kill the officer, and yet he would not have been killed if he had proceeded in the temper and manner agreed upon by yourself and Governor Bradford; but this is past. What is to be done with the family? Why can they not occupy the old home and excite much less opposition to the government than the manifestation of their distress is now doing? If the house is really needed for the public service, or if it has been regularly confiscated and the title transferred, the case is different.

Again, the cases of persons, mostly women, wishing to pass our lines one way or the other. We have in some cases been apparently if not really, inconsistent upon this subject—that is, we have forced some to go who wished to stay, and forced others to stay who wished to go. Suppose we allow all females with ungrown children of either sex to go South, if they desire, upon absolute prohibition against returning during the war; and all to come North upon the same condition of not returning during the war, and the additional condition of taking the oath. . . .

REMARKS AT
A SANITARY FAIR IN WASHINGTON

At the very beginning of the War, at a meeting of women held in Cooper Union in New York City, a Women's Central Association of Relief had been organized and from this grew up the voluntary sanitary commissions which were the forerunners of our present Red Cross. By holding fairs in various cities, these commissions raised money for medical supplies, delicacies and other conveniences. At the fairs people who could not give cash donated merchandise which was sold for the benefit of the soldiers. Nearly five million dollars were raised in this way. The President himself addressed several of these Sanitary Fairs in order to help draw a crowd.

March 18, 1864

LADIES AND GENTLEMEN: I appear to say but a word. This extraordinary war in which we are engaged falls heavily upon all classes of people, but the most heavily upon the soldier. For it has been said, all that a man hath will he give for his life; and while all contribute of their substance, the soldier puts his life at stake, and often yields it up in his country's cause. The highest merit, then, is due to the soldier.

In this extraordinary war, extraordinary developments have manifested themselves, such as have not been seen in former wars; and amongst these manifestations nothing has been more remarkable than these fairs for the relief of suffering soldiers and their families. And the chief agents in these fairs are the women of America.

I am not accustomed to the use of language of eulogy; I have never studied the art of paying compliments to women; but I must say, that if all that has been said by orators and poets since the creation of the world in praise of women were applied to the women of America, it would not do them justice for their conduct during this war. I will close by saying, God bless the women of America.

FROM A REPLY TO A COMMITTEE FROM THE NEW YORK WORKINGMEN'S ASSOCIATION

Lincoln, who was himself descended from a family of working people, and who had worked at manual labor in his youth, was always sympathetic to the working class. He addresses here a New York workingmen's committee and takes the opportunity to impress its members with the importance of the War to the common people of the country.

March 21, 1864

GENTLEMEN OF THE COMMITTEE: The honorary membership in your association, as generously tendered, is gratefully accepted.

You comprehend, as your address shows, that the existing rebellion means more, and tends to more, than the perpetuation of African slavery—that it is, in fact, a war upon the rights of all working people. . . .

None are so deeply interested to resist the present rebellion as the working people. Let them beware of prejudices, working division and hostility among themselves. The most notable feature of a disturbance in your city last summer was the hanging of some working people by other working people.* It should never be so. The strongest bond of human sympathy, outside of the family relation, should be one uniting all working people, of all nations, and tongues, and kindreds. Nor should this lead to a war upon property, or the owners of property. Property is the fruit of labor; property is desirable; is a positive good in the world. That some should be rich shows that others may become rich, and hence is just encouragement to industry and enterprise. Let not him who is houseless pull down the house of another, but let him work diligently and build one for himself, thus by example assuring that his own shall be safe from violence when built.

LETTER TO A. G. HODGES

The elections of 1862 had gone against the administration; those of 1863 had favored it because of the Union victories during the summer of that year; in 1864 the Presidential election was to be held. Lincoln had appointed Grant to the command of all the Union armies early in March, and it was hoped that Grant would win victories during the summer of 1864. Election talk was in the air; but none of the national conventions had yet been held. The border state of Kentucky had stood by the Union throughout the War, although her people were largely in favor of slavery. When Congress ordered that slaves should be enrolled for army service, the news was received with great indignation in that state. Governor Thomas E. Bramlette, ex-Senator Archibald Dixon and Colonel A. G. Hodges went to Washington to protest against this enrollment. Lincoln writes here what is ostensibly a letter to Hodges, but what is actually a public document intended to

* During the draft riots in July, 1863.

interpret the President's attitude on a question that might be expected to cause further trouble in other border states. Although no indication of it appears in the letter itself, the letter was intended to have a definite political influence on the coming election. It is in this letter that Lincoln makes his famous statement: "I claim not to have controlled events, but confess plainly that events have controlled me."

Executive Mansion, April 4, 1864

MY DEAR SIR: You ask me to put in writing the substance of what I verbally said the other day in your presence, to Governor Bramlette and Senator Dixon. It was about as follows:

"I am naturally antislavery. If slavery is not wrong, nothing is wrong. I cannot remember when I did not so think and feel, and yet I have never understood that the Presidency conferred upon me an unrestricted right to act officially upon this judgment and feeling. It was in the oath I took that I would, to the best of my ability, preserve, protect, and defend the Constitution of the United States. I could not take the office without taking the oath. Nor was it my view that I might take an oath to get power, and break the oath in using that power. I understood, too, that in ordinary civil administration this oath even forbade me to practically indulge my primary abstract judgment on the moral question of slavery. I had publicly declared this many times, and in many ways. And I aver that, to this day, I have done no official act in mere deference to my abstract judgment and feeling on slavery. I did understand, however, that my oath to preserve the Constitution to the best of my ability imposed upon me the duty of preserving, by every indispensable means, that government—that nation, of which that Constitution was the organic law. Was it possible to lose the nation and yet preserve the Constitution? By general law, life and limb must be protected, yet often a limb must be amputated to save a life; but a life is never wisely given to save a limb. I felt that measures otherwise unconstitutional might become lawful by becoming indispensable to the preservation of the Constitution through the preservation of the nation. Right or wrong, I assume this ground, and now avow it. I could not feel that, to the best of my ability, I had even tried to preserve the Constitution, if, to save slavery or any minor matter, I should permit the wreck of government, country, and Constitution all together. When, early in the war, General Frémont attempted military emancipation, I forbade it, because I did not then think it an indispensable necessity. When, a little later, General Cameron, then Secretary of War, suggested the arming of the blacks, I objected because I did not yet think it an indispensable necessity. When, still later, General Hunter attempted military emancipation, I again forbade it, because I did not yet think the indispensable necessity had come. When in March and May and July, 1862, I made earnest and successive appeals to the border States to favor compensated emancipation, I believed the indispensable necessity for military emancipation and arming the blacks would come unless averted by that measure. They declined the proposition, and I was, in my best judgment, driven to the alternative of either surrendering the Union, and with it the Constitution, or of laying strong hand upon the colored element. I chose the latter. In choosing it, I hoped for greater gain than loss; but of this, I was not entirely confident. More than a year of trial now shows no loss by it in our foreign relations, none in our home popular sentiment, none in our white military force—no loss by it anyhow or anywhere. On the contrary it shows a gain of quite a hundred and thirty thousand soldiers, seamen, and laborers. These are palpable facts, about which, as facts, there can be no caviling. We have the men; and we could not have had them without the measure.

"And now let any Union man who complains of the measure test himself by writing down in one line that he is for subduing the rebellion by force of arms; and in the next, that he is for taking these hundred and thirty thousand men from the Union side, and placing them where they would be but for the measure he condemns. If he cannot face his case so stated, it is only because he cannot face the truth."

I add a word which was not in the verbal conversation. In telling this tale I attempt no compliment to my own sagacity. I claim not to have controlled events, but confess plainly that events have controlled me. Now, at the end of three years' struggle, the nation's condition is not what either party, or any man, devised or expected. God alone can claim it. Whither it is tending seems plain. If God now wills the removal of a great wrong, and wills also that we of the North, as well as you of the South, shall pay fairly for our complicity in that wrong, impartial history will find therein new cause to attest and revere the justice and goodness of God.

ADDRESS AT SANITARY FAIR IN BALTIMORE

Lincoln again addresses a Sanitary Fair—this time in Baltimore, the city through which he had had to pass secretly almost exactly three years before when he had gone to Washington as President-elect. The Fort Pillow massacre mentioned here was one of the most brutal incidents of the Civil War. The Confederate soldiers who captured the fort ran amok and butchered two hundred and sixty-two Negro soldiers.

April 18, 1864

LADIES AND GENTLEMEN: Calling to mind that we are in Baltimore, we cannot fail to note that the world moves. Looking upon these many people assembled here to serve, as they best may, the soldiers of the Union, it occurs at once that three years ago the same soldiers could not so much as pass through Baltimore. The change from then till now is both great and gratifying. Blessings on the brave men who have wrought the change, and the fair women who strive to reward them for it!

But Baltimore suggests more than could happen within Baltimore. The change within Baltimore is part only of a far wider change. When the war began, three years ago, neither party, nor any man, expected it would last till now. Each looked for the end, in some way, long ere today. Neither did any anticipate that domestic slavery would be much affected by the war. But here we are; the war has not ended, and slavery has been much affected—how much needs not now to be recounted. So true is it that man proposes and God disposes.

But we can see the past, though we may not claim to have directed it; and seeing it, in this case, we feel more hopeful and confident for the future.

The world has never had a good definition of the word liberty, and the American people, just now, are much in want of one. We all declare for liberty; but in using the same word we do not all mean the same thing. With some the word liberty may mean for each man to do as he pleases with himself, and the product of his labor; while with others the same word may mean for some men to do as they please with other men, and the product of other men's labor. Here are two, not only different, but incompatible things, called by the same name, liberty. And it follows that each of the things is, by the respective parties, called by two different and incompatible names—liberty and tyranny.

The shepherd drives the wolf from the sheep's throat, for which the sheep thanks the shepherd as his liberator, while the wolf denounces him for the same act, as the destroyer of liberty, especially as the sheep was a black one. Plainly, the sheep and the wolf are not agreed upon a definition of the word liberty; and precisely the same difference prevails today among us human creatures, even in the North, and all professing to love liberty. Hence we behold the process by which thousands are daily passing from under the yoke of bondage hailed by some as the advance of liberty, and bewailed by others as the destruction of all liberty. Recently, as it seems, the people of Maryland have been doing something to define liberty, and thanks to them that, in what they have done, the wolf's dictionary has been repudiated.

It is not very becoming for one in my position to make speeches at great length; but there is another subject upon which I feel that I ought to say a word.

A painful rumor—true, I fear—has reached us of the massacre by the rebel forces at Fort Pillow, in the west end of Tennessee, on the Mississippi River, of some three hundred colored soldiers and white officers, who had just been overpowered by their assailants. There seems to be some anxiety in the public mind whether the government is doing its duty to the colored soldier, and to the service, at this point. At the beginning of the war, and for some time, the use of colored troops was not contemplated; and how the change of purpose was wrought I will not now take time to explain. Upon a clear conviction of duty I resolved to turn that element of strength to account; and I am responsible for it to the American people, to the Christian world, to history, and in my final account to God. Having determined to use the Negro as a soldier, there is no way but to give him all the protection given to any other soldier. The difficulty is not in stating the principle, but in practically applying it. It is a mistake to suppose the government is indifferent to this matter, or is not doing the best it can in regard to it. . . .

TELEGRAM TO MRS. LINCOLN

The goats mentioned in Lincoln's letter to his wife under date of August 8, 1863 again become a matter for Presidential correspondence.

Executive Mansion, April 28, 1864

Mrs. A. Lincoln, New York: The draft will go to you. Tell Tad the goats and father are very well, especially the goats.

A. Lincoln

LETTER TO GENERAL U. S. GRANT

Lincoln writes to his new chief commander on the eve of his setting out against Richmond. On May 4, Grant crossed the Rapidan and was attacked the next day by Lee in the Battle of the Wilderness. The good wishes that Lincoln extends here were of no avail to Grant. Ahead of him during the next five weeks were the disastrous Battles of the Wilderness, Spotsylvania and Cold Harbor, battles in which he lost 55,000 men.

Executive Mansion, April 30, 1864

Lieutenant-General Grant: Not expecting to see you again before the spring campaign opens, I wish to express in this way my entire satisfaction with what you have done up to this time, so far as I understand it. The particulars of your plans I neither know nor seek to know. You are vigilant and self-reliant; and, pleased with this, I wish not to obtrude any constraints or restraints upon you. While I am very anxious that any great disaster or capture of our men in great numbers shall be avoided, I know these points are less likely to escape your attention than they would be mine. If there is anything wanting which is within my power to give, do not fail to let me know it. And now, with a brave army and a just cause, may God sustain you.

LETTER TO JOHN H. BRYANT

Owen Lovejoy, Illinois abolitionist and brother of Elijah E. Lovejoy, the abolitionist editor who had been killed defending his printing press at Alton, Illinois in 1837, had died on March 25. A monument was being erected to his memory.

Executive Mansion, May 30, 1864

My Dear Sir: Yours of the 14th instant inclosing a card of invitation to a preliminary meeting contemplating the erection of a monument to the memory of Hon. Owen Lovejoy was duly received. As you anticipate, it will be out of my power to attend. Many of you have known Mr. Lovejoy longer than I have, and are better able than I to do his memory complete justice. My personal acquaintance with him commenced only about ten years ago, since when it has been quite intimate, and every step in it has been one of increasing respect and esteem, ending, with his life, in no less than affection on my part. It can truly be said of him that while he was personally ambitious he bravely endured the obscurity which the unpopularity of his principles imposed, and never accepted official honors until those honors were ready to admit his principles with him. Throughout very heavy and perplexing responsibilities here to the day of his death, it would scarcely wrong any other to say he was my most generous friend.

Let him have the marble monument along with the well-assured and more enduring one in the hearts of those who love liberty unselfishly for all men.

REPLY TO THE COMMITTEE NOTIFYING PRESIDENT LINCOLN OF HIS RENOMINATION

Grant had been repulsed at Cold Harbor, and his terrific drive against Richmond had failed. The Republican party, which changed its name for this one occasion to the National Union party, had met in Baltimore, and on June 8, before the full significance of Grant's defeat had been realized by the country, had successfully nominated Abraham Lincoln for a second term as President of the United States. Despite all the opposition that had been shown in his own party, it was finally realized that no other person stood the same chance of election as the President himself. The nomination was made by unanimous vote. Andrew Johnson, War Governor of Tennessee, was nominated as Vice President. A committee called on Lincoln the next day to notify him of his nomination. This is his verbal reply to the committee.

June 9, 1864

MR. CHAIRMAN AND GENTLEMEN OF THE COMMITTEE: I will neither conceal my gratification nor restrain the expression of my gratitude that the Union people, through their convention, in their continued effort to save and advance the nation, have deemed me not unworthy to remain in my present position. I know no reason to doubt that I shall accept the nomination tendered; and yet perhaps I should not declare definitely before reading and considering what is called the platform. I will say now, however, I approve the declaration in favor of so amending the Constitution as to prohibit slavery throughout the nation. When the people in revolt, with a hundred days of explicit notice that they could within those days resume their allegiance without the overthrow of their institution, and that they could not so resume it afterward, elected to stand out, such amendment of the Constitution as now proposed became a fitting and necessary conclusion to the final success of the Union cause. Such alone can meet and cover all cavils. Now the unconditional Union men, North and South, perceive its importance and embrace it. In the joint names of Liberty and Union, let us labor to give it legal form and practical effect.

REPLY TO A DELEGATION FROM THE NATIONAL UNION LEAGUE

The Union League of America had been founded as a secret society during the early days of the War in order that "loyalty be organized, consolidated and be made effective." Its National Grand Council had met in Baltimore at the time of the National Union convention there, and the Union League stood for Lincoln's re-election. This is Lincoln's reply to a delegation from this meeting. In it he makes his often-quoted statement: "It is not best to swap horses while crossing the river."

June 9, 1864

GENTLEMEN: I can only say in response to the kind remarks of your chairman, as I suppose, that I am very grateful for the renewed confidence which has been accorded to me both by the convention and by the National League. I am not insensible at all to the personal compliment there is in this, and yet I do not allow myself to believe that any but a small portion of it is to be appropriated as a personal compliment. That really the convention and the Union League assembled with a higher view—that of taking care of the interests of the country for the present and the great future—and that the part I am entitled to appropriate as a compliment is only that part which I may lay hold of as being the opinion of

the convention and of the League, that I am not entirely unworthy to be intrusted with the place which I have occupied
for the last three years. But I do not allow myself to suppose
that either the convention or the League have concluded to
decide that I am either the greatest or best man in America,
but rather they have concluded that it is not best to swap
horses while crossing the river, and have further concluded
that I am not so poor a horse that they might not make a
botch of it in trying to swap.

FROM A SPEECH AT A SANITARY FAIR IN PHILADELPHIA

*While Grant was withdrawing his troops from their unsuccessful
attack at Cold Harbor to move them south to go into a long siege
at Petersburg, Lincoln speaks at a Sanitary Fair in Philadelphia
and does yeoman-like service for Grant's cause.*

June 16, 1864

WAR, at the best, is terrible, and this war of ours, in its magnitude and in its duration, is one of the most terrible. It has de-
ranged business, totally in many localities, and partially in all
localities. It has destroyed property and ruined homes; it has
produced a national debt and taxation unprecedented, at least
in this country; it has carried mourning to almost every home,
until it can almost be said that the "heavens are hung in
black."

Yet the war continues, and several relieving coincidents have
accompanied it from the very beginning which have not been
known, as I understand, or have any knowledge of, in any
former wars in the history of the world. The Sanitary Commission, with all its benevolent labors; the Christian Commission, with all its Christian and benevolent labors; and the
various places, arrangements, so to speak, and institutions,

have contributed to the comfort and relief of the soldiers. . . .
And lastly, these fairs, which, I believe, began only last August, if I mistake not, in Chicago, then at Boston, at Cincinnati, Brooklyn, New York, and Baltimore, and those at
present held at St. Louis, Pittsburgh, and Philadelphia. The
motive and object that lie at the bottom of all these are most
worthy; for, say what you will, after all, the most is due to the
soldier who takes his life in his hands and goes to fight the
battles of his country. In what is contributed to his comfort
when he passes to and fro, and in what is contributed to him
when he is sick and wounded, in whatever shape it comes,
whether from the fair and tender hand of woman, or from
any other source, it is much, very much. But I think that there
is still that which is of as much value to him in the continual
reminders he sees in the newspapers that while he is absent he
is yet remembered by the loved ones at home. Another view of
these various institutions, if I may so call them, is worthy of
consideration, I think. They are voluntary contributions, given
zealously and earnestly, on top of all the disturbances of business, of all the disorders, of all the taxation, and of all the
burdens that the war has imposed upon us, giving proof that
the national resources are not at all exhausted, and that the
national spirit of patriotism is even firmer and stronger than
at the commencement of the war.

It is a pertinent question, often asked in the mind privately,
and from one to the other, when is the war to end? Surely I
feel as deep an interest in this question as any other can; but I
do not wish to name a day, a month, or year, when it is to end.
I do not wish to run any risk of seeing the time come without
our being ready for the end, for fear of disappointment because the time had come and not the end. We accepted this
war for an object, a worthy object, and the war will end when
that object is attained. Under God, I hope it never will end
until that time. Speaking of the present campaign, General
Grant is reported to have said, "I am going through on this line

if it takes all summer." This war has taken three years; it was begun or accepted upon the line of restoring the national authority over the whole national domain, and for the American people, as far as my knowledge enables me to speak, I say we are going through on this line if it takes three years more.

My friends, I did not know but that I might be called upon to say a few words before I got away from here, but I did not know it was coming just here. I have never been in the habit of making predictions in regard to the war, but I am almost tempted to make one. If I were to hazard it, it is this: That Grant is this evening, with General Meade and General Hancock, and the brave officers and soldiers with him, in a position from whence he will never be dislodged until Richmond is taken. . . .

LETTER TO SECRETARY CHASE

Salmon P. Chase was an ambitious man, so ambitious that he had left nothing undone to push himself forward for the Presidential nomination of 1864. He had favored the Radicals in Congress, and they had supported his candidacy; but, to his great disappointment, Chase had not received the nomination. He had already threatened to resign from the Cabinet three times; this time, over a minor issue as to who was to be appointed Assistant Treasurer at New York, Chase and Lincoln finally disagreed with each other. Chase offered his resignation, and much to his surprise, the President promptly accepted it. Lincoln still felt that Chase was a capable administrator and a good lawyer. After the death of Roger B. Taney, in October, 1864, Lincoln appointed Chase to the position of Chief Justice of the Supreme Court of the United States.

Executive Mansion, June 30, 1864

My Dear Sir: Your resignation of the office of Secretary of the Treasury sent me yesterday is accepted. Of all I have said in commendation of your ability and fidelity I have nothing to unsay; and yet you and I have reached a point of mutual embarrassment in our official relations which it seems cannot be overcome or longer sustained consistently with the public service.

PROCLAMATION
CONCERNING RECONSTRUCTION

When the President had issued his Proclamation of Amnesty and Reconstruction on December 8, 1863, it had been received with great acclaim even by the Radical wing of his own party. As time passed, the Radicals, however, became more and more dissatisfied with the bill, feeling that the terms it offered to the seceded states were much too easy. One after another, and for varying reasons, they parted company with the President. They drafted a bill of their own which passed the House and the Senate under the sponsorship of Henry Winter Davis in the House and Benjamin F. Wade in the Senate. This bill was laid before the President on July 4 for his signature only a few moments before Congress was due to adjourn. Lincoln pocketed the bill, refusing either to sign or to veto it. Four days later, he issued this proclamation in which he shattered all precedent by eliminating those parts of the Wade-Davis Bill to which he could not agree, and by accepting those that were satisfactory to him. He did not want to be committed to any one plan of reconstruction at this time. He was still feeling his way and he was willing to let the people in the Southern states decide for themselves which plan they wished to adopt. Wade and Davis, bitterly disappointed, issued a public denunciation of the President on August 5 in the New York Tribune. This denunciation, which became known as the Wade-Davis Manifesto, was an attack based on the ground that the President had encroached on the authority of Congress.

July 8, 1864

WHEREAS, at the late session, Congress passed a bill to "guarantee to certain States, whose governments have been usurped or overthrown, a republican form of government," a copy of which is hereunto annexed;

And whereas the said bill was presented to the President of the United States for his approval less than one hour before the sine die adjournment of said session, and was not signed by him;

And whereas the said bill contains, among other things, a plan for restoring the States in rebellion to their proper practical relation in the Union, which plan expresses the sense of Congress upon that subject, and which plan it is now thought fit to lay before the people for their consideration.

Now, therefore, I, Abraham Lincoln, President of the United States, do proclaim, declare, and make known, that, while I am (as I was in December last, when by proclamation I propounded a plan for restoration) unprepared, by a formal approval of this bill, to be inflexibly committed to any single plan of restoration; and, while I am also unprepared to declare that the free-State constitutions and governments already adopted and installed in Arkansas and Louisiana shall be set aside and held for nought, thereby repelling and discouraging the loyal citizens who have set up the same as to further effort, or to declare a constitutional competency in Congress to abolish slavery in States, but am at the same time sincerely hoping and expecting that a constitutional amendment abolishing slavery throughout the nation may be adopted, nevertheless I am fully satisfied with the system for restoration contained in the bill as one very proper plan for the loyal people of any State choosing to adopt it, and that I am, and at all times shall be, prepared to give the executive aid and assistance to any such people, so soon as the military resistance to the United States shall have been suppressed in any such State, and the people thereof shall have sufficiently returned to their obedience to the Constitution and the laws of the United States, in which cases military governors will be appointed, with directions to proceed according to the bill.

LETTER TO HORACE GREELEY

Word had come to Horace Greeley, editor of the New York Tribune, that two Confederate commissioners were in Canada, authorized to negotiate for a peaceful settlement of the War. They were willing to meet at Niagara Falls any person in authority sent to them for an interview. Greeley wrote to Lincoln, begging him not to ignore the opportunity. This letter is Lincoln's reply to him. Lincoln later authorized Greeley to go to Niagara Falls to confer with the commissioners, which he unwillingly did. When Greeley arrived at Niagara Falls, he found that the commissioners had no credentials; furthermore, although Lincoln had told him that he would consider such negotiations only on the basis of restoring the Union and abandoning slavery, Greeley ignored the President's conditions and telegraphed to Washington, saying that the commissioners wished to come there to deal with him in person. Lincoln, fearing that such a move might be interpreted as his suing for peace with the South, immediately sent John Hay to Niagara Falls with a note stating his terms in writing. The negotiations promptly collapsed.

Washington, D. C., July 9, 1864

Dear Sir: Your letter of the 7th, with inclosures, received. If you can find any person, anywhere, professing to have any proposition of Jefferson Davis in writing, for peace, embracing the restoration of the Union and abandonment of slavery, whatever else it embraces, say to him he may come to me with you; and that if he really brings such proposition, he shall at the least have safe conduct with the paper (and without publicity, if he chooses) to the point where you shall have met him. The same if there be two or more persons.

TELEGRAM TO GENERAL U. S. GRANT

Grant was settling down for his long siege of Petersburg. Lincoln sends him a characteristic telegram.

Executive Mansion, Washington, August 17, 1864

LIEUTENANT-GENERAL GRANT, CITY POINT, VA.: I have seen your dispatch expressing your unwillingness to break your hold where you are. Neither am I willing. Hold on with a bull-dog grip, and chew and choke as much as possible.

ADDRESS TO THE 164TH OHIO REGIMENT

Lincoln speaks to his soldiers in the midst of the darkest period of the War.

August 18, 1864

SOLDIERS: I am greatly obliged to you, and to all who have come forward at the call of their country. I wish it might be more generally and universally understood what the country is now engaged in. We have, as all will agree, a free government, where every man has a right to be equal with every other man. In this great struggle, this form of government and every form of human right is endangered if our enemies succeed. There is more involved in this contest than is realized by every one. There is involved in this struggle the question whether your children and my children shall enjoy the privileges we have enjoyed. I say this in order to impress upon you, if you are not already so impressed, that no small matter should divert us from our great purpose.

There may be some inequalities in the practical application of our system. It is fair that each man shall pay taxes in exact proportion to the value of his property; but if we should wait before collecting a tax, to adjust the taxes upon each man in exact proportion with every other man, we should never collect any tax at all. There may be mistakes made sometimes; things may be done wrong; while the officers of the government do all they can to prevent mistakes. But I beg of you, as citizens of this great republic, not to let your minds be carried off from the great work we have before us. This struggle is too large for you to be diverted from it by any small matter. When you return to your homes, rise up to the height of a generation of men worthy of a free government, and we will carry out the great work we have commenced.

MEMORANDUM TO HIS CABINET

On August 29, the Democratic National Convention was to be held at Chicago, at which it was almost certain that General McClellan would be nominated to run against Lincoln. During the terrible summer of 1864, everything had gone against the administration, and Lincoln had been told even by his closest advisers that he could not hope for re-election. He presented this memorandum, folded so that it could not be read, to the members of his Cabinet, asking them to sign it. He did not read its contents to them until November 11, after he had been re-elected.

Executive Mansion, August 23, 1864

This morning, as for some days past, it seems exceedingly probable that this administration will not be re-elected. Then it will be my duty to so coöperate with the President-elect as to save the Union between the election and the inauguration; as he will have secured his election on such ground that he cannot possibly save it afterward.

STATEMENT WRITTEN OUT
FOR WARD HILL LAMON

Ever since October, 1862, when Lincoln had gone to visit McClellan at his headquarters at Antietam, the story of his visit there had been used against him in one of the dirtiest whispering campaigns in American politics. The New York World, in particular, had been guilty of printing distorted versions of what had happened during his visit. On September 9, 1864, this piece appeared in the World: "While the President was driving over the field in an ambulance, accompanied by Marshal Lamon, General McClellan, and another officer, heavy details of men were engaged in the task of burying the dead. The ambulance had just reached the neighborhood of the old stone bridge, where the dead were piled highest, when Mr. Lincoln, suddenly slapping Marshal Lamon on the knee, exclaimed: 'Come, Lamon, give us the song about Picayune Butler. McClellan has never heard it.' 'Not now, if you please,' said General McClellan, with a shudder; 'I would prefer to hear it some other place and time!' " The World also published this bit of doggerel:

> *"Abe may crack his jolly jokes*
> *O'er bloody fields of stricken battle,*
> *While yet the ebbing life-tide smokes*
> *From men that die like butchered cattle. . . ."*

Lamon wanted to answer this attack; Lincoln was afraid that his belligerent friend would cause more trouble than good, so he wrote out this account himself. After having written it, however, Lincoln decided against using it.

September [12?], 1864

THE President has known me intimately for nearly twenty years, and has often heard me sing little ditties. The battle of

Antietam was fought on the 17th day of September 1862. On the first day of October, just two weeks after the battle, the President, with some others including myself started from Washington to visit the Army, reaching Harpers' Ferry at noon of that day. In a short while Gen. McClellan came from his Headquarters near the battle-ground, joined the President, and with him, reviewed, the troops at Bolivar Heights that afternoon; and, at night, returned to his Headquarters, leaving the President at Harpers' Ferry. On the morning of the second the President, with Gen. Sumner, reviewed the troops respectively at Loudon Heights and Maryland Heights, and at about noon, started to Gen. McClellan's Headquarters, reaching there only in time to see very little before night. On the morning of the third all started on a review of the three corps, and the Cavalry, in the vicinity of the Antietam battle-ground. After getting through with Gen. Burnsides' Corps, at the suggestion of Gen. McClellan he and the President left their horses to be led, and went into an ambulance or ambulances to go to Gen. Fitz John Porter's Corps, which was two or three miles distant. I am not sure whether the President and Gen. Mc. were in the same ambulance, or in different ones; but myself and some others were in the same with the President. On the way, and on no part of the battle-ground, and on what suggestion I do not remember, the President asked me to sing the little sad song that follows, which he had often heard me sing, and had always seemed to like very much. I sang them. After it was over, some one of the party (I do not think it was the President), asked me to sing something else; and I sang two or three little comic things of which Picayune Butler was one. Porter's Corps was reached and reviewed; then the battle-ground was passed over, and the most noted parts examined; then, in succession the Cavalry, and Franklin's Corps were reviewed, and the President and party returned to Gen. McClellan's Headquarters at the end of a very hard, hot, and dusty day's work. Next day, the 4th, President and Gen. Mc.

visited such of the wounded as still remained in the vicinity, including the now lamented Gen. Richardson; then proceeded to and examined the South-Mountain battle-ground, at which point they parted, Gen. McClellan returning to his Camp, and the President returning to Washington, seeing, on the way, Gen. Hartsoff, who lay wounded at Fredericktown. This is the whole story of the singing and its surroundings. Neither Gen. McClellan or any one else made any objection to the singing; the place was not on the battlefield, the time was sixteen days after the battle, no dead body was seen during the whole time the President was absent from Washington, nor even a grave that had not been rained on since it was made.

PARDON FOR ROSWELL McINTYRE

On the battlefield at Five Forks, Virginia, on April 1, 1865, less than ten days before the end of the War, this note in the handwriting of Abraham Lincoln was found on the body of a soldier.

Executive Mansion, Washington, Oct. 4, 1864

UPON condition that Roswell McIntyre of Co. E. 6th Regt. of New York Cavalry returns to his regiment and faithfully serves out his term, making up for lost time, or until otherwise lawfully discharged, he is fully pardoned for any supposed desertion heretofore committed; and this paper is his pass to go to his regiment.

RESPONSES TO SERENADES
ON THE OCCASION OF HIS RE-ELECTION

On November 8, the people of the Northern states voted for President. Despite the political gloom that had prevailed during the summer of 1864, Lincoln was re-elected with a comfortable margin over his Democratic opponent, George Brinton McClellan. On the two nights following the election, the people of Washington came to the White House to serenade the President.

November 9, 1864

I EARNESTLY believe that the consequences of this day's work, if it be as you assume, and as now seems probable, will be to the lasting advantage, if not to the very salvation, of the country. I cannot at this hour say what has been the result of the election. But, whatever it may be, I have no desire to modify this opinion: that all who have labored today in behalf of the Union have wrought for the best interests of the country and the world; not only for the present, but for all future ages.

I am thankful to God for this approval of the people; but, while deeply grateful for this mark of their confidence in me, if I know my heart, my gratitude is free from any taint of personal triumph. I do not impugn the motives of any one opposed to me. It is no pleasure to me to triumph over any one, but I give thanks to the Almighty for this evidence of the people's resolution to stand by free government and the rights of humanity.

November 10, 1864

IT HAS long been a grave question whether any government, not too strong for the liberties of its people, can be strong enough to maintain its existence in great emergencies. On this point the present rebellion brought our republic to a severe test, and a Presidential election occurring in regular course during the rebellion, added not a little to the strain.

If the loyal people united were put to the utmost of their strength by the rebellion, must they not fail when divided and partially paralyzed by a political war among themselves? But the election was a necessity. We cannot have free government without elections; and if the rebellion could force us to forego or postpone a national election, it might fairly claim to have already conquered and ruined us. The strife of the election is but human nature practically applied to the facts of the case. What has occurred in this case must ever recur in similar cases. Human nature will not change. In any future great national trial, compared with the men of this, we shall have as weak and as strong, as silly and as wise, as bad and as good. Let us, therefore, study the incidents of this as philosophy to learn wisdom from, and none of them as wrongs to be revenged. But the election, along with its incidental and undesirable strife, has done good too. It has demonstrated that a people's government can sustain a national election in the midst of a great civil war. Until now, it has not been known to the world that this was a possibility. It shows, also, how sound and how strong we still are. It shows that, even among candidates of the same party, he who is most devoted to the Union and most opposed to treason can receive most of the people's votes. It shows, also, to the extent yet known, that we have more men now than we had when the war began. Gold is good in its place, but living, brave, patriotic men are better than gold.

But the rebellion continues, and now that the election is over, may not all having a common interest reunite in a common effort to save our common country? For my own part, I have striven and shall strive to avoid placing any obstacle in the way. So long as I have been here I have not willingly planted a thorn in any man's bosom. While I am deeply sensible to the high compliment of a reëlection, and duly grateful, as I trust, to Almighty God for having directed my countrymen to a right conclusion, as I think, for their own good, it adds nothing to my satisfaction that any other man may be disappointed or pained by the result.

May I ask those who have not differed from me to join with me in this same spirit toward those who have? And now let me close by asking three hearty cheers for our brave soldiers and seamen and their gallant and skilful commanders.

LETTER TO MRS. BIXBY, OF BOSTON, MASS.

Just as Gettysburg is the most widely known of all Lincoln's speeches, so this letter to Mrs. Bixby is the most celebrated of all his letters. At the request of Governor Andrew of Massachusetts, Lincoln wrote to Mrs. Lydia Bixby, a Boston widow, to console her for the loss of five sons who were supposed to have died in service. The letter was immediately printed by many newspapers throughout the country. Afterward, it was shown that only two of the boys had actually died in action—one at Fredericksburg, and one at Petersburg. Another, reported to have been killed at Gettysburg, had been taken prisoner. Still another, who also was taken prisoner, enlisted in the Confederate ranks. The youngest son deserted and went to sea. Lincoln, of course, knew nothing of this when he wrote to Mrs. Bixby.

Executive Mansion, November 21, 1864

DEAR MADAM: I have been shown in the files of the War Department a statement of the Adjutant-General of Massachusetts that you are the mother of five sons who have died gloriously on the field of battle. I feel how weak and fruitless must be any words of mine which should attempt to beguile you from the grief of a loss so overwhelming. But I cannot refrain from tendering to you the consolation that may be found in the thanks of the Republic they died to save. I pray that our heavenly Father may assuage the anguish of your bereavement, and leave you only the cherished memory of the loved and lost, and the solemn pride that must be yours to have laid so costly a sacrifice upon the altar of freedom.

Yours very sincerely and respectfully,

ABRAHAM LINCOLN

FROM THE ANNUAL MESSAGE TO CONGRESS

Again the President makes his annual report to Congress. The most remarkable fact brought out in this message is that both population and wealth had increased in the North during the War. For all the blood and gold that had been poured out on the battlefield, the resources of the nation seemed inexhaustible.

December 6, 1864

THE war continues. Since the last annual messages, all the important lines and positions then occupied by our forces have been maintained, and our arms have steadily advanced, thus liberating the regions left in rear; so that Missouri, Kentucky, Tennessee, and parts of other States have again produced reasonably fair crops.

The most remarkable feature in the military operations of the year is General Sherman's attempted march of three hundred miles, directly through the insurgent region. It tends to show a great increase of our relative strength, that our general-in-chief should feel able to confront and hold in check every active force of the enemy, and yet to detach a well-appointed large army to move on such an expedition. The result not yet being known, conjecture in regard to it is not here indulged.

Important movements have also occurred during the year to the effect of molding society for durability in the Union. Although short of complete success, it is much in the right direction that 12,000 citizens in each of the States of Arkansas and Louisiana have organized loyal State governments, with free constitutions, and are earnestly struggling to maintain and administer them. The movements in the same direction, more extensive though less definite, in Missouri, Kentucky, and Tennessee, should not be overlooked. But Maryland presents the example of complete success. Maryland is secure to liberty and Union for all the future. The genius of rebellion will no more claim Maryland. Like another foul spirit, being driven out, it may seek to tear her, but it will woo her no more.

At the last session of Congress a proposed amendment of the Constitution, abolishing slavery throughout the United States, passed the Senate, but failed for lack of the requisite two-thirds vote in the House of Representatives. Although the present is the same Congress, and nearly the same members, and without questioning the wisdom or patriotism of those who stood in opposition, I venture to recommend the reconsideration and passage of the measure at the present session. Of course the abstract question is not changed, but an intervening election shows, almost certainly, that the next Congress will pass the measure if this does not. Hence there is only a question of time as to when the proposed amendment will go to the States for their action. And as it is to so go, at all events, may we not agree that the sooner the better? It is not claimed that the election has imposed a duty on members to change their views or their votes any further than as an additional element to be considered, their judgment may be affected by it. It is the voice of the people now for the first time heard upon the question. In a great national crisis like ours, unanimity of action among those seeking a common end is very desirable—almost indispensable. And yet no approach to such unanimity is attainable unless some deference shall be paid to the will of the majority, simply because it is the will of the majority. In this case the common end is the maintenance of the Union, and among the means to secure that end, such will, through the election, is most clearly declared in favor of such constitutional amendment.

The most reliable indication of public purpose in this country is derived through our popular elections. Judging by the recent canvass and its result, the purpose of the people within the loyal States to maintain the integrity of the Union, was never more firm nor more nearly unanimous than now. The extraordinary calmness and good order with which the millions of voters met and mingled at the polls give strong assurance of this. Not only all those who supported the Union ticket, so called, but a great majority of the opposing party also, may be fairly claimed to entertain, and to be actuated by, the same purpose. It is an unanswerable argument to this effect, that no candidate for any office whatever, high or low, has ventured to seek votes on the avowal that he was for giving up the Union. There has been much impugning of motives, and much heated controversy as to the proper means and best mode of advancing the Union cause; but on the distinct issue of Union or no Union the politicians have shown their instinctive knowledge that there is no diversity among the people. In affording the people the fair opportunity of showing one to another and to the world this firmness and unanimity of purpose, the election has been of vast value to the national cause.

The election has exhibited another fact, not less valuable to be known—the fact that we do not approach exhaustion in the most important branch of national resources—that of living men. While it is melancholy to reflect that the war has filled so many graves, and carried mourning to so many hearts, it is some relief to know that compared with the surviving, the fallen have been so few. While corps, and divisions, and brigades, and regiments have formed, and fought, and dwindled, and gone out of existence, a great majority of the men who composed them are still living. The same is true of the naval service. The election returns prove this. So many voters could not else be found. . . .

It is not material to inquire how the increase has been produced, or to show that it would have been greater but for the war, which is probably true. The important fact remains demonstrated that we have more men now than we had when the war began; that we are not exhausted, nor in process of exhaustion; that we are gaining strength, and may, if need be, maintain the contest indefinitely. This as to men. Material resources are now more complete and abundant than ever.

The national resources, then, are unexhausted, and, as we believe, inexhaustible. The public purpose to reëstablish and maintain the national authority is unchanged, and, as we believe, unchangeable. The manner of continuing the effort remains to choose. On careful consideration of all the evidence accessible, it seems to me that no attempt at negotiation with the insurgent leader could result in any good. He would accept nothing short of severance of the Union—precisely what we will not and cannot give. His declarations to this effect are explicit and oft repeated. He does not attempt to deceive us. He affords us no excuse to deceive ourselves. He cannot voluntarily re-accept the Union; we cannot voluntarily yield it.

Between him and us the issue is distinct, simple, and inflexible. It is an issue which can only be tried by war, and decided by victory. If we yield, we are beaten; if the Southern people fail him, he is beaten. Either way it would be the victory and defeat following war. What is true, however, of him who heads the insurgent cause, is not necessarily true of those who follow. Although he cannot re-accept the Union, they can. Some of them, we know, already desire peace and reunion. The number of such may increase.

They can at any moment have peace simply by laying down their arms and submitting to the national authority under the Constitution. After so much the government could not, if it would, maintain war against them. The loyal people would not sustain or allow it. If questions should remain, we would adjust them by the peaceful means of legislation, conference, courts, and votes, operating only in constitutional and lawful channels. Some certain, and other possible, questions are, and would be, beyond the executive power to adjust; as, for instance, the admission of members into Congress, and whatever might require the appropriation of money. The executive power itself would be greatly diminished by the cessation of actual war. Pardons and remissions of forfeitures, however, would still be within executive control. In what spirit and temper this control would be exercised, can be fairly judged of by the past.

A year ago general pardon and amnesty, upon specified terms, were offered to all except certain designated classes, and it was at the same time made known that the excepted classes were still within contemplation of special clemency. During the year many availed themselves of the general provision, and many more would only that the signs of bad faith in some led to such precautionary measures as rendered the practical process less easy and certain. During the same time, also, special pardons have been granted to individuals of the excepted classes, and no voluntary application has been denied.

Thus, practically, the door has been for a full year open to all, except such as were not in condition to make free choice— that is, such as were in custody or under constraint. It is still so open to all; but the time may come—probably will come— when public duty shall demand that it be closed; and that in lieu more rigorous measures than heretofore shall be adopted.

In presenting the abandonment of armed resistance to the national authority on the part of the insurgents as the only indispensable condition to ending the war on the part of the government, I retract nothing heretofore said as to slavery. I repeat the declaration made a year ago, that "while I remain in my present position I shall not attempt to retract or modify the Emancipation Proclamation, nor shall I return to slavery any person who is free by the terms of that proclamation, or by any of the acts of Congress."

If the people should, by whatever mode or means, make it an executive duty to reënslave such persons, another, and not I, must be their instrument to perform it.

In stating a single condition of peace, I mean simply to say, that the war will cease on the part of the government whenever it shall have ceased on the part of those who began it.

LETTER TO GENERAL W. T. SHERMAN

Early in May when Grant had started his campaign against Richmond, Sherman had marched toward Atlanta which he captured on September 2. He had set the city on fire in the middle of November and then started out across Georgia, marching toward the sea. On December 21, Savannah had fallen to him, and he had sent a message to the President saying that he had taken Savannah as a Christmas gift for him. This is Lincoln's reply to his victorious general.

Executive Mansion, December 26, 1864

MY DEAR GENERAL SHERMAN: Many, many thanks for your Christmas gift, the capture of Savannah.

When you were about leaving Atlanta for the Atlantic coast, I was anxious, if not fearful; but feeling that you were the better judge, and remembering that "nothing risked, nothing gained," I did not interfere. Now, the undertaking being a success, the honor is all yours; for I believe none of us went further than to acquiesce.

And taking the work of General Thomas into the count, as it should be taken, it is indeed a great success. Not only does it afford the obvious and immediate military advantages; but in showing to the world that your army could be divided, putting the stronger part to an important new service, and yet leaving enough to vanquish the old opposing force of the whole—Hood's army—it brings those who sat in darkness to see a great light. But what next?

I suppose it will be safe if I leave General Grant and yourself to decide.

Please make my grateful acknowledgments to your whole army—officers and men.

LETTER TO GENERAL U. S. GRANT

Lincoln writes to Grant to find a place in the army for his son, Robert, who had just been graduated from Harvard. It was Lincoln's plan that his son should serve as a volunteer aide without pay, but Grant told him that it would be better for Robert to become a regularly commissioned officer on an equal footing with his fellow officers. Robert Todd Lincoln thereupon became a captain, and on February 23 was attached to the staff of the general in chief.

Executive Mansion, January 19, 1865

LIEUTENANT-GENERAL GRANT: Please read and answer this letter as though I was not President, but only a friend. My son, now in his twenty-second year, having graduated at Harvard, wishes to see something of the war before it ends. I do not wish to put him in the ranks, nor yet to give him a commission, to which those who have already served long are better entitled and better qualified to hold. Could he, without embarrassment to you or detriment to the service, go into your military family with some nominal rank, I, and not the public, furnishing his necessary means? If no, say so without the least hesitation, because I am as anxious and as deeply interested that you shall not be encumbered as you can be yourself.

INSTRUCTIONS TO SECRETARY SEWARD FOR THE HAMPTON ROADS CONFERENCE

After the failure of several peace conferences with the Confederates, Lincoln had become greatly disillusioned about the possibility of dealing with the Davis government. Nevertheless, when another attempt, originating with the Confederates, was made, he at first decided to send Seward to deal with the commissioners, giving him the instructions listed here. He then decided to take a hand in the conference himself and sailed for Hampton Roads on board the River Queen. He met the three commissioners there; one of them, Alexander Stephens of Georgia, had been in Congress with Lincoln in 1848-49. The conference itself came to nothing since the commissioners had no power to accede to Lincoln's basic conditions.

Executive Mansion, January 31, 1865

HON. WILLIAM H. SEWARD: You will proceed to Fortress Monroe, Virginia, there to meet and informally confer with Messrs. Stephens, Hunter, and Campbell, on the basis of my letter to F. P. Blair, Esq., on January 18, 1865, a copy of which you have. You will make known to them that three things are indispensable—to wit:

1. The restoration of the national authority throughout all the States.

2. No receding by the executive of the United States on the slavery question from the position assumed thereon in the late annual message to Congress, and in preceding documents.

3. No cessation of hostilities short of an end of the war, and the disbanding of all forces hostile to the government.

You will inform them that all propositions of theirs, not inconsistent with the above, will be considered and passed upon in a spirit of sincere liberality. You will hear all they may choose to say and report it to me. You will not assume to definitely consummate anything.

DRAFT OF MESSAGE TO CONGRESS

(Not signed or sent)

At the Hampton Roads Conference on February 3, Lincoln mentioned to the Confederate commissioners that he believed the slaveholders were entitled to some kind of compensation for the loss of their slaves. Compensated emancipation had always been Lincoln's favorite method of disposing of the problem of slavery. Immediately upon his return from Hampton Roads, he drafted this proposed message to Congress, embodying a plan to pay $400,000,000 for the slaves set free in the Southern states This plan, as the endorsement indicates, met with the disapproval of his Cabinet.

February 5, 1865

FELLOW-CITIZENS OF THE SENATE AND HOUSE OF REPRESENTATIVES: I respectfully recommend that a joint resolution, substantially as follows, be adopted so soon as practicable by your honorable bodies: "Resolved by the Senate and House of Representatives of the United States of America, in Congress assembled, That the President of the United States is hereby empowered, in his discretion, to pay $400,000,000 to the States of Alabama, Arkansas, Delaware, Florida, Georgia, Kentucky, Louisiana, Maryland, Mississippi, Missouri, North Carolina, South Carolina, Tennessee, Texas, Virginia, and West Virginia, in the manner and on the conditions following, to wit: The payment to be made in six percent government bonds, and to be distributed among said States *pro rata* on their respective slave populations as shown by the census of 1860, and no part of said sum to be paid unless all resistance to the national authority shall be abandoned and cease, on or before the first day of April next; and upon such abandonment and ceasing of resistance one half of said sum to be paid in manner aforesaid, and the remaining half to be paid only upon the amendment of the National Constitution recently proposed by Congress becoming valid law, on or before the first day of July next, by the action thereon of the requisite number of States."

The adoption of such resolution is sought with a view to embody it, with other propositions, in a proclamation looking to peace and reunion.

Whereas, a joint resolution has been adopted by Congress, in the words following, to wit:

Now, therefore, I, Abraham Lincoln, President of the United States, do proclaim, declare, and make known, that on the conditions therein stated, the power conferred on the executive in and by said joint resolution will be fully exercised; that war will cease and armies be reduced to a basis of peace; that all political offenses will be pardoned; that all property, except slaves, liable to confiscation or forfeiture, will be released therefrom, except in cases of intervening interests of third parties; and that liberality will be recommended to Congress upon all points not lying within executive control.

[Indorsement.]

February 5, 1865. Today these papers, which explain themselves, were drawn up and submitted to the Cabinet and unanimously disapproved by them.

A. Lincoln

SECOND INAUGURAL ADDRESS

This, together with the Gettysburg Address, shows Lincoln's prose at its poetic best. Inauguration Day began with rainy weather, but the day cleared, and the sun came out while Lincoln was speaking. Salmon P. Chase, the new Chief Justice of the Supreme Court, appointed in Taney's stead, administered the oath of office. He noted the spot where Lincoln's lips touched the Bible when he kissed it in taking the oath; it was at a passage from Isaiah, Chapter 5, Verses 27-8: "None shall be weary nor stumble among them; none shall slumber nor sleep; neither shall the girdle of their loins be loosed, nor the latchet of their shoes be broken: whose arrows are sharp, and all their bows bent, their horses' hoofs shall be counted like flint, their wheels like the whirlwind." Charles Francis Adams, Jr., brother of Henry Adams, wrote to his father about the address: "What think you of the inaugural? That rail-splitting lawyer is one of the wonders of the day. Once at Gettysburg and now again on a greater occasion he has shown a capacity for rising to the demands of the hour which we should not expect from orators or men of the schools. This inaugural strikes me in its grand simplicity and directness as being for all time the historical keynote of this War; in it a people seemed to speak in the sublimely simple utterance of ruder times. What will Europe think of this utterance of the rude ruler, of whom they have nourished so lofty a contempt? Not a prince or minister in all Europe could have risen to such an equality with the occasion."

March 4, 1865

FELLOW-COUNTRYMEN: At this second appearing to take the oath of the Presidential office, there is less occasion for an extended address than there was at the first. Then a statement, somewhat in detail, of a course to be pursued, seemed fitting and proper. Now, at the expiration of four years, during which public declarations have been constantly called forth on every point and phase of the great contest which still absorbs the attention and engrosses the energies of the nation, little that is new could be presented. The progress of our arms, upon which all else chiefly depends, is as well known to the public as to myself; and it is, I trust, reasonably satisfactory and en-

couraging to all. With high hope for the future, no prediction
in regard to it is ventured.

On the occasion corresponding to this four years ago, all
thoughts were anxiously directed to an impending civil war.
All dreaded it—all sought to avert it. While the inaugural address was being delivered from this place, devoted altogether
to saving the Union without war, insurgent agents were in the
city seeking to destroy it without war—seeking to dissolve the
Union, and divide effects, by negotiation. Both parties deprecated war; but one of them would make war rather than let the
nation survive; and the other would accept war rather than let
it perish. And the war came.

One-eighth of the whole population were colored slaves, not
distributed generally over the Union, but localized in the
Southern part of it. These slaves constituted a peculiar and
powerful interest. All knew that this interest was, somehow,
the cause of the war. To strengthen, perpetuate, and extend
this interest was the object for which the insurgents would
rend the Union, even by war; while the government claimed
no right to do more than to restrict the territorial enlargement
of it.

Neither party expected for the war the magnitude or the
duration which it has already attained. Neither anticipated
that the cause of the conflict might cease with, or even before,
the conflict itself should cease. Each looked for an easier triumph, and a result less fundamental and astounding. Both
read the same Bible, and pray to the same God; and each invokes His aid against the other. It may seem strange that any
men should dare to ask a just God's assistance in wringing
their bread from the sweat of other men's faces; but let us
judge not, that we be not judged. The prayers of both could
not be answered—that of neither has been answered fully.

The Almighty has His own purposes. "Woe unto the world
because of offenses! for it must needs be that offenses come;
but woe to that man by whom the offense cometh." If we

shall suppose that American slavery is one of those offenses which, in the providence of God, must needs come, but which, having continued through His appointed time, He now wills to remove, and that He gives to both North and South this terrible war, as the woe due to those by whom the offense came, shall we discern therein any departure from those divine attributes which the believers in a living God always ascribe to Him? Fondly do we hope—fervently do we pray—that this mighty scourge of war may speedily pass away. Yet, if God wills that it continue until all the wealth piled by the bondsman's two hundred and fifty years of unrequited toil shall be sunk, and until every drop of blood drawn with the lash shall be paid by another drawn with the sword, as was said three thousand years ago, so still it must be said, "The judgments of the Lord are true and righteous altogether."

With malice toward none; with charity for all; with firmness in the right, as God gives us to see the right, let us strive on to finish the work we are in; to bind up the nation's wounds; to care for him who shall have borne the battle, and for his widow, and his orphan—to do all which may achieve and cherish a just and lasting peace among ourselves, and with all nations.

LETTER TO THURLOW WEED

In this letter to Weed, thanking him for a letter of congratulation on the Second Inaugural Address, can be seen Lincoln's own comment on his celebrated speech.

Executive Mansion, March 15, 1865

DEAR MR. WEED: Every one likes a compliment. Thank you for yours on my little notification speech and on the recent inaugural address. I expect the latter to wear as well as—perhaps better than—anything I have produced; but I believe it is not immediately popular. Men are not flattered by being shown that there has been a difference of purpose between the Almighty and them. To deny it, however, in this case, is to deny that there is a God governing the world. It is a truth which I thought needed to be told, and, as whatever of humiliation there is in it falls most directly on myself, I thought others might afford for me to tell it.

ADDRESS TO AN INDIANA REGIMENT

Lincoln speaks to a regiment from the state in which he had spent his boyhood and adolescence. He explains the part played by the Negroes in the Confederate army.

March 17, 1865

FELLOW-CITIZENS: A few words only. I was born in Kentucky, raised in Indiana, reside in Illinois, and now, here, it is my duty to care equally for the good people of all the States. I am today glad of seeing it in the power of an Indiana regiment to _present this captured flag to the good governor of their State; and yet I would not wish to compliment Indiana above other States, remembering that all have done so well.

There are but few aspects of this great war on which I have not already expressed my views by speaking or writing. There is one—the recent effort of "our erring brethren," sometimes so called, to employ the slaves in their armies. The great question with them has been, "Will the Negro fight for them?" They ought to know better than we, and doubtless do know better than we. I may incidentally remark, that having in my life heard many arguments—or strings of words meant to pass for arguments—intended to show that the Negro ought to be a slave—if he shall now really fight to keep himself a slave, it will be a far better argument why he should remain a slave than I have ever before heard. He, perhaps, ought to be a slave if he desires it ardently enough to fight for it. Or, if one out of four will, for his own freedom, fight to keep the other three in slavery, he ought to be a slave for his selfish meanness. I have always thought that all men should be free; but if any should be slaves, it should be first those who desire it for themselves, and secondly those who desire it for others. Whenever I hear any one arguing for slavery, I feel a strong impulse to see it tried on him personally.

There is one thing about the Negro's fighting for the rebels which we can know as well as they can, and that is that they cannot at the same time fight in their armies and stay at home and make bread for them. And this being known and remembered, we can have but little concern whether they become soldiers or not. I am rather in favor of the measure, and would at any time, if I could, have loaned them a vote to carry it. We have to reach the bottom of the insurgent resources; and that they employ, or seriously think of employing, the slaves as soldiers, gives us glimpses of the bottom. Therefore I am glad of what we learn on this subject.

TELEGRAM TO SECRETARY STANTON

Lincoln had left Washington on March 23 to visit Grant at City Point so that he could confer with Grant and Sherman before the last drive on Petersburg and Richmond began. He describes here to Stanton one of the preliminary battles that were then taking place around the Petersburg redoubts as pressure against the Confederate lines was being increased.

City Point, Va., March 30, 1865

HON. SECRETARY OF WAR: I begin to feel that I ought to be at home and yet I dislike to leave without seeing nearer to the end of General Grant's present movement. He has now been out since yesterday morning, and although he has not been diverted from his program, no considerable effort has yet been produced so far as we know here. Last night at 10.15 p. m. when it was dark as a rainy night without a moon could be, a furious cannonade, soon joined in by a heavy musketry fire, opened near Petersburg and lasted about two hours. The sound was very distinct here as also were the flashes of the guns upon the clouds. It seemed to me a great battle, but the older hands here scarcely noticed it, and sure enough this morning it was found that very little had been done.

TELEGRAM TO SECRETARY STANTON

The Confederate government had fled from Richmond on the night of April 2; the first Union troops entered the city on April 3. Lincoln had never seen Richmond. He announces to Stanton his intention to visit the city on April 4.

City Point, Va., April 3, 1865

HON. EDWIN M. STANTON: Yours received. Thanks for your caution, but I have already been to Petersburg, stayed with General Grant an hour and a half and returned here. It is certain now that Richmond is in our hands, and I think I will go there tomorrow. I will take care of myself.

TELEGRAM TO GENERAL U. S. GRANT

Sheridan and Grant were in pursuit of Lee's army which was in serious straits. Lincoln telegraphs here to his chief commander instructing him to see the matter through to a finish.

Headquarters Armies of the U. S., City Point, April 7, 1865

LIEUTENANT-GENERAL GRANT: Gen. Sheridan says "If the thing is pressed I think that Lee will surrender." Let the thing be pressed.

LAST PUBLIC ADDRESS

Lee surrendered to Grant at Appomattox on April 9. Lincoln returned to Washington where a great celebration of victory was being held. On the evening of April 10, a group of people had come to the White House to serenade him, but he had declined to speak to them at any length, saying that if they would return the next night he would prepare an address for the occasion. He wrote out this speech carefully and read it from a roll of manuscript while standing in one of the windows of the White House. It is not a speech of victory, but a serious analysis of reconstruction plans, particularly as they were being carried out in Louisiana. In this speech, Lincoln prepares to go over the head of Congress to take the issue direct to the people. Among the crowd standing on the White House lawn was John Wilkes Booth, who was reputedly so enraged at what the President had to say about giving the vote to the Negroes, that he then swore that this was the last speech Lincoln would ever make.

April 11, 1865

WE MEET this evening not in sorrow, but in gladness of heart. The evacuation of Petersburg and Richmond, and the surrender of the principal insurgent army, give hope of a righteous and speedy peace, whose joyous expression cannot be restrained. In the midst of this, however, He from whom all blessings flow must not be forgotten. A call for a national thanksgiving is being prepared, and will be duly promulgated. Nor must those whose harder part gives us the cause of rejoicing be overlooked. Their honors must not be parceled out with others. I myself was near the front, and had the high pleasure of transmitting much of the good news to you; but no part of the honor for plan or execution is mine. To General Grant, his skilful officers and brave men, all belongs. The gallant navy stood ready, but was not in reach to take active part.

By these recent successes the reinauguration of the national authority—reconstruction—which has had a large share of thought from the first, is pressed much more closely upon our attention. It is fraught with great difficulty. Unlike a case of war between independent nations, there is no authorized organ for us to treat with—no one man has authority to give up the rebellion for any other man. We simply must begin with and mold from disorganized and discordant elements. Nor is it a small additional embarrassment that we, the loyal people, differ among ourselves as to the mode, manner, and measure of reconstruction. As a general rule, I abstain from reading the reports of attacks upon myself, wishing not to be provoked by that to which I cannot properly offer an answer. In spite of this precaution, however, it comes to my knowledge that I am much censured for some supposed agency in setting up and seeking to sustain the new State government of Louisiana.

In this I have done just so much, and no more than, the public knows. In the annual message of December, 1863, and in the accompanying proclamation, I presented a plan of reconstruction as the phrase goes, which I promised, if adopted by any State, should be acceptable to and sustained by the executive government of the nation. I distinctly stated that this was not the only plan which might possibly be acceptable, and I also distinctly protested that the executive claimed no right to say when or whether members should be admitted to seats in Congress from such States. This plan was in advance submitted to the then Cabinet, and distinctly approved by every member of it. One of them suggested that I should then and in that connection apply the Emancipation Proclamation to the theretofore excepted parts of Virginia and Louisiana; that I should drop the suggestion about apprenticeship for freed people, and that I should omit the protest against my own power in regard to the admission of members to Congress. But even he approved every part and parcel of the plan which has since been employed or touched by the action of Louisiana.

The new constitution of Louisiana, declaring emancipation for the whole State, practically applies the proclamation to the part previously excepted. It does not adopt apprenticeship for freed people, and it is silent, as it could not well be otherwise, about the admission of members to Congress. So that, as it applies to Louisiana, every member of the Cabinet fully approved the plan. The message went to Congress, and I received many commendations of the plan, written and verbal, and not a single objection to it from any professed emancipationist came to my knowledge until after the news reached Washington that the people of Louisiana had begun to move in accordance with it. From about July, 1862, I had corresponded with different persons supposed to be interested [in] seeking a reconstruction of a State government for Louisiana. When the message of 1863, with the plan before mentioned, reached New Orleans, General Banks wrote me that he was confident that the people, with his military coöperation, would reconstruct substantially on that plan. I wrote to him and some of them to try it. They tried it, and the result is known. Such has been my only agency in getting up the Louisiana government.

As to sustaining it, my promise is out, as before stated. But as bad promises are better broken than kept, I shall treat this as a bad promise, and break it whenever I shall be convinced that keeping it is adverse to the public interest; but I have not yet been so convinced. I have been shown a letter on this subject, supposed to be an able one, in which the writer expresses regret that my mind has not seemed to be definitely fixed on the question whether the seceded States, so called, are in the Union or out of it. It would perhaps add astonishment to his regret were he to learn that since I have found professed

Union men endeavoring to make that question, I have pur- posely forborne any public expression upon it. As appears to me, that question has not been, nor yet is, a practically mate- rial one, and that any discussion of it, while it thus remains practically immaterial, could have no effect other than the mischievous one of dividing our friends. As yet, whatever it may hereafter become, that question is bad as the basis of a controversy, and good for nothing at all—a merely pernicious abstraction.

We all agree that the seceded States, so called, are out of their proper practical relation with the Union, and that the sole object of the government, civil and military, in regard to those States, is to again get them into that proper practical relation. I believe that it is not only possible, but in fact easier, to do this without deciding or even considering whether these States have ever been out of the Union, than with it. Finding themselves safely at home, it would be utterly immaterial whether they had ever been abroad. Let us all join in doing the acts necessary to restoring the proper practical relations between these States and the Union, and each forever after innocently indulge his own opinion whether in doing the acts he brought the States from without into the Union, or only gave them proper assistance, they never having been out of it. The amount of constituency, so to speak, on which the new Louisiana government rests, would be more satisfactory to all if it contained 50,000 or 30,000, or even 20,000, instead of only about 12,000, as it does. It is also unsatisfactory to some that the elective franchise is not given to the colored man. I would myself prefer that it were now conferred on the very intelligent, and on those who serve our cause as soldiers.

Still, the question is not whether the Louisiana government, as it stands, is quite all that is desirable. The question is, will it be wiser to take it as it is and help to improve it, or to reject and disperse it? Can Louisiana be brought into proper prac- tical relation with the Union sooner by sustaining or by dis-

carding her new State government? Some twelve thousand
voters in the heretofore slave State of Louisiana have sworn
allegiance to the Union, assumed to be the rightful political
power of the State, held elections, organized a State government, adopted a free-State constitution, giving the benefit of
public schools equally to black and white, and empowering
the legislature to confer the elective franchise upon the colored
man. Their legislature has already voted to ratify the constitutional amendment recently passed by Congress, abolishing
slavery throughout the nation. These 12,000 persons are thus
fully committed to the Union and to perpetual freedom in the
State—committed to the very things, and nearly all the things,
the nation wants—and they ask the nation's recognition and
its assistance to make good their committal.

Now, if we reject and spurn them, we do our utmost to dis-
organize and disperse them. We, in effect, say to the white
man: You are worthless or worse; we will neither help you,
nor be helped by you. To the blacks we say: This cup of liberty which these, your old masters, hold to your lips we will
dash from you, and leave you to the chances of gathering the
spilled and scattered contents in some vague and undefined
when, where, and how. If this course, discouraging and paralyzing both white and black, has any tendency to bring Louisiana
into proper practical relations with the Union, I have so far
been unable to perceive it. If, on the contrary, we recognize
and sustain the new government of Louisiana, the converse of
all this is made true. We encourage the hearts and nerve the
arms of the 12,000 to adhere to their work, and argue for it,
and proselyte for it, and fight for it, and feed it, and grow it,
and ripen it to a complete success. The colored man, too, in
seeing all united for him, is inspired with vigilance, and energy, and daring, to the same end. Grant that he desires the
elective franchise, will he not attain it sooner by saving the
already advanced steps toward it than by running backward
over them? Concede that the new government of Louisiana is

only what it should be as the egg is to the fowl, we shall sooner have the fowl by hatching the egg than by smashing it.

Again, if we reject Louisiana we also reject one vote in favor of the proposed amendment to the national Constitution. To meet this proposition it has been argued that no more than three-fourths of those States which have not attempted secession are necessary to validly ratify the amendment. I do not commit myself against this further than to say that such a ratification would be questionable, and sure to be persistently questioned, while a ratification by three-fourths of all the States would be unquestioned and unquestionable. I repeat the question: Can Louisiana be brought into proper practical relation with the Union sooner by sustaining or by discarding her new State government? What has been said of Louisiana will apply generally to other States. And yet so great peculiarities pertain to each State, and such important and sudden changes occur in the same State, and withal so new and unprecedented is the whole case that no exclusive and inflexible plan can safely be prescribed as to details and collaterals. Such exclusive and inflexible plan would surely become a new entanglement. Important principles may and must be inflexible. In the present situation, as the phrase goes, it may be my duty to make some new announcement to the people of the South. I am considering, and shall not fail to act when satisfied that action will be proper.

LINCOLN'S LAST WRITING

A few moments before the Presidential carriage left the White House on the fatal evening of April 14 to go to Ford's Theater, George Ashmun, Congressman from Massachusetts and chairman of the 1860 National Republican Convention that had nominated Lincoln, asked for an interview with the President. There was no time to go into the matter about which he wished to speak—a cotton claim which one of his clients had against the Government—so Lincoln wrote out this pass to admit Ashmun to the White House in the morning. The carriage then drove off to the theater. There were to be no more tomorrows for the man who had laid down his pen for the last time.

April 14, 1865

ALLOW Mr. Ashmun and friend to come in at 9 A. M. tomorrow.

A. LINCOLN

SUBJECT INDEX

SUBJECT INDEX

ADDRESSES

To General Duff Green, on a slavery amendment to the Constitution, 632

To August Belmont, on the Louisiana situation, 710-711

To John M. Clay, on Henry Clay, 714-715

To Horace Greeley, on Lincoln's stand on slavery, 718-719

To James C. Conkling, on the necessity to win the war, 776-780

To the workingmen of Manchester, England, 748-749

To Henry Winter Davis, running for Congress, 751

To Erastus Corning, on constitutional rights in an emergency, 755-763

To Gov. Horatio Seymour, on the draft law, 768-769

To A. G. Hodges, on emancipation, 807-809

To John H. Bryant, on Owen Lovejoy, 813

LINCOLN, ABRAHAM, THE LIFE OF

Birth, 6; family, 6-8, 11; schooling, 10-12; the Indiana years, 9-13; trips to New Orleans, 13, 14-15; New Salem, Ill., 16-22; Black Hawk War, 18; Ann Rutledge, 19-21; Mary Owens, 21-24; Springfield, Ill., 22-32, 35-42; Mary Todd, 25-30; Sarah Rickard, 28; in Congress, 32-35; slavery issue, 42 et seq.; Stephen A. Douglas, 45-49, 61 et seq.; Republican party, 50, 53-58, 86-91; Lincoln-Douglas debates, 71-77; raid on Harper's Ferry, 80-83; Lincoln nominated for President, 89; elected, 90-91; secession, 91-93, 109 et seq.; journey to Washington, 96-104; Baltimore plot, 102-104; inauguration, 105-106; Cabinet, 107-108; Fort Sumter, 109-110, 112-113; the line-up, 113-115; defense of Washington, 116-119; the Lincolns in the White House, 119-122; economic background for war, 123-124; Bull Run, 127-129; the border states, 130-131; the Trent affair, 131-133; the Radical Republicans, 135-137; death of son Willie, 137; the Monitor and the Merrimac, 138-139; first campaign vs. Richmond, 139-142; proclamation of emancipation, 143-144, 146, 148; McClellan replaced by Burnside, 146-147; humanity of Lincoln, 150-151; Gettysburg, 151-159; a hostile Congress, 159-168; Grant put in charge of army, 160; Mrs. Lincoln, 164, 180-181; presidential campaign of 1864, 168-170; Lincoln re-elected, 170; peace negotiations, 172-174; compensated emancipation, 174-176; second inauguration, 176-178; John Wilkes Booth, 156n, 178-179, 188; a generous peace, 181-183; assassination, 188-189; cross-country funeral procession, 190-191; burial, 191.

MISCELLANEOUS WRITINGS

NOTES

ORDERS

POEMS

PROCLAMATIONS

THE MODERN LIBRARY EDITORIAL BOARD

Maya Angelou

•

Daniel J. Boorstin

•

A. S. Byatt

•

Caleb Carr

•

Christopher Cerf

•

Ron Chernow

•

Shelby Foote

•

Stephen Jay Gould

•

Vartan Gregorian

•

Charles Johnson

•

Jon Krakauer

•

Edmund Morris

•

Elaine Pagels

•

John Richardson

•

Arthur Schlesinger, Jr.

•

Carolyn See

•

William Styron

•

Gore Vidal